SECOND EDITION

Strategic Management

Frank T. Rothaermel

Georgia Institute of Technology

Mc
Graw
Hill
Education

STRATEGIC MANAGEMENT, SECOND EDITION

5 6 7 8 9 0 DOW/DOW 1 0 9 8 7 6 5

ISBN 978-0-07-764506-9 (student edition)
MHID 0-07-764506-5 (student edition)
ISBN 978-0-07-764517-5 (instructor's edition)
MHID 0-07-764517-0 (instructor's edition)

Senior Vice President, Products & Markets: *Kurt L. Strand*
Vice President, Content Production & Technology Services: *Kimberly Meriwether David*
Managing Director: *Paul Ducham*
Executive Brand Manager: *Michael Ablassmeir*
Executive Director of Development: *Ann Torbert*
Senior Development Editor: *Laura Griffin*
Marketing Manager : *Elizabeth Trepkowski*
Director, Content Production: *Terri Schiesl*
Content Project Manager: *Harvey Yep*
Senior Buyer: *Debra R. Sylvester*
Design: *Matt Diamond*
Cover Image: *Veer*
Senior Content Licensing Specialist: *Jeremy Cheshareck*
Typeface: *10/12 Times Roman*
Compositor: *Laserwords Private Limited*
Printer: RR Donnelley

Library of Congress Cataloging-in-Publication Data

Rothaermel, Frank T.
    Strategic management / Frank T. Rothaermel, Georgia Institute of Technology.—Second edition.
        pages cm
    Revised edition of the work, Strategic management : concepts.
    Includes bibliographical references and index.
    ISBN-13: 978-0-07-764506-9 (student edition : alk. paper)
    ISBN-10: 0-07-764506-5 (student edition : alk. paper)
    ISBN-13: 978-0-07-764517-5 (instructor's edition : alk. paper)
    ISBN-10: 0-07-764517-0 (instructor's edition : alk. paper)
    1. Strategic planning. I. Title.
    HD30.28.R6646 2015
    658.4'012—dc23

                                                                    2013044736

www.mhhe.com

DEDICATION

To my eternal family for their love, support, and sacrifice:
Kelleyn, Harris, Winston, Roman, and Adelaide

—FRANK T. ROTHAERMEL

CONTENTS IN BRIEF

MINICASES AND FULL-LENGTH CASES

FULL-LENGTH CASES MARKED WITH A ⇥ WERE AUTHORED OR CO-AUTHORED SPECIFICALLY FOR THIS BOOK BY FRANK T. ROTHAERMEL.

CONTENTS

FULL-LENGTH CASES MARKED WITH A ➤➤ WERE AUTHORED OR CO-AUTHORED SPECIFICALLY FOR THIS BOOK BY FRANK T. ROTHAERMEL.

CHAPTER**CASES AND STRATEGY HIGHLIGHTS**

Frank T. Rothaermel

Georgia Institute of Technology

FRANK T. ROTHAERMEL (PHD) is a professor of strategic management and holds the Russell and Nancy McDonough Chair in the Scheller College of Business at the Georgia Institute of Technology. Frank is also an Alfred P. Sloan Industry Studies Fellow. He received a National Science Foundation (NSF) CAREER award, which "is a Foundation-wide activity that offers the National Science Foundation's most prestigious awards in support of . . . those teacher-scholars who most effectively integrate research and education" (NSF CAREER Award description). Frank is also the area coordinator for Strategic Management.

Frank's research interests lie in the areas of strategy, innovation, and entrepreneurship. To inform his research, he has conducted extensive field work and executive training with leading corporations such as Amgen, Daimler, Eli Lilly, Equifax, GE Energy, GE Healthcare, Hyundai Heavy Industries (South Korea), Kimberly-Clark, Microsoft, McKesson, NCR, Turner (TBS), among others. *BusinessWeek* named Frank one of Georgia Tech's Prominent Faculty in its national survey of business schools. The Kauffman Foundation views Frank as one of the world's 75 thought leaders in entrepreneurship and innovation.

Frank has published some 30 articles in leading academic journals such as the *Academy of Management Journal, Academy of Management Review, Organization Science, Strategic Management Journal,* and elsewhere. Some of his academic articles are highly cited. Frank currently serves (or served) on the editorial boards of the *Academy of Management Journal, Academy of Management Review, Organization Science, Strategic Management Journal,* and *Strategic Organization.* Frank regularly translates his research findings for wider audiences in articles in *Forbes, MIT Sloan Management Review, The Wall Street Journal,* and elsewhere.

He has received several recognitions for his research, including the Sloan Industry Studies Best Paper Award, the Academy of Management Newman Award, the Strategic Management Society Conference Best Paper Prize, the DRUID Conference Best Paper Award, and the Israel Strategy Conference Best Paper Prize. He is also the inaugural recipient of the Byars Faculty Excellence Award.

Frank has a wide range of teaching experience, including at the Georgia Institute of Technology, Georgetown University, ICN Business School (France), Michigan State University, Politecnico di Milano (Italy), St. Gallen University (Switzerland), and the University of Washington. He received numerous teaching awards for excellence in the classroom.

Frank holds a PhD degree in strategic management from the University of Washington, an MBA from the Marriott School of Management at Brigham Young University, and an M.Sc. (Diplom-Volkswirt) in economics from University of Duisburg, Germany. He was a visiting professor at the University of St. Gallen, Switzerland, and an Erasmus Scholar at Sheffield Hallam University, UK. Frank is a member of the Academy of Management, the Industry Studies Association (Founding Member), and the Strategic Management Society.

VISIT THE AUTHOR AT: www.ftrStrategy.com

PREFACE

The market responded very positively to the first edition, and I'm grateful for that strong vote of confidence. In this second edition, I built upon the unique strengths of this text and continue to improve it based on hundreds of insightful reviews and important feedback from professors, students, and professionals. The vision for this text is to provide students with core concepts, frameworks, and analysis techniques in strategy that will integrate their functional course offerings and help them become managers who make well-reasoned strategic decisions. It is a research-based strategy text for the issues that managers face in a globalized and turbulent 21st century, blending theory, empirical research, and practical applications in a student-accessible form.

The competition in the strategy textbook market can be separated into two overarching categories: traditional strategy books, which are the first-generation texts (from the 1980s); and more recent, research-based strategy books, which are the second-generation texts (from the 1990s). This new text is different—a third-generation strategy text, positioned to compete successfully with the primary first- and second-generation incumbents. The third-generation approach you will find here combines the student accessibility and application-oriented frameworks found in first-generation texts with the strategy research in the second-generation texts.

This text synthesizes and integrates theory, empirical research, and practical applications in a unique combination of rigor and relevance. With a single strong voice, the chapters weave together classic and cutting-edge theory with in-chapter cases and strategy highlights, to demonstrate how companies gain and sustain competitive advantage. The strategic intent for the book is to combine quality and value with user-friendliness.

In particular, the content of this product is based on the principles discussed next, each of which provides a value-added dimension for instructors or students, or both.

- **Synthesis and integration of rigorous and relevant strategy material.** For example, the text includes strategy material that has stood the test of time (such as the resource-based view and Porter's five forces model) as well as up-to-date strategy material and current research (such as the dynamic capabilities perspective and the triple bottom line).

  It also includes *student-accessible coverage* of strategic management research. It draws on articles published in the leading academic journals (for instance, *Strategic Management Journal, Academy of Management Journal/Review, Organization Science, Management Science, Journal of Management,* and so on). Although academic theory and empirical research form the foundation of the text, I also have integrated insights from leading practitioner outlets (such as *Harvard Business Review, Sloan Management Review, California Management Review*) to enhance the application of concepts. To weave in current examples and developments, I draw on *The Wall Street Journal, Bloomberg Businessweek, Fortune, Forbes,* and others. In sum, theory is brought to life via the embedded examples within each framework and concept.

- **The comprehensive yet concise presentation of core concepts, frameworks, and techniques.** Although comprehensive, the text does not include every single idea ever introduced to the strategy field. Many students don't read the assigned readings in their strategy textbooks because the books contain *too much* information, presented in a disjointed fashion. Many strategy books read more like a literature review, without addressing *what* the research findings mean and *why* they are important for managers. This jumble prevents students from seeing the bigger strategic picture. They may see the trees, but they fail to see the forest. In contrast, this text will be an *enjoyable* *read* for students—clear, concise, and filled with examples from companies today's students know—while at the same time providing the content and value-add that instructors expect. *It has one vision and one voice!*

- **Combination of traditional and contemporary chapters.** As a review of the chapter-contents listing will demonstrate, the text includes the traditional chapters needed in the core strategy course. In addition, it includes three contemporary *standalone chapters* that reviewers and users have identified as providing additional value:

  - Chapter 2, "Strategic Leadership: Managing the Strategy Process," discusses the roles of leaders in setting strategy within three different models: top-down planning, scenario planning, and strategy as planned emergence. This chapter allows for a thorough discussion of the role of vision, mission, and values; customer versus product-oriented missions; the combination of intended and emergent strategies; and the importance of long-term success in anchoring a firm in ethical values.

  - Chapter 5, "Competitive Advantage, Firm Performance, and Business Models," neatly ends the analysis section of the book by providing five approaches to measuring firm performance and assessing competitive advantage. It looks at three traditional approaches to measure performance (accounting profitability, economic value creation, and shareholder value creation) and at two holistic approaches (the balanced scorecard and the triple bottom line). Instructors can easily cover as many of the approaches as desired for their course and its goals. A new addition is the detailed discussion of business models. Putting strategy into action through innovative business models is becoming more and more important across all types of industries.

  - Chapter 7, *Innovation and Strategic Entrepreneurship,* addresses the important topics of innovation and strategic entrepreneurship as aspects of business strategy. Driven by Schumpeter's "perennial gale of creative destruction," competition seems more heated than ever, with innovation playing a key role in gaining and sustaining competitive advantage. This chapter addresses various aspects of innovation, beginning with the industry life cycle (ILC) and the modes of competition and business-level strategies at various stages in the life cycle. Given the importance of different customer preferences at different stages of the ILC, it introduces the crossing-the-chasm framework and illustrates it with an application to the smartphone industry. Using tools and concepts of strategic management, it explores four types of innovation, social entrepreneurship, and the Internet as a disruptive force. This chapter especially will engage students and provide much food for thought in their jobs and careers.

- **Up-to-date examples and discussion of current topics within a global context.** Having spoken to hundreds of students around the world, I want to minimize the frustration they express in seeing the same, out-of-date examples in so many of their (generic and boiler-plate) business-school textbooks. The book has been written for today's students to reflect the turbulence and dynamism that they will face as managers. I have drawn on up-to-date examples to illustrate how companies apply strategy concepts in today's business world. Although this text contains a standalone chapter on *Global Strategy,* examples throughout the book reflect the global nature of competition and the importance of emerging economies such as the BRIC countries and highlights non-U.S. competitors such as Lenovo, Siemens, the Tata Group, and BYD in globalized industries.

  Each chapter contains two *Strategy Highlight* boxes. These in-chapter examples apply a specific concept to a specific company. They are right-sized for maximum student appeal—long enough to contain valuable insights, and short enough to encourage student reading. For a list of the Strategy Highlight companies and topics, see page xiii.

I also have drawn topics and examples from recent and seminal business bestsellers, such as *The Black Swan; Built to Last; Co-opetition; Crossing the Chasm; Good Strategy, Bad Strategy; Good to Great; Great by Choice; How the Mighty Fall; In the Plex; Innovator's Dilemma (and Solution); Innovator's DNA; Lean In; Playing to Win; Predictably Irrational; Steve Jobs; The Long Tail; The Wide Lens; Wisdom of the Crowds; World 3.0; and Why Smart Executives Fail;* among others. I have included these ideas to expose students to topics that today's managers talk about. Being conversant with these concepts from business bestsellers will help today's students interview better and effortlessly join the discourse in the corporate world.

- *Use of the AFI strategy framework.* The book demonstrates that "less is more" through a focused presentation of the relevant strategy content using *Analysis, Formulation,* and *Implementation* as a guiding framework. This model (see Exhibit 1.5 on page 18) integrates process schools of strategy (based on organization theory, psychology, and sociology) with content schools of strategy (based on economics). Process and content can be viewed as the "yin and yang" of strategy. Current strategy textbooks typically favor one or the other but do not integrate them, which leads to an unbalanced and incomplete treatment of strategic management. The AFI strategy strives for beauty through balance, which is lacking in most current strategy texts on the market. The model also emphasizes that gaining and sustaining competitive advantage is accomplished in an iterative and recursive fashion. The framework offers a repository for theoretical strategy knowledge that is well translated for student consumption, and it provides a toolkit for practicing managers.

- *High-quality cases, well integrated with textbook chapters.* Cases are a fundamental ingredient in teaching strategy. My interactions with colleagues, reviewers, and focus group participants in the course of writing and developing chapters indicate varying instructor needs for top-notch, up-to-date cases that are well-integrated with the content presented. Within this text itself are two types of cases:

  - **ChapterCases** begin and end each chapter, framing the chapter topic and content. The case at the beginning of the chapter highlights a strategic issue that a well-known company faced and relates that company to a concept to be taught in the chapter. The end of each chapter returns to the ChapterCase, in a recapitulation of the case titled "Consider This. . .". Here, we ask students to reconsider the case, applying concepts and information presented in the chapter, along with additional information about the focus company.

  - 20 **MiniCases,** (following Chapter 12), all based on original research, provide a decision scenario that a company's manager might face. With suggested links to related chapters, they offer dynamic opportunities to apply strategy concepts by assigning them as add-ons to chapters, either as individual assignments or as group work, or by using them for class discussion.

  I have taken pride in authoring *all* of the ChapterCases and MiniCases. This additional touch allows quality control and ensures that chapter content and cases use one voice and are closely interconnected. Both types of case materials come with sets of questions to stimulate class discussion or provide guidance for written assignments. The instructor resources offer sample answers that apply chapter content to the cases.

- In addition to these in-text cases, 24 **full-length Cases,** authored or co-authored by me specifically to accompany this textbook, are available through McGraw-Hill's custom-publishing *Create*™ program. Full-length cases NEW to the second edition address strategic issues at Facebook, McDonald's, BlackBerry, and Amazon. Among the others, the cases about BetterWorldBooks, Tesla Motors, Numenta, Best Buy, and Apple have been updated and revised for the new edition. Also available are three full-length cases—about Microsoft, Tropical Salvage, and the movie industry— authored by other strategic-management instructors. Robust case teaching notes and financial data are available for all full-length cases accessed through Create.

■ ***Direct applications of strategy to careers and lives.*** The examples in the book discuss products and services from companies with which students are familiar, such as Facebook, Starbucks, Apple, and Zipcar. Use of such examples aids in making strategy relevant to students' lives and helps them internalize strategy concepts and frameworks.

This edition also provides a stronger focus on practice/applications. Each chapter now closes with a section titled *Implications for the Strategist* that highlights practical implications of the concepts and frameworks discussed and allows the student to build a cumulative toolkit in strategic management. It bridges the gap to practical application and makes the reader more confident in using the tools presented.

In addition, at the end of each chapter's homework materials is an innovative text feature, titled *my*Strategy, which personalizes strategy concepts through direct application of the chapter topic to students' lives. Questions asked in these sections include: *What is your positioning strategy in the job market? How will you differentiate yourself, and at what cost?* and *How much is an MBA worth to you?* Such questions encourage students to think through strategic issues related to their budding careers. You may choose to make this feature a regular part of the course, or you may prefer to let students explore these items outside of the regular coursework. Either way, the *my*Strategy feature demonstrates opportunities to personalize strategy as students plan or enhance careers following completion of the strategy course and their degrees.

For details about changes made in the second edition, see the list that follows.

What's New in the Second Edition

I have revised and updated the second edition in the following ways, many of which were inspired by conversations and feedback from users and reviewers of the first edition.

CHANGES MADE THROUGHOUT

■ ChapterCases and Strategy Highlights throughout have been either completely revised and updated or are new, as detailed in the following chapter-by-chapter entries.

■ All major text examples have been updated or are new, with more in-depth discussion.

■ More global coverage is included throughout, with a stronger China focus (both on the country as well as its global competitors).

■ Additional coverage and discussion of more diverse strategic leaders has been included.

■ Chapters now consistently contain two Strategy Highlight features per chapter.

■ Chapters now contain a stronger practice/application focus throughout. Each chapter now closes with a section discussing practical *Implications for the Strategist*.

■ Following Chapter 12 are 20 MiniCases—13 are brand-new MiniCases, many of which focus on China and Chinese companies competing in the West, and the remaining 7 are updated from the first edition.

- Four brand-new full-length Cases (Facebook, McDonald's, BlackBerry, and Amazon) are available through McGraw-Hill Create (including financial data in e-format for analysis available through McGraw-Hill Connect).
- There is continued focus on providing a streamlined presentation by dropping some material when adding new content. This focus results in a fast-paced, reader-friendly text.

CHAPTER 1

- New ChapterCase about Apple's rise and current challenges to sustain a competitive advantage.
- Draws on Rumelt's insightful book *Good Strategy, Bad Strategy* to more clearly delineate the concept of strategy.
- Sharpened the definitions of strategy and competitive advantage. Part of this involved removing the section on "strategy as a theory of how to compete."
- Moved all stakeholder material (from Chapter 12) into Chapter 1.
- Now includes an extensive discussion of stakeholder strategy and corporate social responsibility in Chapter 1, to provide the foundation for that concept throughout the chapters.
- Moved a revised section of "Formulating Strategy Across Levels" to Chapter 2.
- Moved discussion on business models to Chapter 5, where it could be expanded.
- New Strategy Highlight 1.1 discussing the difficulty JetBlue experienced in trying to combine two different competitive strategies (low cost and differentiation).
- New Strategy Highlight 1.2 about BP's 2010 Gulf Coast oil spill and systemic safety issues over the last decade.
- New discussion and ethical/social issues questions about stakeholder relationships.
- Two new small-group exercises (one on black swan events and the other about the dangers of unclear choice of strategy).

CHAPTER 2

- New ChapterCase, about Indra Yoori as a strategic leader.
- Tightened chapter by moving/deleting section on strategic intent, thereby more closely linking discussions of vision and mission.
- Added extended coverage of strategic leadership (previously in Chapter 12) into Chapter 2, to highlight the role of strategic leaders early on in the chapters.
- Added a revised and updated section on formulating strategy across business levels (from Chapter 1 in 1e), with more examples provided; leads into coverage of the strategic management and types of strategic planning.
- Emphasized the role of strategic leaders in shaping strategy formulation and the strategy process.
- New Strategy Highlight 2.1 on Merck's core values and the development of drugs to treat river blindness and the challenges with the Vioxx recall.
- Added new ethical/social issues question asking students to identify whether actual company vision/mission statements are customer- or product-oriented, or a combination.
- Added a new small-group exercise related to STEM (science, technology, engineering, and math) disciplines and U.S. competitiveness.

CHAPTER 3

- New ChapterCase about Tesla Motors and the U.S. automotive industry.
- Sharpened the PESTEL discussion by subsuming Political/Legal factors and updating examples.
- Added new Strategy Highlight 3.1 on the Eurozone crisis (in the PESTEL discussion).
- Significantly expanded discussion of Porter's five forces to allow for in-depth treatment with current example (including new Strategy Highlight 3.2 on the five forces in the airline industry).
- Added B-section titled "Competition in the Five Forces Model" to highlight two key assumptions in this model.
- Subsumed structure-conduct-performance (SCP) model under "Rivalry among Existing Competitors" following Porter's seminal work in *Competitive Strategy*.
- Expanded discussion of SWOT with application example.
- Added new C-heads under threat of entry: network effects, economies of scale, customer switching costs, capital requirements, advantages independent of size, government policy, and threat of retaliation.
- Expanded the section on rivalry among existing competitors: Moved the discussion of industry structure and types into this section (the fifth force), in the subsection on competitive industry structure.
- Added Exhibit 3.4, "The Five Forces Competitive Analysis Checklist."
- Added small-group exercise (ethical/social issues) asking students to propose new guidelines for helping Kraft promote food to children in a socially responsible way.

CHAPTER 4

- New ChapterCase 4: Nike's Core Competency: The Risky Business of Fairy Tales
- Changes in chapter sequence: (1) Moved the section on how to sustain a competitive advantage to precede the value chain *section.* (2) Also moved the section on dynamic capabilities to earlier in the chapter; now precedes the value chain analysis.
- In the value chain analysis section, provided examples for low-cost and differentiated value chain.
- New Strategy Highlight 4.1: Applying VRIO: The rise and fall of Groupon.
- Discussed Circuit City as an in-text example of what happens when not reinvesting, honing, and upgrading core competencies.
- Expanded discussion of SWOT and added analysis of McDonald's in the implications for the strategist section.
- Used a new example for path dependence—why the U.S. carpet industry is based in Georgia.
- Added *activities, capabilities, dynamic capabilities,* and *isolating mechanisms* as key terms.
- Sharpened definitions and treatment of differences among *resource, capability,* and *core competence* in both text and art.
- New discussion question asks students to conduct a value chain analysis for McDonald's and then analyze whether changes in its priorities affected its value chain.
- Small-Group Exercise 2 asks students to build on the Groupon Strategy Highlight in the chapter in ways that will build dynamic capabilities and make its competencies more difficult to imitate.

CHAPTER 5

- New ChapterCase, focusing on Apple vs. BlackBerry.
- Rearranged topics in first section (on firm performance), to put accounting profitability first, followed by shareholder value creation, and then economic value creation, balanced scorecard, and triple bottom line.
- Used Apple and BlackBerry data to analyze and compare profitability.
- Updated exhibits related to accounting profitability (e.g., stock market valuations of Amazon, Apple, Google, Microsoft, and Samsung; market capitalization of Apple).
- In shareholder value section, added key term *market capitalization*.
- Added section on corporate social responsibility, in triple bottom line section.
- Added section on business models (razor-razor blade; subscription-based; pay as you go; freemium).
- In the business models section, added a detailed discussion of business model innovation, an in-text example about Zipcar, and a Strategy Highlight about Threadless.
- Revised the economic value creation discussion to focus on two companies, with the same costs but slightly different strategies. Added two new exhibits showing economic value creation for two different firms (situations)—Exhibits 5.5 and 5.6.
- New discussion question related to the Threadless Strategy Highlight.
- Added a new small-group exercise asking students to prepare a presentation in support of the triple-bottom-line approach.

CHAPTER 6

- New ChapterCase, about recent strategic initiatives at P&G that were intended to help strengthen its competitive position, including bringing back A. G. Lafley.
- New Strategy Highlight 6.1 on Whole Foods (was the ChapterCase in 1e).
- Revised integration strategy example uses stores (Nordstrom, Target, Walmart) rather than cosmetics companies.
- Moved discussion of integration strategy at the corporate level to Chapter 8.
- Added new heading for stuck in the middle ("Integration Strategy 'Gone Bad'") and used JCPenney as a text example.
- Moved discussion of mass customization into the section on integrated strategy.
- Clarified Exhibit 6.6 on effects of learning and experience.
- Reconceptualized the exhibit on value and cost drivers (now Exhibit 6.10).
- Changed ethical/social issue questions about scale of production and learning curves to a discussion question.
- Added a new ethical/social issue question relating to Whole Foods' business strategy and healthy foods.

CHAPTER 7

- Updated ChapterCase about Wikipedia.
- New section on the innovation process, introducing the "four I's"—idea, invention, innovation, imitation.
- Expanded section on entrepreneurship, including corporate and social entrepreneurship.
- Expanded the discussion of the industry life cycle section, including a subsection on the "shakeout stage."

- Added a new application of the industry life cycle to the smartphone industry in emerging and developed economies.
- Added Geoffrey Moore's "crossing the chasm" framework (unique to this text), including a text example of the application of this model to innovation in the smartphone industry.
- Added a subsection, including exhibits, on closed versus open innovation.
- Updated the discussion on accelerating technological change and moved the exhibit (from Chapter 1 in 1e).
- Clarified the text and retitled the exhibit on product and process innovation and the emergence of an industry standard, to make clear that this concept applies throughout the entire industry life cycle.
- New key terms added: *first-mover advantages, invention, patent, crossing the chasm, innovation ecosystem, organizational inertia, Pareto principle, closed innovation, open innovation.*
- Added a discussion question asking students to think about the effect of the Internet on retailing and how retailers might respond.
- Added a discussion question asking students to explore stories about *low-tech* innovations.
- Added a small-group exercise related to P&G's Connect + Develop open innovation system.

CHAPTER 8

- In the discussion of transaction cost economics, clarified the discussion on economies of scale and economies of scope. Also, changed discussion of the *scope of the firm* to the *boundaries of the firm.*
- Added new Exhibit 8.1 showing internal and external transaction costs, to aid students in understanding this somewhat abstract but critical concept in corporate strategy.
- Moved discussion of integration strategy at the corporate level to this chapter, where it now appears as Strategy Highlight 8.2 on the Tata Group, a multinational conglomerate.
- Added Exhibit 8.12 on dynamic corporate strategy, contrasting Nike and adidas.
- In Exhibit 8.2, added "Transaction-specific investments" in the Advantages/Firm box.
- Deleted all references to *horizontal integration.*
- Added as key terms *internal transaction costs, external transaction costs, core competence-market matrix,* and *strategic alliances.*
- Expanded Discussion Question 2 to apply it to Delta's vertical integration decision.
- Expanded Ethical/Social Issues Question 1 to ask students how firms can outsource HR management systems but continue to show their commitment to employees.

CHAPTER 9

- New ChapterCase about Disney and its serial acquisitions of Pixar, Marvel, and Lucas Films. Expanded and updated the discussion of M&A and its strategic alliances.
- Moved discussion of principal–agent problems to first in the list of reasons for mergers.
- Added discussion of *real-options perspective* into the section on strategic alliances.
- Added discussion of the new build-borrow-or-buy framework (Capron and Mitchell), with accompanying exhibit, in the *Implications for the Strategist* section.

- Added examples of serial acquisitions (e.g., Google bought YouTube; Google bought Waze to pre-empt Apple and FB; Google acquired Motorola's cell phone unit to be able to integrate hardware with software; Facebook bought Instagram; Yahoo bought Tumblr).
- Added as key terms: *co-opetition, build-borrow-or-buy framework.*
- Added discussion question about expected failure rates when merging with competitors as opposed to acquiring smaller companies.
- Added new ethical/social issues question about IKEA's strategic use of nonequity alliances and stakeholder partnerships.
- Added a new small-group exercise about the wave of consolidations in the U.S. office furniture-manufacturing industry located primarily in Michigan.
- Revised the second small-group exercise about social media usage in 2012 by the Fortune Global 100 companies.

CHAPTER 10

- Updated the ChapterCase with new data about the global appeal of Hollywood movies especially in regard to China.
- Revised the discussion of the integration-responsiveness framework to use more traditional terminology: international strategy, multidomestic strategy, global-standardization strategy, transnational strategy.
- Changed discussion of the stages of globalization from a Strategy Highlight box to text.
- Added discussion of Ghemawat's *World 3.0* framework.
- Clarified discussion of the disadvantages of expanding internationally.
- Added the CAGE (cultural, administrative, geographic, and economic) distance framework by Ghemawat (unique to this strategy text), with an accompanying exhibit.
- Streamlined coverage of Hofstede's national culture model.
- Added MTV as an example of an ineffective global-standardization strategy: started with global strategy, moved to multidomestic, now moving to transnational strategy.
- Added new Exhibit 10.6 to show dynamic strategic positioning for MTV Music Channel.
- Added as key terms: *CAGE distance framework, multidomestic strategy.*
- Added Discussion Question 3 about Ghemawat argument that the world isn't "flat" but is "semi-globalized."
- Added a new Ethical/Social Issues section question asking students to predict the persistence of Globalization 3.0 and to project what Globalization 4.0 might look like.
- Added Small-Group Exercise 1 about employment changes as U.S. companies become more globalized.
- Added new *my*Strategy feature about a personal strategy for building the three components of a global mind-set.

CHAPTER 11

- Introduced new model of how to assess strategic initiatives in regard to time horizon and resources required.
- Expanded discussion of SWOT implementation with application example (McDonald's) in the "Implications for the Strategist" section.
- Added and discussed key term: *core rigidity.*
- Added new Discussion Question 2 asking students to describe the values, norms, and artifacts of an organization with which they are familiar.

- Added new Ethical/Social Issues section question about organization culture and sports teams.
- Added a new small-group exercise asking students to think about how a university might apply the ROWE theory.

CHAPTER 12

- New ChapterCase on the continuing boardroom soap opera at Hewlett-Packard (highlighting how much HP deviated from its celebrated HP Way, shown in Exhibit 12.1).
- Strengthened the focus on the board of directors as a key corporate governance mechanism.
- Expanded the discussion of corporate governance and moved it to earlier in the chapter. Expansion includes more on agency theory (with related exhibit), adverse selection, moral hazard.
- Integrated discussion (and related exhibit) of a survey about attitudes toward corporate social responsibility across the globe.
- Added new discussion of Porter's shared value creation framework (unique to this text).
- Added current examples: Galleon Group's founder, Raj Rajaratnam; Carl Icahn's attempted LBO of Dell; Fabrice Tourre of Goldman Sachs.
- Added as key terms: *shared value creation framework, adverse selection, moral hazard, leveraged buyout.*
- Added new Strategy Highlight 12.2 on securities fraud by Fabrice Tourre at Goldman Sachs, and the resulting revision to Goldman's code of conduct.
- Moved section on strategic leadership to Chapter 2.
- Moved stakeholder impact analysis to Chapter 1.
- Moved discussion of corporate social responsibility to Chapters 1 and 5.
- Added new discussion question about the Business Roundtable's recommendation that the CEO not also serve as chairman of the board.
- Added new discussion question about how Nike might apply the shared value creation framework to global economic and social needs.
- Revised questions related to Small-Group Exercise 2 about the female and minority participation on corporate boards.

MINICASES

- Added 13 brand-new MiniCases, many of which focus on China and Chinese companies competing in the West.
- Updated seven MiniCases from the first edition.

FULL-LENGTH CASES

- Added four brand-new, full-length Cases: Facebook, McDonald's, BlackBerry, and Amazon.
- Revised and updated: BetterWorldBooks, Tesla Motors, Numenta, Best Buy, and Apple.
- **All cases**—including the new and revised cases plus all cases from the first edition that were authored by Frank Rothaermel—**are available through McGraw-Hill Create.** Cases include financial data in e-format for analysis.

Instructor Resources

Multiple high-quality, fully integrated resources are available to make your teaching life easier:

- **Connect,** McGraw-Hill's online assignment and assessment system, offers a wealth of content for both students and instructors. Students will find interactive applications, chapter quizzes, templates for financial analysis, video cases, and—new in this edition—SmartBook and LearnSmart. Instructors will find tested and effective tools that enable automatic grading and student-progress tracking and reporting, and a trove of content to support teaching:

  - The **Instructors Manual (IM)** includes thorough coverage of each chapter. New in this edition, we offer two versions of the IM, for newer and experienced faculty. Included in both versions are the appropriate level of theory, recent application or company examples, teaching tips, PowerPoint references, critical discussion topics, and answers to end-of-chapter exercises.

  - The **PowerPoint (PPT)** slides provide comprehensive lecture notes, video links, and company examples not found in the textbook. There will be instructor media-enhanced slides as well as notes with outside application examples.

  - The **Test Bank** includes 100–150 questions per chapter, in a range of formats and with a greater-than-usual number of comprehension, critical-thinking, and application (or scenario-based) questions. It's tagged by learning objective, Bloom's Taxonomy levels, and AACSB compliance requirements.

  - **Links to videos** that relate to concepts from chapters. The video links include sources such as Big Think, Stanford University's Entrepreneurship Corner, *The McKinsey Quarterly,* ABC, BBC, CBS, CNN, ITN/Reuters, MSNBC, NBC, PBS, and YouTube.

- The **Online Learning Center (OLC),** located at www.mhhe.com/ftrStrategy2e, offers resources for both instructors and students:

  - At the **instructors' portion** of the OLC, which is password-protected, instructors can access all of the teaching resources described earlier, a Case Matrix relating cases to concepts within the chapters, and comprehensive Case Teaching Notes, including case financial analysis.

  - At the **students' portion** of the OLC, students can take chapter quizzes to review concepts and click on links to videos that relate back to concepts covered in the chapter and/or cases.

Frank Rothaermel was closely involved in developed all ancillaries, to ensure full integration with the strategy content in the text.

TEGRITY CAMPUS

Tegrity Campus makes class time available 24/7 by automatically capturing every lecture in a searchable format for students to review when they study and complete assignments. With a simple one-click start-and-stop process, you capture all computer screens and corresponding audio. Students can replay any part of any class with easy-to-use browser-based viewing on a PC or Mac.

Tegrity Campus' unique search feature helps students efficiently find what they need, when they need it, across an entire semester of class recordings. Help turn all your students' study time into learning moments immediately supported by your lecture.

To learn more about Tegrity, watch a two-minute Flash demo at http://tegritycampus.mhhe.com.

SIMULATIONS

- McGraw-Hill has two current strategy simulations—Business Strategy Game and GLO-BUS—that can be used with the textbook.
- For more information, contact your local McGraw-Hill sales representative.

MCGRAW-HILL CUSTOMER CARE CONTACT INFORMATION

At McGraw-Hill, we understand that getting the most from new technology can be challenging. That's why our services don't stop after you purchase our products. You can e-mail our Product Specialists 24 hours a day, seven days a week, to get product-training online. Or you can search our knowledge bank of Frequently Asked Questions on our support website. For Customer Support, call **800-331-5094,** e-mail hmsupport@mcgraw-hill.com**,** or visit www.mhhe.com/support**.** One of our Technical Support Analysts will be able to assist you in a timely fashion.

ASSURANCE OF LEARNING READY

Many educational institutions today are focused on the notion of *assurance of learning,* an important element of many accreditation standards. *Strategic Management* is designed specifically to support your assurance of learning initiatives with a simple yet powerful solution.

Each chapter in the book begins with a list of numbered learning objectives, which appear throughout the chapter as well as in the end-of-chapter assignments. Every Test Bank question for *Strategic Management* maps to a specific chapter learning objective in the textbook. Each Test Bank question also identifies topic area, level of difficulty, Bloom's Taxonomy level, and AACSB skill area. You can use our Test Bank software, *EZ Test* and *EZ Test Online,* or *Connect Management* to easily search for learning objectives that directly relate to the learning objectives for your course. You can then use the reporting features of *EZ Test* to aggregate student results in a similar fashion, making the collection and presentation of Assurance of Learning data simple and easy.

AACSB STATEMENT

McGraw-Hill/Irwin is a proud corporate member of AACSB International. Understanding the importance and value of AACSB accreditation, *Strategic Management* recognizes the curricula guidelines detailed in the AACSB standards for business accreditation by connecting selected questions in the Test Bank to the general knowledge and skill guidelines in the AACSB standards.

The statements contained in *Strategic Management* are provided only as a guide for the users of this textbook. The AACSB leaves content coverage and assessment within the purview of individual schools, the mission of the school, and the faculty. While *Strategic Management* and the teaching package make no claim of any specific AACSB qualification or evaluation, we have within *Strategic Management* labeled selected questions according to six of the general knowledge and skills areas.

Acknowledgments

Any list of acknowledgments will almost always be incomplete, but I would like to thank some special people without whom this text would not have been possible. First and foremost, my wife Kelleyn, and our children: Harris, Winston, Roman, and Adelaide. Over the last few years, I have worked longer hours than when I was a graduate student to conduct the research and writing necessary for this text and accompanying case studies and other materials. I sincerely appreciate the sacrifice this has meant for my family.

I was also fortunate to work with McGraw-Hill, and the best editorial and marketing team that one can imagine: Michael Ablassmeir (Executive Brand Manager), Paul Ducham (Managing Director), Ann Torbert (Executive Director of Development), Laura Griffin (Senior Development Editor), Elizabeth Trepkowski (Marketing Manager), Emily Hatteberg (Content Development Editor), Harvey Yep (Content Project Manager), and Matt Diamond (Designer). Thank you to senior management at McGraw-Hill Education who assembled this fine team.

I was more than fortunate to work with a number of great colleagues on various resources that accompany this text. Their names and the resources they helped with follow:

- Marne Arthaud-Day (Kansas State University) on some *Cases* and *Case Teaching Notes*
- John Burr (Purdue University) on some *Cases* and *Teaching Notes*
- Anne Fuller (California State University, Sacramento), *Connect* digital co-author
- Syeda Noorein Inamdar (San Jose State University) on *videos for the chapters and MiniCases*
- Carol Jacobson (Purdue University) on *end-of-chapter material*
- David R. King (Iowa State University) on some *Case Teaching Notes*
- Louise Nemanich (Arizona State University) on the *Instructor Resource Manual*
- Charles Newman (University of Maryland University College), on *videos for the full-length Cases*
- Chris Papenhausen (University of Massachusetts, Dartmouth) on *Strategic Financial Analysis*
- Robert Porter (University of Central Florida) on the *Running Case* in *Connect*
- Marta Szabo White (Georgia State University) on the *PowerPoint Slide Decks*
- Erin Zimmer (Northwood University) on some *Cases* and *Case Teaching Notes*

Over the years, I have been privileged to work with Karyn Lu, a superb copyeditor, on my scholarly research papers, and on this project. Karyn has been much more than a copyeditor, she has been a sounding board for ideas and has helped to make the delivery of the content as user-friendly as possible. Karyn was also instrumental in launching the social media support for professors and students on www.ftrStrategy, the Facebook strategy blog, and the Twitter feed for this text, a novel addition in the strategy content market.

I would also like to thank Kelly Byrom for sharing her expertise in creating a sophisticated graphic design for the exhibits; Melissa Appleyard (Portland State University) and Carol Jacobson (Purdue University) for providing solid content and editorial suggestions; and Andrea Meyer and Laura Winig for superb case content editing.

The Georgia Institute of Technology provided a conducive intellectual environment and superb institutional support to make this project possible. I thank Russell and Nancy McDonough for generously funding the endowed chair that I am honored to hold. I'm grateful for Dean Salbu and Senior Associate Dean Narasimhan for providing the exceptional leadership that allows faculty to fully focus on research, teaching, and service. I have been at Georgia Tech for over a decade, and could not have had better colleagues—all of whom are not only great scholars but also fine individuals whom I'm fortunate to have as friends: Marco Ceccagnoli, Annamaria Conti, Stuart Graham, Matt Higgins, David Ku, Jay Lee, John McIntyre, Alex Oettl, Henry Sauermann, Jerry Thursby, Marie Thursby, and Uriel Stettner at Georgia Tech. We have a terrific group of current and former PhD students, many of whom had a positive influence on this project, including Shanti Agung (Drexel University), Drew Hess (University of Virginia), Kostas Grigoriou (Florida International University), Jaiswal Mayank, Nicola McCarthy, German Retana (INCAE Business School, Costa Rica), Briana Sell, Jose Urbina, Carrie Yang, and Wei Zhang (Singapore Management University).

I'd also like to thank the students at Georgia Tech, in the undergraduate and full-time day MBA, and the evening and executive MBA programs, as well as the executive MBA students from the ICN Business School in Nancy, France, on whom the materials were beta-tested. Their feedback helped fine-tune the content and delivery. Last, but certainly not least, I wish to thank the reviewers and focus group attendees who shared their expertise with us, from the very beginning when we developed the prospectus to the final text and cases that you hold in your hands. The reviewers have given us the greatest gift of all—the gift of time! These very special people are listed starting on page xxxi.

I have long yearned to write a text that shows students and managers how exciting strategic management can be, but that at the same time presents the recent developments in the field, including the rigor upon which concepts and frameworks are now built, to make better strategic decisions in a turbulent and dynamic world. I'm fortunate that I had the support of many people to make this vision become a reality, and I'm truly grateful.

Frank T. Rothaermel
Georgia Institute of Technology

Web: http://ftrStrategy.com
Strategy Blog: http://www.facebook.com/ftrStrategy
Twitter: @ftrStrategy

THANK YOU . . .

This book has gone through McGraw-Hill Education's thorough development process. Over the course of several years, the project has benefited from numerous developmental focus groups and symposiums, from hundreds of reviews from reviewers across the country, and from beta-testing of the first-edition manuscript on a variety of campuses. The author and McGraw-Hill wish to thank the following people who shared their insights, constructive criticisms, and valuable suggestions throughout the development of this project. Your contributions have improved this product.

Second Edition

REVIEWERS

Todd Alessandri
Northeastern University

Cory J. Angert
University of Houston-Downtown

Asli Arikan
The Ohio State University

Jeffery Bailey
University of Idaho

Kevin Banning
Auburn University at Montgomery

Jeff Barden
Oregon State University

Patricia Beckenholdt
University of Maryland University College

John Burr
Purdue University

Richard A. L. Caldarola
Troy University

Brent Clark
University of South Dakota

Timothy S. Clark
Northern Arizona University

Anne N. Cohen
University of Minnesota

Brian Connelly
Auburn University

W. J. Conwell
University of Texas at El Paso

Cynthia S. Cycyota
United States Air Force Academy

Samuel DeMarie
Iowa State University

Irem Demirkan
Northeastern University

Geoffrey Desa
San Francisco State University

Edward Desmarais
Salem State University

Michael E. Dobbs
Eastern Illinois University

William J. Donoher
Missouri State University

Tom Douglas
University of Maryland University College and Colorado State University

Stephen A. Drew
Florida Gulf Coast University

Derrick E. D'Souza
University of North Texas

Helen Eckmann
Brandman University

Linda Edelman
Bentley University

Alan Ellstrand
University of Arkansas-Fayetteville

David Epstein
University of Houston-Downtown

James Fiet
University of Louisville

William Foxx
Troy University

Patrick Greek
Macomb Community College

Shirley A. Green
Indian River State College

Regina A. Greenwood
Nova Southeastern University

Robert D. Gulbro
Athens State University

Craig Gustin
Arizona State University

Ahma Hassan
Morehead State University

Scott D. Hayward
Appalachian State University

Theodore T. Herbert
Rollins College

Scott Hicks
Liberty University

Glenn Hoetker
Arizona State University

R. Michael Holmes, Jr.
Florida State University

Tammy Huffman
Utah Valley University

Syeda Noorein Inamdar
San Jose State University

Ana Elisa Iglesias
Tulane University

Sean Jasso
University of California, Riverside

Mahesh P. Joshi
George Mason University

Brent Kinghorn
Missouri State University

Frank Kozak
Bowling Green State University

Mario Krenn
Louisiana State University

Melody LaPreze
Missouri State University

Hun Lee
George Mason University

Tammy G. Hunt
University of North Carolina Wilmington

Charles J. F. Leflar
University of Arkansas-Fayetteville

Aristotle T. Lekacos
Stony Brook University

Tatiana S. Manolova
Bentley University

Daniel B. Marin
Louisiana State University

Sarah Marsh
Northern Illinois University

Patricia Matuszek
Troy University-Montgomery

Jeffrey E. McGee
The University of Texas at Arlington

Mike Montalbano
Bentley University

Todd Moss
Oregon State University

John Mullane
Middle Tennessee State University

Chandran Mylvaganam
Northwood University-Michigan

Charles Newman
University of Maryland University College

Jill Novak
Indian River State College

Frank Novakowski
Davenport University

Jeffrey R. Nystrom
University of Colorado Denver

Kenny (Kyeungrae) Oh
University of Missouri-St. Louis

Kevin J. O'Mara
Elon University

Eren Ozgen
Troy University-Dothan

Mark Packard
University of Missouri-Columbia

Clifford R. Perry
Florida International University

Antoaneta Petkova
San Francisco State University

Erin Pleggenkuhle-Miles
University of Nebraska-Omaha

Robert Porter
The University of Central Florida

Vasudevan Ramanujam
Case Western Reserve University

Christopher Reutzel
Utah State University

Gary B. Roberts
Kennesaw State University

Elton Scifres
Stephen F. Austin State University

Tim Schoenecker
Southern Illinois University-Edwardsville

Wendell Seaborne
Franklin University

Deborah Searcy
Florida Atlantic University

Jennifer Sexton
Florida State University

Eugene Simko
Monmouth University

Ned Smith
University of Michigan

Mark Starik
San Francisco State University

Mohan Subramaniam
Boston College

Ram Subramanian
Montclair State University

Jing'an Tang
Sacred Heart University

Paul W. Thurston, Jr.
Siena College

Jorge Walter
The George Washington University

Marta Szabo White
Georgia State University

Carolyn Wiethoff
Indiana University

Beth Woodard
Belmont University

Chuanyin Xie
The University of Tampa

SYMPOSIUM ATTENDEES

M. David Albritton
Northern Arizona University

Melissa Appleyard
Portland State University

LaKami T. Baker
Auburn University

James W. Bronson
University of Wisconsin-Whitewater

Barry Bunn
Valencia College

Janice F. Cerveny
Florida Atlantic University

Brian Connelly
Auburn University

John E. Gentner
University of Dayton

Theodore A. Khoury
Portland State University

Jerry Kopf
Radford University

Hun Lee
George Mason University

Rick McPherson
University of Washington

John M. Mezias
University of Miami

Don O. Neubaum
Oregon State University

Charles Newman
University of Maryland University College

Frank Novakowski
Davenport University

Don A. Okhomina
Fayetteville State University

Clifford R. Perry
Florida International University

Carolyn Wiethoff
Indiana University

Scott Williams
Wright State University

Cathy Coleman Wood
University of Tennessee

First Edition
REVIEWERS

Joshua R. Aaron
East Carolina University

Moses Acquaah
University of North Carolina at Greensboro

Garry Adams
Auburn University

Todd Alessandri
Northeastern University

Brent B. Allred
The College of William & Mary

Semiramis Amirpour
University of Texas at El Paso

Melissa Appleyard
Portland State University

Marne Arthaud-Day
Kansas State University

Bindu Arya
University of Missouri-St. Louis

Seung Bach
California State University, Sacramento

David Baker
Kent State University

Dennis R. Balch
University of North Alabama

Edward R. Balotsky
Saint Joseph's University

Kevin Banning
Auburn University at Montgomery

Geoff Bell
University of Minnesota, Duluth

Heidi Bertels
City University of New York

Tim Blumentritt
Kennesaw State University

William C. Bogner
Georgia State University

Dorothy Brawley
Kennesaw State University

Michael G. Brizek
South Carolina State University

James W. Bronson
University of Wisconsin-Whitewater

Jill A. Brown
Bentley University

Clint Chadwick
University of Alabama in Huntsville

Kenneth H. Chadwick
Nicholls State University

Betty S. Coffey
Appalachian State University

Anne N. Cohen
University of Minnesota

Susan K. Cohen
University of Pittsburgh

Parthiban David
American University

Darla Domke-Damonte
Coastal Carolina University

Stephen A. Drew
Florida Gulf Coast University

Arthur J. Duhaime III
Nichols College

David Duhon
University of Southern Mississippi

Danielle Dunne
Fordham University

Alan Ellstrand
University of Arkansas-Fayetteville

David Epstein
University of Houston Downtown

Michael M. Fathi
Georgia Southwestern State University

Kevin Fertig
University of Illinois at Urbana, Champaign

Robert S. Fleming
Rowan University

Daniel Forbes
University of Minnesota

Isaac Fox
University of Minnesota

Susan Fox-Wolfgramm
Hawaii Pacific University

Steven A. Frankforter
Winthrop University

Anne W. Fuller
California State University, Sacramento

Venessa Funches
Auburn University, Montgomery

Jeffrey Furman
Boston University

J. Michael Geringer
California Polytechnic State University, San Luis Obispo

Debbie Gilliard
Metropolitan State College of Denver

Michelle Gittelman
Rutgers University

Devi R. Gnyawali
Virginia Tech

Sanjay Goel
University of Minnesota Duluth

Steve Gove
Virginia Tech

Michael Gunderson
University of Florida

Craig Gustin
American InterContinental University

Stephen F. Hallam
University of Akron

Jon Timothy Heames
West Virginia University

Richard A. Heiens
University of South Carolina, Aiken

Duane Helleloid
University of North Dakota

Andrew M. Hess
University of Virginia

Ken Hess
Metropolitan State University

Phyllis Holland
Valdosta State University

Stephen V. Horner
Arkansas State University

George Hruby
Cleveland State University

Tammy Hunt
University of North Carolina Wilmington

Syeda Noorein Inamdar
San Jose State University

John G. Irwin
Troy University

Carol K. Jacobson
Purdue University

Scott Johnson
Oklahoma State University

Mahesh P. Joshi
George Mason University

Necmi Karagozoglu
California State University, Sacramento

J. Kay Keels
Coastal Carolina University

Franz Kellermanns
University of North Carolina, Charlotte

Jerry Kopf
Radford University

Bruce C. Kusch
Brigham Young University, Idaho

K. Blaine Lawlor
University of West Florida

Marty Lawlor
Rochester Institute of Technology

John Lawrence
University of Idaho

Jon Lehman
Vanderbilt University

David Leibsohn
California State University, Fullerton

Jun Lin
State University of New York (SUNY), New Paltz

Joseph Mahoney
University of Illinois at Urbana-Champaign

Paul Mallette
Colorado State University

Daniel B. Marin
Louisiana State University

Louis Martinette
University of Mary Washington

Anthony U. Martinez
San Francisco State University

David Major
Indiana University

David McCalman
University of Central Arkansas

Jeffrey E. McGee
The University of Texas at Arlington

Michael Merenda
University of New Hampshire

Grant Miles
University of North Texas

Michael Miller
University of Illinois at Chicago

Elouise Mintz
Saint Louis University

Gwen Moore
University of Missouri-St. Louis

James P. Morgan
Webster University, Fort Leonard Wood

Richard T. Mpoyi
Middle Tennessee State University

Chandran Mylvaganam
Northwood University-Michigan

Louise Nemanich
Arizona State University

Frank Novakowski
Davenport University

Kevin J. O'Mara
Elon University

Chris Papenhausen
University of Massachusetts, Dartmouth

James M. Pappas
Oklahoma State University

Ronaldo Parente
Florida International University

Srikanth Paruchuri
Pennsylvania State University

Keith Perry
San Jose State University

Christine Cope Pence
University of California, Riverside

Luis A. Perez-Batres
Central Michigan University

JoDee Phillips
Kaplan University

Michael Pitts
Virginia Commonwealth University

Robert Porter
University of Central Florida

Richard A. Quinn
University of Central Florida

Vasudevan Ramanujam
Case Western Reserve University

Annette L. Ranft
University at Tennessee

Gary B. Roberts
Kennesaw State University

Simon Rodan
San Jose State University

Yassir M. Samra
Manhattan College

Michael D. Santoro
Lehigh University

Gary Scudder
Vanderbilt University

Jim Sena
California Polytechnic State University, San Luis Obispo

Anju Seth
Virginia Tech

Deepak Sethi
Old Dominion University

Mark Sharfman
University of Oklahoma

Thomas Shirley
San Jose State University

Eugene Simko
Monmouth University

Faye A. Sisk
Mercer University, Atlanta

Lise Anne D. Slatten
University of Louisiana, Lafayette

Garry D. Smith
Mississippi State University

James D. Spina
University of Maryland

Jing'an Tang
Sacred Heart University

Linda F. Tegarden
Virginia Tech

Thuhang Tran
Middle Tennessee State University

Kim K. J. Tullis
University of Central Oklahoma

Beverly B. Tyler
North Carolina State University

Isaiah O. Ugboro
North Carolina A&T State University

Bruce Walters
Louisiana Tech University

Jia Wang
California State University, Fresno

Andrew Ward
Lehigh University

Vincent Weaver
Greenville Technical College

Joel West
Claremont Graduate University

Laura Whitcomb
California State University, Los Angeles

Margaret White
Oklahoma State University

Marta Szabo White
Georgia State University

Ross A. Wirth
Franklin University

Michael J. Zhang
Sacred Heart University

Zhe Zhang
Eastern Kentucky University

Yanfeng Zheng
The University of Hong Kong

Arvids A. Ziedonis
University of Oregon

CHAPTER**CASE 3**

Tesla Motors and the U.S. Automotive Industry

THE BIG THREE—GM, Ford, and Chrysler—dominated the U.S. car market throughout most of the 20th century. Having enjoyed protection behind high entry barriers, GM once held more than a 50 percent U.S. market share and was highly profitable for many decades, until about 1980. Ford and Chrysler both also did well during this period. However, as competition in the industry became increasingly global, foreign carmakers entered the U.S. market, at first mainly by importing vehicles from overseas plants. Among the first were German carmakers Volkswagen (now also owner of the Porsche and Audi brands), Daimler, and BMW, as well as Japanese carmakers Honda, Toyota, and Nissan. These foreign entrants intensified competition, threatened the Big Three's market share, and led to political pressure to impose import restrictions in the 1980s. Not to be stopped, the new players responded by buil[...] import restrictions. Hyundai and Kia h[...] ing and selling cars [...]

Although globa[...] the way for signific[...] market, the world[...]

PayPal. The sale of both companies amounted to close to $2 billion, which allowed Musk to focus on his lifelong passions in science, engineering, and space. Musk is founder of and currently runs three different companies: SpaceX (which made history in May 2012 as the first private company to deliver a cargo payload to the International Space Station with its Dragon spacecraft), SolarCity (basically the Walmart of solar panel installations for business and residential customers), and Tesla Motors, an all-electric American car company. It is Tesla where Mr. Musk is currently focusing most of his attention.

As we have discussed, the U.S. automotive industry is characterized by high entry barriers. However,

CHAPTER**CASE 3** / Consider This …

ALTHOUGH TESLA MOTORS has been successful in entering the U.S. automotive market using innovative new technology, its continued success will depend on other firm and industry factors. While industry forces have been favorable for a long time in the U.S. automotive industry, recent dynamics have lowered the profit potential of competing in this industry and thus reduced its attractiveness. Now that Tesla Motors has demonstrated how new technology can be used to circumvent entry barriers, other new ventures may soon follow. Moreover, the incumbent firms are also adopting the new technology by introducing hybrid or all-electric cars, further increasing rivalry in the industry.

Another external industry force that Tesla Motors must address is the bargaining power of suppliers. Lithium-ion battery packs are key components for Tesla's electric engines. They are supplied by only a few technology firms such as Panasonic in Japan. Given that these sources are few, the bargaining power of suppliers in the electric car segment is quite high, further limiting the industry's profit potential. As a consequence of the strong bargaining power of suppliers, combined

In addition, when demand is slowing, excess capacity tends to develop in the automotive industry, and the incumbent car companies begin to initiate a cut-throat price competition to move inventory. Although both GM and Chrysler went into Chapter 11 bankruptcy, neither exited the industry but rather restructured, causing excess capacity to remain in the industry. Finally, complementary products and services such as battery charging and service stations, which are not yet ubiquitous, are needed to help consumers overcome anxieties concerning electric vehicle ownership.

Questions

Thinking about ChapterCase 3, answer the following questions.

1. Which PESTEL factors are the most salient for the electric vehicle segment of the car industry? Do you see a future for electric vehicles in the U.S.? Why or why not?

ChapterCases bookend the chapter topic and focus on companies and industries of interest to students. The opening statement lays out a situation or issue that the chapter will address. The "**Consider This…**" section at the end of the chapter introduces additional information, plus concepts and information from the chapter to extend and complete the ChapterCase example. Questions in the "Consider This…" section are good jumping-off points for class discussion.

Twenty **MiniCases**, with suggested links to related chapters, follow Chapter 12. These short cases focus on a decision scenario that a company's manager might face. They offer dynamic opportunities to apply strategy concepts by assigning them as add-ons to chapters, either as individual assignments or as group work, or by using them for class discussion. In this second edition, half of the MiniCases focus on global companies.

MiniCase 10

From Good to Great to Gone: The Rise and Fall of Circuit City

IN THE 1990S, Circuit City was the largest and most successful consumer-electronics retailer in the United States. Indeed, Circuit City was so successful it was included as one of only 11 companies featured in Jim Collins' bestseller *Good to Great*. To qualify for this august group of high performers, a company had to attain "extraordinary results, averaging cumulative stock returns 6.9 times the general market in the 15 years following their transition points."[1] Indeed, Circuit City was the *best-performing* company on Collins' good-to-great list, outperforming the stock market 18.5 times during the 1982–1997 period.

How did Circuit City become so successful? The company was able to build and refine a set of core competencies that enabled it to create a higher economic value than its competitors. In particular, Circuit City created world-class competencies in efficient and effective logistics expertise. It deployed sophisticated point-of-sale and inventory-tracking technology, supported by IT investments that enabled the firm to connect the flow of information among geographically dispersed stores. This expertise in turn allowed detailed tracking of customer preferences and enabled Circuit City to respond quickly to changing trends. The company also relied on highly motivated, well-trained sales personnel to provide superior service and thus build and maintain customer loyalty. These core competencies enabled Circuit City to implement a "4S business model"—service, selection, savings, and satisfaction—that it applied to big-ticket consumer electronics with an unmatched degree of consistency throughout the United States.

Perhaps even more important during the company's high-performance run, many capable competitors were unable to replicate Circuit City's core competencies. Further underscoring Circuit City's superior performance is the fact, as Jim Collins described it, that "if you had to choose between $1 invested in Circuit

City or $1 invested in General Electric on the day that the legendary Jack Welch took over GE in 1981 and held [that investment] to January 1, 2000, you would have been better off with Circuit City—by [a factor of]

Frank T. Rothaermel prepared this MiniCase from public sources. It is developed for the purpose of class discussion. It is not intended to be used for any kind of endorsement, source of data, or depiction of efficient or inefficient management. All opinions expressed, and all errors and omissions, are entirely the author's. © Rothaermel, 2014.

SOURCE: http://www.wired.com/gadgetlab/2009/03/circuit-city-g/

427

Get Them **Thinking** . . .

Strategy Highlight boxes apply a specific concept to a specific company. Two per chapter, they are long enough to contain valuable insights, yet short enough to encourage student reading.

NEW in this edition, **Implications for the Strategist** sections present practical implications of the concepts and frameworks discussed in the chapter. They enable the student to build a cumulative toolkit in strategic management that bridges the gap between theory and practice.

A variety of end-of-chapter features meet varying course needs:

- **Take-Away Concepts** (chapter summaries) and **Key Terms** help students review important content.
- **Discussion Questions, Social/Ethical Issues,** and **Small-Group Exercises** have been updated to more closely link chapter concepts and provide newly updated examples and applications.
- The **Strategy Term Project** provides an extended, "hands-on" project, divided across chapters into a series of focused, targeted tasks.
- The *my*Strategy feature shows students how to internalize and apply strategy concepts to their lives and careers.

Connect Strategic Management offers a variety of tools and content to enhance productivity and increase student performance.

Available for Rothaermel, 2e, Connect is an integrated technology solution that increases student engagement and comprehension, automates assignment delivery and grading, and through a variety of reports monitors whether learning objectives are met. Connect Strategic Management provides a wide array of tools and content to improve student performance.

LEARNSMART ADVANTAGE

LearnSmart®

LearnSmart is the most widely used and intelligent adaptive learning resource that is proven to strengthen memory recall, improves course retention, and boost grades.

Distinguishing what students know from what they don't, and honing in on concepts they are most likely to forget, LearnSmart continuously adapts to each student's needs by building an individual learning path so students study smarter and retain more knowledge.

Smartbook™

Fueled by LearnSmart—SmartBook is the first and only adaptive reading experience available today.

Assessing what a student knows or doesn't know, and focusing on the concepts the student is likely to forget, SmartBook personalizes content for each student in a continuously adapting reading experience. Reading is no longer a passive and linear experience, but an engaging and dynamic one, through which students are more likely to master and retain important concepts, coming to class better prepared. Valuable reports provide instructors insight as to how students are progressing through textbook content, which is useful for shaping in-class time and assessments.

As a result of the adaptive reading experience found in SmartBook, students are more likely to retain knowledge, stay in class, and get better grades. This revolutionary technology is available only from McGraw-Hill Education and for hundreds of course areas as part of the LearnSmart Advantage series.

CONNECT FEATURES

Running Case

Students will begin by reviewing a specific company and the company's applied strategy using appropriate tools (e.g., PESTEL, Porter's Five Forces, VRIO, SWOT, and others). The analysis will progress from a broad global view, to an industry view, to a strategic group view, and then focus on the company itself, moving from a broad perspective to the appropriate company-level perspective. Students will develop a strategic analysis for the company and consider several scenarios for the company to improve its competitive advantage. The scenarios will include a financial analysis and justification and ultimately provide a specific recommendation.

Interactive Applications

Interactive Applications offer a variety of automatically graded exercises that require students to **apply** key concepts. Whether the assignment includes a *drag and drop, video case, timeline/sequencing,* or *case analysis*, these applications provide instant feedback and progress tracking for students, and detailed results for the instructor.

Resources for Analysis

Resources for student analysis of industries, companies, and strategies include:

- **Templates for strategic financial analysis** and a **How to do a case analysis guide**, complete with financial ratios used to compare performance between firms.
- A **financial review activity**—for students who wish to *refresh* or *extend* their working knowledge of major financial measures in a strategic framework.

Connect Instructor's Manual

New to this edition is a guidebook to walk instructors through the various Connect content available with 2e. It comes complete with general Connect recommendations, screen shots of interactive applications to reference for use with chapters, and suggested follow-up activities.

For more information, contact your McGraw-Hill Learning Technology Consultant or visit

www.McGrawHillConnect.com

Strategy Analysis

The AFI Strategy Framework

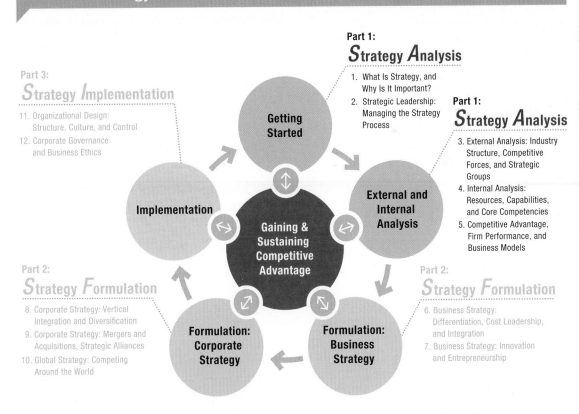

Part 1:
*S*trategy *A*nalysis
1. What Is Strategy, and Why Is It Important?
2. Strategic Leadership: Managing the Strategy Process

Part 1:
*S*trategy *A*nalysis
3. External Analysis: Industry Structure, Competitive Forces, and Strategic Groups
4. Internal Analysis: Resources, Capabilities, and Core Competencies
5. Competitive Advantage, Firm Performance, and Business Models

Part 3:
*S*trategy *I*mplementation
11. Organizational Design: Structure, Culture, and Control
12. Corporate Governance and Business Ethics

Part 2:
*S*trategy *F*ormulation
8. Corporate Strategy: Vertical Integration and Diversification
9. Corporate Strategy: Mergers and Acquisitions, Strategic Alliances
10. Global Strategy: Competing Around the World

Part 2:
*S*trategy *F*ormulation
6. Business Strategy: Differentiation, Cost Leadership, and Integration
7. Business Strategy: Innovation and Entrepreneurship

Getting Started

External and Internal Analysis

Implementation

Gaining & Sustaining Competitive Advantage

Formulation: Corporate Strategy

Formulation: Business Strategy

What Is Strategy, and Why Is It Important?

Learning Objectives

After studying this chapter, you should be able to:

LO 1-1   Explain the role of strategy in a firm's quest for competitive advantage.

LO 1-2   Define competitive advantage, sustainable competitive advantage, competitive disadvantage, and competitive parity.

LO 1-3   Differentiate the roles of firm effects and industry effects in determining firm performance.

LO 1-4   Evaluate the relationship between stakeholder strategy and sustainable competitive advantage.

LO 1-5   Conduct a stakeholder impact analysis.

CHAPTERCASE 1

Apple: Once the World's Most Valuable Company

ON AUGUST 20, 2012, Apple's stock market valuation reached $623 billion, making it the most valuable public company of all time.[1] A mere 15 years earlier, Apple would likely have gone bankrupt if archrival Microsoft (which enjoyed the same position with a valuation of $615 billion in December 1999) had not invested $150 million in Apple. How did Apple become so successful?

Apple became the world's most successful company due to a powerful competitive strategy. That strategy, conceptualized by co-founder Steve Jobs, combines innovation in products, services, and business models. From near-bankruptcy in 1997, Apple's revitalization really took off in the fall of 2001 when it introduced the iPod, a portable digital music player. Eighteen months later, Apple soared even higher when it opened the online store iTunes, quickly followed by its first retail stores. Apple's stores now earn the highest sales per square foot of any retail outlets, including luxury stores such as Tiffany & Co. jewelry or LVMH, purveyor of fine handbags and other luxury goods.

Apple didn't stop there. In 2007, the company revolutionized the smartphone market with the introduction of the iPhone. Just three years later, Apple created the tablet computer industry by introducing the iPad, thus beginning to reshape the publishing and media industries. Further, for each of its iPod, iPhone, and iPad lines of businesses,

Apple followed up with incremental product innovations extending each product category. By combining tremendous brain power, intellectual property, and iconic brand value, Apple has enjoyed dramatic increases in revenues. More traditional firms such as Exxon Mobil and GE—each at one time the world's most valuable company—can now only dream of such results.

In the fall of 2012, investors' expectations of Apple's future growth potential in burgeoning industries such as the mobile Internet, TV, and other media propelled its share price to over $700. Some analysts contend that Apple may become the first $1 trillion company on the planet. What will it take to achieve that? To do so, Apple must continue to find new industries to revolutionize, while at the same time increase its global market penetration in emerging economies such as China and India.[2]

After reading this chapter, you will find more about this case, along with related questions, on page 19.

WHY WAS APPLE so successful? Why did Microsoft's once superior market valuation evaporate? Why did Apple's competitors such as Sony, Dell, Hewlett-Packard (HP), Nokia, and BlackBerry struggle? What must Apple do to sustain its competitive advantage, especially in light of strong performances by competitors such as Google, Amazon, and Samsung? For that matter, why is any company successful? What enables some firms to gain and then sustain their competitive advantage over time? Why do once-great firms fail? How can a firm's managers influence performance? These are the big questions that define strategic management. Answering these questions requires integrating the knowledge you've obtained in your studies of various business disciplines to understand what leads to superior performance.

strategic management
An integrative management field that combines analysis, formulation, and implementation in the quest for competitive advantage.

Strategic management is the integrative management field that combines *analysis, formulation,* and *implementation* in the quest for competitive advantage. Mastery of strategic management enables you to view a firm in its entirety. It also enables you to think like a general manager to help position your firm for superior performance. The *AFI strategy framework* (shown on page 1) embodies this view of strategic management.

In this chapter, we lay the groundwork for the study of strategic management. We'll introduce some foundational ideas about strategy and competitive advantage and then consider the role of business in society. Next, we take a closer look at the components of the AFI framework and provide an overview of the entire strategic management process. We conclude this introductory chapter, as we do with all others in this text, with a section entitled *Implications for the Strategist.* Herein, we provide practical applications and considerations of the material developed in the chapter. Let's begin the exciting journey to understand strategic management and competitive advantage.

1.1 What Strategy Is: Gaining and Sustaining Competitive Advantage

LO 1-1

Explain the role of strategy in a firm's quest for competitive advantage.

strategy The set of goal-directed actions a firm takes to gain and sustain superior performance relative to competitors.

Strategy is a set of goal-directed actions a firm takes to gain and sustain superior performance *relative* to competitors.[3] To achieve superior performance, companies compete for resources: New ventures compete for financial and human capital. Existing companies compete for profitable growth. Charities compete for donations, and social networks compete for members. In any competitive situation, a *good strategy* enables a firm to achieve superior performance.

A *good strategy* consists of three elements:[4]

1. A *diagnosis* of the competitive challenge. This element is accomplished through strategy *analysis* of the firm's external and internal environments (Part 1 of the AFI framework).
2. A *guiding policy* to address the competitive challenge. This element is accomplished through strategy *formulation,* resulting in the firm's corporate, business, and functional strategies (Part 2 of the AFI framework).
3. A *set of coherent actions* to implement the firm's guiding policy. This element is accomplished through strategy *implementation* (Part 3 of the AFI framework).

Let's revisit ChapterCase 1 and see how these three elements manifest themselves in a good strategy.

THE COMPETITIVE CHALLENGE. First, consider the diagnosis of the competitive challenge. ChapterCase 1 briefly traces Apple's renewal from the year 2001, when it hit upon the product and business-model innovations of the iPod/iTunes combination. Prior to that, Apple was merely a niche player in the desktop-computing industry, and struggling financially. Steve Jobs turned the sinking company around by focusing on only two computer models (one laptop and one desktop) in each of two market segments (the professional market and the consumer market) as opposed to dozens of non-differentiated products within each segment. This streamlining of its product lineup enhanced Apple's strategic focus. Even so, the outlook for Apple was grim. Jobs believed that Apple, with less than 5 percent market share, could not win in the personal computer industry where desktops and laptops had become commoditized gray boxes. In that world, Microsoft, Intel, and Dell were the star performers. Jobs needed to create the "next big thing."[5]

A GUIDING POLICY. Next, let's consider the guiding policy. In this case, Apple shifted its competitive focus away from personal computers to mobile devices. In doing so, Apple disrupted several industries through its product and business-model innovations. Simply put, a *business model* explains how the firm intends to make money. Combining hardware (i.e., the iPod) with a complementary service product (i.e., the iTunes Store) enabled Apple to devise a new business model. Users could now download individual songs legally (at 99 cents) rather than buying an entire CD or downloading the songs illegally using Napster and other file-sharing services. The availability of the iTunes Store drove sales of iPods. Along with rising sales for the new iPod and iTunes products, demand rose for iMacs. The new products helped disrupt the existing personal computer market, because people wanted to manage their music and photos on a computer that worked seamlessly with their mobile devices. The success of the iPod/iTunes business model innovation was then leveraged to develop and launch the iPhone and the iPad.

COHERENT ACTIONS. Finally, Apple implemented its guiding policy with a set of coherent actions. Apple's coherent actions took a two-pronged approach: First, it streamlined its product lineup through a simple rule[6]—"we will make only one laptop and one desktop model for each of the two markets we serve, professional and consumer." Second, it disrupted the industry status quo through a potent combination of product and business model innovations, executed at planned intervals. These actions allowed Apple to create a string of temporary competitive advantages. Taken together, this string of temporary competitive advantages enabled the company to sustain its superior performance over a number of years.

A good strategy is more than a mere goal or a company slogan. First, a good strategy defines the competitive challenges facing an organization through a critical and honest assessment of the status quo. Second, a good strategy provides an overarching approach (policy) on how to deal with the competitive challenges identified. Last, a good strategy requires effective implementation through a coherent set of actions.

WHAT IS COMPETITIVE ADVANTAGE?

Competitive advantage is always *relative,* not absolute. To assess competitive advantage, we compare firm performance to a *benchmark*—that is, either the performance of other firms in the same industry or an industry average. A firm that achieves superior performance relative to other competitors in the same industry or the industry average has a **competitive advantage.**[7] Apple, for instance, has achieved a competitive advantage over Google, Samsung, Nokia, and BlackBerry in the smartphone industry and over Microsoft, Amazon, Samsung, and HP in the tablet computer industry. A firm that is able to outperform its competitors or the industry average over a prolonged period of time has a **sustainable competitive advantage.**

However, past performance is no guarantee of future performance. As noted in Chapter-Case 1, Microsoft was once the most valuable company in the world, but has struggled to keep up with Apple. Microsoft, as well as Google, Samsung, Amazon, and others, is working hard to neutralize Apple's competitive advantage. Amazon's Kindle line of tablets and

LO 1-2

Define competitive advantage, sustainable competitive advantage, competitive disadvantage, and competitive parity.

competitive advantage Superior performance relative to other competitors in the same industry or the industry average.

sustainable competitive advantage Outperforming competitors or the industry average over a prolonged period of time.

Microsoft's Surface tablet computer compete against Apple's iPad. The question is whether Apple can continue to maintain a competitive advantage in the face of increasingly strong competition and rapidly changing industry environments. We provide an update on the ChapterCase in the *"Consider This . . ."* section at the end of this chapter.

If a firm underperforms its rivals or the industry average, it has a **competitive disadvantage.** For example, a 15 percent return on invested capital may sound like superior firm performance. In the energy industry, though, where the average return on invested capital is often above 20 percent, such a return puts a firm at a competitive disadvantage. In contrast, if a firm's return on invested capital is 2 percent in a declining industry such as newspaper publishing, where the industry average has been negative (–5 percent) for the last few years, then the firm has a competitive advantage. Should two or more firms perform at the same level, they have **competitive parity.** In Chapter 5, we'll discuss in greater depth how to evaluate and assess competitive advantage and firm performance.

To gain a competitive advantage, a firm needs to provide either goods or services consumers value more highly than those of its competitors, or goods or services similar to the competitors' at a lower price.[8] The rewards of superior value creation and capture are profitability and market share. Steve Jobs wanted to "put a ding in the universe"—making a difference by delivering products and services people love. Mark Zuckerberg built Facebook to make the world more open and connected. Google co-founders Larry Page and Sergey Brin were motivated to create a better search engine in order to make the world's information universally accessible. For Jobs, Zuckerberg, Page, Brin, and numerous other entrepreneurs and businesspeople, creating shareholder value and making money is the *consequence* of filling a need and providing a product, service, or experience consumers wanted, at a price they could afford. The important point here is that strategy is about creating superior value, while containing the cost to create it. Managers achieve this combination of value and cost through *strategic positioning.* That is, they stake out a unique position within an industry that allows the firm to provide value to customers, while controlling costs. The greater the difference between value creation and cost, the greater the firm's *economic contribution* and the more likely it will gain competitive advantage.

Strategic positioning requires *trade-offs,* however. As a low-cost retailer, Walmart has a clear strategic profile and serves a specific market segment. Upscale retailer Nordstrom's has also built a clear strategic profile by providing superior customer service to a specific market segment (luxury). Although these companies are in the same industry, their customer segments overlap very little, and they are not direct competitors. That is because Walmart and Nordstrom's each has chosen a distinct but different strategic position. The managers make conscious trade-offs that enable each company to strive for competitive advantage in the retail industry, using different competitive strategies: leadership versus differentiation. In regard to the customer service dimension, Walmart provides acceptable service by low-skill employees in a big-box retail outlet offering "everyday low prices," while Nordstrom's provides a superior customer experience by professional sales people in a luxury setting. A clear strategic profile—in terms of product differentiation, cost, and customer service—allows each retailer to meet specific customer needs. Competition focuses on creating value for customers (through lower prices or better service and selection, in this example) rather than destroying rivals. Even though Walmart and Nordstrom's compete in the same industry, both can win if they achieve a clear strategic position through a well-executed competitive strategy.

Since clear strategic positioning requires trade-offs, strategy is as much about deciding what *not* to do, as it is about deciding what to do.[9] Because resources are limited, managers must carefully consider their strategic choices in the quest for competitive advantage. Trying to be everything to everybody will likely result in inferior performance.

competitive disadvantage
Underperformance relative to other competitors in the same industry or the industry average.

competitive parity
Performance of two or more firms at the same level.

Strategy Highlight 1.1

JetBlue: "*Stuck in the Middle*"?

Entrepreneur David Neeleman, at the age of 25, co-founded Morris Air, a charter air service that in 1993 was purchased by Southwest Airlines (SWA). Morris Air was a low-fare airline that pioneered many cost-saving practices that later became standard in the industry, such as e-ticketing. After working as an airline executive for SWA, Neeleman founded another airline, JetBlue Airways, in 1998. When Neeleman established JetBlue, his strategy was to provide air travel at even lower costs than SWA. At the same time, he wanted to offer better service and more amenities.

JetBlue copied and improved upon many of SWA's cost-reducing activities. For example, it started out by using just one type of airplane (the Airbus A320) to lower the costs of aircraft maintenance and pilot training. It also chose to fly point to point, directly connecting highly trafficked city pairs. In contrast, legacy airlines such as Delta, United, or American use a hub-and-spoke system; such systems connect many different locations via layovers at airport hubs. The point-to-point business model focuses on directly connecting fewer but more highly trafficked city pairs. The point-to-point system lowers costs by not offering baggage transfers and schedule coordination with other airlines. In addition, JetBlue flew longer distances and transported more passengers per flight than SWA, further driving down its costs. Initially, JetBlue enjoyed the lowest cost per available seat-mile (an important performance metric in the airline industry) in the United States.

At the same time, JetBlue also attempted to enhance its differential appeal by driving up its perceived value. Its intent was to combine high-touch (to enhance the customer experience) and high-tech (to drive down costs). Some of JetBlue's value-enhancing features included high-end 100-seat Embraer regional jets with leather seats, individual TV screens with popular movie and television programming, 100 channels of XM Satellite Radio, and free in-flight Wi-Fi capabilities, along with friendly and attentive on-board service and other amenities. Also, because one-third of customers prefer speaking to a live reservation agent, despite a highly functional website for reservations and other travel-related services, JetBlue decided to employ stay-at-home parents in the United States instead of following industry best practice by outsourcing its reservation system to India. The company suggests this "home sourcing" is more productive than outsourcing; it also says that customers' appreciation of the reservation experience more than makes up for the wage differential between the U.S. and India. To sum it up, JetBlue's "Customer Bill of Rights" declared its dedication to "bringing humanity back to air travel."

In early 2007, however, JetBlue's reputation for outstanding customer service took a major hit: Several flights were delayed due to a snowstorm in which the airline kept passengers on board the aircraft; some sat on the tarmac for up to nine hours. Many wondered whether JetBlue was losing its magic touch. In May 2007, David Neeleman left JetBlue. Ever the entrepreneur, he went on to found Azul, a Brazilian airline, in 2008. For JetBlue, trying to combine a cost-leadership position with a differentiation strategy has meant that despite enjoying some early years of competitive advantage, it is now struggling to maintain that advantage.[10]

Strategy Highlight 1.1 shows how JetBlue ran into trouble by trying to combine two different competitive strategies at the same time—a *cost-leadership* strategy, focused on low cost, and a *differentiation* strategy, focused on delivering unique features and service.

Although the idea of combining different business strategies seems appealing, it is actually quite difficult to execute an *integrated* cost-leadership *and* differentiation position.

Cost leadership and differentiation are distinct strategic positions. Pursuing them at the same time results in trade-offs that work against each other. For instance, higher perceived customer value (e.g., providing leather seats throughout the entire aircraft and free Wi-Fi) comes with higher costs. JetBlue continues to pursue an integration strategy today, attempting to be both a cost leader *and* differentiator. Many firms that attempt such an *integration strategy* end up being *stuck in the middle;* that is, the managers have failed to carve out a clear strategic position. In their attempt to be everything to everybody, these firms end up being neither a low-cost leader nor a differentiator. This common strategic failure contributed to JetBlue's competitive disadvantage in recent years.

The key to successful strategy is to combine a set of activities to stake out a *unique position* within an industry. Competitive advantage has to come from performing different activities or performing the same activities differently than rivals are doing. Ideally, these activities reinforce one another rather than create trade-offs. For instance, Walmart's strategic activities strengthen its position as cost leader: Big retail stores in rural locations, extremely high purchasing power, sophisticated IT systems, regional distribution centers, low corporate overhead, and low base wages and salaries combined with employee profit sharing reinforce each other, to maintain the company's cost leadership.

In addition, operational effectiveness, marketing skills, and other functional expertise all strengthen a unique strategic position. Those capabilities, though, do not substitute for competitive strategy. Competing to be similar but just a bit better than your competitor is likely to be a recipe for cut-throat competition and low profit potential. Let's take this idea to its extreme in a quick thought experiment: If all firms in the same industry pursued a low-cost position through application of competitive benchmarking, all firms would have identical cost structures. None could gain a competitive advantage. Everyone would be running faster, but nothing would change in terms of relative strategic positions. There would be little if any value creation for customers because companies would have no resources to invest in product and process improvements. Moreover, the least-efficient firms would be driven out, further reducing customer choice.

To gain a deeper understanding of what strategy is, it may be helpful to think about what strategy is *not.*[11] Be on the lookout for the following major hallmarks of what strategy is NOT:

1. *Grandiose statements are not strategy.* You may have heard firms say things like, "Our strategy is to win" or "We will be #1." Such statements of desire, on their own, are not strategy. They provide little managerial guidance and frequently fail to address the economic fundamentals. As we will discuss in the next chapter, an effective vision and mission *can* lay the foundation upon which to craft a good strategy. This foundation must be backed up by strategic actions that allow the firm to address a competitive challenge.

2. *A failure to face a competitive challenge is not strategy.* If the firm does not define a clear competitive challenge, managers have no way of assessing whether they are making progress in addressing it. Managers at the now-defunct video rental chain Blockbuster, for example, failed to address the competitive challenges posed by new players such as Netflix, Redbox, Amazon Prime, and Hulu.

3. *Operational effectiveness, competitive benchmarking, or other tactical tools are not strategy.* People casually refer to a host of different policies and initiatives as some sort of strategy: pricing strategy, Internet strategy, alliance strategy, operations strategy, IT strategy, brand strategy, marketing strategy, HR strategy, China strategy,

and so on. All these elements may be a *necessary* part of a firm's functional and global initiatives to support its competitive strategy, but these elements are *not sufficient* to achieve competitive advantage. In this text, though, we will reserve the term *strategy* for describing the firm's overall efforts to *gain and sustain competitive advantage.*

INDUSTRY VS. FIRM EFFECTS IN DETERMINING PERFORMANCE

Firm performance is determined primarily by two factors: industry and firm effects. **Industry effects** describe the underlying economic structure of the industry. They attribute firm performance to the industry in which the firm competes. The structure of an industry is determined by elements common to all industries such as entry and exit barriers, number and size of companies, and types of products and services offered. In a series of empirical studies, academic researchers have found that the industry a firm is in determines about 20 percent of a firm's profitability.[12] In Chapter 3, when studying external analysis, we'll gain a deeper understanding of an industry's underlying structure and how it affects firm performance.

Firm effects attribute firm performance to the actions managers take. In Chapter 4, we'll take a close look inside the firm to understand why firms within the same industry differ, and how differences among firms can lead to competitive advantage.

For now, the key point is that managers' actions tend to be more important in determining firm performance than the forces exerted on the firm by its external environment.[13] Empirical research studies indicate that a firm's strategy can explain up to 55 percent of its performance.[14] Exhibit 1.1 shows these findings.

Although a firm's industry environment is not quite as important as the firm's strategy within its industry, they jointly determine roughly 75 percent of overall firm performance. The remaining 25 percent is partly attributed to business cycles and other effects.

Competition—the ongoing struggle among firms to gain and sustain competitive advantage—does not take place in isolation. Managers therefore must understand the relationship between strategic management and the role of business in society, which we will turn to next.

LO 1-3

Differentiate the roles of firm effects and industry effects in determining firm performance.

industry effects Firm performance attributed to the structure of industry in which the firm competes.

firm effects Firm performance attributed to the actions managers take.

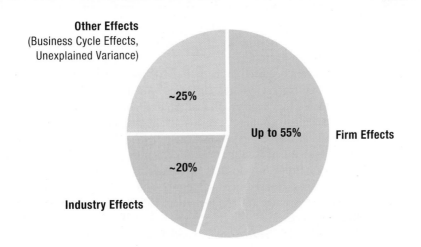

Other Effects (Business Cycle Effects, Unexplained Variance)

~25%

Up to 55% **Firm Effects**

~20%

Industry Effects

EXHIBIT 1.1

Industry, Firm, and Other Effects Explaining Superior Firm Performance

1.2 Stakeholders and Competitive Advantage

Companies with successful strategies generate value for society. When firms compete in their own self-interest while obeying the law and acting ethically, they ultimately create value. In so doing, they make society better.[15] Value creation lays the foundation for the benefits that successful economies can provide: education, public safety, and health care, among others. Superior performance allows a firm to reinvest some of its profits and to grow, which in turn provides more opportunities for employment and fulfilling careers. In ChapterCase 1, we saw that Apple created tremendous value for both its shareholders and customers, along with creating jobs.

In contrast, strategic mistakes can be expensive. Once a leading technology company, Hewlett-Packard was known for innovation, resulting in superior products. The "HP way of management" included lifetime employment, generous benefits, work/life balance, and freedom to explore ideas, among other perks. However, HP has not been able to address the competitive challenges of mobile computing or business IT services effectively. As a result, HP's stakeholders suffered. Shareholder value was destroyed. The company also had to lay off tens of thousands of employees in recent years. Its customers no longer received the innovative products and services that made HP famous.

The examples of Apple and HP illustrate the relationship between individual firms and society at large. Recently, this relationship received more critical scrutiny due to some major shocks to free-market capitalism.

black swan events
Incidents that describe highly improbable but high-impact events.

In the first decade of the 21st century, several **black swan events** eroded the public's trust in business as an institution and capitalism as an economic system.[16] In the past, most people assumed that all swans are white, so when they first encountered swans that were black, they were surprised. Today, the metaphor of a black swan describes the *high impact*

of a highly improbable event. Examples of black swan events include the fall of the Berlin Wall and the subsequent collapse of the Soviet Union, the 9/11 terrorist attacks, the Fukushima nuclear disaster in Japan, and the Arab Spring. Such events were considered to be highly improbable and thus unexpected, but when they did occur, each had a very profound impact.[17]

The implicit trust relationship between the corporate world and society at large has deteriorated due to the arrival of several black swans. One of the first black swan events of the century occurred when the accounting scandals at Enron, Arthur Andersen, WorldCom, Tyco, Adelphia, and Parmalat (of Italy) came to light. Those events led to bankruptcies, large-scale job loss, and billions of dollars in shareholder-value destruction. As a result, the public's trust in business and free-market capitalism began to erode.

Another black swan event occurred in the fall of 2008 with the global financial crisis, which shook the entire free-market system to its core.[18] A real estate bubble had developed in the United States, fueled by cheap credit and the availability of subprime mortgages. When that bubble burst, many entities faced financial stress or bankruptcy—those who had unsustainable mortgages, investors holding securities based on those mortgages, and the financial institutions that had sold the securities. Some went under, and others were sold off at fire-sale prices. Home foreclosures skyrocketed as a large number of borrowers defaulted on their mortgages. House prices in the U.S. plummeted by roughly 30 percent. The Dow Jones Industrial Average (DJIA) lost about half its market value, plunging the United States into a deep recession.

The impact was worldwide. The freezing of capital markets during the global financial crisis triggered a debt crisis in Europe. Some European governments (notably Greece) defaulted on government debt; other countries were able to repay their debts only through the assistance of other, more solvent European countries. This severe financial crisis not only put Europe's common currency, the euro, at risk, but also led to a prolonged and deep recession in Europe.

Back in the United States, the Occupy Wall Street protest movement was born in 2011 out of dissatisfaction with the capitalist system. Issues of income disparity, corporate ethics, corporate influence on governments, and ecological sustainability were key drivers. The Occupy movement, organized through social media platforms such as Twitter and Facebook, eventually expanded around the world.

Although these black swan events differed in their specifics, two common features are pertinent to our study of strategic management.[19] First, these events demonstrate that managerial actions can affect the economic well-being of large numbers of people around the globe.

The second pertinent feature relates to **stakeholders**—organizations, groups, and individuals that can affect or be affected by a firm's actions.[20] This leads us to *stakeholder strategy,* which we discuss next.

stakeholders
Organizations, groups, and individuals that can affect or are affected by a firm's actions.

STAKEHOLDER STRATEGY

Stakeholders have a vested claim or interest in the performance and continued survival of the firm. Stakeholders can be grouped by whether they are internal or external to a firm. As shown in Exhibit 1.2, *internal stakeholders* include stockholders, employees (including executives, managers, and workers), and board members. *External stakeholders* include customers, suppliers, alliance partners, creditors, unions, communities, media, and governments at various levels.

All stakeholders make specific contributions to a firm, which in turn provides different types of benefits to different stakeholders. Employees contribute their time and talents to the firm, receiving wages and salaries in exchange. Shareholders contribute capital in the hope that the stock will rise and the firm will pay dividends. Communities provide real estate, infrastructure, and public safety. In return, they expect that companies will pay taxes, provide employment, and not pollute the environment. The firm, therefore, is embedded in a multifaceted *exchange relationship* with a number of diverse internal and external stakeholders.

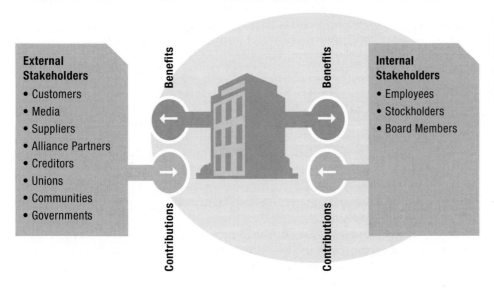

EXHIBIT 1.2

Internal and External Stakeholders in an Exchange Relationship with the Firm

External Stakeholders
- Customers
- Media
- Suppliers
- Alliance Partners
- Creditors
- Unions
- Communities
- Governments

Internal Stakeholders
- Employees
- Stockholders
- Board Members

Benefits

Contributions

If any of the stakeholders withholds participation in the firm's exchange relationships, it can have severe negative performance implications. The aerospace company, Boeing, for example, has a long history of acrimonious labor relations, leading to walk-outs and strikes. This in turn has not only delayed production of airplanes but also raised costs. More recently, borrowers who purchased subprime mortgages are stakeholders (in this case, customers) of financial institutions. When they defaulted in large numbers, they threatened the survival of these financial institutions and, ultimately, of the entire financial system.

stakeholder strategy
An integrative approach to managing a diverse set of stakeholders effectively in order to gain and sustain competitive advantage.

Stakeholder strategy is an integrative approach to managing a diverse set of stakeholders effectively in order to gain and sustain competitive advantage.[21] The unit of analysis is the web of exchange relationships a firm has with its stakeholders (see Exhibit 1.2). Stakeholder strategy allows firms to analyze and manage how various external and internal stakeholders interact to jointly create and trade value.[22] A core tenet of stakeholder strategy is that a single-minded focus on shareholders alone exposes a firm to undue risks that can undermine economic performance and can even threaten the very survival of the enterprise. The strategist's job, therefore, is to understand the complex web of exchange relationships among different stakeholders. By doing so, the firm can proactively shape the various relationships in order to maximize the joint value created, and manage the distribution of this larger pie in a fair and transparent manner. Effective stakeholder management is an example of the actions managers can take in order to improve firm performance, thereby enhancing its competitive advantage and the likelihood of the continued survival of the firm.[23]

The Target Corporation has gathered numerous awards that reflect its strong relationship with its stakeholders. It has been named on lists such as Best Places to Work, Most Ethical Companies, Best in Class for Corporate Governance, and Grassroots Innovation. In 2013, Target again held its position in the top 50 of Fortune's Most Admired Companies List. Since its founding, Target has contributed 5 percent of its profits to education, the arts, and social services in the communities in which it operates and reached the milestone of contributing $4 million per week in 2012. To demonstrate its commitment to minorities and women, Target launched a program to bring minority- and women-owned businesses into its supply chain. Volunteerism and corporate giving strengthen the relationship Target has with its employees, consumers, local communities, and suppliers. These actions, along with many others, can help Target sustain its competitive advantage as a retailer.

Strategy scholars have provided several arguments as to why effective stakeholder management can benefit firm performance:[24]

■ Satisfied stakeholders are more cooperative and thus more likely to reveal information that can further increase the firm's value creation or lower its costs.

■ Increased trust lowers the costs for firms' business transactions.

■ Effective management of the complex web of stakeholders can lead to greater organizational adaptability and flexibility.

■ The likelihood of negative outcomes can be reduced, creating more predictable and stable returns.

■ Firms can build strong reputations that are rewarded in the marketplace by business partners, employees, and customers. Most managers do care about public perception of the firm, as evidenced by high-profile rankings such as the "World's Most Admired Companies" published annually by *Fortune*.[25] As a case in point, Apple has come in first for the last few years.

STAKEHOLDER IMPACT ANALYSIS

The key challenge of stakeholder management is to effectively balance the needs of various stakeholders. The firm of course needs to ensure that its primary stakeholders—the firm's shareholders and other investors—achieve their objectives. At the same time, the firm wants to recognize and address the needs of other stakeholders—employees, suppliers, and customers—in an ethical and fair manner, so that they too are satisfied. This all sounds good in theory, but how can managers go about this in practice?

Stakeholder impact analysis provides a decision tool with which managers can recognize, prioritize, and address the needs of different stakeholders. This tool helps the firm achieve a competitive advantage while acting as a good corporate citizen. Stakeholder impact analysis takes managers through a five-step process of recognizing stakeholders' claims. In each step, managers must pay particular attention to three important stakeholder attributes: *power, legitimacy,* and *urgency.*[26]

- A stakeholder has *power* over a company when it can get the company to do something that it would not otherwise do.
- A stakeholder has a *legitimate claim* when it is perceived to be legally valid or otherwise appropriate.
- A stakeholder has an *urgent claim* when it requires a company's immediate attention and response.

Exhibit 1.3 depicts the five steps in stakeholder impact analysis and the key questions to be asked. Let's look at each step in detail.

STEP 1: IDENTIFY STAKEHOLDERS. In step 1, the firm asks, "Who are our stakeholders?" In this step, the firm focuses on stakeholders that currently have, or potentially can have, a material effect on a company. This prioritization identifies the most powerful stakeholders (both internal and external) and their needs. For public-stock companies, key

LO 1-5

Conduct a stakeholder impact analysis.

stakeholder impact analysis A decision tool with which managers can recognize, prioritize, and address the needs of different stakeholders, enabling the firm to achieve competitive advantage while acting as a good corporate citizen.

EXHIBIT 1.3 / Stakeholder Impact Analysis

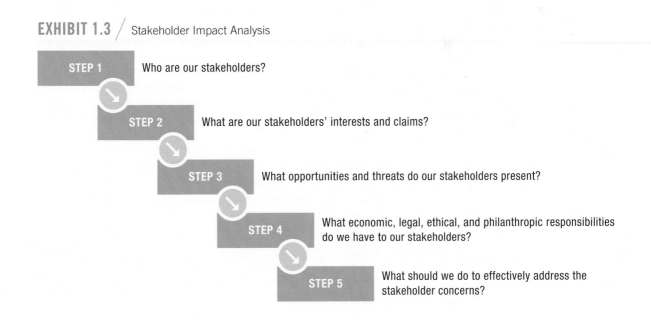

STEP 1 — Who are our stakeholders?

STEP 2 — What are our stakeholders' interests and claims?

STEP 3 — What opportunities and threats do our stakeholders present?

STEP 4 — What economic, legal, ethical, and philanthropic responsibilities do we have to our stakeholders?

STEP 5 — What should we do to effectively address the stakeholder concerns?

stakeholders are the shareholders and other suppliers of capital. If shareholders are not satisfied with returns to investment, they will sell the company's stock, leading to depreciation in the firm's market value.

A second group of stakeholders includes customers, suppliers, and unions. Any of these groups, if their needs are not met, can materially affect the company's operations. For example, the bankruptcy of Hostess Brands—the maker of Twinkies (an American snack cake)—is partially attributed to the unions' unwillingness to accept further concessions.[27] Local communities and the media are also powerful stakeholders that can materially affect the smooth operation of the firm.

STEP 2: IDENTIFY STAKEHOLDERS' INTERESTS.   In step 2, the firm asks, "What are our stakeholders' interests and claims?" Managers need to specify and assess the interests and claims of the pertinent stakeholders using the power, legitimacy, and urgency criteria introduced earlier. As the legal owners, shareholders have the most legitimate claim on a company's profits. However, the separation between ownership (by shareholders) and control of the firm (by professional managers) has been blurring. Many companies incentivize top executives by paying part of their overall compensation with stock options. They also turn employees into shareholders through *employee stock ownership plans (ESOPs)*. These plans allow employees to purchase stock at a discounted rate or use company stock as an investment vehicle for retirement savings. For example, Coca-Cola, Google, Microsoft, Southwest Airlines, Starbucks, Walmart, and Whole Foods all offer ESOPs. Clearly, the claims and interests of stakeholders who are employed by the company, and who depend on the company for salary and other benefits, will be somewhat different from those of stakeholders who merely own stock. The latter are investors who are primarily interested in the increased value of their stock holdings through appreciation and dividend payments. Executives, managers, and workers tend to be more interested in career opportunities, job security, employer-provided health care, paid vacation time, and other perks.

Even within stakeholder groups there can be significant variation in the power a stakeholder may exert on the firm. For example, public companies pay much more attention to large institutional investors than to the millions of smaller, individual investors. Institutional investors have considerable sway because of the size of their assets under management (AUM). For example, TIAA-CREF[28] has assets under management of $440 billion, CalPERS[29] has $220 billion in AUM, and The Vanguard Group has $1.6 trillion. Although both individual and institutional investors can claim the same legitimacy as stockholders, institutional investors have much more power over a firm. They can buy and sell a large number of shares at once, or exercise block-voting rights in the corporate-governance process (which we'll discuss in detail in Chapter 12). These abilities make institutional investors much more potent stakeholders.

STEP 3: IDENTIFY OPPORTUNITIES AND THREATS.   In step 3, the firm asks, "What opportunities and threats do our stakeholders present?" Since stakeholders have a claim on the company, opportunities and threats are two sides of the same coin. Consumer boycotts, for example, can be a credible threat to a company's behavior. Some consumers boycotted Nestlé products due to the firm's promotion of infant formula over breast milk in developing countries. PETA[30] called for a boycott of McDonald's due to alleged animal-rights abuses.

In the best-case scenario, managers transform such threats into opportunities. Sony Corp., for example, was able to do just that.[31] In 2001, the Dutch government blocked

Sony's entire holiday season shipment of PlayStation game systems (valued at roughly $500 million) into the European Union due to a small but legally unacceptable amount of toxic cadmium discovered in one of the system's cables. This incident led to an 18-month investigation in which Sony inspected over 6,000 supplier factories around the world to track down the source of the problem. The findings allowed Sony to redesign and develop a cutting-edge supplier management system that now adheres to a stringent extended value chain responsibility.

STEP 4: IDENTIFY SOCIAL RESPONSIBILITIES. In step 4, the firm asks, "What economic, legal, ethical, and philanthropic responsibilities do we have to our stakeholders?" To identify these responsibilities more effectively, scholars have advanced the notion of **corporate social responsibility (CSR).** This framework helps firms recognize and address the economic, legal, ethical, and philanthropic expectations that society has of the business enterprise at a given point in time.[32] According to the CSR perspective, managers need to realize that society grants shareholders the right and privilege to create a publicly traded stock company. Therefore, the firm owes something to society.[33] Moreover, CSR provides managers with a conceptual model that more completely describes a society's expectations and can guide strategic decision making more effectively. In particular, CSR has four components: economic, legal, ethical, and philanthropic responsibilities.

> **corporate social responsibility (CSR)** A framework that helps firms recognize and address the economic, legal, social, and philanthropic expectations that society has of the business enterprise at a given point in time.

Economic Responsibilities. The business enterprise is first and foremost an economic institution. Investors expect an adequate return for their risk capital. Creditors expect the firm to repay its debts. Consumers expect safe products and services at appropriate prices and quality. Suppliers expect to be paid in full and on time. Governments expect the firm to pay taxes and to manage natural resources such as air and water under a decent stewardship. To accomplish all this, firms must obey the law and act ethically in their quest to gain and sustain competitive advantage.

Legal Responsibilities. Laws and regulations are a society's codified ethics, embodying notions of right and wrong. They also establish the rules of the game. For example, business as an institution can function because property rights exist and contracts can be enforced in courts of law. Managers must ensure that their firms obey all the laws and regulations, including but not limited to labor, consumer, and environmental laws.

One far-reaching piece of U.S. legislation, for example, is the Accounting Reform and Investor Protection Act (commonly known as the Sarbanes–Oxley Act or SOX), passed in response to the accounting scandals mentioned earlier. Among different stipulations, Sarbanes–Oxley increases a CEO's and CFO's personal responsibility for the accuracy of reported accounting data. It also strengthens the independence of accounting firms (they are no longer allowed to provide consulting services to the firms they audit) and affords stronger protection for whistleblowers.

Due to a firm's significant legal responsibilities, many companies appoint compliance officers; some even have an office of corporate citizenship. At GE, for example, a vice president leads the office of corporate citizenship. Its compliance group is comprised of more than 1,000 experienced lawyers, located at the various GE businesses throughout the globe. Their mission is to help GE achieve a competitive advantage with "unyielding integrity and compliance to the law."[34]

Ethical Responsibilities. Legal responsibilities, however, often define only the minimum acceptable standards of firm behavior. Frequently, managers are called upon to go beyond

EXHIBIT 1.4 /

The Pyramid of
Corporate Social
Responsibility

SOURCE: Adapted from
A. B. Carroll (1991), "The
pyramid of corporate social
responsibility: Toward the
moral management of
organizational stakeholders,"
Business Horizons, July–
August: 42.

what is required by law. The letter of the law cannot address or anticipate all possible business situations and newly emerging concerns like Internet privacy or advances in genetic engineering and stem-cell research.

A firm's ethical responsibilities, therefore, go beyond its legal responsibilities. They embody the full scope of expectations, norms, and values of its stakeholders. Managers are called upon to do what society deems just and fair. Starbucks, for example, developed an ethical sourcing policy to help source coffee of the highest quality, while adhering to fair trade and responsible growing practices.

Philanthropic Responsibilities. Philanthropic responsibilities are often subsumed under the idea of *corporate citizenship,* reflecting the notion of voluntarily giving back to society. Over the years, Microsoft's corporate philanthropy program has donated more than $3 billion in cash and software to people who can't afford computer technology.[35]

The pyramid in Exhibit 1.4 summarizes the four components of corporate social responsibility.[36] Economic responsibilities are the foundational building block, followed by legal, ethical, and philanthropic responsibilities. Note that society and shareholders *require* economic and legal responsibilities. Ethical and philanthropic responsibilities result from a society's expectations toward business. The pyramid symbolizes the need for firms to carefully balance their social responsibilities. Doing so ensures not only effective strategy implementation, but also long-term viability.

STEP 5: ADDRESS STAKEHOLDER CONCERNS. Finally, in step 5, the firm asks, "What should we do to effectively address any stakeholder concerns?" In the last step in stakeholder impact analysis, managers need to decide the appropriate course of action for the firm, given all of the preceding factors. Thinking about the attributes of power, legitimacy, and urgency helps to prioritize the legitimate claims and to address them accordingly. Strategy Highlight 1.2 describes how the U.S. government legitimized claims by thousands of businesses and individuals in the aftermath of the BP oil spill in the Gulf of Mexico, causing the claims to become of great urgency to BP.

Strategy Highlight 1.2

BP: "Lack of Business Integrity"?

On April 20, 2010, an explosion occurred on BP's Deepwater Horizon oil drilling rig off the Louisiana coastline, killing 11 workers. The subsequent oil spill continued unabated for over three months. It released an estimated 5 million barrels of crude oil into the Gulf of Mexico, causing the largest environmental disaster in U.S. history. The cleanup alone cost BP $14 billion, and two of its employees even faced manslaughter charges.

Technical problems aside, many experts argued that BP's problems were systemic, because management had repeatedly failed to put an adequate safety culture in place. In 2005, for example, BP experienced a catastrophic accident at a Texas oil refinery, which killed 15 workers. A year later, a leaking BP pipeline caused the largest oil spill ever on Alaska's North Slope. BP's strategic focus on cost reductions, initiated a few years earlier, may have significantly compromised safety across the board.

In the aftermath of the Gulf oil spill, BP faced thousands of claims by many small business owners in the tourism and seafood industries. These business owners were not powerful individually, and pursuing valid legal claims meant facing protracted and expensive court proceedings. As a collective organized in a potential class-action lawsuit, however, they were powerful. Moreover, their claims were backed by the U.S. government, which has the power to withdraw BP's business license or cancel current permits and withhold future ones. Collectively, the small business owners along the Gulf Coast became powerful BP stakeholders, with a legitimate claim that needed to be addressed. In response, BP agreed to pay out $8 billion to settle their claims. Taken together, the monetary damages of the Deepwater Horizon disaster alone have cost BP about $22 billion to date, not to mention the loss in reputation and goodwill.

Even so, this was not the end of the story for BP. Additional fines of up to $20 billion may still come if BP is found to have committed "gross negligence." Moreover, claiming that BP displayed a "lack of business integrity" in handling the Gulf oil spill, the Environmental Protection Agency (EPA) banned BP from any new contracts with the U.S. government. If the EPA decision stands, the ban would put BP at a major competitive disadvantage. It would be unable to acquire new leases for oil field exploration in the U.S., or to continue as a major supplier of refined fuel to the armed forces.[37]

1.3 The AFI Strategy Framework

How do firms go about creating strategies that enhance their chances of achieving superior performance? A successful strategy details a set of actions that managers take to gain and sustain competitive advantage. Effectively managing the strategy process is the result of three broad tasks:

1. Analyze (A)
2. Formulate (F)
3. Implement (I)

The tasks of analyze, formulate, and implement are the pillars of research and knowledge about strategic management. Although we will study each of these tasks one at a time, they are highly interdependent and frequently happen simultaneously. Effective managers do not formulate strategy without thinking about how to implement it, for instance. Likewise, while implementing strategy, managers are constantly analyzing the need to adjust to changing circumstances.

We've captured these interdependent relationships in the **AFI strategy framework** shown in Exhibit 1.5. We want this framework to do two things: (1) to explain and predict differences in firm performance, and (2) to help managers formulate and implement a strategy that results in superior performance. In each of the three broad management tasks, managers focus on specific *questions,* listed below. We address these questions in specific chapters, as indicated.

AFI strategy framework
A model that links three interdependent strategic management tasks—analyze, formulate, and implement—that, together, help managers plan and implement a strategy that can improve performance and result in competitive advantage.

EXHIBIT 1.5 / The AFI Strategy Framework

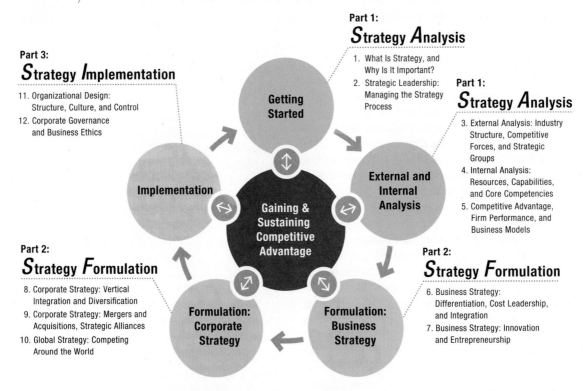

Part 1:
Strategy Analysis

1. What Is Strategy, and Why Is It Important?
2. Strategic Leadership: Managing the Strategy Process

Part 3:
Strategy Implementation

11. Organizational Design: Structure, Culture, and Control
12. Corporate Governance and Business Ethics

Part 1:
Strategy Analysis

3. External Analysis: Industry Structure, Competitive Forces, and Strategic Groups
4. Internal Analysis: Resources, Capabilities, and Core Competencies
5. Competitive Advantage, Firm Performance, and Business Models

Part 2:
Strategy Formulation

8. Corporate Strategy: Vertical Integration and Diversification
9. Corporate Strategy: Mergers and Acquisitions, Strategic Alliances
10. Global Strategy: Competing Around the World

Part 2:
Strategy Formulation

6. Business Strategy: Differentiation, Cost Leadership, and Integration
7. Business Strategy: Innovation and Entrepreneurship

(Circles in diagram: Getting Started; External and Internal Analysis; Implementation; Gaining & Sustaining Competitive Advantage; Formulation: Corporate Strategy; Formulation: Business Strategy)

Strategy Analysis *(A)* Topics and Questions

- Strategic leadership and the strategy process: *What roles do strategic leaders play? What are the firm's vision, mission, and values? What is the firm's process for creating strategy and how does strategy come about?* (Chapter 2)
- External analysis: *What effects do forces in the external environment have on the firm's potential to gain and sustain a competitive advantage?* (Chapter 3)
- Internal analysis: *What effects do internal resources, capabilities, and core competencies have on the firm's potential to gain and sustain a competitive advantage?* (Chapter 4)
- Competitive advantage, firm performance, and business models: *How does the firm make money? How can it assess and measure competitive advantage? What is the relationship between competitive advantage and firm performance?* (Chapter 5)

Strategy Formulation *(F)* Topics and Questions

- Business strategy: *How should the firm compete: cost leadership, differentiation, or integration?* (Chapters 6 and 7)
- Corporate strategy: *Where should the firm compete: industry, markets, and geography?* (Chapters 8 and 9)
- Global strategy: *How and where (local, regional, national, and international) should the firm compete: local, national, or international?* (Chapter 10)

Strategy Implementation *(I)* Topics and Questions

- Organizational design: *How should the firm organize to put the formulated strategy into practice?* (Chapter 11)
- Corporate governance and business ethics: *What type of corporate governance is most effective? How does the firm anchor strategic decisions in business ethics?* (Chapter 12)

The AFI strategy framework shown in Exhibit 1.5 will be repeated at the beginning of each part of this book, to help contextualize where we are in our study of the firm's quest to gain and sustain competitive advantage.

In addition, the *strategy process map,* presented inside the back cover, illustrates the steps in the AFI framework in more detail. The different background shades correspond to each step in the AFI framework. This strategy process map highlights the key strategy concepts and frameworks we'll cover in each chapter. It also serves as a checklist when you conduct a strategic management analysis.

1.4 ◀▶ Implications for the Strategist

The strategist realizes that the difference between success and failure lies in a firm's strategy. Applying the tools and frameworks developed in this text will allow you to help your firm be more successful. Moreover, you can also apply the strategic management toolkit to your own career to pursue your professional goals (see the *my*Strategy modules at the end of each chapter). Basically, *strategy is the science of success and failure.*

The strategist also appreciates the fact that competition is *everywhere.* The strategist knows that the principles of strategic management can be applied universally to all organizations. Strategists work in organizations from government to free enterprise, from publicly owned companies to privately owned ones, from for-profit to nonprofit organizations, and in developed as well as emerging economies. The strategist also knows that firm performance is determined by a set of interdependent factors, including firm and industry effects. The strategist is empowered by the fact that the actions he or she creates have more influence on firm performance than the external environment.

To be more effective, the strategist follows a three-step process:

1. Analyze the external and internal environments.
2. Formulate appropriate business and corporate strategies.
3. Implement the formulated strategies through structure, culture, and controls.

Keep in mind that the strategist is making decisions under conditions of uncertainty and complexity. As the strategist is following the AFI steps, he or she maintains an awareness of key stakeholders and how they can affect or be affected by the decisions that are made. The strategist then monitors and evaluates the progress toward key strategic objectives and makes adjustments by fine-tuning the strategy as necessary. We discuss how this is done in the next chapter where we focus on *strategic leaders* and *the strategic management process.*

CHAPTER**CASE 1** / Consider This . . .

NOT LONG AFTER Apple became the world's most valuable company, signs of trouble emerged. Although Apple enforced its intellectual property in a legal dispute with Samsung, it entered into a licensing agreement with HTC, a Taiwanese maker of mobile phones. Some argue that Apple under Steve Jobs' leadership would never have entered any agreements that would allow direct competitors to benefit from Apple's proprietary technology. Despite Apple's courtroom victory against Samsung, Samsung sold more smartphones than Apple in 2012. With its Galaxy S3 model running on Google's Android system, sales prove that Samsung has a viable competitor against Apple's iPhone 5. In 2013, Samsung introduced the new Galaxy S4 model, further intensifying the head-on competition with Apple.

Uncharacteristically, Apple botched the product launch for the iPhone 5. The embedded Apple map app was far inferior to Google maps, which was used in earlier versions of the iPhone. Subsequently, Apple's top management team also experienced sudden turnover, with some of its executives being forced out. In one instance, CEO Tim Cook asked Scott Forstall, vice president of iPhone and iOS Software and a Steve Jobs protégé, to leave after Forstall refused to sign an apology letter to customers for the shortcomings on the iPhone 5's mapping service. The head of Apple's famed retail operations was also forced out after only six months on the job.

After reaching $658 billion in market valuation and becoming the world's most valuable company, by March 2013 Apple's share price had dropped more than 45 percent, wiping out close to $290 billion in shareholder value. Clearly, while it is difficult to gain a competitive advantage in the first place, it is that much more difficult to sustain it.[38]

Questions

Thinking about ChapterCase 1, answer the following questions.

1. Explain Apple's success over the last decade. Think about which industries it has disrupted and how. Also take a look at Apple's main competitors.

2. Is Apple's success attributable to industry effects or firm effects, or a combination of both? Explain.

3. Apply the three-step process for developing a *good strategy* outlined above (diagnose the competitive challenge, derive a guiding policy, and implement a set of coherent actions) to Apple's situation today. Which recommendations would you have for Apple to outperform its competitors in the future?

4. Why do you think it is so hard not only to gain but also to sustain a competitive advantage?

TAKE-AWAY CONCEPTS

This chapter defined strategy and competitive advantage and discussed the role of business in society. It also set the stage for further study of strategic management, as summarized by the following learning objectives and related take-away concepts.

LO 1-1 / Explain the role of strategy in a firm's quest for competitive advantage.

- Strategy is the set of goal-directed actions a firm takes to gain and sustain superior performance relative to competitors.
- A good strategy enables a firm to achieve superior performance. It consists of three elements:
  1. A diagnosis of the competitive challenge.
  2. A guiding policy to address the competitive challenge.
  3. A set of coherent actions to implement the firm's guiding policy.

- A successful strategy requires three integrative management tasks—analysis, formulation, and implementation.

LO 1-2 / Define competitive advantage, sustainable competitive advantage, competitive disadvantage, and competitive parity.

- Competitive advantage is always judged relative to other competitors or the industry average.
- To obtain a competitive advantage, a firm must either create more value for customers while keeping its cost comparable to competitors, or it must provide the value equivalent to competitors but at a lower cost.
- A firm able to outperform competitors for prolonged periods of time has a sustained competitive advantage.

- A firm that continuously underperforms its rivals or the industry average has a competitive disadvantage.
- Two or more firms that perform at the same level have competitive parity.
- An effective strategy requires that strategic trade-offs be recognized and addressed—for example, between value creation and the costs to create the value.

LO 1-3 / Differentiate the roles of firm effects and industry effects in determining firm performance.

- A firm's performance is more closely related to its managers' actions (firm effects) than to the external circumstances surrounding it (industry effects).
- Firm and industry effects, however, are interdependent. Both are relevant in determining firm performance.

LO 1-4 / Evaluate the relationship between stakeholder strategy and sustainable competitive advantage.

- Stakeholders are individuals or groups that have a claim or interest in the performance and continued survival of the firm. They make specific contributions for which they expect rewards in return.
- *Internal stakeholders* include stockholders, employees (for instance, executives, managers, and workers), and board members.
- *External stakeholders* include customers, suppliers, alliance partners, creditors, unions, communities, and governments at various levels.

- Several recent black swan events eroded the public's trust in business as an institution and free-market capitalism as an economic system.
- The effective management of stakeholders, the organization, groups, or individuals that can materially affect or are affected by the action of a firm, is necessary to ensure the continued survival of the firm and to sustain any competitive advantage.

LO 1-5 / Conduct a stakeholder impact analysis.

- Stakeholder impact analysis considers the needs of different stakeholders, which enables the firm to perform optimally and to live up to the expectations of good citizenship.
- In a stakeholder impact analysis, managers pay particular attention to three important stakeholder attributes: power, legitimacy, and urgency.
- Stakeholder impact analysis is a five-step process that answers the following questions for the firm:
  1. Who are our stakeholders?
  2. What are our stakeholders' interests and claims?
  3. What opportunities and threats do our stakeholders present?
  4. What economic, legal, and ethical responsibilities do we have to our stakeholders?
  5. What should we do to effectively address the stakeholder concerns?

KEY TERMS

AFI strategy framework	Corporate social responsibility (CSR)	Stakeholder impact analysis
Black swan events	Firm effects	Stakeholder strategy
Competitive advantage	Industry effects	Strategic management
Competitive disadvantage	Stakeholder	Strategy
Competitive parity		Sustainable competitive advantage

DISCUSSION QUESTIONS

1. Consider the brief description of Target's stakeholder relationships and combine that information with your experience shopping in a Target store. How might Target's stakeholders (in particular, employees, customers, local communities, and suppliers) influence the manager's decisions about building competitive advantage in the analysis stage of the AFI framework? How might Target gather information from its stakeholders in order to inspire a better customer experience in the formulation stage in order to differentiate? Or in order to lower costs? Brainstorm (by jotting down as many ideas as you can think of) about how key stakeholders may affect (or be affected by) the implementation stage.

2. BP's experience in the Gulf of Mexico has made it the poster company for how *not* to manage stakeholder relationships effectively (see Strategy Highlight 1.2). What advice would you give to BP's managers in order to help them continue to rebuild stakeholder relationships in the Gulf region? How can BP repair its damaged reputation? Brainstorm ways that top management might leverage the experience gained by reacting in the Gulf and use that knowledge to motivate local managers and employees in other locales to build stakeholder relationships proactively so that BP avoids this type of negative publicity.

3. As noted in the chapter, research found that firm effects are more important than industry effects. What does this mean? Can you think of situations where this might not be true?

4. Choose an industry with a clear leader, and then examine the differences between the leader and one or two of the other competitors in the industry. How do the strategies differ? What has the leader done differently? Or what different things has the leader done?

ETHICAL/SOCIAL ISSUES

1. Choose one of the companies discussed in the chapter (such as BP, Target, JetBlue, or Apple). By looking at the company's annual report on its web page or conducting an Internet search for news about the company, identify instances where the company has acted ethically or showed its interest in a key stakeholder—or where it has failed to do so.

2. Corporate leaders are responsible for setting the firm's strategies to gain and sustain a competitive advantage. Should managers be concerned only about the company's financial performance? What responsibility do company managers have for other consequences of their strategies? For example, should Walmart try to mitigate the negative impact its arrival in communities can have on small locally owned stores? Should Apple be concerned about the working conditions at Foxconn (the company that manufactures Apple's devices such as the iPhone and the iPad in China)? Why or why not? Explain.

3. Other than Whole Foods, think of company examples where "doing things right" and acting in the interests of broader stakeholders (rather than just stockholders alone) have produced a stronger competitive advantage. Why was this the case?

SMALL-GROUP EXERCISES

//// **Small-Group Exercise 1**

Form small groups of three to four students. Search the Internet on the following topic and debate your findings.

The chapter includes a discussion of black swan events that were improbable and unexpected yet had an extreme impact on the well-being of individuals, firms, and nations. Nassim Nicholas Taleb, author of

The Black Swan, has argued that policymakers and decision makers need to focus on building more robust organizations or systems rather than on improving predictions of events. This notion is reflected in the response to the predicted increase in powerful storms and storm surges. Hurricanes Katrina (which devastated New Orleans and parts of the Gulf Coast) and Sandy (which wreaked havoc on the New Jersey coast) have stimulated discussions about how to not only build a more resilient infrastructure and buildings, but also develop more flexible and effective responses.

Each group should search the Internet about options and plans to (1) build more sustainable communities that will help threatened areas cope with superstorms, storm surges, or drought conditions, and (2) organize responses to black swan events (such as natural disasters or terrorist attacks) more effectively. Brainstorm additional recommendations that you might make to policymakers.

//// Small-Group Exercise 2

JetBlue was discussed as an example of a company with an unclear strategy. It was *stuck in the middle* because it failed to straddle both a low-cost and differentiated position at the same time (Strategy Highlight 1.1). Scan the current mainstream media for examples of companies that are launching new products or services. Identify whether the company seems to be emphasizing ways that it has lowered costs (and will compete on the basis of price) or ways that it is adding features (and will compete on the basis of uniqueness). Or, does the company seem to be trying to do both? Discuss this within your group and prepare a three-minute summary to present to the class that illustrates the company's approach.

STRATEGY TERM PROJECT

//// Project Overview

The goal of the strategy term project is to give you practical experience with the elements of strategic management. Each end-of-chapter assignment requires data collection and analysis relating the material discussed in the chapter to the firm you select here for study throughout the course. At the end of each chapter, we make additional stages of a strategic analysis available. The goal of this term-long project is to give you a tangible application of many of the concepts discussed in the text. By the end of the project, you will not only have practice in using key strategic management components and processes to increase your understanding of the material, but you will also be able to conduct a complete strategic management analysis of any company.

//// Module 1: Initial Firm Selection and Review

In this first module, you will identify a firm to study for this project. We suggest you select one company and use it for each module in this term project. Choose a firm that you find interesting or one that is part of an industry you would like to know more about. Throughout the modules, you will be required to obtain and analyze a significant amount of data about the firm. Therefore, a key criterion is also to choose a firm that has data available for you to gather.

The primary approach to this project is to select a publicly held firm. Many large firms such as Apple, Coca-Cola, and GE have been widely reported on in the business and popular press, and a wealth of information is available on them. Other medium-sized public firms such as GameStop, Netflix, and Under Armour can be used as example firms for this project. One cautionary note: For firms that are less than three years public or in industries that are not well-defined, it will take some additional reflection to properly identify such items as competitors and suppliers. But if it is a firm you are truly motivated to study, the effort can be quite rewarding.

Relevant data on all public firms can be freely obtained using web services such as Edgar (www.sec.gov/edgar.shtml). (For guidance on how to pull data from the Securities and Exchange Commission [SEC] website, go to the OLC connected with this product at www.mhhe.com/ftrStrategy2e.) Annual reports for firms also are a treasure-trove of information. These reports and other quarterly update materials are often available from the firm's own website (look for "about us" or "investor relations" tabs, often located at the bottom of the company's website). Additionally, most university and public libraries have access to large databases of articles from many trade publications. (Factiva and ABI/Proquest are two examples.) Company profiles of a variety of publicly listed firms are available at reliable websites such as Hoovers.com and finance.yahoo.com. Also, many industries have quite active trade associations that will have websites and publications that can also be useful in this process. Your local librarian can likely provide you with some additional resources that may be licensed for library use or that are otherwise not available online. Examples of these are Value Line Ratings & Reports and Datamonitor.

A second approach to this project is to select a smaller firm in your area. These firms may have coverage in the local press. However, if the firm is not public, you will need to ensure you have access to a wide variety of data from the firm. If this is a firm for which you have worked or where you know people, please check ahead of time to be sure the firm is willing to share its information with you. This approach can work well, especially if the firm is interested in a detailed analysis of its strategic position. But to be successful with this project, be sure you will have access to a broad range of data and information (perhaps including interviews of key managers at the firm).

If you are in doubt on how to select a firm, check with your instructor before proceeding. In some instances, your instructor will assign firms to the study groups.

For this module, complete or answer the following:

1. Provide a brief history of the company.

2. List the top management of the firm and note what experience and leadership skills they bring to the firm. If it is a larger conglomerate, list both the corporate and business managers.

3. What is the principal business model of the firm? (How does the firm make most of its profits?)

---

my STRATEGY

How to Position Yourself for Career Advantage

As the chapter discussed, firm-level decisions have a significant impact on the success or failure of organizations. Industry-level effects, however, can also play an important role (see Exhibit 1.1). Many considerations go into deciding what career choices you make during your working life. The table on the next page provides a sample of revenue growth rates in various industries for a recent five-year period. It shows the data for the top-25 and bottom-25 industries, including the total industry average (out of roughly 100 industries tracked). Using that table, answer the following questions.

1. If you are about to embark on a new career or consider switching careers, what effect should the likelihood of industry growth play in your decision?

2. Why could growth rates be an important consideration? Why not?

3. The data in the table show the most recent five years available. How do you expect this list to look five years from now? Which three to five industries do you expect to top the list, and which three to five industries will be at the bottom of the list? Why?

Top-25 and Bottom-25 Industries (by Revenue Growth Rates), 2007–2011[39]

Rank	Industry Name	Growth in Revenue		Average for All Industries	7.38%
1	Semiconductor equip.	55.88%	75	Telecom. equipment	4.18%
2	Power	43.06%	76	Retail (hardlines)	3.83%
3	Semiconductor	41.30%	77	Shoe	3.50%
4	Public/private equity	39.94%	78	Building materials	2.82%
5	Drug	34.97%	79	Toiletries/cosmetics	2.56%
6	Chemical (basic)	33.40%	80	Restaurant	2.45%
7	Precious metals	32.31%	81	Furn./home furnishings	1.89%
8	Petroleum (producing)	32.22%	82	Automotive	1.66%
9	Metals and mining (div.)	31.59%	83	Cable TV	1.53%
10	Steel	30.89%	84	Electric utility (west)	1.24%
11	Biotechnology	26.94%	85	Funeral services	1.09%
12	Chemical (specialty)	25.69%	86	Human resources	0.01%
13	Electrical equipment	25.14%	87	R.E.I.T.	0.01%
14	Auto parts	23.94%	88	Bank	0.00%
15	Precision instrument	23.36%	89	Bank (midwest)	0.00%
16	Pipeline MLPs	22.83%	90	Insurance (life)	0.00%
17	E-commerce	21.87%	91	Reinsurance	0.00%
18	Petroleum (integrated)	20.81%	92	Thrift	0.00%
19	Property management	19.80%	93	Beverage	−0.59%
20	Foreign electronics	17.51%	94	Natural gas utility	−0.95%
21	Educational services	17.27%	95	Electric utility (east)	−3.29%
22	Diversified co.	17.24%	96	Newspaper	−5.01%
23	Oil field services/equip.	17.02%	97	Telecom. utility	−6.90%
24	Insurance (prop./cas.)	17.00%	98	Publishing	−6.93%
25	Coal	16.91%	99	Homebuilding	−9.29%

ENDNOTES

1. Apple's valuation is in absolute dollars, not in real (inflation-adjusted) dollars. When adjusted for inflation since 1999, Microsoft's record market valuation would be roughly $850 billion in 2012; see "From pipsqueak to powerhouse," *The Economist,* August 21, 2012.

2. This ChapterCase is based on: Isaacson, W. (2011), *Steve Jobs* (New York: Simon & Schuster); "An iPopping phenomenon," *The Economist,* March 24, 2012; "iRational?" *The Economist,* March 24, 2012; "Apple market value hits record high," *The Wall Street Journal,* August 20, 2012; "GiantApple," *The Economist,* August 21, 2012.

3. This section draws on: Porter, M. E. (1980), *Competitive Strategy: Techniques for Analyzing Competitors* (New York: The Free Press); Porter, M. E. (1996), "What is strategy?" *Harvard Business Review,* November–December: 61–78; and Rumelt, R. (2011), *Good Strategy, Bad Strategy: The Difference and Why It Matters* (New York: Crown Business).

4. Rumelt, R. (2011), *Good Strategy, Bad Strategy.*

5. Rumelt, R. (2011), *Good Strategy, Bad Strategy,* p. 14.

6. Sull, D., and K. E. Eisenhardt (2012), "Simple rules for a complex world," *Harvard Business Review,* September.

7. This section draws on: Porter, M. E. (1980), *Competitive Strategy: Techniques for Analyzing Competitors* (New York: The Free Press); Porter, M. E. (1996), "What is strategy?" *Harvard Business Review,* November–December: 61–78; and Porter, M. E. (2008), "The five competitive forces that shape strategy," *Harvard Business Review,* January: 78–93.

8. This section draws on: Porter, M. E. (1980), *Competitive Strategy: Techniques for Analyzing Competitors* (New York: The Free Press); Porter, M. E. (1996), "What is strategy?" *Harvard Business Review,* November–December: 61–78; and Porter, M. E. (2008), "The five competitive forces that shape strategy," *Harvard Business Review,* January: 78–93.

9. Porter, M. E. (1996), "What is strategy?"; and Rumelt, R. (2011), *Good Strategy, Bad Strategy.*

10. Neeleman, D. (2003), Entrepreneurial Thought Leaders Lecture, *Stanford Technology Ventures Program,* April 30; Friedman, T. (2005), *The World Is Flat: A Brief History of the Twenty-First Century* (New York: Farrar, Strauss and Giroux); Bryce, D. J., and J. H. Dyer (2007), "Strategies to crack well-guarded markets," *Harvard Business Review,* May; "Held hostage on the tarmac: Time for a passenger bill of rights?" *The New York Times,* February 16, 2007; and "Can JetBlue weather the storm?" *Time,* February 21, 2007.

11. Porter, M. E. (1980), *Competitive Strategy;* Porter, M. E. (1996), "What is strategy?" *Harvard Business Review,* November–December: 61–78; and Rumelt, R. (2011), *Good Strategy, Bad Strategy.*

12. This interesting debate unfolds in the following articles, among others: Hansen, G. S., and B. Wernerfelt (1989), "Determinants of firm performance: The relative importance of economic and organizational factors," *Strategic Management Journal* 10: 399–411; Rumelt, R. P. (1991), "How much does industry matter?" *Strategic Management Journal* 12: 167–185; Roquebert, J. A., R. L. Phillips, and P. A. Westfall (1996), "Markets vs. management: What 'drives' profitability?" *Strategic Management Journal* 17: 653–664; McGahan, A. M., and M. E. Porter (1997), "How much does industry matter, really?" *Strategic Management Journal* 18: 15–30; Hawawini, G., V. Subramanian, and P. Verdin (2003), "Is performance driven by industry- or firm-specific factors? A new look at the evidence," *Strategic Management Journal* 24: 1–16; and Misangyi, V. F., H. Elms, T. Greckhamer, and J. A. Lepine (2006), "A new perspective on a fundamental debate: A multilevel approach to industry, corporate, and business unit effects," *Strategic Management Journal* 27: 571–590.

13. Ibid.

14. Ibid.

15. Smith, A. (1776), *An Inquiry into the Nature and Causes of the Wealth of Nations,* 5th ed. (published 1904) (London: Methuen and Co.).

16. This discussion draws on: Porter, M. E., and M. R. Kramer (2006), "Strategy and society: The link between competitive advantage and corporate social responsibility," *Harvard Business Review,* December: 80–92; Porter, M. E., and M. R. Kramer (2011), "Creating shared value: How to reinvent capitalism—and unleash innovation and growth," *Harvard Business Review,* January–February; Carroll, A. B., and A. K. Buchholtz (2012), *Business & Society. Ethics, Sustainability, and Stakeholder Management* (Mason, OH: South-Western Cengage); and Parmar, B. L., R. E. Freeman, J. S. Harrison, A. C. Wicks, L. Purnell, and S. De Colle (2010), "Stakeholder theory: The state of the art," *Academy of Management Annals* 4: 403–445.

17. Talib, N. N. (2007), *The Black Swan: The Impact of the Highly Improbable* (New York: Random House).

18. See the discussion by: Lowenstein, R. (2010), *The End of Wall Street* (New York: Penguin Press); Paulson, H. M. (2010), *On the Brink: Inside the Race to Stop the Collapse of the Global Financial System* (New York: Business Plus); and Wessel, D. (2010), *In FED We Trust: Ben Bernanke's War on the Great Panic* (New York: Crown Business).

19. Parmar, B. L., R. E. Freeman, J. S. Harrison, A. C. Wicks, L. Purnell, and S. De Colle (2010), "Stakeholder theory: The state of the art," *Academy of Management Annals* 4: 403–445.

20. Freeman, E. R. (1984), *Strategic Management: A Stakeholder Approach* (Boston, MA: Pitman); Freeman, E. R., and J. McVea (2001), "A stakeholder approach to strategic management," in Hitt, M. A., E. R. Freeman, and J. S. Harrison (eds.), *The Handbook of Strategic Management* (Oxford, UK: Blackwell), pp. 189–207; and Phillips, R. (2003), *Stakeholder Theory and Organizational Ethics* (San Francisco: Berrett-Koehler).

21. To acknowledge the increasing importance of *stakeholder strategy,* the Strategic Management Society (SMS)—the leading association for academics, business executives, and consultants interested in strategic management—has recently created a *stakeholder strategy* division; see http://strategicmanagement.net/. Also see: Anderson, R. C. (2009), *Confessions of a Radical Industrialist: Profits, People, Purpose—Doing Business by Respecting the Earth* (New York: St. Martin's Press); Sisodia, R. S., D. B. Wolfe, and J. N. Sheth (2007), *Firms of Endearment: How World-Class Companies Profit from Passion and Purpose* (Upper Saddle River, NJ: Prentice-Hall Pearson); and Svendsen, A. (1998), *The Stakeholder Strategy: Profiting from Collaborative Business Relationships* (San Francisco: Berrett-Koehler).

22. Parmar, B. L., R. E. Freeman, J. S. Harrison, A. C. Wicks, L. Purnell, and S. De Colle (2010), "Stakeholder theory," p. 406.

23. Ibid.

24. Ibid.

25. *Fortune 2011 The World's Most Admired Companies,* http://money.cnn.com/magazines/fortune/mostadmired/2011/full_list/.

26. Mitchell, R. K., B. R. Agle, and D. J. Wood (1997), "Toward a theory of stakeholder identification and salience," *Academy of Management Review* 22: 853–886; and Eesley, C., and M. J. Lenox (2006), "Firm responses to secondary stakeholder action," *Strategic Management Journal* 27: 765–781.

27. "The media choke on a Twinkie," *The Wall Street Journal,* November 27, 2012.

28. TIAA-CREF is an acronym for Teachers Insurance and Annuity Association–College Retirement Equities Fund.

29. CalPERS is an acronym for California Public Employees' Retirement System.

30. People for the Ethical Treatment of Animals (PETA) is an animal-rights organization.

31. This example is drawn from: Esty, D. C., and A. S. Winston (2006), *Green to Gold: How Smart Companies Use Environmental Strategy to Innovate, Create Value, and Build Competitive Advantage* (Hoboken, NJ: Wiley).

32. This discussion draws on: Carroll, A. B., and A. K. Buchholtz (2012), *Business & Society. Ethics, Sustainability, and Stakeholder Management* (Mason, OH: South-Western Cengage); Carroll, A. B. (1991), "The pyramid of corporate social responsibility: Toward the moral management of organizational stakeholders," *Business Horizons,* July–August: 39–48; and Carroll, A. B. (1979), "A three-dimensional, conceptual model of corporate social performance," *Academy of Management Review* 4: 497–505.

33. For an insightful but critical treatment of this topic, see the 2003 Canadian documentary film *The Corporation.*

34. www.ge.com.

35. Gates, B. (2008), "How to help those left behind," *Time,* August 11.

36. Carroll, A. B. (1991), "The pyramid of corporate social responsibility," pp. 39–48.

37. "BP, plaintiffs reach settlement in Gulf oil spill," *The Wall Street Journal,* March 4, 2012; "BP and the Deepwater Horizon disaster," *The Economist,* November 15, 2012; "BP slapped with record fine," *The Wall Street Journal,* November 15, 2012; "U.S. government slams BP's 'lack of business integrity,'" *The Wall Street Journal,* November 28, 2012.

38. "Apple wins big in patent case," *The Wall Street Journal,* August 24, 2012; "Apple shake-up signals Tim Cook era," *The Wall Street Journal,* October 30, 2012; "Apple, HTC settle patent dispute, sign licensing pact," *The Wall Street Journal,* November 11, 2012; "Eddy Cue: Apple's rising Mr. Fix-It," *The Wall Street Journal,* November 28, 2012.

39. Compiled from Value Line data by A. Damodaran, NYU, http://people.stern.nyu.edu/adamodar/New_Home_Page/datafile/histgr.html.

Chapter 2

Strategic Leadership: Managing the Strategy Process

Chapter Outline

Learning Objectives

After studying this chapter, you should be able to:

LO 2-1 Describe the roles of vision, mission, and values in the strategic management process.

LO 2-2 Evaluate the strategic implications of product-oriented and customer-oriented vision statements.

LO 2-3 Explain why anchoring a firm in ethical values is essential for long-term success.

LO 2-4 Outline how managers become strategic leaders.

LO 2-5 Describe the roles of corporate, business, and functional managers in strategy formulation and implementation.

LO 2-6 Evaluate top-down strategic planning, scenario planning, and strategy as planned emergence.

PepsiCo's Indra Nooyi: "Performance with a Purpose"

AS CHIEF EXECUTIVE Officer (CEO) of PepsiCo, Indra Nooyi is one of the world's most powerful business leaders. A native of Chennai, India, Ms. Nooyi holds multiple degrees: a bachelor's degree in physics, chemistry, and mathematics from Madras Christian College, an MBA from the Indian Institute of Management, and a master's degree from Yale University. Prior to joining PepsiCo in 1994, Ms. Nooyi worked for Johnson & Johnson, Boston Consulting Group, Motorola, and ABB. Ms. Nooyi is not your typical Fortune 500 CEO, though: She is well known for walking around the office barefoot and singing—a remnant from her lead role in an all-girls rock band in high school.

It should come as no surprise, therefore, that Ms. Nooyi has been shaking things up at PepsiCo, a company with roughly $70 billion in annual revenues and some 300,000 employees worldwide. She took the lead role in spinning off Taco Bell, Pizza Hut, and KFC in 1997. Later, she masterminded the acquisitions of Tropicana in 1998 and Quaker Oats (including Gatorade) in 2001. As CEO, Ms. Nooyi declared PepsiCo's vision to be "Performance with a Purpose," as defined by three dimensions:

1. *Human sustainability.* PepsiCo's strategic intent is to make its product portfolio healthier to combat obesity. It wants to reduce the salt and fat in its "fun foods" such as Frito-Lay and Doritos, and to include healthy choices such as Quaker Oats products and Tropicana fruit juices in its lineup. Ms. Nooyi is convinced that if food and beverage companies do not make their products healthier, they will face stricter regulation and lawsuits, as tobacco companies did. Ms. Nooyi's goal is to increase PepsiCo's revenues for nutritious foods from $10 billion today to $30 billion by 2020.

2. *Environmental sustainability.* PepsiCo has instituted various initiatives to ensure that its operations don't harm the natural environment. The company has programs in place to reduce water and energy use, increase recycling, and promote sustainable agriculture. The goal is to transform PepsiCo into a company with a net-zero impact on the environment. Ms. Nooyi believes that young people today will not patronize a company that does not have a strategy that also addresses ecological sustainability.

3. *The whole person at work.* PepsiCo wants to create a corporate culture in which employees do not "just make a living, but also have a life." Ms. Nooyi argues that this type of culture allows employees to unleash both their mental and emotional energies.

PepsiCo's vision of performance with a purpose acknowledges the importance of corporate social responsibility and stakeholder strategy. Ms. Nooyi is convinced that companies have a duty to society to "do better by doing better." She subscribes to a triple-bottom-line approach to competitive advantage, which considers not only economic but also social and environmental performance. Ms. Nooyi declares that the true profits of an enterprise are not just "revenues *minus* costs" but "revenues *minus* costs *minus* costs to society." Problems such as pollution or the increased cost of health care to combat obesity impose costs on society (externalities) that companies typically do not bear. As Indra Nooyi sees it, the time when corporations can just pass on their externalities to society is nearing an end.[1]

After reading this chapter, you will find more about this case, along with related questions, on page 48.

⚫ **HOW DO STRATEGIC LEADERS** like Indra Nooyi develop and implement a vision for their company to achieve strategic goals? How do they use vision, mission, and values to guide and motivate employees? In Chapter 2, we move from thinking about why strategy is important to considering how firms and other organizations define their vision, mission, and values, and how strategic leaders manage the strategy process.

An effective strategy process can lay the foundation on which to build a sustainable competitive advantage. The first step in the strategy process is to define an organization's vision, mission, and values. With those guiding principles in place, we then consider how strategic leaders formulate strategy across different levels: corporate, business, and functional. Next, we introduce three complementary frameworks of the strategy-creation process: strategic planning, scenario planning, and strategy as planned emergence. Finally, we conclude with practical *Implications for the Strategist.*

2.1 Vision, Mission, and Values

LO 2-1

Describe the roles of vision, mission, and values in the strategic management process.

The first steps in the strategic management process are to define a firm's vision, mission, and values. An effective **strategic management process** is the method put in place by strategic leaders to conceive and implement a strategy. It can lay the foundation for a sustainable competitive advantage. **Strategic leadership** pertains to executives' use of power and influence to direct the activities of others when pursuing an organization's goals.[2] As described in ChapterCase 2, Indra Nooyi is demonstrating strategic leadership when defining goals and putting systems, structures, and incentives in place to achieve the vision of "performance with a purpose."

To begin the strategic management process, strategic leaders ask the following questions:

- What do we want to accomplish ultimately? What is our *vision?*
- How do we accomplish our goals? What is our *mission?*
- What guardrails do we put in place to act ethically and legally as we pursue our vision and mission? What are our *values?*

VISION AND MISSION

To answer questions about vision, mission, and values, strategic leaders *need to* begin with the end in mind. Think of building a house. The future owner must communicate her vision to the architect, who draws up a blueprint of the home. The process is iterated a couple of times until all the homeowner's ideas have been translated into the blueprint. Only then does the building of the house begin. The same holds for strategic success. Indra Nooyi has a clear picture in mind of what PepsiCo will look like in the future:

> *Performance with a purpose means delivering sustainable growth by investing in a healthier future for people and our planet. . . . We will continue to build a portfolio of enjoyable and healthier foods and beverages, find innovative ways to reduce the use of energy, water and packaging, and provide a great workplace for our associates. . . . Because a healthier future for all people and our planet means a more successful future for PepsiCo. This is our promise.[3]*

Such a statement about what an organization ultimately wants to accomplish is its **vision.** It captures the company's aspiration. An effective vision pervades the organization with a sense of winning and motivates employees at all levels to aim for the same target, while leaving room for individual and team contributions. Employees in visionary companies tend to feel like part of something bigger than themselves. An inspiring vision helps employees find meaning in their work, beyond monetary rewards. It allows employees to experience a greater sense of purpose and taps into people's intrinsic motivations to make the world a better place through their work activities.[4] This greater individual purpose can in turn lead to higher organizational performance.[5] Basing actions on its vision, a firm will build the necessary resources and capabilities through continuous organizational learning, including learning from failure, to translate into reality what begins as a stretch goal.[6]

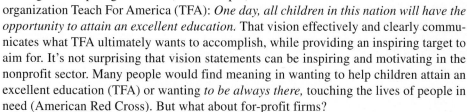

To provide meaning for employees in pursuit of the organization's ultimate goals, vision statements should be forward-looking and inspiring. Consider, for example, the vision of the organization Teach For America (TFA): *One day, all children in this nation will have the opportunity to attain an excellent education.* That vision effectively and clearly communicates what TFA ultimately wants to accomplish, while providing an inspiring target to aim for. It's not surprising that vision statements can be inspiring and motivating in the nonprofit sector. Many people would find meaning in wanting to help children attain an excellent education (TFA) or wanting *to be always there,* touching the lives of people in need (American Red Cross). But what about for-profit firms?

The main difference in the visions of for-profit firms is the metric by which the organization assesses successful performance. TFA measures its organizational success by the impact its teachers have on student performance. In the for-profit sector, many companies measure success primarily by financial performance. Other visionary companies, including 3M, General Electric, Merck, Nordstrom, Procter & Gamble (P&G), and Walmart, provide more aspirational ideas that are not exclusively financial.[7] Visionary companies often are able not only to gain a competitive advantage, but also to outperform their competitors over the long run. Tracking the stock market performance of companies over many decades, strategy scholars found that these visionary companies outperformed their peers by a wide margin. This goes to show that a truly meaningful and inspiring vision makes employees feel they are part of something bigger. In turn, this is highly motivating and can improve financial performance.

Building on the vision, organizations establish a **mission,** which describes what an organization actually does—that is, the products and services it plans to provide, and the markets in which it will compete. Although the terms *vision* and *mission* are often used interchangeably, they are different: Vision defines what an organization wants to accomplish ultimately, and thus the goal can be described by the verb "*to.*" For instance, TFA's vision is *to attain an excellent education for all children.* In contrast, mission describes what an organization does; it defines the means "*by*" which vision is accomplished. Accordingly, TFA's mission is achieved *by enlisting our nation's most promising future leaders in the effort (we will be able to attain an excellent education for all children).* Exhibit 2.1 presents TFA's vision, mission, and values. (See MiniCase 4 for a detailed discussion on how Teach For America inspires future leaders.)

strategic management process Method put in place by strategic leaders to conceive and implement a strategy, which can lay the foundation for a sustainable competitive advantage.

strategic leadership Executives' use of power and influence to direct the activities of others when pursuing an organization's goals.

vision A statement about what an organization ultimately wants to accomplish; it captures the company's aspiration.

mission Description of what an organization actually does—the products and services it plans to provide, and the markets in which it will compete.

EXHIBIT 2.1 / Teach For America: Vision, Mission, and Values

VISION	One day, all children in this nation will have the opportunity to attain an excellent education.
MISSION	Teach For America is growing the movement of leaders who work to ensure that kids growing up in poverty get an excellent education.
CORE VALUES	**Transformational Change:** We seek to expand educational opportunity in ways that are life-changing for children and transforming for our country. Given our deep belief in children and communities, the magnitude of educational inequity and its consequences, and our optimism about the solvability of the problem, we act with high standards, urgency, and a long-term view.

Leadership: We strive to develop and become the leaders necessary to realize educational excellence and equity. We establish bold visions and invest others in working towards them. We work in purposeful, strategic, and resourceful ways, define broadly what is within our control to solve, and learn and improve constantly. We operate with a sense of possibility, persevere in the face of challenges, ensure alignment between our actions and beliefs, and assume personal responsibility for results.

Team: We value and care about each other, operate with a generosity of spirit, and have fun in the process of working together. To maximize our collective impact, we inspire, challenge, and support each other to be our best and sustain our effort.

Diversity: We act on our belief that the movement to ensure educational equity will succeed only if it is diverse in every respect. In particular, we value the perspective and credibility that individuals who share the racial and economic backgrounds of the students with whom we work can bring to our organization, classrooms, and the long-term effort for change.

Respect & Humility: We value the strengths, experiences, and perspectives of others, and we recognize our own limitations. We are committed to partnering effectively with families, schools, and communities to ensure that our work advances the broader good for all children. |

SOURCE: www.teachforamerica.org.

strategic commitments
Actions that are costly, long-term–oriented, and difficult to reverse.

To be effective, firms need to back up their visions and missions with **strategic commitments,** actions that are costly, long-term–oriented, and difficult to reverse.[8] For instance, the vision of EADS, the parent company of Airbus, is *to be the world's leading aerospace company.* Airbus translates this ultimate goal into its mission *by manufacturing the world's best aircraft, with passengers at heart and airlines in mind.* Airbus spent 10 years and $15 billion to develop the A380 super jumbo, which can accommodate over 850 passengers and fly almost 10,000 miles (a sufficient range to fly non-stop from New York to Singapore). The company's vision is backed up by a powerful strategic commitment. Without such commitments, a firm's vision and mission statements are just words. However noble the mission statement, companies will not achieve competitive advantage without strategic actions to back it up.

So, we must ask, do vision statements help firms gain and sustain competitive advantage? The effectiveness of vision statements differs based on whether they are *customer-oriented* or *product-oriented.* Customer-oriented vision statements allow companies to adapt to changing environments, while product-oriented vision statements often do not. Given that our environments are ever-changing, increased strategic flexibility is often a necessary condition to achieve competitive advantage.[9] Let's look at both types of vision statements.

LO 2-2

Evaluate the strategic implications of product-oriented and customer-oriented vision statements.

PRODUCT-ORIENTED VISION STATEMENTS. A product-oriented vision defines a business in terms of a good or service provided. Product-oriented visions tend to force managers to take a more myopic view of the competitive landscape. As an example, let's consider the strategic decisions of U.S. railroad companies. Railroads are in the business of moving goods and people from point A to point B by rail. When they started, their short-distance competition was the horse or horse-drawn carriage. There was little long-distance competition (e.g., ship canals and good roads) to cover the U.S. from coast to coast. Due to their monopoly, especially in long-distance travel, these companies were initially extremely profitable. Not surprisingly, the early U.S. railroad companies saw their vision as being in the railroad business, clearly a product-based definition.

However, the railroad companies' monopoly did not last, as technological innovations changed the transportation business dramatically. After the introduction of the automobile and the commercial jet, consumers had a wider range of choices to meet their long-distance transportation needs. Rail companies were slow to respond; they did not redefine their business in terms of services provided to the consumer. Had they envisioned themselves as serving the full range of transportation needs of people across America (a customer-oriented vision), they might have become successful forerunners of modern logistics companies like FedEx or UPS.

Recently, the railroad companies seem to be learning some lessons: CSX Railroad is now redefining itself as a green-transportation alternative. It claims it can move one ton of freight 423 miles on one gallon of fuel. However, its vision remains product-oriented: *to be the safest, most progressive North American railroad.*

CUSTOMER-ORIENTED VISION STATEMENTS. *A customer-oriented vision* defines a business in terms of providing solutions to customer needs. For example, "We are in the business of providing solutions to professional communication needs." Companies that have customer-oriented visions tend to be more flexible when adapting to changing environments. In contrast, companies that define themselves based on product-oriented statements (e.g., "We are in the typewriter business") tend to be less flexible and thus more likely to fail. The lack of an inspiring need-based vision can cause the long-range problem of failing to adapt to a changing environment.

It is important not to confuse customer-oriented vision statements with listening to your customer. They are not the same thing. Customer-oriented visions identify a critical need but leave open the means of how to meet that need. It is critical not to define *how* a customer need will be met. The future is unknowable, and innovation may provide new ways to meet needs that we cannot fathom today. Even if customer needs are unchanging, the *means* of meeting those needs can certainly change over time. An organization's vision should be flexible, to allow for change and adaptation.

Think about the customer need for personal mobility. A little over 100 years ago, this need was met by horse-drawn buggies, horseback riding, or by trains for long distances. But Henry Ford had a different idea. In fact, he is famous for saying, "If I had listened to my customers, I would have built a better horse and buggy."[10] Instead, Henry Ford's original vision was *to make the automobile accessible to every American.* He succeeded, and the automobile dramatically changed how mobility was achieved.

Fast-forward to today: Ford Motor Company's vision is *to provide personal mobility for people around the world.* Note that it does not even mention the automobile. By focusing on the consumer need for personal mobility, Ford is leaving the door open for exactly how it will fulfill that need. Today, it's mostly with traditional cars and trucks propelled by gas-powered internal combustion engines, with some hybrid electric vehicles in its lineup. In the near future, Ford is likely to provide vehicles powered by alternative energy sources such as electric power or hydrogen. In the far-reaching future, perhaps Ford will get into the business of individual flying devices. Throughout all of this, its vision would still be relevant and compel its managers to engage in future markets. In contrast, a product-oriented vision would have greatly constrained Ford's degree of strategic flexibility.

Sometimes, effective vision statements work through metaphors (implied comparisons). Metaphors can help employees make appropriate decisions when faced with day-to-day situations that can sometimes be novel or stressful. Let's look at Disney's customer-oriented vision— *to make people happy.*[11] Disney translates this vision through the metaphor that its theme parks are like stage performances. Employees are not simply employees, but cast members of a

EXHIBIT 2.2

Companies with
Customer-Oriented
Vision Statements

Amazon: To be earth's most customer centric company; to build a place where people can come to find and discover anything they might want to buy online.

eBay: To provide a global trading platform where practically anyone can trade practically anything.

GE: To turn imaginative ideas into leading products and services that help solve some of the world's toughest problems.

Google: To organize the world's information and make it universally accessible and useful.

IBM: To be the best service organization in the world.

Microsoft: To enable people and businesses throughout the world to realize their full potential.

Nike: To bring inspiration and innovation to every athlete in the world.

Walmart: To give ordinary folk the chance to buy the same thing as rich people.

show. Similarly, visitors to the park are not customers, but audience members. Disney's metaphor has implications for employee behavior. Rather than interviewing for a job, for instance, candidates audition for a role. Any time a Disney park employee is in uniform, he or she is "on stage," delivering a performance. Even street sweepers (often college students on break) are part of the cast. Because they have the closest contact with guests, street sweepers are trained in great detail. They are evaluated not only on street-sweeping performance, but also on their knowledge about rides, parades, and restaurant and restroom locations. Like cast members in a theater company, Disney employees pull off daily performances with a "the show must go on" attitude that allows them to fulfill Disney's vision to make people happy. Exhibit 2.2 provides additional examples of companies with customer-oriented vision statements.

MOVING FROM PRODUCT-ORIENTED TO CUSTOMER-ORIENTED VISION STATEMENTS. In some cases, product-oriented vision statements do not interfere with the firm's success in achieving superior performance and competitive advantage. Consider Intel Corporation, one of the world's leading silicon innovators. Intel's early vision was *to be the preeminent building-block supplier of the PC industry.* Intel designed the first commercial microprocessor chip in 1971 and set the standard for microprocessors in 1978. During the personal computer (PC) revolution in the 1980s, microprocessors became Intel's main line of business. Intel's customers were original equipment manufacturers that produced consumer end-products, such as computer manufacturers HP, IBM, Dell, and Compaq.

In the Internet age, though, the standalone PC as the end-product has become less important. Customers want to stream video and share photos online. These activities consume a tremendous amount of computing power. To reflect this shift, Intel in 1999 changed its vision to focus on being *the preeminent building-block supplier to the Internet economy.* Although its product-oriented vision statements did not impede performance or competitive advantage, in 2008 Intel fully made the shift to a customer-oriented vision: to *delight our customers, employees, and shareholders by relentlessly delivering the platform and technology advancements that become essential to the way we work and live.* Part of this shift was reflected by the hugely successful "Intel Inside" advertising campaign in the 1990s that made Intel a household name worldwide.

Intel accomplished superior firm performance over decades through continuous adaptations to changing market realities. Its formal vision statement lagged behind the firm's strategic transformations. Intel regularly changed its vision statement *after* it had accomplished each successful transformation.[12] In such a case, vision statements and firm performance are clearly not related to one another.

Taken together, empirical research shows that sometimes vision statements and firm performance are *associated* with one another. A positive relationship between vision statements and firm performance is more likely to exist under certain circumstances: if the visions are customer-oriented; if internal stakeholders are invested in defining and revising the visions; and if organizational structures such as compensation systems are aligned with the firm's vision statement.[13] The upshot is that an effective vision statement can lay the foundation upon which to craft a strategy that creates competitive advantage.

LIVING THE VALUES

Organizational values are the ethical standards and norms that govern the behavior of individuals within a firm or organization. Strong ethical values have two important functions. First, they form a solid foundation on which a firm can build its vision and mission, and thus lay the groundwork for long-term success. Second, values serve as the guardrails put in place to keep the company on track when pursuing its vision and mission in its quest for competitive advantage.

The values espoused by a company provide answers to the question, *how do we accomplish our goals?* They help individuals make choices that are both ethical and effective in advancing the company's goals. As discussed in Strategy Highlight 2.1 (next page), the pharmaceutical company Merck provides an example of how values can drive strategic decision making, and what can happen if a company deviates from its core values.

There's one last point to make about organizational values. Without commitment and involvement from top managers, any statement of values remains merely a public relations exercise. Employees tend to follow values practiced by strategic leaders. They observe the day-to-day decisions of top managers and quickly decide whether managers are merely paying lip service to the company's stated values. True values must be lived with integrity, especially by the top management team. Unethical behavior by top managers is like a virus that spreads quickly throughout an entire organization. It is imperative that strategic leaders set an example of ethical behavior by living the values. Since strategic leaders have such a strong influence in setting an organization's vision, mission, and values, we next discuss strategic leadership.

2.2 Strategic Leadership

Executives whose vision and actions enable their organizations to achieve competitive advantage demonstrate **strategic leadership**—the behaviors and styles of executives that influence others to achieve the organization's vision and mission.[14] Merck's then-CEO Raymond Gilmartin, for example, demonstrated strategic leadership in reconfirming the company's core value that patients come before profits by voluntarily withdrawing Vioxx from the market. Strategic leadership typically resides in executives who have overall profit-and-loss responsibility for an entire organization. These executives may be the CEO, or other members of the top-management team.

Although the effect of strategic leaders varies across industries and time, they do matter to firm performance.[15] Just think of great business founders and their impact on the organizations they built: Jack Ma at Alibaba, Jeff Bezos at Amazon, Robin Li at Baidu, Mark Zuckerberg at Facebook, Sergei Brin and Larry Page at Google, Bill Gates at Microsoft, Richard Branson at Virgin Group, and John Mackey at Whole Foods, among many others. There are also strategic leaders who have shaped and revitalized existing businesses: Allan Mulally at Ford, Chung Mong-Koo at Hyundai, Irene Rosenfelt at Kraft Foods, Sheryl Sandberg at Facebook, Don Thompson at McDonald's, Yun Jong-Yong at Samsung, Howard Schultz at Starbucks, Ratan Tata at the Tata Group, and Marissa Mayer at Yahoo.[16]

At the other end of the spectrum, unfortunately, are CEOs whose decisions have led to a massive destruction of shareholder value: Brian Dunn at Best Buy, Charles Prince at Citigroup, Richard Wagoner at GM, Robert Nardelli at The Home Depot (and later Chrysler), Ron Johnson at JCPenney, Richard Fuld at Lehman Brothers, Ed Zander at Motorola, and Gerald Levin at Time Warner.

LO 2-3

Explain why anchoring a firm in ethical values is essential for long-term success.

organizational values Ethical standards and norms that govern the behavior of individuals within a firm or organization.

LO 2-4

Outline how managers become strategic leaders.

strategic leadership The behaviors and styles of executives that influence others to achieve the organization's vision and mission.

executives at headquarters formulate corporate strategy. Examples of corporate executives are Mukesh Ambani (Reliance Industries), Maria das Graças Silva Foster (Petrobras-Petróleo Brasil), Jeffrey Immelt (GE), Virginia Rometty (IBM), and Ursula Burns (Xerox). Corporate executives need to decide in which industries, markets, and geographies their companies should compete. They need to formulate a strategy that can create synergies across business units that may be quite different, and determine the boundaries of the firm by deciding whether to enter certain industries and markets and whether to sell certain divisions. They are responsible for setting overarching strategic objectives and allocating scarce resources among different business divisions, monitoring performance, and making adjustments to the overall portfolio of businesses as needed. The objective of corporate-level strategy is to increase overall corporate value so that it is higher than the sum of the individual business units.

strategic business unit (SBU)
A standalone division of a larger conglomerate, with its own profit-and-loss responsibility.

Business strategy occurs within **strategic business units,** or **SBUs,** the standalone divisions of a larger conglomerate, each with its own profit-and-loss responsibility. General managers in SBUs must answer business strategy questions relating to how to compete in order to achieve superior performance. Within the guidelines received from corporate headquarters, they formulate an appropriate generic business strategy (cost leadership, differentiation, or integration) in their quest for competitive advantage.

Within each strategic business unit are various business *functions:* accounting, finance, human resources, product development, operations, manufacturing, marketing, and customer service. Each *functional manager* is responsible for decisions and actions within a single functional area. These decisions aid in the implementation of the business-level strategy, made at the level above.

In ChapterCase 2, we saw how Indra Nooyi determined PepsiCo's corporate strategy. She wants to reposition PepsiCo toward a more sustainable future by focusing not only on economic but also social and environmental contributions. As chief executive officer, Ms. Nooyi is the corporate executive responsible for the performance of the entire organization. She makes a wide range of corporate strategy decisions:

- What types of products PepsiCo offers
- Where in the value chain (ranging from raw materials to retailing of the final product) to participate
- What industries (e.g., beverages and foods) to compete in
- Where in the world to compete

For the time being, Ms. Nooyi has decided that PepsiCo creates more value when both the beverage and snack foods division are together in one corporation, rather than split up into two companies. In contrast, PepsiCo's archrival, Coca-Cola, focuses on only the non-alcoholic beverages line of business.

As a company, PepsiCo is organized on both a geographic and a product basis. Along the *geographic* dimension, PepsiCo consists of a number of standalone business divisions in the Americas, Europe, Africa, and the Middle East.[26] PepsiCo's revenues are split roughly 50–50 between the U.S. and international sales. Along the *product* dimension, PepsiCo's Americas division is split into two product units, Americas beverages and Americas foods. A general manager leads each geographic and product division. He or she has profit-and-loss (P&L) responsibility for his or her region and product line. These SBU managers in turn report to PepsiCo's CEO.

To implement specific business strategies, PepsiCo's regional and product leaders rely on functional managers, who are responsible for a particular business function such as bottling, supply chain management, marketing, retail, or customer service. The functional managers receive strategic directives from their respective regional and product leaders, and implement these directives within the business activities they are responsible for.

2.3 The Strategic Management Process

We have gained some insight into the corporate, business, and functional levels into which strategy is broken down. Next, we turn to the process or method by which strategic leaders formulate and implement strategy. When strategizing for competitive advantage, managers rely on three different approaches: (1) strategic planning, (2) scenario planning, and (3) strategy as planned emergence. This order also indicates how these approaches were developed over time. Strategic planning was the first framework, before scenario planning was introduced, and strategy as planned emergence is the most recent addition. As you'll see, the first two are relatively formal, "rational" top-down planning approaches. Although the third approach also begins with a strategic plan, it is a less formal and less stylized approach to the development of strategy.

LO 2-6

Evaluate top-down strategic planning, scenario planning, and strategy as planned emergence.

TOP-DOWN STRATEGIC PLANNING

The prosperous decades after World War II resulted in the tremendous growth of corporations. As company executives needed a way to manage ever more complex firms more effectively, they began to use strategic planning. **Top-down strategic planning** is a rational, top-down process through which executives attempt to program future success.[27] In this approach, all strategic intelligence and decision-making responsibilities are concentrated in the office of the CEO. The CEO, much like a military general, leads the company strategically through competitive battles.

Top-down strategic planning A rational, top-down process through which management can program future success; typically concentrates strategic intelligence and decision-making responsibilities in the office of the CEO.

Exhibit 2.6 shows the three steps of analysis, formulation, and implementation in a traditional top-down strategic planning process. Strategic planners provide careful analyses of internal and external data and apply it to all quantifiable areas: prices, costs, margins, market demand, head count, and production runs. Five-year plans, revisited regularly, predict future sales based on anticipated future growth. Top executives tie the allocation of the annual corporate budget to the strategic plan and monitor ongoing performance accordingly. Based on a careful analysis of these data, top managers reconfirm or adjust the company's vision, mission, and values before formulating corporate, business, and functional strategies. Appropriate organizational structures and controls as well as governance mechanisms aid in effective implementation.

In this process, the formulation of strategy is separate from implementation, and thinking about strategy is separate from doing it. Information flows one way only: top-down.

At times, strategic leaders impose their visions onto a company's strategy, structure, and culture from the top down in order to create and enact a desired future state. Under its co-founder and longtime CEO, Steve Jobs, Apple was one of the few successful tech companies using a top-down strategic planning process.[28] Jobs felt that he knew best what the next big thing should be. Under his top-down, autocratic leadership, Apple did not engage in market research, because Jobs firmly believed that "people don't know what they want until you show it to them."[29] Since Jobs' death, Apple's strategy process has become more

EXHIBIT 2.6 / Top-Down Strategic Planning in the AFI Framework

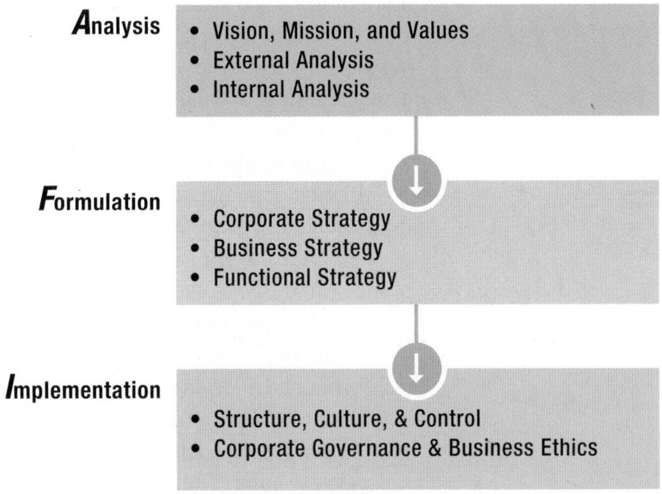

Analysis
- Vision, Mission, and Values
- External Analysis
- Internal Analysis

↓

Formulation
- Corporate Strategy
- Business Strategy
- Functional Strategy

↓

Implementation
- Structure, Culture, & Control
- Corporate Governance & Business Ethics

flexible under its new CEO Tim Cook, and the company is now trying to incorporate the possibilities of different future scenarios and bottom-up strategic initiatives.[30]

Top-down strategic planning rests on the assumption that we can predict the future from the past. The approach works reasonably well when the environment does not change much. One major shortcoming of the strategic planning approach is that we simply cannot know the future. Strategic leaders' visions of the future can be downright wrong; unforeseen events can make even the most scientifically developed and formalized plans obsolete. Thus, many companies are now using a more flexible approach in their strategic management process.

SCENARIO PLANNING

Given that the only constant is change, should managers even try to strategically plan for the future? The answer is yes—but they also need to expect that unpredictable events will happen. We can compare strategic planning in a fast-changing environment to a fire department operation.[31] There is no way to know where and when the next emergency will arise, nor can we know its magnitude beforehand. Nonetheless, fire chiefs put contingency plans in place to address a wide range of emergencies along different dimensions.

scenario planning
Strategy-planning activity in which managers envision different what-if scenarios to anticipate plausible futures.

In the same way, **scenario planning** asks those "what if" questions. Similar to top-down strategic planning, scenario planning also uses a rational, scientific approach to the strategy process. In addition, in scenario planning managers envision different scenarios, to anticipate plausible futures. For example, new laws might restrict carbon emissions or expand employee health care. Demographic shifts may alter the ethnic diversity of a nation; changing tastes or economic conditions will affect consumer behavior. How would any of these changes affect a firm, and how should it respond? Scenario planning takes place at both the corporate and business levels of strategy.

Typical scenario planning addresses both optimistic and pessimistic futures. For instance, strategy executives at UPS recently identified six issues as critical to shaping its future competitive scenarios: (1) the price of oil; (2) climate change; (3) trade barriers (such as "buy American" or "buy Chinese" clauses in new laws around the world); (4) the emerging BRIC (Brazil, Russia, India, and China) economies; (5) political instability; and (6) online commerce worldwide.[32] Managers then formulated strategies they could activate and implement should the envisioned optimistic or pessimistic scenarios begin to appear.

Exhibit 2.7 shows the use of scenario planning with the AFI strategy framework. The goal is to create strategic plans that are more flexible, and thus more effective, than those created through the more static strategic planning approach. In the *analysis stage,* managers brainstorm to identify possible future scenarios. Input from several different hierarchies within the organization and from different functional areas such as R&D, manufacturing, and marketing and sales is critical. UPS executives considered how they would compete if the price of a barrel of oil was $45, or $125, or even $200. Managers may also attach probabilities (highly likely versus unlikely, or 85 percent likely versus 2 percent likely) to different future states.

Although managers often tend to overlook pessimistic future scenarios, it is imperative to consider negative scenarios more carefully. An exporter such as Boeing, Harley-Davidson, or John Deere would want to analyze the impact of shifts in exchange rates on sales and production costs: What if the euro depreciated to $1 per euro, or the Chinese yuan depreciated rather than appreciated? How would Disney and other theme park operators compete if the dollar were to appreciate so much as to make visits by foreign tourists to its California and Florida theme parks prohibitively expensive? Other problems to consider could include how to maintain liquidity when credit and equity markets are tight. Managers might also consider how black swan events (discussed in Chapter 1) might affect their strategic planning. The BP oil spill was such a black swan for many businesses on the Gulf Coast, including the tourism, fishing, and energy industries.

EXHIBIT 2.7

Scenario Planning
Within the AFI
Strategy Framework

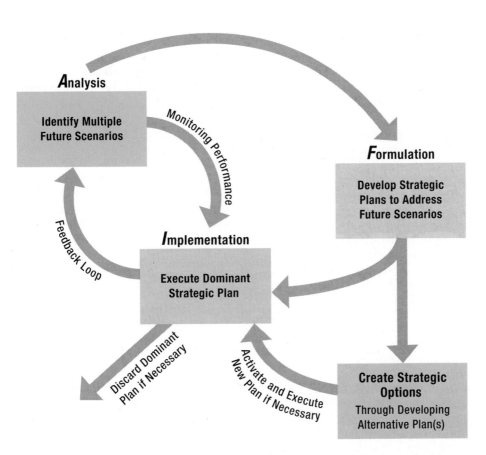

In the *formulation stage* in scenario planning, management teams develop different strategic plans to address possible future scenarios. This kind of what-if exercise forces managers to consider contingency plans before events occur. Each plan relies on an entire set of analytical tools (which will be introduced in upcoming chapters). They capture the firm's internal and external environments and answer several key questions:

- What resources and capabilities do we need to compete successfully in with each future scenario?
- What strategic initiatives should we put in place to respond to each respective scenario?
- How can we shape our expected future environment?

. By formulating responses to the varying scenarios, managers build a portfolio of future options. Managers continue to integrate additional information over time, which in turn influences future decisions. Finally, they transform the most viable options into full-fledged, detailed strategic plans that can be activated and executed as needed. The scenarios and planned responses promote strategic flexibility for the organization.

In the *implementation stage,* managers execute the **dominant strategic plan,** the option that top managers decide most closely matches the current reality. If the situation changes, managers can quickly retrieve and implement any of the alternate plans developed in the formulation stage. The firm's subsequent performance in the marketplace gives managers real-time feedback about the effectiveness of the dominant strategic plan. If performance feedback is positive, managers continue to pursue the dominant strategic plan, fine-tuning it in the process. If performance feedback is negative, or if reality changes, managers consider whether to modify further the dominant strategic plan in order to enhance firm performance, or to activate an alternative strategic plan.

dominant strategic plan The strategic option that top managers decide most closely matches the current reality and which is then executed.

The circular nature of the scenario-planning model in Exhibit 2.7 highlights the continuous interaction among analysis, formulation, and implementation. Through this interactive process, managers can adjust and modify their actions as new realities emerge. The interdependence among analysis, formulation, and implementation also enhances organizational learning and flexibility.

STRATEGY AS PLANNED EMERGENCE: TOP-DOWN *AND* BOTTOM-UP

Critics of top-down and scenario planning argue that *strategic planning* is not the same as *strategic thinking*.[33] In fact, they argue the strategic planning processes are often too regimented and confining. As such, they do not allow for the necessary strategic thinking. Managers doing strategic planning may also fall prey to an *illusion of control*—that is, the hard numbers in a strategic plan can convey a false sense of security. According to critics of strategic planning, in order to be successful, a strategy should be based on an inspiring vision and not on hard data alone. They advise that managers should focus on all types of information sources, including soft sources that can generate new insights, such as personal experience or the experience of front-line employees. The important work, according to this viewpoint, is to synthesize *all available input* from different internal and external sources into an overall strategic vision. This vision in turn should then guide the firm's strategy (as discussed earlier in this chapter).

These critics, most notably Henry Mintzberg, propose a third approach to the strategic management process. In contrast to the two rational planning approaches just discussed, this one is a less formal and less stylized approach to the development of strategy. To reflect the reality that strategy can be planned *or* emerge from the bottom up, Exhibit 2.8 shows a more integrative approach to strategy-making.

According to this more holistic model, the strategy process also begins with a top-down strategic plan. Top-level executives design an **intended strategy**—the outcome of a rational and structured, top-down strategic plan. In today's complex and uncertain world, however, unpredictable events can have tremendous effects. In 1990, online retailing was nonexistent. Today, almost all Internet users have engaged in online retailing. As a total of all sales, online retailing was almost 10 percent (in 2012), and continues to grow fast.[34] Given the dramatic success of Amazon as the world's leading online retailer and eBay as the world's

EXHIBIT 2.8 /

Realized Strategy Is a Combination of Top-Down Intended Strategy and Bottom-Up Emergent Strategy

SOURCE: Adapted from H. Mintzberg and A. McHugh (1985), "Strategy formation in an adhocracy," *Administrative Science Quarterly* 30: 162.

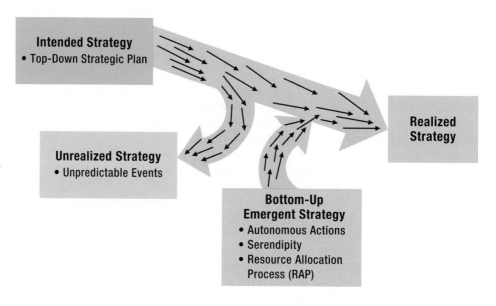

largest online marketplace, brick-and-mortar companies such as Best Buy, Radio Shack, JCPenney, and Sears have all been forced to respond and adjust their strategies in order to avoid bankruptcy. Exhibit 2.8 illustrates how parts of a firm's *intended strategy* fall by the wayside due to unpredictable events and thus turn into *unrealized strategy.*

A firm's **realized strategy** is generally a combination of its top-down strategic intentions and bottom-up emergent strategy. An **emergent strategy** describes any unplanned strategic initiative undertaken by mid-level employees of their own volition. If successful, emergent strategies have the potential to influence and shape a firm's strategy.

The strategic initiative is a key feature in the strategy as a planned emergence model. A **strategic initiative** is any activity a firm pursues to explore and develop new products and processes, new markets, or new ventures. Strategic initiatives can come from anywhere. They could be the result of a response to external trends (such as online retailing) or come from internal sources. As such, strategic initiatives can be the result of top-down planning by executives, or they can also emerge through a *bottom-up process.* (The black arrows in Exhibit 2.8 represent different strategic initiatives.) In particular, strategic initiatives can bubble up from deep within a firm through:

- *Autonomous actions* by lower-level employees
- *Serendipity* (random events, pleasant surprises, accidental happenstances)
- The *resource allocation process (RAP)*[35]

Strategy Highlight 2.2 illustrates that successful emergent strategies are sometimes the result of *serendipity* combined with *autonomous actions* of lower-level employees. (See MiniCase 4, which describes the serendipitous discovery of Viagra.)

Functional managers (such as Diana, the Starbucks store manager featured in Strategy Highlight 2.2) are much closer to the final products, services, and customers than corporate- or business-level managers. As a result, functional managers may initiate strategic initiatives based on autonomous actions that can influence the direction of the company. To be successful, however, top-level executives need to support emergent strategies that they believe fit with the firm's vision and mission. Diana's autonomous actions might not have succeeded (or even got her in trouble) if she did not garner the support of a senior Starbucks executive (Howard Behar). This executive championed her initiative and helped persuade other top executives. Consider the following examples, in which the impetus for strategic initiatives all emerged from the bottom up through *autonomous actions:*

- The Internet company Google organizes the work of its engineers according to a 70-20-10 rule. The majority of the engineers' work time (70 percent) is focused on its main business (search and ads).[36] Google also allows its engineers to spend one day a week (20 percent) on ideas of their own choosing, and the remainder (10 percent) on total wild cards (such as a driverless car). Google reports that half of its new products came from the *20 percent rule.* Examples of innovations that resulted from the 20 percent rule include Gmail, Google Maps, Google News, and Orkut.[37]
- In 2001, a mid-level engineer at General Electric proposed buying Enron Wind, a division that was up for sale as part of Enron's bankruptcy proceedings. Then-CEO Jack Welch didn't want anything with the name Enron on it, given Enron's large-scale

---

intended strategy The outcome of a rational and structured top-down strategic plan.

realized strategy Combination of intended and emergent strategy.

emergent strategy Any unplanned strategic initiative undertaken by mid-level employees of their own volition.

strategic initiative Any activity a firm pursues to explore and develop new products and processes, new markets, or new ventures.

Strategy Highlight 2.2

Starbucks' CEO: "It's Not What We Do"

Diana, a Starbucks store manager in southern California, received several requests a day for an iced beverage offered by a local competitor. After receiving more than 30 requests one day, she tried the beverage herself. Thinking it might be a good idea for Starbucks to offer a similar iced beverage, she requested that headquarters consider adding it to the product lineup. Diana had an internal champion in Howard Behar, then one of Starbucks' top executives. Mr. Behar presented this strategic initiative to the Starbucks executive committee. The committee voted down the idea in a 7:1 vote. Starbucks' CEO Howard Schultz commented, "We do coffee, we don't do iced drinks."

Diana, however, was undeterred. She experimented until she created the iced drink, and then began to offer it in her store. When Howard Behar visited Diana's store, he was shocked to see this new drink on the menu—all

Starbucks stores were supposed to offer only company-approved drinks. But Diana told him the new drink was selling well.

Howard Behar flew Diana's team to Starbucks headquarters in Seattle to serve the iced-coffee drink to the executive committee. They liked its taste, but still said no. Then Behar pulled out the sales numbers that Diana had carefully kept. The drink was selling like crazy: 40 drinks a day the first week, 50 drinks a day the next week, and then 70 drinks a day in the third week after introduction. They had never seen such growth numbers. These results persuaded the executive team to give reluctant approval to introduce the drink in all Starbucks stores.

You've probably guessed by now that we're talking about Starbucks' Frappuccino. Frappuccino is now a billion-dollar business for Starbucks. At one point, this iced-drink brought in more than 20 percent of Starbucks' total revenues (which were $13 billion in 2012).[38]

accounting fraud. When the mid-level engineer kept insisting, even after being rejected several times, GE's leadership relented and bought Enron Wind for $200 million. It turned out to be a huge success, generating revenues over $10 billion in 2012, and opening up other significant opportunities for GE in the alternative-energy industry, including its *ecomagination* initiative. GE's shift from a product-oriented company ("*We bring good things to life*") to a more consumer-oriented one ("*Imagination at work*") was part of the leadership change from Jack Welch to Jeffrey Immelt, who approved the investment in Enron Wind.[39]

Although emergent strategies can arise in the most unusual circumstances, it is important to emphasize the role that top management teams play in this type of strategy process. In the strategy-as-planned-emergence approach, executives need to decide which of the bottom-up initiatives to pursue and which to shut down. This critical decision is made on the basis of whether the strategic initiative fits with the company's vision and mission, and whether it provides an opportunity worth exploiting. In the GE wind energy example, Jeffrey Immelt decided to support this strategic initiative and provided appropriate resources and structures to grow this emergent strategy into a major strategic initiative that's now worth billions of dollars.

In contrast, Google fumbled its social networking opportunity presented by Orkut.[40] In 2002, some two years before Facebook was started (equating to eons in Internet time), Google engineer Orkut Buyukkokten had developed a social network using his 20 percent discretionary time. Marissa Mayer, Google's vice president in charge of this project, liked what she saw and provided initial support. After adding more engineers to further Orkut's development, Google was astonished at the early success of the social network: within the first month alone after release, hundreds of thousands of people signed up. Today, it has a mere 30 million users (mostly in Brazil and India), which pales in comparison to Facebook's over 1 billion users worldwide.

Why did Google fumble its lead over Facebook? Google had a huge opportunity to become the leader in social networking because MySpace imploded after it was acquired by News Corp. Despite initial support, Google's top executives felt that social networking did not fit its vision *to organize the world's information and make it universally accessible and useful.* Google relied on highly complex and proprietary algorithms to organize the knowledge available on the Internet and serve up targeted search ads. Social networking software, in comparison, is fairly pedestrian. Google's co-founders, Sergey Brin and Larry Page, both exceptional computer scientists, looked down on social networking. They felt their Page-Rank algorithm that accounts for hundreds of variables and considers all available websites was far superior in providing *objective* recommendations to users' search queries than *subjective* endorsements by someone's (online) friends. As a consequence, they snubbed social networking. Moreover, given the many different projects Google was pursuing at that time, Orkut was ranked as a low priority by Google's top executives. Starved of further resources, the social networking site withered, making Facebook the undisputed leader.

In 2011, Google launched Google Plus, its newest social networking service. By integrating all its services such as Gmail, YouTube, Chrome, and others into one user interface (and requiring users of even just one Google product to sign in to its portal), the company hopes to catch up with Facebook. Not being able to access Facebook users' activities limits Google's ability to serve targeted ads, and thus cuts into its main line of business. AdWords is Google's main online advertising product and garners some 85 percent of Google's total revenues of $50 billion (in 2012).[41]

Finally, bottom-up strategies can also emerge as a consequence of the firm's resource allocation process (RAP).[42] The way a firm allocates its resources can be critical in shaping its realized strategy.[43] Intel Corp. illustrates this concept.[44] Intel was founded in 1968 to produce DRAM (dynamic random-access memory) chips. From the start, producing these chips was the firm's top-down strategic plan, and initially it worked well. In the 1980s, Japanese competitors brought better-quality chips to the market at lower cost, threatening Intel's position and strategic plan. However, Intel was able to pursue a strategic transformation due to the way it set up its resource allocation process. In a sense, Intel was using functional-level managers to drive business and corporate strategies in a bottom-up fashion. In particular, during this time Intel had only a few "fabs" (fabrication plants to produce silicon-based products). It would have taken several years and billions of dollars to build additional capacity by bringing new fabs online.

With constrained production capacity, Intel had implemented the production-decision rule *to maximize margin-per-wafer-start.* Each time functional managers initiated a new production run, they were to consider the profit margins for DRAM chips and for semiconductors (the "brains" of personal computers); they then could produce *whichever product* delivered the higher margin. By following this simple rule, front-line managers shifted Intel's production capacity away from the lower-margin DRAM business to the higher-margin semiconductor business. The firm's focus on semiconductors emerged from the bottom up, based on resource allocation. Indeed, by the time top management finally approved the de facto strategic switch, the company's market share in DRAM had dwindled to less than 3 percent.[45]

Taken together, a firm's realized strategy is frequently a combination of top-down strategic intent and bottom-up emergent strategies, as Exhibit 2.8 shows. This type of strategy process is called **planned emergence**. In that process, organizational structure and systems allow bottom-up strategic initiatives to emerge and be evaluated and coordinated by top management.[46]

planned emergence
Strategy process in which organizational structure and systems allow bottom-up strategic initiatives to emerge and be evaluated and coordinated by top management.

2.4 ◄► Implications for the Strategist

Two ingredients are needed to create a powerful foundation upon which to formulate and implement a strategy in order to gain and sustain a competitive advantage: First, the firm needs an inspiring vision and mission backed up by ethical values. Second, the firm needs an effective strategic management process.

Each of the three strategy processes introduced in this chapter has its strengths and weaknesses. The effectiveness of the chosen strategy process is *contingent* upon the rate of change in the internal and external environments of the firm. In a slow-moving environment, top-down strategic planning might be the most effective approach. Besides the rate of change, a second dimension is firm size. Larger firms tend to use either a top-down strategic planning process or scenario planning. For a nuclear power provider such as Areva in France that provides over 75 percent of the country's energy and has the long-term backing of the state, for instance, using a top-down strategy approach might work well. Given that nuclear accidents are rare, but when they occur they have a tremendous impact (such as in Chernobyl, Russia, and Fukushima, Japan), Areva might use scenario planning to prepare for black swan events. In fast-moving environments, in contrast, Internet companies such as Alibaba, eBay, Facebook, Google, Dropbox, Pinterest, or Twitter tend to use the strategy-as-planned-emergence process.

Another important implication of our discussion is that all employees should be involved in setting an inspiring vision and mission to create more meaningful work. Belief in a company's vision and mission motivates its employees. Moreover, every employee plays a strategic role. Lower-level employees focus mainly on strategy implementation when a firm is using top-down or scenario planning. As the examples, however, have shown, *any employee* (even at the entry level) can have great ideas that might become *strategic initiatives* with the potential to transform companies.

Here we conclude our discussion of the strategic management process, which marks the end of the "getting started" portion of the AFI framework. The next chapter moves us into the analysis part of the framework, where we begin by studying external and internal analyses.

CHAPTER**CASE 2** / Consider This . . .

MANY OBSERVERS APPLAUD Indra Nooyi for taking a stakeholder strategy approach by making PepsiCo's strategic vision *Performance with a Purpose.* Although Ms. Nooyi has defined an inspiring vision for PepsiCo, financial performance seems to be lagging, especially in comparison with its archrival Coca-Cola, which has done well by continuing to concentrate on its core business in soda and other non-alcoholic beverages. In particular, critics allege that Ms. Nooyi has not paid enough attention to the company's flagship beverage business: Pepsi-Cola fell to No. 3 in U.S. soda sales, behind Coke and Diet Coke. As a result, PepsiCo's stock has underperformed archrival Coca-Cola in recent years.

Some critics even go so far as to call for the replacement of Ms. Nooyi. They also propose splitting PepsiCo into two standalone companies. One would focus on beverages (Pepsi, Gatorade, Tropicana); the other would focus on snack foods (Frito-Lay, Doritos). This move would unlock additional profit potential, the argument goes, because well-performing snack foods would no longer need to subsidize underperforming beverages.

Questions

Thinking about ChapterCase 2, answer the following questions.

1. What "grade" would you give Ms. Nooyi for her job performance as a strategic leader? What are her strengths and weaknesses? Where would you place Ms. Nooyi on the Level-5 pyramid of strategic leadership (see Exhibit 2.4), and why? Support your answers.

2. What should a strategic leader like Ms. Nooyi do if his or her vision does not seem to lead to an immediate (financial) competitive advantage? What would be your top-three recommendations? Support your arguments.

3. If you were a member of PepsiCo's board of directors, would you be concerned with Ms. Nooyi's and/or PepsiCo's performance? If you were concerned, what course of action would you recommend? Would you go so far as to endorse Ms. Nooyi's replacement with a new CEO who would focus more on PepsiCo's stock market performance? Why or why not?

4. Do you agree with Ms. Nooyi's critics that PepsiCo should be split up into two companies—one focusing on beverages, and one focusing on snack foods? What would be the advantages and disadvantages of such a move?

TAKE-AWAY CONCEPTS

This chapter explained the role of vision, mission, and values in the strategic management process. It provided an overview of strategic leadership and explained different processes to create strategy, as summarized by the following learning objectives and related take-away concepts.

LO 2-1 / Describe the roles of vision, mission, and values in the strategic management process.

- A vision captures an organization's aspirations. An effective vision inspires and motivates members of the organization.
- A mission statement describes what an organization actually does—what its business is—and why and how it does it.
- Values define the ethical standards and norms that should govern the behavior of individuals within the firm.

LO 2-2 / Evaluate the strategic implications of product-oriented and customer-oriented vision statements.

- Product-oriented vision statements define a business in terms of a good or service provided.
- Customer-oriented vision statements define business in terms of providing solutions to customer needs.

- Customer-oriented vision statements provide managers with more strategic flexibility than product-oriented missions.
- To be effective, visions and missions need to be backed up by hard-to-reverse strategic commitments.

LO 2-3 / Explain why anchoring a firm in ethical values is essential for long-term success.

- Employees tend to follow values practiced by strategic leaders. Without commitment from top managers, statements of values remain merely public relations exercises.
- Ethical values are the guardrails that help keep the company on track when pursuing its mission and its quest for competitive advantage.

LO 2-4 / Outline how managers become strategic leaders.

- To become an effective strategic leader, a manager needs to develop skills to move sequentially through five different leadership levels: highly capable individual, contributing team member, competent manager, effective leader, and executive.

LO 2-5 / Describe the roles of corporate, business, and functional managers in strategy formulation and implementation.

- Corporate executives must provide answers to the question of *where* to compete (in industries, markets, and geographies), and *how to create synergies* among different business units.

- General managers in strategic business units must answer the strategic question of *how to compete* in order to achieve superior performance. They must manage and align the firm's different functional areas for competitive advantage.

- Functional managers are responsible for *implementing business strategy* within a single functional area.

LO 2-6 / Evaluate top-down strategic planning, scenario planning, and strategy as planned emergence.

- Top-down strategic planning is a sequential, linear process that works reasonably well when the environment does not change much.

- In scenario planning, managers envision what-if scenarios and prepare contingency plans that can be called upon when necessary.

- Strategic initiatives can be the result of top-down planning or can emerge through a bottom-up process from deep within the organization. They have the potential to shape a firm's strategy.

- A firm's realized strategy is generally a combination of its top-down intended strategy and bottom-up emergent strategy, resulting in planned emergence.

KEY TERMS

Dominant strategic plan
Emergent strategy
Intended strategy
Level-5 leadership pyramid
Mission
Organizational values

Planned emergence
Realized strategy
Scenario planning
Strategic business unit (SBU)
Strategic commitments
Strategic initiative

Strategic leadership
Strategic management process
Top-down strategic planning
Upper-echelons theory
Vision

DISCUSSION QUESTIONS

1. What characteristics does an effective mission statement have?

2. In what situations is top-down planning likely to be superior to bottom-up emergent strategy development?

3. This chapter introduces three different levels appropriate for strategic considerations (see Exhibit 2.5). In what situations would some of these levels be more important than others? For example, what issues might be considered by the corporate level? What do you see as the primary responsibilities of corporate-level executives? When might the business-level

managers bear more responsibility for considering how to respond to an issue? In what situations might the functional-level managers have a primary responsibility for considering an issue? How should the organization ensure the proper attention to each level of strategy as needed?

4. Identify an industry that is undergoing intense competition or is being featured in the business press. Discuss how scenario planning might be used by competitors to prepare for future events. Can some industries benefit more than others from this type of process? Explain why.

ETHICAL/SOCIAL ISSUES

1. Over 50,000 people lost their jobs and many their life savings in the Enron debacle. Some of those at Enron who were closely involved in the scandal, such as Jeffrey Skilling (CEO) and Andrew Fastow (CFO), are serving significant prison sentences. Why do you think only one employee initially came forward to report the irregularities and help with the investigation? What responsibility do lower-level executives bear for not reporting such questionable practices by the firm's leadership?

2. The list below shows a sample of various vision/mission statements. Guess the company, and identify whether the statements are customer-oriented, product-oriented, or a combination.

	Vision/Mission Statement	Company	Type of Statement
a.	To be earth's most customer centric company; to build a place where people can come to find and discover anything they might want to buy online.		
b.	To be the most respected global financial services company.		
c.	To provide personal vehicle owners and enthusiasts with the vehicle related products and knowledge that fulfill their wants and needs at the right price.		
d.	To provide technology advancing every company, products enhancing every home, and innovation improving every life.		
e.	To become the Beauty company most women turn to worldwide.		
f.	To provide a global trading platform where practically anyone can trade practically anything.		
g.	To operate the best specialty retail business in America, regardless of the product we sell.		
h.	To combine aggressive strategic marketing with quality products and services at competitive prices to provide the best insurance value for consumers.		
i.	To be the most respected global financial services company.		
j.	To nourish and delight everyone we serve.		
k.	To help our clients make distinctive, lasting, and substantial improvements in their performance and to build a great firm that attracts, develops, excites, and retains exceptional people.		
l.	To be America's best run, most profitable automotive retailer.		
m.	[To] use our pioneering spirit to responsibly deliver energy to the world.		
n.	[To] provide high-quality [chocolate] products while conducting our business in a socially responsible and environmentally sustainable manner.		
o.	Bringing the best to everyone we touch		
p.	[To provide] high value-added supply chain, transportation, business and related information services through focused operating companies.		
q.	[To provide] convenience and low prices.		
r.	To become the first platform of choice for sharing data, to be an enterprise that has the happiest employees, and to last at least 102 years.		
s.	To organize the world's information and make it universally accessible and useful.		
t.	To give ordinary folk the chance to buy the same thing as rich people.		
u.	To give the people the power to share and make the world more open and connected.		

SMALL-GROUP EXERCISES

//// **Small-Group Exercise 1**

A popular topic in education and public policy is the need to support the STEM disciplines (Science, Technology, Engineering, Mathematics) as the key to U.S. competitiveness. These disciplines generate innovative ideas and build new companies—and perhaps new industries. As you have learned in this chapter, innovative ideas can help sustain competitive advantage. Many American businesses, however, are concerned about whether there will be an adequate supply of STEM workers in the future because the growth in job opportunities for STEM occupations is expected to be nearly three times as fast as for non-STEM occupations. A key advocate for federal support for funding STEM education is the STEM Education Coalition, which expresses its mission as "to ensure that STEM education is recognized as a national policy priority."

The skills and expertise of the STEM occupations will be critical in dealing with the National Intelligence Council's Global Trends 2030 initiatives, which will confront the global community over the next 15 years. In particular, the key trends include a need for new communication and manufacturing technologies, cyber-security, health care advances and preparations to manage pandemic threats, innovative and sustainable designs for infrastructure improvements, and improvements in the production and management of food, water, and energy that will meet the needs of a growing population. Business organizations may find opportunities to build sustainable competitive advantages by responding to these trends, but they will need adequate STEM expertise in order to create innovative and appropriate responses to these challenges. With innovation and cooperation, these trends can be confronted peacefully in order to benefit geopolitical stability.

1. Discuss within your group methods that the STEM Education Coalition might use to gain partners, particularly business organizations, that will help them make sure STEM education is a national policy priority. Given the budget crisis, how can they persuade congressional representatives to support funding?

2. How does funding for STEM education affect job opportunities for business majors?

3. Although group members may not be STEM majors, brainstorm ideas about how you might advise businesses to modify their operations or to expand/transform their operations in order to find opportunities in the Global Trends over the next 15 years. Choose a business of interest to the group. Then consider scenarios in which the business may thrive as one of the five trends develop. For example, the majority of businesses might want to ask, "What if threats to cyber-security increase?" Or, "What if water resources become more scarce? How would this affect production or demand for the goods produced?" Your group may also consider businesses or industries that may decline as a result of the trends.

4. What additional developmental opportunities might prepare business majors for playing key roles in facing the Global Trends 2030? What skills will you need in order to manage effectively the STEM employees who are central to innovation?

//// **Small-Group Exercise 2**

In many situations, promising ideas emerge from the lower levels of an organization, only to be discarded before they can be implemented. It was only extraordinary tenacity (and indeed, disregard) for the policy of selling only corporate-approved drinks that permitted the Frappuccino to "bloom" within Starbucks (see Strategy Highlight 2.2).

Some scholars have suggested that companies set aside up to 2 percent of their budgets for *any* manager with budget control to be able to invest in new ideas within the company.[47] Thus, someone with a $100,000 annual budget to manage would be able to invest $2,000 in cash or staff time toward such a project. Multiple managers could go in together for somewhat larger funds or time amounts. Through such a process, the organization could generate a network of "angel investors." Small funds or staff time could be invested into a variety of projects. Approval mechanisms would be easier for these small "seed-stock" ideas, to give them a chance to develop before going for bigger funding at the top levels of the organization.

What would be some problems that would need to be addressed to introduce this angel-network idea into a firm? Use a firm someone in your group has worked for or knows well to discuss possible issues of widely distributing small funding level approvals across the firm.

STRATEGY TERM PROJECT

//// Module 2: Mission, Goals, and the Strategic Management Process

1. Search for a vision, mission statement, and statement of values for your chosen firm. Note that not all organizations publish these statements specifically, so you may need to make inferences from the available information. Relevant information is often available at the firm's website (though it may take some searching) or is contained in its annual reports. You may also interview a manager of the firm or contact Investor Relations. You may also be able to compare the official statement with the business press coverage of the firm.

2. Identify the major goals of the company. What are its short-term versus long-term goals? What resources must the firm acquire to achieve its long-term goals?

3. Trace any changes in strategy that you can identify over time. Try to determine whether the strategic changes of your selected firm are a result of intended strategies, emergent strategies, or some combination of both.

my STRATEGY

How Much Are Your Values Worth to You?

How much are you willing to pay for the job you want? This may sound like a strange question, since your employer will pay you to work, but think again. Consider how much you value a specific type of work, or how much you would want to work for a specific organization because of its values.

A recent study shows scientists who want to continue engaging in research will accept some $14,000 less in annual salary to work at an organization that permits them to publish their findings in academic journals, implying that some scientists will "pay to be scientists." This finding appears to hold in the general business world, too. In a recent survey, 97 percent of Stanford MBA students indicated they would forgo some 14 percent of their expected salary, or about $11,480 a year, to work for a company that matches their own values with concern for stakeholders and sustainability. According to Monster.com, an online career service, about 92 percent of all undergraduates want to work for a "green" company. These diverse examples demonstrate that people put a real dollar amount on pursuing careers in sync with their values.

On the other hand, certain high-powered jobs such as management consulting or investment banking pay very well, but their high salaries come with strings attached. Professionals in these jobs work very long hours, including weekends, and often take little or no vacation time. These workers "pay for pay" in that they are often unable to form stable relationships, have little or no leisure time, and sometimes even sacrifice their health. People "pay for"—make certain sacrifices for—what they value, because strategic decisions require important trade-offs.[48]

1. Identify your personal values. How do you expect these values to affect your work life or your career choice?

2. How much less salary would (did) you accept to find employment with a company that is aligned with your values?

3. How much are you willing to "pay for pay" if your dream job is in management consulting or investment banking?

ENDNOTES

1. This ChapterCase is based on: "PepsiCo shakes it up," *BusinessWeek,* August 14, 2006; "The Pepsi challenge," *The Economist,* August 17, 2006; "Keeping cool in hot water," *BusinessWeek,* June 11, 2007; "Pepsi gets a makeover," *The Economist,* March 25, 2010; "Indra Nooyi on Performance with Purpose 2009," PepsiCo Video, http://bit. ly/Ubhvs8; "Conversation with Indra Nooyi Yale SOM '80"; "PepsiCo wakes up and smells the cola," *The Wall Street Journal,* June 28, 2011; "Should Pepsi break up? *The Economist,* October 11, 2011; "As Pepsi struggles to regain market share, Indra Nooyi's job is on the line," *The Economist,* May 17, 2012; and www.wolframalpha.com.

2. Finkelstein, S., D. C. Hambrick, and A. A. Cannella (2008), *Strategic Leadership: Theory and Research on Executives, Top Management Teams, and Boards* (Oxford, UK: Oxford University Press); and Yulk, G. (1998), *Leadership in Organizations,* 4th ed. (Englewood Cliff, NJ: Prentice-Hall).

3. http://www.pepsico.com/Purpose/ Overview.html.

4. Frankl, V. E. (1984), *Man's Search for Meaning.*

5. Pink, D. H. (2011). *The Surprising Truth About What Motivates Us* (New York: Riverhead Books).

6. Hamel, G., and C. K. Prahalad (1989), "Strategic intent," *Harvard Business Review* (May–June): 64–65; Hamel, G., and C. K. Prahalad (1994), *Competing for the Future* (Boston, MA: Harvard Business School Press); and Collins, J. C., and J. I. Porras (1994), *Built to Last: Successful Habits of Visionary Companies* (New York: Harper Collins).

7. Collins, J. C., and J. I. Porras (1994), *Built to Last: Successful Habits of Visionary Companies.*

8. Dixit, A., and B. Nalebuff (1991), *Thinking Strategically: The Competitive Edge in Business, Politics, and Everyday Life* (New York: Norton); and Brandenburger, A. M., and B. J. Nalebuff (1996), *Co-opetition* (New York: Currency Doubleday).

9. Germain, R., and M. B. Cooper (1990), "How a customer mission statement affects company performance," *Industrial Marketing Management* 19(2), 47–54; Bart, C. K. (1997), "Industrial firms and the power of mission," *Industrial Marketing Management* 26 (4): 371–383; and Bart, C. K. (2001), "Measuring the mission effect in human intellectual capital," *Journal of Intellectual Capital* 2(3): 320–330.

10. "The three habits . . . of highly irritating management gurus," *The Economist,* October 22, 2009.

11. The Disney and Subway discussion is based on: Heath, C., and D. Heath (2007), *Made to Stick,* pp. 60–61.

12. Burgelman, R. A., and A. S. Grove (1996), "Strategic dissonance," *California Management Review* 38: 8–28; and Grove, A. S. (1996), *Only the Paranoid Survive: How to Exploit the Crisis Points that Challenge Every Company* (New York: Currency Doubleday).

13. Bart, C. K., and M. C. Baetz (1998), "The relationship between mission statements and firm performance: An exploratory study," *Journal of Management Studies* 35: 823–853.

14. Finkelstein, S., D. C. Hambrick, and A. A. Cannella (2008), *Strategic Leadership,* p. 4.

15. Hambrick, D. C., and E. Abrahamson (1995), "Assessing managerial discretion across industries: A multimethod approach," *Academy of Management Journal* 38: 1427–1441.

16. "The 100 best performing CEOs in the World," *Harvard Business Review,* January–February 2013.

17. As quoted in: Collins, J. (2009), *How the Mighty Fall. And Why Some Companies Never Give In* (New York: Harper Collins), p. 53.

18. http://www.merck.com/about/featured-stories/mectizan1.html.

19. Gilmartin, R. V. (2011), "The Vioxx recall tested our leadership," *Harvard Business Review Blog Network,* October 6.

20. The Merck River Blindness case and the quote by CEO Kenneth Frazier are drawn from: http://www.merck.com/about/featured-stories/mectizan1.html. This Vioxx example is drawn from: "Jury finds Merck liable in Vioxx death and awards $253 million," *The New York Times,* August 19, 2005; Heal, G. (2008), *When Principles Pay: Corporate Social Responsibility and the Bottom Line* (New York: Columbia Business School); and Collins, J. (2009), *How the Mighty Fall: And Why Some Companies Never Give In* (New York: Harper Collins).

21. Bandiera, O., A. Prat, and R. Sadun (2012), "Managerial capital at the top: Evidence from the time use of CEOs," *London School of Economics and Harvard Business School Working Paper;* and "In defense of the CEO," *The Wall Street Journal,* January 15, 2013. The patterns of how CEOs spend their time have held in a number of different studies across the world.

22. Finkelstein, S., D. C. Hambrick, and A. A. Cannella (2008), *Strategic Leadership,* p. 17.

23. Hambrick, D. C. (2007), "Upper echelons theory: An update," *Academy of Management Review* 32: 334–343; and Hambrick, D. C., and P. A. Mason (1984), "Upper echelons: The organization as a reflection of its top managers," *Academy of Management Review* 9: 193–206.

24. Collins, J. (2001), *Good to Great: Why Some Companies Make the Leap . . . And Others Don't* (New York: HarperCollins), p. 3.

25. Ibid.

26. PepsiCo, Inc. 2011 Annual Report.

27. This discussion is based on: Mintzberg, H. (1993), *The Rise and Fall of Strategic Planning: Reconceiving Roles for Planning, Plans, and Planners* (New York: Simon & Schuster); and Mintzberg, H. (1994), "The fall and rise of strategic planning," *Harvard Business Review* (January–February): 107–114.

28. Isaacson, W. (2011), *Steve Jobs* (New York: Simon & Schuster). See also: Isaacson, W. (2012), "The real leadership lessons of Steve Jobs," *Harvard Business Review* (April).

29. Jobs, S. (1998), "There is sanity returning," *BusinessWeek,* May 25.

30. "CEO Tim Cook pushes employee-friendly benefits long shunned by Steve Jobs," *The Wall Street Journal,* November 12, 2012.

31. Grove, A. S. (1996), *Only the Paranoid Survive.*

32. Personal communication with UPS strategy executives during onsite visit in corporate headquarters, June 17, 2009.

33. Mintzberg, H. (1993), *The Rise and Fall of Strategic Planning;* and Mintzberg, H. (1994), "The fall and rise of strategic planning."

34. Data from the U.S. census bureau, reported in "E-commerce," *The Economist,* April 6, 2013.

35. Arthur, B. W. (1989), "Competing technologies, increasing returns, and lock-in by historical events," *Economic Journal* 99: 116–131; and Brown, S. L., and K. M. Eisenhardt (1998), *Competing on the Edge: Strategy as Structured Chaos* (Boston, MA: Harvard Business School Press); Bower, J. L. (1970), *Managing the Resource Allocation Process* (Boston, MA: Harvard Business School Press); Bower, J. L., and C. G. Gilbert (2005), *From Resource Allocation to Strategy* (Oxford, UK: Oxford University Press); Burgelman, R. A. (1983), "A model of the interaction of strategic behavior, corporate context, and the concept of strategy," *Academy* *of Management Review* 8: 61–71; and Burgelman, R. A. (1983), "A process model of internal corporate venturing in a major diversified firm," *Administrative Science Quarterly* 28: 223–244.

36. Levy, S. (2011), *In the Plex: How Google Thinks, Works, and Shapes Our Lives* (New York: Simon & Schuster).

37. Mayer, M. (2006), "Nine lessons learned about creativity at Google," presentation at Stanford Technology Ventures Program, May 17.

38. Based on Howard Behar (retired President, Starbucks North America and Starbucks International) (2009), Impact Speaker Series Presentation, College of Management, Georgia Institute of Technology, October 14. See also Behar, H. (2007), *It's Not About the Coffee: Leadership Principles from a Life at Starbucks* (New York: Portfolio).

39. John Rice (GE Vice Chairman, President, and CEO, GE Technology Infrastructure) (2009), presentation at Georgia Institute of Technology, May 11.

40. This case vignette is drawn from: Levy, S. (2011), *In the Plex: How Google Thinks, Works, and Shapes Our Lives* (New York: Simon & Schuster).

41. Google's 10-K report. U.S. Securities and Exchange Commission (SEC), Washington, D.C., December 31, 2012.

42. Bower, J. L. (1970), *Managing the Resource Allocation Process* (Boston, MA: Harvard Business School Press); Bower, J. L., and C. G. Gilbert (2005), *From Resource Allocation to Strategy* (Oxford, UK: Oxford University Press); Burgelman, R. A. (1983), "A model of the interaction of strategic behavior, corporate context, and the concept of strategy," *Academy of Management Review* 8: 61–71; and Burgelman, R. A. (1983), "A process model of internal corporate venturing in a major diversified firm," *Administrative Science Quarterly* 28: 223–244.

43. Bower, J. L., and C. G. Gilbert (2005), *From Resource Allocation to Strategy.*

44. Burgelman, R. A. (1994), "Fading memories: A process theory of strategic business exit in dynamic environments," *Administrative Science Quarterly* 39: 24–56.

45. Burgelman, R. A., and A. S. Grove (1996), "Strategic dissonance," *California Management Review* 38: 8–28.

46. Grant, R. M. (2003), "Strategic planning in a turbulent environment: Evidence from the oil majors," *Strategic Management Journal* 24: 491–517; Brown, S. L., and K. M. Eisenhardt (1997), "The art of continuous change: Linking complexity theory and time-based evolution in relentlessly shifting organizations," *Administrative Science Quarterly* 42: 1–34; Farjourn, M. (2002), "Towards an organic perspective on strategy," *Strategic Management Journal* 23: 561–594; Mahoney, J. (2005), *Economic Foundation of Strategy* (Thousand Oaks, CA: Sage); and Burgelman, R. A., and A. S. Grove (2007), "Let chaos reign, then rein in chaos – repeatedly: Managing strategic dynamics for corporate longevity," *Strategic Management Journal* 28: 965–979.

47. Hamel, G. (2007), *The Future of Management* (Boston, MA: Harvard Business School Publishing).

48. This *my*Strategy module is based on: Stern, S. (2004), "Do scientists pay to be scientists?" *Management Science* 50(6): 835–853; and Esty, D. C., and A. S. Winston (2009), *Green to Gold: How Smart Companies Use Environmental Strategy to Innovate, Create Value, and Build Competitive Advantage,* revised and updated (Hoboken, NJ: John Wiley).

Chapter 3

External Analysis: Industry Structure, Competitive Forces, and Strategic Groups

Chapter Outline

Learning Objectives

After studying this chapter, you should be able to:

LO 3-1 Generate a PESTEL analysis to evaluate the impact of external forces on the firm.

LO 3-2 Apply Porter's five competitive forces to explain the profit potential of different industries.

LO 3-3 Explain how competitive industry structure shapes rivalry among competitors.

LO 3-4 Describe the strategic role of complements in creating positive-sum co-opetition.

LO 3-5 Appraise the role of industry dynamics and industry convergence in shaping the firm's external environment.

LO 3-6 Generate a strategic group model to reveal performance differences between clusters of firms in the same industry.

CHAPTER**CASE 3**

Tesla Motors and the U.S. Automotive Industry

THE BIG THREE—GM, Ford, and Chrysler—dominated the U.S. car market throughout most of the 20th century. Having enjoyed protection behind high entry barriers, GM once held more than a 50 percent U.S. market share and was highly profitable for many decades, until about 1980. Ford and Chrysler both also did well during this period. However, as competition in the industry became increasingly global, foreign carmakers entered the U.S. market, at first mainly by importing vehicles from overseas plants. Among the first were German carmakers Volkswagen (now also owner of the Porsche and Audi brands), Daimler, and BMW, as well as Japanese carmakers Honda, Toyota, and Nissan. These foreign entrants intensified competition, threatened the Big Three's market share, and led to political pressure to impose import restrictions in the 1980s. Not to be stopped, the new players responded by building U.S. plants in order to avoid import restrictions. More recently, Korean carmakers Hyundai and Kia have also joined in and begun making and selling cars in the United States.

Although globalization and deregulation paved the way for significant new entry into the U.S. auto market, the worldwide car manufacturing industry has been exposed to few new entrants. In fact, no new major car manufacturers have emerged in the last couple of decades simply because few industrial products (save for commercial airplanes and nuclear power plants) are as complex to build as cars powered by internal combustion engines. Car manufacturers also require large-scale production in order to be cost-competitive. Taken together, these factors create significant entry barriers into the car manufacturing industry. Would you say, then, that a Silicon Valley technology startup attempting to break into this industry might be running a fool's errand?

Serial entrepreneur Elon Musk, who creates and runs new ventures to address not only economic but also social and environmental challenges, begs to differ. During the Internet boom, Musk made his name (and fortune) by developing an early version of Google maps and by co-founding the online payment system PayPal. The sale of both companies amounted to close to $2 billion, which allowed Musk to focus on his lifelong passions in science, engineering, and space. Musk is founder of and currently runs three different companies: SpaceX (which made history in May 2012 as the first private company to deliver a cargo payload to the International Space Station with its Dragon spacecraft), SolarCity (basically the Walmart of solar panel installations for business and residential customers), and Tesla Motors, an all-electric American car company. It is Tesla where Mr. Musk is currently focusing most of his attention.

As we have discussed, the U.S. automotive industry is characterized by high entry barriers. However, rather than attempting to overcome these barriers through large-scale entry using traditional internal combustion technology, Mr. Musk uses new technology to sidestep them altogether. In particular, Tesla Motors develops all-electric powertrains and cars, and currently offers three models. Unlike complex gasoline engines, electric cars are powered by relatively simple motors and gearboxes that have few parts. In fact, the Tesla Roadster, an expensive sports car, has already successfully demonstrated that electric vehicles can be more than mere golf carts by outperforming a Porsche 911 on key metrics such as acceleration. In a move to appeal to a more mass market and to reach a larger production scale to drive down unit costs, Tesla next developed the Model S, a four-door family sedan. The Model S received an outstanding market reception, and was awarded the 2013 *MotorTrend* Car of the Year. Tesla is also working on a newly designed seven-seat electric vehicle—the Model X—in an attempt to combine the best features of an SUV with the benefits of a minivan.[1]

After reading the chapter, you will find more about this case, with related questions, on page 88.

57

THE TESLA MOTORS ChapterCase illustrates that competitive forces in an industry have a direct bearing on a firm's profit potential. Globalization led to extensive entry by foreign car manufacturers, increasing the number of competitors in the U.S. auto industry, and with it, competitive rivalry. The Japanese automakers, for example, were successful in the U.S. market because their cars were generally of better quality, their production systems were more efficient, and they were more responsive to changes in customer preferences. Today, Korean carmakers are attempting to duplicate this feat. At the same time, U.S. automakers Ford and GM are experiencing a resurgence. Moreover, technological innovations have allowed startups such as Tesla Motors to enter the electric car segment (or strategic group), effectively circumventing high entry barriers into the broader automotive market. With more firms vying for a share of the U.S. auto market, competitive intensity is sure to increase.

In this chapter, we present a set of frameworks to analyze the firm's *external environment*—that is, the industry in which the firm operates, and the competitive forces that surround the firm from the outside. We move from a more macro perspective to a more micro understanding of how the external environment affects a firm's quest for competitive advantage.

We begin with the PESTEL framework, which allows us to scan, monitor, and evaluate changes and trends in the firm's macroenvironment. Next, we study Porter's five forces model of competition, which allows us to determine an industry's profit potential. Depending on the firm's strategic position, these forces can affect its performance in a positive or negative fashion. We then move from a static analysis of a firm's industry environment to a dynamic understanding of how industries and competition change over time. Finally, we will introduce the strategic group model as a final framework to help us understand performance differences between clusters of firms in the same industry before developing practical *Implications for the Strategist*.

3.1 The PESTEL Framework

LO 3-1

Generate a PESTEL analysis to evaluate the impact of external forces on the firm.

PESTEL model
A framework that categorizes and analyzes an important set of external forces (political, economic, sociocultural, technological, ecological, and legal) that might impinge upon a firm. These forces are embedded in the global environment and can create both opportunities and threats for the firm.

A firm's external environment consists of all the forces that can affect its potential to gain and sustain a competitive advantage. By analyzing the forces in the external environment, managers can mitigate threats and leverage opportunities. One common approach to understanding how external forces impinge upon a firm is to consider the source or proximity of these forces. For example, external forces in the firm's *general environment* are ones that managers have little direct influence over, such as macroeconomic factors (e.g., interest or currency exchange rates). In contrast, external factors in the firm's *task environment* are ones that managers do have some influence over, such as the composition of their strategic groups (a set of close rivals) or the structure of the industry. We will now take a look at each of these environmental layers in detail, moving from a firm's general environment to its task environment (following along in Exhibit 3.1, we will be working from the outer ring to the inner ring).

The **PESTEL model** groups the forces in the firm's general environment into six segments: *political, economic, sociocultural, technological, ecological,* and *legal,* which together form the acronym PESTEL. Although many of the PESTEL factors are interdependent, the PESTEL model provides a relatively straightforward way to *scan, monitor,* and *evaluate* the important external factors and trends that might impinge upon a firm. As markets have opened up and international trade has increased

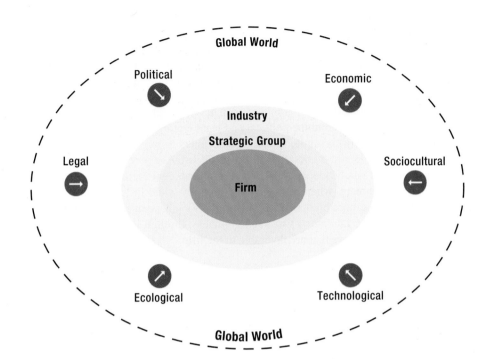

EXHIBIT 3.1

The Firm Embedded in Its External Environment: Global World, PESTEL Forces, Industry, and Strategic Group

in recent decades, the PESTEL forces have become more global. As a consequence, these forces are embedded in the global environment and can create both opportunities and threats.

POLITICAL/LEGAL FACTORS

Since they are closely related, we will consolidate the discussion of political and legal factors. The *political environment* describes the processes and actions of government bodies that can influence the decisions and behavior of firms.[2] Governments, for example, can affect firm performance by exerting political pressure on companies. In Strategy Highlight 1.2, we saw how the U.S. government exerted political pressure upon BP in the aftermath of the Gulf of Mexico oil spill. In overseas markets, BP also faced political pressure. After a disagreement with its Russian partners, the government exerted political pressure upon BP to sell its stake in its joint venture with TNK, a local Russian oil company. State-owned Rosneft, a large, fully integrated oil company, then acquired the TNK-BP joint venture, originally formed to explore new oil reserves in Siberia.[3]

The *legal environment* captures the official outcomes of political processes as manifested in laws, mandates, regulations, and court decisions—all of which can have a direct bearing on a firm's profit potential. In fact, regulatory changes tend to affect entire industries at once. Many industries in the United States have been deregulated over the last few decades, including airlines, telecom, energy, and trucking, among others. In theory, removing or reducing government regulations tends to lead to new firm entry, intensified competition, innovation, and higher value at lower prices for consumers. One exception to this rule is the finance industry, where the repeal of the Glass–Steagall Act in 1999 removed any separation between traditional and investment banking. This led to skewed incentives and undue risk-taking by many of the world's largest financial institutions, contributing to the global financial crisis. As a political and legal response, the finance industry was re-regulated when the Dodd–Frank Wall Street Reform and Consumer Protection Act was signed into law in 2010.

Taken together, political/legal environments can have a direct bearing on a firm's performance. Governments often combine political and legal factors to achieve desired changes in consumer behavior. For example, to induce consumers to buy zero-emission vehicles, the U.S. government offers a $7,500 federal tax credit with the purchase of a new electric vehicle such as the Tesla Model S. While these political/legal factors are located in the firm's general environment, where managers traditionally wield little influence, firms are nevertheless becoming more proactive in their attempts to shape and influence this realm. They do so by applying *non-market strategies*—that is, through lobbying, contributions, litigation, and so on, in ways that are favorable to the firm.[4]

ECONOMIC FACTORS

Economic factors in a firm's external environment are largely macroeconomic, affecting economy-wide phenomena. Managers need to consider how the following five macroeconomic factors can affect firm strategy:

- Growth rates
- Interest rates
- Levels of employment
- Price stability (inflation and deflation)
- Currency exchange rates

GROWTH RATES. The overall economic *growth rate* is a measure of the change in the amount of goods and services produced by a nation's economy. It indicates what stage of the business cycle the economy is in—that is, whether business activity is expanding (boom) or contracting (recession). In periods of economic expansion, consumer and business demands are rising, and competition among firms frequently decreases. Basically, the rising tide of economic growth "lifts all boats." During these economic boom cycles, businesses expand operations to satisfy demand and are more likely to be profitable. The reverse is generally true for recessionary periods, although certain companies that focus on low-cost solutions may benefit from economic contractions because demand for their products or services rises in such times. For customers, expenditures on luxury products are often the first to be cut during recessionary periods (for instance, you might switch from a $4 Venti latte at Starbucks to a $2 alternative from McDonald's).

Occasionally, boom periods can overheat and lead to speculative bubbles. Between 1995 and 2000, for example, the United States witnessed such a bubble, propelled by new companies seeking to capture business opportunities on the Internet. The market for dot-com companies was characterized by "irrational exuberance,"[5] with the NASDAQ stock index peaking at its all-time high of 5,132 points on March 10, 2000. Hundreds of dot-com businesses were founded during this time, but very few survived the burst of the bubble. Among the survivors are today's powerhouses of the Internet economy including Google, Amazon, and eBay.

In the early 2000s, the United States saw yet another bubble—this time in housing.[6] Easy credit, made possible by the availability of subprime mortgages and other financial innovations, fueled an unprecedented demand in housing. Real estate, rather than stocks, became the investment vehicle of choice for many Americans, propelled by the common belief that house prices could only go up. When the housing bubble burst, the economic recession of 2008–2009 began, impacting in some way nearly all businesses in the United States and worldwide.

INTEREST RATES. Another key macroeconomic variable for managers to track is *interest rates*—the amount that savers are paid for use of their money and the amount that borrowers pay for that use. The economic boom during the early years in the 21st century, for example, was fueled by cheap credit. Low interest rates have a direct bearing on consumer demand. When credit is cheap (because interest rates are low), consumers buy homes, automobiles, computers, and even vacations on credit; in turn, all of this demand fuels economic growth. During periods of low interest rates, firms can easily borrow money to finance future growth. Borrowing at lower rates lowers the cost of capital and enhances a firm's competitiveness. These effects reverse, however, when interest rates are high. Consumer demand slows down, credit is harder to come by, and firms find it more difficult to borrow money to support operations and might defer investments.

LEVELS OF EMPLOYMENT. The state of the economy directly affects the *level of employment*. In boom times, unemployment is low, and skilled human capital becomes a scarce and more expensive resource. In economic downturns, unemployment rises. As more people search for employment, skilled human capital is abundant and wages usually fall.

A period of high unemployment could be a good time for firms to expand or upgrade their human capital base. Although U.S. companies generally lay off people during recessions, some Japanese companies, such as Toyota, prefer to use downturns to train their workers on the latest manufacturing techniques.[7] Clearly, this human resource management strategy is a short-term expense for Toyota, yet it positions the company well when the economy picks up again. Moreover, periods of higher unemployment often spur an uptick in entrepreneurship as the opportunity cost of starting a new venture falls. Need proof? Now-famous companies that began during recessionary periods include Microsoft, FedEx, GE, Revlon Cosmetics, and Hyatt Hotels.

PRICE STABILITY. *Price stability*—the lack of change in price levels of goods and services—is rare. Therefore, companies will often have to deal with changing price levels, which is a direct function of the amount of money in any economy. When there is too much money in an economy, we tend to see rising prices—*inflation*. Indeed, a popular economic definition of inflation is *too much money chasing too few goods and services.*[8] Inflation tends to go along with higher interest rates and lower economic growth. Countries such as Argentina, Brazil, Mexico, and Poland experienced periods of extremely high inflation rates in recent decades.

Deflation describes a decrease in the overall price level. A sudden and pronounced drop in demand generally causes deflation, which in turn forces sellers to lower prices to motivate buyers. Because many people automatically think of lower prices from the buyer's

Strategy Highlight 3.1

How the Eurozone Crisis Is Hurting Companies

In the wake of the recent global financial crisis (2008–2012), the European sovereign-debt crisis has taken center stage. It is negatively affecting companies across the globe. What is the Eurozone crisis, and how does it affect business? The euro is the common currency used by 17 of the 27 member states of the European Union (EU), an economic and political union of more than 500 million people. In the 1950s, in response to extreme forms of nationalism and the resulting world wars that had devastated the continent, the first steps were taken to create a supra-national EU. Heavy industries such as coal and steel became economically integrated. In 1992, after almost 40 years of continued economic integration, peace, and prosperity, the European leaders initiated further steps toward political and economic integration. In 1999, the euro was introduced as a common currency and a single EU market was created, allowing for free movements of people and capital, as well as goods and services. At the time, the vision was to create a "United States of Europe" with far-reaching economic and political integration to subsume individual nation states.

Although the euro is a common currency administered by the European Central Bank (ECB), the EU does not have budgetary authority. Each nation state runs its own fiscal budget. By 2009, it was clear that several European countries had taken on too much debt and were unable to repay their credit obligations. Borrowing costs and interest rates for the most indebted countries (Portugal, Italy, Ireland, Greece, and Spain—combined under the unfortunate moniker PIIGS) skyrocketed. With the risk of sovereign countries defaulting on their debts, investors panicked. Moreover, if one or more of the indebted countries were to be forced out of the Eurozone, they would likely fall

point of view, a decreasing price level seems at first glance to be attractive. However, deflation is actually a serious threat to economic growth because it distorts expectations about the future.[9] For example, once price levels start falling, companies will not invest in new production capacity or innovation because they expect a further decline in prices. In recent decades, the Japanese economy has been plagued with persistent deflation.

CURRENCY EXCHANGE RATES. The *currency exchange rate* determines how many dollars one must pay for a unit of foreign currency. It is a critical variable for any company that either buys or sells products and services across national borders. If the U.S. dollar depreciates (declines in value), for example, it takes more dollars to buy one euro, which in turn makes European imports such as LVMH luxury accessories or BMW automobiles more expensive for U.S. buyers. By the same token, U.S. exports such as Boeing aircraft or John Deere tractors benefit from a weaker U.S. dollar, because it makes their products relatively cheaper when exported to Europe. This process reverses when the dollar appreciates (increases in value) against the euro. In a similar fashion, as the Chinese yuan appreciates in value, it will make Chinese goods imported into the U.S. relatively more expensive. At the same time, Chinese purchasing power increases, which in turn allows their businesses to purchase more U.S. capital goods such as sophisticated machinery and other cutting-edge technologies.

In summary, economic factors affecting businesses are ever-present and rarely static. Managers need to fully appreciate the power of these factors, in both domestic and global markets, in order to assess their effects on firm performance. Strategy Highlight 3.1 shows how the European debt crisis—an external economic factor—is hurting large and small companies alike across the globe.

into economic isolation and decline. The combined effect of the unpaid loans and economic decline could lead to a collapse of the banking system, not only in Europe but also with repercussions in the United States due to the interdependencies of world finance.

Because the euro is a common currency, the affected countries could no longer devalue their own currencies in order to improve competitiveness. To get a handle on the budget deficit, European countries, with help from the International Monetary Fund (IMF), enacted strict austerity programs. As government budgets tightened, public sector workers such as teachers and police were laid off, public services were cut drastically, and pensions were renegotiated. Tightened capital markets made it difficult, if not impossible, for private sector companies to finance their continued operations. In the deep recession that followed, demand for goods and services collapsed, and some countries faced depression-like unemployment figures. In most EU countries, unemployment has been persistently above 10 percent in recent years; in Spain and Greece, that number rose to above 20 percent. Youth unemployment (for those under 25) in Spain soared to over 50 percent. It is not uncommon to see Spanish medical doctors working in low-level nursing home jobs in Germany.

When banks are not providing credit to companies, their continued operation is threatened and recession deepens. Major European airlines such as Air France rely on debt financing to purchase new aircraft. However, due to the current credit crunch, European orders for Airbus, Boeing, and Embraer (a Brazilian aerospace company) have collapsed. Even companies located as far away as China have been hurt by the Eurozone crisis as their European orders for goods ranging from sneakers and toys to scooters and electronics have evaporated. The credit crunch has also had a negative impact on the majority of small and medium-sized enterprises in Europe, which find it difficult to obtain bank loans. This situation is particularly harmful because most of the firms are private and rely on debt rather than equity financing. As we can see, the macroeconomic effects of the Eurozone crisis have significant microeconomic consequences.[11]

SOCIOCULTURAL FACTORS

Sociocultural factors capture a society's cultures, norms, and values. Because sociocultural forces not only are constantly in flux but also differ across groups, managers need to closely monitor such trends and consider the implications for firm strategy. In recent years, for example, a growing number of U.S. consumers have become more health-conscious about what they eat. This trend led to a boom for businesses such as Subway and Whole Foods. At the same time, traditional fast-food companies such as McDonald's and Burger King, along with grocery chains such as Albertsons and Kroger, have all had to scramble to provide healthier choices in their product offerings.

Demographic trends are also important sociocultural forces. These trends capture population characteristics related to age, gender, family size, ethnicity, sexual orientation, religion, and socioeconomic class. Like other sociocultural factors, demographic trends present opportunities but can also pose threats. The most recent U.S. census revealed that 51 million Americans (16.4 percent of the total population) are Hispanic. It is now the second-largest ethnic group in the United States, and growing fast. On average, Hispanics are also younger and their incomes are climbing quickly. This trend is not lost on companies trying to benefit from this opportunity. For example, MundoFox and ESPN Deportes (specializing in soccer) have joined Univision and NBC's Telemundo in the Spanish-language television market. In the United States, Univision is now the fifth most popular network overall, just behind the four major English-language networks (ABC, NBC, CBS, and Fox). Likewise, advertisers are pouring dollars into the Spanish-language networks to promote their products and services.[10]

TECHNOLOGICAL FACTORS

Technological factors capture the application of knowledge to create new processes and products. Recent innovations in process technology include lean manufacturing, Six Sigma quality, and biotechnology. The nanotechnology revolution, which is just beginning, promises major upheaval for a vast array of industries ranging from tiny medical devices to new-age materials for earthquake-resistant buildings.[12] Recent product innovations include the smartphone, computer tablets, and high-performing electric cars such as the Tesla Roadster. Recent service innovations include social media and online search engines. If one thing seems certain, technological progress is relentless and seems to be picking up speed over time.[13] Not surprisingly, changes in the technological environment bring both opportunities and threats for companies.

Let's think about the rapid progress in mobile computing. BlackBerry, once an undisputed leader in the smartphone industry, did not recognize early enough or act upon changes in the external environment. Consumer preferences changed quickly as the iPhone and later the iPad became available. Professionals brought their own Apple devices to work instead of using company-issued BlackBerrys. Although the Canadian technology company made a valiant effort to make up lost ground with its new BlackBerry 10 operating system and several new models, it was too little, too late. Given the importance of a firm's innovation strategy to competitive advantage, we discuss the effect of technological factors in greater detail in Chapter 7.

ECOLOGICAL FACTORS

Ecological factors concern broad environmental issues such as the natural environment, global warming, and sustainable economic growth. Organizations and the natural environment coexist in an interdependent relationship. Managing these relationships in a responsible and sustainable way directly influences the continued existence of human societies and the organizations we create. Managers can no longer separate the natural and the business worlds; they are inextricably linked.[14]

Business organizations have contributed to the pollution of air, water, and land, as well as depletion of the world's natural resources. BP's infamous oil spill in the Gulf of Mexico destroyed fauna and flora along the U.S. shoreline from Texas to Florida. This disaster led to a decrease in fish and wildlife populations, triggered a decline in the fishery and tourism industries, and threatened the livelihood of thousands of people. It also cost BP more than $40 billion and one half of its market value (see Strategy Highlight 1.2).

The relationship between organizations and the natural environment does not necessarily need to be in conflict, however. Ecological factors can also provide business opportunities. As we saw in ChapterCase 3, Tesla Motors is addressing environmental concerns regarding the carbon emissions of gasoline-powered cars by building zero-emission battery-powered vehicles. The question of how to generate the power needed to charge the batteries in a sustainable way, however, still needs to be addressed.

3.2 Industry Structure and Firm Strategy: The Five Forces Model

LO 3-2

Apply Porter's five competitive forces to explain the profit potential of different industries.

We now move one step closer to the firm (in the center of Exhibit 3.1) and come to the industry in which it competes. An **industry** is a group of (incumbent) companies that face more or less the same set of suppliers and buyers. Firms competing in the same industry tend to offer similar products or services to meet specific customer needs. Although the

PESTEL framework allows us to scan, monitor, and evaluate the external environment to identify opportunities and threats, **industry analysis** provides a more rigorous basis not only to identify an industry's profit potential (the level of profitability that can be expected for the *average* firm), but also to derive implications for one firm's strategic position within an industry. A firm's **strategic position** relates to its ability to create value for customers (V) while containing the cost to do so (C). Competitive advantage flows to the firm that is able to create as large a gap as possible between the value the firm's product or service generates and the cost required to produce it ($V - C$).

Michael Porter developed the highly influential **five forces model** to help managers understand the profit potential of different industries and how they can position their respective firms to gain and sustain competitive advantage.[15] By combining theory from industrial organization economics with hundreds of detailed case studies, Porter derived two key insights that form the basis of his seminal five forces model:

1. Rather than defining competition narrowly as the firm's closest competitors to explain and predict a firm's performance, competition must be viewed more broadly to encompass not only direct rivals but also a set of other forces in an industry: buyers, suppliers, potential new entry of other firms, and the threat of substitutes.

2. The profit potential of an industry is neither random nor entirely determined by industry-specific factors. Rather, it is a function of the five forces that shape competition: *threat of entry, power of suppliers, power of buyers, threat of substitutes,* and *rivalry among existing firms.*

COMPETITION IN THE FIVE FORCES MODEL

The first major insight this model provides is the fact that while a firm's ability to create as large a gap as possible between the value (V) the firm's product or service generates and the cost (C) to produce it is essential to create economic value ($V - C$), the firm must also be able to capture a significant share of it to gain and sustain competitive advantage. What does this mean? In Porter's five forces model, competition is *not* defined narrowly as the firm's closest competitors (e.g., Nike versus Under Armour, Amazon versus Netflix, Merck versus Pfizer, and so on) but rather more broadly to include other forces in an industry: buyers, suppliers, potential new entry of other firms, and the threat of substitutes. Competition describes the tug-of-war between these forces to capture as much as possible of the economic value created in an industry. The focal firm's managers, therefore, must be concerned not only about the intensity of rivalry among direct competitors, but also about the strength of the other competitive forces that are attempting to extract part or all of the economic value the firm creates. When faced with competition in this broader sense, strategy explains how a firm is able to achieve superior performance. The airline industry provides an illustrative example in Strategy Highlight 3.2.[16]

---

industry A group of (incumbent) companies that face more or less the same set of suppliers and buyers; these firms tend to offer similar products or services to meet specific customer needs.

industry analysis A method to (1) identify an industry's profit potential and (2) derive implications for a firm's strategic position within an industry.

strategic position A firm's strategic profile based on value creation and cost. The goal is to generate as large a gap as possible between the value the firm's product or service creates and the cost required to produce it ($V - C$).

five forces model A framework developed by Michael Porter that identifies five forces that determine the profit potential of an industry and shape a firm's competitive strategy.

Strategy Highlight 3.2

The Five Forces in the Airline Industry

Although many of the mega airlines such as American, Delta, and United have lost billions of dollars over the last few decades and continue to struggle to make a profit, other players in this industry have been quite profitable because they were able to extract some of the value created. The nature of rivalry among airlines is incredibly intense, as consumers primarily make decisions based on price. In inflation-adjusted dollars, ticket prices have been falling since industry deregulation in 1978. Thanks to Internet travel sites such as Orbitz, Travelocity, and Kayak, price comparisons are effortless. Consumers benefit from cut-throat price competition between carriers and capture significant value. Low switching costs and nearly perfect information combine to strengthen buyer power. Moreover, large corporate customers such as McKinsey or IBM, which contract with airlines to serve all of their employees' travel needs, are rather powerful buyers and further reduce profit margins for air carriers.

Entry barriers are relatively low, resulting in a number of new airlines popping up. To enter the industry (on a small scale, serving a few select cities), a prospective new entrant needs only a couple of airplanes which can be rented, a few pilots and crew members, some routes connecting city pairs, and gate access in airports. Indeed, despite notoriously low industry profitability, Virgin America entered the U.S. market in 2007. Virgin America is the brainchild of Sir Richard Branson, founder and chairman of the Virgin Group, a UK conglomerate of hundreds of companies using the Virgin brand, including the international airline Virgin Atlantic. Its business strategy is to offer low-cost service between major metropolitan cities on the American East and West Coasts.

In the airline industry, the supplier power is also strong. The providers of airframes (e.g., Boeing or Airbus), makers of aircraft engines (e.g., GE or Rolls-Royce), aircraft maintenance companies (e.g., Goodrich), caterers (e.g., Marriott), labor unions, and airports controlling gate access all bargain away the profitability of airlines.

To make matters worse, substitutes are also readily available: If prices are seen as too high, customers can drive their cars or use the train or bus. As an example, the route between Atlanta and Orlando (roughly 400 miles) used to be one of the busiest and most profitable ones for Delta. Given the increasing security delays at airports, more and more people now prefer to drive. Taken together, the competitive forces are quite unfavorable for generating a profit potential in the airline industry: low entry barriers, high supplier power, high buyer power combined with low customer switching costs, and the availability of low-cost substitutes. This type of hostile environment leads to intense rivalry among existing airlines and low overall industry profit potential.

As we have seen, despite all this, the surprise finding is that while the mega airlines themselves (i.e., American, Delta, and United) frequently struggle to make a profit, the other players in the industry—such as the suppliers of aircraft engines, aircraft maintenance companies, IT companies providing reservation and logistics services, caterers, airports, and so on—are actually quite profitable, all extracting significant value from the air transportation industry.[17] Customers also are better off, as ticket prices have decreased and travel choices increased.

The air transportation industry in the Strategy Highlight 3.2 example shows that the five forces framework is a powerful and versatile tool to analyze industries because it takes a broader perspective and enables managers to evaluate fundamental forces beyond direct rivalry that shape firm-level performance outcomes. The five forces model allows managers to analyze all players using a wider industry lens, which in turn enables a deeper understanding of an industry's profit potential. Moreover, a five forces analysis provides the basis for how a firm should position itself to gain and sustain a competitive advantage. We are now ready to take a closer look at each of the five competitive forces.

The five forces model enables managers to not only understand their industry environment but also shape their firm's strategy. As a rule of thumb, *the stronger the five forces, the lower the industry's profit potential*—making the industry less attractive for competitors. The reverse is also true: *the weaker the five forces, the greater the industry's profit*

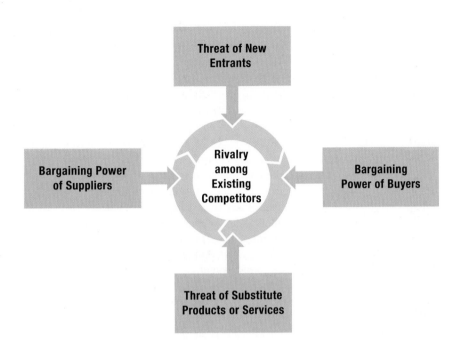

EXHIBIT 3.2

Porter's Five Forces Model

SOURCE: Michael E. Porter, "The five competitive forces that shape strategy," *Harvard Business Review,* January 2008.

potential—making the industry more attractive. Therefore, from the perspective of a manager of an existing (incumbent) firm competing for advantage in an established industry, the company should be positioned in a way that relaxes the constraints of strong forces and leverages weak forces. The goal of crafting a strategic position is of course to improve the firm's ability to achieve a competitive advantage.

We next discuss each of the five competitive forces in detail, and will take up the topic of competitive positioning in Chapter 6 when studying business-level strategy. As Exhibit 3.2 shows, Porter's model identifies five key competitive forces that managers need to consider when analyzing the industry environment and formulating competitive strategy:

1. Threat of entry
2. Power of suppliers
3. Power of buyers
4. Threat of substitutes
5. Rivalry among existing competitors

THE THREAT OF ENTRY

The **threat of entry** describes the risk that potential competitors will enter the industry. Potential new entry depresses industry profit potential in two major ways.

First, with the threat of additional capacity coming into an industry, incumbent firms may lower prices to make entry appear less attractive to the potential new competitors, which would in turn reduce the overall industry's profit potential, especially in industries with slow or no overall growth in demand. For example, demand for new microwaves is more or less constrained by the replacement rate for older models and how many new households are created. Since this market grows slowly, if at all, any additional entry would likely lead to excess capacity and lower prices overall.

threat of entry The risk that potential competitors will enter an industry.

Second, the threat of entry by additional competitors may force incumbent firms to spend more to satisfy their existing customers. Larger investments in value creation further reduce an industry's profit potential if prices cannot be raised. For example, entry barriers to specialty coffee retailing are relatively low, which explains the large number of smaller, regional chains such as Peet's Coffee (with less than 200 stores, mostly on the West Coast) and a few smaller national players such as Caribou Coffee (with 415 stores throughout most of the United States). Low entry barriers in turn force large incumbent firms such as Starbucks (with over 13,000 stores in the U.S.) to constantly spend more money on upgrading the ambience and service offerings in their stores. While this raises the value of Starbucks' offering in the eyes of the consumers, it lowers the company's profit margin. Rather than lowering prices, Starbucks has chosen to constantly upgrade and refresh its stores and service offerings to prevent others from entering the industry or from rapidly expanding (i.e., moving beyond a small niche competitor like Peet's to become a national competitor like Caribou Coffee). In terms of existing national competitors, Starbucks also attempts to prevent the smaller entities from becoming larger, because this would increase competitive rivalry and erode industry profit potential.

Of course, the more profitable an industry, the more attractive it is for new competitors to enter. There are, however, a number of important barriers to entry that raise the costs for potential competitors, which reduces the threat of entry. **Entry barriers,** which are advantageous for incumbent firms, are obstacles that determine how easily a firm can enter an industry. Incumbent firms can benefit from several important sources of entry barriers:

entry barriers
Obstacles that determine how easily a firm can enter an industry. Entry barriers are often one of the most significant predictors of industry profit potential.

- Economies of scale
- Network effects
- Customer switching costs
- Capital requirements
- Advantages independent of size
- Government policy
- Credible threat of retaliation

ECONOMIES OF SCALE. *Economies of scale* are cost advantages that accrue for firms with larger output because they can spread fixed costs over more units, can employ technology more efficiently, can benefit from a more specialized division of labor, and can demand better terms from their suppliers. These factors in turn drive down the cost per unit, allowing large incumbent firms to enjoy a cost advantage over new entrants who cannot muster such scale.

Take the example of the car industry in ChapterCase 3. Entry barriers into the broad automobile industry seem almost insurmountable because of the need for large-scale production in order to be efficient. Many industry analysts argue that to be viable, a car company must be able to produce and sell some 5 million cars per year.[18] This fact explains in part why Fiat, an Italian carmaker selling an estimated 2.5 million vehicles per year, purchased a majority of the shares in Chrysler, selling less than 2 million vehicles per year. Given the industry structure in the automobile business, entering the auto manufacturing industry doesn't seem advisable. Yet Tesla Motors is joining the fray. How can it sidestep such insurmountable entry barriers? The answer: technology. Rather than attempting to compete head-on in internal combustion engines, Tesla Motors is entering the all-electric car segment, a much less crowded niche in the overall car industry. Expanding its product lineup beyond the Roadster (over $100K sticker price) by offering a seven-seat family sedan (Model S, roughly $50K) with a much broader customer appeal, Tesla is hoping to benefit from economies of scale in this market niche.

New entry into the automotive industry, even in niche segments, has significant competitive implications for the existing firms within the industry. Competitive intensity increases when new firms such as Tesla Motors enter the industry. Incumbent firms such as GM and Nissan are responding to the new entrants by introducing innovations of their own, such as the Chevy Volt (a plug-in hybrid) and the Nissan Leaf (an all-electric car). Consumers are likely to benefit from an increase in competitive intensity if more innovative and efficient electric cars are introduced with lower prices. Only time will tell if these new entrants will mature to become full-fledged industrial enterprises and be strong enough to push some incumbents out of the industry, or whether they themselves will vanish.

NETWORK EFFECTS. The threat of potential entry is reduced when network effects are present. *Network effects* describe the positive effect that one user of a product or service has on the value of that product or service for other users. When network effects are present, the value of the product or service increases with the number of users.

For example, customers of online auctions are attracted to eBay because they can benefit from network effects. With more than 100 million active users, buyers are more likely to find the item they are looking for on eBay, while at the same time sellers are more likely to find buyers for the items they are offering. The ability to create markets where supply and demand will clear (where quantity supplied and quantity demanded are equal) is a positive function of the number of users. Having secured a larger number of users, network effects give eBay an advantage over any potential new entrant. In a similar fashion, Facebook, with over one billion active users worldwide, enjoys tremendous network effects, making it difficult for new entrants such as Google Plus to compete effectively. We will discuss network effects in more detail in Chapter 7.

CUSTOMER SWITCHING COSTS. *Switching costs* are incurred by moving from one supplier to another. Changing vendors may require the buyer to alter product specifications, retrain employees, and/or modify existing processes. Switching costs are therefore one-time sunk costs, which can be quite significant and a formidable barrier to entry.

For example, when a firm has been using enterprise resource planning (ERP) software from SAP for many years, it will incur significant switching costs when implementing a new ERP system from Oracle. Likewise, switching from using a PC with a Microsoft Windows operating system to a Mac with Apple iOS will require many hours of learning the new operating system and software applications. Since Apple has been the smaller player in the PC market for many decades, it invested much more to entice users to switch from Microsoft Windows to Apple iOS than the other way around. Lowering customer switching costs allowed Apple to gain market share at the expense of Microsoft and PC makers such as Dell and HP. In a similar fashion, the threat of potential new entry is high when customer switching costs are low. When entering the smartphone market with its iPhone, Apple was able to lower switching costs with an intuitive interface and user-friendly design.

CAPITAL REQUIREMENTS. Capital requirements describe the "price of the entry ticket" into a new industry. How much capital is required to compete in this industry, and which companies are willing and able to make such investments? Frequently related to economies of scale, capital requirements may encompass investments to set up plants with dedicated machinery, run a production process, and cover start-up losses.

In the aircraft manufacturing industry, at least for large commercial jets, Boeing and Airbus are the only competitors. There is not a significant threat of entry because entering the airframe manufacturing industry requires huge capital investments. In fact, Airbus was only able to overcome these tremendous barriers to entry with the help of direct subsidies from several European governments including France, Germany, Spain, and the UK.

In such cases, the likelihood of entry is determined by not only the level of capital investment required to enter the industry, but also the expected return on investment. The potential new entrant must carefully weigh the required capital investments, the cost of financing, and the expected return.

For example, in the southeastern United States, TV cable company Comcast has entered the business for residential and commercial telephone services and Internet connectivity (as an ISP, Internet service provider), emerging as a direct competitor for AT&T. Comcast also acquired NBC Universal, combining delivery and content. AT&T responded to Comcast's threat by introducing U-verse, a product combining high-speed Internet access with cable TV and telephone service, all provided over its super-fast fiber-optic network.

Taken together, the threat of entry is high when capital requirements are low in comparison to the expected returns. If an industry is attractive enough, efficient capital markets are likely to provide the necessary funding to enter an industry. Capital, unlike proprietary technology and industry-specific know-how, is a resource that can be relatively easily acquired in the face of attractive returns.

ADVANTAGES INDEPENDENT OF SIZE. Incumbent firms often possess cost and quality advantages that are independent of size. These advantages can be based on brand loyalty, proprietary technology, preferential access to raw materials and/or distribution channels, favorable geographic locations, and cumulative learning and experience effects.

Apple's Mac-brand customers are among the most loyal product fans. New entrants will have great difficulty attracting Mac users to their computer products, because Mac fans seem to have a personal identification and bond with the products that goes beyond the product features.

Patents and trade secrets, such as the original Coke formula, are examples of proprietary technology and know-how that can also reduce the threat of entry. The value of trade secrets to a firm is reflected in the efforts to improve cyber-security so that trade secrets cannot be stolen by hacking into corporate computers.

Preferential access to raw materials such as diamond mines can bestow absolute cost advantages on incumbent companies. For many decades, De Beers, a global diamond mining and trading company, held a virtual monopoly in both access to diamond mines and the distribution channels in the diamond trade, which in turn reduced the threat of entry.

Favorable locations, such as Silicon Valley for software companies, often present advantages that other locales cannot match easily, such as access to human and venture capital, as well as world-class research and engineering institutions.

Finally, incumbent firms often benefit from cumulative learning and experience effects accrued over long periods of time. Leading industrial engineering companies such as Siemens and GE have many decades of experience in solving the toughest engineering problems. Attempting to obtain such deep knowledge within a shorter time frame is often costly, if not impossible, which in turn constitutes a formidable barrier to entry.

GOVERNMENT POLICY. Frequently government policies restrict or prevent new entrants. Until recently, India did not allow foreign retailers such as Walmart or IKEA to own stores and compete with domestic companies, in order to protect the country's millions of small vendors and wholesalers. China frequently requires foreign companies to enter joint ventures with domestic ones and to share technology. In the U.S., many states have restrictive licensing policies that limit the sale of liquor. City agencies such as the New York City Taxi and Limousine Commission severely limit operating licenses, thereby preventing entry into an industry with otherwise low entry barriers.

In contrast, deregulations in industries such as airlines, telecommunications, and trucking have generated significant new entries. Therefore, the threat of entry is high when restrictive government policies do not exist, or when industries become deregulated.

CREDIBLE THREAT OF RETALIATION. Potential new entrants must also anticipate how incumbent firms will react. A credible threat of retaliation by incumbent firms often deters entry. Should entry still occur, however, incumbents are able to retaliate quickly, through initiating a price war, for example. The industry profit potential can in this case easily fall below the cost of capital. Incumbents with deeper pockets than new entrants are able to withstand price competition for a longer time and wait for the new entrants to exit the industry—then raise prices again. Other weapons of retaliation include increased product and service innovation, advertising, sales promotions, and litigation.

Potential new entrants should expect a strong and vigorous response beyond price competition by incumbent firms in several scenarios: if the current competitors have made large-scale specific investments that are of little use in other industries; unused excess capacity; substantial resources; reputational clout with industry suppliers and buyers; and a history of vigorous retaliation during earlier entry attempts. Moreover, if industry growth is slow or stagnant, incumbents are more likely to retaliate against new entrants in order to protect their market share, often initiating a price war with the goal of driving out these new entrants. In contrast, the threat of entry is high when new entrants expect that incumbents will not or cannot retaliate.

THE POWER OF SUPPLIERS

The bargaining power of suppliers captures pressures that industry suppliers can exert on an industry's profit potential. This force reduces a firm's ability to obtain superior performance for two reasons: powerful suppliers can raise the cost of production by demanding higher prices for their inputs, or by reducing the quality of the input factor or service level delivered. Powerful suppliers are a threat to firms because they reduce the industry's profit potential by capturing part of the economic value created.

To compete effectively, companies generally need a wide variety of inputs into the production process, including raw materials and components, labor (may be individuals or labor unions, when the industry faces collective bargaining), and services. The relative bargaining power of suppliers is high when:

- The suppliers' industry is more concentrated than the industry it sells to.
- Suppliers do not depend heavily on the industry for a large portion of their revenues.
- Incumbent firms face significant switching costs when changing suppliers.
- Suppliers offer products that are differentiated.
- There are no readily available substitutes for the products or services that the suppliers offer.
- Suppliers can credibly threaten to forward integrate into the industry.

In Strategy Highlight 3.2, we briefly mentioned that the airline industry faces strong supplier power. Let's take a closer look at one important supplier group to this industry: Boeing and Airbus, the makers of large commercial jets. Many of the factors that determine supplier power are strong, while some are moderate. The reason why airframe manufacturers are powerful suppliers to airlines is because their industry is much more concentrated (only two firms) than the industry it sells to (there are hundreds of commercial airlines across the world). Given the trend of large airlines merging to create even larger mega-airlines, however, increasing buyer power may eventually balance this out a bit. Nonetheless, the airlines face non-trivial switching costs when changing suppliers (from Boeing to Airbus, or vice versa) because pilots and crew would need to be retrained to fly a new type of aircraft, maintenance capabilities would need to be expanded, and some routes may even need to be reconfigured due to differences in aircraft range and passenger capacity. Moreover, while some of the aircraft can be used as substitutes, Boeing and Airbus offer differentiated products. This fact becomes clearer when considering the most recent models from each company. Boeing introduced the 787 Dreamliner to capture long-distance point-to-point travel (close to 8,000-mile range, sufficient to fly non-stop from Los Angeles to Sydney), while Airbus introduced the A-380 Superjumbo to focus on high-volume transportation (close to 900 passengers) between major airport hubs (e.g., Tokyo's Haneda Airport and Singapore's International Airport). When considering long-distance travel, there are no readily available substitutes for commercial airliners, a fact that strengthens supplier power.

All in all, the vast strengths of these factors lead us to conclude that the supplier power of commercial aircraft manufacturers is quite significant. This puts Boeing and Airbus in a strong position to extract profits from the airline industry, thus reducing the profit potential of the airlines themselves.

Although the supplier power of Boeing and Airbus is strong, three factors moderate their bargaining positions somewhat. First, the suppliers of commercial airliners depend heavily on commercial airlines for their revenues. Second, Boeing and Airbus are unlikely to threaten forward integration and become commercial airlines themselves. Finally, industry structures are not static, but can change over time. In the last few years, several of the remaining large domestic U.S. airlines have merged (Delta and Northwest, United and Continental, and American and U.S. Airways), which changed the industry structure in their favor. There are now fewer but even larger airlines remaining. This fact increases their buyer power, which we turn to next.

THE POWER OF BUYERS

In many ways, the bargaining power of buyers is the flip side of the bargaining power of suppliers. Buyers are the customers of an industry. The power of buyers concerns the pressure an industry's customers can put on the producer's margins in the industry by demanding a lower price or higher product quality. When buyers successfully obtain price discounts, it reduces a firm's top line (revenue). When buyers demand higher quality and more service, it generally raises production costs. Strong buyers can therefore reduce industry profit potential and with it, a firm's profitability. Powerful buyers are a threat to the producing firms because they reduce the industry's profit potential by capturing part of the economic value created.

As with suppliers, an industry may face many different types of buyers. The buyers of an industry's product or service may be individual consumers—like you or me when we decide which provider we want to use for our wireless devices. In many areas, you can choose between several providers such as AT&T, Sprint, or Verizon. Although we might be able to play different providers against one another when carefully comparing their individual service plans, as individual consumers we generally do not have significant buyer power. On the other hand, large institutions such as businesses or universities have significant buyer power when deciding which provider to use for their wireless services, because they are able to sign up or move several thousand employees at once.

The power of buyers is high when:

- There are a few buyers and each buyer purchases large quantities relative to the size of a single seller.
- The industry's products are standardized or undifferentiated commodities.
- Buyers face low or no switching costs.
- Buyers can credibly threaten to backwardly integrate into the industry.

In addition, companies need to be aware of situations when buyers are especially price sensitive. This is the case when:

- The buyer's purchase represents a significant fraction of its cost structure or procurement budget.
- Buyers earn low profits or are strapped for cash.
- The quality (cost) of the buyers' products and services is not affected much by the quality (cost) of their inputs.

For instance, Google faces strong buyer power from Samsung because Samsung products account for 40 percent of Google's Android operating system use in smartphones and roughly 30 percent in tablets (in 2012). Google benefits from Samsung's strong performance, allowing the Android operating system to capture more than 70 percent market share in smartphones. This large installed base of mobile operating systems enables Google to capture revenues from use of its search engine. However, leveraging its buyer power, Samsung is now demanding a larger share of revenues from Google's online searches, and may also demand specialized Google apps designed for Samsung smartphones exclusively.[19]

The retail giant Walmart provides perhaps the most potent example of tremendous buyer power. Walmart is not only the largest retailer worldwide (with over 10,000 stores and 2.2 million employees); it is also one of the largest companies in the world (with roughly $450 billion in revenues in 2012). Walmart is one of few large big-box global retail chains and frequently purchases large quantities from its suppliers. Walmart leverages its buyer power by exerting tremendous pressure on its suppliers to lower prices and to increase quality or risk losing access to shelf space at the largest retailer in the world. Walmart's buyer power is so strong that many suppliers co-locate offices directly next to Walmart's headquarters in Bentonville, Arkansas, because such proximity enables Walmart's managers to test the supplier's latest products and negotiate prices.

The bargaining power of buyers also increases when their switching costs are low. Having multiple suppliers of a product category located close to its headquarters allows Walmart to demand further price cuts and quality improvements because it can easily switch from one supplier to the next. This threat is even more pronounced if the products are non-differentiated commodities from the consumers' perspective. For example, Walmart can easily switch from Rubbermaid plastic containers to Sterlite containers by offering more shelf space to the producer that offers the greatest price cut or quality improvement.

Buyers are also powerful when they can credibly threaten backward integration. Backward integration occurs when a buyer moves upstream in the industry value chain, into the seller's business. Walmart has exercised the threat to backward integrate by producing a number of products as private-label brands such as Equate health and beauty items, Ol'Roy dog food, and Parent's Choice baby products. This situation is also observed in the auto-component supply industry, in which car manufacturers such as GM, Toyota, or Volkswagen have the capability to backward-integrate in order to produce their components in-house if their demands for lower prices and higher product quality are not met by their suppliers. Taken together, powerful buyers have the ability to extract a significant amount of the value created in the industry, leaving little or nothing for producers.

In regard to any of the five forces that shape competition, it is important to note that their relative strengths are context-dependent. For example, the Mexican multinational CEMEX, one of the world's leading cement producers, faces very different buyer power in the U.S. versus in its domestic market. Cement is an undifferentiated commodity product. In the U.S., cement buyers consist of a few large and powerful construction companies that account for a significant percentage of CEMEX's output. This results in razor-thin margins in the U.S. In contrast, the vast majority of CEMEX's customers in its Mexican home market are numerous, small, individual customers facing a few large suppliers, with CEMEX being the biggest. Not surprisingly, CEMEX earns high profit margins in its home market. This example provides the context to show that CEMEX actually competes in two different industry conditions (albeit offering the same product), because it faces two very different competitive forces in the U.S. and Mexico.

THE THREAT OF SUBSTITUTES

Substitutes meet the same basic customer needs as the industry's product but in a different way. The threat of substitutes is the idea that products or services available from *outside the given industry* will come close to meeting the needs of current customers.[20] For example, many software products are substitutes to professional services, at least at the lower end. Tax preparation software such as Intuit's TurboTax is a substitute for professional services offered by H&R Block and others. Legal Zoom, an online legal documentation service, is a threat to professional law firms. Other examples of substitutes are energy drinks versus coffee, videoconferencing versus business travel, e-mail versus express mail, gasoline versus biofuel, and wireless telephone services versus Voice over Internet Protocol (VoIP), offered by Skype or Vonage.

A high threat of substitutes reduces industry profit potential by limiting the price the industry's competitors can charge for their products and services. The threat of substitutes is high when:

- The substitute offers an attractive price-performance trade-off.
- The buyer's cost of switching to the substitute is low.

The movie rental company Redbox, which uses over 42,000 kiosks in the U.S. to make movie rentals available for just $1, is a substitute for buying movie DVDs. For buyers, video rental via Redbox offers an attractive price-performance trade-off with low switching costs in comparison to DVD ownership.

In addition to a lower price, substitutes may also become more attractive by offering a higher value proposition.[21] In Spain, some six million travelers commute annually between Madrid and Barcelona. Traditionally, the travel choices to cover these roughly 400 miles were to fly, drive, or take a slow train. Given that a car ride or train take most of the day, it was not surprising that roughly 90 percent of commuters chose to fly, creating a highly profitable business for local airlines. This all changed when the Alta Velocidad Española (AVE), an ultra-modern high-speed train, was completed in 2008. Train travel offers amenities that air travel cannot. Most notably, taking into account total travel time, high-speed trains are faster than short-haul flights. Moreover, train passengers not only travel in greater comfort than passengers in air travel, but they also commute from one city center to the next, with only a short walk or cab ride to their final destinations.

The AVE example highlights the two fundamental insights provided by Porter's five forces framework. First, competition must be defined more broadly to go beyond direct industry competitors. In this case, rather than defining competition narrowly as the firm's closest competitors, airline executives in Spain must look beyond other airlines and consider substitute offerings such as high-speed trains. Second, any of the five forces on its own, if sufficiently strong, can extract industry profitability. In the AVE example, the threat of substitutes is limiting the airline industry's profit potential. With the arrival of the AVE, the airlines' monopoly on fast transportation between Madrid and Barcelona vanished as did the airlines' high profits. The strong threat of substitutes in this case increased the rivalry among existing competitors (in the airline industry), to which we now turn.

RIVALRY AMONG EXISTING COMPETITORS

Rivalry among existing competitors describes the intensity with which companies within the same industry jockey for market share and profitability. It can range from genteel to cut-throat. The other four forces—threat of entry, the power of buyers and suppliers, and the threat of substitutes—all exert pressure upon this rivalry (as indicated by the arrows pointing toward the center in Exhibit 3.2). The stronger the forces, the stronger the expected competitive intensity, which in turn limits the industry's profit potential.

LO 3-3

Explain how competitive industry structure shapes rivalry among competitors.

Competitors can lower prices to attract customers from rivals. When intense rivalry among existing competitors brings about price discounting, industry profitability erodes. Alternatively, competitors can use non-price competition to create more value in terms of product features and design, quality, promotional spending, and after-sales service and support. When non-price competition is the primary basis of competition, costs increase, which can also have a negative impact on industry profitability. However, when these moves create unique products with features tailored closely to meet customer needs and willingness to pay, then average industry profitability tends to increase because producers are able to raise prices and thus increase revenues and profit margins.

The intensity of rivalry among existing competitors is determined largely by the following factors:

- Competitive industry structure
- Industry growth
- Strategic commitments
- Exit barriers

COMPETITIVE INDUSTRY STRUCTURE. The **competitive industry structure** refers to elements and features common to all industries. The structure of an industry is largely captured by:

- The number and size of competitors in an industry
- Whether the firms possess some degree of pricing power
- The type of product or service the industry offers (commodity or differentiated product)
- The height of entry barriers[22]

competitive industry structure Elements and features common to all industries, including the number and size of competitors in an industry, whether the firms possess some degree of pricing power, and the type of product or service the industry offers.

Exhibit 3.3 shows different industry types along a continuum from fragmented to consolidated structures. At one extreme, a *fragmented industry* consists of many small firms

EXHIBIT 3.3 / Industry Competitive Structures along the Continuum from Fragmented to Consolidated

Industry Competitive Structure

Perfect Competition	Monopolistic Competition	Oligopoly	Monopoly
• Many small firms	• Many firms	• Few (large) firms	• One firm
• Firms are price takers	• Some pricing power	• Some pricing power	• Considerable pricing power
• Commodity product	• Differentiated product	• Differentiated product	• Unique product
• Low entry barriers	• Medium entry barriers	• High entry barriers	• Very high entry barriers

Fragmented
Low Profit Potential

Consolidated
High Profit Potential

and tends to generate low profitability. At the other end of the continuum, a *consolidated industry* is dominated by a few firms, or even just one firm, and has the potential to be highly profitable. The four main competitive industry structures are (1) perfect competition, (2) monopolistic competition, (3) oligopoly, and (4) monopoly.

Perfect Competition. A *perfectly competitive* industry is characterized as fragmented and has many small firms, a commodity product, ease of entry, and little or no ability for each individual firm to raise its prices. The firms competing in this type of industry are approximately similar in size and resources. Consumers make purchasing decisions solely on price, because the commodity product offerings are more or less identical. The resulting performance of the industry shows low profitability. Under these conditions, firms in perfect competition have difficulty achieving even a temporary competitive advantage and can achieve only competitive parity. Although perfect competition is a rare industry structure in its pure form, markets for commodities such as natural gas, copper, and iron tend to approach this structure.

Modern high-tech industries are also not immune to the perils of perfect competition. Many Internet entrepreneurs learned the hard way that it is difficult to beat the forces of perfect competition. Fueled by eager venture capitalists, about 100 e-tailers such as *pets.com*, *petopia.com*, and *pet-store.com* had sprung up by 1999, at the height of the Internet bubble.[23] Cut-throat competition ensued, with online retailers selling products below cost. To make matters worse, at the same time, category-killers such as PetSmart and PetCo were expanding rapidly, opening some 2,000 brick-and-mortar stores in the United States and Canada. As a consequence, most online pet supply retailers went out of business. Taking a look at the competitive industry structures depicted in Exhibit 3.3, we might have predicted that online pet supply stores were unlikely to be profitable. When there are many small firms offering a commodity product in an industry that is easy to enter, no one is able to increase prices and generate profits. The ensuing price competition led to an industry shakeout, leaving online retailers in the dust.

Monopolistic Competition. A *monopolistically competitive* industry is characterized by many firms, a differentiated product, some obstacles to entry, and the ability to raise prices for a relatively unique product while retaining customers. The key to understanding this industry structure is that the firms now offer products or services with unique features.

The computer hardware industry provides one example of monopolistic competition. Many firms compete in this industry, and even the largest of them (such as Acer, Apple,

Dell, HP, or Lenovo) have less than 20 percent market share. Moreover, while products between competitors tend to be similar, they are by no means identical. As a consequence, managers selling a product with unique features tend to have some ability to raise prices. When a firm is able to differentiate its product or service offerings, it carves out a niche in the market in which it has some degree of monopoly power over pricing, thus the name "monopolistic competition." Firms frequently communicate the degree of product differentiation through advertising.

Oligopoly. The term *oligopoly* comes from the Greeks and means "few sellers." An *oligopolistic* industry is consolidated with few (large) firms, differentiated products, high barriers to entry, and some degree of pricing power. The degree of pricing power depends, just as in monopolistic competition, on the degree of product differentiation.

A key feature of an oligopoly is that the competing firms are *interdependent.* With only a few competitors in the mix, the actions of one firm influence the behaviors of the others. Each competitor in an oligopoly, therefore, must consider the strategic actions of the other competitors. This type of industry structure is often analyzed using *game theory,* which attempts to predict strategic behaviors by assuming that the moves and reactions of competitors can be anticipated.[24] Due to their strategic interdependence, companies in oligopolies have an incentive to coordinate their strategic actions to maximize joint performance. Although explicit coordination such as price fixing is illegal in the United States, tacit coordination such as "an unspoken understanding" is not.

The express-delivery industry is an example of an oligopoly. The main competitors in this space are FedEx and UPS. Any strategic decision made by FedEx (e.g., to expand delivery services to ground delivery of larger-size packages) directly affects UPS; likewise, any decision made by UPS (e.g., to guarantee next-day delivery before 8:00 a.m.) directly affects FedEx. Other examples of oligopolies include the soft drink industry (Coca-Cola versus Pepsi), airframe manufacturing business (Boeing versus Airbus), home-improvement retailing (The Home Depot versus Lowe's), toys and games (Hasbro versus Mattel), and detergents (P&G versus Unilever).[25]

Companies in an oligopoly tend to have some pricing power if they are able to differentiate their product or service offerings from those of their competitors. However, *non-price competition* is the preferred mode of competition. This means competing by offering unique product features or services rather than competing based on price alone. When one firm in an oligopoly cuts prices to gain market share from its competitor, the competitor typically will respond in kind and also cut prices. This process initiates a price war, which can be especially detrimental to firm performance if the products are close rivals.

In the early years of the soft drink industry, for example, whenever Pepsi lowered prices, Coca-Cola followed suit. These actions only resulted in reduced profitability for both companies. In recent decades, both Coca-Cola and Pepsi have repeatedly demonstrated that they have learned this lesson. They shifted the basis of competition from price-cutting to new product introductions and lifestyle advertising. Any price adjustments are merely short-term promotions. By leveraging innovation and advertising, managers from Coca-Cola and Pepsi have moved to non-price competition, which in turn allows them to charge higher prices and to improve industry and company profitability.[26]

Monopoly. An industry is a *monopoly* when there is only one (large) firm supplying the market. "Mono" means *one,* and thus a monopolist is the only seller in a market. The firm may offer a unique product, and the challenges to moving into the industry tend to be high. The monopolist has considerable pricing power. As a consequence, firm (and thus industry) profitability tends to be high.

In some instances, the government will grant one firm the right to be the sole supplier of a product or service. This is often done to incentivize a company to engage in a venture that would not be profitable if there was more than one supplier. For example, public utilities incur huge fixed costs to build plants and to supply a certain geographic area. Public utilities supplying water, gas, and electricity to businesses and homes are frequently monopolists. For example, Georgia Power is the only supplier of electricity for over 2.25 million customers in the southeastern United States. Philadelphia Gas Works is the only supplier of natural gas in the city of Philadelphia, Pennsylvania, serving some 500,000 customers. These are so-called *natural monopolies.* Without them, the governments involved believe the market would not supply these products or services at all. In the past few decades, however, more and more of these natural monopolies have been deregulated in the United States, including airlines, telecommunications, railroads, trucking, and ocean transportation. This deregulation has allowed competition to emerge, which frequently leads to lower prices, better service, and more innovation.

While natural monopolies appear to be disappearing from the competitive landscape, so-called *near monopolies* are of much greater interest to strategists. These are firms that have accrued significant market power, for example, by owning valuable patents or proprietary technology. In the process, they are changing the industry structure in their favor, generally from monopolistic competition or oligopolies to near monopolies. These near monopolies are firms that have accomplished product differentiation to such a degree that they are in a class by themselves, just like a monopolist. The European Union, for example, views Intel (with its 80 percent market share in semiconductors) as a near monopoly. This is an enviable position in terms of the ability to extract profits, so long as Intel can steer clear of monopolistic behavior, which may attract antitrust regulators and lead to legal repercussions.

INDUSTRY GROWTH. Industry growth directly affects the intensity of rivalry among competitors. In periods of high growth, consumer demand is rising, and price competition among firms frequently decreases. Because the pie is expanding, rivals are focused on capturing part of that larger pie rather than taking market share and profitability away from one another. The demand for knee replacements, for example, is a fast-growing segment in the medical products industry. In the United States, robust demand is driven by the need for knee replacements for an aging population as well as for an increasingly obese population. The leading competitors are Zimmer, DePuy, and Stryker, but significant share is held by Smith & Nephew and Biomet. Competition is primarily based on innovative design, improved implant materials, and differentiated products such as gender solutions and a range of high-flex knees. With improvements to materials and procedures, younger patients are also increasingly choosing early surgical intervention. Competitors are able to avoid price competition and, instead, focus on differentiation that allows premium pricing.

In contrast, rivalry among competitors becomes fierce during slow or even negative industry growth. Price discounts, frequent new product releases with minor modifications, intense promotional campaigns, and fast retaliation by rivals are all tactics indicative of an industry with slow or negative growth. Competition is fierce because rivals can only gain at the expense of others; therefore, companies are focused on taking business away from one another. Demand for traditional fast-food providers such as McDonald's, Burger King, and Wendy's has been declining in recent years. Consumers have become more health conscious and demand has shifted to alternative restaurants such as Subway, Chick-fil-A, and Chipotle. Attempts by McDonald's and Wendy's to steal customers from one another include frequent discounting tactics such as dollar menus. Such competitive tactics are indicative of cut-throat competition and a low profit potential in the traditional hamburger fast-food industry.

Competitive rivalry based solely on cutting prices is especially destructive to profitability because it transfers most, if not all, of the value created in the industry to the customers—leaving little, if anything, for the firms in the industry. While this may appear attractive to customers, firms that are not profitable are not able to make the investments necessary to upgrade their product offerings or services to provide higher value, and eventually leave the industry altogether. Destructive price competition can lead to limited choices, lower product quality, and higher prices for consumers in the long run if only a few large firms survive.

STRATEGIC COMMITMENTS. If firms make strategic commitments to compete in an industry, rivalry among competitors is likely to be more intense. We defined *strategic commitments* (in Chapter 2) as firm actions that are costly, long-term oriented, and difficult to reverse. Strategic commitments to a specific industry can stem from large fixed cost requirements, but also from non-economic considerations.

For example, significant strategic commitments are required to compete in the airline industry when using a hub-and-spoke system to provide not only domestic but also international coverage. The traditional U.S. airlines Delta, United, and American have large fixed costs to maintain their network of routes that affords global coverage, frequently in conjunction with foreign partner airlines. These fixed costs (in terms of aircrafts, gate leases, hangars, maintenance facilities, baggage sorting facilities, and ground transportation) all accrue before the airlines sell any tickets. High fixed costs create tremendous pressures to fill empty seats. An airline seat on a specific flight is perishable, just like hotel rooms not filled. Empty airline seats are often filled through price-cutting. Given similar high fixed costs, other airlines respond in kind. Eventually, a vicious cycle of price-cutting ensues, driving average industry profitability to zero, or even negative numbers (where the companies are losing money). To make matters worse, given their strategic commitments airlines are unlikely to exit an industry. Excess capacity remains, further depressing industry profitability.

In other cases, strategic commitments to a specific industry may be the result of more political than economic considerations. Airbus, for example, was created by a number of European governments through direct subsidies in order to provide a countervailing power to Boeing. The European Union in turn claims that Boeing is subsidized by the U.S. government indirectly via defense contracts. Given these political considerations (and large-scale commitments), neither Airbus nor Boeing is likely to exit the aircraft manufacturing industry even if industry profit potential falls to zero.

Likewise, the French government owns and supports Areva, an industrial conglomerate in the nuclear power industry, because it views nuclear power to be essential to the country's energy independence (75 percent of the country's electricity is from nuclear power). Strategic and employment considerations ensure Areva's continued survival, while making it difficult, if not impossible, for non-subsidized companies to compete.

EXIT BARRIERS. The rivalry among existing competitors is also a function of an industry's **exit barriers,** the obstacles that determine how easily a firm can leave that industry. Exit barriers are comprised of both economic and social factors. They include fixed costs that must be paid regardless of whether the company is operating in the industry or not. A company exiting an industry may still have contractual obligations to suppliers, such

exit barriers
Obstacles that determine how easily a firm can leave an industry.

as employee health care and retirement benefits, as well as severance pay. Social factors include elements such as emotional attachments to certain geographic locations. In Michigan, entire communities depend on GM, Ford, and Chrysler. If any of those carmakers were to exit the industry altogether, communities would suffer. Other social and economic factors include ripple effects through the supply chain. When one major player in an industry shuts down, its suppliers are adversely impacted as well.

An industry with low exit barriers is more attractive because it allows underperforming firms to exit more easily. This in turn reduces competitive pressure on the remaining firms because excess capacity is removed. In contrast, an industry with high exit barriers reduces its profit potential because excess capacity still remains. All of the large airlines featured in Strategy Highlight 3.2 (American, Delta, and United) have filed for bankruptcy at one point or another. Due to a unique feature of U.S. Chapter 11 bankruptcy law, however, companies may continue to operate and reorganize while being temporarily shielded from their creditors and other obligations until renegotiated. This implies that excess capacity is not removed from the industry, and by putting pressure on prices further reduces industry profit potential.

To summarize our discussion of the five forces model, Exhibit 3.4 provides a check-list that you can apply to any industry when assessing the underlying competitive forces that shape strategy. The key take-away from the five forces model is that the stronger (weaker) the forces, the lower (greater) the industry's ability to earn above-average profits, and correspondingly, the lower (greater) the firm's ability to gain and sustain a competitive advantage. Therefore, managers need to craft a strategic position for their company that leverages weak forces into opportunities, and mitigates strong forces because they are potential threats to the firm's ability to gain and sustain a competitive advantage.

ADDING A SIXTH FORCE: THE STRATEGIC ROLE OF COMPLEMENTS

LO 3-4

Describe the strategic role of complements in creating positive-sum co-opetition.

complement
A product, service, or competency that adds value to the original product offering when the two are used in tandem.

complementor
A company that provides a good or service that leads customers to value your firm's offering more when the two are combined.

As valuable as the five forces model is for explaining the profit potential and attractiveness of industries, some have suggested extensions of it. Intel's former chairman and CEO, Andy Grove, as well as strategy scholars, have suggested that the value of Porter's five forces model can be further enhanced if one also considers the availability of complements.[27]

A **complement** is a product, service, or competency that adds value to the original product offering when the two are used in tandem.[28] Complements increase demand for the primary product, thereby enhancing the profit potential for the industry and the firm. A company is a **complementor** to your company if customers value your product or service offering more when they are able to combine it with the other company's product or service.[29] Firms may choose to provide the complements themselves or work with another company to accomplish this. Several examples illustrate this point:

■ In the smartphone industry, Google is a complementor to Samsung. The Korean high-tech company's smartphones are more valuable when they come with Google's Android system pre-installed. Customers buying a Samsung smartphone have access to roughly the same number of apps in Google's Play store as users of Apple's iPhone. We noted earlier that Google is facing strong buyer power from Samsung because it accounts for a large quantity of Google's overall sales of its Android operating system. Samsung is attempting to leverage its increased buyer power to request a larger share of online search revenues from Google and to obtain other preferential treatment, such as the development of Google apps tailored exclusively for Samsung smartphones and tablets.

The threat of entry is high when:

√ The minimum efficient scale to compete in an industry is low.

√ Network effects are not present.

√ Customer switching costs are low.

√ Capital requirements are low.

√ Incumbents do not possess:

    ○ Brand loyalty.

    ○ Proprietary technology.

    ○ Preferential access to raw materials.

    ○ Preferential access to distribution channels.

    ○ Favorable geographic locations.

    ○ Cumulative learning and experience effects.

√ Restrictive government regulations do not exist.

√ New entrants expect that incumbents will not or cannot retaliate.

The power of suppliers is high when:

√ Suppliers' industry is more concentrated than the industry it sells to.

√ Suppliers do not depend heavily on the industry for their revenues.

√ Incumbent firms face significant switching costs when changing suppliers.

√ Suppliers offer products that are differentiated.

√ There are no readily available substitutes for the products or services that the suppliers offer.

√ Suppliers can credibly threaten to forward integrate into the industry.

The power of buyers is high when:

√ There are a few buyers and each buyer purchases large quantities relative to the size of a single seller.

√ The industry's products are standardized or undifferentiated commodities.

√ Buyers face low or no switching costs.

√ Buyers can credibly threaten to backwardly integrate into the industry.

The threat of substitutes is high when:

√ The substitute offers an attractive price-performance trade-off.

√ The buyers' cost of switching to the substitute is low.

The rivalry among existing competitors is high when:

√ There are many competitors in the industry.

√ The competitors are roughly of equal size.

√ Industry growth is slow, zero, or even negative.

√ Exit barriers are high.

√ Incumbent firms are highly committed to the business.

√ Incumbent firms cannot read or understand each other's strategies well.

√ Products and services are direct substitutes.

√ Fixed costs are high and marginal costs are low.

√ Excess capacity exists in the industry.

√ The product or service is perishable.

EXHIBIT 3.4 /

The Five Forces
Competitive Analysis
Checklist

SOURCE: Adapted from Porter, M. E. (2008), "The five competitive forces that shape strategy," *Harvard Business Review,* January.

At the same time, Google and Samsung are increasingly becoming competitors as well. With Google's acquisition of Motorola Mobility, the online search company is planning to launch its own line of smartphones under the Google brand. This development illustrates the process of **co-opetition,** which is cooperation by competitors to achieve a strategic objective. Samsung and Google cooperate as complementors to compete against Apple's strong position in the mobile device industry, while at the same time Samsung and Google are increasingly becoming competitive with one another.

■ Illegal music downloads created a powerful substitute for CD record sales, which plummeted with the availability of file-sharing software such as Napster. Seeing a strategic opportunity, Apple established the iTunes music store to complement its iPod music player. Apple makes money by selling the hardware (iPod or iPhone), while providing the complement (iTunes software) for free. That combination allows you to load your device with thousands of songs that can be selected from more than 28 million offered from the iTunes music store at a reasonable price (beginning at $0.69 each). Similarly, when Apple launched the iPad, it had already established relationships with several major publishing houses as complementors to fill its iBook online store with millions of e-books. Moreover, since the iPad runs on the same operating system as the iPhone (iOS), the over 800,000 apps for the iPhone are also available for the iPad through Apple's App store.

3.3 Changes over Time: Industry Dynamics

LO 3-5

Appraise the role of industry dynamics and industry convergence in shaping the firm's external environment.

Although the five-forces-plus-complements model is useful in understanding an industry's profit potential, it provides only a point-in-time snapshot of a moving target. With this model (as with other static models), one cannot determine the changing speed of an industry or the rate of innovation. This drawback implies that managers must repeat their analysis over time in order to create a more accurate picture of their industry. It is therefore important that managers consider industry dynamics.

Industry structures are not stable over time. Rather, they are dynamic. Since a consolidated industry tends to be more profitable than a fragmented one (see Exhibit 3.3), firms have a tendency to change the industry structure in their favor, making it more consolidated through (horizontal) mergers and acquisitions. Having fewer competitors generally equates to higher industry profitability. Industry incumbents, therefore, have an incentive to reduce the number of competitors in the industry. With fewer but larger competitors, incumbent firms can mitigate the threat of strong competitive forces such as supplier or buyer power more effectively. The U.S. domestic airline industry (featured in Strategy Highlight 3.2) has witnessed several large, horizontal mergers between competitors, including Delta and Northwest, United and Continental, Southwest and AirTran, as well as American and U.S. Airways. These moves in turn allow the remaining carriers to enjoy a more benign industry structure. It also allows them to retire some of the excess capacity in the industry as the merged airlines consolidate their networks of routes. The merger activity in the airline industry provides one example of how firms can proactively reshape industry structure in their favor. A more consolidated airline industry is likely to lead to higher ticket prices and fewer choices for customers, but also more profitable airlines.

In contrast, consolidated industry structures may also break up and become more fragmented. This generally happens when there are external shocks to an industry such as deregulation, new legislation, technological innovation, or globalization. For example, the emergence of the Internet moved the stock brokerage business from an oligopoly controlled by full-service firms such as Merrill Lynch and Morgan Stanley to monopolistic competition with many generic online brokers such as Ameritrade, E*TRADE, and Scottrade.

Another dynamic to be considered is **industry convergence,** a process whereby formerly unrelated industries begin to satisfy the same customer need. Industry convergence is often brought on by technological advances. For years, many players in the media industries have been converging due to technological progress in IT, telecommunications, and digital media. Media convergence unites computing, communications, and content, thereby causing significant upheaval across previously distinct industries. Content providers in industries such as newspapers, magazines, TV, movies, radio, and music are all scrambling to adapt. Many standalone print newspapers are closing up shop, while others are trying to figure out how to offer online news content for which consumers are willing to pay.[30] As a consequence of media convergence, annual online ad spending is predicted to reach $130 billion in 2015, overtaking print advertising and closing in fast on TV advertising.[31] Internet companies such as Google, Facebook, Twitter, and Pinterest are changing the industry structure by constantly morphing their capabilities and forcing old-line media companies such as News Corp., Time Warner, and Disney to adapt. Amazon's Kindle e-reader, Apple's iPad, or Samsung's Galaxy Tab provide a new form of content delivery that has the potential to make print media obsolete.

3.4 Explaining Performance Differences Within the Same Industry: Strategic Groups

In further analyzing the firm's external environment in order to explain performance differences, we now move to firms *within the same industry.* As noted earlier in the chapter, a firm occupies a place within a **strategic group,** a set of companies that pursue a similar strategy within a specific industry in their quest for competitive advantage (see Exhibit 3.1).[32] Strategic groups differ from one another along important dimensions such as expenditures on research and development, technology, product differentiation, product and service offerings, pricing, market segments, distribution channels, and customer service.

To explain differences in firm performance within the same industry, scholars offer the **strategic group model,** which clusters different firms into groups based on a few key strategic dimensions.[33] They find that even within the same industry, firm performances differ depending on strategic group membership. Some strategic groups tend to be more profitable than others. This difference implies that firm performance is determined not only by the industry to which the firm belongs, but also by its strategic group membership.

The distinct differences across strategic groups reflect the business strategies that firms pursue. Firms in the same strategic group tend to follow a similar strategy. Companies in the same strategic group, therefore, are direct competitors. The rivalry among firms of the same strategic group is generally more intense than the rivalry between strategic groups: *intra-group rivalry exceeds inter-group rivalry.* The number of different business strategies

LO 3-6

Generate a strategic group model to reveal performance differences between clusters of firms in the same industry.

---

co-opetition
Cooperation by competitors to achieve a strategic objective.

industry convergence
A process whereby formerly unrelated industries begin to satisfy the same customer need.

strategic group The set of companies that pursue a similar strategy within a specific industry.

strategic group model
A framework that explains differences in firm performance within the same industry by clustering different firms into groups based on a few key strategic dimensions.

pursued within an industry determines the number of strategic groups in that industry. In most industries, strategic groups can be identified along a fairly small number of dimensions. In many instances, two strategic groups are in an industry based on two different business strategies: one that pursues a low-cost strategy (e.g., in the car industry: the South Korean carmaker Kia, the Chinese manufacturers BYD and Geely, the Indian Tata Motors with its Nano car line, and others, that make up one group), and a second that pursues a differentiation strategy (e.g., BMW, Mercedes, Audi, Porsche, and others). We'll discuss each of these generic business strategies in detail in Chapter 6.

MAPPING STRATEGIC GROUPS

To understand competitive behavior and performance within an industry, we can map the industry competitors into strategic groups. When mapping strategic groups, it is important to focus on several factors:

- Identify the most important strategic dimensions (such as expenditures on research and development, technology, product differentiation, product and service offerings, pricing, market segments, distribution channels, and customer service).

- Choose two key dimensions for the horizontal and vertical axes, which expose important differences among the competitors. The dimensions chosen for the axes should *not* be highly correlated.

- Graph the firms in the strategic group, indicating each firm's market share by the size of the bubble with which it is represented.[34]

Again, the U.S. domestic airline industry provides an illustrative example. Exhibit 3.5 maps the companies active within this industry. The two strategic dimensions on the axes are prices charged and routes serviced. As a result of this mapping, two strategic groups become apparent, as indicated by the dashed lines: low-cost, point-to-point airlines (Virgin Atlantic, Alaska Airlines, JetBlue, and Southwest Airlines) versus differentiated airlines using a hub-and-spoke system (American, Delta, and United). As we can see, the low-cost, point-to-point airlines are clustered in the lower-left corner because they tend to offer lower ticket prices but generally service a smaller number of routes due to their point-to-point operating system.

The differentiated airlines offering full services using a hub-and-spoke route system are the so-called legacy carriers. This second strategic group clusters in the upper-right corner because their ticket prices tend to be somewhat higher due to frequently higher cost structures. They usually offer many more routes than the point-to-point low-cost carriers, made possible by use of the hub-and-spoke system. This functional-level strategy allows the legacy airlines to offer many different destinations. For example, Delta's main hub is in Atlanta, Georgia.[35] If you were to fly from Seattle, Washington, to Miami, Florida, you would stop to change planes in Delta's Atlanta hub on your way.

The strategic group mapping in Exhibit 3.5 provides some additional insights:

- *Competitive rivalry is strongest between firms that are within the same strategic group.* The closer firms are on the strategic group map, the more directly and intensely they are in competition with one another. After a wave of mergers, the remaining mega-airlines—American, Delta, and United—are competing head to head, not only in the U.S. domestic market but also globally. They tend to monitor one another's strategic actions closely. While Delta does face competition from low-cost carriers such as Southwest Airlines (SWA) on some domestic routes, its primary competitive rivals are the other legacy carriers. This is because they compete more on providing seamless

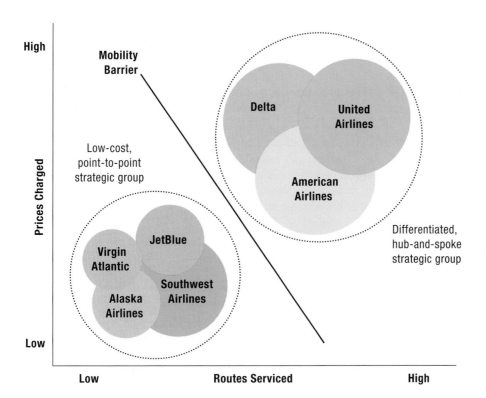

global services within their respective airline alliances (Skyteam for Delta, Oneworld for American, and Star Alliance for United) than on low-cost airfares for particular city pairs in the U.S. Nonetheless, when Delta is faced with direct competition from SWA on a particular domestic route (e.g., from Atlanta to Chicago), both tend to offer similar low-cost fares.

■ *The external environment affects strategic groups differently.* During times of economic downturn, for example, the low-cost airlines tend to take market share away from the legacy carriers. Moreover, given their higher cost structure, the legacy carriers are often unable to be profitable during recessions (at least on domestic routes). This implies that external factors such as recessions or high oil prices favor the companies in the low-cost strategic group. On the other hand, given a number of governmental restrictions on international air travel, the few airlines that are able to compete globally usually make a tidy profit in this specific industry segment.

■ *The five competitive forces affect strategic groups differently.* Let's look at the five competitive forces discussed earlier. *Barriers to entry,* for example, are higher in the hub-and-spoke (differentiated) airline group than in the point-to-point (low-cost) airline group. Following deregulation, many airlines entered the industry, but all of these new players used the point-to-point system. Since hub-and-spoke airlines can offer worldwide service and are protected from foreign competition by regulation, they often face weaker *buyer power,* especially from business travelers. While the hub-and-spoke airlines compete head-on with the point-to-point airlines when they are flying the same or similar routes, the *threat of substitutes* is stronger for the point-to-point airlines. This is because they tend to be regionally focused and also compete with car, train, or bus travel, which are viable substitutes. The threat of *supplier power* tends to be stronger for the airlines in the point-to-point, low-cost strategic group because they are much smaller and thus have weaker negotiation power when acquiring new aircraft, for example. To get around this, these airlines frequently purchase used aircraft from legacy carriers. This brief application of the five forces model leads us to conclude that rivalry among existing competitors in the low-cost, point-to-point strategic group is likely to be more intense than within the differentiated, hub-and-spoke strategic group.

■ *Some strategic groups are more profitable than others.* Historically, airlines clustered in the lower-left corner tend to be more profitable (when considering the U.S. domestic market only). Why? Because they create similar, or even higher, value for their customers in terms of on-time departure and arrival, safety, and fewer bags lost, while keeping ticket costs below those of the legacy carriers. The point-to-point airlines are able to offer their services at a lower cost and a higher perceived value, thus creating the basis for a competitive advantage.

MOBILITY BARRIERS

mobility barriers
Industry-specific
factors that separate
one strategic group
from another.

Although some strategic groups tend to be more profitable and therefore more attractive than others, **mobility barriers** restrict movement between groups. These are industry-specific factors that separate one strategic group from another.[36]

The two groups identified in the U.S. airline industry map in Exhibit 3.5 are separated by the fact that the group using a hub-and-spoke operational model offers international routes, while the point-to-point airlines generally do not. Offering international routes necessitates the hub-and-spoke model. Frequently, the international routes tend to be the only remaining profitable routes left for the legacy carriers. This economic reality implies that if carriers in the lower-left cluster, such as SWA or JetBlue, would like to compete globally, they would likely need to change their point-to-point operating model to a hub-and-spoke model. Or, they could select a few profitable international routes and service them with long-range aircrafts such as Boeing 787s or Airbus A-380s. However, adding international service to the low-cost model would require significant capital investments, and a likely departure from a well-functioning business model. Additional regulatory hurdles reinforce these mobility barriers, such as the difficulty of securing landing slots at international airports around the world. From the perspective of the legacy carriers whose profits tend to be generated primarily from international routes, mobility barriers protect this *profit sanctuary* for the time being.

3.5 ◄► Implications for the Strategist

At the start of the strategic management process, it is critical for managers to conduct a thorough analysis of the firm's external environment to identify threats and opportunities. The initial step is to apply a PESTEL analysis to scan, monitor, and evaluate changes and trends in the firm's macroenvironment. This versatile framework allows managers to track important trends and developments based on the *source* of the external factors: political, economic, sociocultural, technological, ecological, and legal. When applying a PESTEL analysis, the guiding consideration for managers should be the question of how the external factors identified affect the firm's industry environment.

Exhibit 3.1 further delineates external factors based on the *proximity* of these external factors by gradually moving from the general to the task environment. The next layer for managers to understand is the industry. Applying Porter's five forces model allows managers to understand the profit potential of an industry and to obtain clues on how to carve out a strategic position that makes gaining and sustaining a competitive advantage more likely. Follow these steps to apply the five forces model:[37]

1. *Define the relevant industry.* In the five forces model, industry boundaries are drawn by identifying a group of incumbent companies that face more or less the same suppliers and buyers. This group of competitors is likely to be an industry if it also has the same entry barriers and a similar threat from substitutes. In this model, therefore, an industry is defined by commonality and overlap in the five competitive forces that shape competition.

2. *Identify the key players in each of the five forces and attempt to group them into different categories.* This step aids in assessing the relative strength of each force. For example, while makers of jet engines (GE, Rolls Royce, Pratt & Whitney) and local catering services are all suppliers to airlines, their strengths vary widely. Segmenting different players within each force allows you to assess each force in a more fine-grained manner.

3. *Identify the underlying drivers of each force.* Which forces are strong, and which are weak? Why? Keeping with the airline example, why is the supplier power of jet engine manufacturers strong? Because they are supplying a mission-critical, highly differentiated product for airlines. Moreover, there are only a few suppliers of jet engines worldwide, and no viable substitutes.

4. *Assess the overall industry structure.* What is the industry's profit potential? Here you need to identify forces that directly influence industry profit potential, because not all forces are likely to have an equal effect. Focus on the most important forces that drive industry profitability.

The final step in industry analysis is to draw a strategic group map. This exercise allows the strategist to unearth and explain *performance differences within the same industry.* When analyzing a firm's external environment, it is critical to apply the three frameworks introduced in this chapter (PESTEL, Porter's five forces, and strategic group mapping). Taken together, the external environment can determine up to one half of the performance differences across firms (see Exhibit 1.2).

Although the different models discussed in this chapter are an important step in the strategic management process, they are not without shortcomings. First, all of the models presented are *static.* They provide a snapshot of what is actually a moving target and do not allow for consideration of industry dynamics. However, changes in the external environment can appear suddenly, for example, through the appearance of black swan events. Industries can be revolutionized by innovation. Strategic groups can be made obsolete through deregulation or technological progress. To overcome this important shortcoming, managers must conduct external analyses at different points in time to gain a sense of the underlying *dynamics.* The frequency with which these tools need to be applied is a function of the rate of change in the industry. The mobile app industry is changing extremely fast, while the railroad industry experiences a less volatile environment.

Second, the models presented in this chapter do not allow managers to fully understand *why* there are performance differences among firms in the *same* industry or strategic group. To better understand differences in firm performance, we must look *inside the firm* to study its resources, capabilities, and core competencies. We do this in the next chapter by moving from external to internal analysis.

CHAPTER**CASE 3** / Consider This . . .

ALTHOUGH TESLA MOTORS has been successful in entering the U.S. automotive market using innovative new technology, its continued success will depend on other firm and industry factors. While industry forces have been favorable for a long time in the U.S. automotive industry, recent dynamics have lowered the profit potential of competing in this industry and thus reduced its attractiveness. Now that Tesla Motors has demonstrated how new technology can be used to circumvent entry barriers, other new ventures may soon follow. Moreover, the incumbent firms are also adopting the new technology by introducing hybrid or all-electric cars, further increasing rivalry in the industry.

Another external industry force that Tesla Motors must address is the bargaining power of suppliers. Lithium-ion battery packs are key components for Tesla's electric engines. They are supplied by only a few technology firms such as Panasonic in Japan. Given that these sources are few, the bargaining power of suppliers in the electric car segment is quite high, further limiting the industry's profit potential. As a consequence of the strong bargaining power of suppliers, combined with the weak demand for its $100K sports car, Fisker Automotive, another American automaker of plug-in hybrid sports cars based in Anaheim, California, filed for bankruptcy.

In this segment, the bargaining power of buyers is also strong. Individual buyers have many choices, and electric cars tend to be priced at a steep premium due to low production runs. Large-scale buyers such as rental car companies Avis and Hertz or the New York City taxi fleet all have significant purchasing power, further driving down profit potential.

In addition, when demand is slowing, excess capacity tends to develop in the automotive industry, and the incumbent car companies begin to initiate a cut-throat price competition to move inventory. Although both GM and Chrysler went into Chapter 11 bankruptcy, neither exited the industry but rather restructured, causing excess capacity to remain in the industry. Finally, complementary products and services such as battery charging and service stations, which are not yet ubiquitous, are needed to help consumers overcome anxieties concerning electric vehicle ownership.

Questions

Thinking about ChapterCase 3, answer the following questions.

1. Which PESTEL factors are the most salient for the electric vehicle segment of the car industry? Do you see a future for electric vehicles in the U.S.? Why or why not?

2. Looking at Porter's five forces of competition, how would you assess the profit potential of the U.S. car industry?

3. Using the five forces model, what implications can we derive for how Tesla Motors should compete in the U.S. car industry? What would be your top three recommendations for Elon Musk? Support your arguments.

4. Draw a strategic group map for the U.S. automotive industry. What are your conclusions?

TAKE-AWAY CONCEPTS

This chapter demonstrated various approaches to analyzing the firm's *external environment*, as summarized by the following learning objectives and related take-away concepts.

LO 3-1 / **Generate a PESTEL analysis to evaluate the impact of external forces on the firm.**

■ A firm's macroenvironment consists of a wide range of political, economic, sociocultural, technological, ecological, and legal (PESTEL) factors that can affect industry and firm performance. These external forces have both domestic and global aspects.

- The political environment describes the influence government bodies can have on firms.
- The economic environment is mainly affected by five factors: growth rates, interest rates, levels of employment, price stability (inflation and deflation), and currency exchange rates.
- Sociocultural factors capture a society's cultures, norms, and values.
- Technological factors capture the application of knowledge to create new processes and products.
- Ecological factors concern a firm's regard for environmental issues such as the natural environment, global warming, and sustainable economic growth.
- Legal environment factors capture the official outcomes of the political processes that manifest themselves in laws, mandates, regulations, and court decisions.

LO 3-2 / Apply Porter's five competitive forces to explain the profit potential of different industries.

- Competition must be viewed more broadly to encompass not only direct rivals but also a set of other forces in an industry: buyers, suppliers, the potential new entry of other firms, and the threat of substitutes.
- The profit potential of an industry is a function of the five forces that shape competition: (1) threat of entry, (2) power of suppliers, (3) power of buyers, (4) threat of substitutes, and (5) rivalry among existing competitors.
- The stronger a competitive force, the greater the threat it represents. The weaker the competitive force, the greater the opportunity it presents.
- A firm can shape an industry's structure in its favor through its strategy.

LO 3-3 / Explain how competitive industry structure shapes rivalry among competitors.

- The competitive structure of an industry is largely captured by the number and size of competitors in an industry, whether the firms possess some degree of pricing power, the type of product or

service the industry offers (commodity or differentiated product), and the height of entry barriers.

- A perfectly competitive industry is characterized by many small firms, a commodity product, low entry barriers, and no pricing power for individual firms.
- A monopolistic industry is characterized by many firms, a differentiated product, medium entry barriers, and some pricing power.
- An oligopolistic industry is characterized by few (large) firms, a differentiated product, high entry barriers, and some degree of pricing power.
- A monopoly exists when there is only one (large) firm supplying the market. In such instances, the firm may offer a unique product, the barriers to entry may be high, and the monopolist usually has considerable pricing power.

LO 3-4 / Describe the strategic role of complements in creating positive-sum co-opetition.

- Co-opetition (co-operation among competitors) can create a positive-sum game, resulting in a larger pie for everyone involved.
- Complements increase demand for the primary product, enhancing the profit potential for the industry and the firm.
- Attractive industries for co-opetition are characterized by high entry barriers, low exit barriers, low buyer and supplier power, a low threat of substitutes, and the availability of complements.

LO 3-5 / Appraise the role of industry dynamics and industry convergence in shaping the firm's external environment.

- Industries are dynamic—they change over time.
- Different conditions prevail in different industries, directly affecting the firms competing in these industries and their profitability.
- In industry convergence, formerly unrelated industries begin to satisfy the same customer need. It is often brought on by technological advances.

LO 3-6 / Generate a strategic group model to reveal performance differences between clusters of firms in the same industry.

- A strategic group is a set of firms within a specific industry that pursue a similar strategy in their quest for competitive advantage.

- Generally, there are two strategic groups in an industry based on two different business strategies: one that pursues a low-cost strategy and a second that pursues a differentiation strategy.

- Rivalry among firms of the same strategic group is more intense than the rivalry between strategic groups: intra-group rivalry exceeds inter-group rivalry.

- Strategic groups are affected differently by the external environment and the five competitive forces.

- Some strategic groups are more profitable than others.

- Movement between strategic groups is restricted by mobility barriers—industry-specific factors that separate one strategic group from another.

KEY TERMS

Competitive industry structure

Complement

Complementor

Co-opetition

Entry barriers

Exit barriers

Five forces model

Industry

Industry analysis

Industry convergence

Mobility barriers

PESTEL model

Strategic group

Strategic group model

Strategic position

Threat of entry

DISCUSSION QUESTIONS

1. Why is it important for an organization to study and understand its external environment?

2. How do the five competitive forces in Porter's model affect the average profitability of the industry? For example, in what way might weak forces increase industry profits, and in what way do strong forces reduce industry profits? Identify an industry in which many of the competitors seem to be having financial performance problems. Which of the five forces seems to be strongest?

3. What is a strategic group? How can studying such groups be useful in industry analysis?

4. How do mobility barriers affect the structure of an industry? How do they help us explain firm differences in performance?

ETHICAL/SOCIAL ISSUES

1. UBS, a venerable Swiss banking institution with global business activities, experienced the significant implications that political factors can have on the bottom line. The U.S. government alleged that by advertising its "tax savings" advantages to U.S. clients, UBS aided wealthy Americans in siphoning off billions of dollars to a safe haven that the IRS cannot touch. The government requested from UBS the names of 52,000 U.S. citizens who it suspected were tax evaders. Initially, UBS declined to release names, citing Swiss banking laws and regulations that guarantee the privacy of customers. However, UBS was in a lose–lose situation: If it resisted the IRS, it risked losing its U.S. banking license. If it disclosed names of its customers, it would break the traditional Swiss banking secrecy and potentially violate Swiss law, which makes it a felony to improperly disclose client information. In 2009, after multiple rounds of intense negotiations, UBS finally relented to significant pressure by the U.S. government and released the names of 4,450 U.S. citizens who are suspected to have evaded taxes.

The U.S. government's case against UBS was helped immensely by a former employee at UBS who cooperated with prosecutors on details of how such transactions occur. The "whistle-blower," a U.S. citizen, has been lauded for his help in the investigation. Yet, in January 2010 he also began serving a 40-month prison sentence for his own guilty plea for helping his clients at UBS evade taxes.[38] Some in the industry believe such a surprisingly long prison term, despite his cooperation with investigators, will dramatically reduce motivation for other potential whistleblowers to come forward.

a. What is the proper role for a multinational firm in cases where government regulations across countries are in conflict? For example, UBS executives claimed that releasing *any* names of U.S. customers would violate Swiss banking laws. A compromise was later reached that only the names of customers suspected of illegal activity were released.

b. What is the responsibility of individual employees to their employers and to their governments when there seems to be a conflict?

SMALL-GROUP EXERCISES

//// Small-Group Exercise 1
(Ethical/Social Issues)

Your group is a team of Kraft (www.kraftfoodsgroup .com) marketing interns. The company has asked you to propose new guidelines for helping it promote food to children in a socially responsible way. As the fourth-largest consumer packaged food and beverage company in the U.S., its 2012 sales were over $18 billion. The company projects steady growth but would like your help in boosting growth. One of Kraft's largest brands is Oscar Mayer Lunchables, described as making lunch fun and targeted to busy parents who want a quick lunch to send with their children to school or keep on hand as an after-school snack. One of the options is Lunchables with Juice, Nachos Cheese Dip, and Salsa. However, there is a growing controversy about the social responsibility of directly marketing to children when the food is unhealthy—high in fat, sugar, and salt, but low in nutrition. There is a societal concern with the growing rate of obesity in children and the increased incidence in diabetes that results from childhood obesity. In response, most food and beverage companies have agreed to follow voluntary guidelines created by the Better Business Bureau, termed the Children's Food and Beverage Advertising Initiative (CFBAI). The guidelines ask for participating companies to pledge to advertise only healthy choices during children's programs, defined as those with an audience of 35 percent or more children under 12.

Kraft would like to have a reputation as a socially responsible company. Accordingly, Kraft would like to create internal guidelines that will help it market Lunchables (as well as other packaged food items) responsibly and gain the approval of medical professionals, parents, and watchdog groups.[39]

1. Visit the Kraft website (www.kraftfoodcompanies .com) and review the Lunchables products, as well as other packaged food products that Kraft offers. Discuss among group members the extent to which product options are healthy choices.

2. What changes would you recommend to the CFBAI pledge in order to ensure that the primary audience watching advertisements for Kraft packaged foods will not be children? Describe alternative guidelines that Kraft might adopt.

3. Identify other actions that Kraft might take in order to demonstrate that it is a food company that genuinely cares about children's health and a company that would like to help reverse the trend of increasing childhood obesity.

4. If your group believes that the company is not responsible for personal choices that consumers make to eat unhealthy food, then describe how the company should respond to activist groups and public health officials that are urging companies to stop producing and marketing unhealthy foods.

//// Small-Group Exercise 2

One industry with an impact on both undergraduate and MBA students is textbook publishing. Traditional printed textbooks are being challenged by the growing demand for electronic versions of these materials. E-readers such as the Amazon Kindle and Apple iPad are examples of devices that are likely to drive industry convergence. Millions of e-readers are sold each year.[40]

Use the five forces model to think through the various impacts such technology shifts may have on the textbook industry. Include in your response answers to the following questions.

1. How should managers of a textbook publishing company respond to such changes?

2. Will the shifts in technology be likely to raise or lower the textbook industry–level profits? Explain.

STRATEGY TERM PROJECT

//// Module 3: External Analysis

In this section, you will study the external environment of the firm you have previously selected for this project.

1. Are any changes taking place in the macroenvironment that might have a positive or negative impact on the industry in which your company is based? Apply the PESTEL framework to identify which factors may be the most important in your industry. What will be the effect on your industry?

2. Apply the five forces model to your industry. What does this model tell you about the nature of competition in the industry?

3. Identify any strategic groups that might exist in the industry. How does the intensity of competition differ across the strategic groups you have identified?

4. How dynamic is the industry in which your company is based? Is there evidence that industry structure is reshaping competition, or has done so in the recent past?

my STRATEGY

Is My Job the Next One Being Outsourced?

The outsourcing of IT programming jobs to India is now commonly understood after years of this trend. However, more recently some accounting functions have also begun to flow into India's large technically trained and English-speaking work force. For example, the number of U.S. tax returns completed in India rose dramatically from 2003 to 2011 (25,000 in 2003 to 1.6 million in 2011). Some estimate that over 20 million U.S. tax returns will be prepared in India within the next few years. Outsourcing in the accounting functions may affect the job and career prospects for accounting-oriented business school graduates. Tax accountants in Bangalore, India, are much cheaper than those in Boston or Baltimore. Moreover, tax accountants in India often work longer hours and can therefore process many more tax returns than only U.S.-based CPAs and tax accountants during the crunch period of the U.S. tax filing system.[41]

1. Which aspects of accounting do you think are more likely to resist the outsourcing trends just discussed? Think about what aspects of accounting are the high-value activities versus the routine standardized ones. (If it's been a while since you took your accounting courses, reach out for information to someone in your strategy class who is an accounting major.)

2. What industries do you think may offer the best U.S. (or domestic) job opportunities in the future? Which industries do you think may offer the greatest job opportunities in the global market in the future? Use the PESTEL framework and the five forces model to think through a logical set of reasons that some fields will have higher job growth trends than others.

3. Do these types of macroenvironmental and industry trends affect your thinking about selecting a career field after college? Why or why not? Explain.

ENDNOTES

1. For an in-depth discussion of Tesla Motors and the car industry, see Case MHE-FTR-017-0077645065, "Tesla Motors: Will sparks fly in the U.S. automobile industry?" in F. T. Rothaermel (2015), *Strategic Management,* 2nd ed. Burr Ridge, IL: McGraw-Hill.

2. For a detailed treatise on how institutions shape the economic climate and with it firm performance, see: North, D. C. (1990), *Institutions, Institutional Change, and Economic Performance* (New York: Random House).

3. "BP and Rosneft," *The Economist,* October 20, 2012; and "Rosneft completes $55 billion takeover of TNK-BP," *The Wall Street Journal,* March 21, 2013.

4. Hillman, A. J., Keim, G. D., and D. Schuler (2004), "Corporate political activity: A review and research agenda," *Journal of Management* 30: 837–857; and De Figueireo, R.J.P., and G. Edwards (2007), "Does private money buy public policy? Campaign contributions and regulatory outcomes in telecommunications," *Journal of Economics & Management Strategy* 16: 547–576.

5. This phrase was used in a speech to the American Enterprise Institute on December 5, 1996, by the former Chairman of the Federal Reserve Bank, Alan Greenspan, to describe the mood in the equity markets.

6. Lowenstein, R. (2010), *The End of Wall Street* (New York: Penguin Press).

7. "Toyota keeps idled workers busy honing their skills," *The Wall Street Journal,* October 13, 2008.

8. "Professor Emeritus Milton Friedman dies at 94," University of Chicago press release, November 16, 2006.

9. Lucas, R. (1972), "Expectations and the neutrality of money," *Journal of Economic Theory* 4: 103–124.

10. "Media companies are piling into the Hispanic market. But will it pay off?" *The Economist,* December 15, 2012.

11. "Crisis in Europe tightens credit across the globe," *The New York Times,* November 28, 2011; "The European debt crisis: A beginner's guide," *The Huffington Post,* December 21, 2011; "European debt crisis," *The New York Times,* January 10, 2013.

12. Rothaermel, F. T., and M. Thursby (2007), "The nanotech vs. the biotech revolution: Sources of incumbent productivity in research," *Research Policy* 36: 832–849; and Woolley, J. L., and R. M. Rottner (2008), "Innovation policy and nanotech entrepreneurship," *Entrepreneurship Theory and Practice* 32: 791–811.

13. Bettis, R., and M. A. Hitt (1995), "The new competitive landscape," *Strategic Management Journal* 16 (Special Issue): 7–19; Hill, C.W.L., and F. T. Rothaermel (2003), "The performance of incumbent firms in the face of radical technological innovation," *Academy of Management Review* 28: 257–274; and Afuah, A. (2009), *Strategic Innovation: New Game Strategies for Competitive Advantage* (New York: Routledge).

14. Academy of Management, ONE Division, 2013 domain statement; Anderson, R. C. (2009), *Confessions of a Radical Industrialist: Profits, People, Purpose—Doing Business by Respecting the Earth* (New York: St. Martin's Press); and Esty, D. C., and A. S. Winston (2009), *Green to Gold: How Smart Companies Use Environmental Strategy to Innovate, Create Value, and Build Competitive Advantage,* revised and updated (Hoboken, NJ: John Wiley).

15. The discussion in this section is based on: Porter, M. E. (1979), "How competitive forces shape strategy," *Harvard Business Review,* March–April: 137–145; Porter, M. E. (1980), *Competitive Strategy: Techniques for Analyzing Industries and Competitors* (New York: Free Press); Porter, M. E. (2008), "The five competitive forces that shape strategy," *Harvard Business Review,* January; and Magretta, J. (2012), *Understanding Michael Porter: The Essential Guide to Competition and Strategy* (Boston, MA: Harvard Business Review Press).

16. Porter, M. E. (2008), "The five competitive forces that shape strategy"; *An Interview with Michael E. Porter: The Five Competitive Forces that Shape Strategy,* Harvard Business Publishing video; author's interviews with Delta executives.

17. "Everyone else in the travel business makes money off airlines. The carriers are trying to fight back," *The Economist,* August 25, 2012; "How airline ticket prices fell 50% in 30 years (and nobody noticed)," *The Atlantic,* February 28, 2013.

18. "Fiat nears stake in Chrysler that could lead to takeover," *The Wall Street Journal,* January 20, 2009.

19. "Samsung Sparks Anxiety at Google," *The Wall Street Journal,* February 25, 2013.

20. Whether a product is a substitute (complement) can be estimated by the cross-elasticity of demand. The cross-elasticity estimates the percentage change in the quantity demanded of good X resulting from a 1 percent change in the price of good Y. If the cross-elasticity

of demand is greater (less) than zero, the products are substitutes (complements). For a detailed discussion, see: Allen, W. B., K. Weigelt, N. Doherty, and E. Mansfield (2009), *Managerial Economics.*

21. This example, as with some others in the section on the five forces, is drawn from Magretta, J. (2012), *Understanding Michael Porter: The Essential Guide to Competition and Strategy* (Boston, MA: Harvard Business Review Press).

22. Because the threat of entry is one of the five forces explicitly recognized in Porter's model, we discuss barriers to entry when introducing the threat of entry above. The competitive industry structure framework is frequently referred to as the Structure-Conduct-Performance (SCP) model. For a detailed discussion, see: Bain, J. S. (1968), *Industrial Organization* (New York: John Wiley); Scherer, F. M., and D. Ross (1990), *Industrial Market Structure and Economic Performance,* 3rd ed. (Boston, MA: Houghton-Mifflin); Carlton, D. W., and J. M. Perloff (2000), *Modern Industrial Organization,* 3rd ed. (Reading, MA: Addison-Wesley); and Allen, W. B., K. Weigelt, N. Doherty, and E. Mansfield (2009), *Managerial Economics: Theory, Application, and Cases,* 7th ed. (New York: Norton).

23. Besanko, D., E. Dranove, M. Hanley, and S. Schaefer (2010), *The Economics of Strategy,* 5th ed. (Hoboken, NJ: Wiley).

24. Dixit, A., S. Skeath, and D. H. Reiley (2009), *Games of Strategy,* 3rd ed. (New York: Norton).

25. When there are only two main competitors, it's called a *duopoly,* and is a special case of oligopoly.

26. Yoffie, D. B., and Y. Wang (2009), *Cola Wars Continue.*

27. Brandenburger, A. M., and B. Nalebuff (1996), *Co-opetition* (New York: Currency Doubleday); and Grove, A. S. (1999), *Only the Paranoid Survive* (New York: Time Warner).

28. Milgrom, P., and J. Roberts (1995), "Complementarities and fit strategy, structure, and organizational change in manufacturing," *Journal of Accounting and Economics* 19(2-3): 179–208; and Brandenburger, A. M., and B. Nalebuff (1996), *Co-opetition.*

29. In this recent treatise, Porter also highlights positive-sum competition. See Porter, M. E. (2008), "The five competitive forces that shape strategy," *Harvard Business Review,* January.

30. "Reading between the lines," *The Economist,* March 26, 2009; and "New York Times is near web charges," *The Wall Street Journal,* January 19, 2010.

31. "Global online ad spending forecast to exceed print in 2015," *MarketingCharts,* December 3, 2012.

32. Hunt, M. S. (1972), *Competition in the Major Home Appliance Industry, 1960–1970,* unpublished doctoral dissertation, Harvard University; Hatten, K. J., and D. E. Schendel (1977), "Heterogeneity within an industry: Firm conduct in the U.S. brewing industry," *Journal of Industrial Economics* 26: 97–113; and Porter, M. E. (1980), *Competitive Strategy: Techniques for Analyzing Industries and Competitors* (New York: Free Press).

33. This discussion is based on: Hunt, M. S. (1972), *Competition in the Major Home Appliance Industry, 1960–1970;* Hatten, K. J., and D. E. Schendel (1977), "Heterogeneity within an industry: Firm conduct in the U.S. brewing industry"; Porter, M. E. (1980), *Competitive Strategy;* Cool, K., and D. Schendel (1988), "Performance differences among strategic group members," *Strategic Management Journal* 9: 207–223; Nair, A., and S. Kotha (2001), "Does group membership matter? Evidence from the Japanese steel industry," *Strategic Management Journal* 22: 221–235; and McNamara, G., D. L. Deephouse, and R. Luce (2003), "Competitive positioning within and across a strategic group structure: The performance of core, secondary, and solitary firms," *Strategic Management Journal* 24: 161–181.

34. In Exhibit 3.5, United Airlines is the biggest bubble, because it merged with Continental in 2010, creating the largest airline in the United States. Delta is the second-biggest airline in the U.S. after merging with Northwest Airlines in 2008.

35. American's hub is at Dallas–Fort Worth; Continental's is at Newark, New Jersey; United's is at Chicago, Illinois; and U.S. Airways' is at Charlotte, North Carolina.

36. Caves, R. E., and M. E. Porter (1977), "From entry barriers to mobility barriers," *Quarterly Journal of Economics* 91: 241–262.

37. Porter, M. E. (2008), "The five competitive forces that shape strategy," *Harvard Business Review,* January; and Magretta, J. (2012), *Understanding Michael Porter: The Essential Guide to Competition and Strategy,* pp. 56–57.

38. "Crying foul, ex-UBS banker starts prison term," *The Wall Street Journal,* January 9, 2010.

39. Sources: Corporate website; Orciari, M. (2013), "Industry self-regulation permits junk food ads in programming popular with children," *Yale News,* March 12. Accessed online; Moss, M. (2013), "How the fast food industry creates and keeps selling the crave," *New York Times Magazine,* February 24.

40. "E-Readers everywhere: The inevitable shakeout," *Bloomberg BusinessWeek,* January 11, 2010.

41. The *my*Strategy module is based on: Friedman, T. (2005), *The World Is Flat: A Brief History of the Twenty-first Century* (New York: Farrar, Strauss & Giroux); and Value-Notes, http://www.sourcingnotes.com/content/view/197/54/.

Chapter 4

Internal Analysis: Resources, Capabilities, and Core Competencies

Learning Objectives

After studying this chapter, you should be able to:

LO 4-1 Differentiate among a firm's resources, capabilities, core competencies, and activities.

LO 4-2 Compare and contrast tangible and intangible resources.

LO 4-3 Evaluate the two critical assumptions behind the resource-based view.

LO 4-4 Apply the VRIO framework to assess the competitive implications of a firm's resources.

LO 4-5 Evaluate different conditions that allow firms to sustain their competitive advantage.

LO 4-6 Outline how dynamic capabilities can help a firm sustain competitive advantage.

LO 4-7 Apply a value chain analysis to understand which of the firm's activities in the process of transforming inputs into outputs generate differentiation and which drive costs.

LO 4-8 Conduct a SWOT analysis to combine external and internal analysis and derive strategic implications.

CHAPTER**CASE 4**

Nike's Core Competency: The Risky Business of Fairy Tales

Kobe Bryant

WITH ANNUAL REVENUES doubling during the last decade to over $25 billion and having a globally recognized brand, Nike is the undisputed leader in the athletic shoe and apparel industry. The number two adidas has some $15 billion in sales, while recent entrant Under Armour reports revenues of less than $1 billion. Nike is tremendously successful, holding close to a 60 percent market share in running and nearly a 90 percent market share in basketball.

The Beaverton, Oregon, company has come a long way from its humble beginnings. It was founded by University of Oregon track and field coach Bill Bowerman and middle-distance runner Phil Knight in 1964 originally as Blue Ribbon Sports. In 1971, the company was renamed Nike (the "goddess of victory" in Greek mythology) and the now iconic "swoosh" was designed by a Portland State University student.

Coach Bowerman was a true innovator because he constantly sought ways to give his athletes a competitive edge. He experimented with many factors affecting running performance, from different track surfaces to rehydration drinks. Coach Bowerman's biggest focus, however, was on providing a better running shoe for his athletes. While sitting at the breakfast table one Sunday morning and absentmindedly looking at his waffle iron, Coach Bowerman had an epiphany. He began pouring hot, liquid urethane into the waffle iron—ruining it in the process—but coming up with the now famous waffle-type sole that not only provided better traction but was also lighter than traditional running shoes.

After completing his undergraduate degree at the University of Oregon and serving in the U.S. Army, Phil Knight entered the MBA program at Stanford. One entrepreneurship class required him to come up with a business idea. So, he wrote a term paper on how to disrupt the leading athletic shoe maker adidas. The research question he came up with was "Can Japanese sports shoes do to German sports shoes what Japanese cameras have done to German cameras?"[1] At that time,

adidas athletic shoes were the gold standard. They were also expensive and hard to find in the U.S. After several failed attempts to interest Japanese sneaker makers, Phil Knight was able to strike a distribution agreement with Tiger Shoes. After his first shipment arrived in the U.S., Phil Knight sent some of the running shoes to his former coach Bill Bowerman, hoping to make a sale. To his surprise, Bill Bowerman replied that he was interested in becoming a business partner and contributing his innovative ideas on how to improve running shoes, including the waffle design. With an investment of $500 each and a handshake, the venture commenced.

Based on a highly successful string of innovations including Nike Air, by 1979 the company had captured more than a 50 percent market share for running shoes in the United States. A year later, Nike went public. In 1984, Nike signed Michael Jordan—whom many consider the greatest basketball player of all time—with an unprecedented multimillion-dollar endorsement deal. Rather than spreading its marketing budget more widely as was common in the sports industry at that time, Nike made the unorthodox move to spend basically its entire budget for a specific sport on a *single* star athlete. Nike sought to sponsor future superstars that embodied an unlikely success story. Michael Jordan's story is that he had been cut from his high school basketball team only to become the greatest basketball player ever.

In the 1990s and 2000s, Nike continued to sponsor track and field sports stars such as Marion Jones, as well as Kobe Bryant in basketball. With the help of major celebrity endorsements, Nike was also able to move on to different sports and their superstars,

EXHIBIT 4.1 / Some of Nike's (Past and Current) Celebrity Endorsements

Oscar Pistorious

Lance Armstrong

including golf with Tiger Woods, cycling with Lance Armstrong, soccer with Wayne Rooney, and football with Michael Vick.

Over time, Nike developed a deep expertise in *creating heroes.* It picked athletes that succeeded against the odds—cancer survivor Lance Armstrong, double amputee "blade runner" Oscar Pistorius, and other athletes hailing from disadvantaged backgrounds. Although this core competency made Nike highly successful, it has not been without considerable risks. Time and time again, Nike's heroes have become unmasked as cheaters, frauds, and criminals, some of whom have committed serious felonies, such as (alleged) homicide. As Nike veers from one public relations disaster to the next, disappointment with the brand and its promise may eventually set in causing customers to go elsewhere.[2]

After reading the chapter, you will find more about this case, with related questions, on page 120.

🔺 **ONE OF THE KEY** messages of this chapter is that a firm's ability to gain and sustain competitive advantage is partly driven by *core competencies*—unique strengths that are embedded deep within a firm. Core competencies allow a firm to differentiate its products and services from those of its rivals, creating higher value for the customer or offering products and services of comparable value at lower cost. Nike is less about running shoes or sports apparel than about unlocking human potential. This is captured in Nike's mission *"to bring inspiration and innovation to every athlete in the world"* (and *"if you have a body, you are an athlete"*).[3] Nike uses its heroes to tell a story whose moral is that through sheer will, tenacity, and hard work, anyone can unlock the hero within and achieve amazing things. Nike will help everyone become a hero. *Just Do It!* This type of mythical brand image has allowed Nike to not only enter but often dominate one sport after another, from running to ice hockey.

Nike's unique strength, built over many decades and embedded deep within the firm, allows it to differentiate its products from its rivals and create more perceived value for its customers. To hone and refine this core competency, Nike spent some $4 billion, or 16 percent of annual revenues, in 2012 alone on sponsoring athletes. Its iconic brand alone is worth some $16 billion, making it one of the most valuable in the world.[4]

In this chapter, we study analytical tools to explain why differences in firm performance exist even within the *same* industry. For example, why does Nike outperform adidas, ASICS, Li Ning, New Balance, Mizuno, Puma, Skechers, and Under Armour in the athletic shoe and apparel industry? Since these companies compete in the same industry and face the same external opportunities and threats, the source for some of the observable performance difference must be found *inside the firm.* When discussing industry, firm, and other effects in explaining superior performance, we noted that up to 55 percent of the overall performance differences is explained by firm-specific effects (see Exhibit 1.1).

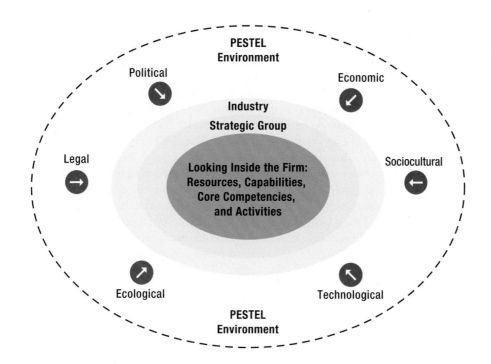

EXHIBIT 4.2 /

Looking Inside the
Firm for Competitive
Advantage:
Resources,
Capabilities, Core
Competencies, and
Activities

Looking inside the firm to analyze its resources, capabilities, and core competencies allows us to understand the firm's strengths and weaknesses. Linking these insights from a firm's internal analysis to the ones derived in the prior chapter on external analysis allows managers to determine their strategic options. Ideally, firms want to leverage their internal strengths to exploit external opportunities, and to mitigate internal weaknesses and external threats.

Exhibit 4.2 depicts how we move from the firm's external environment to its internal environment. To formulate and implement a strategy that enhances the firm's chances of gaining and sustaining competitive advantage, the firm must have certain types of resources and capabilities that combine to form core competencies. The goal should be to develop resources, capabilities, and competencies that create a *strategic fit* with the firm's environment. Rather than creating a static fit, the firm's internal strengths should change with its external environment in a *dynamic* fashion. The chapter will provide a deeper understanding of the sources of competitive advantage that reside within a firm.

To gain a better understanding of why and how firm differences explain competitive advantage, we begin this chapter by taking a closer look at *core competencies*. Next, we introduce the *resource-based view* of the firm to provide an analytical model that allows us to assess resources, capabilities, and competencies and their potential for creating a sustainable competitive advantage. We then discuss the *dynamic capabilities perspective,* a more recent model that emphasizes a firm's ability to modify and leverage its resource base to gain and sustain a competitive advantage in a constantly changing environment. We finally turn our attention to the *value chain analysis* to gain a deeper understanding of the internal activities a firm engages in when transforming inputs into outputs. We conclude with *Implications for the Strategist,* with a particular focus on how to use the *SWOT analysis* to combine external and internal analysis.

core competencies
Unique strengths, embedded deep within a firm, that allow a firm to differentiate its products and services from those of its rivals, creating higher value for the customer or offering products and services of comparable value at lower cost.

4.1 Looking Inside the Firm for Core Competencies

LO 4-1

Differentiate among a firm's resources, capabilities, core competencies, and activities.

Let's begin by taking a closer look at **core competencies.** These are unique strengths, embedded deep within a firm. Core competencies allow a firm to differentiate its products and services from those of its rivals, creating higher value for the customer or offering products and services of comparable value at lower cost. The important point here is that competitive advantage can be driven by core competencies.[5]

Company examples of core competencies abound: Honda's life began with a small two-cycle motorbike engine. Through continuous learning over several decades, and often from lessons learned from failure, Honda built the core competency to design and manufacture small but powerful and highly reliable engines for which it now is famous. This core competency results from superior engineering know-how and skills carefully nurtured and honed over several decades. Today, Honda engines can be found everywhere: in cars, SUVs, vans, trucks, motorcycles, ATVs, boats, airplanes, generators, snow blowers, lawn mowers and other yard equipment, and so on. Due to their superior performance, Honda engines have been the only ones used in the Indy Racing League (IRL) since 2006. Not coincidentally, this was also the first year in its long history that the Indy 500 was run without a single engine problem. One way to look at Honda is to view it as a company with a distinct competency in engines and a business model of finding places to put its engines. That is, underneath the products and services that make up the *visible* side of competition lies a diverse set of *invisible* competencies that make this happen. These invisible core competencies reside deep within the firm. Companies, therefore, compete as much in the product and service markets as they do in developing and leveraging core competencies. Although invisible by themselves, core competencies find their expression in superior products and services. Exhibit 4.3 identifies the core competencies of a number of companies, with application examples.

EXHIBIT 4.3 / Company Examples of Core Competencies and Applications

Company	Core Competencies	Application Examples
Amazon.com	Providing the largest selection of items online, combined with superior IT systems and customer service.	Expansion to cover most electronic media, digital downloads, tablet computers (Kindle series), as well as apparel, toys, electronics, tools, etc. Offering cloud computing services.
Apple	Leveraging industrial design to integrate hardware and software in innovative and category-defining mobile devices that take the user's experience to a new level.	iMac, iPhone, iPod, iPad, iTunes, Apple TV.
Coca-Cola	Leveraging one of the world's most recognized brand names (based on its original "secret formula") into a diverse lineup of soft drinks and other beverages.	Coke, Coke Zero, Diet Coke, Fanta, Fresca, Sprite, Dasani, Powerade, etc.
ExxonMobil	Discovering and exploring fossil-fuel–based energy sources globally.	Oil and gas.
Facebook	Connecting over one billion social media users worldwide.	News feed, timeline, and graph search.
General Electric	Designing and implementing efficient management processes, developing and training leaders, leveraging deep industrial engineering expertise.	Energy, health care, airplane jet engines, finance.

Company	Core Competencies	Application Examples
Google	Creating proprietary algorithms to develop software products and services for the Internet and mobile computing.	Online search, Android mobile operating system, Chrome OS, Chrome web browser, Google Play, AdWords, AdSense, Google docs, Gmail, Goog411, Google Maps/Earth, Google Books, Google Scholar, etc.
Honda	Designing and manufacturing of small but powerful and highly reliable internal combustion engines.	Motorcycles, cars, ATVs, sporting boats, snow mobiles, lawn mowers, small aircraft, etc.
IKEA	Designing modern functional home furnishings at low prices offered in a unique retail experience.	Fully furnished room setups, practical tools for all rooms, do-it-yourself.
McKinsey	Developing practice-relevant knowledge, insights, and frameworks.	Management; in particular, strategy consulting targeted toward company and government leaders.
Netflix	Proprietary algorithms to track individual customer preferences.	DVD-by-mail rentals, streaming media (including proprietary) content, connection to game consoles.
Starbucks	Providing high-quality beverages and selected food items, combined with superior customer service in a friendly and welcoming environment.	Customized handcrafted (coffee) beverages; warm/cold, seasonal, and fruit drinks; comfortable and convenient ambience in retail outlets; free Wi-Fi Internet connections.
Tesla Motors	Designing high-performance battery-powered motors and power trains.	Tesla Roadster, Tesla Model S, Tesla Model X.
UPS	Providing superior supply chain management services and solutions at low cost.	Package tracking and delivery, transportation, ecommerce, consulting services.

Since core competencies are critical to gaining and sustaining competitive advantage, it is important to understand how they are created. Core competencies are built through the interplay of resources and capabilities. Exhibit 4.4 shows this relationship. **Resources** are any assets such as cash, buildings, machinery, or intellectual property that a company can draw on when crafting and executing a strategy. Resources can be either tangible or intangible. **Capabilities** are the organizational and managerial skills necessary to orchestrate a diverse set of resources and to deploy them strategically. Capabilities are by nature intangible. They find their expression in a company's structure, routines, and culture. **Activities** are distinct and fine-grained business processes such as order taking, the physical delivery of products, or invoicing customers. Each distinct activity enables firms to add incremental value by transforming inputs into goods and services. In the interplay of resources and capabilities, resources reinforce core competencies, while capabilities allow managers to orchestrate their core competencies. Strategic choices find their expression in a set of specific firm activities, which leverage core competencies for competitive advantage. The arrows leading back from performance to resources and capabilities indicate that superior performance in the marketplace generates profits that can be reinvested into the firm (retained earnings) to further hone and upgrade a firm's resources and capabilities in its pursuit of achieving and maintaining a strategic fit within a dynamic environment.

Core competencies that are not continuously nourished will eventually lose their ability to yield a competitive advantage. In the consumer electronics industry, Best Buy

resources Any assets that a firm can draw on when formulating and implementing a strategy.

capabilities Organizational and managerial skills necessary to orchestrate a diverse set of resources and deploy them strategically.

activities Distinct and fine-grained business processes that enable firms to add incremental value by transforming input into goods and services.

EXHIBIT 4.4

Linking Resources,
Capabilities, Core
Competencies,
and Activities
to Competitive
Advantage and
Superior Firm
Performance

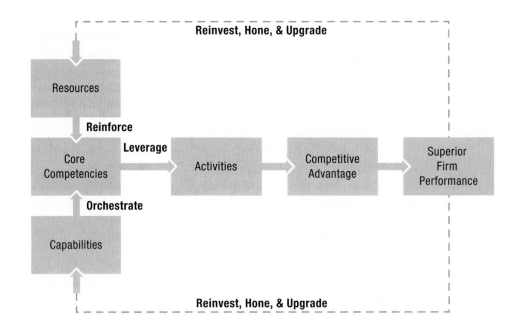

outperformed Circuit City based on its strengths in customer-centricity (segmenting customers based on demographic, attitudinal, and value tiers, and configuring stores to serve the needs of the customer segments in that region), employee development, and exclusive branding. Although Best Buy outperformed Circuit City (which filed for bankruptcy in 2009), more recently Best Buy did not hone and upgrade its core competencies sufficiently to compete effectively against Amazon.com, the world's largest online retailer. As such, Amazon does not have the overhead expenses associated with maintaining buildings or human sales forces, and can therefore undercut in-store retailers on price. When a firm does not invest in continual upgrading or improving core competencies, its competitors are more likely to develop equivalent or superior skills, as did Amazon. This insight will allow us to explain differences between firms in the same industry, as well as competitive dynamics, over time. It also will help us identify strategies with which firms gain and sustain a competitive advantage and weather an adverse external environment.

4.2 The Resource-Based View

LO 4-2

Compare and contrast
tangible and intangible
resources.

To gain a deeper understanding of how resources, capabilities, and competencies can be a source of competitive advantage, we turn to the **resource-based view** of the firm to provide a model that systematically aids in identifying core competencies.[6] As the name suggests, this model sees resources as key to superior firm performance. As Exhibit 4.5 illustrates, resources fall broadly into two categories: tangible and intangible. **Tangible resources** have physical attributes and are visible. Examples of tangible resources are labor, capital, land, buildings, plant, equipment, and supplies. **Intangible resources** have no physical attributes and thus are invisible. Examples of intangible resources are a firm's culture, its knowledge, brand equity, reputation, and intellectual property.

Let's take Apple as an example. Its tangible resources ("fixed assets"), valued at $15 billion, include its headquarters (a campus with multiple buildings) on Infinite Loop in Cupertino,

California, and some cutting-edge machinery and equipment, including product tooling and manufacturing process equipment.[7] The Apple brand, an intangible resource, is valued at over $180 billion (#1 worldwide)—which is 12 times higher than the value of its tangible assets.[8] This relationship is even more skewed if we look at Google. Its tangible resources ("fixed assets"), valued at $8 billion, include its headquarters ("The Googleplex") in Mountain View, California, and numerous server farms (clusters of computer servers) across the globe.[9] The Google brand, an intangible resource, is valued at over $110 billion (No. 3 worldwide)—which is 14 times higher than the value of its tangible assets.[10]

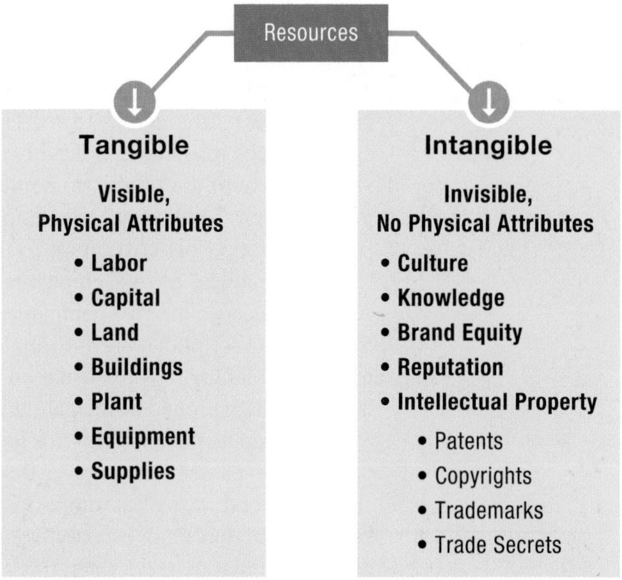

Google's headquarters provides examples of both tangible and intangible resources. The Googleplex is a piece of land with a futuristic building, and thus a tangible asset. The *location* of the company in the heart of Silicon Valley is an *intangible resource* that provides access to a valuable network of contacts and gives the company several benefits. It allows Google to tap into a large and computer-savvy work force and access graduates and knowledge spillovers from a large number of universities, including San Francisco State University, San Jose State University, Santa Clara University, Stanford, and the University of California, Berkeley, among others, which adds to Google's technical and managerial capabilities.[11] Another benefit stems from Silicon Valley's designation as having the largest concentration of venture capital in the United States, which is beneficial because venture capitalists tend to prefer local investments to ensure closer monitoring.[12] Google received initial funding from the famous venture capital firms Kleiner Perkins Caufield & Byers and Sequoia Capital, both located in Silicon Valley.

Competitive advantage is more likely to spring from intangible rather than tangible resources. Tangible assets, such as buildings or computer servers, can be bought on the open market by any comers who have the necessary cash. However, a brand name must be built, often over long periods of time. Google (founded in 1998) accomplished its enormous brand valuation fairly quickly due to its ubiquitous Internet presence, while most of the other companies in the global top-10 most valuable brands—Apple, IBM, McDonald's, Microsoft, Coca-Cola, Marlboro, AT&T, and Verizon—took much longer.[13] The telecom provider China Mobile rounds out the top-10 brands with a valuation at roughly $50 billion. This state-owned telecommunications company also rose fairly quickly to prominence (it was founded in 1997), because it is the world's largest mobile phone operator with over 710 million subscribers.[14] In comparison, AT&T Mobility, the largest mobile operator in the United States, has about 110 million subscribers.[15]

It is important to note that the resource-based view of the firm uses the term *resource* much more broadly than previously defined. In the resource-based view of the firm, a resource includes any assets as well as any capabilities and competencies that a firm can draw upon when formulating and implementing strategy. In addition, the usefulness of the resource-based view to explain and predict competitive advantage rests upon two critical assumptions about the nature of resources, to which we turn next.

EXHIBIT 4.5 / Tangible and Intangible Resources

Resources

Tangible
Visible, Physical Attributes
- Labor
- Capital
- Land
- Buildings
- Plant
- Equipment
- Supplies

Intangible
Invisible, No Physical Attributes
- Culture
- Knowledge
- Brand Equity
- Reputation
- Intellectual Property
  - Patents
  - Copyrights
  - Trademarks
  - Trade Secrets

resource-based view A model that sees certain types of resources as key to superior firm performance. If a resource exhibits VRIO attributes (see the section "The VRIO Framework" below), the resource enables the firm to gain and sustain a competitive advantage.

tangible resources Resources that have physical attributes and thus are visible.

intangible resources Resources that do not have physical attributes and thus are invisible.

TWO CRITICAL ASSUMPTIONS

LO 4-3

Evaluate the two critical assumptions behind the resource-based view.

Two assumptions are critical in the resource-based model: (1) *resource heterogeneity* and (2) *resource immobility.*[16] What does this mean? In the resource-based view, a firm is assumed to be a bundle of resources, capabilities, and competencies. The first critical assumption—**resource heterogeneity**—is that bundles of resources, capabilities, and competencies differ across firms. The insight that the resource-based view brings to strategy is that the resource bundles of firms competing in the *same* industry (or even the same strategic group) are unique to some extent and thus differ from one another. For example, although Southwest Airlines (SWA) and Alaska Airlines both compete in the same strategic group (low-cost, point-to-point airlines, see Exhibit 3.5), they draw on different resource bundles. SWA's employee productivity tends to be higher than that of Alaska Airlines, because the two companies differ along human and organizational resources. At SWA, job descriptions are informal and employees pitch in to "get the job done." Pilots may help load luggage to ensure an on-time departure; flight attendants clean airplanes to help turn them around at the gate within 15 minutes from arrival to departure. This allows SWA to keep its planes flying for longer and lowers its cost structure, savings which SWA passes on to passengers in lower ticket prices.

The second critical assumption—**resource immobility**—is that resources tend to be "sticky" and don't move easily from firm to firm. Because of that stickiness, the resource differences that exist between firms are difficult to replicate and, therefore, can last for a long time. For example, SWA has enjoyed a sustained competitive advantage, allowing it to outperform its competitors over several decades. That resource difference is not due to a lack of imitation attempts, though. Continental and Delta both attempted to copy SWA, with Continental Lite and Song airline offerings, respectively. Neither Continental nor Delta, however, was able to successfully imitate the resource bundles and firm capabilities that make SWA unique. The important point is that resource bundles are different across firms, and these differences can persist for long periods of time. These two assumptions about resources that firms may control are critical to explaining superior firm performance in the resource-based model.

Note, by the way, that the critical assumptions of the resource-based model are fundamentally different from the way in which a firm is viewed in the perfectly competitive industry structure introduced in Chapter 3. In perfect competition, all firms have access to the *same* resources and capabilities, ensuring that any advantage that one firm has will be short-lived. That is, when resources are freely available and mobile, competitors can move quickly to acquire resources that are utilized by the current market leader. Although some commodity markets approach this situation, most other markets include firms whose resource endowments differ from one another. The resource-based view, therefore, provides useful insights to managers in a firm's quest for competitive advantage.

THE VRIO FRAMEWORK

LO 4-4

Apply the VRIO framework to assess the competitive implications of a firm's resources.

We are now in a position to evaluate a firm's resource endowments and answer the question of what resource attributes underpin competitive advantage. In the resource-based model, certain *types of resources* are seen as key to superior firm performance.[17] For a resource to be the basis of a competitive advantage, it must be valuable (V), rare (R), and costly to imitate (I), and the firm must organize (O) to capture the value of the resource. Following the lead of Jay Barney, one of the pioneers of the resource-based view of the firm, we call this model the **VRIO framework.**[18] According to this model, a firm can gain

EXHIBIT 4.6 / Applying the Resource-Based View: A Decision Tree Revealing Competitive Implications

Is the Resource, Capability, or Competency...　　　　　　　　**and Is the Firm...**

Valuable	→YES	Rare	→YES	Costly to Imitate	→YES	Organized to Capture Value?	→YES	Sustained Competitive Advantage

NO ↓ Competitive Disadvantage

NO ↓ Competitive Parity

NO ↓ Temporary Competitive Advantage

NO ↓ Temporary Competitive Advantage

and sustain a competitive advantage only when it has resources that satisfy all of the VRIO criteria. Keep in mind that resources in the VRIO framework are broadly defined to include any assets *as well as* any capabilities and competencies that a firm can draw upon when formulating and implementing strategy.

Exhibit 4.6 captures the VRIO framework. You can use this decision tree to decide if the resource, capability, or competency under consideration fulfills the VRIO requirements. As you study the following discussion of each of the VRIO attributes, you will see that the attributes accumulate. Only if a firm's managers are able to answer "yes" four times to the attributes listed in the decision tree is the resource in question a core competency that underpins a firm's sustainable competitive advantage.

VALUABLE (V). A resource is **valuable** if it helps a firm increase the perceived value of its product or service in the eyes of consumers, either by adding attractive features or by lowering price because the resource helps the firm lower its costs. By raising the perceived value of the product, the resource increases the firm's revenues, in turn increasing the firm's profitability (assuming costs are not increasing). If the resource allows the firm to lower its cost, it also increases profitability (assuming perceived value is not decreasing).

Honda's competency in designing and producing efficient engines increases the perceived value of its products for consumers. That competency, supported by its lean manufacturing system, enables quality to be designed and built directly into the product and also helps Honda lower its costs. Thus, Honda's competency in designing and building engines is considered a valuable resource in the VRIO framework.

In our quest for competitive advantage, we next need to find out if the resource is also rare.

---

resource heterogeneity Assumption in the resource-based view that a firm is a bundle of resources and capabilities that differ across firms.

resource immobility Assumption in the resource-based view that a firm has resources that tend to be "sticky" and that do not move easily from firm to firm.

VRIO framework A theoretical framework that explains and predicts firm-level competitive advantage. A firm can gain a competitive advantage if it has resources that are valuable (V), rare (R), and costly to imitate (I). The firm also must organize (O) to capture the value of the resources.

valuable resource One of the four key criteria in the VRIO framework. A resource is valuable if it helps a firm increase the perceived value of its product or service, either by adding attractive features or lowering costs.

rare resource One of the four key criteria in the VRIO framework. A resource is rare if the number of firms that possess it is less than the number of firms it would require to reach a state of perfect competition.

RARE (R). A resource is **rare** if only one or a few firms possess it. If the resource is common, it will result in perfect competition where no firm is able to maintain a competitive advantage. A firm is on the path to competitive advantage only if it possesses a valuable resource that is also rare. As Toyota built its initial position as a global auto manufacturer, its lean manufacturing system was a valuable and rare resource. As the leading innovator in developing an efficient and effective approach to manufacturing, Toyota was the first carmaker to resolve a trade-off that had existed for many decades: to lower production costs *and* increase the quality of essentially "mass-customized" cars.

Looking again at Exhibit 4.6, we can see the result of a resource being *both* valuable *and* rare: During the time period when lean manufacturing was a valuable and rare resource, Toyota was able to gain a *temporary competitive advantage.* However, as knowledge about lean manufacturing diffused throughout the car industry, Toyota was not able to sustain its competitive advantage. *Knowledge diffusion* can occur through benchmarking studies, new methods taught in college courses, and consultants. After some time, use of lean manufacturing to produce mass-customized cars with high quality and low cost became a necessary but not sufficient condition for competitive advantage. Once lean manufacturing became an industry standard, the best that firms could do was to achieve competitive parity. Over time, lean manufacturing had become a valuable but common resource, leading to competitive parity.

Tiffany & Co. has developed a core competency—elegant jewelry design and craftsmanship delivered through a superior customer experience—that is valuable, rare, and costly for competitors to imitate. Since the mid-1800s, its trademarked Tiffany Blue Box has stood as a symbol of its core competency.

costly-to-imitate resource One of the four key criteria in the VRIO framework. A resource is costly to imitate if firms that do not possess the resource are unable to develop or buy the resource at a comparable cost.

COSTLY TO IMITATE (I). A resource is **costly to imitate** if firms that do not possess the resource are unable to develop or buy the resource at a reasonable price. If the resource in question is valuable, rare, and costly to imitate, then it is an internal strength and a core competency. If the firm's competitors fail to duplicate the strategy based on the valuable, rare, and costly-to-imitate resource, then the firm can achieve a temporary competitive advantage. Google's core competency in creating proprietary algorithms to develop software products and services for the Internet and mobile computing is valuable, rare, and costly to imitate. Although Microsoft clearly has a strength in developing operating system and application software for the PC, it lacks Google's ability to create a superior web search engine despite its efforts with Bing. Google's core competency in developing proprietary algorithms that underlie its web-based products and services is thus costly and difficult for Microsoft (and others) to imitate. The combination of the three resource attributes ($V + R + I$) has allowed Google to enjoy a competitive advantage.

A firm that enjoys a competitive advantage, however, attracts significant attention from its competitors. They in turn will attempt to negate a firm's resource advantage. A competing firm can succeed in this effort through directly imitating the resource in question (*direct imitation*) or through working around it to provide a comparable product or service (*substitution*).

Take Crocs Shoes, the maker of a plastic clog, as an example. Launched in 2002 as a spa shoe at the Ft. Lauderdale, Florida, boat show, Crocs experienced explosive growth selling tens of millions of pairs each year and reaching over $650 million in revenue in 2008. Crocs are worn by people in every age group and walk of life, including celebrities such as Heidi Klum, Adam Sandler, Matt Damon, and Brooke Shields. To protect its unique shoe design, the company owns several patents. Given its explosive growth, however, numerous cheap imitators of Crocs have sprung up to copy its colorful and comfortable plastic clog. Despite its patents and celebrity endorsements, other firms were able to more or less directly copy the shoe, taking a big bite into Crocs' profits. Indeed,

Crocs' share price plunged from a high of $74.75 to $0.94 in little over one year.[19] This example illustrates that competitive advantage cannot be sustained if the underlying capability (i.e., creating molds to imitate the shape, look, and feel of the original Crocs shoe) can easily be replicated and can thus be *directly imitated.* Any competitive advantage in a fashion-driven industry, moreover, is notoriously short-lived if the company fails to continuously innovate or build such brand recognition that imitators won't gain a foothold in the market. Crocs Shoes was more or less a "one-trick pony." Nike, on the other hand, was able to do both—continuously innovate *and* build tremendous brand recognition—and thus provides a counter-example of how to avoid losing a competitive advantage through direct imitation. As Nike continues to innovate and moves into different sports, it is a moving target. This makes it much harder for competitors to imitate Nike directly.

The second avenue of imitation for a firm's valuable and rare resource is through *substitution.* This is often accomplished through *strategic equivalence.* Take the example of Jeff Bezos launching and developing Amazon.com. Prior to inception, the retail book industry was dominated by a few large chains and many independent mom-and-pop bookstores. Bezos realized that he could not compete with the big-box book retailers directly and needed a different business model. The emergence of the Internet allowed him to come up with a new distribution system that negated the need for retail stores (and thus high real-estate costs). Bezos' new business model of ecommerce not only substituted for the traditional (fragmented) supply chain in book retailing, but also allowed Amazon to offer lower prices due to its lower operating costs. Amazon uses a strategic equivalent substitute to satisfy a customer need previously met by brick-and-mortar retail stores.

In some instances, firms are able to combine direct imitation and substitution when attempting to mitigate the competitive advantage of a rival. With its smartphones in the Galaxy line of models, Samsung has been able to imitate successfully the look and feel of Apple's iPhones. Samsung's Galaxy smartphones use Google's Android operating system and apps from Google Play as an alternative to Apple's iOS and iTunes store. Although a U.S. court has found that Samsung infringed on some of Apple's patents in its older models, apparently Samsung has found a way to successfully imitate the look and feel of Apple's iPhones in its newer models. Samsung achieved this through a combination of *direct imitation* (look and feel) and *substitution* (using Google's mobile operating system and app store).[20]

ORGANIZED TO CAPTURE VALUE (O). The final criterion of whether a rare, valuable, and costly-to-imitate resource can form the basis of a sustained competitive advantage depends on the firm's ability to capture the resource's value-creating potential. To fully exploit the competitive potential of its resources, capabilities, and competencies, a firm must be **organized to capture value**—that is, it must have in place an effective organizational structure and coordinating systems. (We will study organizational design in detail in Chapter 11.)

Before Apple, HP, Lenovo, or Microsoft had any significant share of the personal computer market, Xerox PARC invented and developed an early word-processing application, the graphical user interface (GUI), the Ethernet, the mouse as a pointing device, and even the first personal computer. These technology breakthroughs laid the foundation of the desktop-computing industry.[21] Xerox's invention competency built through a unique combination of resources and capabilities was clearly valuable, rare, and costly to imitate with the potential to create a competitive advantage.

organized to capture value One of the four key criteria in the VRIO framework. The characteristic of having in place an effective organizational structure, processes, and systems to fully exploit the competitive potential of the firm's resources, capabilities, and competencies.

Due to a lack of appropriate organization, however, Xerox failed to appreciate and exploit the many breakthroughs made by its Palo Alto Research Center (PARC) in computing software and hardware. Xerox failed to exploit the value of these innovative products originating from PARC's underlying core competency in research and engineering, because the innovations did not fit within the Xerox business focus on photocopiers. Under pressure in its core photocopier business from Japanese low-cost competitors, Xerox's top management was busy looking for innovations in the photocopier business. The organization of the company's innovation system did not allow it to appreciate the competitive potential of the valuable, rare, and inimitable resources generated at PARC. The organizational problems were accentuated by the fact that Xerox headquarters is on the East Coast in Norwalk, Connecticut, while PARC is on the West Coast in Palo Alto, California.[22] Nor did it help that development engineers at Xerox headquarters had a disdain for the scientists engaging in basic research at PARC.

If a firm is not effectively organized to exploit the competitive potential of a valuable, rare, and costly-to-imitate *(VRI)* resource, the best-case scenario is a temporary competitive advantage. In the case of Xerox, where management was not supportive of the resource, even a temporary competitive advantage would not be realized even though the resource obeys the *VRI* attributes.

In summary, for a firm to gain and sustain a competitive advantage, its resources and capabilities need to interact in such a way as to create unique core competencies (again, see Exhibit 4.4). Ultimately, though, only a few competencies may turn out to be *core* competencies that fulfill the VRIO requirements.[23] A company cannot do everything equally well and must carve out a unique strategic position for itself, making necessary trade-offs.[24] Strategy Highlight 4.1 demonstrates application of the VRIO framework.

HOW TO SUSTAIN A COMPETITIVE ADVANTAGE

LO 4-5

Evaluate different conditions that allow firms to sustain their competitive advantage.

Do specific conditions exist—above and beyond core competencies obeying the *VRIO* attributes—that might help a firm protect and sustain its competitive advantage? Although no competitive advantage can be sustained indefinitely, several conditions can offer some protection to a successful firm by making it more difficult for competitors to imitate the resources, capabilities, or competencies that underlie its competitive advantage: (1) better expectations of future resource value (or simply luck), (2) path dependence, (3) causal ambiguity, and (4) social complexity.[25] These *barriers to imitation* are important examples of **isolating mechanisms** because they prevent rivals from competing away the advantage a firm may enjoy.[26] If one, or any combination, of these isolating mechanisms is present, a firm may strengthen its basis for competitive advantage, increasing its chance to be sustainable over a longer period of time.

isolating mechanisms
Barriers to imitation that prevent rivals from competing away the advantage a firm may enjoy.

BETTER EXPECTATIONS OF FUTURE RESOURCE VALUE. Sometimes firms can acquire resources at a low cost, which lays the foundation for a competitive advantage later when expectations about the future of the resource turn out to be more accurate. *To create heroes,* Nike needs to not only consistently identify and sign athletes that have succeeded against the odds, but do so *before* these athletes have become world-renowned superstars. Right after ending his college career with the University of North Carolina Tar Heels, Nike signed Michael Jordan. Nike's Air Jordan basketball shoes are all-time classics that remain popular to this day. Having consistently better expectations of the future value of resources allows Nike not only to shape the desired image of the athlete, but to capture some of the value these athletes create as resources that obey the *VRI* criteria.

Strategy Highlight 4.1

Applying VRIO: The Rise and Fall of Groupon

After graduating with a degree in music from Northwestern University, Andrew Mason spent a couple of years as a web designer. In 2008, the then 27-year-old founded Groupon, a daily-deal website that connects local retailers and other merchants to consumers by offering goods and services at a discount. Groupon creates marketplaces by bringing the brick-and-mortar world of local commerce onto the Internet. The company basically offers a "group-coupon." If more than a pre-determined number of Groupon users sign up for the offer, the deal is extended to all Groupon users. For example, a local spa may offer a massage for $40 instead of the regular $80. If more than say 10 people sign up, the deal becomes reality. The users pre-pay $40 for the coupon, which Groupon splits 50-50 with the local merchant. Inspired by how Amazon.com has become the global leader in ecommerce, Mason's strategic vision for Groupon was *to be the global leader in local commerce.*

Measured by its explosive growth, Groupon is one of the most successful recent Internet startups. It has over 200 million subscribers and works with over 500,000 merchants in the United States and some 50 international countries. Indeed, Groupon's success attracted a $6 billion buyout offer by Google in early 2011, which Andrew Mason declined. In November 2011, just three years after its founding, Groupon held a successful initial public offering (IPO) and was valued at more than $16 billion with a share price of over $26. Just a year later, Groupon's share price had fallen 90 percent to just $2.63. In early 2013, Mason posted a letter for Groupon employees on the web, arguing that it would leak anyway, stating "After four and a half intense and wonderful years as CEO of Groupon, I've decided that I'd like to spend more time with my family. Just kidding – I was fired today."

What went wrong? The implosion of Groupon's market value can be explained by an application of the VRIO framework. Its competency to drum up more business for local retailers by offering lower prices for its users was certainly *valuable.* Before Groupon, local merchants used online and classified ads, direct mail, yellow pages, and other venues to reach customers. Rather than using one-way communication, Groupon facilitates the meeting of supply and demand in local markets. When Groupon was

first launched, this type of local market-making competency was also *rare.* Groupon enjoyed a first-mover advantage. Its ability to use technology to spur local commerce was considered so valuable and rare that Google offered $6 billion to buy the company—just a little over two years after Groupon's founding! Things started to go wrong soon after that.

The multibillion-dollar Google offer drew the attention of many potential competitors to Groupon's business model. As it turned out, Groupon was more of a sales company than a tech venture, even though it was perceived as such in the wake of the Web 2.0 boom. To target and fine-tune its local deals, Groupon relies heavily on human labor to do the selling. Barriers to entry in this type of business are nonexistent because Groupon's competency is built more on a tangible resource (labor) than on an intangible one (proprietary technology). Given that Groupon's valuable and rare competency was *not hard to imitate,* hundreds of new ventures (so-called "Groupon clones") rushed in to take advantage of this opportunity. Existing online giants such as Google, Amazon (via LivingSocial), and Facebook also moved in. Spurned, Google almost immediately created its own daily-deal version with Google Offers. Also, note that the ability to imitate a rare and valuable resource is directly linked to barriers of entry, which is one of the key elements in Porter's five forces model *(threat of new entrants).* This allows linking internal analysis using the resource-based view to external analysis with the five forces model (which also would have predicted low industry profit potential given low or no barriers to entry).

To make matters worse, these Groupon clones are often able to better serve the needs of local markets and specific population groups. Some daily-deal sites focus only on a specific geographic area. As an example, Conejo Deals meets the needs of customers and retailers in Southern California's Conejo Valley, a cluster of suburban communities. These hyper-local sites tend to have much deeper relationships and expertise with merchants in their specific areas. Since they are mostly matching local customers with local businesses, moreover, they tend to foster more repeat business than the one-off bargain hunters that use Groupon (based in Chicago). In addition, some daily-deal sites often target specific groups. They have greater expertise in matching their users with local retailers (e.g., Daily Pride serving LGBT communities; Black Biz Hookup serving African-American business owners and operators; Jdeal, a Jewish group-buying site in New York City, and so on).

"Finding your specific group" or "going hyper local" allows these startups to increase the perceived value added for their users over and above what Groupon can offer. The problem is that although Groupon aspires to be the *global leader,* there is really no advantage to global scale in serving local markets. This is because daily-deal sites are best suited to market *experience goods,* such as

haircuts at a local barber shop or a meal in a specific Thai restaurant. The quality of these goods and services cannot be judged unless they are consumed. Since the creation of experience goods and their consumption happens in the *same geographic space,* there is really no advantage to having global scale.

Once imitated, Groupon's competency to facilitate local commerce using an Internet platform was neither valuable nor rare. As an application of the VRIO model would have predicted, Groupon's competitive advantage as a first mover would only be temporary at best (see Exhibit 4.6).[27]

A real estate developer also provides an illustrative example of the role that better expectations of a future resource value can play. One important decision she must make is to decide when and where to buy land for future development. Her firm may gain a competitive advantage if she buys a parcel of land for a low cost in an undeveloped rural area 40 miles north of San Antonio, Texas. Several years later, an interstate highway is built right near her firm's land. With the highway, suburban growth explodes as many new neighborhoods and shopping malls are built. Her firm is now able to develop this particular piece of property to build high-end office or apartment buildings. The value creation far exceeds the cost, and her firm gains a competitive advantage. The resource has suddenly become valuable, rare, and costly to imitate, allowing the developer's firm a competitive advantage. Other developers could have bought the land, but once the highway was announced, the cost of the developer's land and that of adjacent land would have risen drastically, reflecting the new reality and thus negating any potential for competitive advantage. In this case, the developer had better expectations than her competitors of the future value of the resource (the land she purchased). If this developer can repeat such "better expectations" over time, she will have a sustained competitive advantage. If she cannot, she was simply lucky. The role of luck in gaining an initial advantage is illustrated in the story in Strategy Highlight 4.2 about Bill Gates and Microsoft.

path dependence
A situation in which the options one faces in the current situation are limited by decisions made in the past.

PATH DEPENDENCE. **Path dependence** describes a process in which the options one faces in a current situation are limited by decisions made in the past.[28] Often, early events—sometimes even random ones—have a significant effect on final outcomes. The U.S. carpet industry provides an example of path dependence.[29] It is quite striking how geographically concentrated the economic activity of carpet making is in the U.S. Carpet mills located within a 65-mile radius of Dalton, Georgia, produce roughly 85 percent of all carpets in the U.S. and almost one half of all carpets sold worldwide. While the U.S. manufacturing sector has suffered in recent decades, the carpet industry has flourished. Companies not located in this regional cluster around Dalton are at a disadvantage because they cannot access the required know-how, skilled labor, suppliers, low-cost infrastructure, and so on needed to be competitive.

Two more or less random events combined to result in the geographic concentration of carpet making in the U.S. These events contributed to path dependence in this specific industry. First, with the boom after World War II, many manufacturers moved south to

Strategy Highlight 4.2

Bill "Lucky" Gates

Taking a closer look at one of the richest people in the world shows that the co-founder of Microsoft, Bill Gates, was lucky on more than one occasion (as he himself freely admits). He was lucky to be born as William H. Gates III, into a well-to-do Seattle family. His father was a prominent attorney and co-founder of what is today the law firm K&L Gates LLC (one of the largest law firms in the world). His mother hailed from a banker's family in Nebraska. As a graduate from the University of Washington, Mrs. Mary Gates worked as a teacher and was active in civic affairs.

Young Bill was lucky to be enrolled in Lakeside School, an exclusive preparatory school in Seattle. In 1968, when Bill was in eighth grade, the Mothers Club at Lakeside School used proceeds of a rummage sale to buy a computer terminal along with time-share programming from GE. Suddenly, Lakeside School had more computer power than many premier research universities at that time. Bill fell in love with programming and spent every free minute he had on the computer, writing software programs. In 1973, he enrolled at Harvard, where he met Steve Ballmer, who later became Microsoft's CEO. The first mini-computer, the MITS Altair 8800, appeared on the cover of *Popular Electronics* magazine in January 1975. Paul Allen and Bill Gates wrote the Altair BASIC program and sold it to MITS of Albuquerque, New Mexico. In the same year, 19-year-old Bill Gates dropped out of Harvard and founded Microsoft with 22-year-old Paul Allen, a Washington State University college dropout.

Microsoft's biggest break came in 1980 when IBM asked Microsoft to write the operating system for its PC. How did IBM, the world leader in computing, know about a fledgling startup? Here Bill Gates was lucky again. Mary Gates was the first woman to chair the United Way's national executive committee, and IBM's CEO, John Akers, also served on the charity's prestigious board. At one of the board meetings, Mr. Akers shared with Mrs. Gates the fact that IBM was looking for an operating system for its soon-to-be-released PC that would set the standard in the industry. Mrs. Gates in turn suggested that her son's company would be the right partner.

The only catch was that Bill Gates didn't have an operating system that would meet IBM's needs, but he knew that a small computer outfit in Seattle had developed an operating system called Q-DOS, short for "quick and dirty operating system." On short notice, Bill Gates borrowed $50,000 (approximately $140,000 in today's value) from his father to buy Q-DOS from Seattle Computer Products, which did not know that IBM was looking for an operating system. Gates then turned around and sold a license of what is now MS-DOS to IBM, but he did not transfer the copyright to the operating system as part of the sale because he correctly believed that other hardware vendors would want to adopt IBM's open standard. It is important to note that while Bill Gates got some lucky breaks during Microsoft's early days, luck cannot be sustained over time. Microsoft leveraged these initial breaks into a dominant position in the personal computer industry for several decades through an effective strategy. As technological change continued at an unrelenting pace, however, Microsoft is no longer the dominant player in the mobile computing industry.[30]

escape restrictions placed upon them in the North such as through unionized labor and higher taxation. Second, and perhaps more important, was technological progress that allowed industrial-scale production of tufted textiles to be used as substitutes for the more expensive wool. This technology emerged in the northwest region of Georgia, in and near Dalton. This historical accident explains why today almost all the carpet mills in the U.S. are located in a relatively small region, including world leaders such as Shaw Industries and Mohawk Industries.

Path dependence also rests on the notion that time cannot be compressed at will. When attempting to compress lots of effort and resources such as R&D into a short time period, it will not be as effective as when a firm spreads out its effort and investments over a longer period of time. Trying to achieve the same outcome in a short time period, even with higher investments, tends to lead to inferior results. The disappointing results are due to *time compression diseconomies.*[31]

GM's problems in providing a competitive alternative to the highly successful Toyota Prius, a hybrid electric vehicle, highlight path dependence and time compression issues. The California Air Resource Board (CARB) in 1990 passed a mandate for introducing zero-emissions cars, which stipulated that 10 percent of new vehicles sold by carmakers must have zero emissions by 2003. This mandate not only accelerated research in alternative energy sources for cars, but also led to the development of the first fully electric production car, GM's EV1. GM launched the car in California and Arizona in 1996. Competitive models followed, with the Toyota RAV EV and the Honda EV. In this case, regulations in the legal environment fostered innovation in the automobile industry (see discussion of PESTEL forces in Chapter 3).

Companies not only are influenced by forces in their environment but can also influence the development of those forces. The California mandate on zero emissions, for example, did not stand. Several stakeholders, including the car and oil companies, fought it through lawsuits and other actions. CARB ultimately gave in to the pressure and abandoned its zero-emissions mandate. When the mandate was revoked, GM recalled and destroyed its EV1 electric vehicles and terminated its electric-vehicle program. This decision turned out to be a strategic error that would haunt GM a decade or so later. Although GM was the leader among car companies in electric vehicles in the mid-1990s, it did not have a competitive model to counter the Toyota Prius when its sales took off in the early 2000s. The Chevy Volt (a plug-in hybrid), GM's first major competition to the Prius, was delayed by over a decade because GM had to start its electric-vehicle program basically from scratch. Not having an adequate product lineup during the early 2000s, GM's U.S. market share dropped below 20 percent in 2009 (from over 50 percent a few decades earlier), the year it filed for bankruptcy. (GM reorganized under Chapter 11 of the U.S. bankruptcy code, and relisted on the New York Stock Exchange in 2010.) While GM sold about 40,000 Chevy Volts worldwide, Toyota sold over 3.5 million Prius cars. This example shows that firms cannot compress time at will; indeed, learning and improvements must take place over time.

Strategic decisions have long-term consequences due to path dependence and time-compression diseconomies; they are not easily reversible. A competitor cannot imitate or create core competencies quickly, nor can one go out and buy a reputation for quality or innovation on the open market. These types of valuable, rare, and costly-to-imitate resources, capabilities, and competencies must be built and organized effectively over time, often through a painstaking process that frequently includes learning from failure.

causal ambiguity
A situation in which the cause and effect of a phenomenon are not readily apparent.

CAUSAL AMBIGUITY. **Causal ambiguity** describes a situation in which the cause and effect of a phenomenon are not readily apparent. To formulate and implement a strategy that enhances a firm's chances of gaining and sustaining a competitive advantage, managers need to have a hypothesis or theory of how to compete. This implies that managers need to have some kind of understanding about causes for superior and inferior performance. Understanding the underlying reasons of observed phenomena is far from trivial, however. Everyone can see that Apple has had several hugely successful innovative products such as the iMac, iPod, iPhone, and the iPad, combined with its hugely popular iTunes services. These successes stem from Apple's set of *V, R, I,* and *O* core competencies that supports its ability to continue to offer a variety of innovative products.

A deep understanding, however, of exactly *why* Apple has been so successful is very difficult. Even Apple's managers themselves may not be able to clearly pinpoint the sources of their success. Is it the visionary role that the late Steve Jobs played? Is it the rare skills of Apple's uniquely talented design team within Apple? Is it the timing of the company's product introductions? Or is it Apple's former Chief Operating Officer Tim Cook (now its CEO) who adds superior organizational skills and puts all the pieces together when running the day-to-day operations? If the link between cause and effect is ambiguous for Apple's managers, it is that much more difficult for others seeking to copy a valuable resource, capability, or competency.

SOCIAL COMPLEXITY. **Social complexity** describes situations in which different social and business systems interact with one another. There is frequently no causal ambiguity as to how the *individual* systems such as supply chain management or new product development work in isolation. They are often managed through standardized business processes such as Six Sigma or ISO 9000. Social complexity, however, emerges when two or more such systems are *combined*. Copying the emerging complex social systems is difficult for competitors because neither direct imitation nor substitution is a valid approach. The interactions between different systems create too many possible permutations for a system to be understood with any accuracy. The resulting social complexity makes copying these systems difficult, if not impossible, resulting in a valuable, rare, and costly-to-imitate resource that the firm is organized to exploit.

> **social complexity**
> A situation in which different social and business systems interact with one another.

A simple thought experiment can illustrate this point. A group with three people has three relationships, connecting every person directly with one another. Adding a fourth person to this group doubles the number of direct relationships to six. Just introducing one more person increases the number of relationships to 10.[32] This gives you some idea of how complexity might increase when we combine different systems with many different parts.

In reality, firms are often made up of thousands of employees from all walks of life. Their interactions within the firm's processes, procedures, and norms make up its culture. Although an observer may conclude that Zappos' culture, with its focus on providing superior customer service, might be the basis for its competitive advantage, engaging in reverse social engineering to crack Zappos' code of success might be much more difficult. Moreover, an organizational culture that works for Zappos, an online retailer for shoes and clothing, might cause havoc for Lockheed Martin, an aerospace and defense company. This implies that one must understand competitive advantage within its organizational and industry context. Looking at individual elements of success without taking social complexity into account is a recipe for inferior performance, if not worse.

Taken together, a firm may be able to protect its competitive advantage (even for long periods of time) when its managers have consistently better expectations about the future value of resources, it has accumulated a resource advantage that can be imitated only over long periods of time, or when the source of its competitive advantage is causally ambiguous or socially complex.

> **dynamic capabilities**
> A firm's ability to create, deploy, modify, reconfigure, upgrade, or leverage its resources in its quest for competitive advantage.

4.3 The Dynamic Capabilities Perspective

> **LO 4-6**
> Outline how dynamic capabilities can help a firm sustain competitive advantage.

A firm's external environment is rarely stable (as discussed in Chapter 3). Rather, in many industries, change is fast and ferocious. Firms that fail to adapt their core competencies to a changing external environment not only lose a competitive advantage but may go out of business altogether. This is the reason why reinvesting, honing, and upgrading resources and capabilities is so crucial (see Exhibit 4.4). **Dynamic capabilities** describe a firm's ability to create, deploy, modify, reconfigure, upgrade, or leverage its resources over time in its quest for competitive advantage. Dynamic capabilities are essential to move beyond a short-lived advantage and create a sustained competitive advantage. For a firm to sustain its advantage, any fit between its internal strengths and the external environment must be dynamic. That is, the firm must be able to change its resource base as the external environment changes. The goal should be to develop resources, capabilities, and competencies that create a *strategic fit* with the firm's environment. Rather than creating a static fit, the firm's internal strengths should change with its external environment in a *dynamic* fashion.

Not only do dynamic capabilities allow firms to adapt to changing market conditions; they also enable firms to *create market changes* that can strengthen their strategic position. These market changes implemented by proactive firms introduce altered circumstances, to which more reactive rivals might be forced to respond. Apple's dynamic capabilities allowed it to redefine the markets for mobile devices and computing, in particular in music, smartphones, and media content. For the portable music market through its iPod (and iTunes store), Apple generated environmental change to which Sony and others had to respond. With its iPhone, Apple redefined the market for smartphones, again creating environmental change to which competitors such as Samsung, BlackBerry, Nokia, or Google (with its Motorola unit) must respond. Apple's introduction of the iPad is redefining the media and tablet computing market, forcing competitors such as Amazon and Microsoft to respond. Dynamic capabilities are especially relevant for surviving and competing in markets that shift quickly and constantly, such as the high-tech space in which firms such as Apple, Google, and Amazon compete.

dynamic capabilities perspective A model that emphasizes a firm's ability to modify and leverage its resource base in a way that enables it to gain and sustain competitive advantage in a constantly changing environment.

In the **dynamic capabilities perspective,** competitive advantage is the outflow of a firm's capacity to modify and leverage its resource base in a way that enables it to gain and sustain competitive advantage in a constantly changing environment. Given the accelerated pace of technological change, in combination with deregulation, globalization, and demographic shifts, dynamic markets today are the rule rather than the exception. As a response, a firm may create, deploy, modify, reconfigure, or upgrade resources so as to provide value to customers and/or lower costs in a dynamic environment. The essence of this perspective is that competitive advantage is not derived from static resource or market advantages, but from a *dynamic reconfiguration* of a firm's resource base. Today, consumers value reliable, gas-powered engines made by Honda. If consumers start to value electric motors more (because they produce zero emissions), the value of Honda's engine competency will decrease. If this happens, the Chinese automaker BYD, which morphed from a battery maker to a car company, might gain an advantage over Honda. While Honda views itself as an engineering-driven automotive company, startup BYD views its core competency as batteries. This in turn can be leveraged into a strong strategic position in electric-power systems for cars, cell phones, laptops, cameras, medical devices, and so on. Imitation by competitors is especially difficult in such a case because it requires hitting a moving target.

resource stocks The firm's current level of intangible resources.

resource flows The firm's level of investments to maintain or build a resource.

One way to think about developing dynamic capabilities and other intangible resources is to distinguish between resource stocks and resource flows.[33] **Resource stocks** are the firm's current level of intangible resources. **Resource flows** are the firm's level of investments to maintain or build a resource. A helpful metaphor to explain the differences between resource stocks and resource flows is a bathtub that is being filled with water (see Exhibit 4.7).[34] The amount of water in the bathtub indicates a company's level of a specific *intangible resource stock*—such as its dynamic capabilities, new product development, engineering expertise, innovation capability, reputation for quality, and so on.

Intangible-resource stocks are built through investments over time. These resource flows are represented in the drawing by the different faucets, from which water flows into the tub. These different faucets indicate investments the firm can make in different intangible resources. Investments in building an innovation capability, for example, differ from investments made in marketing expertise. Each investment flow would be represented by a different faucet.

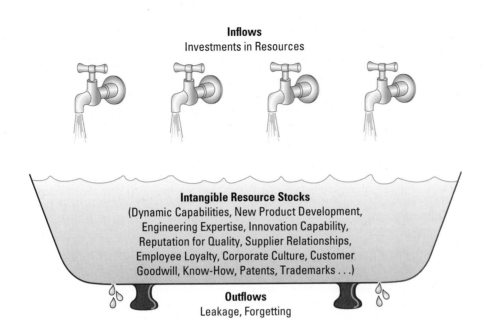

Inflows
Investments in Resources

Intangible Resource Stocks
(Dynamic Capabilities, New Product Development,
Engineering Expertise, Innovation Capability,
Reputation for Quality, Supplier Relationships,
Employee Loyalty, Corporate Culture, Customer
Goodwill, Know-How, Patents, Trademarks . . .)

Outflows
Leakage, Forgetting

EXHIBIT 4.7

The Bathtub
Metaphor: The
Role of Inflows and
Outflows in Building
Stocks of Intangible
Resources

SOURCE: Figure based on
metaphor used in I. Dierickx
and K. Cool (1989), "Asset
stock accumulation and
sustainability of competitive
advantage," *Management
Science* 35: 1504–1513.

How fast a tub fills depends on how much water comes out of the faucets and how long the faucets are left open. Intangible resources are built through continuous investments and experience over time. Many intangible resources, such as Hyundai's reputation for quality or Ritz-Carlton's excellence in customer responsiveness, take a long time to build. Organizational learning also fosters the buildup of intangible-resource stocks.

How fast the bathtub fills, however, also depends on how much water leaks out of the tub. The outflows represent a reduction in the firm's intangible-resource stocks. Resource leakage might occur through employee turnover, especially if key employees leave. Significant resource leakage can erode a firm's competitive advantage. A reduction in resource stocks can occur if a firm does not engage in a specific activity for some time and forgets how to do this activity well.

According to the dynamic capabilities perspective, the managers' task is to decide which investments to make over time (i.e., which faucets to open and how far) in order to best position the firm for competitive advantage in a changing environment. Moreover, managers also need to monitor the existing intangible-resource stocks and their attrition rates due to leakage and forgetting. This perspective provides a dynamic understanding of capability development to allow a firm's continuous adaptation to a changing external environment.

4.4 The Value Chain Analysis

The **value chain** describes the internal activities a firm engages in when transforming inputs into outputs.[35] Each activity the firm performs along the horizontal chain adds incremental value—raw materials and other inputs are transformed into components that are finally assembled into finished products or services for the end consumer. Each activity the firm performs along the value chain also adds incremental costs. A careful analysis of the value chain allows managers to obtain a more detailed and fine-grained understanding of how the firm's *economic value creation (V − C)* breaks down into a distinct set of activities that help determine perceived value *(V)* and the costs *(C)* to create it. The value

value chain The internal activities a firm engages in when transforming inputs into outputs; each activity adds incremental value. Primary activities directly add value; support activities add value indirectly.

LO 4-7

Apply a value chain analysis to understand which of the firm's activities in the process of transforming inputs into outputs generate differentiation and which drive costs.

chain concept can be applied to basically any firm, from those in manufacturing industries to those in high-tech ones or service firms.

A firm's activities are one of the key internal drivers of performance differences across firms, as highlighted by their place in the center of Exhibit 4.2. *Activities* are distinct actions that enable firms to add incremental value at each step by transforming input into goods and services. Managing a supply chain, running the company's IT system and websites, or providing customer support are all examples of distinct activities. Activities are narrower than functional areas such as marketing, because each functional area is made up of a set of distinct activities. *To create heroes,* Nike has to engage in a number of activities: find athletes that succeed against the odds; identify them before they are well-known superstars; sign the athletes; create products that are closely linked with the athlete; promote the athletes and their Nike products through TV ads and social media in order to create the desired image, and so on. Each activity contributes to the relative value the product and service offering has in the eyes of potential customers and the firm's relative cost position vis-à-vis its rivals. The value chain transformation process is composed of a set of distinct activities; Exhibit 4.8 displays a generic value chain. When a firm's set of distinct activities are able to generate value greater than the costs to create them, the firm obtains a profit margin (as shown in Exhibit 4.8), assuming the market price the firm is able to command exceeds the costs of value creation.

A generic value chain (as displayed in Exhibit 4.8) needs to be modified to capture the activities of a specific business. A retail chain such as American Eagle Outfitters, for example, needs to identify suitable store locations, either build or rent stores, purchase goods and supplies, manage distribution and store inventories, operate stores (both in the brick-and-mortar world and online), hire and motivate a sales force, create payment and IT systems or partner with vendors, engage in promotions, and ensure after-sales services including returns. A maker of semiconductor chips such as Intel, on the other hand, needs to engage in R&D, design and engineer semiconductor chips and their production processes, purchase silicon and other ingredients, set up and staff chip fabrication plants, control quality and throughput, engage in marketing and sales, and provide after-sales customer support.

EXHIBIT 4.8

A Generic Value
Chain: Primary and
Support Activities

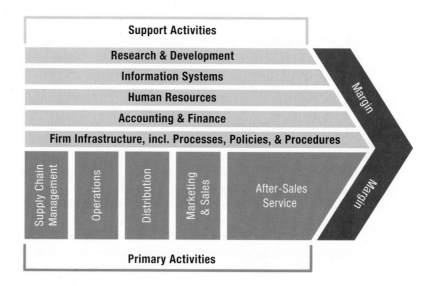

As shown in Exhibit 4.8, the value chain is divided into primary and support activities. The **primary activities** add value directly as the firm transforms inputs into outputs—from raw materials through production phases to sales and marketing and finally customer service. Primary activities are supply chain management, operations, distribution, marketing and sales, and after-sales service. Other activities, called **support activities,** add value indirectly. These activities—such as research and development (R&D), information systems, human resources, accounting and finance, and firm infrastructure including processes, policies, and procedures—*support* each of the primary activities.

To help a firm achieve a competitive advantage, each distinct activity performed needs to either add incremental value to the product or service offering or lower its relative cost. Discrete and specific firm activities are the basic units with which to understand competitive advantage because they are the drivers of the firm's relative costs and level of differentiation the firm can provide to its customers. Although the resource-based view of the firm helps identify the integrated set of resources and capabilities that are the building blocks of core competencies, the value chain perspective enables managers to see how competitive advantage flows from the firm's distinct set of activities. This is because a firm's core competency is generally found in a network linking different but distinct activities, each contributing to the firm's strategic position as either low-cost leader or differentiator.

Let's consider The Vanguard Group, one of the world's largest investment companies, with $2 trillion of assets under management.[36] It serves individual investors, financial professionals, and institutional investors such as state retirement funds. Vanguard's mission is *to help clients reach their financial goals by being their highest-value provider of investment products and services.*[37] It therefore emphasizes low-cost investing and quality service for its clients. Vanguard's average expense ratio (fees as a percentage of total net assets paid by investors) is generally the lowest in the industry.[38] Vanguard's core competency of low-cost investing while providing acceptable quality service for its clients is accomplished through a unique set of interconnected primary and support activities including strict cost control, direct distribution, low expenses with savings passed on to clients, offering a broad array of mutual funds, an efficient investment management approach, and straightforward client communication and education.

4.5 ◄► Implications for the Strategist

We've now reached a significant point: Combining tools for external analysis from Chapter 3 with the frameworks for internal analysis introduced in this chapter allows you, as the strategist, to begin formulating a strategy that matches the firm's internal resources and capabilities to the demands of the external industry environment. Ideally, managers want to leverage a firm's internal strengths to exploit external opportunities, while mitigating internal weaknesses and external threats. This approach allows the formulation of a strategy that is tailored to their company, creating a unique fit between the company's internal resources and the external environment. A *strategic fit* increases the likelihood that a firm is able to gain a competitive advantage. If a firm achieves a *dynamic* strategic fit, it is likely to be able to sustain its advantage over time.

USING SWOT ANALYSIS TO COMBINE EXTERNAL AND INTERNAL ANALYSIS

We synthesize insights from an internal analysis of the company's *strengths* and *weaknesses* with those from an analysis of external *opportunities* and *threats* using the **SWOT analysis.** Internal strengths (S) and weaknesses (W) concern resources, capabilities, and

---

primary activities
Firm activities that add value directly by transforming inputs into outputs as the firm moves a product or service horizontally along the internal value chain.

support activities
Firm activities that add value indirectly, but are necessary to sustain primary activities.

SWOT analysis
A framework that allows managers to synthesize insights obtained from an internal analysis of the company's strengths and weaknesses (S and W) with those from an analysis of external opportunities and threats (O and T).

LO 4-8

Conduct a SWOT analysis to combine external and internal analysis and derive strategic implications.

EXHIBIT 4.9

Strategic Questions
Within the SWOT
Matrix

Strategic Questions	Opportunities	Threats
Strengths	*How can managers use strengths to take advantage of opportunities?*	*How can managers use strengths to reduce the likelihood and impact of threats?*
Weaknesses	*How can managers overcome weaknesses that prevent the firm from taking advantage of opportunities?*	*How can managers overcome weaknesses that will make threats a reality?*

competencies. Whether they are strengths or weaknesses can be determined by applying the VRIO framework (discussed in this chapter). External opportunities (O) and threats (T) are in the firm's general environment and can be captured by PESTEL and Porter's five forces analyses (discussed in the previous chapter).

A SWOT analysis allows managers to evaluate a firm's current situation and future prospects by simultaneously considering internal and external factors. The SWOT analysis encourages managers to scan the internal and external environments, looking for any relevant factors that might affect the firm's current or future competitive advantage. The focus is on internal and external factors that can affect—in a positive or negative way—the firm's ability to gain and sustain a competitive advantage. To facilitate a SWOT analysis, managers use a set of strategic questions that link the firm's internal environment to its external environment, as shown in Exhibit 4.9. In this SWOT matrix, the horizontal axis is divided into factors that are *external to the organization* (the focus of Chapter 3) and the vertical axis into factors that are *internal to the organization* (the focus of this chapter).

In a first step, managers gather information for a SWOT analysis in order to link internal factors *(Strengths and Weaknesses)* to external factors *(Opportunities and Threats).* Next, managers use the SWOT matrix shown in Exhibit 4.9 to develop *strategic alternatives* for the firm using a four-step process:

1. Focus on the *Strengths–Opportunities* quadrant (top left) to derive "offensive" alternatives by using an internal strength in order to exploit an external opportunity.

2. Focus on the *Weaknesses–Threats* quadrant (bottom right) to derive "defensive" alternatives by eliminating or minimizing an internal weakness in order to mitigate an external threat.

3. Focus on the *Strengths–Threats* quadrant (top right) to use an internal strength to minimize the effect of an external threat.

4. Focus on the *Weaknesses–Opportunities* quadrant (bottom left) to shore up an internal weakness to improve its ability to take advantage of an external opportunity.

In a final step, managers need to carefully evaluate the pros and cons of each strategic alternative to select one or more alternatives to implement. Managers need to carefully explain their decision rationale, including why other strategic alternatives were rejected. To further facilitate application of the SWOT framework, Exhibit 4.10 shows a hypothetical example for McDonald's, the world's largest chain of hamburger fast-food restaurants, operating more than 34,000 restaurants in some 120 countries.[39]

Opportunities	Threats
1. Growth in emerging economies	1. Possible increase in minimum wage
2. Health consciousness of U.S. population	2. Popularity of easy-to-prepare grocery items

	Strategic Alternatives:
Strengths 1. Financial resources 2. Brand name 3. Consistency	1. Launch new locations in China & Mexico (S1, S2, O1) 2. New ads showing ease and speed of drive-thru for take-home orders (W1, T2) 3. Launch McDonald's frozen foods in grocery outlets (S2, S3, T2)
Weaknesses 1. Market share decline 2. Dependence on fried foods on menu	4. Develop and emphasize more healthy food menu items (W1, W2, O2)

EXHIBIT 4.10

Applying SWOT: Hypothetical Example for McDonald's

Based on the SWOT analysis shown in Exhibit 4.10, McDonald's developed four strategic alternatives:

1. By combining its internal strengths in financial resources (S1) and brand name (S2) with external opportunities due to growth in emerging economies (O1), it developed an offensive strategic option to launch new restaurants in China and Mexico.
2. By combining an internal weakness due to market share decline and thus a loss of market power (W1) with the external threat of the increasing popularity of easy-to-prepare grocery items (T2), it developed the defensive strategic option to develop and air new ads showing the ease and speed of McDonald's drive-thru for take-home orders.
3. The third strategic option is to leverage internal strengths in brand name (S2) and consistency (S3) to minimize the external threat of easy-to-prepare grocery items (T2) by launching a McDonald's line of frozen foods in grocery stores.
4. The final strategic alternative is to overcome internal weaknesses due to market share decline (W1) and dependence on fried foods on its menu (W2) in order to develop and market more healthy food items. Shoring up these internal weaknesses would improve McDonald's chances to take advantage of the external opportunity provided by the increased health consciousness of the U.S. population (O2).

Although the SWOT analysis is a widely used management framework, however, a word of caution is in order. A problem with this framework is that a strength can also be a weakness, and that an opportunity can also simultaneously be a threat. Earlier in this chapter, we discussed the location of Google's headquarters in Silicon Valley and near several universities as a key resource for the firm. Most people would consider this a strength for the firm. However, California has a high cost of living and is routinely ranked among the worst of the states in the U.S. in terms of "ease of doing business." In addition, this area of California is along major earthquake fault lines and is more prone to natural disasters than many other parts of the country. So is the location a strength or a weakness? The answer is "it depends." In a similar fashion, is global warming an opportunity or threat for car manufacturers? If governments enact higher gasoline taxes and make driving more expensive, it can be a threat. If, however, carmakers respond to government regulations by developing more fuel-efficient cars as well as low- or zero-emission engines such as hybrid or electric vehicles, it may create more demand for new cars and lead to higher sales.

To make the SWOT analysis an effective management tool, the strategist must first conduct a thorough external and internal analysis, as laid out in Chapters 3 and 4. This sequential process enables the strategist to ground the analysis in rigorous theoretical frameworks before using SWOT to synthesize the results from the external and internal analyses in order to derive a set of strategic options.

You have now acquired the toolkit with which to conduct a complete strategic analysis of a firm's internal and external environments. In the next chapter, we consider various ways to assess and measure competitive advantage. That chapter will complete Part 1, on strategy analysis, in the AFI framework (see Exhibit 1.5).

CHAPTER**CASE** 4 / Consider This . . .

ALTHOUGH NIKE'S CO-FOUNDER and chairman Phil Knight declared that scandals surrounding its superstar endorsement athletes are "part of the game," its marketing strategy is not without risks.[40] In some instances, Nike continued to sponsor its athletes involved in various scandals, while in others it terminated its lucrative endorsement contracts. Nike continued to sponsor LA Lakers' Kobe Bryant who was cleared of alleged rape charges. After Tiger Woods was engulfed in an infidelity scandal, Nike continued to sponsor the golf superstar. In 2007, Nike ended its endorsement deal contract with NFL quarterback Michael Vick after a public outcry and his subsequent felony conviction of running a dog-fighting ring and engaging in animal cruelty. In 2011, after serving a prison sentence and restarting his career at the Philadelphia Eagles, Nike signed a new endorsement deal with Michael Vick. In 2012, Nike terminated its long-term relationship with disgraced cyclist Lance Armstrong. Just before Armstrong's public admission to doping in an interview with Oprah Winfrey, Phil Knight answered "never say never" when asked if Nike would sponsor Lance Armstrong again in the future. In 2013, Nike removed its ads with Oscar Pistorius and the unfortunate tag line "I am the bullet in the chamber," after the alleged homicide charges against the South African track-and-field athlete.

Time and time again Nike's heroes have fallen from grace. Clearly, Nike's approach in building its core

competency of creating heroes is not without risks. Too many of these public relations disasters combined with too severe shortcomings of some of Nike's most celebrated heroes could damage the company's reputation and lead to a loss of competitive advantage.

Questions

Thinking about ChapterCase 4, answer the following questions.

1. The case indicates that Nike's core competency is *to create heroes*. What does this mean? How did Nike build its core competency? Does it obey the *VRIO* attributes?

2. What would it take for Nike's approach to turn from a strength into a weakness? Did this tipping point already occur? Why or why not?

3. What recommendations would you have for Phil Knight and Nike? Can you identify a way to "reframe" the competency of creating heroes? Or a new way to think of heroes that would continue to build the brand?

4. If you are a competitor of Nike (such as adidas, Under Armour, New Balance, or Li Ning), how could you exploit Nike's apparent vulnerability? Provide a set of concrete recommendations.

TAKE-AWAY CONCEPTS

This chapter demonstrated various approaches to analyzing the firm's *internal environment,* as summarized by the following learning objectives and related take-away concepts.

LO 4-1 / Differentiate among a firm's resources, capabilities, core competencies, and activities.

- *Core competencies* are unique, deeply embedded, firm-specific strengths that allow companies to differentiate their products and services and thus create more value for customers than their rivals, or offer products and services of acceptable value at lower cost.

- *Resources* are any assets that a company can draw on when crafting and executing strategy.

- *Capabilities* are the organizational and managerial skills necessary to orchestrate a diverse set of resources to deploy them strategically.

- *Activities* are distinct and fine-grained business processes that enable firms to add incremental value by transforming input into goods and services.

LO 4-2 / Compare and contrast tangible and intangible resources.

- *Tangible resources* have physical attributes and are visible.

- *Intangible resources* have no physical attributes and are invisible.

- Competitive advantage is more likely to be based on intangible resources.

LO 4-3 / Evaluate the two critical assumptions behind the resource-based view.

- The first critical assumption—*resource heterogeneity*—is that bundles of resources, capabilities, and competencies differ across firms. The resource bundles of firms competing in the same industry (or even the same strategic group) are unique to some extent and thus differ from one another.

- The second critical assumption—*resource immobility*—is that resources tend to be "sticky" and don't move easily from firm to firm. Because

of that stickiness, the resource differences that exist between firms are difficult to replicate and, therefore, can last for a long time.

LO 4-4 / Apply the VRIO framework to assess the competitive implications of a firm's resources.

- For a firm's resource to be the basis of a competitive advantage, it must have *VRIO* attributes: *valuable (V), rare (R),* and *costly to imitate (I).* The firm must also be able to *organize (O) in order to capture the value of the resource.*

- A resource is *valuable (V)* if it allows the firm to take advantage of an external opportunity and/or neutralize an external threat.

- A resource is *rare (R)* if the number of firms that possess it is less than the number of firms it would require to reach a state of perfect competition.

- A resource is *costly to imitate (I)* if firms that do not possess the resource are unable to develop or buy the resource at a comparable cost.

- The firm is *organized (O) to capture the value* of the resource if it has an effective organizational structure, processes, and systems in place to fully exploit the competitive potential.

LO 4-5 / Evaluate different conditions that allow firms to sustain their competitive advantage.

- Several conditions make it costly for competitors to imitate the resources, capabilities, or competencies that underlie a firm's competitive advantage: (1) *better expectations of future resource value (or simply luck),* (2) *path dependence,* (3) *causal ambiguity,* and (4) *social complexity.*

- These *barriers to imitation* are isolating mechanisms because they prevent rivals from competing away the advantage a firm may enjoy.

LO 4-6 / Outline how dynamic capabilities can help a firm sustain competitive advantage.

- To sustain a competitive advantage, any fit between a firm's internal strengths and the external environment must be dynamic.

- *Dynamic capabilities* allow a firm to create, deploy, modify, reconfigure, or upgrade its resource base to gain and sustain competitive advantage in a constantly changing environment.

LO 4-7 / Apply a value chain analysis to understand which of the firm's activities in the process of transforming inputs into outputs generate differentiation and which drive costs.

- The value chain describes the internal activities a firm engages in when transforming inputs into outputs.
- Each activity the firm performs along the horizontal chain adds incremental value and incremental costs.
- A careful analysis of the value chain allows managers to obtain a more detailed and fine-grained understanding of how the firm's economic value created breaks down into a distinct set of activities that help determine perceived value and the costs to create it.

- When a firm's set of distinct activities is able to generate value greater than the costs to create it, the firm obtains a profit margin (assuming the market price the firm is able to command exceeds the costs of value creation).

LO 4-8 / Conduct a SWOT analysis to combine external and internal analysis and derive strategic implications.

- Formulating a strategy that increases the chances of gaining and sustaining a competitive advantage is based on synthesizing insights obtained from an internal analysis of the company's strengths (S) and weaknesses (W) with those from an analysis of external opportunities (O) and threats (T).
- The strategic implications of a SWOT analysis should help the firm to leverage its internal strengths to exploit external opportunities, while mitigating internal weaknesses and external threats.

KEY TERMS

Activities	Isolating mechanisms	Resource stocks
Capabilities	Organized to capture value	Resources
Causal ambiguity	Path dependence	Social complexity
Core competencies	Primary activities	Support activities
Costly-to-imitate resource	Rare resource	SWOT analysis
Dynamic capabilities	Resource-based view	Tangible resources
Dynamic capabilities perspective	Resource flows	Valuable resource
	Resource heterogeneity	Value chain
Intangible resources	Resource immobility	VRIO framework

DISCUSSION QUESTIONS

1. Why is it important to study the internal resources, capabilities, and activities of firms? What insights can be gained?

2. **a.** Conduct a value chain analysis for McDonald's. What are its primary activities? What are its support activities? Identify the activities that add the most value for

   the customer. Why? Which activities help McDonald's to contain cost? Why?

   b. In the last few years, McDonald's has made a lot of changes to its menu, adding more healthy choices and more higher-priced items, such as those offered in McCafé (e.g., premium roast coffee, frappé, and fruit smoothies), and has also enhanced its in-restaurant services (e.g., free, unlimited Wi-Fi, newer interiors). Did McDonald's new priorities—in terms of a broader, healthier menu and an improved in-restaurant experience—require changes to its traditional value chain activities? If so, how? Try to be as specific as possible in comparing the McDonald's from the recent past (focusing on low-cost burgers) to the McDonald's today.

3. The resource-based view of the firm identifies four criteria that managers can use to evaluate whether particular resources and capabilities are core competencies and can, therefore, provide a basis for sustainable competitive advantage. Are these measures independent or interdependent? Explain. If (some of) the measures are interdependent, what implications does that fact have for managers wanting to create and sustain a competitive advantage?

ETHICAL/SOCIAL ISSUES

1. As discussed in this chapter, resources that are valuable, rare, and costly to imitate can help create a competitive advantage. In many cases, firms try to "reverse-engineer" a particular feature from a competitor's product for their own uses. It is commonplace, for example, for cell phone manufacturers to buy the newest phones of their competitors on the market and take them apart to see what new components/features the new models have implemented.

    As the competition between Google (www. google.com) and Baidu (www.ir.baidu.com) over Internet searches in China makes clear, however, this sort of corporate behavior does not stop with hardware products. With hundreds of millions of users and growing fast, China is considered to be one of the most lucrative online markets worldwide. Baidu, a Chinese web services company, has allegedly adapted many of the search tools that Google uses. Baidu, however, modifies its searches inside China (its major market) to accommodate government guidelines. In protest over these same guidelines, in 2010 Google left the Chinese market and is running its Chinese search operations from Hong Kong. Google no

longer censors its online searches as requested by the Chinese government. Baidu has some 75 percent market share in online search in China, and Google less than 20 percent.[41]

    It is legal to take apart publicly available products and services and try to replicate them and even develop work-arounds for relevant patents. But is it ethical? If a key capability protected by patents or trademarks in your firm is being reverse-engineered by the competition, what are your options for a response? Also, how do you evaluate Google's decision to move its servers to Hong Kong? For Google's values, see http://www.google.com/about/company/philosophy/.

2. The chapter mentions that one type of resource flow is the loss of key personnel who move to another firm. Assume that the human resources department of your firm has started running ads and billboards for open positions near the office of your top competitor. Your firm is also running Google ads on a keyword search for this same competitor. Is there anything unethical about this activity? Would your view change if this key competitor had just announced a major layoff?

SMALL-GROUP EXERCISES

//// Small-Group Exercise 1

Brand valuations were mentioned in the chapter as a potential key intangible resource for firms. Some product brands are so well-established the entire category of products (including those made by competitors) may

be called by the brand name rather than the product type. In your small group, develop two or three examples of this happening in the marketplace. In any of the cases noted, does such brand valuation give the leading brand a competitive advantage? Or does it produce confusion in the market for all products or services in that category? Provide advice to the leading brand as to how the firm can strengthen the brand name.

//// Small-Group Exercise 2

Strategy Highlight 4.1 explains the rise and fall of Groupon. The company's strategic vision was *to be a global leader in local commerce,* based on a core competency that could be described as "local market-making." Numerous competitors took advantage of low barriers to entry and the easy imitation of Groupon's combined competency of some technology skills with sales skills, so that Groupon found that its

competitive advantage was only temporary. Groupon continues to compete but needs your advice on how to build dynamic capabilities that might help it pursue the vision of becoming a global leader in local commerce. How might Groupon reinvest or upgrade its technology and sales skills so it builds a global customer base? For example, are there new products or services that would meet the needs of global clients in each of the local markets where the client does business? Brainstorm ways that Groupon might add value for its customers. How might Groupon build relationships with clients that are more socially complex, making Groupon's competencies more difficult to imitate?

STRATEGY TERM PROJECT

//// Module 4: Internal Analysis

In this section, you will study the internal resources, capabilities, core competencies, and value chain of your selected firm.

1. A good place to start with an internal firm analysis is to catalog the assets a firm has. Make a list of the firm's tangible assets. Then, make a separate list of its intangible assets.

2. Now extend beyond the asset base and use the VRIO framework to identify the competitive position held by your firm. Which, if any, of these resources are helpful in sustaining the firm's competitive advantage?

3. Identify the core competencies that are at the heart of the firm's competitive advantage. (Remember, a firm will have only one, or at most a few, core competencies, by definition.)

4. Perform a SWOT analysis for your firm. Remember that strengths and weaknesses (S, W) are internal to the firm, and opportunities and threats (O, T) are external. Prioritize the strategic actions that you would recommend to your firm. Refer to the *Implications for the Strategist* section on how to conduct a SWOT analysis and provide recommendations.

my STRATEGY

Looking Inside Yourself: What Is My Competitive Advantage?

Here, we encourage you to take what you have learned about competitive advantage and apply it to your personal career. Spend a few minutes looking at yourself to discover *your own* competitive advantage.

1. Write down your own personal strengths and weaknesses. What sort of organization will permit you to really leverage your strengths and keep you highly

engaged in your work (person–organization fit)? Do some of your weaknesses need to be mitigated through additional training or mentoring from a more seasoned professional?

2. Personal capabilities also need to be evaluated over time. Are your strengths and weaknesses different today from what they were five years ago? What are you doing to make sure your capabilities are dynamic? Are you upgrading skills, modifying behaviors, or otherwise seeking to change your future strengths and weaknesses?

3. Are some of your strengths valuable, rare, and costly to imitate? How can you organize your work to help capture the value of your key strengths (or mitigate your weaknesses)? Are your strengths specific to one or a few employers, or are they more generally valuable in the marketplace? In general, should you be making investments in your human capital in terms of company-specific or market-general skills? Why should that distinction matter?

4. As an employee, how could you persuade your boss that you could be a vital source of sustainable competitive advantage? What evidence could you provide to make such an argument? If you are currently or previously employed, consider how your professional activities can help reinforce the key value added activities in your department or organization.

ENDNOTES

1. As quoted in: "Knight the king: The founding of Nike," *Harvard Business School Case Study,* 9-810-077, p. 2.

2. This ChapterCase is based on: Nike, Inc., *History and Heritage,* http://nikeinc.com/pages/history-heritage; "Knight the king: The founding of Nike," "Social strategy at Nike;" *Harvard Business School Case Study,* 9-712-484; "The big business of fairy tales," *The Wall Street Journal,* February 14, 2013; and Sachs, J. (2012), *Winning the story wars. Why those who tell—and live—the best stories will rule the future* (Boston, MA: Harvard Business School Press).

3. http://help-en-us.nike.com/app/answers/detail/a_id/113/p/3897.

4. "Top 100 most valuable global brands 2012," report by Millward Brown, WPP.

5. Prahalad, C. K., and G. Hamel (1990), "The core competence of the corporation," *Harvard Business Review,* May–June.

6. This discussion is based on: Amit, R., and P.J.H. Schoemaker (1993), "Strategic assets and organizational rent," *Strategic Management Journal* 14: 33–46; Barney, J. (1991), "Firm resources and sustained competitive advantage," *Journal of Management* 17: 99–120; Peteraf, M. (1993), "The cornerstones of competitive advantage," *Strategic Management Journal* 14: 179–191; and Wernerfelt, B. (1984), "A resource-based view of the firm," *Strategic Management Journal* 5: 171–180.

7. Apple Annual Report, 2012.

8. "Top 100 most valuable global brands 2012," report by Millward Brown, WPP.

9. Google Annual Report, 2012

10. "Top 100 most valuable global brands 2012."

11. For a discussion on the benefits of being located in a technology cluster, see: Saxenian, A. L. (1994), *Regional Advantage: Culture and Competition in Silicon Valley and Route 128* (Cambridge, MA: Harvard University Press); and Rothaermel, F. T., and D. Ku (2008), "Intercluster innovation differentials: The role of research universities," *IEEE Transactions on Engineering Management* 55: 9–22.

12. Stuart, T., and O. Sorenson (2003), "The geography of opportunity: Spatial heterogeneity in founding rates and the performance of biotechnology firms," *Research Policy* 32: 229–253.

13. Ibid.

14. http://www.chinamobileltd.com.

15. http://www.att.com.

16. This discussion is based on: Amit, R., and P.J.H. Schoemaker (1993), "Strategic assets and organizational rent"; Barney, J. (1991), "Firm resources and sustained competitive advantage"; Peteraf, M. (1993), "The cornerstones of competitive advantage"; and Wernerfelt, B. (1984), "A resource-based view of the firm."

17. This discussion is based on: Amit, R., and P.J.H. Schoemaker (1993), "Strategic assets and organizational rent"; Barney, J. (1991), "Firm resources and sustained competitive advantage"; Barney, J., and W. Hesterly (2009), *Strategic Management and Competitive Advantage,* 3rd ed. (Upper Saddle River, NJ: Pearson Prentice Hall); Peteraf, M. (1993), "The cornerstones of competitive advantage"; and Wernerfelt, B. (1984), "A resource-based view of the firm."

18. Barney, J. (1991), "Firm resources and sustained competitive advantage"; and Barney, J., and W. Hesterly (2009), *Strategic Management and Competitive Advantage,* 3rd ed.

19. Crocs' share price hit an all-time high of $74.75 on October 31, 2007. By November 20, 2008, the Crocs share price had fallen to $0.94.

20. "Apple wins big in patent case," *The Wall Street Journal,* August 24, 2012; and "U.S. judge reduces Apple's patent award in Samsung case," *The Wall Street Journal,* March 1, 2013.

21. Chesbrough, H. (2006), *Open Innovation: The New Imperative for Creating and Profiting from Technology* (Boston, MA: Harvard Business School Press).

22. In 1968, Xerox moved its headquarters from Rochester, New York, to Norwalk, Connecticut.

23. Prahalad, C. K., and G. Hamel (1990), "The core competence of the corporation."

24. Porter, M. E. (1996), "What is strategy?" *Harvard Business Review,* November–December: 61–78.

25. This discussion is based on: Barney, J. (1986), "Strategic factor markets: Expectations, luck, and business strategy," *Management Science* 32: 1231–1241; Barney, J. (1991), "Firm resources and sustained competitive advantage," *Journal of Management* 17: 99–120; Dierickx, I., and K. Cool (1989), "Asset stock accumulation and sustainability of competitive advantage," *Management Science* 35: 1504–1513; and Mahoney, J. T., and J. R. Pandian (1992), "The resource-based view within the conversation of strategic management," *Strategic Management Journal* 13: 363–380.

26. Lippman, S. A., and R. P. Rumelt (1982), "Uncertain imitability: An analysis of interfirm differences in efficiency under competition," *The Bell Journal of Economics* 13: 418–438.

27. Groupon Annual Report, 2012; Groupon investor deck, March 2013; "In Groupon's $6 billion wake, a fleet of start-ups," *The New York Times,* March 9, 2011; "The economics of Groupon," *The Economist,* October 22, 2011; "Groupon: Deep discount," *The Economist,* August 14, 2012; "Why Groupon is over and Facebook and Twitter should follow," *Forbes,* August 20, 2012; "Groupon CEO fired as daily-deals biz bottoms out," *WIRED,* February 28, 2013; "Struggling Groupon ousts its quirky CEO," *The Wall Street Journal,* February 28, 2013; "Don't weep for Groupon ex-CEO Andrew Mason," *The Wall Street Journal,* March 1, 2013; and Godin, S. (2008), *Tribes: We Need You to Lead Us* (New York: Portfolio).

28. Arthur, W. B. (1989), "Competing technologies, increasing returns, and lock-in by historical events," *Economics Journal* 99: 116–131; and Dierickx, I., and K. Cool (1989), "Asset stock accumulation and sustainability of competitive advantage," *Management Science* 35: 1504–1513.

29. Krugman, P. (1993), *Geography and Trade* (Cambridge, MA: MIT Press); and Patton, R. L. (2010), "A history of the U.S. carpet industry," *Economic History Association Encyclopedia,* http://eh.net/encyclopedia/article/patton.carpet.

30. Manes, S., and P. Andrews (1994), *Gates: How Microsoft's Mogul Reinvented an Industry and Made Himself the Richest Man in America* (New York: Doubleday); and Gladwell, M. (2008), *Outliers: The Story of Success* (New York: Little, Brown, and Company).

31. Dierickx, I., and K. Cool (1989), "Asset stock accumulation and sustainability of competitive advantage," *Management Science* 35: 1504–1513.

32. More formally, the number of relationships (r) in a group is a function of its group members (n), with $r = n(n − 1)/2$. The assumption is that two people, A and B, have only one relationship (A ← → B), rather than two relationships (A → B and A ← 1 B). In the latter case, the number of relationships (r) in a group with n members doubles, where $r = n(n − 1)$.

33. Dierickx, I., and K. Cool (1989), "Asset stock accumulation and sustainability of competitive advantage," *Management Science* 35: 1504–1513.

34. Ibid.

35. This discussion is based on: Porter, M. E. (1985), *Competitive Advantage: Creating and Sustaining Superior Performance* (New York:

Free Press); Porter, M. E. (1996), "What is strategy?"; Siggelkow, N. (2001), "Change in the presence of fit: The rise, the fall, and the renaissance of Liz Claiborne," *Academy of Management Journal* 44: 838–857; and Magretta, J. (2012), *Understanding Michael Porter. The Essential Guide to Competition and Strategy.*

36. This discussion draws on: Porter, M. E. (1996), "What is strategy?"; and Siggelkow, N. (2002), "Evolution toward fit," *Administrative Science Quarterly* 47: 125–159.

37. https://careers.vanguard.com/vgcareers/why_vgi/story/mission.shtml.

38. "Funds: How much you're really paying," *Money* (November 2005); and https://personal.vanguard.com/us/content/Home/WhyVanguard/AboutVanguardWhoWeAreContent.jsp.

39. http://www.aboutmcdonalds.com.

40. According to Reuters, cited in: http://www.sportbusiness.com December 15, 2009.

41. "How Baidu won China," *Bloomberg Businessweek,* November 11, 2010; "Special report: China and the Internet," *The Economist,* April 6, 2013.

Chapter 5

Competitive Advantage, Firm Performance, and Business Models

Learning Objectives

After studying this chapter, you should be able to:

LO 5-1 Conduct a firm profitability analysis using accounting data.

LO 5-2 Apply shareholder value creation to assess and evaluate competitive advantage.

LO 5-3 Explain economic value creation and different sources of competitive advantage.

LO 5-4 Apply a balanced scorecard to assess and evaluate competitive advantage.

LO 5-5 Apply a triple bottom line to assess and evaluate competitive advantage.

LO 5-6 Outline how business models put strategy into action.

Assessing Competitive Advantage: Apple vs. BlackBerry

WE BEGAN OUR JOURNEY into strategic management (in Chapter 1) by looking at how Apple achieved a sustainable competitive advantage (until the end of 2012), while its various competitors struggled to keep up. Prior to the introduction of the iPhone in 2007, however, the Canadian high-tech company BlackBerry was a global leader in wireless communication. As an early innovator, BlackBerry defined the smartphone category and changed the way millions of people around the world live and work. At one point, the BlackBerry smartphone was a corporate status symbol.

As we discussed in Chapter 1, *strategy* is a set of goal-directed actions a firm takes to gain and sustain competitive advantage. Since *competitive advantage* is defined as superior performance *relative* to other competitors in the same industry or the industry average, a firm's managers must be able to accomplish two critical tasks:

1. Accurately assess the performance of their firm.
2. Compare and benchmark their firm's performance to other competitors in the same industry or against the industry average.

One of the most commonly used metrics in assessing firm financial performance is *return on invested capital (ROIC),* where ROIC = (Net profits/Invested capital).[1] ROIC is a popular metric because it is a good proxy for *firm profitability.* In particular, the ratio measures how effectively a company uses its *total invested capital,* which consists of two components: (1) *shareholders' equity* through the selling of shares to the public, and (2) *interest-bearing debt* through borrowing from financial institutions and bond holders.

As a rule of thumb, if a firm's ROIC is greater than its *cost of capital,* it generates value; if it is less than the cost of capital, the firm destroys value. To be more precise and to be able to derive strategic implications, however, managers must compare their ROIC to other competitors.

Let's compare the financial performance of Apple and BlackBerry, direct competitors in the smartphone and mobile device industry. Exhibit 5.1 shows the ROIC for Apple and BlackBerry (as of fiscal year 2012). It further breaks down ROIC into its constituent components. This provides important clues for managers concerning what areas to focus on when attempting to improve firm performance.

Apple's ROIC was 35.0 percent, which was more than 21 percentage points higher than BlackBerry's (14.1 percent). This means that for every $1.00 invested into Apple, the company returned almost $1.35, while for every $1.00 invested in the company, BlackBerry returned $1.14. Since Apple was 2.5 times more efficient than BlackBerrry at generating a return on invested capital, Apple had a clear competitive advantage over BlackBerry.[2]

After reading the chapter, you will find more about this case, with related questions, on page 152.

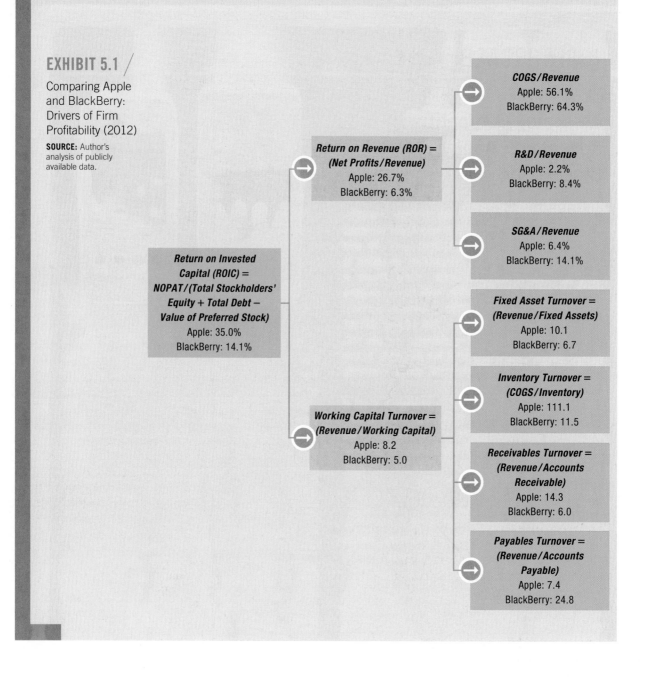

EXHIBIT 5.1

Comparing Apple and BlackBerry: Drivers of Firm Profitability (2012)

SOURCE: Author's analysis of publicly available data.

Return on Invested Capital (ROIC) =
NOPAT/(Total Stockholders'
Equity + Total Debt −
Value of Preferred Stock)
Apple: 35.0%
BlackBerry: 14.1%

Return on Revenue (ROR) =
(Net Profits/Revenue)
Apple: 26.7%
BlackBerry: 6.3%

Working Capital Turnover =
(Revenue/Working Capital)
Apple: 8.2
BlackBerry: 5.0

COGS/Revenue
Apple: 56.1%
BlackBerry: 64.3%

R&D/Revenue
Apple: 2.2%
BlackBerry: 8.4%

SG&A/Revenue
Apple: 6.4%
BlackBerry: 14.1%

Fixed Asset Turnover =
(Revenue/Fixed Assets)
Apple: 10.1
BlackBerry: 6.7

Inventory Turnover =
(COGS/Inventory)
Apple: 111.1
BlackBerry: 11.5

Receivables Turnover =
(Revenue/Accounts
Receivable)
Apple: 14.3
BlackBerry: 6.0

Payables Turnover =
(Revenue/Accounts
Payable)
Apple: 7.4
BlackBerry: 24.8

GAINING AND SUSTAINING competitive advantage is the defining goal of strategic management. Competitive advantage leads to superior firm performance. To explain differences in firm performance and to derive strategic implications, therefore, we must think hard about how to best measure and assess it. We therefore devote this chapter to studying how to measure and assess firm performance. In particular, we introduce three different frameworks to capture the multifaceted nature of competitive advantage. The three traditional frameworks to measure and assess firm performance are *accounting profitability, shareholder value creation,* and *economic value creation.* We then will introduce two integrative frameworks, combining quantitative data with qualitative assessments: *the* *balanced scorecard* and *the triple bottom line.* Next, we take a closer look at *business models,* to understand more deeply how firms put their strategy into action in order to make money. We conclude the chapter with a practical *Implications for the Strategist* section.

5.1 Competitive Advantage and Firm Performance

Since competitive advantage is always *relative*—measured in relation to other firms—how do we know when a firm has a competitive advantage? How do we measure and assess competitive advantage? What strategic implications for managerial actions do we derive from our assessments? Surprisingly, these apparently simple questions do not have simple answers. Strategic management researchers have debated them intensely for at least 30 years.[3]

We, too, will consider these key questions. We will develop a *multidimensional perspective* to assessing competitive advantage. Let's begin by focusing on the three standard performance dimensions, asking:[4]

1. What is the firm's *accounting profitability?*
2. How much *shareholder value* does the firm create?
3. How much *economic value* does the firm generate?

These three performance dimensions tend to be correlated, particularly when considered over longer time periods. That is, accounting profitability and economic value creation tend to be reflected in the firm's stock price.

ACCOUNTING PROFITABILITY

Using accounting data to assess competitive advantage and firm performance is standard managerial practice. When assessing competitive advantage by measuring accounting profitability, we use financial data and ratios derived from publicly available accounting data such as income statements and balance sheets.[5] In ChapterCase 5, we noted that to measure competitive advantage, we must be able to (1) accurately assess firm performance and (2) compare and benchmark the focal firm's performance to other competitors in the same industry or against the industry average.

Standardized financial metrics derived from publicly available accounting data such as income statements and balance sheets fulfill both these conditions. Public companies are required by law to release these data, which must be in compliance with the generally accepted accounting principles (GAAP) set by the Financial Accounting Standards Board (FASB) and be audited by certified public accountants. Publicly traded firms are required to file the Form 10-K (or 10-K report) annually with the U.S. Securities and Exchange Commission (SEC), a federal regulatory agency. The 10-K reports are the primary source of companies' accounting data available to the public. In the wake of the Sarbanes–Oxley Act of 2002, accounting data released to the public must now comply with more stringent requirements. This in turn enhances the data's usefulness for comparative analysis.

Accounting data enable us to conduct direct performance comparisons between different companies. Some of the profitability ratios most commonly used in strategic management are *return on invested capital (ROIC)*, *return on equity (ROE)*, *return on assets (ROA)*, and *return on revenue (ROR)*. In five tables in the "How to Conduct a Case Analysis" module (following the MiniCases at the back of the text), you will find a complete presentation of accounting measures and financial ratios, how they are calculated, and a brief description of their strategic characteristics.

To demonstrate the usefulness of accounting data in assessing competitive advantage and to derive strategic implications, let's revisit the comparison between Apple and

LO 5-1

Conduct a firm profitability analysis using accounting data.

BlackBerry that we began in ChapterCase 5. As shown in Exhibit 5.1, Apple had a distinct competitive advantage over BlackBerry (in 2012) because Apple's ROIC was much higher than BlackBerry's. Although this is an important piece of information, managers need to know the underlying factors driving differences in firm profitability. Why is the ROIC for these two companies so different?

Much like detectives, managers look for clues to solve that mystery: They break down ROIC into its constituent parts (as shown in Exhibit 5.1)—*return on revenue* and *working capital turnover*—to discover the underlying drivers of the marked difference in firm profitability. *Return on revenue (ROR)* indicates how much of the firm's sales is converted into profits. Apple's ROR was more than 20 percentage points higher than that of Black-Berry. For every $100 in revenues, Apple earns $26.70 in profit, while BlackBerry earns only $6.30 in profit. To explore further drivers of this difference, return on revenue is then broken down into three additional financial ratios: *Cost of goods sold (COGS)/Revenue; Research & development (R&D) expense/Revenue;* and *Selling, general, & administrative (SG&A) expense/Revenue.*

The first of these three ratios, *COGS/Revenue,* indicates how efficiently a company can produce a good. Apple is more efficient than BlackBerry (by more than 8 percentage points). This implies that Apple's profit margin is higher than that of BlackBerry because Apple is able to command a greater price premium (higher markup) for its products. In the eyes of the consumer, Apple's products are seen as creating a higher value. Apple is more successful than BlackBerry in differentiating its products through user-friendliness and offering complementary services such as iTunes.

The next ratio, *R&D/Revenue,* indicates how much of each dollar that the firm earns in sales is invested to conduct research and development. A higher percentage is generally an indicator of a stronger focus on innovation to improve current products and services, and to come up with new ones. The third ratio, *SG&A/Revenue,* indicates how much of each dollar that the firm earns in sales is invested in sales, general, and administrative (SG&A) expenses. Generally, this ratio is an indicator of the firm's focus on marketing to promote its products and services. Interestingly, Apple's R&D intensity and marketing intensity are much less than BlackBerry's. Apple spent 2.2 percent on R&D for every dollar of revenue, while BlackBerry spent almost four times as much (8.4 percent R&D intensity). Although BlackBerry's R&D and marketing intensities were multiples of Apple's (in 2012), keep in mind that Apple was spending much more in absolute dollar terms because it had a much larger revenue. Adjusting financial metrics by size (e.g., revenue), however, allows a direct comparison between different competitors.

Historically, Apple has spent much less on research and development than other firms in the industry, in both absolute and relative terms. Apple's co-founder and CEO, the late Steve Jobs, defined Apple's R&D philosophy as follows: "Innovation has nothing to do with how many R&D dollars you have. When Apple came up with the Mac, IBM was spending at least 100 times more on R&D. It's not about money. It's about the people you have, how you're led, and how much you get it."[6]

In contrast, BlackBerry's R&D and marketing spending has been elevated in 2012 (thus reducing its profitability) in order to complete the development and subsequent launch (in early 2013) of its new mobile operating system (BlackBerry 10) and its newest touchscreen-based smartphone, the BlackBerry Z10. In terms of marketing intensity, BlackBerry spent more than twice as much as Apple (14.1 percent vs. 6.4 percent). The marketing-intensity ratio (SG&A/Revenue) indicates how much of each dollar the company takes in as revenue is spent on advertising and sales support.

In January 2012, Thorsten Heins was named the new CEO of BlackBerry. To reinvigorate the company's lackluster reputation for innovation in the smartphone arena, Mr. Heins almost immediately increased Black-Berry's marketing budget to get out its message in preparation for the rollout of its latest smartphone and operating system.[7] To improve its "cool-factor," BlackBerry even hired Alicia Keys, a Grammy Award–winning singer, as its Global Creative Director.[8]

The second component of ROIC is *working capital turnover* (see Exhibit 5.1), which is a measure of how effectively capital is being used to generate revenue. For every dollar that BlackBerry puts to work, it realizes $5.00 of sales; for Apple, the conversion rate is more than 1.6 times higher, at $8.20. This relatively large difference provides an important clue for BlackBerry's managers to dig deeper to find the underlying drivers in working capital turnover. This

Thorsten Heins, BlackBerry CEO, left, with Alicia Keys, right.
SOURCE: Getty Images.

enables managers to uncover which levers to pull in order to improve firm financial performance. In a next step, therefore, managers break down working capital turnover into other ratios, including *fixed asset turnover, inventory turnover, receivables turnover,* and *payables turnover.* Each of these metrics is a measure of how effective a particular item on the balance sheet is contributing to revenue.

Fixed asset turnover (Revenue/Fixed assets) measures how well a company leverages its fixed assets, particularly property, plant, and equipment (PPE). BlackBerry's fixed assets contribute $6.70 of revenue for every dollar spent on PPE, while each dollar of Apple's fixed assets generate $10.10. This ratio indicates how much of a firm's capital is tied up in its fixed assets. Higher fixed assets often go along with lower firm valuations (more on this in the section "Shareholder Value Creation" later in this chapter).

The performance difference between Apple and BlackBerry in regard to *inventory turnover (COGS/Inventory)* is even more striking. Cost of goods sold (COGS) captures the firm's production cost of merchandise it *has sold.* Inventory is the cost of the firm's merchandise *to be* sold. This ratio indicates how much of a firm's capital is tied up in its inventory. Apple turned over its inventory 111 times during 2012, which implies that the company had very little capital tied up in its inventory. Apple benefited from strong demand for its products, as well as an effective management of its global supply chain. The vast majority of Apple's manufacturing is done in China by low-cost producer Foxconn, which employs over 1.2 million people. In contrast, BlackBerry has likely higher production costs because it uses higher-cost suppliers than Apple. BlackBerry's suppliers are located in the U.S. (e.g., Qualcomm and Jabil Circuit) and Luxembourg, countries with a much higher cost structure than that of Foxconn in China.[9]

In stark contrast, BlackBerry turned over its inventory only 11.5 times. In comparison to BlackBerry, Apple turned over its inventory almost 10 times faster! This big difference can be explained by a pronounced decline in demand for BlackBerry products and disappointing new product launches. Consumers continued to migrate away from BlackBerry smartphones to Apple iPhones and Android-based devices. Apple benefited from greater *economies of scale* (a decrease in per-unit cost as output increased) because it sold more than four times as many iPhones as BlackBerry sold smartphones in 2012 (136 million iPhones vs. 33 million BlackBerrys).[10] Moreover, BlackBerry's new product launches such as the Playbook (a tablet computer) flopped. At the same time, demand for the Apple iPad soared.

The final set of financial ratios displayed in Exhibit 5.1 concerns the effectiveness of a company's receivables and payables. These are part of a company's cash flow management; they indicate the company's efficiency in extending credit, as well as collecting debts. Higher ratios of *receivables turnover (Revenue/Accounts receivable)* imply more efficient management in collecting accounts receivable and shorter durations of interest-free loans to customers (i.e., time until payments are due). In contrast, *payables turnover (Revenue/ Accounts payable)* indicates how fast the firm is paying its creditors and how much it benefits from interest-free loans extended by its suppliers. A lower ratio indicates more efficient management in paying creditors and generating interest-free loans from suppliers. In the two dimensions of cash flow management, Apple displays a clear advantage over BlackBerry. Apple is paid much faster than BlackBerry. This might be explained by the fact that Apple's customers are mainly individual consumers (who tend to pay with cash or credit cards at the time of purchase), while BlackBerry's most important customers are corporate IT departments and governments (who request to be invoiced, and thus pay later). On the other hand, Apple is taking quite a bit longer to pay its creditors. Due to its stronger negotiating power, Apple might also be able to extend its payment periods, while BlackBerry is required to pay its creditors more quickly.

A deeper understanding of the underlying drivers for differences in firm profitability allows managers to derive strategic implications. Given its higher *COGS/Revenue* ratio, BlackBerry needs to think hard about how to drive down costs, while increasing revenues. With increased marketing spending, BlackBerry is clearly hoping that each dollar spent on marketing and advertising will generate more than one dollar in profits. Since BlackBerry has just completed a major refresh of its mobile phone hardware and operating system, it might reduce R&D intensity going forward. This in turn should improve firm profitability. One of the key pivot points for BlackBerry will be to turn over its inventory much faster. This is, of course, closely tied to consumer demand for its products. Having more attractive products in its lineup and improving its supply chain and logistics should help BlackBerry improve its inventory turnover, and with it, its profitability.

Although accounting data tend to be readily available and we can easily transform them into financial ratios to assess and evaluate competitive performance, they also exhibit some important limitations:

- *All accounting data are historical data and thus backward-looking.* Accounting profitability ratios show us only the outcomes from past decisions, and the past is no guarantee of future performance. Dell Computer, for example, clearly outperformed its competition based on accounting data in the first few years in the last decade, but more recently it has fallen on hard times, exhibiting a distinct competitive disadvantage. Also, there is a significant time delay before accounting data become publicly available. Some strategy scholars have even gone so far as to suggest that using accounting data to make strategic decisions is like driving a car by looking in the rearview mirror.[11]

- *Accounting data do not consider off–balance sheet items.* Off–balance sheet items, such as pension obligations (quite large in some U.S. companies) or operating leases in the retail industry, can be significant factors. For example, one retailer may own all its stores, which would properly be included in the firm's assets; a second retailer may lease all its stores, which would *not be* listed as assets. All else being equal, the second retailer's return on assets (ROA) would be higher. We address this shortcoming by adjusting accounting data to obtain an *equivalent* economic capital base, so that we can compare companies with different capital structures.

■ *Accounting data focus mainly on tangible assets, which are no longer the most important.*[12] This limitation of accounting data is nicely captured in the adage: *Not everything that can be counted counts. Not everything that counts can be counted.*[13] Although accounting data capture some intangible assets, such as the value of intellectual property (patents, trademarks, and so on) and customer goodwill, many key intangible assets are not captured. Today, the most competitively important assets tend to be intangibles such as innovation, quality, and customer experience, which are not included in a firm's balance sheets. For example, Hyundai's reputation for quality, Honda's core competency in designing highly reliable engines, and Zappos' superior customer experience are not balance sheet items.

Indeed, intangibles that are not captured in accounting data have become much more important in firms' stock market valuations over the last few decades. Look at Exhibit 5.2, which shows the firm's book value (accounting data capturing the firm's actual costs of assets minus depreciation) as part of a firm's total stock market valuation (number of outstanding shares times share price). The firm's book value captures the historical cost of a firm's assets, whereas market valuation is based on future expectations for a firm's growth potential and performance. For the firms in the S&P 500 (the 500 largest publicly traded companies by market capitalization in the U.S. stock market, as determined by Standard & Poor's, a rating agency), the importance of a firm's book value has declined dramatically over time. At the same time, the importance of intangibles that contribute to growth potential and yet are not captured in a firm's accounting data has increased commensurately (see Exhibit 5.2). In 1980, about 80 percent of a firm's stock market valuation was based on its book value with 20 percent based on the market's expectations concerning the firm's future performance. This almost reversed by 2002 (in the aftermath of the Internet bubble), when firm valuations were based only 25 percent on assets captured by accounting data. The important take-away is that intangibles not captured in firms' accounting data have become much more important to a firm's competitive advantage (about 70 percent in 2010, for example). The importance of intangibles becomes clearer if you think, for example, about market valuations of Internet-based firms such as Facebook or Google.

Key financial ratios based on accounting data give us an important tool with which to assess competitive advantage. In particular, they help us measure *relative* profitability, which is useful when comparing firms of different sizes over time. While not perfect, these ratios are an important starting point when analyzing the competitive performance of firms (and thus are critical tool for case analysis). Again, see the "How to Conduct a Case

EXHIBIT 5.2 / The Declining Importance of Book Value in a Firm's Stock Market Valuation, 1980–2010

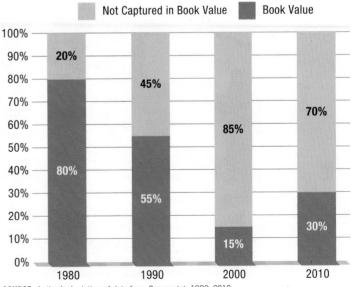

SOURCE: Author's depiction of data from Compustat, 1980–2010.

Analysis" module. We next turn to *shareholder value creation,* as a second traditional way to measure and assess competitive advantage.

SHAREHOLDER VALUE CREATION

LO 5-2

Apply shareholder value creation to assess and evaluate competitive advantage.

shareholders
Individuals or organizations that own one or more shares of stock in a public company. They are the legal owners of public companies.

risk capital The money provided by shareholders in exchange for an equity share in a company; it cannot be recovered if the firm goes bankrupt.

Shareholders—individuals or organizations that own one or more shares of stock in a public company—are the legal owners of public companies. From the shareholders' perspective, the measure of competitive advantage that matters most is the return on their **risk capital,**[14] which is the money they provide in return for an equity share, money that they cannot recover if the firm goes bankrupt. In September 2008, the shareholders of Lehman Brothers, a global financial services firm, lost their entire investment of about $40 billion when the firm declared bankruptcy.

Investors are primarily interested in a company's **total return to shareholders,** which is the return on risk capital, including stock price appreciation plus dividends received over a specific period. Unlike accounting data, total return to shareholders is an *external* performance metric. It essentially indicates how the stock market views all available public information about a firm's past, current state, and expected future performance (with most of the weight on future growth expectations). The idea that all available information about a firm's past, current state, and expected future performance is embedded in the market price of the firm's stock is called the *efficient-market hypothesis.*[15] In this perspective, a firm's share price provides an objective performance indicator. When assessing and evaluating competitive advantage, a comparison of rival firms' share price development or market capitalization provides a helpful yardstick when used over the *long term.* **Market capitalization** (or market cap) captures the total dollar market value of a company's outstanding shares at any given point in time *(Market cap = Number of outstanding shares × Share price).* If a company has 50 million shares outstanding, and each share is traded at $200, the market capitalization is $10 billion (50,000,000 × $200 = $10,000,000,000, or $10 billion).[16]

All public companies in the United States are required to report total return to shareholders annually in the statements they file with the Securities and Exchange Commission (SEC). In addition, companies must also provide benchmarks, usually one comparison to the industry average and another to a broader market index (which is relevant for more diversified firms).[17] Since competitive advantage is defined in relative terms, these benchmarks allow us to assess whether a firm has a competitive advantage. In its annual reports, Microsoft, for example, compares its performance to two stock indices: the NASDAQ computer index and the S&P 500. The computer index includes over 400 high-tech companies traded on the NASDAQ, such as Apple, Dell, Google, Intel, and Oracle. It provides a comparison of Microsoft to the computer industry—broadly defined. The S&P 500 offers a comparison to the wider stock market beyond the computer industry. In its

2012 annual report, Microsoft shows that it *outperformed* the S&P 500 over the last five years but *underperformed* in comparison to the NASDAQ computer index.[18]

Effective strategies to grow the business can increase a firm's profitability and thus its stock price.[19] Indeed, investors and Wall Street analysts expect continuous growth. A firm's stock price generally increases only if the firm's rate of growth exceeds investors' expectations. This is because investors discount into the present value of the firm's stock price whatever growth rate they foresee in the future. If a low-growth business like Comcast (in cable TV) is expected to grow 2 percent each year but realizes 4 percent growth, its stock price will appreciate. In contrast, if a fast-growing business like Apple in mobile computing is expected to grow by 10 percent annually but delivers "only" 8 percent growth, its stock price will fall.

Investors also adjust their expectations over time. Since the business in the slow-growth industry surprised them by delivering higher than expected growth, they adjust their expectations upward. The next year, they expect this firm to again deliver 4 percent growth. On the other hand, if the industry average is 10 percent a year in the high-tech business, the firm that delivered 8 percent growth will again be expected to deliver at least the industry average growth rate; otherwise, its stock will be further discounted.

In ChapterCase 1, we noted that Apple was once the most valuable company on the planet. Considering *stock market valuations (Share price × Number of outstanding shares)* over the *long term* provides a useful metric to assess competitive advantage. Exhibit 5.3 shows the stock market valuations for Apple and a set of its closest competitors from 1990 until the end of 2012. Microsoft was once the most valuable company worldwide (in December 1999), but since then its market valuation has dropped by more than 50 percent. This is because investors now have lower expectations concerning Microsoft's ability to deliver profitable growth in the future. In particular, Microsoft is struggling with the transition away from desktop to mobile computing. *Competitive advantage is clearly transitory!*

total return to shareholders Return on risk capital that includes stock price appreciation plus dividends received over a specific period.

market capitalization A firm performance metric that captures the total dollar market value of all of a company's outstanding shares at any given point in time (Market cap = Number of outstanding shares × Share price).

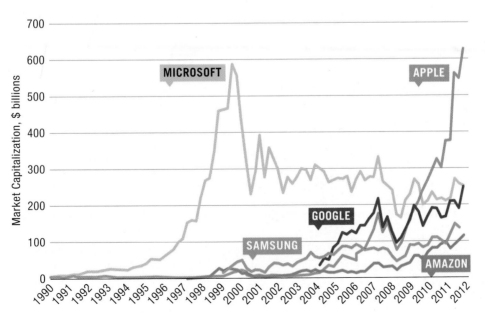

EXHIBIT 5.3

Stock Market Valuations of Amazon, Apple, Google, Microsoft, and Samsung

SOURCE: Author's depiction of data from Bloomberg.

Exhibit 5.3 also shows the resurgence of Samsung and the strong performance of up-and-coming newer competitors such as Google and Amazon. Samsung's rise is driven by a set of successful smartphones, while Google and Amazon continue to have tremendous growth opportunities as they find new areas to apply their core competencies. As demonstrated by Exhibit 5.3, market capitalization over the long run is a valuable tool to assess competitive advantage and firm performance.

In contested industries, it is difficult to gain a competitive advantage, and even more difficult to sustain it over time. As Exhibit 5.4 shows, only a few short months after reaching its all-time high market cap of $658 billion in the fall of 2012, Apple's market capitalization fell by about 45 percent, wiping out close to $290 billion in shareholder value. Within a short 16-months' time, Apple's market cap rose from $370 billion in December 2011 to its all-time high of $658 billion in September 2012, only to fall back to $370 billion by April 2013.

Although measuring firm performance through total return to shareholders and firm market capitalization has many advantages, it is not without problems:

■ *Stock prices can be highly volatile, making it difficult to assess firm performance, particularly in the short term.* This volatility implies that total return to shareholders is a better measure over the long term due to the "noise" introduced by market volatility, external factors, and investor sentiment.

■ *Overall macroeconomic factors such as the unemployment rate, economic growth or contraction, and interest and exchange rates all have a direct bearing on stock*

EXHIBIT 5.4

Apple's Market Cap (December 2011– April 2013)

SOURCE: Author's depiction of data from Bloomberg.

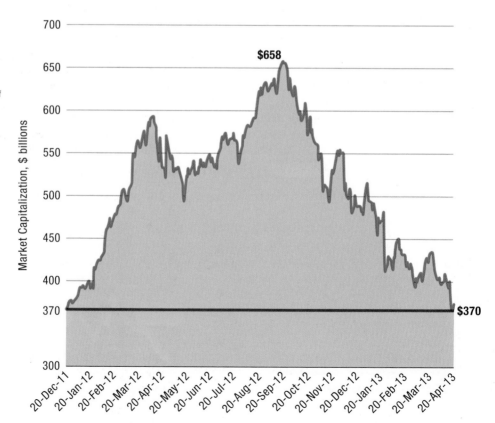

prices. It can be difficult to ascertain the extent to which a stock price is influenced more by external macroeconomic factors (as discussed in Chapter 3) than by the firm's strategy.

■ *Stock prices frequently reflect the psychological mood of investors, which can at times be irrational.* Stock prices can overshoot expectations based on economic fundamentals amidst periods like the Internet boom, during which former Federal Reserve Chairman Alan Greenspan described investors' buoyant sentiments as "irrational exuberance."[20] Similarly, stock prices can undershoot expectations during busts like the 2008–2009 worldwide financial crisis, during which investors' sentiment was described as "irrational gloom."[21]

ECONOMIC VALUE CREATION

The relationship between *economic value creation* and competitive advantage is fundamental in strategic management. It provides the foundation upon which to formulate a firm's competitive strategy of cost leadership or differentiation (discussed in detail in the next chapter). For now, it is important to note that a firm has a competitive advantage when it creates more *economic value* than rival firms. What does that mean?

Economic value created is the difference between a buyer's willingness to pay for a product or service and the firm's total cost to produce it. Let's assume you consider buying a laptop computer and you have a budget of $1,200. You have narrowed your search down to two models, one offered by Firm A, the other by Firm B. Your subjective assessment of the benefits derived from owning Firm A's laptop is $1,000—this is the absolute maximum you'd be willing to pay for it, or the *reservation price.* In contrast, you value Firm B's laptop model at $1,200 because it has somewhat higher performance, is more user-friendly, and definitely has a higher "coolness-factor." Given that you value Firm B's laptop by $200 more than Firm A's model, you will purchase a laptop from Firm B.

Let's move now from your individual considerations to the overall market for laptop computers in order to derive implications for firm-level competitive advantage. To simplify this illustration, only Firm A and Firm B are competing in the market for laptops. Assuming that both Firm A and Firm B have the same total unit cost of producing the particular laptop model under consideration ($400) and the market at large has similar preferences as you do, then Firm B will have a competitive advantage. This is because Firm B creates more economic value than Firm A (by $200), but has the same total cost. This situation is depicted in Exhibit 5.5. The amount of *total perceived consumer benefits*

LO 5-3

Explain economic value creation and different sources of competitive advantage.

economic value created Difference between value (*V*) and cost (*C*), or (*V* − *C*); sometimes also called *economic contribution.*

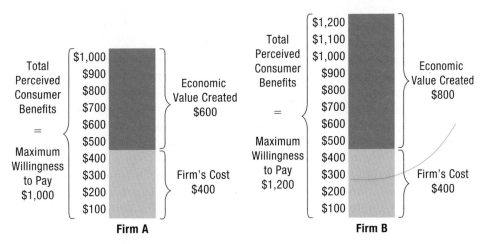

EXHIBIT 5.5

Firm B's Competitive Advantage: Same Cost as Firm A but Firm B Creates More Economic Value

equals the *maximum willingness to pay*. This amount is then split into economic value creation and the firm's total unit cost. Firm A and Firm B have identical total unit cost ($400 per laptop). However, Firm B's laptop is perceived to provide more utility than Firm A's laptop, which implies that Firm B creates more economic value ($800) than Firm A ($600). Taken together, Firm B has a competitive advantage over Firm A because Firm B creates more economic value. This is because Firm B's offering has greater total perceived consumer benefits than Firm A's, while the firms have the same total cost. In short, Firm B's advantage is based on superior *differentiation* leading to higher perceived value. Further, the competitive advantage can be quantified: It is $200 per laptop sold for Firm B over Firm A.

Exhibit 5.5 shows that Firm B's competitive advantage is based on greater economic value creation due to superior product differentiation. Competitive advantage, however, can also result from a relative *cost advantage* over rivals, assuming both firms can create the same total perceived consumer benefits. As shown in Exhibit 5.6, both laptop makers now offer a model that has the same perceived consumer benefits ($1,200). Firm A, however, creates economic value greater ($800) than that of Firm B ($600). This is because Firm A's total unit cost ($400) is lower than Firm B's ($600) due to Firm A's relative cost advantage. As Exhibit 5.6 shows, Firm A has a competitive advantage over Firm B (in the amount of $200 each time Firm A sells a laptop). Here, the source of the competitive advantage is a relative cost advantage over rivals.

value The dollar amount (*V*) a consumer would attach to a good or service; the consumer's *maximum willingness to pay;* sometimes also called *reservation price.*

Three components are needed to further explain *total perceived consumer benefits* and *economic value created* in more detail: (1) *value (V),* (2) *price (P),* and (3) *cost (C).* **Value** denotes the dollar amount (*V*) a consumer would attach to a good or service. Value captures a consumer's willingness to pay and is determined by the perceived benefits a good or service provides to the buyer. The cost (*C*) to produce the good or service matters little to the consumer, but it matters a great deal to the producer (supplier) of the good or service since it has a direct bearing on the profit margin. Continuing with the laptop example, total perceived *value* ($1,200) splits into *economic value created* ($V - C = \$800$) plus *total unit cost* ($C = \$400$), or: $V = (V - C) + C$.

profit (producer surplus) Difference between price charged (*P*) and the cost to produce (*C*), or (*P − C*).

The difference between the price charged (*P*) and the cost to produce (*C*) is the **profit,** or **producer surplus.** In the laptop example, if the price charged is $900, the profit is $P - C = \$900 - \$400 = \$500$. The firm captures this amount as profit per unit sold. As

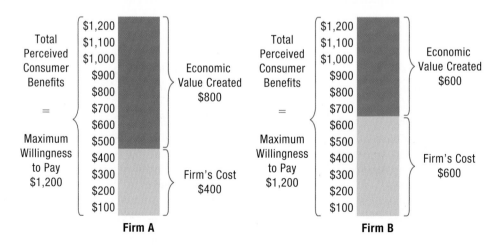

EXHIBIT 5.6

Firm A's Competitive Advantage: Same Total Perceived Consumer Benefits as Firm B but Firm A Creates More Economic Value

the consumer, you capture the difference between what you would have been willing to pay (V) and what you paid (P), called **consumer surplus.** In our example, the consumer surplus is $V - P = \$1,200 - \$900$, or $300. *Economic value creation* therefore equals *consumer surplus plus firm profit*, or $(V - C) = (V - P) + (P - C)$. In the laptop example, economic value created $(\$1,200 - \$400) =$ Consumer surplus $(\$1,200 - \$900) +$ Producer surplus $(\$900 - \$400) = \$300 + \$500 = \$800$.

The relationship between consumer and producer surplus is the reason trade happens: Both transacting parties capture *some* of the overall value created. Note, though, that the distribution of the value created between parties need not be equal to make trade worthwhile. By applying this framework, strategy is about (1) *creating economic value* and (2) *capturing as much of it as possible.*

Exhibit 5.7 graphically illustrates how these concepts fit together. On the left side of the graph, V represents the total perceived consumer benefits, as captured in the consumer's maximum willingness to pay. In the lower part of the center bar, C is the cost to produce the product or service (the unit cost). It follows that the difference between the consumers' maximum willingness to pay and the firm's cost $(V - C)$ is the economic value created. The price of the product or service (P) is indicated in the dashed line. The economic value created $(V - C)$, as shown in Exhibit 5.7, is split between producer and consumer: $(V - P)$ is the value the consumer captures *(consumer surplus)*, and $(P - C)$ is the value the producer captures *(producer surplus,* or *profit).*

Competitive advantage goes to the firm that achieves the largest economic value created, which is the difference between V, the consumer's willingness to pay, and C, the cost to produce the good or service. The reason is that a large difference between V and C gives the firm two distinct pricing options: (1) It can charge higher prices to reflect the higher value and thus increase its profitability, or (2) it can charge the same price as competitors and thus gain market share. Given this, the strategic objective is to maximize $(V - C)$, or the economic value created.

consumer surplus
Difference between the value a consumer attaches to a good or service (V) and what he or she paid for it (P), or $(V - P)$.

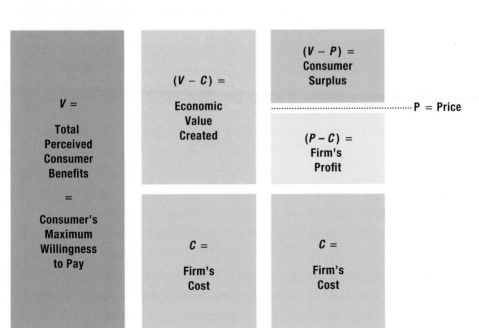

EXHIBIT 5.7

Competitive Advantage and Economic Value Created: The Role of Value, Cost, and Price

Applying the notion of *economic value creation* also has direct implications for firm financial performance. Revenues are a function of the value created for consumers and the price of the good or service, which together drive the volume of goods sold. In this perspective, profit (Π) is defined as total revenues (TR) minus total costs (TC):

$\Pi = TR - TC$, where $TR = P \times Q$, or price times quantity sold

Total costs include both fixed and variable costs. *Fixed costs* are independent of consumer demand—for example, the cost of capital to build computer manufacturing plants or an online retail presence to take direct orders. *Variable costs* change with the level of consumer demand—for instance, components such as LCD screens, microprocessors, hard drives, display screens, and keyboards.

Rather than merely relying on historical costs, as done when taking the perspective of *accounting profitability* (introduced earlier), in the *economic value creation* perspective, *all costs,* including *opportunity costs,* must be considered. **Opportunity costs** capture the value of the best forgone alternative use of the resources employed.

opportunity costs
The value of the best forgone alternative use of the resources employed.

An entrepreneur, for example, faces two types of opportunity costs: (1) forgone wages she could be earning if she was employed elsewhere and (2) the cost of capital she invested in her business, which could instead be invested in, say, the stock market or U.S. Treasury bonds. At the end of the year, the entrepreneur considers her business over the last 12 months. She made an *accounting profit* of $70,000, calculated as total revenues minus expenses (which include all historical costs but not opportunity costs). But she also realizes she has forgone $60,000 in salary she could have earned at another firm. In addition, she knows she could have earned $20,000 in interest if she had bought U.S. Treasury bills with a 4 percent return instead of investing $500,000 in her business. The opportunity cost of being an entrepreneur was $80,000 ($60,000 + $20,000). Therefore, when considering all costs, including opportunity costs, she actually experienced an economic loss of $10,000 ($80,000 − $70,000). When considering her future options, she should stay in business only if she values her independence as an entrepreneur more than $10,000 or thinks business will be better next year.

As with any tool to assess competitive advantage, the economic value creation framework also has some limitations:

■ *Determining the value of a good in the eyes of consumers is not a simple task.* One way to tackle this problem is to look at consumers' purchasing habits for their revealed preferences, which indicate how much each consumer is willing to pay for a product or service. In the earlier example, the value (V) you placed on the laptop—the highest price you were willing to pay, or your reservation price—was $1,200. If the firm is able to charge the reservation price ($P = \$1,200$), it captures all the economic value created ($V - C = \$800$) as producer surplus or profit ($P - C = \$800$).

■ *The value of a good in the eyes of consumers changes based on income, preferences, time, and other factors.* If your income is high, you are likely to place a higher value on some goods (e.g., business-class air travel) and a lower value on other goods (e.g., Greyhound bus travel). In regard to preferences, you may place a higher value on a ticket for a Lady Gaga concert than on one for the New York Philharmonic orchestra (or vice versa). As an example of time value, you place a higher value on an airline ticket that will get you to a business meeting tomorrow than on one for a planned trip to take place eight weeks from now.

■ *To measure firm-level competitive advantage, we must estimate the economic value created for all products and services offered by the firm.* This estimation may be a relatively easy task if the firm offers only a few products or services. However, it becomes much more complicated for diversified firms such as General Electric, Unilever, or the Tata Group that may offer hundreds or even thousands of different products and services across many different industries and geographies. Although the performance of individual strategic business units (SBUs) can be assessed along the dimensions described here, it becomes more difficult to make this assessment at the corporate level. Yet, assessing corporate-level performance is critical in order to justify the existence of diversified conglomerates (more on this in our discussion on diversification strategy in Chapter 8).

In summary, the economic value creation perspective gives us one useful way to assess competitive advantage. This approach is conceptually quite powerful, and it lies at the center of many strategic management frameworks (such as the generic business strategies we discuss in the next chapter). However, it falls short when managers are called upon to operationalize competitive advantage. When the need for "hard numbers" arises, managers and analysts frequently rely on firm financials such as *accounting profitability* or *shareholder value creation* to measure firm performance.

We've now completed our consideration of the three standard dimensions for measuring competitive advantage—economic value, accounting profitability, and shareholder value. Although each provides unique insights for our assessment of a firm's performance, one drawback is that they are more or less one-dimensional metrics. Focusing on just one performance metric when assessing competitive advantage, however, can lead to significant problems, because each metric has its shortcomings, as listed earlier. We now turn to two conceptual frameworks—the balanced scorecard and the triple bottom line—that attempt to provide a more holistic perspective on firm performance.

balanced scorecard
Strategy implementation tool that harnesses multiple internal and external performance metrics in order to balance financial and strategic goals.

THE BALANCED SCORECARD

Just as airplane pilots rely on a number of instruments to provide constant information about key variables such as altitude, airspeed, fuel, position of other aircraft in the vicinity, and destination in order to ensure a safe flight, so should managers rely on multiple yardsticks to more accurately assess company performance in an integrative way. Kaplan and Norton proposed a framework to help managers achieve their strategic objectives more effectively.[22] Called the **balanced scorecard,** this approach harnesses multiple internal and external performance metrics in order to balance both financial and strategic goals.

Exhibit 5.8 depicts the balanced-scorecard framework. Managers using the balanced scorecard develop strategic objectives and appropriate metrics by answering four key questions that Kaplan and Norton, during a yearlong research project with a number of different companies, identified as the most salient.[23] Brainstorming answers to these questions (ideally) results in a set of measures that give managers a quick but also comprehensive view of the firm's current state. The four key questions are:

LO 5-4

Apply a balanced scorecard to assess and evaluate competitive advantage.

1. *How do customers view us?* The customer's perspective concerning the company's products and services is linked directly to its revenues and profits. The perceived value of a product or service determines how much the customer is willing to pay for it. The question, "How do customers view us?" is therefore directly linked to how much

EXHIBIT 5.8 / A Balanced-Scorecard Approach to Creating and Sustaining Competitive Advantage

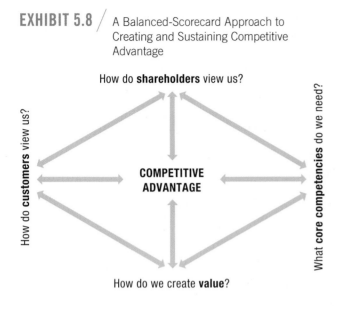

economic value a firm can create. If the customer views the company's offering favorably, she is willing to pay more for a certain product or service, enhancing its competitive advantage (assuming production costs are well below the asking price).

To learn how customers view a company's products or services, managers collect data to identify areas to improve, with a focus on speed, quality, service, and cost. In the air-express industry, for example, managers learned from their customers that many don't really need next-day delivery for most of their documents and packages; rather what they really cared about was the ability to track the shipments. This discovery led to the development of steeply discounted second-day delivery by UPS and FedEx, combined with sophisticated online tracking tools.

2. *How do we create value?* Answering this question challenges managers to come up with strategic objectives that ensure future competitiveness, innovation, and organizational learning. It focuses on the business processes and structures that allow a firm to create economic value. One useful metric, for example, is the percentage of revenues obtained from new product introductions. 3M, for example, requires that 30 percent of revenues must come from products introduced within the last four years.[24] A second metric, aimed at assessing a firm's external learning and collaboration capability, is to stipulate that a certain percentage of new products must originate from outside the firm's boundaries.[25] Through its Connect + Develop program, the consumer products company Procter & Gamble has raised the percentage of new products that originated (at least partly) from outside P&G, from 15 to 35 percent.[26]

3. *What core competencies do we need?* This question focuses managers internally, to identify the core competencies needed to achieve their objectives, and the accompanying business processes that support, hone, and leverage those competencies. Robert Clarke, former president of performance development at Honda, argues that Honda is at its heart an engine company (not a car company).[27] Beginning with motorcycles in 1948, Honda nurtured this core competency over many decades, and today is leveraging it to reach stretch goals in the design, development, and manufacture of small airplanes.

4. *How do shareholders view us?* The final perspective in the balanced scorecard is the shareholders' view of financial performance. Some of the measures in this area rely on accounting data such as cash flow, operating income, ROIC, ROE, and, of course, total returns to shareholders. Understanding the shareholders' view of value creation leads managers to a more future-oriented evaluation.

By relying on both an internal and an external view of the firm, the balanced scorecard combines the strengths provided by the individual approaches to assessing competitive advantage discussed earlier: accounting profitability, shareholder value creation, and economic value creation.

ADVANTAGES OF THE BALANCED SCORECARD. The balanced-scorecard approach is popular in managerial practice because it has several advantages. In particular, the balanced scorecard allows managers to:

- Communicate and link the strategic vision to responsible parties within the organization.
- Translate the vision into measureable operational goals.
- Design and plan business processes.
- Implement feedback and organizational learning in order to modify and adapt strategic goals when indicated.

The balanced scorecard can accommodate both short- and long-term performance metrics. It provides a concise report that tracks chosen metrics and measures and compares them to target values. This approach allows managers to assess past performance, identify areas for improvement, and position the company for future growth. Including a broader perspective than financials allows managers and executives a more balanced view of organizational performance—hence its name. In a sense, the balanced scorecard is a broad diagnostic tool. It complements the common financial metrics with operational measures on customer satisfaction, internal processes, and the company's innovation and improvement activities.

Let's look at FMC Corporation, a chemical manufacturer employing some 5,000 people in different SBUs and earning over $3 billion in annual revenues, as an example of how to implement the balanced-scorecard approach.[28] To achieve its vision of becoming "the customer's most valued supplier," FMC's managers initially had focused solely on financial metrics such as return on invested capital (ROIC) as performance measures. FMC is a multibusiness corporation with several standalone profit-and-loss strategic business units; its overall performance was the result of both over- and underperforming units. FMC's managers had tried several approaches to enhance performance, but they turned out to be more or less ineffective. Perhaps even more significant, short-term thinking by general managers was a major obstacle in the attempt to implement a business strategy.

Searching for improved performance, FMC's CEO decided to adopt a balanced-scorecard approach. It enabled the managers to view FMC's challenges and shortcomings from a holistic, company perspective, which was especially helpful to the general managers of different business units. In particular, the balanced scorecard allowed general managers to focus on market position, customer service, and new product introductions that could generate long-term value. Using the framework depicted in Exhibit 5.8, general managers had to answer tough follow-up questions such as: How do we become the customer's most valued supplier, and how can my division create this value for the customer? How do we become more externally focused? What are my division's core competencies and contributions to the company goals? What are my division's weaknesses?

Implementing a balanced scorecard allowed FMC's managers to align their different perspectives to create a more focused corporation overall. General managers now review progress along the chosen metrics every month, and corporate executives do so on a quarterly basis. Although successful for FMC, implementing a balanced-scorecard approach is not a one-time effort, but requires continuous tracking of metrics and updating of strategic objectives, if needed. It is a continuous process, feeding performance back into the strategy process to assess its effectiveness (see Chapter 2).

DISADVANTAGES OF THE BALANCED SCORECARD. Though widely implemented by many businesses, the balanced scorecard is not without its critics.[29] It is important to note that the balanced scorecard is a tool for *strategy implementation,* not for *strategy* *formulation.* It is up to a firm's managers to formulate a strategy that will enhance the chances of gaining and sustaining a competitive advantage. In addition, the balanced-scorecard approach provides only limited guidance about which metrics to choose. Different situations call for different metrics. All of the three approaches to measuring competitive advantage—accounting profitability, shareholder value creation, and economic value creation—in addition to other quantitative and qualitative measures, can be helpful when using a balanced-scorecard approach.

When implementing a balanced scorecard, managers need to be aware that a failure to achieve competitive advantage is not so much a reflection of a poor framework but of a strategic failure. The balanced scorecard is only as good as the skills of the managers who use it: They first must devise a strategy that enhances the odds of achieving competitive advantage. Second, they must accurately translate the strategy into objectives that they can measure and manage within the balanced-scorecard approach.[30]

Once the metrics have been selected, the balanced scorecard tracks chosen metrics and measures and compares them to target values. It does not, however, provide much insight into how metrics that deviate from the set goals can be put back on track.[31]

THE TRIPLE BOTTOM LINE

Today, managers are frequently asked to maintain and improve not only the firm's economic performance but also its social and ecological performance. As we saw in ChapterCase 2, CEO Indra Nooyi responded by declaring PepsiCo's vision to be *Performance with a Purpose* defined by goals in the social dimension (*human sustainability* to combat obesity by making its products healthier, and the *whole person at work* to achieve work-life balance) and ecological dimension (*environmental sustainability* in regard to clean water, energy, recycling, and so on), in addition to firm financial performance.

Noneconomic factors can have a significant impact on a firm's financial performance, not to mention its reputation and customer goodwill. We saw in Strategy Highlight 1.2 how BP's infamous oil spill in the Gulf of Mexico put the company on the brink of financial collapse. It also threatened to destroy fauna and flora along the U.S. shoreline from Texas to Florida, as well as the livelihood of hundreds of thousands of people in the tourism and fishing industries. BP's estimated legal damages could be over $40 billion; the loss of its reputation and customer goodwill is likely to be much higher.

In contrast, being proactive along noneconomic dimensions can make good business sense. In anticipation of industry regulation in terms of "extended producer responsibility," which requires the seller of a product to take it back for recycling at the end of its life, the German carmaker BMW was proactive. It not only lined up the leading car-recycling companies but also started to redesign its cars using a modular approach. The modular parts allow for quick car disassembly and reuse of components in the after-sales market (so-called "refurbished or rebuilt auto parts").[32]

triple bottom line
Combination of economic, social, and ecological concerns that can lead to a sustainable strategy.

Three dimensions—*economic, social, and ecological*—make up the **triple bottom line.** As the intersection of the three ovals in Exhibit 5.9 suggests, achieving positive results in all three areas can lead to a sustainable strategy—a strategy that can endure over time. A *sustainable strategy* produces not only positive financial results, but also positive results along the social and ecological dimensions. Like the balanced scorecard, the triple bottom line takes a more integrative and holistic view in assessing a company's performance.[33] Using a triple-bottom-line approach, managers audit their company's fulfillment of its social and ecological obligations to stakeholders such as employees, customers, suppliers, and communities as conscientiously as they track its financial performance.[34] In this sense, the triple-bottom-line framework is related to *stakeholder theory,* an approach to understanding a firm as embedded in a network of internal and external constituencies that each make contributions and expect consideration in return (see the discussion in Chapter 1). For an example of how carpet manufacturer Interface uses a triple-bottom-line approach to gain and sustain a competitive advantage, read Strategy Highlight 5.1.

Since the emergence of strategic management as a field of research and practice, the focus has been on firm economic performance. More recently, however, society and investors require companies to also address social and ecological concerns. This discussion is captured under the notion of *corporate social responsibility,* to which we turn next.

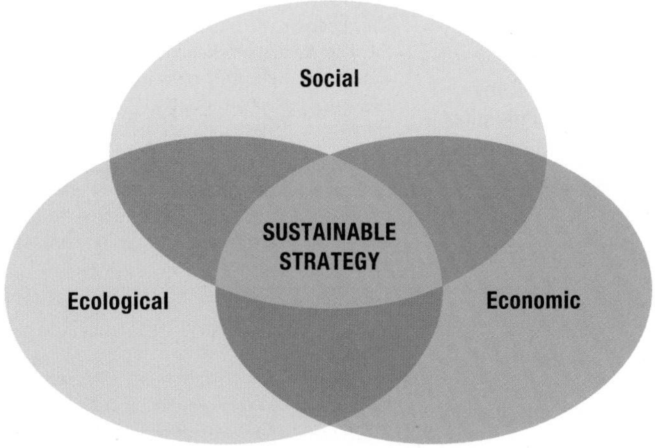

CORPORATE SOCIAL RESPONSIBILITY.

Corporate social responsibility (introduced in Chapter 1) helps firms recognize and address society's expectations of the business enterprise at a given point in time. The notion of corporate social responsibility is rapidly gaining ground. Millennials, defined as those born between 1980 and 1991, tend to expect

EXHIBIT 5.9 / The Triple Bottom Line

The simultaneous pursuit of performance along social, economic, and ecological dimensions provides a basis for a sustainable strategy.

Strategy Highlight 5.1

Interface: The World's First Sustainable Company

Interface Inc. is a leader in modular carpeting, with annual sales of roughly $1 billion. What makes the company unique is its strategic intent to become the world's first *fully sustainable* company. In 1994, founder Ray Anderson set a goal for the company to be "off oil" entirely by 2020. That included not using any petroleum-based raw materials or oil-related energy to fuel the manufacturing plants.

According to Collins and Porras in *Built to Last,* their classic study of high-performing companies over long periods of time, this is a *"BHAG—a big hairy audacious goal."* BHAGs are bold missions declared by visionary companies and are a "powerful mechanism to stimulate progress."[35] Weaning Interface off oil by 2020 is indeed a BHAG. Many see the carpet industry as an extension of the petrochemical industry, given its heavy reliance on fossil fuels and chemicals in the manufacturing, shipping, and installation of its products.

Today, Interface is a leader in both modular carpet and sustainability. The company estimates that between 1996 and 2008, it saved over $400 million due to its energy efficiency and use of recycled materials. Its business model is changing the carpet industry. Speaking of sustainability as a business model, Mr. Anderson stated in 2009:

Sustainability has given my company a competitive edge in more ways than one. It has proven to be the most powerful marketplace differentiator I have known in my long career. Our costs are down, our profits are up, and our products are the best they have ever been. Sustainable design has provided an unexpected wellspring of innovation, people are galvanized around a shared higher purpose, better people are applying, the best people are staying and working with a purpose, the goodwill in the marketplace generated by our focus on sustainability far exceeds that which any amount of advertising or marketing expenditure could have generated—this company believes it has found a better way to a bigger and more legitimate profit—a better business model.[36]

EXHIBIT 5.10

Defining Three
Generations: Baby
Boomers, Generation
Xers, and Millennials

SOURCE: Based on "Talent
Report: What Workers Want
in 2012," published by The
MacArthur Foundation
(p. 2), www.netimpact.org/
whatworkerswant.

Baby Boomers (born between 1947 and 1963) now make up the oldest cohort of the work force. This group was parented by prosperity, and shares a presumption of entitlement to their world view. Shaping political experiences were the civil rights movement, Vietnam, and Watergate, not to mention rock music, drugs, and the sexual revolution. The Boomer cohort has always been big enough to force the culture to adapt to them. For years they have dictated politics, culture, and policy by their sheer number in a market-driven economy.

Generation X, or Xers (born between 1964 and 1979). This group's formative experiences were framed by familial and financial insecurity. They grew up amidst rising rates of divorce and recession. Where the sexual revolution of the Boomers brought free expression and experimentation, the threat of AIDS brought Xers fear and caution. During adolescence and early adulthood, their political world view was shaped by, well, pretty much nothing. Described as "slackers," and scorned for a world view that begins and ends with themselves, even their moniker is about something that never happened.

Millennials (born between 1980 and 1991) are much more like Boomers than Xers. They grew up as an affirmed generation, with a re-focus on the family, and are generally thought of as having high self-esteem and self-confidence. They are racially and ethnically diverse and tolerant of a variety of lifestyles. They are occasionally called Generation Y, or Millennials, because one of their defining characteristics is having come of age along with the Internet. Information has always been virtually costless and universally available to them; technology cheap and easily mastered; community as much a digital place of common interest as a shared physical space. They may also be self-centered as a generation, defined a bit by the technology of iPods and iPhones, Facebook and YouTube.

companies to be socially responsible and have expressed a strong interest to work for companies that match their values.[37] Exhibit 5.10 provides a brief description of Baby Boomers, Generation Xers, and Millennials. According to a recent U.S. survey, over half of the student population (58 percent) would accept a 15 percent lower pay to "work for an organization whose values are like my own."[38] Among the many research studies looking at the relationship between CSR and firm performance, some find CSR improves financial performance, while others conclude superior financial performance makes CSR possible.[39]

5.2 Business Models: Putting Strategy into Action

LO 5-6

Outline how business
models put strategy into
action.

business model
Organizational plan
that details the firm's
competitive tactics and
initiatives; in short,
how the firm intends to
make money.

Strategy is a set of goal-directed actions a firm takes to gain and sustain superior performance relative to competitors or the industry average. The translation of strategy into action takes place in the firm's **business model**, which details the firm's competitive tactics and initiatives. Simply put, the firm's business model explains how the firm intends to make money. The business model stipulates how the firm conducts its business with its buyers, suppliers, and partners.[40]

How companies do business can sometimes be as important to gaining and sustaining competitive advantage as what they do. This also implies that *business model innovation* might be as important achieving superior performance as product or process innovation. A company might come up with a better MP3 player than Apple's iPod (or the one embedded in the iPhone and iPad), but few of the 500 million iTunes users are likely to switch brands. As discussed in ChapterCase 1, for most of its history Apple was a personal computer company. The introduction of the iPod and the iTunes Store were aspects of Apple's business model innovation. Apple's innovation not only offered hardware and software but also enabled digital music distribution, linking music content owners with end consumers in a legal, scalable, and profitable fashion. Strategy Highlight 5.2 shows another example of business model innovation: how the online startup Threadless has used the Internet to craft a new business model.

Strategy Highlight 5.2

Threadless: Leveraging Crowdsourcing to Design Cool T-Shirts

Threadless, a community-centered online apparel store (www.threadless.com), was founded in 2000 by Jake Nickell, then a student at the Illinois Institute of Art, and Jacob DeHart, then a student at Purdue University, with $1,000 as startup capital. After Jake had won an online T-shirt design contest, the two entrepreneurs came up with a business model to leverage user-generated content. The idea is to let consumers "work for you" and turn consumers into *prosumers,* a hybrid between producers and consumers.

Members of the Threadless community do most of the work, which they consider fun: They submit T-shirt designs online, and community members vote on which designs they like best. The designs receiving the most votes are put in production, printed, and sold online. Threadless leverages **crowdsourcing,** a process in which a group of people voluntarily perform tasks that were traditionally being completed by a firm's employees. Rather than outsourcing its work to other companies, Threadless

outsources its T-shirt design to its website community. The concept of leveraging a firm's own customers via Internet-enabled technology to help produce better products is explicitly included in Threadless' business model.

Threadless' business model translates real-time market research and design contests into quick sales. Threadless produces only T-shirts that were approved by its community. Moreover, it has a very good understanding of market demand because it knows the number of people who participated in each design contest. In addition, when scoring each T-shirt design in a contest, Threadless users have the option to check "*I'd buy it.*" These features give the Threadless community a voice in T-shirt design and also coax community members into making a pre-purchasing commitment. Threadless does not make any significant investments until the design and market size are determined, minimizing its downside. Not surprisingly, Threadless has sold every T-shirt that it has printed. Moreover, it has a cult-like following and is outperforming established companies such as Old Navy and Urban Outfitters with their more formulaic T-shirt designs.

To come up with an effective business model, the firm's managers first transform their strategy of how to compete into a blueprint of actions and initiatives that support the overarching goals. In a second step, managers implement this blueprint through structures, processes, culture, and procedures. If the company fails to translate a strategy into a profitable business model, the firm will run into trouble.

Take Zipcar, a member-based car-sharing company, as an example.[41] Zipcar came up with a new business model: It allows its members to rent a vehicle online that is already in their vicinity for a few hours or a day. Users are charged for the duration of use of the car, and gas and insurance are included in the rental fees. Zipcar appeals to urban dwellers and Millennials who prefer not to own a vehicle, but have a need for a car on occasion. The Zipcar member just pays for the service of access to a car as needed. The downside of Zipcar's business model is that it requires a large amount of up-front investment to build the rental car fleet. Although Zipcar has excelled in customer experience and technology, it was unable to obtain the capital necessary to scale its operation in order to be profitable. Given low barriers to imitation, numerous competitors (some with prior capital investment in the rental car industry) have sprung up. The new competitors include traditional car rental companies and others that created Zipcar clones such as Hertz on Demand, Enterprise's WeCar, U-Haul's U Car Share, Avis On Location, and Daimler's Car2Go. Since the member-based car-sharing business model works best in highly populated areas, several regional competitors have also entered the industry, including City CarShare in the San Francisco Bay Area, I-GO in Chicago, and Mint in New York and Boston. Additional

crowdsourcing
A process in which a group of people voluntarily performs tasks that were traditionally completed by a firm's employees.

imitators with a slightly different business model include peer-to-peer car-sharing startups such as Getaround and RelayRides. As a consequence, Zipcar's stock price fell rapidly. Zipcar was eventually acquired by rental car company Avis, which plans to combine its vast rental fleet with Zipcar's mobile technology and customer experience.

DIFFERENT BUSINESS MODELS

Given their critical importance to achieving competitive advantage, business models are constantly evolving. It is helpful, however, to introduce some of the more popular business models today in order to increase the strategy toolkit at your disposal:

- *Razor–Razor-Blade.* The initial product is often sold at a loss or given away for free in order to drive demand for complementary goods. The company makes its money on the replacement part needed. As the name indicates, it was invented by Gillette, which gave away its razors and sold the replacement cartridges for relatively high prices. The razor–razor-blade model is found in many business applications today. For example, HP charges little for its laser printers but imposes high prices for its replacement cartridges. Another example is current-generation video game consoles that are sold at a loss to drive demand for games which are sold at a premium to recoup the loss on the consoles.

- *Subscription-Based.* The subscription-based model has been traditionally used for (print) magazines and newspapers. Users pay for access to a product or service whether they use the product or service during the payment term or not. Industries that use this model presently are cable television, cellular service providers, satellite radio, Internet service providers, and health clubs.

    With the help of a hilarious promotional video that went viral with over 10 million views,[42] the entrepreneur Michael Dubin launched Dollar Shave Club, an ecommerce startup that delivers razors by mail. It uses a subscription-based business model.[43] As the company's name suggests, its entry-level membership plan delivers a razor and five cartridges a month for just $1 (plus $2 shipping). The member selects an appropriate plan, pays a monthly fee, and will receive razors every month in the mail. The entrepreneur identified the need in the market for serving people who don't like to go shopping for razors and certainly don't like to pay the high prices commanded by market leaders in razors. The company seems to be off to a great start. After the promotional video was uploaded on YouTube in March 2012, some 12,000 people signed up for Dollar Shave membership within the first 48 hours. It also raised over $10 million in venture capital funding from prominent firms such as Kleiner Perkins Caufield & Byers and Andreessen Horowitz. It remains to be seen, however, if Dollar Shave Club can disrupt the $13 billion razor-blade industry where Procter & Gamble's subsidiary Gillette holds two-thirds of the world market.

    Some companies combine different business models. Telecommunications companies such as AT&T or Verizon, for example, combine the *razor–razor-blade* model with the *subscription-based business model.* They provide a basic cell phone at no charge or significantly subsidize high-end smartphones when you sign up for a two-year wireless service plan. Telecom providers recoup the subsidy provided for the smartphone by requiring customers to sign up for lengthy service plans. This is why it is so critical for telecom providers to keep their *churn rate*—the proportion of subscribers that leave, especially prior to the end of the contractual term—as low as possible.

- *Pay-as-You-Go.* In the *pay-as-you-go business model,* the user pays for only the services he or she consumes. The pay-as-you-go model is most widely used by utilities providing power and water and cell phone service plans, but is gaining momentum in other areas such as rental cars (i.e., Zipcar) and cloud computing. News providers such as *The New York Times* and *The Wall Street Journal* have created "pay walls" as a pay-as-you-go option.

- **Freemium.** The *freemium (= free + premium) business model* is a model in which the basic features of a product or service are provided *free* of charge, but the user must pay for *premium* services such as advanced features or add-ons.[44] For example, companies provide a minimally supported version of their software as a trial (e.g., business application or video game) to give users the chance to try the product. Users later have the option of purchasing a supported version of software, which includes a full set of product features and product support. The freemium business model is used extensively by open-source software companies such as Red Hat, mobile app companies, and other Internet businesses. Many of the free versions of applications include advertisements to make up for the cost of supporting non-paying users. In addition, the paying premium users subsidize the free users. The freemium model is often used to build a consumer base when the marginal cost of adding another user is low or even zero (such as in software sales). Some examples are Adobe Acrobat, Dropbox, Evernote, LinkedIn, Microsoft Office 365, and Spotify.

5.3 ◀▶ Implications for the Strategist

In this chapter, we discussed how to measure and assess competitive advantage using three traditional approaches: accounting profitability, shareholder value, and economic value creation. We then introduced two conceptual frameworks to help us understand competitive advantage in a more holistic fashion: the balanced scorecard and the triple bottom line. Exhibit 5.11 summarizes the concepts discussed.

Several managerial implications emerged from our discussion of competitive advantage and firm performance:

- No *best* strategy exists—only *better* ones (better in comparison with others). We must interpret any performance metric relative to those of competitors and the industry average. True performance can be judged only in comparison to other contenders in the field or the industry average, not on an absolute basis.

- The goal of strategic management is to integrate and align each business function and activity to obtain superior performance at the business unit and corporate levels. Therefore, competitive advantage is best measured by criteria that reflect *overall business unit performance* rather than the performance of specific departments. For example, although the functional managers in the marketing department may (and should) care

---

Competitive advantage is reflected in superior firm performance.

>> We always assess competitive advantage *relative* to a benchmark, either using competitors or the industry average.

>> Competitive advantage is a multifaceted concept.

>> We can assess competitive advantage by measuring accounting profit, shareholder value, or economic value.

>> The balanced-scorecard approach harnesses multiple internal and external performance dimensions to balance a firm's financial and strategic goals.

>> More recently, competitive advantage has been linked to a firm's triple bottom line, the ability to maintain performance in the economic, social, and ecological contexts to achieve a *sustainable strategy*.

EXHIBIT 5.11

How Do We Measure and Assess Competitive Advantage?

greatly about the success or failure of their recent ad campaign, the *general* manager cares most about the performance implications of the ad campaign at the business unit level for which she has profit-and-loss responsibility. Metrics that aggregate upward and reflect overall firm and corporate performance are most useful to assess the effectiveness of a firm's competitive strategy.

- Both *quantitative and qualitative* performance dimensions matter in judging how effective a firm's strategy is. Those who focus on only one metric will risk being blindsided by poor performance on another. Rather, managers need to rely on a more holistic perspective when assessing firm performance, measuring different dimensions over different time periods.

- A firm's business model is critical to achieving a competitive advantage. How a firm does business is as important as what it does.

This concludes our discussion of competitive advantage, firm performance, and business models as well as Part 1—strategy analysis—of the AFI framework. In Part 2, we turn our attention to the next steps in the AFI framework—strategy formulation. In Chapters 6 and 7, we focus on business strategy: *How should the firm compete (cost leadership, differentiation, or integration)?* In Chapters 8 and 9, we study corporate strategy: *Where should the firm compete (industry, markets, and geography)?* Chapter 10, which concludes Part 2, looks at global strategy: *How and where (local, regional, national, and international) should the firm compete around the world?*

CHAPTER**CASE 5** / Consider This . . .

CHAPTERCASE 5 presents a firm profitability analysis for Apple and BlackBerry in fiscal year 2012. Although the analysis presented therein allows us to answer the two key questions we set out to accomplish (accurately assess firm performance and compare it to competitors), keep in mind that this is a *static* analysis. It covers only one fiscal year. We basically take a snapshot of a moving target. To obtain a more complete picture, managers need to engage in a *dynamic* analysis, repeating this over a number of years. This will allow managers to identify when and where things went wrong (in the case for BlackBerry) and how to get back on track.

Questions

Exhibit 5.12 shows key financial data for Apple and BlackBerry for the three fiscal years 2010–2012. (Five years' worth of data, 2008–2012, and related analysis are available online in *Connect*.) Using the financial ratios presented in the five tables in the "How to Conduct a Case Analysis" module (near the back of the text, after the MiniCases), do the following.

1. Calculate some key profitability, activity, leverage, liquidity, and market ratios for Apple and BlackBerry over time.

2. Conduct a *dynamic* firm profitability analysis over time (fiscal years 2008–2012) as shown in Exhibit 5.1. Can you find signs of performance differentials between these two firms that may have indicated problems at BlackBerry? When did BlackBerry's performance problems become apparent?

3. Make a recommendation to Thorsten Heins, the CEO of BlackBerry, about actions he could take to improve firm performance.

4. Make a recommendation to Tim Cook, the CEO of Apple, about actions he could take to improve firm performance.

EXHIBIT 5.12 / Key Financial Data for Apple and BlackBerry (fiscal years 2010–2012)

In millions of US$ (except for per share items)	Apple Y/E Sept. 2012	Apple Y/E Sept. 2011	Apple Y/E Sept. 2010	BlackBerry Y/E Mar. 2013	Blackberry Y/E Mar. 2012	Blackberry Y/E Mar. 2011
Total revenue	156,508	108,249	65,225	11,073	18,423	19,907
Cost of revenue, total	87,846	64,431	39,541	7,639	11,848	11,082
Gross profit	68,662	43,818	25,684	3,434	6,575	8,825
Selling/general/admin. expenses, total	10,040	7,599	5,517	2,111	2,600	2,400
Total operating expense	13,421	10,028	7,299	4,669	5,078	4,189
Operating income	55,241	33,790	18,385	−1,235	1,497	4,636
Income before tax	55,763	34,205	18,540	−1,220	1,518	4,644
Income after tax	41,342	25,607	13,896	0	1,429	3,405
Net income	41,733	25,922	14,013	−646	1,164	3,411
Diluted weighted average shares	945	937	925	524	524	538
Dividends per share—common stock	3	0	0	0	0	0
Diluted normalized EPS	44	28	15	−1	2	6
Cash and equivalents	10,746	9,815	11,261	1,549	1,527	1,791
Short-term investments	18,383	16,137	14,359	1,105	247	330
Cash and short-term investments	29,129	25,952	25,620	2,654	1,774	2,121
Accounts receivable—trade, net	10,930	5,369	5,510	2,353	3,062	3,955
Total receivables, net	18,692	11,717	9,924	2,625	3,558	4,279
Total inventory	791	776	1,051	603	1,027	618
Total current assets	57,653	44,988	41,678	7,101	7,071	7,488
Property/plant/equipment, total—net	15,452	7,777	4,768	2,395	2,733	2,504
Accumulated depreciation, total						
Goodwill, net	1,135	896	741	0	304	508
Intangibles, net	4,224	3,536	342	3,448	3,286	1,798
Long-term investments	92,122	55,618	25,391	221	337	577
Other long-term assets, total	5,478	3,556	2,263			
Total assets	176,064	116,371	75,183	13,165	13,731	12,875
Accounts payable	21,175	14,632	12,015	1,064	744	832
Accrued expenses	11,414	9,247	5,723	1,842	2,382	2,511
Other current liabilities, total	5,953	4,091	2,984	542	263	108
Total current liabilities	38,542	27,970	20,722	3,448	3,389	3,630
Total long-term debt	0	0	0	0	0	0

In millions of US$ (except for per share items)	Apple Y/E Sept. 2012	Apple Y/E Sept. 2011	Apple Y/E Sept. 2010	BlackBerry Y/E Mar. 2013	Blackberry Y/E Mar. 2012	Blackberry Y/E Mar. 2011
Total debt	0	0	0	0	0	0
Other liabilities, total	22,617	14,191	8,515	542	263	108
Total liabilities	57,854	39,756	27,392	3,705	3,631	3,937
Common stock, total	667	381	283	13	14	66
Additional paid-in capital	0	0	0	0	0	0
Retained earnings (accumulated deficit)	101,289	62,841	37,169	7,267	7,913	6,749
Total equity	118,210	76,615	47,791	9,460	10,100	8,938
Total liabilities and shareholders' equity	176,064	116,371	75,183	13,165	13,731	12,875
Total common shares outstanding	939	929	916	2,431	2,446	2,359

TAKE-AWAY CONCEPTS

This chapter demonstrated three traditional approaches for assessing and measuring firm performance and competitive advantage, as well as two conceptual frameworks designed to provide a more holistic, albeit more qualitative, perspective on firm performance. We also discussed the role of business models in translating a firm's strategy into actions.

LO 5-1 / Conduct a firm profitability analysis using accounting data.

- To measure competitive advantage, we must be able to (1) accurately assess firm performance, and (2) compare and benchmark the focal firm's performance to other competitors in the same industry or the industry average.

- To measure accounting profitability, we use standard metrics derived from publicly available accounting data.

- Commonly used profitability metrics in strategic management are *return on assets (ROA), return on equity (ROE), return on invested capital (ROIC),* and *return on revenue (ROR).* See the

key financial ratios in five tables in the "How to Conduct a Case Analysis" module.

- All accounting data are historical and thus backward-looking. They focus mainly on tangible assets, and do not consider intangibles that are hard or impossible to measure and quantify, such as an innovation competency.

LO 5-2 / Apply shareholder value creation to assess and evaluate competitive advantage.

- Investors are primarily interested in total return to shareholders, which includes stock price appreciation plus dividends received over a specific period.

- Total return to shareholders is an external performance metric; it indicates how the market views all publicly available information about a firm's past, current state, and expected future performance.

- Applying a shareholders' perspective, key metrics to measure and assess competitive advantage are the return on (risk) capital and market capitalization.

- Stock prices can be highly volatile, which makes it difficult to assess firm performance. Overall macroeconomic factors have a direct bearing on stock prices. Also, stock prices frequently reflect the psychological mood of the investors, which can at times be irrational.

- Shareholder value creation is a better measure of competitive advantage over the *long term* due to the "noise" introduced by market volatility, external factors, and investor sentiment.

LO 5-3 / Explain economic value creation and different sources of competitive advantage.

- The relationship between economic value creation and competitive advantage is fundamental in strategic management. It provides the foundation upon which to formulate a firm's competitive strategy of cost leadership or differentiation.

- Three components are critical to evaluating any good or service: value (*V*), price (*P*), and cost (*C*). In this perspective, cost includes opportunity costs.

- Economic value created is the difference between a buyer's willingness to pay for a good or service and the firm's cost to produce it ($V - C$).

- A firm has a competitive advantage when it is able to create more economic value than its rivals. The source of competitive advantage can stem from higher perceived value creation (assuming equal cost) or lower cost (assuming equal value creation).

LO 5-4 / Apply a balanced scorecard to assess and evaluate competitive advantage.

- The balanced-scorecard approach attempts to provide a more integrative view of competitive advantage.

- Its goal is to harness multiple internal and external performance dimensions to balance financial and strategic goals.

- Managers develop strategic objectives for the balanced scorecard by answering four key questions: (1) How do customers view us? (2) How do we create value? (3) What core competencies do we need? (4) How do shareholders view us?

LO 5-5 / Apply a triple bottom line to assess and evaluate competitive advantage.

- Noneconomic factors can have a significant impact on a firm's financial performance, not to mention its reputation and customer goodwill.

- Managers are frequently asked to maintain and improve not only the firm's economic performance but also its social and ecological performance.

- Three dimensions—economic, social, and ecological—make up the triple bottom line. Achieving positive results in all three areas can lead to a *sustainable strategy*—a strategy that can endure over time.

- A sustainable strategy produces not only positive financial results, but also positive results along the social and ecological dimensions.

- Using a triple-bottom-line approach, managers audit their company's fulfillment of its social and ecological obligations to stakeholders such as employees, customers, suppliers, and communities in as serious a way as they track its financial performance.

- The triple-bottom-line framework is related to *stakeholder theory,* an approach to understanding a firm as embedded in a network of internal and external constituencies that each make contributions and expect consideration in return.

LO 5-6 / Outline how business models put strategy into action.

- The translation of a firm's strategy *(where and how to compete for competitive advantage)* into action takes place in the firm's business model *(how to make money)*.

- A business model details how the firm conducts its business with its buyers, suppliers, and partners.

- How companies do business is as important to gaining and sustaining competitive advantage as what they do.

- Some important business models include *razor–razor-blade, subscription-based, pay-as-you-go,* and *freemium.*

KEY TERMS

Balanced scorecard	Market capitalization	Total return to shareholders
Business model	Opportunity costs	Triple bottom line
Consumer surplus	Profit (or producer surplus)	Value
Crowdsourcing	Risk capital	
Economic value created	Shareholders	

DISCUSSION QUESTIONS

1. Domino's Pizza has been in business over 50 years and claimed to be "#1 Worldwide in Pizza Delivery" in 2013. Visit the company's business-related website (www.dominosbiz.com) and read the company profile under the "Investors" tab. Does the firm focus on the accounting, shareholder, or economic perspective in describing its competitive advantage in the profile?

2. For many people, the shareholder perspective is perhaps the most familiar measure of competitive advantage for publicly traded firms. What are some of the disadvantages of using shareholder value as the sole point of view for defining competitive advantage?

3. Interface Inc. is discussed in Strategy Highlight 5.1. It may seem unusual for a business-to-business (B2B) carpet company to be using a triple-bottom-line approach for its strategy. What other industries do you think could productively use this approach? How would it change customers' perceptions if it did?

4. Threadless (in Strategy Highlight 5.2) is an example of a firm building on its customer base to use new products and also to participate in the design and vetting of popular designs. In the spring of 2013, Disney and Pixar Animation announced an expansion of its partnership with Threadless. Previous successes have been shirts for Disney villains, *Toy Story,* and the Muppets, made from designs based on winning submissions of an art contest. The current launch is for T-shirts designed to coincide with the summer 2013 sequel of *Monsters University* by Disney and Pixar Animation. The designs were chosen from 487 submissions by artists around the world. With Disney's long history of expertise in designing clothing to coincide with movie launches, why do you think the company has decided to partner with Threadless? How does this help Disney build competitive advantage? What other firms use this crowdsourcing technique? Where else might this type of business model show up in the future?

ETHICAL/SOCIAL ISSUES

1. You work as a supervisor in a manufacturing firm. The company has implemented a balanced-scorecard performance-appraisal system and a financial bonus for exceeding goals. A major customer order for 1,000 units needs to ship to a destination across the country by the end of the quarter, which is two days away from its close. This shipment, if it goes well, will have a major impact on both your customer-satisfaction goals and your financial goals.

   With 990 units built, a machine breaks down. It will take two days to get the parts and repair the machine. You realize there is an opportunity to load the finished units on a truck tomorrow with paperwork for the completed order of 1,000 units. You can have an employee fly out with the 10 remaining parts and meet the truck at the destination city once the machinery has been repaired. The 10 units can be added to the pallet and delivered as a complete shipment of 1,000 pieces, matching the customer's order and your paperwork. What do you do?

2. The chapter mentions that accounting data do not consider off–balance sheet items. A retailer that owns its stores will list the value of that property as an asset, for example, while a firm that leases

its stores will not. What are some of the accounting and shareholder advantages of leasing compared to owning retail locations?

3. How does this issue play out when comparing brick-and-mortar stores to online businesses (e.g., Best Buy versus Amazon; Barnes & Noble versus Amazon; Home Depot versus Amazon; The Gap versus Threadless; Nordstrom versus Zappos; and so on)? Make recommendations to brick-and-mortar stores as to how they can build competitive advantage over the online competitors. What conclusions do you draw?

SMALL-GROUP EXERCISES

//// Small-Group Exercise 1

As discussed in the chapter, a balanced scorecard views the performance of an organization through four lenses: customer, innovation and learning, internal business, and financial. According to surveys from Bain & Company (a consulting firm), in recent years about 60 percent of firms in both public and private sectors have used a balanced scorecard for performance measures.[45]

With your group, create a balanced scorecard for the business school at your university. You might start by looking at your school's web page for a mission or vision statement. Then divide up the four perspectives among the team members to develop some key elements for each one. It may be helpful to remember the four key balanced-scorecard questions from the chapter:

1. How do customers view us? (Hint: First discuss the following: Who are the customers? The students? The companies that hire students? Others?)

2. How do we create value?

3. What core competencies do we need?

4. How do shareholders view us? (For public universities, the shareholders are the taxpayers who invest their taxes into the university. For private universities, the shareholders are the people or organizations that endow the university.)

//// Small-Group Exercise 2

At the next big family gathering, you want to impress your grandparents with the innovative ideas you have learned in business school. They have decades of experience in investing in the stock market and, from their college days, believe that economic profitability is the primary responsibility of business. You would like to convince them that a triple-bottom-line approach is the modern path to stronger economic performance. With your group members, prepare a casual yet informative speech that you can use to persuade them. They probably will not listen for more than two minutes, so you know you have to be clear and concise with interesting examples. You may want to reinforce your argument by consulting "The Bottom Line of Corporate Good," published in *Forbes*.[46] Present your speech in whatever way your instructor requests—to your group, the entire class, or post a video on YouTube.

STRATEGY TERM PROJECT

//// Module 5: Competitive Advantage Perspectives

1. Based on information in the annual reports or published on the firm's website, summarize what the firm views as the reasons for its successes (either past or expected in the future). Search for both quantitative and qualitative success factors provided in the report.

2. Does the firm seem most focused on accounting profitability, shareholder value creation, or economic value creation? Give quotes or information from these sources to support your view.

3. Many firms are now including annual corporate social responsibility (CSR) reports on their websites. See whether your firm does so. If it does not, are there other indications of a triple-bottom-line approach, including social and ecological elements, in the firm's strategies?

my STRATEGY

How Much Is an MBA Worth to You?

The *my*Strategy box at the end of Chapter 2 asked how much you would be willing to pay for the job you want—for a job that reflects your values. Here, we look at a different issue relating to worth: How much is an MBA worth over the course of your career?

Alongside the traditional two-year full-time MBA program, many business schools also offer evening MBAs and executive MBAs. Let's assume you know you want to pursue

an advanced degree, and you need to decide which program format is better for you (or you want to evaluate the choice you already made). You've narrowed your options to either (1) a two-year full-time MBA program, or (2) an executive MBA program at the same institution that is 18 months long with classes every other weekend. Let's also assume the price for tuition, books, and fees is $30,000 for the full-time program and $90,000 for the executive MBA program.

Which MBA program should you choose? Consider in your analysis the value, price, and cost concepts discussed in this chapter. Pay special attention to opportunity costs attached to different MBA program options.

ENDNOTES

1. *(Net profits / Invested capital)* is shorthand for *(Net operating profit after taxes [NOPAT]/ Total stockholders' equity + Total debt − Value of preferred stock).* See discussion of profitability ratios in Table 1, "When and How to Use Financial Measures to Assess Firm Performance," of the "How to Conduct a Case Analysis" module at the back of the text.

2. This ChapterCase is based on: 2012 SEC 10-K reports for Apple and BlackBerry.

3. This debate takes place in the following discourses, among others: Schmalensee, R. (1985), "Do markets differ much?" *American Economic Review* 75: 341–351; Rumelt, R. P. (1991), "How much does industry matter?" *Strategic Management Journal* 12: 167–185; Rumelt, R. P. (2003), "What in the world is competitive advantage?" *Policy Working Paper 2003-105,* UCLA; Porter, M. E. (1985), *Competitive Advantage: Creating and Sustaining Superior Performance* (New York: Free Press); McGahan, A. M., and M. E. Porter (1997), "How much does industry matter, really?" *Strategic Management Journal* 18: 15–30; McGahan A. M., and M. E. Porter (2002), "What do we know about variance in accounting profitability?" *Management Science* 48: 834–851; Hawawini, G., V. Subramanian, and P. Verdin (2003), "Is performance driven by industry- or firm-specific factors? A new look at the evidence," *Strategic Management Journal* 24: 1–16; McNamara, G., F. Aime, and P. Vaaler (2005), "Is performance driven by industry- or firm-specific factors? A reply to Hawawini, Subramanian, and

Verdin," *Strategic Management Journal* 26: 1075–1081; Hawawini, G., V. Subramanian, and P. Verdin (2005), "Is performance driven by industry- or firm-specific factors? A new look at the evidence: A response to McNamara, Aime, and Vaaler," *Strategic Management Journal* 26: 1083–1086; and Misangyi, V. F., H. Elms, T. Greckhamer, and J. A. Lepine (2006), "A new perspective on a fundamental debate: A multilevel approach to industry, corporate, and business unit effects," *Strategic Management Journal* 27: 571–590.

4. Rumelt, R. P. (2003), "What in the world is competitive advantage?"

5. For a discussion see: McGahan, A. M., and M. E. Porter (2002), "What do we know about variance in accounting profitability?" *Management Science,* 48: 834–851.

6. "The second coming of Apple through a magical fusion of man—Steve Jobs—and company, Apple is becoming itself again: The little anticompany that could," *Fortune,* November 9, 1998.

7. "RIM's new CEO sticks with strategy," *The Wall Street Journal,* January 24, 2012.

8. "Meet your new BlackBerry global creative director: Alicia Keys," *The Wall Street Journal,* January 30, 2013.

9. "RIM squeezes BlackBerry suppliers as economy stalls," *BusinessWeek,* April 13, 2009; and "Do you know who manufactured your BlackBerry?" *Forbes,* January 13, 2011.

10. http://aaplinvestors.net/stats/iphone/bbvsiphone/.

11. Hamel, G., and C. K. Prahalad (1994), *Competing for the Future* (Boston, MA: Harvard Business School Press).

12. Baruch, L. (2001), *Intangibles: Management, Measurement, and Reporting* (Washington, DC: Brookings Institution Press).

13. Cameron, W. B. (1967), *Informal Sociology: A Casual Introduction to Sociological Thinking* (New York: Random House).

14. Friedman, M. (2002), *Capitalism and Freedom,* 40th anniversary edition (Chicago, IL: University of Chicago Press).

15. Fama, E. (1970), "Efficient capital markets: A review of theory and empirical work," *Journal of Finance* 25: 383–417; Beechy, M., D. Gruen, and J. Vickrey (2000), "The efficient market hypothesis," a survey Research Discussion Paper, Federal Reserve Bank of Australia.

16. The three broad categories of companies by market cap are large cap (over $10 billion), mid cap ($2 billion to $10 billion), and small cap (less than $2 billion).

17. Alexander, J. (2007), *Performance Dashboards and Analysis for Value Creation* (Hoboken, NJ: Wiley-Interscience).

18. Microsoft 2012 Annual Report.

19. This section draws on: Christensen, C. M, and M. E. Raynor (2003), *The Innovator's Solution: Creating and Sustaining Successful*

Growth (Boston, MA: Harvard Business
School Press).

20. Speech given by Alan Greenspan on
December 5, 1996, at the American Enterprise
Institute.

21. "Irrational gloom," *The Economist,*
October 11, 2002.

22. Kaplan, R. S., and D. P. Norton (1992),
"The balanced scorecard: Measures that drive
performance," *Harvard Business Review,*
January–February: 71–79.

23. Ibid.

24. Govindarajan, V., and J. B. Lang (2002),
3M Corporation, case study, Tuck School of
Business at Dartmouth.

25. Rothaermel, F. T., and A. M. Hess (2010),
"Innovation strategies combined," *MIT Sloan
Management Review,* Spring: 12–15.

26. Huston, L., and N. Sakkab (2006), "Connect & Develop: Inside Procter & Gamble's
new model for innovation," *Harvard Business
Review,* March: 58–66.

27. Clarke, R. (2009), "Failure: The secret to
success," at http://dreams.honda.com/#/video_
fa; and see also: Prahalad, C. K., and G. Hamel
(1990), "The core competence of the corporation," *Harvard Business Review,* May–June.

28. Kaplan, R. S. (1993), "Implementing the
balanced scorecard at FMC Corporation: An
interview with Larry D. Brady," *Harvard
Business Review,* September–October:
143–147.

29. Norreklit, H. (2000), "The balance on
the balanced scorecard—A critical analysis
of some of its assumptions," *Management
Accounting Research* 11: 65–88; Jensen, M. C.
(2002), "Value Maximization, Stakeholder
Theory, and the Corporate Objective Function," in *Unfolding Stakeholder Thinking,*
Andriof, J., et al. (eds.) (Sheffield, UK:
Greenleaf Publishing).

30. Kaplan, R. S., and D. P. Norton (1992),
"The balanced scorecard: Measures that drive

performance"; Kaplan, R. S., and D. P. Norton
(2007), "Using the balanced scorecard as a
strategic management system," *Harvard Business Review,* July–August.

31. Lawrie, G., and I. Cobbold (2002),
"Development of the 3rd generation
balanced scorecard: Evolution of the balanced scorecard into an effective strategic
performance management tool," 2GC Working Paper, 2GC Limited, Albany House,
Market Street, Maidenhead, Berkshire, SL6
8BE UK.

32. Senge, P. M., B. Bryan Smith,
N. Kruschwitz, J. Laur, and S. Schley, (2010),
*The Necessary Revolution: How Individu-
als and Organizations Are Working Together
to Create a Sustainable World* (New York:
Crown).

33. Anderson, R. C. (2009), *Confessions
of a Radical Industrialist: Profits,
People, Purpose—Doing Business by
Respecting the Earth* (New York: St. Martin's
Press).

34. Norman, W., and C. MacDonald (2004),
"Getting to the bottom of 'triple bottom line,'"
Business Ethics Quarterly 14: 243–262.

35. Collins, J. C., and J. I. Porras (1994),
*Built to Last: Successful Habits of
Visionary Companies* (New York:
HarperBusiness), p. 93.

36. Anderson, R. C. (2009), *Confessions
of a Radical Industrialist,* p. 5; TED talk,
"Ray Anderson on the business logic of
sustainability," www.ted.com; and Perkins,
J. (2009), *Hoodwinked: An Economic Hit
Man Reveals Why the World Financial
Markets Imploded—and What We Need to
Do to Remake Them* (New York: Crown
Business), p. 107.

37. "Talent Report: What Workers Want
in 2012," published by The MacArthur
Foundation, www.netimpact.org/
whatworkerswant, defines three different
generations and describes their attributes

(on page 2) as shown in this chapter's
Exhibit 5.10.

38. Ibid.

39. Orlitzky, M., F. L. Schmidt, and
S. L. Rynes (2003), "Corporate social and
financial performance: A meta-analysis,"
Organization Studies 24: 403–441;
Margolis, J. D., and J. P. Walsh (2001), *People
and Profits? The Search for a Link between
a Company's Social and Financial Performance* (Mahwah, NJ: Erlbaum). However,
this relationship may not be linear, but rather
U-shaped, as shown in Barnett, M., and
R. M. Salomon (2012), "Does it pay to be
really good? Addressing the shape of the
relationship between social and financial performance," *Strategic Management Journal* 33:
1304–1320.

40. This discussion is based on: Adner,
R. (2012), *The Wide Lens. A New Strategy for
Innovation* (New York: Portfolio/Penguin);
and Amit, R., and C. Zott (2012), "Creating
value through business model innovation,"
MIT Sloan Management Review, Spring:
41–49.

41. "Zipcar: Entrepreneurial genius, public-
company failure," *The Wall Street Journal,*
January 2, 2013.

42. Dollar Shave Video: http://www.youtube
.com/dollarshaveclub.

43. "A David and Gillette story," *The
Wall Street Journal,* April 12, 2012; and
"Riding the momentum created by a
cheeky video," *The New York Times,* April
10, 2013.

44. Anderson, C. (2009), *Free: The Future of
a Radical Price* (New York: Hyperion).

45. See www.thepalladiumgroup.com for
examples.

46. http://www.forbes.com/sites/
causeintegration/2012/09/14/
the-bottom-line-of-corporate-good/.

Chapter 6

Business Strategy: Differentiation, Cost Leadership, and Integration

Learning Objectives

After studying this chapter, you should be able to:

LO 6-1 Define business-level strategy and describe how it determines a firm's strategic position.

LO 6-2 Examine the relationship between value drivers and differentiation strategy.

LO 6-3 Examine the relationship between cost drivers and the cost-leadership strategy.

LO 6-4 Assess the benefits and risks of cost-leadership and differentiation business strategies vis-à-vis the five forces that shape competition.

LO 6-5 Evaluate value and cost drivers that may allow a firm to pursue an integration strategy.

LO 6-6 Explain why it is difficult to succeed at an integration strategy.

LO 6-7 Describe and evaluate the dynamics of competitive positioning.

P&G's Strategic Position Weakens

WITH REVENUES OF $85 billion and business in over 180 countries, Procter & Gamble (P&G) is a global leader in consumer goods. Some of its category-defining brands include Ivory soap, Tide detergent, Crest toothpaste, Iams pet food, and Pampers diapers. Among its many offerings, P&G has 22 consumer brands in its lineup that each achieve over $1 billion in annual sales. P&G's iconic brands are a result of a clearly formulated and effectively implemented business strategy. The company pursues a differentiation strategy and attempts to create higher perceived value for its customers than its competitors by delivering products with unique features and attributes. Creating higher perceived value generally goes along with higher product costs due to greater R&D and promotion expenses, among other things. Successful differentiators, however, are able to command a premium price for their products.

In the summer of 2009, after 30 years with P&G, Robert McDonald was appointed CEO. Since then, P&G's strategic position has weakened considerably, and profit has declined for three straight years. P&G also lost market share in key "product-country combinations," including beauty in the U.S. and oral care in China. So what happened?

Some of today's problems are the result of P&G's $57 billion acquisition of Gillette in 2005, engineered by then-CEO A. G. Lafley. Although Gillette holds two-thirds market share of the $15 billion shaving industry, future incremental revenue growth for the entire company is now harder to achieve given P&G's larger base. Perhaps even more troubling is that Mr. Lafley focused P&G mainly on the U.S. market. Rather than inventing new product categories, P&G added more features to its existing brands such as Olay's extra-moisturizing creams and ultra-soft and sensitive Charmin toilet paper. The strategic decision to focus on the domestic market and to incrementally add more features to its existing products created two serious problems for P&G.

First, with the deep recession of 2008–2009, U.S. consumers moved away from higher-priced brands, such as those offered by P&G, to lower-cost private-label alternatives. Moreover, P&G's direct rivals in branded goods, such as Colgate-Palmolive, Kimberly-Clark, and Unilever, were faster in cutting costs and prices in response to more frugal customers. P&G also fumbled recent launches of reformulated products such as Tide Pods (detergent sealed in single-use pouches) and the Pantene line of shampoos and conditioners. The decline in U.S. demand hit P&G especially hard because the domestic market delivers about one-third of sales, but almost two-thirds of profits. Second, by focusing on the U.S. market, P&G not only missed out on the booming growth years that the emerging economies experienced, but it also left these markets to its rivals. As a consequence, Colgate-Palmolive, Kimberly-Clark, and Unilever all outperformed P&G in recent years.

To strengthen its competitive position, Mr. McDonald launched two strategic initiatives. First, P&G began to refocus its portfolio on the company's 40 most lucrative product-market combinations, which are responsible for about half of P&G's revenues but almost 70 percent of its profits. Part of this initiative was to expand P&G's presence in large emerging economies. Recently, P&G launched Tide in India and Pantene shampoos in Brazil. Moreover, P&G began to leverage its Crest brand globally, to take on Colgate-Palmolive's global dominance in toothpaste. Second, P&G implemented strict cost-cutting measures through eliminating all spending not directly related to selling. It also planned to shed 4,000 jobs, among other cost-reduction moves. Taken together, it hopes to cut costs by $10 billion by 2016.

The hope was that these two initiatives would strengthen P&G's strategic position by improving its differentiated appeal to command premium prices, while lowering its cost structure. By spring 2013, however, P&G's performance had further deteriorated. The company's board of directors brought back A. G. Lafley as CEO to replace Mr. McDonald. It remains to be seen if Mr. Lafley can turn around P&G, because some of the strategic decisions that led to a weakening of P&G's strategic position were made under his watch.[1]

After reading the chapter, you will find more about this case, with related questions, on page 189.

THE P&G CHAPTERCASE raises a number of issues that we will address in this chapter. P&G differentiates itself from competitors by offering branded consumer product goods with distinct features and attributes. This business strategy implies that P&G focuses on increasing the perceived value created for customers, which allows it to charge a premium price. This approach proved successful, especially in rich countries such as the United States. Over time, though, in response to changes in the external environment, the strategy needed to be fine-tuned. P&G took a fresh look at reinvigorating its business-level strategy in order to strengthen its competitive position. Future growth seems to lie with more cost-conscious consumers, both in the U.S. and global markets. Moreover, P&G needs to focus on consumers in large emerging economies, which it has traditionally neglected.

The two strategic initiatives launched were intended to strengthen P&G's competitive position. The first strategic initiative—refocusing P&G's brand portfolio on the company's 40 most lucrative product-market combinations—aimed at further enhancing its differentiated appeal. P&G's value proposition needs to be more compelling for its consumers. Top-line growth should also come from expanding into large emerging markets such as China, India, and Brazil with products especially reformulated and promoted to meet local preferences. To reduce pressures on profit margins, however, P&G must also control its cost structure, which is higher than that of its competitors. To address this problem, the company implemented strict cost-reduction measures.

The goal of the two strategic initiatives is to increase the perceived value of P&G's brands in the minds of the consumer, while lowering production costs. The combined effort should—if successful—increase P&G's economic value creation $(V - C;$ also called the *value gap)*. The expectation is that P&G's revised business strategy featured in the ChapterCase would strengthen its strategic position and help it regain its competitive advantage.

This chapter, the first in Part 2 on *strategy formulation,* takes a close look at business-level strategy. It deals with *how* to compete for advantage. Based on the analysis of the external and internal environments (presented in Part 1), the second step in the *AFI Strategy Framework* (see the strategy framework on page 161) is to formulate a business strategy that enhances the firm's chances of achieving a competitive advantage.

We begin our discussion of strategy formulation by defining *business-level strategy, strategic position,* and *generic business strategies.* We then take a close look at two key generic business strategies, introduced briefly in Chapter 1: *differentiation* and *cost leadership.* We pay special attention to value and cost drivers that managers can use to carve out a clear strategic profile. Next, we relate the two business-level strategies to the five forces in order to highlight their respective benefits and risks. We then introduce the notion of *integration strategy*—combining a differentiation and cost-leadership strategic position—and explain why trade-offs make this difficult to implement effectively. We look at changes in competitive positioning over time before concluding with practical *Implications for the Strategist.*

6.1 Business-Level Strategy: How to Compete for Advantage

Business-level strategy details the goal-directed actions managers take in their quest for competitive advantage when competing in a single product market.[2] It may involve a single product or a group of similar products that use the same distribution channel. It concerns the broad question, "How should we compete?" To formulate an appropriate business-level strategy, managers must answer the "who-what-why-and-how" questions of competition:

LO 6-1

Define business-level strategy and describe how it determines a firm's strategic position.

- *Who*—which customer segments—will we serve?
- *What* customer needs, wishes, and desires will we satisfy?
- *Why* do we want to satisfy them?
- *How* will we satisfy our customers' needs?[3]

business-level strategy The goal-directed actions managers take in their quest for competitive advantage when competing in a single product market.

To formulate an effective business strategy, managers need to keep in mind that competitive advantage is determined jointly by *industry* and *firm* effects. As shown in Exhibit 6.1, one route to competitive advantage is shaped by *industry effects,* while a second route is determined by *firm effects.* As discussed in Chapter 3, an industry's profit potential can be assessed using the five forces framework plus the availability of complements. Managers need to be certain that the business strategy is aligned with the five forces that shape competition. They can evaluate performance differences among clusters of firms in the same industry by conducting a strategic-group analysis. The concepts introduced in Chapter 4 are key in understanding *firm effects* because they allow us to look inside firms and explain why they differ based on their resources, capabilities, and competencies. It is also important to note that industry and firm effects are not independent, but rather they are *interdependent,* as shown by the two-pointed arrow connecting industry effects and firm effects.

At the firm level, performance is determined by value and cost positions *relative* to competitors. This is the firm's *strategic position.* Although P&G was once the global leader in branded consumer products, recently its value position relative to competitors declined because consumers did not value additional incremental features and reformulations as

EXHIBIT 6.1 / Industry and Firm Effects Jointly Determine Competitive Advantage

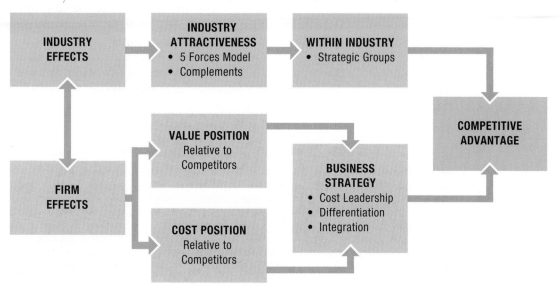

much as they valued lower prices. Moreover, P&G's relative cost position is weaker due to its higher cost structure, thereby reducing its ability to compete on price. As a consequence, P&G's strategic position weakened and it experienced a competitive disadvantage.

STRATEGIC POSITION

We noted (in Chapter 5) that competitive advantage is based on the difference between the *perceived value* a firm is able to create for consumers (V), captured by how much consumers are willing to pay for a product or service, and the total cost (C) the firm incurs to create that value. The greater the *economic value created* ($V - C$), the greater the firm's competitive advantage. To answer the business-level strategy question of how to compete, managers have two primary competitive levers at their disposal: value (V) and cost (C).

A firm's business-level strategy determines its *strategic position*—its strategic profile based on value creation and cost—in a specific product market. A firm attempts to stake out a valuable and unique position that meets customer needs while simultaneously creating as large a gap as possible between the value the firm's product creates and the cost required to produce it. Higher value tends to require higher cost. To achieve a desired strategic position, managers must make **strategic trade-offs**—choices between a cost *or* value position. Managers must address the tension between value creation (which tends to generate higher cost) and the pressure to keep cost in check so as not to erode the firm's economic value creation and profit margin. A business strategy is more likely to lead to a competitive advantage if it allows firms to either *perform similar activities differently,* or *perform different activities* than their rivals that result in creating more value or offering similar products or services at lower cost.[4]

GENERIC BUSINESS STRATEGIES

There are two fundamentally different generic business strategies—*differentiation* and *cost leadership*. A **differentiation strategy** seeks to create higher value for customers than the value that competitors create, by delivering products or services with unique features while keeping costs at the same or similar levels. A **cost-leadership strategy**, in contrast, seeks to create the same or similar value for customers by delivering products or services at a lower cost than competitors, enabling the firm to offer lower prices to its customers.

These two strategies are called *generic strategies* because they can be used by any organization—manufacturing or service, large or small, for-profit or nonprofit, public or private, U.S. or non-U.S.—in the quest for competitive advantage, independent of industry context. Differentiation and cost leadership require distinct strategic positions in order to increase a firm's chances to gain and sustain a competitive advantage.[5] Because value creation and cost tend to be positively correlated, there exist important trade-offs between value creation and low cost.

---

strategic trade-offs Choices between a cost *or* value position. Such choices are necessary because higher value tends to require higher cost.

differentiation strategy Generic business strategy that seeks to create higher value for customers than the value that competitors create, by delivering products or services with unique features while keeping the firm's cost structure at the same or similar levels.

cost-leadership strategy Generic business strategy that seeks to create the same or similar value for customers by delivering products or services at a lower cost than competitors, enabling the firm to offer lower prices to its customers.

Different generic strategies can lead to competitive advantage, even in the *same industry*. For example, Rolex and Timex both compete in the market for wristwatches, yet they follow different business strategies. Rolex follows a differentiation strategy: It creates a higher value for its watches by making higher-quality timepieces with unique features that last a lifetime and that bestow a perception of prestige and status upon their owners. Customers are willing to pay a steep premium for these attributes. Timex, in contrast, follows a cost-leadership strategy: It uses lower-cost inputs and efficiently produces a wristwatch of acceptable quality, highlights reliability and accuracy, and prices its timepieces at the low end of the market. The issue is not to compare Rolex and Timex directly—they compete in different market segments of the wristwatch industry. Both can achieve a competitive advantage using diametrically opposed business strategies. This is because both have a clear strategic profile. Rather, the idea is to compare Rolex's strategic position with the next-best differentiator (e.g., Ebel), and Timex's strategic position with the next-best, low-cost producer (e.g., Swatch).

When considering different business strategies, managers also must define the **scope of competition**—whether to pursue a specific, narrow part of the market or go after the broader market.[6] In the preceding example, Rolex focuses on a small market segment: affluent consumers who want to present a certain image. Timex offers watches for many different segments of the mass market.

Now we can combine the dimensions describing a firm's strategic position (*differentiation vs. cost*) with the scope of competition *(narrow vs. broad)*. As shown in Exhibit 6.2, by doing so we get the two major generic (or broad) business strategies *(cost leadership* and *differentiation)*, shown as the top two boxes in the matrix, and what are termed the *focused* version of each (shown as the bottom two boxes in the matrix). The focused versions of the strategies—**focused cost-leadership strategy** and **focused differentiation strategy**—are essentially the same as the broad generic strategies *except* that the competitive scope is narrower. The manufacturing company BIC pursues a focused cost-leadership strategy, offering disposable pens and cigarette lighters at a very low price (often free promotional giveaways by companies), while Mont Blanc pursues a focused differentiation strategy, offering exquisite pens priced at several hundred dollars.

The automobile industry provides an example of the *scope of competition.* Alfred P. Sloan, long-time president and CEO of GM, defined the carmaker's mission as providing *a car for every purse and purpose.* GM was one of the first to implement a multidivisional

EXHIBIT 6.2 / Strategic Position and Competitive Scope: Generic Business Strategies

SOURCE: Adapted from M. E. Porter (1980), *Competitive Strategy. Techniques for Analyzing Industries and Competitors* (New York: Free Press).

---

scope of competition The size—narrow or broad—of the market in which a firm chooses to compete.

focused cost-leadership strategy Same as the cost-leadership strategy except with a narrow focus on a niche market.

focused differentiation strategy Same as the differentiation strategy except with a narrow focus on a niche market.

structure in order to separate the brands into strategic business units, allowing each brand to create its unique strategic position within the broad automotive market. For example, the current GM product lineup ranges from the low-cost-positioned Chevy Spark, starting at a price of $12,000, to the highly differentiated Cadillac Escalade SUV priced at $74,000.

Tesla Motors, the maker of electric cars (featured in ChapterCase 3), offers a highly differentiated product and pursues only a small market segment. It uses a *focused differentiation strategy.* Tesla focuses on environmentally conscious consumers that are willing to pay a premium price. It offered its sporty Roadster for a base price of $110,000. In 2012, Tesla launched the Model S, a four-door sedan, starting at $62,000 (after a $7,500 federal tax credit). The company plans to sell only 20,000 vehicles a year,[7] equal to less than 0.20 percent U.S. market share of auto sales. Although Tesla Motors continues to broaden its product lineup with the new Model X (an SUV) and increase its scale, the company maintains its focused-differentiation strategy.

6.2 Differentiation Strategy: Understanding Value Drivers

LO 6-2

Examine the relationship between value drivers and differentiation strategy.

The goal of a generic differentiation strategy is to add unique features that will increase the perceived value of goods and services in the minds of the consumers so they are willing to pay a higher price. Ideally, a firm following a differentiation strategy aims to achieve in the minds of consumers a level of value creation that its competitors cannot easily match. The focus of competition in a differentiation strategy tends to be on unique product features, service, and new product launches, or on marketing and promotion rather than price. For example, the carpet company Interface is a leader in sustainability and offers innovative products such as its Cool Carpet, the world's first carbon-neutral floor covering. Interface's customers reward it with a willingness to pay a higher price for its environmentally friendly products.[8]

A company that uses a differentiation strategy can achieve a competitive advantage as long as its economic value created $(V - C)$ is greater than that of its competitors. Panel (a) in Exhibit 6.3 shows that Firm B, a differentiator, achieves a competitive advantage over Firm A. Firm B not only offers greater value than Firm A, but also achieves *cost parity* (meaning it has the same costs as Firm A). However, even if Firm B fails to achieve cost parity (which is often the case since higher value tends to go along with higher costs in terms of higher-quality raw materials, research and development, employee training to

EXHIBIT 6.3

Differentiation Strategy: Achieving Competitive Advantage

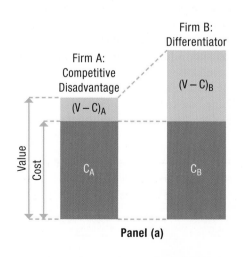

Panel (a)

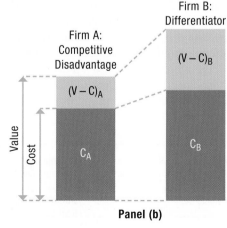

Panel (b)

provide superior customer service, and so on), it can still gain a competitive advantage if its economic value creation exceeds that of its competitors. This situation is depicted in Panel (b) of Exhibit 6.3. In both situations, Firm B's economic value creation, $(V - C)_B$, is greater than that of Firm A $(V - C)_A$. Firm B, therefore, achieves a competitive advantage because it has a higher value gap $[(V - C)_B > (V - C)_A]$ which allows it to charge a premium price, reflecting its higher value creation.

Although increased value creation is a defining feature of a differentiation strategy, managers must also control costs. Rising costs reduce economic value created and erode profit margins. Indeed, if cost rises too much as the firm attempts to create more perceived value for customers, its value gap shrinks, negating any differentiation advantage. Strategy Highlight 6.1 (next page) details how Whole Foods lost its competitive advantage mainly because of a failure to control costs effectively.

Although a differentiation strategy is generally associated with premium pricing, managers have an important second pricing option. When a firm is able to offer a differentiated product or service and can control its costs at the same time, it is able to gain market share from other firms by charging a similar price but offering more perceived value. By leveraging its differentiated appeal of superior customer service and quality, for example, Marriott offers a line of different hotels: its flagship Marriott full-service business hotel equipped to host large conferences; Residence Inn for extended stay; Marriott Courtyard for business travelers; and Marriott Fairfield Inn for inexpensive leisure and family travel.[9] Although these hotels are roughly comparable to competitors in price, they generally offer a higher perceived value. This difference between price and value allows Marriott to gain market share and post superior performance.

Managers can adjust a number of different levers to improve a firm's strategic position. These levers either increase perceived value or decrease costs. Here, we will study the most salient *value drivers* that managers have at their disposal (we look at cost drivers later).[10] They are:

- Product features
- Customer service
- Complements

These value drivers are related to a firm's expertise in, and organization of, different internal value chain activities. Although these are the most important value drivers, no such list can be complete. Applying the concepts introduced in this chapter should allow managers to identify other important value and cost drivers unique to their business.

When attempting to increase the perceived value of the firm's product or service offerings, managers must remember that the different value drivers contribute to competitive advantage *only if* their increase in value creation (ΔV) exceeds the increase in costs (ΔC). The condition of $\Delta V > \Delta C$ must be fulfilled if a differentiation strategy is to strengthen a firm's strategic position and thus enhance its competitive advantage.

PRODUCT FEATURES

One of the obvious but most important levers that managers can adjust are the product features and attributes, thereby increasing the perceived value of the product or service offering. Adding unique product features allows firms to turn commodity products into differentiated products commanding a premium price. Strong R&D capabilities are often needed to create superior product features. The luxury car maker BMW follows a differentiation strategy. It has a strong reputation for superior engineering, built through decades of continued R&D investments. As a result, a BMW M3, a sports coupé, comes with many

Strategy Highlight   6.1

Trimming Fat at Whole Foods Market

When four young entrepreneurs opened a small natural-foods store in Austin, Texas, in 1980, they never imagined it would one day turn into an international supermarket chain with stores in the United States, Canada, and the United Kingdom. Some 30 years later, with the acquisition of a close competitor, Wild Oats, Whole Foods now has 350 stores, employs more than 72,000 people, and earned $12 billion in revenue in 2012. Its mission is to offer the finest natural and organic foods available, maintain the highest quality standards in the grocery industry, and remain firmly committed to sustainable agriculture.

Whole Foods differentiates itself from competitors by offering top-quality foods obtained through sustainable agriculture. This business strategy implies that Whole Foods focuses on increasing the perceived value created for customers, which allows it to charge a premium price. In addition to natural and organic foods, it also offers a wide variety of prepared foods and luxury food items, such as $400 bottles of wine. The decision to sell high-ticket items incurs higher costs for the company because such products require more expensive in-store displays and more highly skilled workers, and many fresh items are perishable and require high turnover. Moreover, sourcing natural and organic food is generally done locally, limiting any scale advantages. Taken together, these actions reduce efficiency and drive up costs.

Given its unique strategic position as an upscale grocer offering natural, organic, and luxury food items, Whole Foods enjoyed a competitive advantage during the economic boom through early 2008. But as consumers became more budget conscious during the recession of 2008–2009, the company's financial performance deteriorated. Competitive intensity also increased markedly because basically every supermarket chain now offers organic food.

To revitalize Whole Foods, co-founder and co-CEO John Mackey decided to "trim fat" on two fronts: First, the supermarket chain refocused on its mission to offer wholesome and healthy food options. In Mackey's words, Whole Foods' offerings had included "a bunch of junk," including candy. Mackey is passionate about helping U.S. consumers overcome obesity in order to help reduce heart disease and diabetes. Given that, the new strategic intent at Whole Foods is to become the champion of healthy living not only by offering natural and organic food choices, but also by educating consumers with its new Healthy Eating initiative. Whole Foods Market now has "Take Action Centers" in every store to educate customers on many food-related topics such as genetic engineering, organic foods, pesticides, and sustainable agriculture.

Second, Whole Foods will trim fat by reducing costs. For example, it has expanded its private-label product line by 5 percent and now includes over 2,300 products at lower prices. Moreover, to attract more customers who buy groceries for an entire family or group, Whole Foods now offers volume discounts to compete with Costco and Sam's Club, the two largest membership chains in the U.S.

To offer its private-label line and volume-discount packages, Whole Foods is beginning to rely more on low-cost suppliers and is improving its logistics system to cover larger geographic areas more efficiently. By continuing to open new stores and thus increase scale, Whole Foods is hoping to drive costs down further. Co-CEO Walter Robb emphasizes how cost-cutting allows Whole Foods to lower its prices to bring in new customers, while maintaining its profit margin: "The only impediment you hear [from people about why they don't shop at Whole Foods] is that it's more expensive, right? Which is less true than it used to be, and if we can get through the price thing, then we can talk about what we want to talk about, which is the quality of the food."[11]

The strategic initiatives put in place to strengthen Whole Foods' strategic profile by clarifying its value proposition, and perhaps more importantly by reducing its cost, seem to be paying off. Whole Foods is now again experiencing superior performance in comparison to old-line grocery stores such as Kroger, Safeway, and even Walmart (the largest grocery retailer in the United States). A more clearly formulated business strategy allows Whole Foods to increase the value gap by improving its differentiated appeal to command premium prices, while keeping its cost structure in check at the same time.[12]

more performance features than regular sedans. The high-performance capabilities of an M3 also come with a premium price. In the kitchen-utensil industry, OXO also follows a differentiation strategy, highlighting product features. By following its "philosophy of making products that are easy to use for the widest spectrum of possible users,"[13] OXO differentiates its kitchen utensils through its patent-protected ergonomically designed soft black rubber grips.

CUSTOMER SERVICE

Managers can increase the perceived value of their firms' product or service offerings by focusing on customer service and responsiveness. For example, the online retailer Zappos earned a reputation for superior customer service by offering free shipping both ways: to the customer and for returns.[14] Zappos' managers didn't view this as an additional expense but rather as part of their marketing budget. Moreover, Zappos does not outsource its customer service and its associates do not use predetermined scripts. They are instead encouraged to build a relationship of trust with each individual customer. There seemed to be a good return on investment as word spread through the online shopping community. Competitors took notice, too; Amazon bought Zappos for over $1 billion.[15]

L.L.Bean was founded in 1912 to sell the waterproof "Maine Hunting Shoe"—a unique product that came with a guarantee of 100 percent satisfaction. The company built its business on superior customer service and customer satisfaction. Today, L.L.Bean's policy of "Shipped for Free. Guaranteed to Last." continues to focus on these strengths.

The hotel industry provides a second example of superior customer service. Following its mission, "We are Ladies and Gentlemen serving Ladies and Gentlemen," the Ritz-Carlton has become one of the world's leaders in providing a personalized customer experience based on sophisticated analysis of data gathered about each guest, including past choices. It offers personalized customer service that few hotel chains can match.

COMPLEMENTS

When studying industry analysis in Chapter 3, we identified the availability of complements as an important force determining the profit potential of an industry. Complements add value to a product or service when they are consumed in tandem. Finding complements, therefore, is an important task for managers in their quest to enhance the value of their offerings.

The introduction of AT&T U-verse is a recent example of managers leveraging complements to increase the perceived value of a service offering.[16] AT&T's U-verse service bundles high-speed Internet access, phone, and TV services. Service bundles can be further enhanced by DVR capabilities that allow users to pause live TV, to record up to four live TV shows at once, and to access video on demand. A DVR by itself is not very valuable, but included as a "free" add-on to subscribers, it turns into a complement that significantly enhances the perceived value of the service bundle. Leveraging complementary products allowed AT&T to break into the highly competitive television services market, significantly enhancing the value of its service offerings.

By choosing the differentiation strategy as the strategic position for a product, managers focus their attention on adding value to the product through its unique features that respond to customer preferences, customer service during and after the sale, or an effective marketing campaign that communicates the value of the product's features to the target market. Although this positioning involves increased costs (for example, higher-quality inputs or innovative research and development activities), customers will be willing to pay a premium price for the product or service that satisfies their needs and preferences. In the next section, we will discuss how managers formulate a cost-leadership strategy.

6.3 Cost-Leadership Strategy: Understanding Cost Drivers

LO 6-3

Examine the relationship between cost drivers and the cost-leadership strategy.

The goal of a cost-leadership strategy is to reduce the firm's cost below that of its competitors while offering adequate value. The *cost leader*, as the name implies, focuses its attention and resources on reducing the cost to manufacture a product or deliver service in order to offer lower prices to its customers. The cost leader optimizes all of its value chain activities to achieve a low-cost position. Although staking out the lowest-cost position in the industry is the overriding strategic objective, a cost leader still needs to offer products and services of acceptable value. As an example, GM and Korean car manufacturer Kia offer some models that compete directly with one another, yet Kia's cars tend to be produced at lower cost, thus providing a similar value proposition.

A cost leader can achieve a competitive advantage as long as its economic value created $(V - C)$ is greater than that of its competitors. Panel (a) in Exhibit 6.4 shows that Firm B, a cost leader, achieves a competitive advantage over Firm A because Firm B not only has lower cost than Firm A, but also achieves *differentiation parity* (meaning it creates the same value as Firm A). Thus, Firm B's economic value creation, $(V - C)_B$, is greater than that of Firm A $(V - C)_A$.

What if Firm B fails to create differentiation parity? Such parity is often hard to achieve because value creation tends to go along with higher costs, and Firm B's strategy is aimed at lower costs. Firm B can still gain a competitive advantage as long as its economic value creation exceeds that of its competitors. This situation is depicted in Panel (b) of Exhibit 6.4: Even with lower value (no differentiation parity) but lower cost, Firm B's economic value creation, $(V - C)_B$, still is greater than that of Firm A, $(V - C)_A$. For example, as the low-cost leader, Walmart was able to take market share from Kmart, which filed for bankruptcy in 2002.

In both situations in Exhibit 6.4, Firm B's economic value creation is greater than that of Firm A. Firm B achieves a competitive advantage in both cases. Either it can charge prices similar to its competitors and benefit from a greater profit margin per unit, or it can charge lower prices than its competition and gain higher profits from higher volume. Both variations of a cost-leadership strategy can result in competitive advantage.

Although companies successful at cost leadership must excel at controlling costs, this doesn't mean they can neglect value creation. Kia signals the quality of its cars with a five-year, 60,000-mile warranty, one of the more generous warranties in the industry. Walmart offers products of acceptable quality, including many brand-name products. Within the airline industry, Strategy Highlight 6.2 shows how Ryanair has been able to devise and implement a cost-leadership strategy.

EXHIBIT 6.4

Cost-Leadership Strategy: Achieving Competitive Advantage

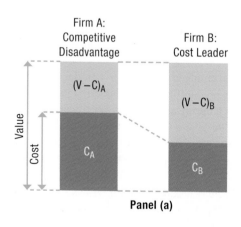

Panel (a)

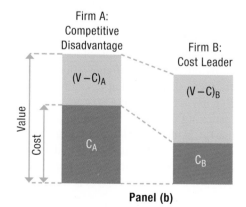

Panel (b)

Strategy Highlight 6.2

Ryanair: Lower Cost than the Low-Cost Leader!

Southwest Airlines is a classic example of a company pursuing a cost-leadership strategy.[17] Ryanair took a page out of Southwest Airlines' playbook and copied much of its business strategy. Ryanair is pursuing, however, an even more refined version in Europe. Headquartered in Dublin, Ireland, Ryanair proudly calls itself "the nastiest airline in the world" because of its relentless effort to drive down costs in order to offer rock-bottom air fares. In fact, Ryanair is the lowest-cost airline in the world. It flies some 300 Boeing 737 aircraft to over 175 destinations across Europe and North Africa, dozens of them priced as low as $20.

How can this be possible? Ryanair is the epitome of a no-frills airline: The seats don't recline, they have no seat-back pockets (safety cards are printed on the back of the seat in front of you), the older planes have no window shades, life jackets are in the overhead compartment, and thus only one very small carry-on bag is allowed. These choices lower aircraft-purchase costs and allow faster cleaning and turnaround. Ryanair has explored other ideas to further reduce costs, such as removing two toilets to add six more seats, removing rows of seats to offer standing-only areas (thus increasing capacity), charging

for the use of toilets, charging a premium for overweight passengers, having passengers carry their luggage to and from the airplane, and so on.

Although Ryanair's tickets are cheap, "extras" such as pillows, blankets, and a bottle of water require an additional fee. It costs $10 to check in online, but if you forget to do so, Ryanair will check you in at the airport for $100. The costs to check bags is above the industry standard ($80 per bag), and a whopping $125 per bag during the peak summer season (June 1 to September 30). Ryanair offers many other amenities, and its website has been described as a bazaar: You can book a hotel room, rent a car, get a credit card, buy insurance, and even gamble. In flight, attendants sell merchandise such as digital cameras ($137.50) and MP3 players ($165). It is estimated that more than 20 percent of Ryanair's revenues flow from such ancillary services, unusual for an airline. If you want to contact Ryanair, you can't via the website or e-mail; instead, you must use a premium-rate phone line.

Ryanair has pushed unbundling air travel into its many components furthest. Traditionally, air travel was sold at one price as a bundle of different services, which included "free" checking of bags as well as meals served on board. Ryanair offers the basic service (air travel only) for a low price, but charges a steep premium for all other items and upgrades.[18]

The most important *cost drivers* that managers can manipulate to keep their costs low are:

- Cost of input factors
- Economies of scale
- Learning-curve effects
- Experience-curve effects

However, this list is only a starting point; managers may consider other cost drivers, depending on the unique situation.

COST OF INPUT FACTORS

One of the most basic advantages a firm can have over its rivals is access to lower-cost input factors such as raw materials, capital, labor, and IT services. The South African company De Beers has long held a very strong position in the market for diamonds because it tightly controls the supply of raw materials. The aluminum producer Alcoa has access to lower-cost bauxite mines in the United States, which supply a key ingredient for aluminum. GE, through its GE Capital division, has a lower cost of capital than other industrial conglomerates such as Siemens, Philips, or ABB. To lower labor costs for some types of tasks, some companies outsource certain activities to India, known for its low-cost IT and accounting services, call centers, and medical-image reading.[19]

ECONOMIES OF SCALE

Firms with greater market share might be in a position to reap **economies of scale**, decreases in cost per unit as output increases. This relationship between unit cost and output is depicted in the first (left-hand) part of Exhibit 6.5: Cost per unit falls as output increases up to point Q_1. A firm whose output is closer to Q_1 has a cost advantage over other firms with less output. In this sense, bigger is better.

In the airframe-manufacturing industry, for example, reaping economies of scale and learning is critical for cost-competitiveness. The market for commercial airplanes is often not large enough to allow more than one competitor to reach sufficient scale to drive down unit cost. Boeing chose not to compete with Airbus in the market for superjumbo jets; rather, it decided to focus on a smaller, fuel-efficient airplane (the 787 Dreamliner, priced at roughly $225 million) that allows for long-distance, point-to-point connections. By early 2013, it had built over 100 Dreamliners with more than 800 orders for the new airplane.[20] Boeing can expect to reap significant economies of scale and learning, which will lower per-unit cost. At the same time, Airbus had delivered over 100 A380 superjumbos (sticker price: $390 million) with a total of 262 orders on its books.[21] If both companies would have chosen to compete head-on in each market segment, the resulting per-unit cost for each airplane would have been much higher because neither could have achieved significant economies of scale (overall their market share split is roughly 50–50).

What causes per-unit cost to drop as output increases (up to point Q_1)? Economies of scale allow firms to:

- Spread their fixed costs over a larger output.
- Employ specialized systems and equipment.
- Take advantage of certain physical properties.

EXHIBIT 6.5

Economies of Scale, Minimum Efficient Scale, and Diseconomies of Scale

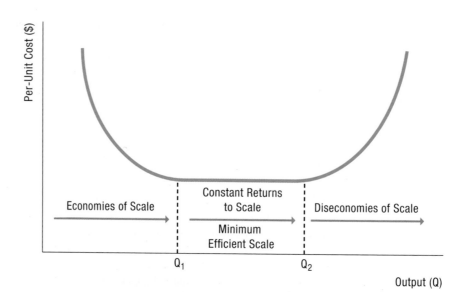

SPREADING FIXED COSTS OVER LARGER OUTPUT. Larger output allows firms to spread their fixed costs over more units. That is why gains in market share are often critical to drive down per-unit cost. Between 2007 and 2009, Microsoft spent approximately $25 billion on R&D, a significant portion of it on its new Windows 7 operating system.[22] This R&D expense was a fixed cost Microsoft had to incur before a single copy of Windows 7 was sold. However, once the initial version of the new software was completed, the marginal cost of each additional copy was basically zero, especially for copies sold in digital form online. Given that Microsoft dominates the operating system market for personal computers (PCs) with more than 90 percent market share, it sold several hundred million copies of Windows 7, thereby spreading its huge fixed cost of development over a large output. Microsoft's large installed base of Windows operating systems throughout the world provided it with competitive advantage, because it could leverage its economies of scale to drive down the per-unit cost for each additional copy of Windows 7.

Microsoft's advantage due to its large installed base on personal computers, however, is no longer as valuable.[23] Due to the shift to mobile computing, demand for PCs has been in free-fall in recent years. Before 2010, growth in the PC industry often exceeded more than 20 percent a year. Since then, the market for PCs has declined rapidly. The launch of Microsoft's newest operating system—Windows 8—was disappointing. A key feature of Windows 8 was the ability to straddle both personal computers and mobile devices by providing a dual interface, but the feature left consumers confused. In mobile operating systems, Google (Android) and Apple (iOS) are the clear leaders, while Microsoft's (Windows) market share is miniscule (3 percent in smartphones and 7 percent in tablets).

EMPLOYING SPECIALIZED SYSTEMS AND EQUIPMENT. Larger output also allows firms to invest in more specialized systems and equipment, such as enterprise resource planning (ERP) software or manufacturing robots. GM introduced the Chevy Volt in the 2011 model year, its first plug-in hybrid vehicle. It is priced at about $40,000, almost twice as expensive as a Toyota Prius. Yet GM is counting on selling the Chevy Volt in large numbers so that specialized robotics equipment can be employed in a cost-effective fashion. This in turn should drive down production costs, and allow GM to lower the price for the Chevy Volt.[24]

TAKING ADVANTAGE OF CERTAIN PHYSICAL PROPERTIES. Economies of scale also occur because of certain physical properties. One such property is known as the *cube-square rule:* The volume of a body such as a pipe or a tank increases disproportionately more than its surface. This same principle makes big-box retail stores such as Walmart, Best Buy, the Home Depot, and Toys"R"Us cheaper to build and run. They can also stock much more merchandise and handle inventory more efficiently. Their huge size makes it difficult for department stores or small retailers to compete on cost and selection.

Look again at Exhibit 6.5. The output range between Q_1 and Q_2 in the figure is considered the **minimum efficient scale (MES)** in order to be cost-competitive. Between Q_1 and Q_2, the returns to scale are constant. It is the output range needed to bring the cost per unit down as much as possible, allowing a firm to stake out the lowest-cost position achievable through economies of scale. If the firm's output range is less than Q_1 or more than Q_2, the firm is at a cost disadvantage.

With more than four million Prius cars sold since its introduction in 1997, Toyota has been able to reach the minimum efficient scale part of the per-unit cost curve. This allows the company to offer the car at a relatively low price and still make a profit.

The concept of minimum efficient scale applies not only to manufacturing processes but also to managerial tasks such as how to organize work. Due to investments in specialized technology and equipment (e.g., electric arc furnaces), Nucor is able to reach MES

minimum efficient scale (MES) Output range needed to bring down the cost per unit as much as possible, allowing a firm to stake out the lowest-cost position that is achievable through economies of scale.

with much smaller batches of steel than larger, fully vertically integrated steel companies using older technology. Nucor's optimal plant size is about 500 people, which is much smaller than at larger integrated steel makers such as U.S. Steel (which often employs thousands of workers per plant).[25] Of course, minimum efficient scale depends on the specific industry: The average per-unit cost curve, depicted conceptually in Exhibit 6.5, is a reflection of the underlying production function, which is determined by technology and other input factors.

Benefits to scale cannot go on indefinitely, though. Bigger is not always better; in fact, sometimes bigger is worse. Beyond Q_2 in Exhibit 6.5, firms experience **diseconomies of scale**—increases in cost as output increases. Why? As firms get too big, the complexity of managing and coordinating raises the cost, negating any benefits to scale. Large firms tend to become overly bureaucratic, with too many layers of hierarchy. They grow inflexible and slow in decision making. To avoid problems associated with diseconomies of scale, Gore Associates, maker of GORE-TEX fabric, Glide dental floss, and many other innovative products, breaks up its company into smaller units. Managers at Gore Associates found that employing about 150 people per plant allows them to avoid diseconomies of scale. Gore's Ben Hen uses a simple rule: "We put 150 parking spaces in the lot, and when people start parking on the grass, we know it's time to build a new plant."[26]

Finally, there are also physical limits to scale. Airbus is pushing the envelope with its A380 aircraft, which can hold more than 850 passengers and fly up to 8,200 miles (enough to travel non-stop from Boston to Hong Kong at about 600 mph). The goal, of course, is to drive down the cost of the average seat-mile flown (CASM, a standard cost metric in the airline industry). It remains to be seen whether the A380 superjumbo will enable airlines to reach minimum efficient scale or will simply be too large to be efficient. For example, boarding and embarking procedures must be streamlined in order to accommodate more than 850 people in a timely and safe manner. Many airports around the world will need to be retrofitted with longer and wider runways to allow the superjumbo to take off and land.

Taken together, *scale economies* are critical to driving down a firm's cost and strengthening a cost-leadership position. Although managers need to increase output to operate at a minimum efficient scale (between Q_1 and Q_2 in Exhibit 6.5), they also need to be watchful not to drive scale beyond Q_2, where they would encounter diseconomies. Monitoring the firm's cost structure closely over different output ranges allows managers to fine-tune operations and benefit from economies of scale.

LEARNING CURVE

Learning by doing can also drive down cost. As individuals and teams engage repeatedly in an activity, whether writing computer code, developing new medicines, or building submarines, they learn from their cumulative experience.[27] *Learning curves* were first documented in aircraft manufacturing as the United States ramped up production in the 1930s, prior to its entry into World War II.[28] Every time production was doubled, the per-unit cost dropped by a predictable and constant rate (approximately 20 percent).[29] This important relationship is captured in Exhibit 6.6, where different colors denote different levels of learning curves: 90 percent (blue), 80 percent (green), and 70 percent (brown). As learning occurs, you move down the learning curve. The steeper the learning curve, the more learning takes place. For example, a 90 percent learning curve indicates that per-unit cost drops 10 percent every time output is doubled. A 70 percent learning curve indicates a 30 percent drop every time output is doubled.

diseconomies of scale Increases in cost per unit when output increases.

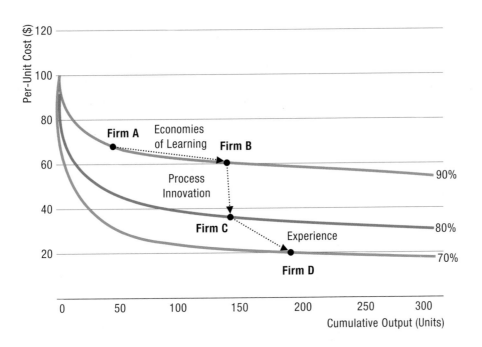

EXHIBIT 6.6

Gaining Competitive Advantage Through Leveraging Learning- and Experience-Curve Effects

It is not surprising that a learning curve was first observed in aircraft manufacturing. An aircraft is an extremely complex industrial product; a modern commercial aircraft can contain more than five million different parts, compared with a few thousand for a car. The more complex the production process, the more learning effects we can expect. As cumulative output increases, managers learn how to optimize the process and workers improve their performance through repetition. Learning curves are a robust phenomenon that have been observed in many industries, not only in manufacturing processes such as building airplanes, cars, ships, and semiconductors, but also in alliance management, franchising, and health care.[30] For example, physicians who perform only a small number of cardiac surgeries per year can have a patient mortality rate five times higher than physicians who perform the same surgery more frequently.[31]

There are some important differences between economies of scale and learning effects:

- Learning effects occur *over time* as output is accumulated, while economies of scale are captured at *one point in time* when output is increased. Although learning declines at some point (as shown in Exhibit 6.6, learning curves flatten out), there are no *diseconomies to learning* (unlike *diseconomies to scale* as shown in Exhibit 6.5's past output Q_2).

- In some production processes (e.g., a simple one-step process in the manufacture of steel rods), effects from economies of scale can be quite significant, while learning effects are minimal. In contrast, in some professions (brain surgery or the practice of estate law), learning effects can be substantial, while economies of scale are minimal. Managers need to understand this subtle but important difference in order to calibrate their business-level strategy. For example, if a firm's cost advantage is due to economies of scale, a manager should be less concerned about employee turnover (and thus a potential loss in learning) and more concerned with drops in production runs. In contrast, if the firm's low-cost position is based on complex learning, managers should be much more concerned if a key employee (e.g., a star researcher at a pharmaceutical company) was to leave.

EXPERIENCE CURVE

The concept of an *experience curve* attempts to capture both learning effects *and* process improvements.[32] In this perspective, economies of learning allow movement down a *given* learning curve based on current production technology. By moving further down a given learning curve than competitors, a firm can gain a competitive advantage. For example, Exhibit 6.6 shows that Firm B is further down the blue (90 percent) learning curve than Firm A. Firm B leverages economies of learning due to larger cumulative output to gain an advantage over Firm A.

As we know, however, technology and production processes do not stay constant. *Process innovation*—a new method or technology to produce an existing product—may initiate a new and steeper learning curve. If Firm C is able to implement a new production process (such as lean manufacturing), it initiates an entirely new and steeper learning curve. In Exhibit 6.6, Firm C is able to gain a competitive advantage over B through process innovation. This allows Firm C to jump down to the green (80 percent) learning curve, reflecting the new and lower-cost production process introduced.

Also as shown in Exhibit 6.6, by capturing *experience-curve effects* (learning effects plus process innovation), Firm D is breaking away from Firm C, gaining a competitive advantage. Firm D is able to implement a cost-leadership strategy and enjoy a competitive advantage over Firms A, B, and C. Taken together, learning by doing allows a firm to lower its per-unit costs by moving down a given learning curve, while combining experience-based learning *and* process innovation allows the firm to leapfrog to a steeper learning curve, thereby further driving down its per-unit costs.

In summary, by choosing a cost-leadership strategy, managers must focus their attention on lowering the overall costs of producing the product or service while maintaining an acceptable level of quality that will serve the needs of the customer. Cost leaders appeal to the price-conscious buyer, whose main criterion is the price of the product or service. By attending to the reduction of costs in each value chain activity, managers aim to achieve the lowest cost position in the industry. This provides the ability to offer the lowest price in the market and the consequent ability to attract an increased volume of sales. As successful cost leaders such as Walmart illustrate (*"Every Day Low Prices"*), this strategic position can be a very profitable business.

6.4 Business-Level Strategy and the Five Forces: Benefits and Risks

LO 6-4

Assess the benefits and risks of cost-leadership and differentiation business strategies vis-à-vis the five forces that shape competition.

The business-level strategies introduced in this chapter allow firms to carve out strong strategic positions that enhance the likelihood of gaining and sustaining competitive advantage. The five forces model introduced in Chapter 3 helps managers assess the forces—threat of entry, power of suppliers, power of buyers, threat of substitutes, and rivalry among existing competitors—that make some industries more attractive than others. With this understanding of industry dynamics, managers use one of the generic business-level strategies to protect themselves against the forces that drive down profitability.[33] Exhibit 6.7 details the relationship between competitive positioning and the five forces. In particular, it highlights the benefits and risks of cost-leadership and differentiation business strategies, which we discuss next.

COST-LEADERSHIP STRATEGY: BENEFITS AND RISKS

A cost-leadership strategy is defined by obtaining the lowest-cost position in the industry while offering acceptable value. The cost leader, therefore, is protected from other competitors because of having the lowest cost. If a price war ensues, the low-cost leader will be the last firm standing; all other firms will be driven out as margins evaporate. Since reaping

EXHIBIT 6.7 / Competitive Positioning and the Five Forces: Benefits and Risks
of Cost-Leadership and Differentiation Business Strategies

Competitive Force	Cost Leadership		Differentiation	
	Benefits	**Risks**	**Benefits**	**Risks**
Threat of entry	• Protection against entry due to economies of scale	• Erosion of margins • Replacement	• Protection against entry due to intangible resources such as a reputation for innovation, quality, or customer service	• Erosion of margins • Replacement
Power of suppliers	• Protection against increase in input prices, which can be absorbed	• Erosion of margins	• Protection against increase in input prices, which can be passed on to customers	• Erosion of margins
Power of buyers	• Protection against decrease in sales prices, which can be absorbed	• Erosion of margins	• Protection against decrease in sales prices, because well-differentiated products or services are not perfect imitations	• Erosion of margins
Threat of substitutes	• Protection against substitute products through further lowering of prices	• Replacement, especially when faced with innovation	• Protection against substitute products due to differential appeal	• Replacement, especially when faced with innovation
Rivalry among existing competitors	• Protection against price wars because lowest-cost firm will win	• Focus of competition shifts to non-price attributes • Lowering costs to drive value creation below acceptable threshold	• Protection against competitors if product or service has enough differential appeal to command premium price	• Focus of competition shifts to price • Increasing differentiation of product features that do not create value but raise costs • Increasing differentiation to raise costs above acceptable threshold

SOURCE: Based on M. E. Porter, "The five competitive forces that shape strategy," *Harvard Business Review,* January 2008; and M. E. Porter (1980), *Competitive Strategy: Techniques for Analyzing Industries and Competitors* (New York: Free Press).

economies of scale is critical to reaching a low-cost position, the cost leader is likely to have a large market share, which in turn reduces the threat of entry.

A cost leader is also fairly well isolated from threats of powerful suppliers to increase input prices, because it is more able to absorb price increases through accepting lower profit margins. Likewise, a cost leader can absorb price reductions more easily when demanded by powerful buyers. Should substitutes emerge, the low-cost leader can try to fend them off by further lowering its prices to reinstall relative value with the substitute. For example, Walmart tends to be fairly isolated from these threats. Walmart's cost structure combined with its large volume allows it to work with suppliers in keeping prices low, to the extent that suppliers are often the party who experiences a profit margin squeeze.

Although a cost-leadership strategy provides some protection against the five forces, it also carries some risks. If a new entrant with new and relevant expertise enters the market, the low-cost leader's margins may erode due to loss in market share while it attempts to learn new capabilities. For example, Walmart faces challenges to its cost leadership: Target has had success due to its superior merchandising capabilities. The Dollar Store has drawn customers who prefer a smaller format than the big box of Walmart. The risk of replacement is particularly pertinent if a potent substitute emerges due to an innovation. Leveraging e-commerce, Amazon has become a potent substitute and thus a powerful threat to many brick-and-mortar retail outlets including Barnes & Noble, Best Buy, The Home Depot, and even Walmart. Powerful suppliers and buyers may be able to reduce margins so much that the low-cost leader could have difficulty covering the cost of capital, and lose the potential for a competitive advantage.

The low-cost leader also needs to stay vigilant to keep its cost the lowest in the industry. Over time, competitors can beat the cost leader by implementing the same business strategy, but more effectively. Although keeping its cost the lowest in the industry is imperative, the cost leader must not forget that it needs to create an acceptable level of value. If continuously lowering costs leads to a value proposition that falls below an acceptable threshold, the low-cost leader's market share will evaporate. Finally, the low-cost leader faces significant difficulties when the focus of competition shifts from price to non-price attributes.

DIFFERENTIATION STRATEGY: BENEFITS AND RISKS

A differentiation strategy is defined by establishing a strategic position that creates higher perceived value while controlling costs. The successful differentiator is able to stake out a unique strategic position, where it can benefit from imperfect competition (as discussed in Chapter 3), and command a premium price. A well-executed differentiation strategy reduces rivalry among competitors.

A successful differentiation strategy is likely to be based on unique or specialized features of the product, on an effective marketing campaign, or on intangible resources such as a reputation for innovation, quality, and customer service. A rival would need to improve the product features as well as build a similar or more effective reputation in order to gain market share. The threat of entry is reduced: Competitors will find such intangible advantages time-consuming and costly, and maybe impossible, to imitate. If the source of the differential appeal is intangible rather than tangible (e.g., reputation rather than observable product and service features), a differentiator is even more likely to sustain its advantage.

Moreover, if the differentiator is able to create a significant difference between perceived value and current market prices, the differentiator will not be so threatened by increases in input prices due to powerful suppliers. Although an increase in input factors could erode margins, a differentiator is likely able to pass on price increases to its customers as long as its value creation exceeds the price charged. Since a successful differentiator creates perceived value in the minds of consumers and builds customer loyalty, powerful buyers demanding price decreases are unlikely to emerge. A strong differentiated position also reduces the threat of substitutes, because the unique features of the product have been created to appeal to customer preferences, keeping them loyal to the product. By providing superior quality beverages and other food items combined with a great customer experience and a global presence, Starbucks has built a strong differentiated appeal. It has cultivated a loyal following of customers who reward it with repeat business.

The viability of a differentiation strategy is severely undermined when the focus of competition shifts to price rather than value-creating features. This can happen when differentiated products become commoditized and an acceptable standard of quality has emerged across rival firms. Although the iPhone was a highly differentiated product when first introduced in 2007, touch-based screens and other once-innovative features are now standard in smartphones. Indeed, Android-based smartphones held 70 percent market share in 2012.[34] A differentiator also needs to be careful not to overshoot its differentiated appeal by adding product features that raise costs but not the perceived value in the minds of consumers. Finally, a differentiator needs to be vigilant that its costs of providing uniqueness do not rise above the customer's willingness to pay.

It is important to note that none of the business-level strategies depicted in Exhibit 6.2 (cost leadership, differentiation, and focused variations thereof) is inherently superior. The success of each is context-dependent and relies on two factors:

- How well the strategy leverages the firm's internal strengths while mitigating its weaknesses; and
- How well it helps the firm exploit external opportunities while avoiding external threats.

There is no single correct generic strategy for a specific industry. The deciding factor is that the chosen business strategy provides a strong position that attempts to maximize economic value creation and is effectively implemented.

6.5 Integration Strategy: Combining Cost Leadership and Differentiation

Competitive conditions in an industry may require firms to develop skills in lowering costs as well as adding uniqueness—particularly in globalized industries. For example, success may require lowering costs in order to compete with firms in countries with lower labor costs and may require adding special features to respond to local customer preferences in individual country markets. Since either increasing perceived value or lowering production costs can increase a firm's competitive advantage, it is tempting to conclude that managers should be focusing on *both efforts*. To accomplish this, they would need to integrate two different strategic positions: differentiation *and* low cost.[35] Managers should not pursue this complex strategy unless they are able to reconcile the conflicting requirements of each generic strategy.

A successful **integration strategy** requires that trade-offs between differentiation and low cost are reconciled. This is often difficult because differentiation and low cost are distinct strategic positions that require the firm to effectively manage internal value chain activities that are fundamentally different from one another. For example, a cost leader would focus research and development on process technologies in order to improve efficiency, but a differentiator would focus research and development on product technologies in order to add uniqueness. When successful, investments in differentiation and low cost are not substitutes but are complements, providing important spill-over effects. An integration strategy allows a firm to offer a differentiated product or service at low cost. Exhibit 6.8 shows how a successfully formulated integration strategy combines both a differentiation and low-cost position. Exhibit 6.8 also shows the consequence of an integration strategy gone bad—the firm ends up being "stuck in the middle," meaning the firm has neither a clear differentiation nor a clear cost-leadership profile. We discuss the potential pitfalls of an integration strategy in detail next.

integration strategy
Business-level strategy that successfully combines differentiation and cost-leadership activities.

EXHIBIT 6.8 / Integration Strategy vs. "Stuck in the Middle"

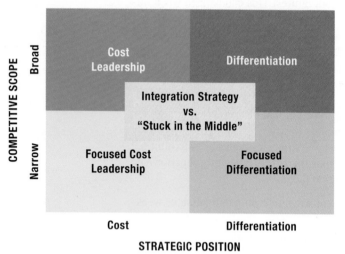

Being successful at an integration strategy doesn't imply that the firm must be the highest-value creator *and* the lowest-cost producer in its respective industry. Whether an integration strategy can lead to competitive advantage depends on the *difference* between value creation (V) and cost (C), and on the resulting magnitude of economic value created ($V - C$). What matters in gaining competitive advantage is the *relative* difference in economic value creation in comparison to industry rivals. The goal of an integration strategy is therefore to achieve a larger economic value created than that of rivals pursuing a differentiation or low-cost–leadership strategy. This is what Target, a large retailer with some 2,000 stores in North America, is attempting to accomplish. Exhibit 6.9 compares the value and cost positions of three retail chains: Nordstrom, Target, and Walmart. Each of these companies has succeeded in carving out a well-defined strategic position within the cosmetics world: Nordstrom is a differentiator; Walmart is a cost leader; Target is an integrator.

Nordstrom is an upscale retailer pursuing a differentiation strategy by focusing on a superior customer experience in a luxury department store setting. Target has been able to effectively compete with Nordstrom mostly by achieving a much lower cost position, while offering an acceptable shopping experience when compared with Nordstrom. On the other hand, Target has been able to compete with Walmart by building equivalent skills in efficient logistics expertise. Target almost achieves cost parity with Walmart. At the same time, Target outdoes Walmart in product selection, merchandising, and store layout so that its stores offer a higher-quality shopping experience for the customer. Target creates significantly more value in the minds of customers than does Walmart with its no-frills approach. The key point is that if Target is successful with its integration strategy, it achieves the highest economic value [in Exhibit 6.9, $(V - C)_{Nordstrom} < (V - C)_{Target} > (V - C)_{Walmart}$].

A successfully implemented integration strategy allows firms two pricing options: First, the firm can charge a higher price than the cost leader, reflecting its higher value creation and thus generating greater profit margins. Second, the firm can lower its price below that of the differentiator because of its lower-cost structure. If the firm offers lower prices than the differentiator, it can gain market share and make up the loss in margin through increased sales.

EXHIBIT 6.9 / Target's Attempt at Achieving Competitive Advantage by Pursuing an Integration Strategy

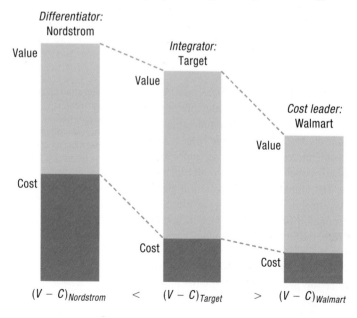

VALUE AND COST DRIVERS OF INTEGRATION STRATEGY

For an integration strategy to succeed, managers must resolve trade-offs between the two generic strategic positions—low cost and differentiation. Some possible levers they can use to overcome these challenges include quality, economies of scope, innovation, and the firm's structure, culture, and routines. These are critical: They allow managers to simultaneously *increase* perceived value and *lower* cost. Although we discuss each of these value and cost drivers individually, they are *interdependent*. For example, process innovations such as lean manufacturing contribute to better quality and customer service, which reinforce one another and enhance the brand of a product or service. Here, we will study the most salient value *and* cost drivers that managers can use to pursue an integration strategy. They are:

LO 6-5

Evaluate value and cost drivers that may allow a firm to pursue an integration strategy.

- Quality
- Economies of scope
- Customization
- Innovation
- Structure, culture, and routines

QUALITY. The quality of a product denotes its durability and reliability. Quality not only can increase a product's perceived value, but also can lower its cost. Through techniques such as total quality management, companies design and build products with quality in mind, while increasing their differentiated appeal. By building in better quality, companies lower the cost of both production and after-sale service requirements. From the customer's perspective, the product has increased value because it reduces the total cost of ownership. Quality is a two-pronged activity: It raises economic value creation $(V - C)$ by simultaneously increasing V and lowering C.

ECONOMIES OF SCOPE. We saw that economies of scale allow a firm to lower its per-unit cost as its output increases. The concept **economies of scope** describes the savings that come from producing two (or more) outputs at less cost than producing each output individually, even though using the same resources and technology. Starbucks, for example, is already set up to boil purified water for its hot coffee beverages; thus, it reaps economies of scope when it offers tea in addition to coffee. As a result, Starbucks lowers its cost structure by sharing its production assets over multiple outputs, while increasing its menu and thus its differentiated appeal.

economies of scope
Savings that come from producing two (or more) outputs at less cost than producing each output individually, despite using the same resources and technology.

mass customization
The manufacture of a large variety of customized products or services at a relatively low unit cost.

CUSTOMIZATION. Customization allows firms to go beyond merely adding differentiating features to tailoring products and services for specific customers. Advances in manufacturing and information technology have made feasible **mass customization**—the manufacture of a large variety of customized products or services done at a relatively low unit cost.[36] Customization and low cost were once opposing goals—you could have one or the other, but not both. In the car industry, Toyota was the first to introduce lean manufacturing, allowing it to mass customize vehicles and produce higher quality at a lower per-unit cost. Other companies are able to conquer this trade-off by using the Internet. You can design your own T-shirts at threadless.com or create customized sneakers at nike.com. BMW allows you to design your customized vehicle online and then follow the manufacturing progress in real time.

INNOVATION. Broadly defined, *innovation* describes any new product and process, or any modification of existing ones.[37] Innovation is frequently required to resolve existing trade-offs when companies pursue an integration strategy.

International furniture retailer IKEA orchestrates different internal value chain activities to reconcile the tension between differentiation and cost leadership in order to carve out a unique strategic position. IKEA uses innovation in furniture design, engineering, and store design to solve the trade-offs between value creation and production cost. Josephine Rydberg-Dumont, president of IKEA Sweden, highlights how difficult resolving this trade-off is: "Designing beautiful-but-expensive products is easy. Designing beautiful products that are inexpensive and functional is a huge challenge."[38] IKEA leverages its deep design and engineering expertise to offer furniture that is stylish and functional and that can be easily assembled by the consumer. IKEA also focuses on lowering cost by displaying its products in a warehouse-like setting, thus reducing inventory cost. Customers serve themselves, and then transport the furniture to their homes in IKEA's signature flat-packs for assembly. In this way, IKEA is able to pursue an integration strategy, leveraging innovation to increase the perceived value of its products, while simultaneously lowering its cost.

Given its importance in a firm's quest for competitive advantage, we'll discuss innovation as a business strategy in depth in Chapter 7.

STRUCTURE, CULTURE, AND ROUTINES.

A firm's structure, culture, and routines are critical when pursuing an integration strategy. The challenge that managers face is to structure their organizations so that they both control cost *and* allow for creativity that can lay the basis for differentiation. Doing the two together is hard to accomplish. Achieving a low-cost position requires an organizational structure that relies on strict budget controls, while differentiation requires an organizational structure that allows creativity and customer responsiveness to thrive, which typically necessitates looser organizational structures and controls.

ambidextrous organization An organization able to balance and harness different activities in trade-off situations.

The goal for managers who want to pursue an integration strategy should be to build an **ambidextrous organization**, one that enables managers to balance and harness different activities in trade-off situations.[39] Here, the trade-offs to be addressed involve the simultaneous pursuit of low-cost and differentiation strategies. Notable management practices that companies use to resolve this trade-off include flexible and lean manufacturing systems, total quality management, just-in-time inventory management, and Six Sigma.[40] Other management techniques that allow firms to reconcile cost and value pressures are the use of teams in the production process, as well as decentralized decision making at the level of the individual customer.

Ambidexterity describes a firm's ability to address trade-offs not only at one point but also over time. It encourages managers to balance *exploitation* (applying current knowledge to enhance firm performance in the short term) with *exploration* (searching for new knowledge that may enhance a firm's future performance).[41] For example, while Intel focuses on maximizing sales from its *current* cutting-edge microprocessors, it also has several different teams with different time horizons working on *future* generations of microprocessors.[42] In ambidextrous organizations, managers constantly analyze their existing business processes and routines, looking for ways to change them in order to resolve trade-offs across internal value chain activities and time.[43] Given the importance of a firm's structure, culture, and routines to gaining and sustaining competitive advantage, we dedicate Part 3, Strategy Implementation, to discussing this important topic in detail.

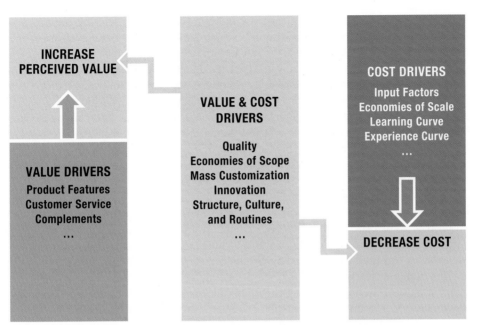

EXHIBIT 6.10 /

Value and Cost
Drivers

Exhibit 6.10 provides a summary of these drivers and their effects. In particular, the exhibit highlights drivers that uniquely affect either value creation or low cost (used for differentiation *or* cost-leadership strategies) and drivers that simultaneously increase value while lowering cost (used for integration strategies).

INTEGRATION STRATEGY GONE BAD: "STUCK IN THE MIDDLE"

Although appealing in a theoretical sense, an integration strategy is actually quite difficult to translate into reality. The reason is that differentiation and cost leadership are distinct strategic positions that require important trade-offs.[44] An integration strategy is difficult to implement because it requires the reconciliation of fundamentally different strategic positions—differentiation and low cost—which in turn require distinct internal value chain activities (see Chapter 4) in order to allow the firm to increase value *and* lower cost at the same time.

Many firms that attempt to pursue an integration strategy fail because they end up being *stuck in the middle:* They succeed at neither a differentiation nor a cost-leadership strategy. In a world of strategic trade-offs, increasing value and lowering cost have opposite effects. Improved product features, customer services, and customization all result in higher cost, while offering a no-frills product reduces perceived value. It happens quite often that a firm can't do both but must choose to be *either* a differentiator *or* a cost leader. We began our discussion of strategy by showing (in Strategy Highlight 1.1) how JetBlue ended up being stuck in the middle by trying to combine two different strategic positions: cost leadership and differentiation. The result was inferior performance relative to its competitors.

More recently, JCPenney under its CEO, Ron Johnson, learned the hard way how difficult it is to change a strategic position.[45] When hired as JCPenney's CEO in 2011, Mr. Johnson was hailed as a star executive. He was poached from Apple, where he had created and led Apple's retail stores since 2000. Apple's stores are the most successful retail outlets globally in terms of sales per square foot. No other retail outlet, not even luxury jewelers, achieves more sales.

Once on board with JCPenney, Mr. Johnson immediately began to change the company's strategic position from a cost-leadership to an integration strategy. In particular,

LO 6-6

Explain why it is difficult to succeed at an integration strategy.

he tried to reposition the department store more toward the high end by providing an improved customer experience and more exclusive merchandise through in-store boutiques. Mr. Johnson ordered all clearance racks with steeply discounted merchandise, common in JCPenney stores, to be removed. He also did away with JCPenney's long-standing practice of mailing discount coupons to its customers. Rather than following industry best practice by testing the more drastic changes to JCPenney's strategic positioning in a small number of selected stores, Mr. Johnson implemented them in all 1,800 stores at once. When one executive raised the issue of pre-testing, Mr. Johnson bristled and responded: "We didn't test at Apple." Under his leadership, JCPenney also got embroiled in a legal battle with Macy's because of Mr. Johnson's attempt to lure away homemaking maven Martha Stewart and her exclusive merchandise collection.

The envisioned integration strategy failed badly, and JCPenney ended up being stuck in the middle. Within 12 months of having Mr. Johnson at the helm, JCPenney's sales dropped by 25 percent. In a hypercompetitive industry such as retailing where every single percent of market share counts, this was a landslide. Less than 18 months into his new job, Mr. Johnson was fired and replaced by his predecessor, Myron Ullman.

This example clearly shows the perils of attempting an integration strategy due to the inherent trade-off in the underlying generic business strategies of cost leadership and differentiation. Moreover, it highlights the need but also the risk of changing a company's strategic position *too abruptly*. It is therefore critical for managers to understand the dynamics of competitive positioning to which we now turn.

6.6 The Dynamics of Competitive Positioning

LO 6-7

Describe and evaluate the dynamics of competitive positioning.

Companies that successfully implement one of the generic business strategies (differentiation or cost leadership) are more likely to attain competitive advantage. To do so, companies seek to reach the so-called **productivity frontier**, which is the value-cost relationship that captures the result of performing best practices at any given time.[46] Firms that exhibit effectiveness and efficiency reach the productivity frontier; others are left behind. Moreover, the productivity frontier represents a set of best-in-class strategic positions the firm can take relating to value creation and low cost *at a given point in time*. A firm's business strategy determines which strategic position it aspires to along the productivity frontier.

productivity frontier
Relationship that captures the result of performing best practices at any given time; the function is concave (bulging outward) to capture the trade-off between value creation and production cost.

Strategic positions, however, are not fixed, but can—and need to—change as the environment changes. It is critical for managers, therefore, to understand *the dynamics of competitive positioning*—or how strategy shapes a firm's position over time. Reaching the productivity frontier at a given point in time increases the likelihood of achieving a competitive advantage. Falling behind the productivity frontier, in contrast, results in a competitive disadvantage. Changes in the industry environment, however, allow firms to stake out more valuable positions and turn inferior performance into a competitive advantage. By the same token, as industries change, once-leading companies that held strategic positions along the productivity frontier may fall behind. Since competition is never static, understanding changes as the industry evolves is critical in staking out valuable competitive positions and to sustain a competitive advantage.

To illustrate this concept, let's look at the competitive dynamics in the $350 billion PC industry between 2010 and 2013.[47] Computer hardware has historically been a highly competitive industry. Many components are commodities. Until 2010, the industry experienced double-digit growth each year. Since 2010, however, the industry has been in decline with a pronounced drop in sales in the most recent years. Part of the declining demand is the result of an ongoing substitution effect: Consumers buy tablet computers or smartphones

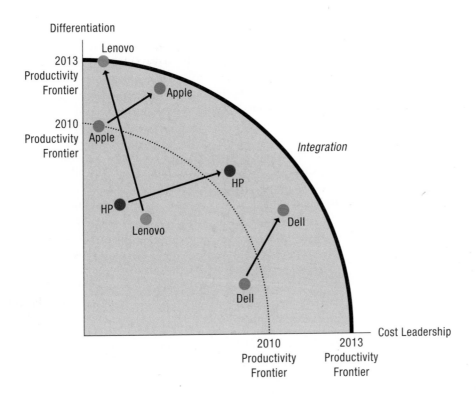

EXHIBIT 6.11

The Dynamics
of Competitive
Positioning in the
PC Industry: Apple,
Lenovo, HP, and Dell

(with larger screens) to use for mobile computing rather than personal computers such as laptops or desktops. By 2013, declining demand combined with a shrinking market size created an intensely competitive rivalry in the PC industry.

We demonstrate the dynamics of competitive positioning by visualizing the different competitive positions of Apple, Dell, HP, and Lenovo over time. These are the main competitors in the PC industry, jointly capturing the majority of the market share. At a given time, the horizontal axis in Exhibit 6.11 indicates best practice in cost leadership, and the vertical axis indicates best practice in differentiation.[48] Combining both cost leadership and differentiation, the company that seeks an integration strategy stakes out a position in the center part in the best-practice frontier (somewhere between the axes). The dotted line shows the productivity frontier in 2010. It indicates a set of best possible strategic positions a firm could occupy on the productivity frontier at that point in time.

Let's take a look at Exhibit 6.11. As a differentiator, Apple had carved out a strong strategic position. Its business-level strategy of differentiation was best-in-class at this time. Using superior hardware and software integration capabilities in combination with excellent marketing, Apple turned a commodity into a differentiated product. Consumers paid a premium price for a superior user experience. By 2010, consumer preferences in the PC industry had moved to value-added features such as seamless integration of PCs with mobile devices (e.g., MP3 music player, digital cameras, video, and so on) that left the other competitors (HP, Lenovo, and Dell) behind the productivity frontier. Apple's successful serial innovations in mobile devices (iPod, iPhone, and the iPad combined with the iTunes Store) drove up demand for Apple's Macs because consumers wanted one central hub to manage all their mobile devices and content conveniently. This clearly formulated and well-executed strategy allowed Apple to reach the productivity frontier.

Given their stronger focus on corporate IT departments than the consumer market, HP, Dell, and Lenovo were hit harder by the 2008–2009 recession than Apple. In particular, both HP and Lenovo were "stuck in the middle" in 2010. When compared with Apple and Dell, respectively, they were able to offer neither value-creating differentiation nor low cost, ending up with strategic positions below the productivity frontier.

HP had acquired Compaq in 2002 for $25 billion. This merger, which created the world's largest computer PC manufacturer, was intended to stake out a strategic position as integrator, providing "high-tech at low cost." By 2010, however, HP was not able to reconcile the thorny cost-differentiation trade-off. HP was unable to reach the productivity frontier. HP's board replaced CEO Mark Hurd (partly due to an ethics scandal) with Leo Apotheker in 2010, who in turn was replaced by Meg Whitman in 2011.

In 2010, the Chinese technology company Lenovo was still working on integrating IBM's fledgling PC business, which it had acquired in 2005. At this point in time, the company did not yet have a clear strategic profile as either a differentiator or low-cost leader. Nor did it have a strong presence outside China and other Asian markets. Lagging behind the productivity frontier in 2010, Lenovo experienced a competitive disadvantage.

Once the leader in low-cost PCs, Dell had enjoyed a strong strategic position on the productivity frontier for over a decade. By 2006, however, Dell's performance began to decline. In 2007, founder Michael Dell returned from retirement to take over as CEO. Dell attempted to reposition the company by moving more toward IT service and by providing more differentiation in its PCs, to go beyond "grey boxes." In 2008, Dell hired an industrial designer from Nike to come up with colorful futuristic designs for its product offerings.[49] In 2009, Dell purchased Perot Systems, an IT service provider, for $3.9 billion to further enhance its differential appeal by adding services and to better compete with HP, which acquired EDS, another IT service provider, for $13 billion in 2008.[50] By 2010, however, Dell's strategic position as cost leader appeared no longer as valuable as in the early 2000s, because one of the key competitive success factors became differentiation. Dell fell behind the productivity frontier as market demand shifted to more value-added features in the PC industry such as the seamless integration between computers and mobile devices which Dell could not offer. Taken together, in 2010, Apple enjoyed a clear competitive advantage over Dell, HP, and Lenovo.

Fast-forward to 2013 . . . Now the competitive dynamics look quite different. Apple has been struggling to continue its innovation home runs (the iPod, iTunes Store, iPhone, and the iPad) it enjoyed for a decade beginning in 2001. In an attempt to capture more of the low end of the market, Apple introduced lower-cost variations of its products, such as the iPad Mini (in 2012). It changed its strategic position more toward integration, but fell behind the productivity frontier as demand for its Macs dropped by roughly 10 percent annually.

After reversing a 2011 decision to spin out its PC business, HP continues to push forward with an integration strategy. However, it continues to have severe problems. An $11 billion acquisition of software company Autonomy (which ended in a $9 billion write-down) and the continued difficulty to transform itself into a software and service company have contributed to HP's sustained competitive disadvantage.[51] Partly as a consequence of a failure to clearly formulate a business and corporate strategy, demand for HP computer hardware has fallen by as much as 25 percent per year. HP continues to underperform and falls short of the productivity frontier in 2013.

Likewise, Dell continues to experience difficulties in changing its strategic position, moving from a well-executed cost-leadership strategy toward more integration, combined with a stronger focus on IT services. As consumer preferences changed toward demanding more value-added differentiation, Dell's cost-leadership strategy was no longer as valuable. In response, Dell decided to change its strategic position. What Dell's attempt at strategic repositioning shows, however, is that reconciling the trade-offs inherent in pursuing low cost and differentiation simultaneously is difficult to achieve. By 2013, Dell experienced a sustained competitive disadvantage. Demand for its PCs dropped by as much as 15 percent per year. As a consequence, Dell's market share in the PC industry dropped from 25 percent a few years ago to 11 percent in 2013.

By 2013, Lenovo was able to carve out the clearest strategic profile. It executed well on its strategic decision to focus on the higher end of the market by providing laptops and desktops with outstanding performance. Lenovo moved to the productivity frontier, occupying the position of a clear differentiator. Demand for PCs was in free-fall during this time period, and all competitors—except Lenovo—lost significant market share. Lenovo was the only PC maker whose demand did not fall despite the industry shrinking by double digits. Indeed, Lenovo holds 40 percent market share in high-end PCs (over $900) that run a Windows operating system (which are the vast majority of PCs in the high-end category). Lenovo's decision to carve out a clear strategic profile by following a well-crafted and executed differentiation strategy rewarded the company with a competitive advantage.

6.7 ◄► Implications for the Strategist

Strategic positioning is critical to gaining competitive advantage. Well-formulated and implemented generic business strategies (i.e., low cost *or* differentiation) enhance the firm's chances of obtaining superior performance. Strategic positioning requires making important trade-offs (think Walmart versus J. Crew in clothing).

In rare instances, a few exceptional firms might be able to reconcile the significant trade-offs between increasing value and lowering production cost by pursuing both business strategies simultaneously. These integration strategies tend to be successful only if a firm is able to rely on an innovation that allows it to reconcile the trade-offs mentioned (such as Toyota in the 1980s and 1990s with its lean-manufacturing approach, before that approach diffused widely).

Given the dynamics of competitive positioning, firms cannot stand still but must constantly refine and improve their strategic position over time. The goal is to not fall behind the productivity frontier, which is defined by the theoretically possible best practice at any given time. Since innovation is such an essential part of business strategy and competitive advantage, we now turn to discussing innovation in much more detail in the next chapter.

CHAPTER**CASE 6** / Consider This . . .

Reflecting higher value creation based on its differentiation strategy, P&G generally charges a 20–40 percent premium for its products in comparison to retailers' private-label brands. For instance, a 150-oz. container of liquid Tide detergent is $18 at Target, while the retailer's private-label brand is priced at $15. Given recent recessionary pressures on disposable household incomes, many consumers switched to private-label brands that they felt

did just as fine a job. Not only has P&G lost market share because of its higher prices to consumers; its profit margins have also been squeezed by rising costs of input factors.

One underlying problem that P&G is facing is that rather than creating new product categories that it is famous for, it is tweaking existing products incrementally.

P&G's recent major product breakthroughs such as Swiffer cleaning devices and supplies, Crest Whitestrips, and Febreze odor fresheners were all launched over a decade ago. In an attempt to bring in more innovation from the outside through its Connect+Develop initiative, P&G has slashed its R&D spending in recent years by as much as 50 percent, and is now spending less than some of its rivals. The Connect+Develop initiative was put in place by A. G. Lafley during his first term as P&G's CEO.

Questions

1. The ChapterCase states that P&G is pursuing a differentiation strategy. Looking at the value and cost drivers discussed in this chapter and the table entitled "Competitive Positioning and the Five Forces: Benefits and Risks of Cost-Leadership and Differentiation Business Strategies" in Exhibit 6.7, identify the factors causing P&G's business strategy to lose its luster. Why is P&G's differentiation strategy no longer as potent as it once was?

2. Given the discussion in the ChapterCase about P&G slashing its R&D spending and cutting costs and jobs more generally, does the firm risk being "stuck in the middle"? Why or why not? If yes, why would being "stuck in the middle" be a bad strategic position?

3. Your task is to help Mr. Lafley sharpen P&G's strategic position. Which strategic position along the productivity frontier should P&G stake out? Which value and/or cost drivers would you focus on to improve P&G's strategic profile? How would you go about it? What results would you expect?

TAKE-AWAY CONCEPTS

This chapter discussed two generic business-level strategies (*differentiation* and *cost leadership*); some factors that companies can use to drive those strategies; *integration strategy,* the attempt to find a competitive advantage by reconciling the trade-offs between the two generic business strategies; and the dynamics of competitive positioning as summarized by the following learning objectives and related take-away concepts.

LO 6-1 / Define business-level strategy and describe how it determines a firm's strategic position.

- Business-level strategy determines a firm's strategic position in its quest for competitive advantage when competing in a single industry or product market.
- Strategic positioning requires that managers address strategic trade-offs that arise between value and cost, because higher value tends to go along with higher cost.
- Differentiation and cost leadership are distinct strategic positions.
- Besides selecting an appropriate strategic position, managers must also define the scope of competition—whether to pursue a specific market niche or go after the broader market.

LO 6-2 / Examine the relationship between value drivers and differentiation strategy.

- The goal of a differentiation strategy is to increase the perceived value of goods and services so that customers will pay a higher price for additional features.
- In a differentiation strategy, the focus of competition is on value-enhancing attributes and features, while controlling costs.
- Some of the unique value drivers managers can manipulate are product features, customer service, customization, and complements.
- Value drivers contribute to competitive advantage only if their increase in value creation (ΔV) exceeds the increase in costs (ΔC).

LO 6-3 / Examine the relationship between cost drivers and the cost-leadership strategy.

- The goal of a cost-leadership strategy is to reduce the firm's cost below that of its competitors.

- In a cost-leadership strategy, the focus of competition is achieving the lowest possible cost position, which allows the firm to offer the lowest price while maintaining acceptable value.
- Some of the unique cost drivers that managers can manipulate are the cost of input factors, economies of scale, and learning- and experience-curve effects.
- No matter how low the price, if there is no acceptable value proposition, the product or service will not sell.

LO 6-4 / Assess the benefits and risks of cost-leadership and differentiation business strategies vis-à-vis the five forces that shape competition.

- The five forces model helps managers use generic business strategies to protect themselves against the industry forces that drive down profitability.
- Differentiation and cost-leadership strategies allow firms to carve out strong strategic positions, not only to protect themselves against the five forces, but also to benefit from them in their quest for competitive advantage.
- Exhibit 6.7 details the benefits and risks of each business strategy.

LO 6-5 / Evaluate value and cost drivers that may allow a firm to pursue an integration strategy.

- To address the trade-offs between differentiation and cost leadership at the business level, managers may leverage quality, economies of scope,

innovation, and the firm's structure, culture, and routines.
- The trade-offs between differentiation and low cost can be addressed either at the business level or at the corporate level.

LO 6-6 / Explain why it is difficult to succeed at an integration strategy.

- A successful integration strategy requires that trade-offs between differentiation and low cost be reconciled.
- Integration strategy often is difficult because the two distinct strategic positions require internal value chain activities that are fundamentally different from one another.
- When firms fail to resolve strategic trade-offs between differentiation and cost, they end up being "stuck in the middle." They then succeed at neither strategy, leading to a competitive disadvantage.

LO 6-7 / Describe and evaluate the dynamics of competitive positioning.

- The productivity frontier represents a set of best-in-class strategic positions the firm can take relating to value creation and low cost *at a given point in time*.
- Reaching the productivity frontier enhances the likelihood of obtaining a competitive advantage.
- Not reaching the productivity frontier implies competitive disadvantage if other firms *are* positioned at the productivity frontier.
- Strategic positions need to change *over time* as the environment changes.

KEY TERMS

Ambidextrous organization	Economies of scale	Mass customization
Business-level strategy	Economies of scope	Minimum efficient scale (MES)
Cost-leadership strategy	Focused cost-leadership strategy	Productivity frontier
Differentiation strategy	Focused differentiation strategy	Scope of competition
Diseconomies of scale	Integration strategy	Strategic trade-offs

DISCUSSION QUESTIONS

1. What are some drawbacks and risks to a broad generic business strategy? To a focused strategy?

2. How can a firm attempting to have an integrated business-level strategy manage to avoid being "stuck in the middle"?

3. In Chapter 4, we discussed the internal value chain activities a firm can perform in its business model (see Exhibit 4.8). The value chain priorities can be quite different for firms taking different business strategies. Create examples of value chains for three firms: one using cost leadership, another using differentiation, and a third using an integration business-level strategy.

4. A company such as Intel has a complex design and manufacturing process. This should lead Intel management to be concerned with scale of production and learning curves. When do you think managers should be more concerned with large-scale production runs, and when do you think they should be most concerned with practices that would foster or hinder the hiring, training, and retention of key employees?

ETHICAL/SOCIAL ISSUES

1. Suppose Procter & Gamble (P&G) learns that a relatively new startup company Method (www.methodhome.com) is gaining market share with a new laundry detergent in West Coast markets. In response, P&G lowers the price of its Tide detergent from $18 to $9 for a 150-oz. bottle only in markets where Method's product is for sale. The goal of this "loss leader" price drop is to encourage Method to leave the laundry detergent market. Is this an ethical business practice? Why or why not?

2. Whole Foods Market continues to seek ways to differentiate itself from the competition (see Strategy Highlight 6.1). The firm spends 5 percent of its net profits on a variety of charities, and it also provides opportunities for patrons to contribute to such causes.

   In 2010, Whole Foods enhanced a "back-to-school" project it started a year earlier. It set a goal to put 300 salad bars in public schools within a 50-mile radius of any Whole Foods store. The firm solicited contributions from customers for this cause. In February 2011, Whole Foods announced the fund-raising had surpassed the original $750,000 goal. With over $1.4 million in collections, the company expanded the program to more than 500 elementary, middle, and high schools across the United States. Whole Foods is also expanding its in-store educational efforts with "wellness clubs" in some stores. These dedicated areas of the store give customers a chance to learn firsthand about healthy cooking and eating.[52]

   Co-CEO John Mackey noted that 100 years ago Americans spent about half their disposable income on food. Today that figure is about 8 percent. Additionally, Mackey said that "really healthy eating" should cost around $200 per month, noting that it is the processing of foods that drives up food prices. The least-expensive way to eat, Mackey advised, is by sticking with whole grains, beans, seasonal plants and produce, and proper home cooking.[53]

   a. What value drivers is Whole Foods using to remain differentiated in the face of Walmart and other competitors now selling organic foods? (Looking back at Exhibit 6.9 may be useful.)

   b. Given the discussion in Strategy Highlight 6.1 about Whole Foods trimming its cost structure, does the firm risk being "stuck in the middle"? Why or why not?

   c. What other methods could Whole Foods use to successfully drive its business strategy?

SMALL-GROUP EXERCISES

//// Small-Group Exercise 1

Ryanair (see Strategy Highlight 6.2) is noted as a firm that can make a profit on a $20 ticket by imposing numerous fees and surcharges.

1. Generally, an ethical business practice is to disclose fees to potential customers to permit effective cost comparisons. Log on to www.ryanair.com and determine if Ryanair has transparent disclosure of these fees.

2. If you were a competitor in the European market, such as British Airways or Lufthansa, how would you compete against Ryanair knowing your cost structure would not allow price parity? If you were a low-cost leader like Easy Jet, how would you compete against Ryanair?

//// Small-Group Exercise 2

1. In the accompanying table is a list of prominent firms. Place each firm you know (or research online) in one of the five categories of generic business-level strategies—broad cost leadership, focused cost leadership, broad differentiation, focused differentiation, and integration. Explain your choices.

2. What are some common features of the firms you have placed within each category?

Ann Taylor	Martin Guitars
BIC	McKinsey & Co.
Big Lots	Netflix
Black & Decker	Nike
Clif Bar	Patek Philippe
Coca-Cola	Porsche
Dollar Stores	Rhapsody
Ferrari	Rolls-Royce
Google	Ryanair
Goya Foods	Samuel Adams
Greyhound Lines	Singapore Airlines
Hyundai	Target
Kia Motors	Toyota
JetBlue	Vanguard
Lands' End	Victoria's Secret
Liberty Mutual	WellPoint
LVMH	Zara

STRATEGY TERM PROJECT

//// Module 6: Business Strategy

In this module, we will look at the business model your selected company uses and analyze its business-level strategy to see if it is appropriate for the strategic position. If your firm is a large multibusiness entity, you will need to choose one of the major businesses (strategic business unit, or SBU) of the firm for this analysis. In prior chapters, we collected information about this firm's external environment and some of its internal competitive advantages. Using this information and any other you have gathered, address the following questions.

1. Does your selected business have differentiated products or services? If so, what is the basis for this differentiation from the competition?

2. Does your firm have a cost-leadership position in this business? If so, can you identify which cost drivers it uses effectively to hold this position?

3. What is your firm's approach to the market? If it segments the market, identify the scope of competition it is using.

4. Using the answers to the preceding questions, identify which generic business strategies your firm is employing. Is the firm leveraging the appropriate value and cost drivers for the business strategy you identified? Explain why or why not.

5. As noted in the chapter, each business strategy is context-dependent. What do you see as positives and negatives with the selected business strategy of your firm in its competitive situation?

6. In Chapter 3, we identified strategic groups in the industry relevant to your firm. Review the firms listed in the same strategic group as your selected firm. See if there is a similarity with the generic business strategy used by each. In most strategic groups, there will be market and (some) strategy similarities across the firms.

7. What suggestions do you have to improve the firm's business strategy and strategic position?

my STRATEGY

Different Value and Cost Drivers—What Determines *Your* Buying Decisions?

Firms communicate their strategy to their customers through advertising and promotions. What role does a firm's approach to communicating with you have on *your* buying decision? Do you understand how a firm's message influences your decision? Greater awareness of how firms try to influence customers can help you understand strategic positioning. On a personal level, greater understanding of your buying decisions can help you manage your disposable income more wisely. For example, to stay within your budget, conscious awareness that your choice of a high-priced beverage has been influenced by product placement in a TV show or movie may cause you to reconsider the expenditure and choose a lower-priced alternative or even forgo the purchase.

In the following table, the columns show some optional advertising approaches used by companies to communicate the value of their product in order to influence your buying decisions, and the rows list some familiar product categories. Referring to the table, do the following:

1. For each product category, first consider how each type of advertising might influence you; then rank from 1 (not at all) to 5 (strong influence) and enter that number in the cell. Most consumers use different criteria to make purchase decisions for different categories of product. Compare your rankings with those of other students in the class. What approaches not included here have a stronger influence on your buying decisions?

2. Second, for each advertising approach, decide whether you think it would be more likely to be used for products sold by a company using a differentiation (D), cost-leadership (CL), or integration (I) strategy and enter the letter abbreviation of that strategy under the column heading. Compare your responses with those of other students and discuss why differentiators and cost leaders may choose similar or different advertising approaches.

How Different Advertising Approaches Influence Consumer Buying Decisions

	Product Placement in TV or Movies	Celebrity Endorsement	Sustainability Claims	Comments on Social Media	Point of Purchase Displays	Print Media Ads	Low-Price Assurances
Mobile device							
Shoes for professional wear							
Clothing for casual wear							
Clothing for formal event							
Sporting goods							
Airline ticket							
Car							
Food and beverages							
Computer							

ENDNOTES

1. This ChapterCase is based on: "A David and Gillette story," *The Wall Street Journal,* April 12; "P&G's stumbles put CEO on hot seat for turnaround," *The Wall Street Journal,* September 27, 2012; "At Procter & Gamble, the innovation well runs dry," *BusinessWeek,* September 6, 2012; "Embattled P&G chief replaced by old boss," *The Wall Street Journal,* May 23, 2013; Lafley, A. G., and R. L. Martin (2013), *Playing to Win: How Strategy Really Works* (Boston, MA: Harvard Business Review Press); and "P&G's Billion-Dollar Brands: Trusted, Valued, Recognized," Fact Sheet, www.pg.com.

2. This discussion is based on: Porter, M. E. (1980), *Competitive Strategy: Techniques for Analyzing Industries and Competitors* (New York: Free Press); Porter, M. E. (1985), *Competitive Advantage: Creating and Sustaining Superior Performance* (New York: Free Press); Porter, M. E. (1996), "What is strategy?" *Harvard Business Review,* November–December; and Porter, M. E. (2008), "The five competitive forces that shape strategy," *Harvard Business Review,* January.

3. These questions are based on: Abell, D. F. (1980), *Defining the Business: The Starting Point of Strategic Planning* (Englewood Cliffs, NJ: Prentice-Hall); Porter, M. E. (1996), "What is strategy?"; and Priem, R. (2007), "A consumer perspective on value creation," *Academy of Management Review* 32: 219–235.

4. Porter, M. E. (1996), "What is strategy?"

5. The discussion of generic business strategies is based on: Porter, M. E. (1980), *Competitive Strategy. Techniques for Analyzing Industries and Competitors;* Porter, M. E. (1985), *Competitive Advantage: Creating and Sustaining Superior Performance;* Porter, M. E. (1996), "What is strategy?"; and Porter, M. E. (2008), "The five competitive forces that shape strategy."

6. To decide if and how to divide up the market, you can apply the market segmentation techniques you have acquired in your marketing and microeconomics classes.

7. Elon Musk in "Uber Entrepreneur: An Evening with Elon Musk," Churchill Club, Mountain View, CA, April 7, 2009 (available at ForaTV: http://fora.tv/2009/04/07/ Uber_Entrepreneur_An_Evening_with_Elon_ Musk).

8. Anderson, R. C., and R. White (2009), *Confessions of a Radical Industrialist: Profits, People, Purpose—Doing Business by Respecting the Earth* (New York: St. Martin's Press).

9. Christensen, C. M., and M. E. Raynor (2003), *The Innovator's Solution: Creating and Sustaining Successful Growth* (Boston, MA: Harvard Business School Press).

10. The interested reader is referred to the strategy, marketing, and economics literatures. A good start in the strategy literature is the classic work of M. E. Porter: Porter, M. E. (1980), *Competitive Strategy: Techniques for Analyzing Industries and Competitors;* Porter, M. E. (1985), *Competitive Advantage: Creating and Sustaining Superior Performance;* and Porter, M. E. (2008), "The five competitive forces that shape strategy."

11. "Walter Robb: Whole Foods' other CEO on organic growth," *Fortune,* May 6, 2013.

12. "Frank talk from Whole Foods' John Mackey," *The Wall Street Journal,* August 4, 2009; "As sales slip, Whole Foods tries to push health," *The Wall Street Journal,* August 5, 2009; "The conscience of a capitalist," *The Wall Street Journal,* October 3, 2009; "Walter Robb on Whole Foods' recession lessons," *BusinessWeek,* August 9, 2012; "Walter Robb: Whole Foods' other CEO on organic growth," *Fortune,* May 6, 2013; "Whole Foods profits by cutting 'whole paycheck' reputation," *BusinessWeek,* May 8, 2013; www.whole foodsmarket.com.

13. www.oxo.com/about.jsp.

14. Hsieh, T. (2010), *Delivering Happiness: A Path to Profits, Passion, and Purpose* (New York: Business Plus).

15. "Amazon opens wallet, buys Zappos," *The Wall Street Journal,* July 23, 2009.

16. www.att.com/u-verse/.

17. See a discussion of Southwest Airlines' cost-leadership strategy in Porter, M. E. (1996), "What is strategy?" *Harvard Business Review,* November–December: 61–78.

18. Anderson, C. (2009), *Free: The Future of a Radical Price* (New York: Hyperion); "Walmart with wings," *BusinessWeek,* November 27, 2006; "Snarling all the way to the bank," *The Economist,* August 23, 2007; and "Ryanair's O'Leary: The duke of discomfort," *Bloomberg Businessweek,* September 2, 2010, www.ryanair.com.

19. Friedman, T. (2005), *The World Is Flat: A Brief History of the Twenty-First Century* (New York: Farrar, Strauss and Giroux).

20. "Boeing looks beyond Dreamliner's first flight," *The Wall Street Journal,* December 15, 2009, www.boeing.com.

21. www.airbus.com/en/aircraftfamilies/a380/ home/.

22. Kevin Turner, COO Microsoft. Keynote Speech at Microsoft's Worldwide Partner Conference, New Orleans, July 15, 2009.

23. "Microsoft Concedes Windows 8 Misses Expectations," *The Wall Street Journal,* May 7, 2013; "Windows 8 is only the beginning of Microsoft's problems," *The Economist,* May 11, 2013.

24. "GM hopes Volt juices its future," *The Wall Street Journal,* August 12, 2009.

25. "Nucor's new plant project still on hold," *Associated Press,* July 23, 2009, www.nucor. com.

26. Gladwell, M. (2002), *The Tipping Point: How Little Things Can Make a Big Difference* (New York: Back Bay Books) p. 185.

27. Levitt, B., and J. G. March (1988), "Organizational learning," in Scott, W. R. (ed.), *Annual Review of Sociology* 14: 319–340 (Greenwich, CT: JAI Press).

28. For insightful reviews and syntheses on the learning-curve literature, see: Yelle, L. E. (1979), "The learning curve: Historical review and comprehensive survey," *Decision Sciences* 10: 302–308; and Argote, L., and G. Todorova (2007), "Organizational learning: Review and future directions," in Hodgkinson, G. P., and J. K. Ford (eds.), *International Review of Industrial and Organizational Psychology* 22: 193–234 (New York: Wiley).

29. Wright, T. P. (1936), "Factors affecting the cost of airplanes," *Journal of Aeronautical Sciences* 3: 122–128.

30. This discussion is based on: Darr, E. D., L. Argote, and D. Epple (1995), "The acquisition, transfer and depreciation of knowledge in service organizations: Productivity in franchises," *Management Science* 42: 1750–1762; King, A. W., and A. L. Ranft (2001), "Capturing knowledge and knowing through improvisation: What managers can learn from the thoracic surgery board certification process," *Journal of Management* 27: 255–277; Zollo, M., J. J. Reuer, and H. Singh (2002), "Interorganizational routines and performance in strategic alliances," *Organization Science* 13: 701–713; Hoang, H., and F. T. Rothaermel (2005), "The effect of general and partner-specific alliance experience on joint R&D project performance," *Academy of Management Journal* 48: 332–345; Rothaermel, F. T., and D. L. Deeds (2006), "Alliance type, alliance experience, and alliance management capability in high-technology ventures," *Journal of Business Venturing* 21: 429–460; Pisano, G. P., R. M. Bohmer, and A. C. Edmondson

(2001), "Organizational differences in rates of learning: Evidence from the adoption of minimally invasive cardiac surgery," *Management Science* 47: 752–768; Edmondson, A. C., R. M. Bohmer, and G. P. Pisano (2001), "Disrupted routines: Team learning and new technology implementation in hospitals," *Administrative Science Quarterly* 46: 685–716; Thompson, P. (2001), "How much did the liberty shipbuilders learn? New evidence from an old case study," *Journal of Political Economy* 109: 103–137; and Gulati, R., D. Lavie, and H. Singh (2009), "The nature of partnering experience and the gain from alliances," *Strategic Management Journal* 30: 1213–1233.

31. Ramanarayanan, S. (2008), "Does practice make perfect: An empirical analysis of learning-by-doing in cardiac surgery." Available at SSRN: http://ssrn.com/abstract=1129350.

32. Boston Consulting Group (1972), *Perspectives on Experience* (Boston, MA: Boston Consulting Group).

33. This discussion is based on: Porter, M. E. (1979), "How competitive forces shape strategy," *Harvard Business Review,* March–April: 137–145; Porter, M. E. (1980), *Competitive Strategy. Techniques for Analyzing Industries and Competitors;* and Porter, M. E. (2008), "The five competitive forces that shape strategy."

34. "Samsung sparks anxiety at Google," *The Wall Street Journal,* February 25, 2013.

35. This discussion is based on: Hill, C.W.L. (1988), "Differentiation versus low cost or differentiation and low cost: A contingency framework," *Academy of Management Review* 13: 401–412; and Miller, A., and G. G. Dess (1993), "Assessing Porter's model in terms of its generalizability, accuracy, and simplicity," *Journal of Management Studies* 30: 553–585.

36. Davis, S. M. (1987), *Future Perfect* (Reading, MA: Addison-Wesley).

37. This discussion is based on: Afuah, A. (2009), *Strategic Innovation. New Game Strategies for Competitive Advantage* (New York: Routledge); Hill, C.W.L., and F. T. Rothaermel (2003), "The performance of incumbent firms in the face of radical technological innovation," *Academy of Management Review* 28: 257–274; Rothaermel, F. T., and A. Hess, "Finding an innovation strategy that works," *The Wall Street Journal,* August 17, 2009; and Rothaermel, F. T., and A. Hess (2010), "Innovation strategies combined," *MIT Sloan Management Review,* Spring: 12–15.

38. "IKEA: How the Swedish retailer became a global cult brand," *BusinessWeek,* November 14, 2005.

39. This discussion is based on: O'Reilly, C. A., III, and M. L. Tushman (2007), "Ambidexterity as dynamic capability: Resolving the innovator's dilemma," *Research in Organizational Behavior* 28: 1–60; Raisch, S., and J. Birkinshaw (2008), "Organizational ambidexterity: Antecedents, outcomes, and moderators," *Journal of Management* 34: 375–409; and Rothaermel, F. T., and M. T. Alexandre (2009), "Ambidexterity in technology sourcing: The moderating role of absorptive capacity," *Organization Science* 20: 759–780.

40. Hamel, G. (2006), "The why, what, and how of management innovation," *Harvard Business Review,* February.

41. March, J. G. (1991), "Exploration and exploitation in organizational learning," *Organization Science* 2: 319–340; and Levinthal, D. A., and J. G. March (1993), "The myopia of learning," *Strategic Management Journal* 14: 95–112.

42. Author's interviews with Intel managers and engineers.

43. Brown, S. L., and K. M. Eisenhardt (1997), "The art of continuous change: Linking complexity theory and time-paced evolution in relentlessly shifting organizations," *Administrative Science Quarterly* 42: 1–34;

and O'Reilly, C. A., B. Harreld, and M. Tushman (2009), "Organizational ambidexterity: IBM and emerging business opportunities," *California Management Review* 51: 75–99.

44. This discussion is based on: Porter, M. E. (1980), *Competitive Strategy;* and Porter, M. E. (1996), "What is strategy?" *Harvard Business Review,* November–December: 61–78.

45. "For Penney's heralded boss, the shine is off the apple," *The Wall Street Journal,* February 24, 2013; "Macy's CEO: Penney, Martha Stewart deal made me 'sick,'" *The Wall Street Journal,* February 25, 2013; and "Penney CEO out, old boss back in," *The Wall Street Journal,* April 8, 2013.

46. Porter, M. E. (1996), "What is strategy?"

47. This discussion is based on: "Lenovo aims higher in U.S.," *The Wall Street Journal,* January 10, 2013; "Dell: From PC king to buyout fodder," *The Wall Street Journal,* January 15, 2013; "Lenovo closes in on HP, Dell as PC sales plummet," *Bloomberg Businessweek,* April 11, 2013. Data reported are from industry research firms Gartner and IDC.

48. The shape of the productivity frontier is concave to indicate the trade-offs between low cost and differentiation.

49. "Taking the dull out of Dell," *BusinessWeek,* November 3, 2008.

50. "Dell to buy Perot in catch-up deal," *The Wall Street Journal,* September 22, 2009.

51. "HP affirms commitment to Autonomy," *The Wall Street Journal,* April 10, 2013.

52. Material for this case discussion is from: "More than 500 schools awarded grants for salad bars," Whole Foods Market Press Release, February 1, 2011, www.wholefoodsmarket.com/backtoschool/; and "ECO:nomics: Whole Foods CEO says eating healthy costs less," WSJ Video, March 3, 2011.

53. "ECO:nomics: Whole Foods CEO says eating healthy costs less."

Chapter 7

Business Strategy:
Innovation and Entrepreneurship

Learning Objectives

After studying this chapter, you will be able to:

LO 7-1 Outline the four-step innovation process from idea to imitation.

LO 7-2 Apply strategic management concepts to entrepreneurship and innovation.

LO 7-3 Describe the competitive implications of different stages in the industry life cycle.

LO 7-4 Derive strategic implications of the crossing-the-chasm framework.

LO 7-5 Categorize different types of innovations in the markets-and-technology framework.

LO 7-6 Explain the long-tail concept and derive its strategic implications.

LO 7-7 Compare and contrast closed and open innovation.

Wikipedia:
The Free Encyclopedia

WIKIPEDIA IS OFTEN the first source consulted for information about an unfamiliar topic, but this was not always the case. For almost 250 years, Encyclopedia Britannica was the gold standard for authoritative reference works, delving into more than 65,000 topics with articles by some 4,000 scholarly contributors, including many by Nobel Laureates. The beautiful leather-bound, multivolume set of books made a nice decorative item in many homes. In the early 1990s, when total sales for encyclopedias were over $1.2 billion annually, Encyclopedia Britannica was the undisputed market leader, holding more than 50 percent market share and earning some $650 million in revenues. Not surprisingly, its superior differentiated appeal was highly correlated with cost, reflected in its steep sticker price of up to $2,000.

Innovation changed all that. Banking on the widespread diffusion of the personal computer, Microsoft launched its electronic encyclopedia Encarta in 1993 at a price of $99. Although some viewed it as merely a CD-version of the lower-cost and lower-quality Funk & Wagnall's Encyclopedia sold in supermarkets, Encarta still took a big bite out of Britannica's market. Within only three years, the market for printed encyclopedias had shrunk by half, along with Britannica's revenues, while Microsoft sold over $100 million worth of Encarta CDs.

In 2001, Internet entrepreneur Jimmy Wales launched Wikipedia, the free online multilanguage encyclopedia. In Hawaiian, *wiki* means quick, referring to the instant do-it-yourself editing capabilities of the site. Wikipedia is a nonprofit venture supported by the Wikimedia Foundation, which obtains its funding from donations. Wikipedia now has 26 million articles in 285 languages, including over 4.2 million items in English.

Wikipedia's slogan is "*the Free Encyclopedia that anyone can edit.*" Since it is open source, any person, expert or novice, can contribute content and edit pages using the handy "edit this page" button. It also draws on tens of thousands of volunteer editors, who monitor and validate content by consensus. Although Wikipedia's volume of English entries is almost 65 times greater than that of Britannica, the site is not as error-prone as you might think. The free online encyclopedia relies on the *wisdom of the crowds,* which assumes "the many" often know more than "the expert." Moreover, user-generated content needs to be verifiable by reliable sources such as links to reputable websites. A peer-reviewed study by *Nature* of selected science topics found that the error rate of Wikipedia and *Britannica* was roughly the same. Yet, Wikipedia's crowdsourcing approach to display user-generated content is not without criticism. The most serious are that the content may be unreliable and unauthoritative, that it could exhibit systematic bias, and that group dynamics might prevent objective and factual reporting.[1]

After reading the chapter, you will find more about this case, with related questions, on page 231.

INNOVATION—the successful introduction of a new product, process, or business model—is a powerful driver in the competitive process. The ChapterCase provides an example of how advancements in technology can render traditional business models obsolete. With introduction of its CD-based Encarta, Microsoft destroyed about half the value created by Britannica. In turn, Wikipedia moved away from Britannica's and Microsoft's proprietary business models to an open-source model powered by user-generated content and available to anyone on the Internet. In doing so, it destroyed Encarta's business, which Microsoft shut down in 2009. At the same time, Wikipedia created substantial benefits for users by shifting to the open-source model for content. Because Wikipedia was able to create value for consumers by driving the price for the end user to zero and making the information instantly accessible on the Internet, there is no future for printed or CD-based encyclopedias. Sales of the beautiful leather-bound Encyclopedia Britannica volumes declined from a peak of 120,000 sets in 1990 to a mere 12,000 sets in 2010. As a consequence, Encyclopedia Britannica announced in 2012 that it no longer would print its namesake books. Its content is now accessible via a paid subscription through its website and apps for mobile devices.

Innovation allows firms to redefine the marketplace in their favor and achieve a competitive advantage.[2] As a powerful competitive weapon for business strategy formulation, innovation and the related topic of entrepreneurship are the focus of this chapter. We begin this chapter by detailing how competition is a process driven by continuous innovation. Next we discuss strategic and social entrepreneurship. We then take a deep dive into the industry life cycle. This helps us to formulate a more dynamic business strategy as the industry changes over time. We also introduce the crossing-the-chasm framework, highlighting the difficulties in transitioning different stages of the industry life cycle. We then move into a detailed discussion of different types of innovation and derive their strategic implications. We also present different ways to organize for innovation. As with every chapter, we conclude with practice-oriented *Implications for the Strategist*.

7.1 Competition Driven by Innovation

Competition is a process driven by the "perennial gale of creative destruction," in the words of famed economist Joseph Schumpeter.[3] The continuous waves of market leadership changes in the encyclopedia business, detailed in the ChapterCase, demonstrate the potency of innovation as a competitive weapon: It can simultaneously create and destroy value. Firms must be able to innovate while also fending off competitors' imitation attempts. A successful strategy requires both an effective offense and a hard-to-crack defense.

Many firms have dominated an early wave of innovation only to be destroyed by the next wave. Examples include:

- *The move from typewriters to computers:* Wang Laboratories, a computer company that led the market for word-processing machines, destroyed typewriter companies such as Smith Corona and Underwood. It then was undone by computer makers such as IBM and Compaq. Today, IBM has exited the personal computer market, selling its PC division to the Chinese technology company Lenovo, and Compaq has been acquired by HP. The computer industry, however, has not been standing still either. Once-successful PC makers such as HP and Dell are now under threat by companies that are innovating in the mobile device space, such as Amazon, Apple, and Samsung.

- *The explosion of television-viewing options:* The traditional television networks (ABC, CBS, and NBC) have been struggling to maintain viewers and advertising revenues as cable and satellite providers have offered innovative programming. Those same cable and satellite providers are trying hard to hold on to viewers as more and more people gravitate toward customized content online. To exploit such opportunities, Google acquired YouTube, while Comcast, the largest cable operator in the U.S., purchased NBC Universal from GE.[4] Comcast's acquisition helps it integrate delivery services and content, with the goal of establishing itself as a new player in the media industry. In turn, both traditional TV and cable networks are currently under threat from content providers that stream via the Internet, such as Netflix, YouTube, Vimeo, Hulu, and Amazon Instant Video.

As the adage goes, change is the only constant—and the rate of technological change has accelerated dramatically over the last hundred years. Changing technologies spawn new industries, while others die out. This makes innovation a powerful strategic weapon in order to gain and sustain competitive advantage. Exhibit 7.1 shows how many years it took for different technological innovations to reach 50 percent of the U.S. population (either through ownership or usage). As an example, it took 84 years for half of the U.S. population to own a car, but only 28 years for half the population to own a TV. The pace of the adoption rate of recent innovations continues to accelerate. It took 19 years for the

EXHIBIT 7.1 / Accelerating Speed of Technological Change

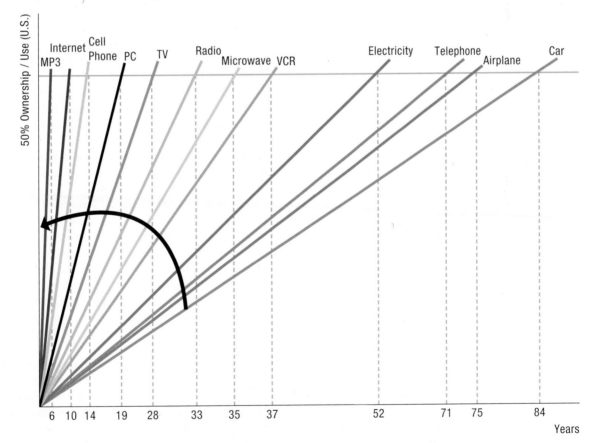

SOURCE: Author's depiction of data from the U.S. Census Bureau, the Consumer Electronics Association, *Forbes*, and the National Cable and Telecommunications Association.

PC to reach 50 percent ownership, but only 6 years for MP3 players to accomplish the same diffusion rate.

What factors explain increasingly rapid technological diffusion and adoption? One determinant is that initial innovations such as the car, airplane, telephone, and the use of electricity provided the necessary infrastructure for newer innovations to diffuse more rapidly. Another reason is the emergence of new business models that make innovations more accessible. For example, Dell's direct-to-consumer distribution system improved access to low-cost PCs, and Walmart's low-price, high-volume model utilized its sophisticated IT logistics system to fuel explosive growth. In addition, satellite and cable distribution systems facilitated the ability of mass media such as radio and TV to deliver advertising and information to a wider audience. The speed of technology diffusion has accelerated further with the emergence of the Internet, social networking sites, and viral messaging. The accelerating speed of technological changes has significant implications for the competitive process and firm strategy. We will now take a closer look at the innovation process unleashed by technological changes.

THE INNOVATION PROCESS

Outline the four-step innovation process from idea to imitation.

Broadly viewed, innovation describes the discovery and development of new knowledge in a four-step process captured in the *4-I's: idea, invention, innovation,* and *imitation* (see Exhibit 7.2).[5]

The innovation process begins with an *idea.* The idea is often presented in terms of abstract concepts or as findings derived from basic research. Basic research is conducted to discover new knowledge. This may be done to enhance the fundamental understanding of nature, without any commercial application or benefit in mind. In the long run, however, basic research is often transformed into applied research with commercial application. For example, wireless communication technology is built upon the fundamental science breakthroughs Albert Einstein accomplished in his research on the nature of light.[6]

invention The transformation of an idea into a new product or process, or the modification and recombination of existing ones.

patent A form of intellectual property that gives the inventor exclusive rights to benefit from commercializing a technology for a specified time period in exchange for public disclosure of the underlying idea.

In a next step, **invention** describes the transformation of an idea into a new product or process, or the modification and recombination of existing ones. The practical application of basic knowledge in a particular area frequently results in new technology. If an invention is *useful, novel,* and *non-obvious* as assessed by the U.S. Patent and Trademark Office, it can be patented.[7] A **patent** is a form of *intellectual property,* and gives the inventor exclusive rights to benefit from commercializing a technology for a specified time period in exchange for public disclosure of the underlying idea. In the U.S., the time period for the right to exclude others from the use of the technology is 20 years from the filing date of a patent application. Exclusive rights often translate into a *temporary monopoly position* until the patent expires. For instance, many pharmaceutical drugs are patent protected. Moreover, patents can be enforced in court. In the smartphone industry, Apple won a patent infringement lawsuit against Samsung. A federal jury found that some of Samsung's older mobile devices had infringed on several Apple patents.[8]

Innovation concerns the *commercialization* of an invention by entrepreneurs.[9] **Entrepreneurs** are the agents who introduce change into the competitive system. They do this not only by figuring out how to use inventions, but also by introducing new products or services, new production processes, and new forms of organization. Entrepreneurs can introduce change by starting new ventures, such as Jimmy Wales with Wikipedia or Mark Zuckerberg with Facebook. Or they can be found within existing firms, such as A. G. Lafley at Procter & Gamble (P&G), who implemented an *open-innovation model* (which we'll discuss later). When innovating within existing companies, change agents are often called *intrapreneurs:* those pursuing *corporate entrepreneurship.*[10]

According to Schumpeter, entrepreneurs who drive innovation need just as much skill, commitment, and daring as inventors who are responsible for the process of invention. As an example, the engineer Nikola Tesla invented the alternating-current (AC) electric motor, and was granted a patent in 1888 by the U.S. Patent and Trademark Office.[11] Although this breakthrough technology was neglected for much of the time during the 20th century, the entrepreneur Elon Musk is commercializing Tesla's invention with Tesla Motors, a new venture formed to design and manufacture all-electric automobiles. Tesla Motors (a name that Elon Musk chose to honor Nikola Tesla) launched several all-electric vehicles based on Tesla's original invention.

The successful commercialization of a new product or service allows a firm to extract temporary monopoly profits. Apple's innovation by launching the iPhone reshaped the smartphone industry in its favor, resulting in a temporary competitive advantage. To sustain a competitive advantage, however, a firm must continuously innovate—that is, it must produce a string of successful new products or services over time. In this spirit, not only has Apple introduced incrementally improved iPhones, but also the firm has launched other innovative mobile devices such as the iPad line of products, multimedia tablet computers created with the intent to drive convergence in computing, telecommunications, and media content.

Successful innovators can benefit from a number of **first-mover advantages**,[12] including economies of scale as well as experience and learning-curve effects (as discussed in Chapter 6). First movers may also benefit from *network effects* (see Strategy Highlight 7.1 later in this chapter). Moreover, first movers may hold important intellectual property such as critical patents. They may also be able to lock in key suppliers as well as customers through increasing switching costs. For example, users of Microsoft Word might find the switching costs entailed in moving to a different word-processing software prohibitive. Not only would they need to spend many hours learning the new software, but collaborators would also need to have compatible software installed and be familiar with the program to open and revise shared documents.

Google (by offering Google Docs, a free web-based suite of application software such as word-processing, spreadsheet, and presentation programs) is attempting to minimize switching costs by leveraging *cloud computing*—a real-time network of shared computing resources via the Internet. Rather than requiring each user to have the appropriate

EXHIBIT 7.2 / The 4-I's: Idea, Invention, Innovation, and Imitation

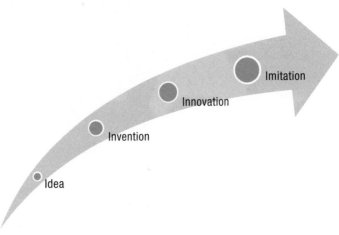

---

innovation The commercialization of any new product or process, or the modification and recombination of existing ones. To drive growth, innovation also needs to be useful and successfully implemented.

entrepreneurs The agents that introduce change into the competitive system. They do this not only by figuring out how to use inventions, but also by introducing new products or services, new production processes, and new forms of organization.

first-mover advantages Competitive benefits that accrue to the successful innovator.

EXHIBIT 7.3 / Innovation: A Novel and Useful Idea That Is Successfully Implemented

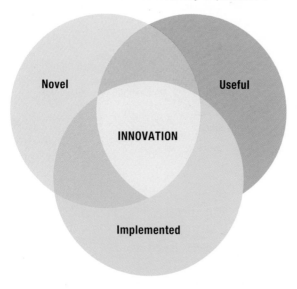

software installed on his or her personal computer, the software is maintained and updated in the cloud. Files are also saved in the cloud, which allows collaboration in real time globally wherever one can access an Internet connection.

It is important to note that innovation need not be high-tech in order to be a potent competitive weapon, as P&G's history of innovative new product launches such as the Swiffer line of cleaning products shows. P&G uses the *razor–razor-blade business model* (introduced in Chapter 5), where the consumer purchases the handle at a low price, but must pay a premium for replacement refills and pads over time. As shown in Exhibit 7.3, an innovation needs to be novel, useful, and successfully implemented in order to help firms gain and sustain a competitive advantage.

The innovation process ends with *imitation.* If an innovation is successful in the marketplace, competitors will attempt to imitate it. As discussed in detail when introducing the VRIO framework in Chapter 4, Samsung's Galaxy line of smartphones has been able to imitate successfully the look and feel of Apple's iPhones. As featured in the Chapter-Case, Wikipedia has some 500 million readers monthly, making it one of the most-visited websites. This success has not gone unnoticed. Scholarpedia, a competitor to Wikipedia, combines features from Wikipedia such as open-source content submission with features from Britannica such as strict quality control by leading scholarly experts.

7.2 Strategic and Social Entrepreneurship

Apply strategic management concepts to entrepreneurship and innovation.

entrepreneurship The process by which people undertake economic risk to innovate—to create new products, processes, and sometimes new organizations.

Entrepreneurship describes the process by which change agents undertake economic risk to innovate—to create new products, processes, and sometimes new organizations.[13] Entrepreneurs innovate by commercializing ideas and inventions.[14] They seek out or create new business opportunities and then assemble the resources necessary to exploit them.[15] If successful, entrepreneurship not only drives the competitive process, it also creates value for the individual entrepreneurs and society at large.

Although many new ventures fail, some achieve spectacular success. Examples of successful entrepreneurs are:

■ Jeff Bezos is the founder of Amazon.com, the world's largest online retailer. The stepson of a Cuban immigrant, Bezos graduated from Princeton and then worked as a financial analyst on Wall Street. In 1994, after reading that the Internet was growing by 2,000 percent a month, he set out to leverage the Internet as a new distribution channel. Listing products that could be sold online, he finally settled on books because that retail market was fairly fragmented, with huge inefficiencies in its distribution system. Perhaps even more important, books represent a perfect commodity, because they are identical regardless of where a consumer buys them. This reduced uncertainty when introducing online shopping to consumers. In a comprehensive research study that evaluated the long-term performance of CEOs globally, Jeff Bezos was ranked #2, just behind the late Steve Jobs (Apple), but ahead of Yun Jong-Yong (Samsung).[16]

- Oprah Winfrey, best-known for her self-titled TV talk show, is also founder and CEO of Harpo Productions, a multimedia company. Some of Harpo's well-known products include *The Oprah Winfrey Show, Dr. Phil, The Rachael Ray Show, The Dr. Oz Show, Oprah.com, O, The Oprah Magazine,* and *O at Home.* In January 2011, she launched a new cable-TV channel jointly with Discovery Communications: *OWN, The Oprah Winfrey Network.*[17] A graduate of Tennessee State University, Oprah used her entrepreneurial talents to rise from poverty and an abusive childhood to become one of the most successful entrepreneurs in the multimedia business, with a net worth of over $2 billion.[18] In 2011, Oprah Winfrey ended her all-time record-setting talk show to devote her entrepreneurial talents to *OWN* (which is yet to turn a profit—it has lost more than $330 million since inception). To make *OWN* more successful, Oprah Winfrey took over the position as CEO in addition to Chief Creative Officer. Her skillful interview with Lance Armstrong, in which the disgraced cyclist confessed for the first time publicly to the use of doping, drew a record 4.3 million viewers.

- Elon Musk is an engineer and serial entrepreneur with a deep passion to "solve environmental, social and economic challenges."[19] Elon Musk left his native South Africa at age 17. He went to Canada and then to the United States, where he completed a bachelor's degree in economics and physics at the University of Pennsylvania. After only two days in a PhD program in applied physics and material sciences at Stanford University, Mr. Musk left graduate school to found Zip2, an online provider of content publishing software for news organizations. Four years later, in 1999, computer maker Compaq acquired Zip2 for $341 million (and was in turn acquired by HP in 2002). Elon Musk moved on to co-found PayPal, an online payment processor. When eBay acquired PayPal for $1.5 billion in 2002, Elon Musk had the financial resources to pursue his passion to use science and engineering to solve social and economic challenges. He is leading three new ventures simultaneously: electric cars with Tesla Motors (featured in ChapterCase 3), renewable energy with SolarCity, and space exploration with SpaceX.

Strategic entrepreneurship describes the pursuit of innovation using tools and concepts from strategic management.[20] We can leverage innovation for competitive advantage by applying a strategic management lens to entrepreneurship. The fundamental question of strategic entrepreneurship, therefore, is how to combine entrepreneurial actions, creating new opportunities or exploiting existing ones with strategic actions taken in the pursuit of competitive advantage.[21] This can take place within new ventures such as Tesla Motors or within established firms such as Samsung. Samsung's continued innovation in mobile devices is an example of strategic entrepreneurship: Samsung's managers use strategic analysis, formulation, and implementation when deciding which type of mobile device to research and develop, when to launch it, and how to implement the necessary organizational changes to support the new product launch. Each new release is an innovation; each is therefore an act of entrepreneurship—planned and executed using strategic management concepts. This approach allowed Samsung to take the lead in smartphones from Apple in terms of worldwide units sold.[22]

Social entrepreneurship describes the pursuit of social goals by using entrepreneurship. Social entrepreneurs evaluate the performance of their ventures not only by financial metrics but also by ecological and social contribution. They use a *triple-bottom-line* approach to assess performance (as discussed in Chapter 5). Examples of social entrepreneurship ventures include Teach For America (whose vision, mission, and values we discussed in Chapter 2), TOMS Shoes (which gives a pair of shoes to an economically disadvantaged child for every pair of shoes it sells), BetterWorldBooks (an online bookstore that "harnesses the power of capitalism to bring literacy and opportunity to people around the world"),[23] and Wikipedia (discussed in the ChapterCase).

strategic entrepreneurship The pursuit of innovation using tools and concepts from strategic management.

social entrepreneurship The pursuit of social goals by using entrepreneurship.

The founder of Wikipedia, Jimmy Wales, is a social entrepreneur.[24] Raised in Alabama, Wales was educated by his mother and grandmother who ran a nontraditional school. In 1994, he dropped out of a doctoral program in economics at Indiana University to take a job at a stock brokerage firm in Chicago. In the evenings he wrote computer code for fun and built a web browser. During the late 1990s Internet boom, Wales was one of the first to grasp the power of an open-source method to provide knowledge on a very large scale. What differentiates Jimmy Wales from other web entrepreneurs is his idealism: Wikipedia is free for the end user and supports itself solely by donations (and not, for example, by online advertising). Jimmy Wales' idealism is a form of social entrepreneurship: His vision is to make the entire repository of human knowledge available to anyone, anywhere for free.

Since entrepreneurs and the innovations they unleash frequently create entire new industries, we now turn to a discussion of the industry life cycle to derive implications for competitive strategy.

7.3 Innovation and the Industry Life Cycle

LO7-3

Describe the competitive implications of different stages in the industry life cycle.

industry life cycle
The five different stages—introduction, growth, shakeout, maturity, and decline—that occur in the evolution of an industry over time.

Innovations frequently lead to the birth of new industries. Innovative advances in IT and logistics facilitated the creation of the overnight express delivery industry by FedEx and that of big-box retailing by Walmart. The Internet set online retailing in motion, with new companies such as Amazon and eBay taking the lead, and revolutionized the advertising industry through Google and Facebook. Advances in nanotechnology are revolutionizing many different industries, ranging from medical diagnostics and surgery to lighter and stronger airplane components.[25]

Industries tend to follow a predictable **industry life cycle**: As an industry evolves over time, we can identify five distinct stages: *introduction, growth, shakeout, maturity,* and *decline.*[26] We illustrate how the type of innovation changes at each stage of the life cycle as well as how innovation can initiate and drive a new life cycle.

The number and size of competitors change as the industry life cycle unfolds, and different types of consumers enter the market at each stage. That is, both the supply and demand sides of the market change as the industry ages. Each stage of the industry life cycle requires different competencies for the firm to perform well and to satisfy that stage's unique customer group. We first introduce the life cycle model before discussing different customer groups in more depth when introducing the *crossing-the-chasm* concept later in this chapter.[27]

Exhibit 7.4 depicts a typical industry life cycle, focusing on the smartphone industry in emerging and developed economies. In a stylized industry life cycle model, the horizontal axis shows time (in years) and the vertical axis market size. In Exhibit 7.4, however, we are taking a snapshot of the global smartphone industry in the year 2014. This implies that we are joining two different life cycles (one for emerging economies and one for developed economies) in the same exhibit at one point in time.

The development of most industries follows an S-curve. Initial demand for a new product or service is often slow to take off, then accelerates, before decelerating, and eventually turning to zero, and even becoming negative as a market contracts.

As shown in Exhibit 7.4, in emerging economies such as Argentina, Brazil, China, India, Indonesia, Mexico, and Russia, the smartphone industry is in the growth stage (in 2014). The market for smartphones in these countries is expected to grow rapidly over the next few years. More and more of the consumers in these countries with very large populations are expected to upgrade from a simple mobile phone to a smartphone such as the iPhone or Galaxy.

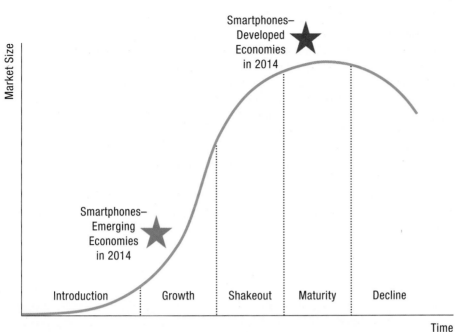

EXHIBIT 7.4

Industry Life Cycle:
The Smartphone
Industry in Emerging
and Developed
Economies

In contrast, the market for smartphones is in the maturity stage (in 2014) in developed economies such as Australia, Canada, Germany, Japan, South Korea, the United Kingdom, and the United States. This implies that developed economies moved through the prior three stages of the industry life cycle (introductory, growth, and shakeout) some years earlier. Because the smartphone industry is mature in these markets, little or no growth in market size is expected over the next few years because most consumers own smartphones. This implies that any market share gain by one firm comes at the expense of others. Competitive intensity is expected to be high.

Each stage of the industry life cycle—introduction, growth, shakeout, maturity, and decline—has different strategic implications for competing firms. We now discuss each stage in detail.

INTRODUCTION STAGE

When an individual inventor or company launches a successful innovation, a new industry may emerge. In this introductory stage, the innovator's core competency is R&D, which is necessary to creating a new product category that will attract customers. This is a capital-intensive process, in which the innovator is investing in designing a unique product, trying new ideas to attract customers, and producing small quantities—all of which contribute to a high price when the product is launched. The initial market size is very small, and growth is slow.

In this introductory stage, when barriers to entry tend to be high, generally only a few firms are active in the market. In their competitive struggle for market share, they emphasize unique product features and performance rather than price.

Although there are some benefits to being early in the market (as previously discussed), innovators also may encounter some *first-mover disadvantages*. They must educate potential customers about the product's intended benefits, find distribution channels and complementary assets, and continue to perfect the fledgling product. Although a core competency in R&D is necessary to create or enter an industry in the introductory stage, some competency in marketing also is helpful in achieving a successful product launch and market acceptance. Competition can be intense, and early winners are well-positioned to stake out a strong position for the future. As one of the main innovators in software for mobile devices, Google's Android operating system for smartphones is enjoying a strong market position and substantial lead over competitors.

The strategic objective during the introductory stage is to achieve market acceptance and seed future growth. One way to accomplish these objectives is to initiate and leverage **network effects,**[28] the positive effect that one user of a product or service has on the value of that product for other users. Network effects occur when the value of a product or service increases, often exponentially, with the number of users. If successful, network effects propel the industry to the next stage of the life cycle, the growth stage (which we discuss next). Strategy Highlight 7.1 describes how Apple leveraged the network effects generated by numerous complementary software applications (apps) to achieve a strong position in the smartphone industry.

network effects The positive effect (externality) that one user of a product or service has on the value of that product for other users.

Strategy Highlight 7.1

Apple Leverages Network Effects to Propel Growth

Apple launched its enormously successful iPhone in the summer of 2007. A year later, it followed up with the Apple App Store, which boasts that, for almost anything you might need, "there's an app for that." *Apps* are small software programs developed to provide mobile users with inexpensive business and personal services wherever they may be. Popular apps allow iPhone users to access their business contacts via LinkedIn, call colleagues overseas via Skype, check delivery of their Zappos packages shipped via UPS, get the latest news on Twitter, and engage in customer relationship management using Salesforce.com. You can stream music via Pandora, watch YouTube videos, access Facebook to check on your friends, post the latest photos using Instagram, or pin the latest fads about home décor on Pinterest.

Even more important is the effect that apps have on the value of an iPhone. Arguably, the explosive growth of the iPhone is due to the fact that the Apple App Store offers the largest selection of apps to its users. Almost 1 million apps were downloaded 50 billion times as of spring 2013. Moreover, Apple argues that users have a better experience because the apps take advantage of the tight integration of hardware and software provided by the iPhone. The availability of apps, in turn, leads to network effects that increase the value of the iPhone for its users. Exhibit 7.5 shows how. Increased value creation, as we know from Chapter 6, is positively related to demand, which in turn increases the installed base, meaning the number of people using an iPhone. This in turn incentivizes software developers to write more apps. Making apps widely available strengthened Apple's position in the smartphone industry. Based on positive feedback loops, a virtuous cycle emerges where one factor positively reinforces another.[29]

EXHIBIT 7.5 / Leveraging Network Effects to Drive Demand: Apple's iPhone

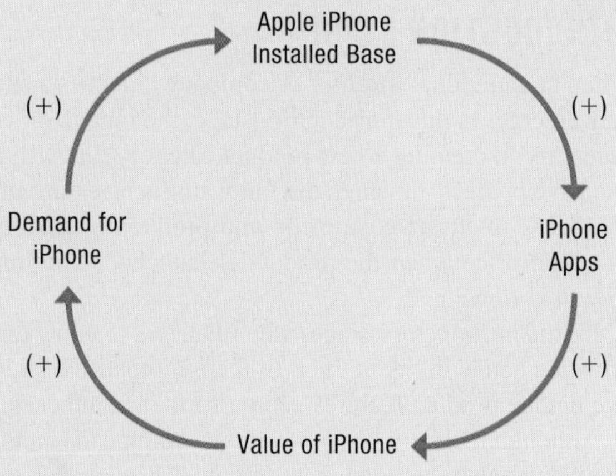

GROWTH STAGE

Market growth accelerates in the growth stage of the industry life cycle (see Exhibit 7.4). After the initial innovation has gained some market acceptance, demand increases rapidly as first-time buyers rush to enter the market, convinced by the proof-of-concept demonstrated in the introductory stage.

As the size of the market expands, a **standard** signals the market's agreement on a common set of engineering features and design choices.[30] Standards can emerge bottom-up through competition in the marketplace, or be imposed top-down by government or other standard-setting agencies such as the Institute of Electrical and Electronics Engineers (IEEE) that develops and sets industrial standards in a broad range of industries, including energy, electric power, biomedical and health care technology, IT, telecommunications, consumer electronics, aerospace, and nanotechnology.

An agreed-upon standard, such as the IBM PC, ensures that all components of the system work well together, regardless of who developed them. It also helps legitimize the new technology by reducing uncertainty and confusion. A standard tends to capture a larger market share and can persist for a long time. The Wintel standard (a portmanteau of Windows and Intel) marked the beginning of exponential growth in the personal computer industry; it still holds some 90 percent of market share.

An example of a recent standards war that was fought in the marketplace is high-definition format Blu-ray versus the HD-DVD format. Blu-ray, backed by an association of electronics companies including Sony, Panasonic, Philips, LG, Hitachi, and Samsung, bested the HD-DVD format backed by Toshiba. Some argue that Sony's PlayStation 3 acted as a catalyst for adopting the Blu-ray format. A tipping point in favor of the Blu-ray format was reached when Warner Bros. decided to release discs only in Blu-ray format beginning in the summer of 2008. Within weeks, leading retailers such as Walmart, Best Buy, and the now-defunct Circuit City began carrying DVDs in Blu-ray format and did not stock as large a selection in the HD-DVD format; Netflix and Blockbuster began renting Blu-ray DVDs predominantly. As a consequence, thousands of titles are now available on high-definition Blu-ray discs, while production has ceased on HD-DVDs. The competitive implications are tremendous: Industry agreement on the format has opened a new market for both Blu-ray disc players and titles. Barriers to entry fell as technological uncertainties were overcome, and many new and established firms rushed to participate in the growth opportunity.

Government bodies or industry associations can also set standards by making top-down decisions. The European Union determined in the 1980s that GSM (Global System for Mobile Communications) should be the standard for cell phones in Europe. The United States relied instead on a market-based approach, and CDMA (code division multiple access), a proprietary standard developed by Qualcomm, emerged as an early leader. While North American manufacturers and service providers such as AT&T, Verizon, Motorola, and others were fighting a format war, Scandinavian companies such as Nokia and Ericsson faced no such uncertainty, and they leveraged their early lead into market dominance. Today, about 80 percent of the global mobile market uses the GSM standard.

Since demand is strong during the growth phase, both efficient and inefficient firms thrive; the rising tide lifts all boats. Moreover, prices begin to fall, often rapidly, as standard business processes are put in place and firms begin to reap economies of scale and learning. Distribution channels are expanded, and complementary assets become widely available.[31]

After a standard is established in an industry, the basis of competition tends to move away from product innovations toward process innovations.[32] **Product innovations**, as the name suggests, are new or recombined knowledge embodied in new products—the jet airplane, electric vehicle, MP3 player, smartphones, and tablet computers. On the other

---

standard An agreed-upon solution about a common set of engineering features and design choices.

product innovations New or recombined knowledge embodied in new products.

process innovations
New ways to produce existing products or deliver existing services.

hand, **process innovations** are new ways to produce existing products or to deliver existing services. Process innovations are made possible through advances such as the Internet, lean manufacturing, Six Sigma, biotechnology, nanotechnology, and so on.

Process innovation must not be high-tech to be impactful, however. The invention of the standardized shipping container, for instance, has transformed global trade.[33] By loading goods into uniform containers that could easily be moved between trucks, rail, and ships, significant savings in cost and time were accomplished. Before containerization was invented some 60 years ago, it cost almost $6 to load a ton of (loose) cargo, and theft was rampant. After containerization, the cost for loading a ton of cargo had plummeted to $0.16 and theft all but disappeared (because containers are sealed at the departing factory). Efficiency gains in terms of labor and time were even more impressive. Before containerization, dock labor could move 1.7 tons per hour onto a cargo ship. After containerization, this had jumped to 30 tons per hour. Ports are now able to accommodate much larger ships, and travel time across the oceans has fallen in half. As a consequence, costs for shipping goods (such as cars) across the globe have fallen rapidly. Moreover, containerization enabled optimization of global supply chains and set the stage for subsequent process innovations such as *just-in-time (JIT) operations management.* Taken together, a set of research studies estimated that containerization alone more than tripled international trade within five years of adopting this critical process innovation.[34]

Exhibit 7.6 shows the level of product and process innovation throughout the entire life cycle.[35] In the introductory stage, the level of *product* innovation is at a maximum because new features increasing perceived consumer value are critical to gaining traction in the market. In contrast, process innovation is at a minimum in the introductory stage because companies only produce a small number of products, often just prototypes or beta versions. The main concern is to commercialize the invention—that is, to demonstrate that the product works and that a market exists.

The relative importance, however, reverses over time. Frequently, a standard emerges during the growth stage of the industry life cycle (indicated by the dashed line in Exhibit 7.6). At that point, most of the technological and commercial uncertainties about the new product are gone. After the market accepts a product innovation, and a standard for the new technology has emerged, *process innovation rapidly becomes more important than product innovation.* As market demand increases, economies of scale kick in: Firms establish and optimize standard business processes through applications of lean manufacturing, Six Sigma, and so on. As a consequence, product improvements become incremental, while the level of process innovation rises rapidly.

The core competencies for competitive advantage in the growth stage tend to shift toward manufacturing and marketing capabilities, with an R&D emphasis on process innovation in order to improve efficiency. Competitive rivalry is muted because the market is growing fast. Since market demand is robust in this stage and more competitors have entered the market, there tends to be more strategic variety: Some competitors will

EXHIBIT 7.6 / Product and Process Innovation and the Emergence of an Industry Standard Throughout an Industry Life Cycle

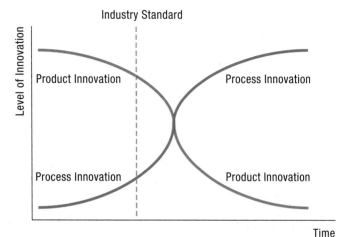

continue to follow a *differentiation* strategy, emphasizing unique features, product functionality, and reliability. Other firms employ a *cost-leadership strategy* in order to offer an acceptable level of value but lower prices to consumers. They realize that lower cost is likely a key success factor in the future, because this will allow the firm to lower prices and attract more consumers into the market. When introduced in the spring of 2010, for example, Apple's first-generation iPad was priced at $829 for 64GB with a 3G Wi-Fi connection.[36] Just three years later, in spring 2013, the same model was priced at only one-third of the original price, or $275.[37] Access to efficient and large-scale manufacturing operations (such as those offered by Foxconn in China, the company that assembles most of Apple's products) and effective supply-chain capabilities are key success factors when market demand increases rapidly.

The key objective for firms during the growth phase is to stake out a strong strategic position not easily imitated by rivals. In the fast-growing shapewear industry, startup company Spanx has staked out a strong position. In 1998, Florida State University graduate Sara Blakely decided to cut the feet off her pantyhose to enhance her looks when wearing pants.[38] Soon after she obtained a patent for her bodyshaping undergarments, and Spanx began production and retailing of its shapewear in 2000. Sales grew exponentially after Blakely appeared on *The Oprah Winfrey Show.* By 2010, Spanx had grown to 100 employees and sold millions of Spanx "power panties," with revenues exceeding $1 billion. To stake out a strong position and to preempt competitors, Spanx now offers over 200 products ranging from slimming apparel and swimsuits to bras and activewear. Moreover, it now designs and manufactures body-shaping undergarments for men ("Spanx for Men – MANX"). Spanx products are now available in over 50 countries globally via the Internet. Moreover, to strengthen its strategic position and brand image in the United States, Spanx is opening retail stores across the country.

The shapewear industry's explosive growth has attracted several other players: Flexees by Maidenform, Body Wrap, and Miraclesuit, to name a few. They are all attempting to carve out positions in the new industry. Given Spanx's ability to stake out a strong position during the growth stage of the industry life cycle and the fact that it continues to be a moving target, it might be difficult for competitors to dislodge the company.

Also, taking risk as an entrepreneur paid off for Spanx's founder Sara Blakely: After investing an initial $5,000 into her startup, she became the world's youngest self-made female billionaire. In 2012, Sara Blakely was also listed in the *Time 100,* the annual list of the most influential people in the world.

SHAKEOUT STAGE

Rapid industry growth and expansion cannot go on indefinitely. As the industry moves into the next stage of the industry life cycle, the rate of growth declines (see Exhibit 7.4). Demand was largely satisfied in the prior growth stage. Given the large market size achieved from the growth stage, any additional market demand in the next stage is limited. Demand now consists of replacement or repeat purchases only. This limited market demand in turn increases competitive intensity within the industry. Firms begin to compete directly against one another for market share, rather than trying to capture a share of an increasing pie. As rivals vie for a shrinking pie and competitive intensity is increasing, the weaker firms are forced out of the industry. This is the reason why this phase of the industry life cycle is called the shakeout stage: Only the strongest competitors survive increasing rivalry as firms begin to cut prices and offer more services, all in an attempt to capture more of a shrinking market. This type of cut-throat competition erodes profitability of all but the most efficient firms in the industry. As a consequence, the industry often consolidates, as the weakest competitors either are acquired by stronger firms or exit through bankruptcy.

The winners in this increasingly competitive environment are generally firms that stake out a strong position as cost leaders. Key success factors at this stage are the manufacturing and process engineering capabilities that can be used to drive costs down. As discussed earlier, following the emergence of a standard during the growth stage, the importance of process innovation increases rapidly and the importance of product innovation diminishes quickly.

Assuming an acceptable value proposition, price is the dominant competitive weapon in the mature stage; product features and performance requirements are now well established. A few firms may be able to implement an integration strategy, combining differentiation and low cost, but given the intensity of competition, many weaker firms are forced to exit. Any firm that does not have a clear strategic profile is likely to not survive the shakeout phase.

MATURITY STAGE

Generally, the larger firms enjoying economies of scale are the ones that survived the shakeout phase as the industry consolidated and most excess capacity was removed. After the shakeout is completed and a few firms remain, the industry enters the maturity stage. During the fourth stage of the industry life cycle, the industry structure morphs into an oligopoly with only a few large firms. The market has reached its maximum size, and industry demand is likely to be zero or even negative going forward. As shown in Exhibit 7.4, the smartphone industry in the U.S. and other developed economies is just entering the maturity stage. Competitive intensity is likely to increase going forward.

The domestic airline industry has been in the maturity stage for a long time. The large number of bankruptcies, as well as the wave of mega-mergers such as those of Delta and Northwest, United and Continental, and American Airlines and US Airways are a consequence of low or zero growth in a mature market characterized by significant excess capacity.

DECLINE STAGE

Changes in the external environment (such as those discussed in Chapter 3 when presenting the PESTEL framework) often take industries from maturity to decline. In this final stage of the industry life cycle, the size of the market contracts as demand falls.

At the end of a life cycle, the level of process innovation reaches its maximum as firms attempt to lower cost as much as possible, while the level of incremental product innovation reaches its minimum, as Exhibit 7.6 shows. If an innovation emerges that opens up a new industry, then this dynamic interplay between product and process innovation starts anew.

If there is any remaining excess industry capacity in the decline stage, this puts strong pressure on prices and can further increase competitive intensity, especially if the industry has high exit barriers. At this stage, managers generally have four strategic options: *exit, harvest, maintain,* or *consolidate:*[39]

- Some firms are forced to *exit* the industry by bankruptcy or liquidation. The U.S. textile industry has experienced a large number of exits over the last few decades, mainly due to low-cost foreign competition.

- In pursuing a *harvest strategy,* the firm reduces investments in product support and allocates only a minimum of human and other resources. While several companies such as IBM, Brother, Olivetti, and Nakajima still offer typewriters, they don't invest much in future innovation. Instead, they are maximizing cash flow from their existing typewriter product line.

- Philip Morris, on the other hand, is following a *maintain strategy* with its Marlboro brand, continuing to support marketing efforts at a given level despite the fact that U.S. cigarette consumption has been declining.

- Although market size shrinks in a declining industry, some firms may choose to *consolidate* the industry by buying rivals (those who choose to exit). This allows the consolidating firm to stake out a strong position—possibly approaching monopolistic market power, albeit in a declining industry.

Although chewing tobacco is a declining industry, the Swedish Match company has pursued a number of acquisitions to consolidate its strategic position in the industry. It acquired, among other firms, the Pinkerton Tobacco company of Owensboro, Kentucky, maker of the Red Man brand. Red Man is the leading chewing tobacco brand in the United States. Red Man has carved out a strong strategic position built on a superior reputation for a quality product and by past endorsements of major league baseball players since 1904. Despite a federally mandated prohibition on marketing and gory product warnings detailing the health risk of chewing tobacco, the Red Man brand has remained not only popular, but also profitable.

CROSSING THE CHASM

The industry life cycle model assumes a more or less smooth transition from one stage to another. This holds true for most continuous innovations that require little or no change in consumer behavior.

LO7-4

Derive strategic implications of the crossing-the-chasm framework.

In the influential bestseller *Crossing the Chasm*[40] Geoffrey Moore documented that many innovators, however, were unable to successfully transition from one stage of the industry life cycle to the next. Based on empirical observations, Moore's core argument is that each stage of the industry life cycle is dominated by a different customer group. Different customer groups with distinctly different preferences enter the industry at each stage of the industry life cycle. Each customer group responds differently to a technological innovation. This is due to differences in the psychological, demographic, and social attributes observed in each unique customer segment. Moore's main contribution is that the significant differences between the customer groups that enter early during the introductory stage of the industry life cycle versus customers that enter later during the growth stage make a firm's smooth transition between the different parts of the industry life cycle difficult. That is, these distinct differences between customer groups lead to a big gulf or *chasm* into which companies and their innovations frequently fall. Only companies that recognize these differences and are able to apply the appropriate competencies at each stage of the industry life cycle will have a chance to transition successfully from stage to stage.

Exhibit 7.7 shows the *chasm framework* and the different customer segments. The industry life cycle model (shown in Exhibit 7.4) follows an S-curve leading up to 100 percent

EXHIBIT 7.7 /

The Crossing-the-
Chasm Framework

SOURCE: Adapted from
G. A. Moore (1991), *Crossing
the Chasm: Marketing and
Selling Disruptive Products to
Mainstream Customers* (New
York: HarperCollins), p. 17.

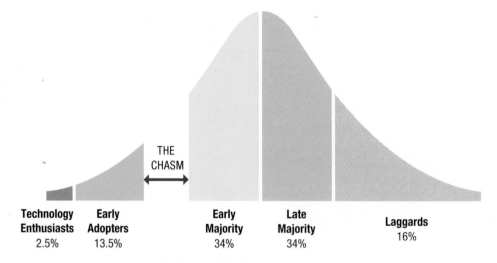

total market potential that can be reached during the maturity stage. In contrast, the *chasm framework,* breaks down the 100 percent market potential into different customer segments, highlighting the *incremental* contribution each specific segment can bring into the market. This results in the familiar Bell curve. Note the big gulf, or *chasm,* separating the early adopters from the early and late majority that make up the mass market. Each stage customer segment is also separated by smaller chasms. Both the large competitive chasm and the smaller ones have strategic implications, which we'll discuss next.

Both new technology ventures and innovations introduced by established firms have a high failure rate. This can be explained as a failure to successfully cross the chasm from the early users to the mass market because the firm does not recognize that the business strategy needs to be fine-tuned for each customer segment. Formulating a business strategy for each segment guided by the "*who-what-why-and-how*" questions of competition (Who to serve? What needs to satisfy? Why and how to satisfy them?), first introduced in Chapter 6, the firm will find that the core competencies to satisfy each of the different customer segments are quite different. If not recognized and addressed, this will lead to the demise of the innovation as it crashes into the chasm between life cycle stages.

We first introduce each customer group and map it to the respective stage of the industry life cycle. To illustrate, we then apply the chasm framework to a historical analysis of the smartphone industry.

TECHNOLOGY ENTHUSIASTS. The customer segment in the introductory stage of the industry life cycle is called *technology enthusiasts.*[41] This is the smallest market segment, and makes up no more than 2.5 percent of the total market potential. Technology enthusiasts often have an engineering mindset and pursue new technology proactively. They frequently seek out new products before the products are officially introduced into the market. Technology enthusiasts enjoy using beta versions of products, tinkering with the product's imperfections and providing (free) feedback and suggestions to companies. For example, many software companies such as Google and Microsoft launch beta versions to accumulate customer feedback to work out bugs prior to the official launch. Moreover, technology enthusiasts are often willing to pay a premium price to have the latest gadget. The endorsement by technology enthusiasts validates the fact that the new product does in fact work.

A recent example of an innovation that appeals to technology enthusiasts is Google Glass, a mobile computer that is worn like a pair of regular glasses. Instead of a lens, however, one side displays a small, high-definition computer screen. Google Glass allows the wearer to use the Internet and smartphone-like applications via voice commands (e.g., conduct online search, stream video, and so on). It was developed as part of Google's wildcard program (introduced in Chapter 2). Technology enthusiasts were eager to get a hold of Google Glass when made available in a beta testing program in 2013. Those interested had to compose a Google+ or Twitter message of 50 words or less explaining why they would be a good choice to test the device, and include the hash tag #ifihadglass. Some 150,000 people applied and 8,000 winners were chosen. They were required to attend a Google Glass event and pay $1,500 for the developer version of Google Glass. Although many industry leaders, including Apple's CEO Tim Cook, agree that wearable computers like the Nike+ fuel band (a physical activity tracker that is worn on the wrist; data are integrated into an online community and phone app) are important mobile devices, they suggest that there is a very large chasm between the current technology for computerized eyeglasses and a successful product for the mass market.[42]

EARLY ADOPTERS. The customers entering the market in the growth stage are *early adopters*. They make up roughly 13.5 percent of the total market potential. Early adopters, as the name suggests, are eager to buy in early into a new technology or product concept. Unlike technology enthusiasts, however, their demand is driven by their imagination and creativity rather than by the technology per se. They recognize and appreciate the possibilities the new technology can afford them in their professional and personal lives. Early adopters' demand is fueled more by intuition and vision rather than technology concerns. These are the people that lined up at Toyota dealerships in 2000 when the Prius, a hybrid electric vehicle, was first introduced in the United States. Users of Skype (a VoIP service) when it was first released in 2003 were early adopters, recognizing the possibility that Skype's service allowing free communication over the Internet anywhere in the world would have value in their personal and professional lives. Since early adopters are not influenced by standard technological performance metrics but by intuition and imagination (What can this new product do for me or my business?), the firm needs to communicate the product's potential applications in a more direct way than it attracted the initial technology enthusiasts. Attracting the early adopters to the new offering is critical to opening up any new high-tech market segment.

EARLY MAJORITY. The customers coming into the market in the growth stage are called *early majority*. Their main consideration in deciding whether or not to adopt a new technological innovation is a strong sense of practicality. They are pragmatists and are most concerned with the question of what the new technology can do for them. Before adopting a new product or service, they weigh the benefits and costs carefully. Customers in the early majority are aware that many hyped new product introductions will fade away, so they prefer to wait and see how things shake out. They like to observe how early adopters are using the product. Early majority customers rely on endorsements by others. They seek out reputable references such as reviews in prominent trade journals or in magazines such as *Consumer Reports*.

Because the early majority makes up roughly one-third of the entire market potential, winning them over is critical to the commercial success of the innovation. They are on the cusp of the mass market. Bringing the early majority on board is the key to catching the growth wave of the industry life cycle. Once they decide to enter the market, a *herding effect* is frequently observed: the early majority enters in large numbers.[43]

To summarize, the significant differences in the attitudes toward technology of the early majority when compared to the early adopters signify the wide competitive gulf—*the*

Tesla Motors CEO Elon Musk, left, in front of a Tesla Roadster; Fisker Automotive CEO Henrik Fisker, right, in front of a Fisker Karma.

chasm—between these two consumer segments (see Exhibit 7.7). Without adequate demand from the early majority, most innovative products wither away.

Fisker Automotive, a California-based designer and manufacturer of premium plug-in hybrid vehicles, fell into the chasm because it was unable to transition to the mass market. Between its founding in 2007 and 2012, Fisker sold some 1,800 vehicles of its Karma model, a $100K sports car, to early adopters. It was unable, however, to follow up with a lower-cost model to attract the early majority into the market. In addition, technology and reliability issues for the Karma could not be overcome. By 2013, Fisker had crashed into a chasm.[44]

In contrast, Tesla Motors, the maker of all-electric vehicles introduced in ChapterCase 3, and a fierce rival of Fisker at one point in time, was able to overcome the chasm by successfully launching a mass-market car (the Model S, a family sedan). Critical to attracting the early majority, Tesla's Model S received a strong endorsement as the 2013 *MotorTrend* Car of the Year and the highest test scores ever awarded by *Consumer Reports*. This made the early majority feel more comfortable in considering and purchasing a Tesla vehicle.

LATE MAJORITY. The next wave of growth comes from buyers in the *late majority* entering the market. Like the early majority, they are a large customer segment, making up approximately 34 percent of the total market potential. Combined, the early adopters and early majority make up the lion's share of the market potential. Most industry growth and firm profitability, therefore, are driven by demand coming from just two groups—early and late majority.

Members of the early and late majority are also quite similar in their attitudes toward new technology. The late majority shares all the concerns of the early majority. In addition, there is one important difference. Although the early majority is confident in their ability to master the new technology, the late majority is not. They prefer to wait until standards have emerged and are firmly entrenched, so that uncertainty is much reduced. The late majority also prefers to buy from well-established firms with a strong brand image rather than from unknown new ventures.

LAGGARDS. Finally, *laggards*—customers who adopt a new product only if it is absolutely necessary, such as first-time cell phone adopters in the U.S. today—are the last consumer segment to come into the market. These customers generally don't want new technology, either for personal or economic reasons. Given their reluctance to adopt new technology, they are generally not considered worth pursuing. Laggards make up no more than 16 percent of the total market potential. They tend to enter the market after it is completely mature and frequently during the decline stage. Their demand is far too small to compensate for reduced demand from the early and late majority (jointly almost 70 percent of total market demand), who are moving on to different products and services.

CROSSING THE CHASM: APPLICATION TO THE SMARTPHONE INDUSTRY.

Let's apply the crossing-the-chasm framework to one specific industry. Keep in mind that in this model, the transition from stage to stage in the industry life cycle is characterized by different competitive chasms that open up because of important differences between customer groups. Although the large chasm between early adopters and the early majority is the main cause of demise for technological innovations, other smaller mini-chasms open up between each stage.

Exhibit 7.8 shows the application of the chasm model to the smartphone industry. The first victim was Motorola's Iridium, an ill-fated satellite-based telephone system.[45] Development began in 1992 after the spouse of a Motorola engineer complained that they couldn't get any data or voice access to check on clients while vacationing on a remote island. Motorola's solution was to launch 66 satellites into low orbit to provide global voice and data coverage. In late 1998, Motorola began offering its satellite phone service, charging $5,000 per handset (which was almost too heavy to carry around) and up to $14 per minute for calls.[46] Problems in consumer adoption beyond the few technology enthusiasts became rapidly apparent. The Iridium phone could not be used inside buildings or in cars. Rather, to receive a satellite signal, the phone needed an unobstructed line of sight to a satellite. Iridium crashed into the first chasm, never moving beyond technology enthusiasts. For Motorola, it was a billion-dollar business blunder. Iridium was soon displaced by cell phones that relied on earth-based networks of radio towers. The global satellite telephone industry never moved beyond the introductory stage of the industry life cycle.

The first Treo, a fully functioning smartphone combining voice and data capabilities, was released in 2002 by Handspring. The Treo fell into the main chasm that arises between early adopters and the early majority (see Exhibit 7.8). Technical problems, combined with a lack of apps and an overly rigid contract with Sprint as its sole service provider, prevented the Treo from gaining traction in the market beyond early adopters.

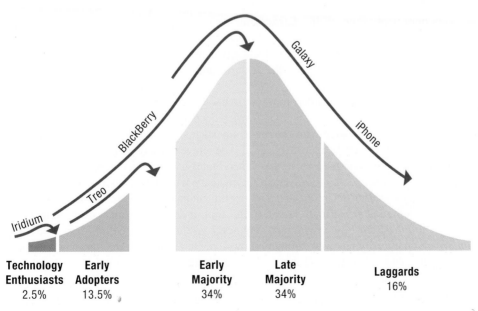

EXHIBIT 7.8

Crossing the Chasm: The Smartphone Industry

| Technology Enthusiasts 2.5% | Early Adopters 13.5% | Early Majority 34% | Late Majority 34% | Laggards 16% |

For these reasons, the Treo was not an attractive product for the early majority, who rejected it. This caused the Treo to plunge into the chasm. Just a year later, Handspring was folded into Palm, which in turn was acquired by HP for $1bn in 2010.[47] HP shut down Palm in 2011 and wrote off the acquisition.[48]

Research in Motion (RIM)[49] introduced its first fully functioning BlackBerry smartphone in 2000. It was a huge success—especially with two key consumer segments. First, corporate IT managers were early adopters. They became product champions for the BlackBerry because of its encrypted security software and its reliability in always staying connected to a company's network. This allowed users to receive e-mail and other data in real time, anywhere in the world where wireless service was provided. Second, corporate executives were the early majority pulling the BlackBerry over the chasm because it allowed 24/7 access to data and voice. RIM was able to create a *beachhead* to cross the chasm between the technology enthusiasts and early adopters on one side and the early majority on the other.[50] RIM's managers were able to identify the needs of not only early adopters (e.g., IT managers) but also the early majority (e.g., executives), who pulled the BlackBerry over the chasm. By 2005, the BlackBerry had become a corporate executive status symbol. As a consequence of capturing the first three stages of the industry life cycle, between 2002 and 2007, RIM enjoyed no less than 30 percent year-over-year revenue growth as well as double-digit growth in other financial performance metrics such as return on equity. RIM enjoyed a temporary competitive advantage.

In 2007, RIM's dominance over the smartphone market began to erode quickly. The main reason was Apple's introduction of the iPhone. Although technology enthusiasts and early adopters argue that the iPhone is an inferior product to the BlackBerry based on technological criteria, the iPhone enticed not only the early majority, but also the late majority to enter the market. For the late majority, encrypted software security was much less important than having fun with a device that allowed users to surf the web, take pictures, play games, and send and receive e-mail. Moreover, the Apple iTunes Store soon provided thousands of apps for basically any kind of service. While the BlackBerry couldn't cross the gulf between the early and the late majority, Apple's iPhone captured the mass market rapidly. Moreover, consumers began to bring their personal iPhone to work, which forced corporate IT departments to open up their services beyond the BlackBerry. Apple rode the wave of this success to capture each market segment. Likewise, Samsung with its Galaxy line of phones is enjoying a similar success across the different market segments.

This brief application of the chasm framework to the smartphone industry shows its usefulness. It provides insightful explanations of why some companies failed, while others succeeded—and thus goes at the core of strategy management.

In summary, Exhibit 7.9 details the features and strategic implications of the entire industry life cycle at each stage.

A word of caution is in order, however: Although the industry life cycle is a useful framework to guide strategic choice, industries do not *necessarily evolve* through these stages. Moreover, innovations can emerge at any stage of the industry life cycle, which in turn can initiate a new cycle. Industries can also be rejuvenated, often in the declining stage. Although the motorcycle industry in the United States had been declining for a long time, Harley Davidson was able to rejuvenate the industry with new designs and an extended lineup of bikes, greater reliability, and a more efficient and professional dealer network.

Although the industry life cycle is a useful tool, it does not explain everything about changes in industries. Some industries may never go through the entire life cycle, while others are continually renewed through innovation. Be aware, too, that other factors such as fads in fashion, changes in demographics, or deregulation can affect the dynamics of industry life cycles.

EXHIBIT 7.9 / Features and Strategic Implications of the Industry Life Cycle

	Life Cycle Stages				
	Introduction	**Growth**	**Shakeout**	**Maturity**	**Decline**
Core Competency	R&D, some marketing	R&D, some manufacturing, marketing	Manufacturing, process engineering	Manufacturing, process engineering, marketing	Manufacturing, process engineering, marketing, service
Type and Level of Innovation	Product innovation at a maximum; process innovation at a minimum	Product innovation decreasing; process innovation increasing	After emergence of standard: product innovation decreasing rapidly; process innovation increasing rapidly	Product innovation low; process innovation high	Product innovation at a minimum; process innovation at a maximum
Market Growth	Slow	High	Moderate and slowing down	None to moderate	Negative
Market Size	Small	Moderate	Large	Largest	Small to moderate
Price	High	Falling	Moderate	Low	Low to high
Number of Competitors	Few, if any	Many	Fewer	Moderate, but large	Few, if any
Mode of Competition	Non-price competition	Non-price competition	Shifting from non-price to price competition	Price	Price or non-price competition
Type of Buyers	Technology enthusiasts	Early adopters	Early majority	Late majority	Laggards
Business-Level Strategy	Differentiation	Differentiation	Differentiation, or integration strategy	Cost-leadership or integration strategy	Cost-leadership, differentiation, or integration strategy
Strategic Objective	Achieving market acceptance	Staking out a strong strategic position; generating "deep pockets"	Surviving by drawing on "deep pockets"	Maintaining strong strategic position	Exit, harvest, maintain, or consolidate

7.4 Types of Innovation

Because of the importance of innovation to industry life cycles and as a critical component in formulating business strategy, we now turn to a discussion of different types of innovation and the strategic implications of each. We need to know, in particular, along which dimensions we should assess innovations. This will allow us to formulate a business strategy that can leverage innovation for competitive advantage.

LO7-5

Categorize different types of innovations in the markets-and-technology framework.

One insightful way to categorize innovations is to measure their degree of newness in terms of *technology* and *markets*.[51] Here, *technology* refers to the methods and materials used to achieve a commercial objective.[52] For example, Amazon integrates different types of technologies (hardware, software, microprocessors, the Internet, logistics, and so on) to

EXHIBIT 7.10 / Types of Innovation: Combining Markets and Technologies

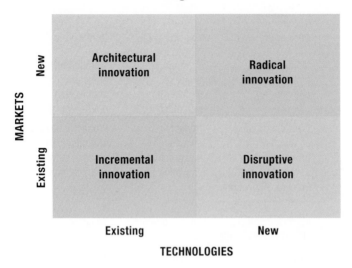

provide not only the largest selection of retail goods online, but also an array of services and mobile devices (e.g., cloud computing, Kindle tablets, Prime, and so on). We also want to understand the *market* for an innovation—e.g., whether an innovation is introduced into a new or an existing market—because an invention turns into an innovation only when it is successfully commercialized.[53] Measuring an innovation along the technology and market dimensions gives us the framework depicted in Exhibit 7.10. Along the horizontal axis, we ask whether the innovation builds on existing technologies or creates a new one. On the vertical axis, we ask whether the innovation is targeted toward existing or new markets. Four types of innovations emerge: incremental, radical, architectural, and disruptive innovations. As indicated by the color coding in Exhibit 7.10, each diagonal forms a pair: incremental versus radical innovation and architectural versus disruptive innovation.

INCREMENTAL VS. RADICAL INNOVATION

Although radical breakthroughs such as smartphones and magnetic resonance imaging (MRI) radiology capture most of our attention, the vast majority of innovations are actually incremental ones. An **incremental innovation** squarely builds on an established knowledge base and steadily improves an existing product or service offering.[54] It targets existing markets using existing technology.

On the other hand, **radical innovation** draws on novel methods or materials, is derived either from an entirely different knowledge base or from a recombination of existing knowledge bases with a new stream of knowledge, or targets new markets by using new technologies.[55] Well-known examples of radical innovations include the introduction of the mass-produced automobile (the Ford Model T), the X-ray, the airplane, and more recently biotechnology breakthroughs such as genetic engineering and the decoding of the human genome.

Many firms get their start by successfully commercializing radical innovations, some of which, such as the airplane, even give birth to new industries. Although the British firm de Havilland first commercialized the jet-powered passenger airplane, Boeing was the company that rode this radical innovation to industry dominance. More recently, Boeing's leadership has been contested by Airbus; each company has approximately half the market. This stalemate is now being challenged by aircraft manufacturers such as Bombardier of Canada and Embraer of Brazil, which are moving up-market by building larger luxury jets that are competing with some of the smaller airplane models offered by Boeing and Airbus.

A predictable pattern of innovation is that firms (often new ventures) use radical innovation to create a temporary competitive advantage. They then follow up with a string of incremental innovations to sustain that initial lead. Gillette is a prime example for this pattern of strategic innovation. In 1903, entrepreneur Mr. King C. Gillette invented and began selling the safety razor with a disposable blade. This *radical innovation* launched the

incremental innovation An innovation that squarely builds on an established knowledge base, and steadily improves an existing product or service offering; targets existing markets by using existing technology.

radical innovation An innovation that draws on novel methods or materials, is derived either from an entirely different knowledge base or from a recombination of the existing knowledge bases with a new stream of knowledge, or targets new markets by using new technologies.

Gillette company (now a brand of Procter & Gamble). To sustain its competitive advantage, Gillette not only made sure that its razors were inexpensive and widely available (by introducing the "razor and razor blade" business model), but also continually improved its razor blades. In a classic example of a string of *incremental innovations,* Gillette kept adding an additional blade with each new version of its razor until the number had gone from one to six! Though this innovation strategy seems predictable, it worked. In 2013, Gillette held 66 percent market share for razors and blades of the $13 billion industry globally. Gillette's newest razor, the Fusion ProGlide Power, costs around $12, plus $19.99 for a four-pack of cartridges. With each new razor introduction, Gillette is able to push up its per-unit cartridge price.[56]

The Gillette example shows how radical innovation created a competitive advantage that the company sustained by follow-up incremental innovation. Such an outcome is not a foregone conclusion, though. In some instances, the innovator might be outmaneuvered by low-cost disruption. As discussed in Chapter 5, the Dollar Shave Club is attempting to establish a low-cost subscription business model in order to invade Gillette's market from the bottom up.

In other instances, the innovator is outcompeted by second movers that quickly introduce a similar incremental innovation to continuously improve their own offering. For example, although CNN was the pioneer in 24-hour cable news, today Fox News is the most watched cable news network in the U.S. (although the entire industry is in decline as viewers now consume much more content online).

Once firms have achieved market acceptance of a breakthrough innovation, they tend to follow up with incremental rather than radical innovations. Over time, these companies morph into industry incumbents. Future radical innovations are generally introduced by new entrepreneurial ventures. Why is this so? The reasons concern *economic incentives, organizational inertia,* and the firm's embeddedness in an *innovation ecosystem.*[57]

ECONOMIC INCENTIVES. Economists highlight the role of *incentives* in strategic choice. Once an innovator has become an established incumbent firm (such as Google has today), it has strong incentives to defend its strategic position and market power. An emphasis on incremental innovations strengthens the incumbent firm's position and thus maintains high entry barriers. A focus on incremental innovation is particularly attractive once an industry standard has emerged and technological uncertainty is reduced. As a result, the incumbent firm uses incremental innovation to extend the time it can extract profits based on a favorable industry structure (see the discussion in Chapter 3). Any potential radical innovation threatens the incumbent firm's dominant position.

The incentives for entrepreneurial ventures, however, are just the opposite. Successfully commercializing a radical innovation is frequently the only option to enter an industry protected by high entry barriers. One of the first biotech firms, Amgen, used newly discovered drugs based on genetic engineering to overcome entry barriers to the pharmaceutical industry, in which incumbents had enjoyed notoriously high profits for several decades. Because of differential economic incentives, incumbents often push forward with incremental innovations, while new entrants focus on radical innovations.

ORGANIZATIONAL INERTIA. From an organizational perspective, as firms become established and grow, they rely more heavily on formalized business processes and structures. In some cases, the firm may experience **organizational inertia**—resistance to changes in the status quo. Incumbent firms, therefore, tend to favor incremental innovations

organizational inertia A firm's resistance to changes in the status quo.

that reinforce the existing organizational structure and power distribution while avoiding radical innovation that could disturb the existing power distribution (e.g., between different functional areas, such as R&D and marketing). New entrants, however, do not have formal organizational structures and processes, giving them more freedom to launch an initial breakthrough. (We discuss the link between organizational structure and firm strategy in depth in Chapter 11.)

INNOVATION ECOSYSTEM. A final reason incumbent firms tend to be a source of incremental rather than radical innovations is that they become embedded in an **innovation ecosystem**: a network of suppliers, buyers, complementors, and so on.[58] They no longer make independent decisions but must consider the ramifications on other parties in their innovation ecosystem. Continuous incremental innovations reinforce this network and keep all its members happy, while radical innovations disrupt it. Again, new entrants don't have to worry about preexisting innovation ecosystems, since they will be building theirs around the radical innovation they are bringing to a new market.

ARCHITECTURAL VS. DISRUPTIVE INNOVATION

Firms can also innovate by leveraging *existing technologies* into *new markets*. Doing so generally requires them to reconfigure the components of a technology, meaning they alter the overall "architecture" of the product.[59] An **architectural innovation**, therefore, is a new product in which known components, based on existing technologies, are reconfigured in a novel way to create new markets.

As a radical innovator commercializing the xerography invention, Xerox was long the most dominant copier company worldwide.[60] It produced high-volume, high-quality, and high-priced copying machines that it leased to its customers through a service agreement. Although these machines were ideal for the high end of the market such as Fortune 100 companies, Xerox ignored small and medium-sized businesses. By applying an architectural innovation, the Japanese entry Canon was able to redesign the copier so that it didn't need professional service—reliability was built directly into the machine, and the user could replace parts such as the cartridge. This allowed Canon to apply the *razor–razor-blade business model* (introduced in Chapter 5), charging relatively low prices for its copiers but adding a steep markup to its cartridges. What Xerox had not envisioned was the possibility that the components of the copying machine could be put together in an altogether different way that was more user-friendly. More importantly, Canon addressed a need in a specific consumer segment—small and medium-sized businesses and individual departments or offices in large companies—that Xerox neglected.

Finally, a **disruptive innovation** leverages *new technologies* to attack *existing markets*. It invades an existing market from the bottom up, as shown in Exhibit 7.11.[61] The dashed blue lines represent different market segments, from segment 1 at the low end to segment

---

innovation ecosystem A firm's embeddedness in a complex network of suppliers, buyers, and complementors, which requires interdependent strategic decision making.

architectural innovation A new product in which known components, based on existing technologies, are reconfigured in a novel way to attack new markets.

disruptive innovation An innovation that leverages new technologies to attack existing markets from the bottom up.

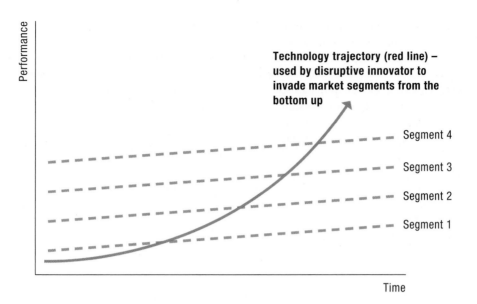

EXHIBIT 7.11 /

Disruptive Innovation: Riding the Technology Trajectory to Invade Different Market Segments from the Bottom Up

4 at the high end. As first demonstrated by Clayton Christensen, the dynamic process of disruptive innovation begins when a firm, frequently a startup, introduces a new product based on a new technology to meet existing customer needs. To be a disruptive force, however, this new product or technology has to have additional characteristics:

1. It begins as a low-cost solution to an existing problem.
2. Initially, its performance is inferior to the existing technology, but its rate of technological improvement over time is faster than the rate of performance increases required by different market segments. In Exhibit 7.11, the red line captures the new technology's trajectory, or rate of improvement over time.

The following examples illustrate disruptive innovations:

■ Japanese carmakers successfully followed a strategy of disruptive innovation by first introducing small fuel-efficient cars, and then leveraging their low-cost and high-quality advantages into high-end luxury segments, captured by brands such as Lexus, Infiniti, and Acura. More recently, the South Korean carmakers Kia and Hyundai have followed a similar strategy.

■ Digital photography improved enough over time to provide higher-definition pictures. As a result, it has been able to replace film photography, even in most professional applications.

■ Laptop computers disrupted desktop computers; now tablets and larger-screen smartphones are disrupting laptops.

■ Educational organizations such as Coursera and Udacity are disrupting traditional universities by offering *massive open online courses* (MOOCs), using the web to provide large-scale, interactive online courses with open access.

One factor favoring the success of disruptive innovation is that it relies on stealth attack: It invades the market from the bottom up, by first capturing the low end. Many times, incumbent firms fail to defend (and sometimes are even happy to cede) the low end of the market, because it is frequently a low-margin business. Google, for example, is using its mobile operating system, Android, as a *beachhead* to challenge Microsoft's dominance in the personal computer industry, where 90 percent of machines run Windows.[62] Google's Android, in contrast, is optimized to run on mobile devices, the fastest-growing segment in computing. To appeal to users who spend most of their time on the web accessing e-mail and other online applications, for instance, it is designed to start up in a few seconds. Moreover, Google provides Android free of charge.[63] In contrast to Microsoft's proprietary Windows operating system, Android is open-source software, freely accessible to anyone for further development and refinement. In this sense, Google is leveraging *crowdsourcing* in its new product development, just as Threadless uses crowdsourcing to design and market T-shirts, and Wikipedia uses the wisdom of the crowds to collectively edit encyclopedia entries.

Another factor favoring the success of disruptive innovation is that incumbent firms often are slow to change. Incumbent firms tend to listen closely to their current customers and respond by continuing to invest in the existing technology and in incremental changes to the existing products. When a newer technology matures and proves to be a better solution, those same customers will switch over. At that time, however, the incumbent firm does not yet have a competitive product ready that is based on the disruptive technology. Although customer-oriented mission statements are more likely to guard against firm obsolescence than product-oriented ones (see Chapter 2), they are no guarantee that a firm can hold out in the face of disruptive innovation. One of the counterintuitive findings that Clayton Christensen unearthed in his studies is that it can hurt incumbents to listen (too closely) only to their existing customers. Apple is famous for not soliciting customer feedback because it believes it knows what customers need before they even realize it.

Although these examples show that disruptive innovations are a serious threat for incumbent firms, some have devised strategic initiatives to counter them:

1. *Continue to innovate in order to stay ahead of the competition.* Being a moving target is much harder to hit than standing still and resting on existing (innovation) laurels. Apple has done this well during the decade from 2001–2011 (as detailed in Chapter-Case 1). Amazon is another example of a company that has continuously morphed through innovation,[64] from a simple online book retailer to the largest e-commerce company. It now also offers consumer electronics (Kindle tablets), cloud computing, and content streaming, among other offerings.

2. *Guard against disruptive innovation by protecting the low end of the market* (segment 1 in Exhibit 7.11) by introducing low-cost innovations to preempt stealth competitors. Intel introduced the Celeron chip, a stripped-down, budget version of its Pentium chip, in 1998. More recently, Intel followed up with the Atom chip, a new processor that is inexpensive and consumes little battery power, to power low-cost mobile devices.[65] Nonetheless, Intel also listened too closely to its existing personal computer customers such as Dell, HP, Lenovo, and so on, and allowed ARM Holdings, a British semiconductor design company (that supplies its technology to Apple, Samsung, HTC, and others) to take the lead in providing high-performing, low-power-consuming processors for smartphones and other mobile devices.

3. *Disrupt yourself, rather than wait for others to disrupt you.* A firm may develop products specifically for emerging markets such as China and India, and then introduce these innovations into developed markets such as the United States, Japan, or the European Union.[66] Strategy Highlight 7.2 describes how GE Healthcare invented and commercialized a disruptive innovation in China that is now entering the U.S. market (riding the steep technology trajectory of disruptive innovation shown in Exhibit 7.11).

Strategy Highlight 7.2

GE's New Innovation Mantra: Disrupt Yourself!

GE Healthcare is a leader in diagnostic devices. Realizing that the likelihood of disruptive innovation increases over time, GE decided to disrupt itself. A high-end ultrasound machine found in cutting-edge research hospitals in the United States or Europe costs $250,000. There is no market for these high-end, high-price products in developing countries. Given their large populations, however, there is a strong medical need for ultrasound devices.

In 2002, a GE team in China, through a bottom-up strategic initiative, developed an inexpensive, portable ultrasound device, combining laptop technology with a probe and sophisticated imaging software. This lightweight device (11 pounds) was first used in rural China. In the spring of 2009, GE unveiled the new medical device under the name Venue 40 in the United States, at a price of less than $30,000. There was also high demand from many American general practitioners, who could not otherwise afford the quarter of a million dollars needed to procure a high-end machine (that weighed about 400 pounds).

In the fall of 2009, GE's chairman and CEO Jeff Immelt unveiled the Vscan, an even smaller device that looks like a cross between an early iPod and a flip phone. This wireless ultrasound device is priced at less than $10,000. GE views the Vscan as the "stethoscope of the 21st century," which a primary care doctor can hang around her neck when visiting patients.[67]

Jeffrey Immelt, GE CEO and Chairman, unveils the Vscan.

THE INTERNET AS DISRUPTIVE FORCE: THE LONG TAIL

To harness the power of the Internet, firms digitize their offerings. This process acts as an especially disruptive force.[68] We are all familiar with the impact that the digitization of music, books, and movies has had on brick-and-mortar sellers. Web applications such as TurboTax and LegalZoom are replacing professional tax accountants and attorneys. Online gaming is the fastest-growing segment in the $55 billion video game industry.[69] One thing is for sure: Everything that can go digital will—creating some losers and some winners. Online digitization is thus both a threat and an opportunity.

> **LO7-6**
> Explain the long-tail concept and derive its strategic implications.

These observations and their strategic implications have been explained by Chris Anderson in his bestseller *The Long Tail.*[70] The *long-tail* phenomenon is that 80 percent of offerings in a category are *not* big hits (see Exhibit 7.12). It turns out that 80 percent of sales in a given product category (such as movies, books, and songs) come from "blockbusters" in the "short head" of the distribution curve, which represents only 20 percent of the offerings in a category. This phenomenon is captured by the **Pareto principle,** also known as the *80-20 rule,* which says that roughly 80 percent of effects come from 20 percent of the causes.

> **Pareto principle**
> Roughly 80 percent of effects come from 20 percent of the causes.

The *short head* represents the mainstream, where all the blockbusters, bestsellers, and hits are to be found. These products tend to appeal to the largest segment of the market with homogenous tastes. In the physical world of brick-and-mortar retail stores, these

EXHIBIT 7.12

The Short Head and
the Long Tail

SOURCE: Adapted from
C. Anderson (2006), *The
Long Tail: Why the Future of
Business Is Selling Less of
More* (New York: Hyperion).

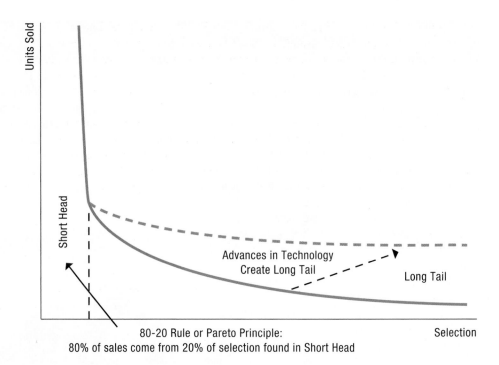

product selections are often the only choice on display, because there are significant costs to carrying broader inventory to meet a wider variety of consumer needs.

The disruptive force of the Internet provides an opportunity to online retailers to benefit from marketing the long tail, which is the remaining 80 percent of offerings. Online retailers can "sell less of more" by taking advantage of low-cost virtual shelf space, which is basically unlimited. The Internet, combined with sophisticated search engines and inventory-management software, allows firms to drive down transaction costs to match individual consumer demand with supply. As shown by the dashed line in Exhibit 7.12, the combined effects of these advances in technology make it possible to increase the number of units sold—that is, to create the long tail. The **long-tail** business model is one in which companies can obtain a large part of their revenues by selling a small number of units from among almost unlimited choices.

The long tail allows online retailers to overcome the problem of **thin markets**, in which transactions are likely not to take place because there are only a few buyers and a few sellers and they have difficulty finding each other. We can look at eBay with 100 million users worldwide as an example of an online retailer with an innovative approach to retailing, enabling buyers and sellers to meet online to exchange any good, no matter how exotic, at no search cost to the buyer. Google also benefits from the long tail, because it is able to match even small advertisers with their specific target demographics.

In any distribution, the short tail captures only the tip of the iceberg. The long tail, in contrast, captures the bottom of the iceberg, the non-obvious choices. By leveraging sophisticated IT systems, online retailers such as Rhapsody, Netflix, and Amazon are able to aggregate these choices. Even Walmart, the world's largest retailer, carries only about 55,000 music tracks. In contrast, Rhapsody's inventory contains over 16 million tracks. The average retail store in the now defunct Blockbuster chain carried no more

long tail Business model in which companies can obtain a large part of their revenues by selling a small number of units from among almost unlimited choices.

thin markets A situation in which transactions are likely not to take place because there are only a few buyers and sellers who have difficulty finding each other.

than 1,000 DVD titles; Netflix carries more than 100,000. The typical Barnes & Noble superstore holds some 100,000 book titles; on Amazon you can find 5 million. All in all, the leading online retailers carry an inventory 50 to 100 times larger than those of their largest brick-and-mortar competitors. Between 25 and 45 percent of all revenues for Rhapsody, Netflix, and Amazon come from the long tail, or products not available in offline retail stores.

The Internet as a disruptive innovation enables companies to solve important strategic trade-offs. It lowers the costs of shelf space, inventory, and distribution to near zero and enables firms to aggregate non-hits and match unique consumer preferences to supply. Although the early experiences of media and entertainment industries illustrate the long-tail business model, it is expected that the model can be used to build a business in any product or service that can be digitized.

OPEN INNOVATION

During the 20th century, the *closed innovation* approach was the dominant research and development (R&D) approach for most leading industrial corporations: They tended to discover, develop, and commercialize new products internally.[71] Although this approach was costly and time-consuming, it allowed firms to fully capture the returns to their own innovations.

LO7-7

Compare and contrast closed and open innovation.

Several factors led to a shift in the knowledge landscape from closed innovation to open innovation. They include:

- The increasing supply and mobility of skilled workers
- The exponential growth of venture capital
- The increasing availability of external options (such as spinning out new ventures) to commercialize ideas that were previously shelved or in-source promising ideas and inventions
- The increasing capability of external suppliers

Taken together, these factors have led more and more companies to adopt an open innovation approach to research and development. **Open innovation** is a framework for R&D that proposes permeable firm boundaries to allow a firm to benefit not only from internal ideas and inventions, but also from ideas and innovation from external sources. The sharing goes both ways: some external R&D is in-sourced (and further developed in-house) while the firm may spin out internal R&D that does not fit its strategy in order to allow others to commercialize it. Even the largest companies, such as AT&T, IBM, and GE, are shifting their innovation strategy toward a model that blends internal with external knowledge-sourcing via licensing agreements, strategic alliances, joint ventures, and acquisitions.[72]

Exhibit 7.13 depicts the closed and open innovation models. In the closed innovation model (left panel), the firm is conducting all research and development in-house, using a traditional funnel approach. The boundaries of the firm are impenetrable. Outside ideas and projects cannot enter, nor does the firm allow its own research ideas and development projects to leave the firm. Firms in the closed innovation model are extremely protective of their intellectual property. This not only allows the firm to capture all the benefits from its own R&D, but also prevents competitors from benefitting from it. The mindset of firms in the closed innovation model is that to profit from R&D, the firm must come up with its own discoveries, develop them on its own, and control the distribution channels. Strength in R&D is equated with a high likelihood of benefitting from first-mover advantages. Firms following the closed innovation model, however, are much more likely to fall prone to the

open innovation A framework for R&D that proposes permeable firm boundaries to allow a firm to benefit not only from internal ideas and inventions, but also from external ones. The sharing goes both ways: some external ideas and inventions are in-sourced while others are spun-out.

EXHIBIT 7.13 / Closed Innovation vs. Open Innovation

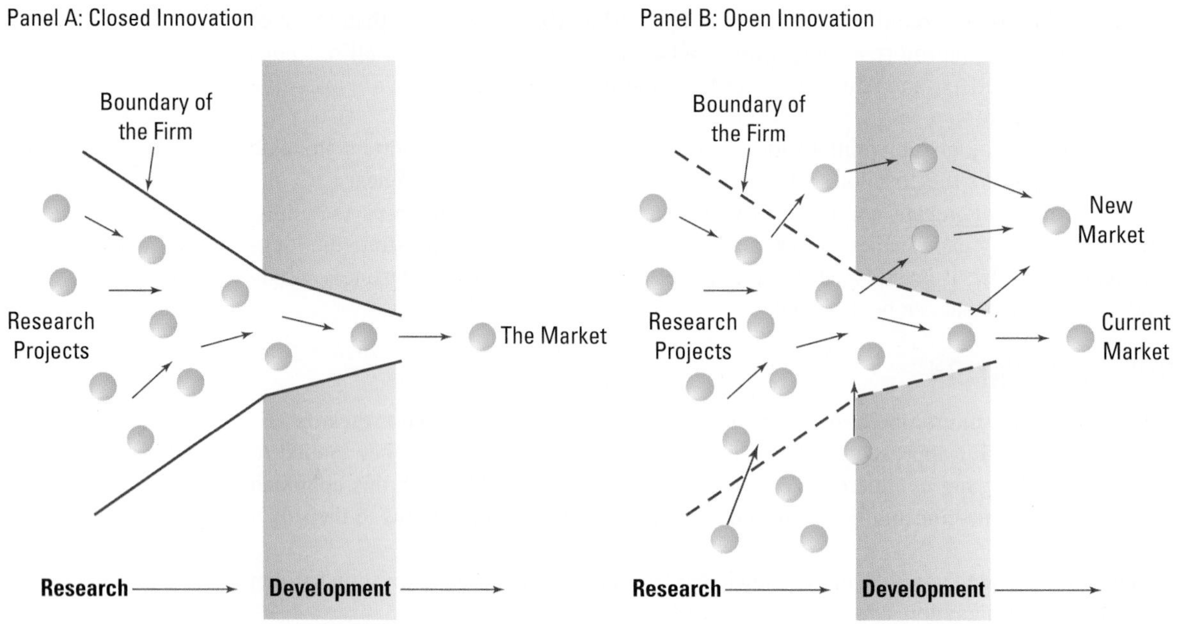

Panel A: Closed Innovation

Panel B: Open Innovation

SOURCE: Adapted from H. Chesbrough (2003), "The area of open innovation," *MIT Sloan Management Review,* Spring: 35–41.

not-invented-here syndrome:[73] "If the R&D leading to a discovery and a new development project was not conducted in-house, it cannot be good."

As documented in a detailed case study, the pharmaceutical company Merck suffers from the *not-invented-here syndrome,* meaning that if a product was not created and developed at Merck, it could not be good enough.[74] Merck's culture and organizational systems perpetuate this logic, which assumes that since they hired the best people, the smartest people in the industry must work for Merck, and so the best discoveries must be invented at Merck. The company leads the industry in terms of R&D spending, because Merck believes that if it is the first to discover and develop a new drug, it would be the first to market. Merck is one of the most successful companies by total number of active R&D projects. Perhaps even more important, Merck's researchers had been awarded several Nobel Prizes for their breakthrough research, a considerable point of pride for Merck's personnel.

In the open innovation model, in contrast, a company attempts to commercialize both its own ideas and research from other firms. It also finds external alternatives such as spin-out ventures or strategic alliances to commercialize its internally developed R&D. The boundary of the firm has become porous (as represented by the dashed lines in the right panel in Exhibit 7.13), allowing the firm to spin out some R&D projects while in-sourcing other promising projects. Companies using an open innovation approach realize that great ideas can come from both inside and outside the company. Significant value can be had by commercializing external R&D and letting others commercialize internal R&D that does not fit with the firm's strategy. The focus is on building a more effective *business model* to commercialize (internal and external) R&D, rather than focusing on being first to market.

EXHIBIT 7.14 / Contrasting Principles of Closed and Open Innovation

Closed Innovation Principles	Open Innovation Principles
The smart people in our field work for us.	Not all the smart people work for us. We need to work with smart people inside *and* outside our company.
To profit from R&D, we must discover it, develop it, and ship it ourselves.	External R&D can create significant value; internal R&D is needed to claim (absorb) some portion of that value.
If we discover it ourselves, we will get it to market first.	We don't have to originate the research to profit from it; we can still be first if we successfully commercialize new research.
The company that gets an innovation to market first will win.	Building a better business model is often more important than getting to market first.
If we create the most and best ideas in the industry, we will win.	If we make the best use of internal and external ideas, we will win.
We should control our intellectual property (IP), so that our competitors don't profit from it.	We should profit from others' use of our IP, and we should buy others' IP whenever it advances our own business model.

SOURCE: Adapted from H. W. Chesbrough (2003), *Open Innovation: The New Imperative for Creating and Profiting from Technology* (Boston: Harvard Business School Press).

One key assumption underlying the open innovation model is that combining the best of internal and external R&D will more likely lead to a competitive advantage. This requires that the company must continuously upgrade its internal R&D capabilities to enhance its **absorptive capacity**—its ability to understand external technology developments, evaluate them, and integrate them into current products or create new ones.[75] Exhibit 7.14 compares and contrasts open-innovation and closed-innovation principles.

An example of open innovation is Procter & Gamble's "Connect+Develop," or C+D (a play on research and development, or R&D).[76] Because of the maturing of its products and markets, P&G's CEO A. G. Lafley decided it was time to look outside for new ideas. P&G is an $85-billion company whose investors expect it to grow at least 4–6 percent a year, which implies generating between $3 and $5 billion in incremental revenue annually. P&G was no longer able to generate this amount of growth through closed innovation. By 2000, P&G's closed innovation machine had stalled, and the company lost half its market value. It needed a change in innovation strategy to drive organic growth.

P&G's Connect+Develop is a web-based interface that connects the company's internal-innovation capability with the distributed knowledge in the global community. From that external community, researchers, entrepreneurs, and consumers can submit ideas that might solve some of P&G's toughest innovation challenges. The C+D model is based on the realization that innovation was increasingly coming from small entrepreneurial ventures and even from individuals. Universities also became much more proactive in commercializing their inventions. The Internet now enables access to widely distributed knowledge from around the globe.

External collaborations fostered through the worldwide Connect+Develop network now play a role in roughly 50 percent of P&G's new products, up from about 15 percent in 2000. Successful product innovations that resulted from P&G's open innovation model include "Pringles meets Print" (sold for $1.5 billion in 2011), Mr. Clean Magic Eraser, Swiffer Dusters, Crest SpinBrush, and Olay Regenerist.

absorptive capacity
A firm's ability to understand external technology developments, evaluate them, and integrate them into current products or create new ones.

As discussed in ChapterCase 6, however, the open innovation model did not prevent P&G from being "stuck in the middle" as it focused too much on incremental innovation rather than on radical innovation by creating new product categories. This, combined with a neglect of emerging economies, weakened P&G's strategic position considerably.

7.5 ◀▶ Implications for the Strategist

An effective innovation strategy is critical in formulating a business strategy that affords the firm a competitive advantage. The competitive process is driven by innovation. Successful innovation affords firms a temporary monopoly, with the corresponding pricing power. *Fast Company* has named Nike, Amazon, Square, Splunk, Fab, Uber, Sproxil, Pinterest, Safaricom, and Target as its *2013 Most Innovative Companies.*[77] Continuous innovation fuels the success of these companies.

Entrepreneurs are the agents that introduce change into the competitive system. They do this not only by figuring out how to use inventions, but also by introducing new products or services, new production processes, and new forms of organization. Entrepreneurs frequently start new ventures, but they may also be found in existing firms.

The industry life cycle model and the crossing-the-chasm framework have critical implications for how you as the strategist manage innovation. To overcome the chasm, you need to formulate a business strategy guided by the "who-what-why-and-how" questions of competition to ensure you meet the distinctly different customer needs inherent along the industry life cycle. You also need to be mindful that to do so you need to bring different competencies and capabilities to bear at different stages of the industry life cycle.

Many of the more successful companies have either adopted or are moving toward an open innovation model. As a strategist, you must actively manage a firm's internal and external innovation activities. Internally, you can *induce innovation* through a top-down process or motivate innovation through *autonomous behavior,* a bottom-up process.[78] In induced innovation, you need to put a structure and system in place to foster innovation. 3M puts structures and systems to foster induced innovation: "A core belief of 3M is that creativity needs freedom. That's why, since about 1948, we've encouraged our employees to spend 15 percent of their working time on their own projects. To take our resources, to build up a unique team, and to follow their own insights in pursuit of problem-solving."[79] We discussed *autonomous behavior* in detail in Chapter 2. To not only motivate and support innovations through autonomous behavior, but also ensure their possible success, *internal champions* need to be willing to support promising projects. In Strategy Highlight 2.2, we detailed how Howard Behar, at that time a senior executive at Starbucks, was willing to support the bottom-up idea of Frappuccino.

Externally, you must manage innovation through cooperative strategies such as licensing, strategic alliances, joint ventures, and acquisitions. These are the vehicles of *corporate strategy* discussed in the next two chapters.

In conclusion, in this and the previous chapter, we discussed how firms can use *business-level strategy*—differentiation, cost leadership, integration, and innovation—to gain and sustain competitive advantage. We now turn our attention to *corporate-level strategy* to help us understand how executives make decisions about where to compete (in terms of industries, value chains, and geography) and how to execute it through strategic alliances as well as mergers and acquisitions. A thorough understanding of business and corporate strategy is necessary to formulate and sustain a winning strategy.

CHAPTER**CASE 7** / Consider This . . .

WIKIPEDIA, AS DISCUSSED in ChapterCase 7, leverages technological innovation afforded by the Internet combined with a crowdsourcing approach to content development and maintenance. Beyond the technical challenges of web interfaces, servers, and bandwidth for delivery is a sometimes-overlooked capability: the Wikipedians themselves. Over 32 million people have registered accounts to contribute edits to Wikipedia. More than 300,000 users provide edits to the website at least once a month. These volunteers build the content for the site, using a creative commons license that ensures free access to any of the 500 million unique visitors each month.[80] This crowdsourcing and its legal underpinnings are successful only as long as individuals are willing to spend their own time contributing to the site for no pay or other extrinsic benefits. The ability to attract and utilize legions of interested individuals is vital to the success of Wikipedia both today and into the future.

Moreover, Wikipedia is a nonprofit, free-of-advertising social entrepreneurship venture that is exclusively financed by donations. Wikipedia runs regular calls for donations using slogans such as:[81] "Please help us feed the servers," "We make the Internet not suck. Help us out," and "We are free, our bandwidth isn't!" Calls for donations also come in the form of personal appeals by co-founder Jimmy Wales. The question arises whether the donation model is sustainable given not only the increasing demand for Wikipedia's services, but also the emergence of competitors.

Wikipedia might not be as error-prone in science topics as shown in the *Nature* study mentioned earlier, because most entries on Wikipedia are not about science. Wikipedia maintains that it fosters a "neutral point of view." A recent research study tested this claim. In particular, a study of 28,000 articles about U.S.

politics revealed a significant bias.[82] On average, Wikipedia entries lean left of center. Initial entries arrive with a slant, and change little over time. This bias is more pronounced in earlier Wikipedia articles. The authors call this the "vintage bias." Although the degree of slant in Wikipedia articles changes little over time, more recent political entries are more balanced. One reason the authors put forth to explain the vintage effect is that in the early days of Wikipedia only technology enthusiasts and early adopters participated, and this demographic tends to lean left. The shift toward a more "neutral point of view" over the years has arisen from the growth of Wikipedia, bringing in the early and late majority as contributors.

Questions

1. How can Wikipedia maintain and grow its ability to harness the crowdsourcing of its "Wikipedians" to maintain high-quality (and quickly updated) content?

2. As Wikipedia keeps growing, do you think it can continue to rely exclusively on donations (in time and money)? Why or why not? What other "business models" could be considered? Would any of those "violate the spirit of Wikipedia"? Why or why not?

3. What, if anything, should Wikipedia do to ensure that its articles indeed present a "neutral point of view"? Shouldn't the crowdsourcing approach ensure an objectivity? Does a "neutral point of view" matter to Wikipedia's sustainability? Why or why not?

4. How has the "long tail" affected Wikipedia?

TAKE-AWAY CONCEPTS

This chapter discussed various aspects of innovation and entrepreneurship as a business-level strategy, as summarized by the following learning objectives and related take-away concepts.

LO 7-1 / Outline the four-step innovation process from idea to imitation.

■ Innovation describes the discovery and development of new knowledge in a four-step process captured in the 4-I's: *idea, invention, innovation,* and *imitation.*

- The innovation process begins with an idea.
- An invention describes the transformation of an idea into a new product or process, or the modification and recombination of existing ones.
- Innovation concerns the commercialization of an invention by entrepreneurs (within existing companies or new ventures).
- If an innovation is successful in the marketplace, competitors will attempt to imitate it.

LO 7-2 / Apply strategic management concepts to entrepreneurship and innovation.

- Entrepreneurship describes the process by which change agents undertake economic risk to innovate—to create new products, processes, and sometimes new organizations.
- Strategic entrepreneurship describes the pursuit of innovation using tools and concepts from strategic management.
- Social entrepreneurship describes the pursuit of social goals by using entrepreneurship. Social entrepreneurs use a triple-bottom-line approach to assess performance.

LO 7-3 / Describe the competitive implications of different stages in the industry life cycle.

- Innovations frequently lead to the birth of new industries.
- Industries generally follow a predictable industry life cycle, with five distinct stages: introduction, growth, shakeout, maturity, and decline.
- Exhibit 7.9 details features and strategic implications of the industry life cycle

LO 7-4 / Derive strategic implications of the crossing-the-chasm framework.

- The core argument of the crossing-the-chasm framework is that each stage of the industry life cycle is dominated by a different customer group, which responds differently to a new technological innovation.
- There exists a significant difference between the customer groups that enter early during the introductory stage of the industry life cycle and customers that enter later during the growth stage.

- This distinct difference between customer groups leads to a big gulf or chasm which companies and their innovations frequently fall into.
- To overcome the chasm, managers need to formulate a business strategy guided by the "who-what-why-and-how" questions of competition.

LO 7-5 / Categorize different types of innovations in the markets-and-technology framework.

- Four types of innovation emerge when applying the existing versus new dimensions of technology and markets: incremental, radical, architectural, and disruptive innovations (see Exhibit 7.10).
- An incremental innovation squarely builds on an established knowledge base, and steadily improves an existing product or service offering (existing market / existing technology).
- A radical innovation draws on novel methods or materials, is derived either from an entirely different knowledge base or from the recombination of the existing knowledge base with a new stream of knowledge (new market / new technology).
- An architectural innovation is an embodied new product in which known components, based on existing technologies, are reconfigured in a novel way to attack new markets (new market / existing technology).
- A disruptive innovation is an innovation that leverages new technologies to attack existing markets from the bottom up (existing market / new technology).

LO 7-6 / Explain the long-tail concept and derive its strategic implications.

- Firms digitize their offerings to leverage the Internet as a disruptive force.
- The long tail describes a business model in which companies can obtain a significant part of their revenues by selling a small number of units from among almost unlimited choices.

LO 7-7 / Compare and contrast closed and open innovation.

- Closed innovation is a framework for R&D that proposes impenetrable firm boundaries. Key to success in the closed innovation model is that the firm discovers, develops, and commercializes new products internally.

- Open innovation is a framework for R&D that proposes permeable firm boundaries to allow a firm to benefit not only from internal ideas and inventions, but also from external ones. The sharing goes both ways: some external ideas

and inventions are in-sourced while others are spun-out.

- Exhibit 7.14 compares and contrasts principles of closed and open innovation.

KEY TERMS

Absorptive capacity	Innovation	Patent
Architectural innovation	Innovation ecosystem	Process innovations
Disruptive innovation	Invention	Product innovations
Entrepreneurs	Long tail	Radical innovation
Entrepreneurship	Network effects	Social entrepreneurship
First-mover advantages	Open innovation	Standard
Incremental innovation	Organizational inertia	Strategic entrepreneurship
Industry life cycle	Pareto principle	Thin markets

DISCUSSION QUESTIONS

1. Select an industry and consider how the industry life cycle has affected business strategy for the firms in that industry over time. Detail your answer based on each stage: introduction, growth, shakeout, maturity, and decline.

2. Describe a firm you think has been highly innovative. Which of the four types of innovation—radical, incremental, disruptive, or architectural—did it use? Did the firm use different types over time?

3. The chapter discussed the Internet as a disruptive innovation that has facilitated online retailing. It also, however, has presented challenges to brick-and-mortar retailers. How might retailers such as Nordstrom, Neiman Marcus, or Macy's need to change their in-store experience in order to continue to attract a flow of customers into their

stores to expand sales using direct selling and store displays of the actual merchandise? If the Internet continues to grow and sales of brick-and-mortar retailers decline, how might the retailers attract, train, and retain high-quality employees if the industry is perceived as in decline?

4. Much has been said about competitive advantage gained from innovations such as the Internet, high-technology gadgets, and apps. The chapter points out, however, that low-technology innovations such as the razor–razor-blade business model can also create value. Think of other low-technology innovations that are/were novel, useful, and successfully implemented so that the innovating firm gained a competitive advantage. Find information about the entrepreneurial story behind the innovation.

ETHICAL/SOCIAL ISSUES

1. You are a co-founder of a startup firm making electronic sensors. After a year of sales, your business is not growing rapidly, but you have some steady customers keeping the business afloat. A major supplier has informed you it can

no longer supply your firm because it is moving to serve large customers only, and your volume does not qualify. Though you have no current orders to support an increased commitment to this supplier, you do have a new version of your sensor coming out that you hope will increase the purchase volume by over 75 percent and qualify you for continued supply. This supplier is important to your plans. What do you do?

2. GE's development of the Vscan provides many benefits as a lower-cost and portable ultrasound device (see Strategy Highlight 7.2). Cardiologists, obstetricians, and veterinarians will be able to use the device in rural areas and developing countries. One of the criticisms of the device, however, is that it also facilitates the use of the technology for gender-selective abortion. In India, for example, there is a cultural preference for males, and the Vscan has been used to identify gender in order to abort an unwanted female fetus. Some argue that gender selection is also used for economic reasons—specifically, to alleviate the financial strain of the common dowry practice. A daughter would require the family to pay a dowry of cash and gifts to the bridegroom's family in order to arrange a suitable marriage, while a son would bring in a dowry of cash, jewelry, gifts, and household items to help the couple start their home. In addition, even though there has been some progress for women in India, others attribute the use of gender selection to women's lack of social, political, and economic empowerment.[83]

To what extent is GE ethically responsible for how—and why—the Vscan is used? (To what extent is any company ethically responsible for how—and why—its product is used?) Note that GE's website states that it is an "Agent of Good." Consider ways that GE might become involved in communities in India to show the company's concern for the underlying problems by improving conditions for women. What other ways might GE influence the way that its equipment is used?

SMALL-GROUP EXERCISES

//// Small-Group Exercise 1

Your group works for Warner Music Group (www.wmg.com), a large music record label whose sales are declining largely due to piracy. Your supervisor assigns you the task of developing a strategy for improving this situation.

1. What are the key issues you must grapple with to improve the position of Warner Music Group (WMG)?

2. In what phase of the life cycle is the record-label industry?

3. How does this life cycle phase affect the types of innovation that should be considered to help WMG be successful?

//// Small-Group Exercise 2

The chapter compares and contrasts closed versus open innovation. It also describes Procter & Gamble's Connect+Develop open innovation system. With your group members, brainstorm to prepare a brief memo with a set of talking points regarding the following questions:

1. What are some of the risks of an open innovation approach that a company should consider before embarking on it?

2. Do you believe P&G's Connect+Develop (C+D) open innovation system has the potential to create a competitive advantage for the firm? How might P&G's capabilities be strengthened as a result? If you believe that C+D does have the potential to create a competitive advantage, do you believe it is sustainable? Why or why not?

3. Larry Huston and Nabil Sakkab, (former) executives at P&G, proclaimed that "Connect+Develop will become the dominant innovation model in the 21st century."[84] Do you agree with their statement? Why or why not? If C+D did become the dominant innovation model, how would this affect its potential to create a competitive edge for a firm?

4. Introducing the C+D innovation model requires tremendous organizational change. As Huston and Sakkab described the change effort: "We needed to move the company's attitude from resistance to innovations *'not invented here'* to enthusiasm for those *'proudly found elsewhere.'* And we needed to change how we defined, and perceived, our R&D organization—from 7,500 people inside to 7,500 plus 1.5 million outside, with a permeable boundary between them."[85] Identify some of

the major obstacles a manager would encounter attempting this kind of organizational change. For example, how might P&G's research employees react? Although you have not been formally introduced to organizational structure, consider some recommendations for how to accomplish such large-scale organizational change successfully.

STRATEGY TERM PROJECT

//// Module 7: Innovation Strategy

In this section, you will study the environment of the firm you have selected for the strategy term project and the firm's susceptibility to technological disruptions from new entrants.

1. Where is your firm's industry on the life cycle as shown in Exhibit 7.4? What are the strategic implications?

2. What is the firm's innovation strategy? Does it rely on incremental or radical innovations? Disruptive or architectural? What are the competitive implications of the firm's innovation strategies?

3. Are intellectual property rights important for your firm? Can you find what strategies the firm is implementing to protect its proprietary position? Identify a recent innovation by your firm. What is your firm's strategy to cross the chasm(s) to achieve mass market adoption of its innovation?

4. What attributes describe the current major customer segment for your firm? Are these changing? If so, is your firm prepared to meet these new customer demands?

5. How does your firm organize for innovation? Does it use a closed or an open innovation approach? Is its current approach working out well, or does it need changing? If yes, how?

my STRATEGY

Do You Want to Be an Entrepreneur?

Some 50–75 percent of MBA students from the leading programs are becoming entrepreneurs within 15 years of graduation. Moreover, economic downturns appear to be the best time to start a company. Many of today's *Fortune-100* and high-tech success stories were launched in economic downturns. The global depression of 1873–1895 witnessed the founding of today's industry giants such as AT&T, GE, Hershey's, Gillette, Johnson & Johnson, Abbott, Lilly, Merck, and Bristol-Myers. Similarly, Hewlett-Packard (HP), Texas Instruments, and United Technologies got their starts during the Great Depression of 1929–1939 in the United States.

The success story of Silicon Valley began with the founding of HP in Palo Alto, California. This cluster of high-tech innovators, venture capitalists, and entrepreneurs took off during a time when the stock market had crashed by some 90 percent and almost one in three U.S. workers were unemployed. Apple, Microsoft, LexisNexis, FedEx, and Genentech began their corporate lives during the oil price shocks and subsequent recession in the mid-1970s. During the early 1980s, inflation raged and mortgage rates were over 20 percent. Still, during this period entrepreneurs founded Amgen, CNN, MTV, E*Trade, AOL, Adobe, and Autodesk.[86]

1. Why do you think recessions are a good time to start a business? Wouldn't that seem counterintuitive?

2. Thinking about today's business climate, would you say that now is a good time to start a business? Why or why not?

3. If you were to start a business, what type of business would you want to start, and why? What idea or invention would you be commercializing?

4. Does it matter *where* (in terms of geography) you start your business? Why or why not?

5. Explain how you would apply the strategic management framework to enhance your startup's chances to gain and sustain a competitive advantage.

ENDNOTES

1. This ChapterCase is based on: Surowiecki, J. (2004), *The Wisdom of Crowds* (New York: Bantam Dell); "Internet encyclopedias go head-to-head," *Nature,* December 15, 2005; Anderson, C. (2006), *The Long Tail. Why the Future of Business Is Selling Less of More* (New York: Hyperion); Anderson, C. (2009), *Free. The Future of a Radical Price* (New York: Hyperion); Greenstein, S., and F. Zhu (2012), "Is Wikipedia biased?" *American Economic Review* 102: 343–348; "Wikipedia's old-fashioned revolution," *The Wall Street Journal,* April 6, 2009; "End of era for Encyclopaedia Britannica," *The Wall Street Journal,* March 14, 2012; "How Jimmy Wales' Wikipedia harnessed the web as a force for good," *Wired,* March 19, 2013; www.encyclopediacenter.com; www.alexa.com/topsites; and, of course, various Wikipedia sources.

2. Rothaermel, F. T., and A. Hess (2010), "Innovation strategies combined," *MIT Sloan Management Review,* Spring: 12–15.

3. Schumpeter, J. A. (1942), *Capitalism, Socialism, and Democracy* (New York: Harper & Row); Foster, R., and S. Kaplan (2001), *Creative Destruction: Why Companies That Are Built to Last Underperform the Market— and How to Successfully Transform Them.*

4. "Comcast, GE strike deal; Vivendi to sell NBC stake," *The Wall Street Journal,* December 4, 2009.

5. Stokes, D. E. (1997), *Pasteur's Quadrant: Basic Science and Technological Innovation* (Washington, DC: Brookings Institute Press); Madhavan, R., and R. Grover (1998), "From embedded knowledge to embodied knowledge: New product development as knowledge management," *Journal of Marketing* 62: 1–12; and Rothaermel, F. T., and D. L. Deeds (2004), "Exploration and exploitation alliances in biotechnology: A system of new product development," *Strategic Management Journal* 25: 201–221.

6. Isaacson, W. (2007), *Einstein: His Life and Universe* (New York: Simon & Schuster).

7. A detailed description of patents can be found at the U.S. Patent and Trademark Office's website at http://www.uspto.gov/.

8. "U.S. judge reduces Apple's patent award in Samsung case," *The Wall Street Journal,* March 1, 2013.

9. Schumpeter, J. A. (1942), *Capitalism, Socialism, and Democracy.* For an updated and insightful discussion, see Foster, R., and S. Kaplan (2001), *Creative Destruction: Why Companies That Are Built to Last Underperform the Market—and How to Successfully*

Transform Them. For a very accessible discussion, see McCraw, T. (2007), *Prophet of Innovation: Joseph Schumpeter and Creative Destruction* (Boston: Harvard University Press).

10. Burgelman, R. A. (1983), "Corporate entrepreneurship and strategic management: Insights from a process study," *Management Science* 29: 1349–1364; Zahra, S. A., and J. G. Covin, "Contextual influences on the corporate entrepreneurship-performance relationship: A longitudinal analysis," *Journal of Business Venturing* 10: 43–58.

11. U.S. Patent 381968, see http://www.google.com/patents/US381968.

12. Lieberman, M. B., and D. B. Montgomery (1988), "First-mover advantages," *Strategic Management Journal* 9: 41–58 (Summer Special Issue).

13. Schramm, C. J. (2006), *The Entrepreneurial Imperative* (New York: HarperCollins). Dr. Carl Schramm is president of the Kauffman Foundation, the world's leading foundation for entrepreneurship.

14. Schumpeter, J. A. (1942), *Capitalism, Socialism, and Democracy;* Foster, R., and S. Kaplan (2001), *Creative Destruction: Why Companies That Are Built to Last Underperform the Market—and How to Successfully Transform Them.*

15. Shane, S., and S. Venkataraman (2000), "The promise of entrepreneurship as a field of research," *Academy of Management Review* 25: 217–226; Alvarez, S., and J. B. Barney (2007), "Discovery and creation: Alternative theories of entrepreneurial action," *Strategic Entrepreneurship Journal* 1: 11–26.

16. Hansen, M. T., Ibarra, H., and U. Peyer (2013), "The best-performing CEOs in the world," *Harvard Business Review,* January.

17. "Oprah Winfrey to end her program in 2011," *The Wall Street Journal,* November 19, 2009.

18. *Forbes Special Edition: "Billionaires,"* March 29, 2010.

19. http://elonmusk.com/.

20. Hitt, M. A., R. D. Ireland, S. M. Camp, and D. L. Sexton (2002), "Strategic entrepreneurship: Integrating entrepreneurial and strategic management perspectives," in Hitt, M. A., R. D. Ireland, S. M. Camp, and D. L. Sexton (eds.), *Strategic Entrepreneurship: Creating a New Mindset* (Oxford, UK: Blackwell Publishing); Rothaermel, F. T. (2008), "Strategic management and strategic entrepreneurship," *Presentation at the Strategic Management Society Annual International Conference,* Cologne, Germany, October 12.

21. Ibid; Bingham, C. B., K. M. Eisenhardt, and N. R., Furr (2007), "What makes a process a capability? Heuristics, strategy, and effective capture of opportunities," *Strategic Entrepreneurship Journal* 1: 27–47.

22. "Apple iPhone5 #2 to Samsung's 213 million shipped phones," *Forbes,* January 28, 2013.

23. http://www.betterworldbooks.com/info.aspx?f=corevalues.

24. This discussion is based on: "How Jimmy Wales' Wikipedia harnessed the web as a force for good," *Wired,* March 19, 2013.

25. Rothaermel, F. T., and M. Thursby (2007), "The nanotech vs. the biotech revolution: Sources of incumbent productivity in research," *Research Policy* 36: 832–849; and Woolley, J. (2010), "Technology Emergence through Entrepreneurship across Multiple Industries," *Strategic Entrepreneurship Journal* 4: 1–21.

26. This discussion is built on the seminal work by Rogers, E. (1962), *Diffusion of Innovations* (New York: Free Press). For a more recent treatise, see Baum, J.A.C., and A. M. McGahan (2004), *Business Strategy over the Industry Lifecycle,* Advances in Strategic Management, Volume 21 (Bingley, United Kingdom: Emerald).

27. Moore, G. A. (1991), *Crossing the Chasm. Marketing and Selling Disruptive Products to Mainstream Customers* (New York: HarperCollins).

28. This discussion is based on: Arthur, W. B. (1989), "Competing technologies, increasing returns, and lock-in by historical events," *Economics Journal* 99: 116–131; Hill, C.W.L. (1997), "Establishing a standard: Competitive strategy and winner-take-all industries," *Academy of Management Executive* 11: 7–25; Shapiro, C., and H. R. Varian (1998), *Information Rules. A Strategic Guide to the Network Economy* (Boston, MA: Harvard Business School Press); and Schilling, M. A. (2002), "Technology success and failure in winner-take-all markets: Testing a model of technological lockout," *Academy of Management Journal* 45: 387–398.

29. This Strategy Highlight is based on: "Inside the app economy," *BusinessWeek,* October 22, 2009; Adner, R. (2012), *The Wide Lens. A New Strategy for Innovation* (New York: Portfolio); "The 10 most popular iPhone Apps of all time," *PCMag.com,* May 3, 2013; and http://www.apple.com/iphone/from-the-app-store/.

30. This discussion is based on: Utterback, J. M. (1994), *Mastering the Dynamics of Innovation* (Boston, MA: Harvard Business School Press); Anderson, P., and M. Tushman (1990), "Technological discontinuities and dominant designs: A cyclical model of technological change," *Administrative Science Quarterly* 35: 604–634; and Schilling, M. A. (1998), "Technological lockout: An integrative model of the economic and strategic factors driving technology success and failure," *Academy of Management Review* 23: 267–284.

31. This discussion is based on: Teece, D. J. (1986), "Profiting from technological innovation: Implications for integration, collaboration, licensing and public policy," *Research Policy* 15: 285–305; and Ceccagnoli, M., and F. T. Rothaermel (2008), "Appropriating the returns to innovation," *Advances in Study of Entrepreneurship, Innovation, and Economic Growth* 18: 11–34.

32. Abernathy, W. J., and J. M. Utterback (1978), "Patterns of innovation in technology," *Technology Review* 80: 40–47; Benner, M., and M. A. Tushman (2003), "Exploitation, exploration, and process management: The productivity dilemma revisited," *Academy of Management Review* 28: 238–256.

33. "Containers have been more important for globalization than freer trade," *The Economist,* May 18, 2013.

34. The article "Containers have been more important for globalization than freer trade," *The Economist,* May 18, 2013, presents findings from the following research studies: Hummels, D. (2007), "Transportation costs and international trade in the second era of globalization," *Journal of Economic Perspectives* 21: 131–154; Baldwin, R. (2011), "Trade and industrialization after globalization's 2nd unbundling: How building and joining a supply chain are different and why it matters," *NBER Working Paper 17716;* and Bernhofen, D., Z. El-Sahli, and R. Keller (2013), "Estimating the Effects of the Container Revolution on World Trade," *Working Paper,* Lund University.

35. This discussion is based on: Abernathy, W. J., and J. M. Utterback (1978), "Patterns of innovation in technology," *Technology Review* 80: 40–47; Benner, M., and M. A. Tushman (2003), "Exploitation, exploration, and process management: The productivity dilemma revisited," *Academy of Management Review* 28: 238–256.

36. www.apple.com/ipad/pricing/.

37. www.geeks.com.

38. The history of Spanx is documented at www.spanx.com.

39. Harrigan, K. R. (1980), *Strategies for Declining Businesses* (Lexington, MA: Heath).

40. Moore, G. A. (1991), *Crossing the Chasm. Marketing and Selling Disruptive Products to Mainstream Customers* (New York: HarperCollins).

41. We follow the customer type category originally introduced by E. M. Rogers (1962), *Diffusion of Innovations* (New York: Free Press) and also used by G. Moore (1991): technology enthusiasts (~2.5%), early adopters (~13.5%), early majority (~34%), late majority (~34%), and laggards (~16%). Rogers' book originally used the term *innovators* rather than *technology enthusiasts* for the first segment. Given the specific definition of innovation as commercialized invention in this chapter, we follow Moore (1991, page 30) and use the term *technology enthusiasts.*

42. "For wearable computers, future looks blurry," *The Wall Street Journal,* May 30, 2013.

43. Shiller, R. (1995), "Conversation, information, and herd behavior," *American Economic Review* 85: 181–185.

44. "A year of few dull moments," *The New York Times,* December 21, 2012; "How the wheels came off for Fisker," *The Wall Street Journal,* April 24, 2013.

45. The Iridium example is drawn from: Finkelstein, S. (2003), *Why Smart Executives Fail: And What You Can Learn from Their Mistakes* (New York: Portfolio).

46. In inflation-adjusted 2012 U.S. dollars. The original price in 1998 was $3,000 and the cost per minute up to $8.

47. "HP gambles on ailing Palm," *The Wall Street Journal,* April 29, 2010.

48. "What's gone wrong with HP?" *The Wall Street Journal,* November 6, 2012.

49. In 2013, RIM adopted BlackBerry as company name.

50. Moore, G. A. (1991), *Crossing the Chasm. Marketing and Selling Disruptive Products to Mainstream Customers* (New York: HarperCollins).

51. Shuen, A. (2008), *Web 2.0: A Strategy Guide* (Sebastopol, CA: O'Reilly Media); Thursby, J., and M. Thursby (2006), *Here or There? A Survey in Factors of Multinational R&D Location* (Washington, DC: National Academies Press).

52. Byers, T. H., R. C. Dorf, and A. J. Nelson (2011), *Technology Entrepreneurship: From Idea to Enterprise* (Burr Ridge, IL: McGraw-Hill).

53. This discussion is based on: Schumpeter, J. A. (1942), *Capitalism, Socialism, and Democracy;* Freeman, C., and L. Soete (1997), *The Economics of Industrial Innovation* (Cambridge, MA: MIT Press); and Foster, R., and S. Kaplan (2001), *Creative Destruction: Why Companies That Are Built to Last Underperform the Market—and How to Successfully Transform Them.*

54. The discussion of incremental and radical innovations is based on: Hill, C.W.L., and F. T. Rothaermel (2003), "The performance of incumbent firms in the face of radical technological innovation," *Academy of Management Review* 28: 257–274.

55. Hill, C.W.L., and F. T. Rothaermel (2003), "The performance of incumbent firms in the face of radical technological innovation," *Academy of Management Review* 28: 257–274.

56. "A David and Gillette story," *The Wall Street Journal,* April 12, 2012.

57. This discussion is based on: Hill, C.W.L., and F. T. Rothaermel (2003), "The performance of incumbent firms in the face of radical technological innovation."

58. Brandenburger, A. M., and B. J. Nalebuff (1996), *Co-opetition* (New York: Currency Doubleday); and Christensen, C. M., and J. L. Bower (1996), "Customer power, strategic investment, and the failure of leading firms," *Strategic Management Journal* 17: 197–218; Adner, R. (2012), *The Wide Lens. A New Strategy for Innovation* (New York: Portfolio)

59. Henderson, R., and K. B. Clark (1990), "Architectural innovation: The reconfiguration of existing technologies and the failure of established firms," *Administrative Science Quarterly* 35: 9–30.

60. This example is drawn from: Chesbrough, H. (2003), *Open Innovation. The New Imperative for Creating and Profiting from Technology* (Boston, MA: Harvard Business School Press).

61. The discussion of disruptive innovation is based on: Christensen, C. M. (1997), *The Innovator's Dilemma: When New Technologies Cause Great Firms to Fail* (Boston, MA: Harvard Business School Press); and Christensen, C. M., and M. E. Raynor (2003), *The Innovator's Solution: Creating and Sustaining Successful Growth* (Boston, MA: Harvard Business School Press).

62. Android here is used to include Chrome OS. "Introducing the Google Chrome OS," *The Official Google Blog,* July 7, 2009, http://googleblog.blogspot.com/2009/07/introducing-google-chrome-os.html.

63. See discussion on Business Models in Chapter 1. See also: Anderson, C. (2009), *Free. The Future of a Radical Price.*

64. Rindova, V., and S. Kotha (2001), "Continuous 'morphing': Competing through dynamic capabilities, form, and function," *Academy of Management Journal* 44: 1263–1280.

65. The new processor not only is inexpensive but also consumes little battery power. Moreover, it marks a departure from the Wintel (Windows and Intel) alliance, because Microsoft did not have a suitable operating system ready for the low-end netbook market. Many of these computers are using free software such as Google's Android operating system and Google Docs for applications.

66. This approach is referred to as *reverse innovation* in the literature; see Govindarajan, V. and C. Trimble (2012), *Reverse Innovation: Create Far from Home, Win Everywhere* (Boston, MA: Harvard Business Review Press).

67. This Strategy Highlight is based on: Immelt, J. R., V. Govindarajan, and C. Trimble (2009), "How GE is disrupting itself," *Harvard Business Review*, October; author's interviews with Michael Poteran of GE Healthcare (10/30/09 and 11/04/09); and "Vscan handheld ultrasound: GE unveils 'stethoscope of the 21st century,'" *The Huffington Post*, October 20, 2009.

68. This section is based on: Anderson, C. (2006), *The Long Tail. Why the Future of Business Is Selling Less of More;* and Anderson, C. (2009), *Free. The Future of a Radical Price.*

69. "A giant sucking sound," *The Economist,* November 5, 2009.

70. Anderson, C. (2006), *The Long Tail. Why the Future of Business Is Selling Less of More.*

71. The discussion in this section draws mainly on Chesbrough's seminal work, but also on the other insightful sources referenced here. Chesbrough, H. W. (2003), *Open Innovation: The New Imperative for Creating and Profiting from Technology* (Boston, MA: Harvard Business School Press); Chesbrough, H. (2003), "The area of open innovation," *MIT Sloan Management Review,* Spring: 35–41; Chesbrough, H. (2007), "Why companies should have open business models," *MIT Sloan Management Review,* Winter: 22–28; Chesbrough, H. W., and M. M. Appleyard (2007), "Open innovation and strategy," *California Management Review,* Fall 50: 57–76; Laursen, K., and A. Salter (2006), "Open for innovation: The role of openness

in explaining innovation performance among U.K. manufacturing firms," *Strategic Management Journal* 27: 131–150; and West, J., and S. Gallagher (2006), "Challenges of open innovation: The paradox of firm investment in open-source software," *R&D Management* 36: 319–331.

72. Rothaermel, F. T., and M. T. Alexandre (2009), "Ambidexterity in technology sourcing: The moderating role of absorptive capacity," *Organization Science* 20: 759–780; Rothaermel, F. T., and A. M. Hess (2010), "Innovation strategies combined," *MIT Sloan Management Review,* Spring 51: 13–15.

73. Katz, R., and T. J. Allen (1982), "Investigating the Not Invented Here (NIH) syndrome: A look at the performance, tenure, and communication patterns of 50 R&D project groups," *R&D Management* 12: 7–20.

74. Horbaczewski, A., and F. T. Rothaermel (2013), "Merck: Open for innovation?" Case Study MH-FTR-009-0077645065, available at: http://create.mcgraw-hill.com.

75. Cohen, W. M., and D. A. Levinthal (1990), "Absorptive capacity: New perspective on learning and innovation," *Administrative Science Quarterly* 35: 128–152; Zahra, S. A., and G. George (2002), "Absorptive capacity: A review, reconceptualization, and extension," *Academy of Management Review* 27: 185–203; and Rothaermel, F. T., and M. T. Alexandre (2009), "Ambidexterity in technology sourcing: The moderating role of absorptive capacity," *Organization Science* 20: 759–780.

76. Huston, L., and N. Sakkab (2006), "Connect & Develop: Inside Procter & Gamble's new model for innovation," *Harvard Business Review,* March: 58–66; Lafley, A. G., and R. L. Martin (2013), *Playing to Win: How Strategy Really Works* (Boston, MA: Harvard Business Review Press); Rothaermel, F. T., and M. T. Alexandre (2009), "Ambidexterity in technology sourcing: The moderating role of absorptive capacity," *Organization Science* 20: 759–780; Rothaermel, F. T., and A. M. Hess (2010), "Innovation strategies combined," *MIT Sloan Management Review,* Spring 51: 13–15; and "Diamond buys P&G's Pringles," *The Wall Street Journal,* April 6, 2011.

77. http://www.fastcompany.com/section/most-innovative-companies-2013.

78. Burgelman, R. A. (1983), "Corporate entrepreneurship and strategic management:

Insights from a process Study," *Management Science* 29: 1349–1364; Burgelman, R. A. (1991), "Intraorganizational ecology of strategy making and organizational adaptation: Theory and field research," *Organization Science* 2: 239–262; and Burgelman, R. A., and A. Grove (2007), "Let chaos reign, then rein in chaos—repeatedly: Managing strategic dynamics for corporate longevity," *Strategic Management Journal* 28: 965–979.

79. http://solutions.3m.com/innovation/en_US/stories/time-to-think.

80. Data from Wikipedia, www.wikipedia.org/wiki/wikipedia:about.

81. http://en.wikipedia.org/wiki/Wikipedia:Donation_appeal_ideas.

82. Greenstein, S., and F. Zhu (2012), "Is Wikipedia biased?" *American Economic Review* 102: 343–348.

83. "Gendercide in India," *The Economist,* April 7, 2011; "Sex-selective abortion," *The Economist,* June 28, 2011; "India women: One dishonourable step backwards," *The Economist,* May 11, 2012; and "India's skewed sex ratios," *The Economist,* December 18, 2012.

84. Huston, L., and N. Sakkab (2006), "Connect & Develop: Inside Procter & Gamble's new model for innovation," *Harvard Business Review,* March: 58–66; Lafley, A. G., and R. L. Martin (2013), *Playing to Win: How Strategy Really Works* (Boston, MA: Harvard Business Review Press).

85. Huston, L., and N. Sakkab (2006), "Connect & Develop: Inside Procter & Gamble's new model for innovation," *Harvard Business Review,* March: 58–66; Lafley, A. G., and R. L. Martin (2013), *Playing to Win: How Strategy Really Works* (Boston, MA: Harvard Business Review Press).

86. This *my*Strategy example is based on: "14 big businesses that started in a recession," www.insidecrm.com, November 11, 2008; "Full-time MBA programs: Stanford University," *BusinessWeek,* November 13, 2008; "Start-ups that thrive in a recession," *The Wall Street Journal,* February 4, 2009; "Why great companies get started in the downturns," www.vcconfidential.com, February 24, 2009; and "M.B.A. students shift focus toward entrepreneurship," *U.S. News & World Report,* April 29, 2011.

Chapter 8

Corporate Strategy: Vertical Integration and Diversification

Learning Objectives

After studying this chapter, you should be able to:

LO 8-1 Define corporate strategy and describe the three dimensions along which it is assessed.

LO 8-2 Describe and evaluate different options firms have to organize economic activity.

LO 8-3 Describe the two types of vertical integration along the industry value chain: backward and forward vertical integration.

LO 8-4 Identify and evaluate benefits and risks of vertical integration.

LO 8-5 Describe and examine alternatives to vertical integration.

LO 8-6 Describe and evaluate different types of corporate diversification.

LO 8-7 Apply the core competence–market matrix to derive different diversification strategies.

LO 8-8 Explain when a diversification strategy creates a competitive advantage and when it does not.

Refocusing GE: A Future of Clean-Tech and Health Care?

healthy**magination**
better health for more people.

JEFFREY IMMELT WAS APPOINTED chairman and CEO of General Electric (GE) on September 7, 2001. Since then, the external environment has experienced continuous and dramatic change: first, the social and economic effects of the 9/11 terrorist attacks, followed later by the 2008–2009 global financial crisis. Although GE is a diversified conglomerate that spans many industries and markets, the recession in 2001 and the even deeper recession of 2008–2009 hit the company especially hard. One reason was the financial blow that GE Capital took, since more than half of GE's profits came from that unit. In a critical 17 months, GE's share price fell 84 percent, from $42.12 (on October 2, 2007) to $6.66 (on March 5, 2009), equating to a loss in shareholder value of $378 billion. To compound matters, GE also lost its AAA credit rating, and the company had to ask for a $15 billion liquidity injection from famed investor Warren Buffett. Between 2008 and 2013, GE significantly underperformed the Dow Jones Industrial Index.

The need for change was clear to Mr. Immelt. In 2009, GE's five business units (Technology Infrastructure, Energy Infrastructure, Capital Finance, Consumer and Industrial, and NBC Universal) brought in $157 billion in annual revenues. More than 50 percent of those revenues came from outside the United States, and GE employed more than 300,000 people in over 100 countries. Mr. Immelt decided to refocus GE's portfolio of businesses to reduce its exposure to capital markets and to achieve reliable and sustainable future growth by leveraging its core competency in industrial engineering. GE sold NBC Universal to Comcast, the largest U.S. cable operator, and also put its century-old appliance unit up for sale. GE had identified the clean-technology sector and, more recently, health care as major future-growth industries. To capitalize on these opportunities, GE launched two strategic initiatives: *ecomagination* and *healthymagination*.

Ecomagination is GE's clean-tech strategic initiative, launched in 2005 and renewed in 2010 by adding another $10 billion in investments. As Mr. Immelt explains, its strategic intent is "to focus our unique energy, technology, manufacturing, and infrastructure capabilities to develop tomorrow's solutions such as solar energy, hybrid locomotives, fuel cells, lower-emission aircraft engines, lighter and stronger materials, efficient lighting, and water purification technology."[1] The *ecomagination* initiative generates roughly $25 billion in annual revenues for GE.

Healthymagination, launched in 2009, is GE's newest strategic initiative. Its goal is to increase the quality of, and access to, health care while lowering its cost. Investing $6 billion by 2015, GE's strategic intent is to reduce the cost of health care by 15 percent, increase access to essential health care services worldwide by 15 percent, reach a minimum of 100 million people a year, and improve health care quality by 15 percent by streamlining health care procedures, processes, and standards.[2]

These two strategic initiatives are tools with which GE's top executives are attempting to drive change within their large multinational corporation. In particular, Mr. Immelt hopes that the two new strategic initiatives not only position GE to take advantage of opportunities in future industries, but also facilitate more lateral cooperation between the disparate GE strategic business units to share R&D, technology, management processes, and talent.

After reading the chapter, you will find more about this case, with related questions, on page 267.

🔺 **AS A MULTIBUSINESS** enterprise, GE has been changing its corporate strategy in several ways. One, it has moved away from slow-growing businesses, such as appliances and entertainment, and turned to future-growth industries, such as clean-tech and health care. Two, Jeffrey Immelt reduced GE's exposure to the financial markets by trimming the GE Capital unit. Although during the first decade of the 2000s GE Capital produced roughly half of GE's profits based on one-third of its revenues, it made GE more vulnerable to changes in the macro environment such as the 2008–2009 financial crisis. Three, GE is also focusing more on faster growing international markets such as those in Asia, Eastern Europe, and the Middle East.

These changes in GE's portfolio of businesses and geographic focus illustrate that firms must decide in which industries and global markets to compete. Moreover, these choices are likely to change over time in response to opportunities and threats in the external environment. Answers to the important question of *where to compete* are captured in a firm's *corporate strategy,* which we cover in the next three chapters. In this chapter, we define corporate strategy and then look at two fundamental corporate strategy topics: vertical integration and diversification. We conclude the chapter with *Implications for the Strategist* that provide a practical application of dynamic corporate strategy at Nike and adidas.

8.1 What Is Corporate Strategy?

Define corporate strategy and describe the three dimensions along which it is assessed.

Strategy formulation centers around the key questions of where and how to compete. *Business strategy* concerns the question of *how to compete* in a *single product market.* As discussed in Chapter 6, the two generic business strategies that firms can pursue in their quest for competitive advantage are to increase differentiation (while containing cost) *or* lower costs (while maintaining differentiation). If trade-offs can be reconciled, some firms might be able to pursue an integration strategy by increasing differentiation *and* lowering costs. As firms grow, they are frequently expanding their business activities through seeking out new markets both by offering new products and services and by competing in different geographies. When this happens, managers must formulate a corporate strategy. To gain and sustain competitive advantage, therefore, any corporate strategy must align with and strengthen a firm's business strategy, whether it is differentiation, cost leadership, or an integration strategy.

corporate strategy
The decisions that senior management makes and the goal-directed actions it takes to gain and sustain competitive advantage in several industries and markets simultaneously; addresses *where to compete* along three dimensions: products and services, industry value chain, and geography (regional, national, or global markets).

Corporate strategy comprises the decisions that senior management makes and the goal-directed actions it takes in the quest for competitive advantage in several industries and markets simultaneously.[3] It provides answers to the key question of *where to compete.* Corporate strategy determines the boundaries of the firm along three dimensions: industry value chain, products and services, and geography (regional, national, or global markets). Executives must decide:

1. *In what stages of the industry value chain to participate.* The industry value chain describes the transformation of raw materials into finished goods and services along distinct vertical stages. This decision determines the firm's vertical integration.
2. *What range of products and services to offer.* This decision determines the firm's level of diversification.
3. *Where to compete* in terms of regional, national, or international markets. This decision determines the firm's geographic scope.

Although many managers have input to this important decision-making process, the responsibility for corporate strategy ultimately rests with the CEO. We noted in ChapterCase 8, for example, General Electric CEO Immelt's attempt to refocus the conglomerate on future-growth industries through the *ecomagination* and *healthymagination* strategic initiatives. In his 2010 letter to shareholders, Mr. Immelt confirmed GE's back-to-its-roots corporate strategy: "As we grew, financial services became too big and added too much volatility. GE must be an industrial company first. We have increased our investment in industrial growth."[4]

Where to compete in terms of industry value chain, products and services, and geography are the fundamental corporate strategic decisions. The underlying strategic management concepts that will guide our discussion of vertical integration, diversification, and geographic competition are *core competencies, economies of scale, economies of scope,* and *transaction costs.*

- *Core competencies* are unique strengths embedded deep within a firm (as discussed in Chapter 4). Core competencies allow a firm to differentiate its products and services from those of its rivals, creating higher value for the customer or offering products and services of comparable value at lower cost. According to the *resource-based view of the firm,* a firm's boundaries are delineated by its knowledge bases and competencies.[5] Activities that draw on what the firm knows how to do well (e.g., Honda's core competency in small, highly reliable engines, or Google's core competency in developing proprietary search algorithms) should be done in-house, while non-core activities such as payroll and facility maintenance can be outsourced. In this perspective, the internally held knowledge underlying a core competency determines a firm's boundaries.

- *Economies of scale* occur when a firm's average cost per unit decreases as its output increases (as discussed in Chapter 6). Anheuser-Busch InBev, the largest global brewer (producer of brands such as Budweiser, Bud Light, Stella Artois, and Beck's), reaps significant economies of scale. Given its size, it is able to spread its fixed costs over the millions of gallons of beer it brews each year, in addition to the significant buyer power its large market share affords. Larger market share, therefore, often leads to lower costs.

- *Economies of scope,* in turn, are the savings that come from producing two (or more) outputs or providing different services at less cost than producing each individually, though using the same resources and technology (as discussed in Chapter 6). Leveraging its online retailing expertise, for example, Amazon benefits from economies of scope: It can offer a large range of different product and service categories at a lower cost than it would take to offer each product line individually.

- *Transaction costs* are all costs associated with an economic exchange. The concept is developed in transaction cost economics, a strategic management framework, and enables managers to answer the question of whether it is cost-effective for their firm to expand its boundaries through vertical integration or diversification. This implies taking on greater ownership of the production of needed inputs or of the channels by which it distributes its outputs, or adding business units that offer new products and services.

We begin our study of corporate strategy by drawing on transaction cost economics to explain vertical integration, meaning the choices a firm makes concerning its boundaries. Later, we will explore managerial decisions relating to diversification, which directly affect the firm's range of products and services in multi-industry competition.

8.2 The Boundaries of the Firm

LO 8-2

Describe and evaluate different options firms have to organize economic activity.

Determining the boundaries of the firm so that it is more likely to gain and sustain a competitive advantage is the critical challenge in corporate strategy.[6] A theoretical framework in strategic management called **transaction cost economics** explains and predicts the boundaries of the firm. Insights gained from transaction cost economics help managers decide what activities to do in-house versus what services and products to obtain from the external market. This stream of research was first initiated by Nobel Laureate Ronald Coase, who asked a fundamental question: Given the efficiencies of free markets, why do firms even exist? The key insight of transaction cost economics is that different *institutional arrangements*—markets versus firms—have different costs attached.

To start, we need to identify **transaction costs**: these are all internal and external costs associated with an economic exchange, whether it takes place within the boundaries of a firm or in markets.[7] Exhibit 8.1 visualizes the notion of transaction costs. It shows the respective internal transactions costs within Firm A and Firm B, as well as the external transactions that occur when Firm A and Firm B do business with one another.

The total costs of transacting consist of external and internal transaction costs, as follows:

■ When companies transact in the open market, they incur **external transaction costs**: the costs of searching for a firm or an individual with whom to contract, and then negotiating, monitoring, and enforcing the contract.

■ Transaction costs can occur within the firm as well. Considered **internal transaction costs**, these include costs pertaining to organizing an economic exchange within a firm—for example, the costs of recruiting and retaining employees, paying salaries and benefits, setting up a shop floor, providing office space and computers, and organizing, monitoring, and supervising work. Internal transaction costs also include administrative costs associated with coordinating economic activity between different business units of the same corporation such as transfer pricing for input factors, and between

EXHIBIT 8.1

Internal and External Transaction Costs

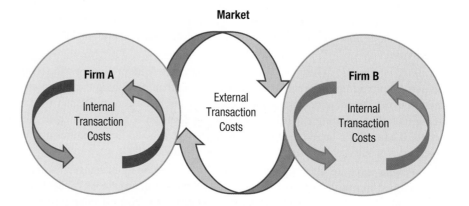

transaction cost economics A theoretical framework in strategic management to explain and predict the boundaries of the firm, which is central to formulating a corporate strategy that is more likely to lead to competitive advantage.

transaction costs All internal and external costs associated with an economic exchange, whether within a firm or in markets.

external transaction costs Costs of searching for a firm or an individual with whom to contract, and then negotiating, monitoring, and enforcing the contract.

internal transaction costs Costs pertaining to organizing an economic exchange within a hierarchy; also called *administrative costs*.

business units and corporate headquarters including important decisions pertaining to resource allocation, among others. Internal transaction costs tend to increase with organizational size and complexity.

FIRMS VS. MARKETS: MAKE OR BUY?

Transaction cost economics allows us to explain which activities a firm should pursue in-house ("make") versus which goods and services to obtain externally ("buy"). These decisions help determine the boundaries of the firm. In some cases, costs of using the market such as search costs, negotiating and drafting contracts, monitoring work, and enforcing contracts when necessary may be higher than integrating the activity within a single firm and coordinating it through an organizational hierarchy. When the costs of pursuing an activity in-house are less than the costs of transacting for that activity in the market ($C_{in\text{-}house} < C_{market}$), then the firm should *vertically integrate* by owning production of the needed inputs or the channels for the distribution of outputs. In other words, when *firms* are more efficient in organizing economic activity than are *markets,* which rely on contracts among many independent actors, firms should vertically integrate.[8]

For example, rather than contracting in the open market for individual pieces of software code, Google hires programmers to write code in-house. Owning these software-development capabilities is valuable to the firm because its costs such as salaries and employee benefits to in-house computer programmers are less than what they would be in the open market. More importantly, Google gains economies of scope in software development resources and capabilities and reduces the monitoring costs. This is because skills acquired in writing software code for its different Internet-based service offerings are transferable to new offerings. Programmers working on the original proprietary software code for the Google search engine leveraged these skills in creating a highly profitable online advertising business (AdWords and AdSense).[9] Although some of Google's software products are open source, such as the Android operating system, many of the company's Internet services are based on closely guarded and proprietary software code. Google, like many leading high-tech companies such as Amazon, Apple, Facebook, and Microsoft, relies on proprietary software code and algorithms, because using the open market to transact for individual pieces of software would be prohibitively expensive. Also, the firms would need to disclose the underlying software code to outside developers, thus negating the value-creation potential.

Firms and markets, as different institutional arrangements for organizing economic activity, have their own distinct advantages and disadvantages, summarized in Exhibit 8.2.

The advantages of firms include:

■ The ability to make *command-and-control decisions* by fiat along clear hierarchical lines of authority.

EXHIBIT 8.2 / Organizing Economic Activity: Firms vs. Markets

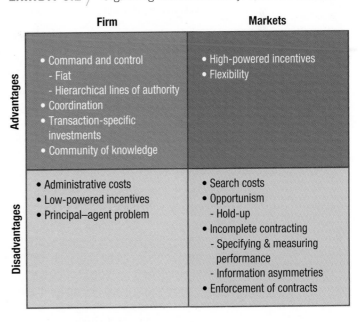

	Firm	**Markets**
Advantages	• Command and control - Fiat - Hierarchical lines of authority • Coordination • Transaction-specific investments • Community of knowledge	• High-powered incentives • Flexibility
Disadvantages	• Administrative costs • Low-powered incentives • Principal–agent problem	• Search costs • Opportunism - Hold-up • Incomplete contracting - Specifying & measuring performance - Information asymmetries • Enforcement of contracts

- Coordination of highly complex tasks to allow for *specialized division of labor.*
- *Transaction-specific investments,* such as specialized robotics equipment that is highly valuable within the firm, but of little or no use in the external market.
- Creation of a *community of knowledge.*

The disadvantages of organizing economic activity within firms include:

- *Administrative costs* because of necessary bureaucracy.
- *Low-powered incentives,* such as hourly wages and salaries. These often are less attractive motivators than the entrepreneurial opportunities and rewards that can be obtained in the open market.
- The *principal–agent problem.*

The **principal–agent problem** is a major disadvantage of organizing economic activity within firms, as opposed to within markets. It can arise when an agent such as a manager, performing activities on behalf of the principal (the owner of the firm), pursues his or her own interests.[10] Indeed, the *separation of ownership and control* is one of the hallmarks of a publicly traded company, and so some degree of the principal–agent problem is almost inevitable.[11] For example, a manager may pursue his or her own interests such as job security and managerial perks (e.g., corporate jets and golf outings) that conflict with the principal's goals—in particular, creating shareholder value. One potential way to overcome the principal–agent problem is to give stock options to managers, thus making them owners. We will revisit the principal–agent problem, with related ideas, in Chapters 11 and 12.

The advantages of markets include:

- *High-powered incentives.* Rather than work as a salaried engineer for an existing firm, for example, an individual can start a new venture offering specialized software. High-powered incentives of the open market include the entrepreneur's ability to capture the venture's profit, to take a new venture through an initial public offering (IPO), or to be acquired by an existing firm. In these so-called *liquidity events,* a successful entrepreneur can make potentially enough money to provide financial security for life.[12]
- *Increased flexibility.* Transacting in markets enables those who wish to purchase goods to compare prices and services among many different providers.

The disadvantages of markets include:

- *Search costs.* On a very fundamental level, perhaps the biggest disadvantage of transacting in markets, rather than owning the various production and distribution activities within the firm itself, entails non-trivial *search costs.* In particular, a firm faces search costs when it must scour the market to find reliable suppliers from among the many firms competing to offer similar products and services. Even more difficult can be the search to find suppliers when the specific products and services needed are not offered at all by firms currently in the market. In this case, production of supplies would require transaction-specific investments, an advantage of firms.
- *Opportunism by other parties. Opportunism* is behavior characterized by self-interest seeking with guile (we'll discuss this in more detail later).
- *Incomplete contracting.* Although market transactions are based on implicit and explicit contracts, all contracts are incomplete to some extent, because not all future contingencies can be anticipated at the time of contracting. It is also difficult to specify expectations (e.g., What stipulates "acceptable quality" in a graphic design project?) or to measure performance and outcomes (e.g., What does "excess wear and tear" mean when returning a leased car?). Another serious hazard inherent in contracting is *information asymmetry* (which we discuss next).

- *Enforcement of contracts.* It often is difficult, costly, and time-consuming to enforce legal contracts. Not only does litigation absorb a significant amount of managerial resources and attention, but it can easily amount to several million dollars in legal fees. Legal exposure is one of the major hazards in using markets rather than integrating an activity within a firm's hierarchy.

Frequently, sellers have better information about products and services than buyers, which in turn creates **information asymmetries**, situations in which one party is more informed than another, because of the possession of private information. When firms transact in the market, such unequal information can lead to a *lemons problem.* Nobel Laureate George Akerlof first described this situation using the market for used cars as an example.[13] Assume only two types of cars are sold: good cars and bad cars (lemons). Good cars are worth $8,000 and bad ones are worth $4,000. Moreover, only the seller knows whether a car is good or is a lemon. Assuming the market supply is split equally between good and bad cars, the probability of buying a lemon is 50 percent. Buyers are aware of the general possibility of buying a lemon and thus would like to hedge against it. Therefore, they split the difference and offer $6,000 for a used car. This discounting strategy has the perverse effect of crowding out all the good cars because the sellers perceive their value to be above $6,000. Assuming that to be the case, all used cars offered for sale will be lemons.

The important take-away here is *caveat emptor*—buyer beware. Information asymmetries can result in the crowding out of desirable goods and services by inferior ones. This has been shown to be true in many markets, not just for used cars, but also in e-commerce (e.g., eBay), mortgage-backed securities, and even collaborative R&D projects.[14]

> **information asymmetries**
> Situations in which one party is more informed than another, because of the possession of private information.

ALTERNATIVES ON THE MAKE-OR-BUY CONTINUUM

The "make" and "buy" choices *anchor each end of a continuum* from markets to firms, as depicted in Exhibit 8.3. Several alternative hybrid arrangements are in fact available between these two extremes.[15] Moving from transacting in the market ("buy") to full integration ("make"), alternatives include short-term contracts as well as various forms of strategic alliances (long-term contracts, equity alliances, and joint ventures) and parent–subsidiary relationships.

SHORT-TERM CONTRACTS. When engaging in *short-term contracting,* a firm sends out *requests for proposals (RFPs)* to several companies, which initiates competitive bidding for contracts to be awarded with a short duration, generally less than one year.[16]

EXHIBIT 8.3 / Alternatives on the Make-or-Buy Continuum

Buy		Strategic Alliances			Make	
Arm's-length market transactions	Short-term contracts	Long-term contracts • Licensing • Franchising	Equity alliances	Joint ventures	Parent– subsidiary relationship	Activities performed in-house

Less integrated   More integrated

The benefit to this approach lies in the fact that it allows a somewhat longer planning period than individual market transactions. Moreover, the buying firm can often demand lower prices due to the competitive bidding process. The drawback, however, is that firms responding to the RFP have no incentive to make any transaction-specific investments (e.g., buy new machinery to improve product quality) due to the short duration of the contract. This is exactly what happened in the U.S. automotive industry when GM used short-term contracts for standard car components to reduce costs. When faced with significant cost pressures, suppliers reduced component quality in order to protect their eroding margins. This resulted in lower-quality GM cars, contributing to a competitive advantage vis-à-vis competitors, most notably Toyota but also Ford, which used a more cooperative, longer-term partnering approach with their suppliers.[17]

STRATEGIC ALLIANCES. As we move toward greater integration on the make-or-buy continuum, the next organizational forms are strategic alliances. **Strategic alliances** are voluntary arrangements between firms that involve the sharing of knowledge, resources, and capabilities with the intent of developing processes, products, or services to lead to competitive advantage.[18] Alliances have become a ubiquitous phenomenon, especially in high-tech industries. Moreover, strategic alliances can facilitate investments in transaction-specific assets without encountering the internal transaction costs involved in owning firms in various stages of the industry value chain.

strategic alliances Voluntary arrangements between firms that involve the sharing of knowledge, resources, and capabilities with the intent of developing processes, products, or services to lead to competitive advantage.

Strategic alliances is an umbrella term that denotes different hybrid organizational forms—among them, long-term contracts, equity alliances, and joint ventures. Given their prevalence in today's competitive landscape, as a key vehicle to execute a firm's corporate strategy, we take a quick look at strategic alliances here and then study them in more depth in Chapter 9.

Long-Term Contracts. We noted that firms in short-term contracts have no incentive to make transaction-specific investments. *Long-term contracts,* which work much like short-term contracts but with a duration generally greater than one year, help overcome this drawback. Long-term contracts help facilitate transaction-specific investments. **Licensing**, for example, is a form of long-term contracting in the manufacturing sector that enables firms to commercialize intellectual property such as a patent. The first biotechnology drug to reach the market, Humulin (human insulin), was developed by Genentech and commercialized by Eli Lilly based on a licensing agreement.

licensing A form of long-term contracting in the manufacturing sector that enables firms to commercialize intellectual property.

In service industries, **franchising** is an example of long-term contracting. In these arrangements, a franchisor such as McDonald's, Burger King, 7-Eleven, H&R Block, or Subway grants a franchisee (usually an entrepreneur owning no more than a few outlets) the right to use the franchisor's trademark and business processes to offer goods and services that carry the franchisor's brand name. Besides providing the capital to finance the expansion of the chain, the franchisee generally pays an up-front (buy-in) lump sum to the franchisor plus a percentage of revenues.

franchising A long-term contract in which a franchisor grants a franchisee the right to use the franchisor's trademark and business processes to offer goods and services that carry the franchisor's brand name; the franchisee in turn pays an up-front buy-in lump sum and a percentage of revenues.

Equity Alliances. Yet another form of strategic alliance is an *equity alliance*—a partnership in which at least one partner takes partial ownership in the other partner. A partner purchases an ownership share by buying stock, and thus making an equity investment. The taking of equity tends to signal greater commitment to the partnership.

Strategy Highlight 8.1 describes an equity alliance between Toyota and Orocobre Ltd., an Australian mineral-resource company, to facilitate specialized investments for the exploration and mining of lithium, a critical input for lithium-ion batteries used in hybrid and electric vehicles.

In a contract arrangement, one transaction partner could attempt to *hold up* the other, by demanding lower prices or threatening to walk away from the agreement altogether (with whatever financial penalties might be included in the contract). To assuage Orocobre's

Strategy Highlight 8.1

Toyota Locks Up Lithium for Car Batteries

In 2012, 40 percent of all Toyota cars sold in Japan and 14 percent sold globally were hybrid electric vehicles. Since the introduction of the first Prius model in 1997, Toyota has sold more than 5 million hybrid cars. It should come as no surprise then that global demand for lithium-ion batteries to propel hybrid electric cars has grown almost a hundred-fold, to $25 billion in 2014, up from a mere $278 million in 2009. Moreover, this type of battery requires large amounts of high-quality lithium, which is difficult and costly to extract. Given the specific geological conditions, the company mining the lithium must deploy highly specialized equipment, which is of little use in alternative applications.

Given the strong demand for its hybrid vehicles, Toyota Motor Corporation was interested in securing a long-term supply of lithium. It approached Orocobre, which holds the exploration rights to a large salt-lake area in northwestern

Argentina. Although lithium is found in several rock formations across the globe, large quantities can be extracted in a cost-effective manner only below the surfaces of salt flats. Initial investments in specialized equipment worth several hundred million dollars, however, are required even to understand the *quality* of the deposits. If the findings are positive, more investments would be needed to exploit them commercially.

Should Orocobre make the investment in the specialized equipment? What if the lithium is not of the quality expected, or a new technology emerges that is superior to lithium-ion batteries? If Toyota were merely to transact for the lithium in the market—by simply signing a contract with Orocobre that it would purchase any lithium it mined—Toyota could walk away from the exploratory project undertaken by Orocobre if the results were not what it had expected, or if the forecasted demand for lithium-ion batteries did not materialize. To mitigate Orocobre's concerns, Toyota took an equity stake worth an estimated $120 million in this project.[19]

---

concerns, Toyota made a **credible commitment**—a long-term strategic decision that is both difficult and costly to reverse. Alternatively, Toyota could have acquired Orocobre outright, thus engaging in backward vertical integration as well as in unrelated diversification. This would have been, however, a much more costly and riskier strategic move.

Joint Ventures. In a **joint venture**, which is another special form of strategic alliance, two or more partners create and jointly own a new organization. Since the partners contribute equity to a joint venture, they make a long-term commitment, which in turn facilitates transaction-specific investments. Dow Corning, owned jointly by Dow Chemical and Corning, is an example of a joint venture. Dow Corning, which focuses on silicone-based technology, employs roughly 10,000 people and has $5 billion in annual revenues, which shows that some joint ventures can be quite large.[20] Hulu, which offers web-based streaming video of TV shows and movies, is also a joint venture, owned by NBC, Fox, and Disney. With three million users in 2013, Hulu is a smaller competitor to Netflix with some 30 million users. We will further discuss joint ventures in Chapter 9.

PARENT–SUBSIDIARY RELATIONSHIP. The *parent–subsidiary relationship* describes the most-integrated alternative to performing an activity within one's own corporate family. The corporate parent owns the subsidiary and can direct it via command and control. Transaction costs that arise are frequently due to political turf battles, which may include the capital budgeting process and transfer prices, among other areas. For example, although GM owns its European carmakers (Opel in Germany and Vauxhall in the United Kingdom), it had problems bringing some of their know-how and design of small fuel-efficient cars back into the U.S. This failure put GM at a competitive disadvantage vis-à-vis the Japanese competitors when they were first entering the U.S. market with more

credible commitment
A long-term strategic decision that is both difficult and costly to reverse.

joint venture
Organizational form in which two or more partners create and jointly own a new organization.

fuel-efficient cars. In addition, the Japanese carmakers were able to improve the quality and design of their vehicles faster, which in turn enabled them to gain a competitive advantage, especially in an environment of rising gas prices.

The GM versus Opel and Vauxhall parent–subsidiary relationship was burdened by political problems because managers in Detroit did not respect the engineering behind the small, fuel-efficient cars that Opel and Vauxhall made. They were not very interested in using European know-how for the U.S. market and didn't want to pay much or anything for it. Moreover, Detroit was tired of subsidizing the losses of Opel and Vauxhall, and felt that its European subsidiaries were manipulating the capital budgeting process.[21] In turn, the Opel and Vauxhall subsidiaries felt resentment toward their parent company: GM had initially planned to shut them down as part of its bankruptcy restructuring, whereas they instead hoped to be divested as independent companies.[22]

Having laid a strong theoretical foundation by fully considering transaction cost economics and the boundaries of the firm, we now turn our attention to the firm's position along the vertical industry value chain.

vertical integration
The firm's ownership of its production of needed inputs or of the channels by which it distributes its outputs.

industry value chain Depiction of the transformation of raw materials into finished goods and services along distinct vertical stages, each of which typically represents a distinct *industry* in which a number of different firms are competing.

8.3 Vertical Integration along the Industry Value Chain

The first key question when formulating corporate strategy is: In what stages of the industry value chain should the firm participate? Deciding whether to make or buy the various activities in the industry value chain involves the concept of vertical integration. **Vertical integration** is the firm's ownership of its production of needed inputs or of the channels by which it distributes its outputs. Vertical integration can be measured by a firm's value added: What percentage of a firm's sales is generated within the firm's boundaries?[23] The degree of vertical integration tends to correspond to the number of industry value chain stages in which a firm directly participates.

Exhibit 8.4 depicts a generic **industry value chain**. Industry value chains are also called *vertical value chains,* because they depict the transformation of raw materials into finished goods and services along distinct vertical stages. Each stage of the vertical value chain typically represents a distinct *industry* in which a number of different firms are competing. This is also why the movement of a firm backward or forward along the *vertical* industry value chain is called *vertical* integration.

To understand the concept of vertical integration along the different stages of the industry value chain more fully, let's use your cell phone as an example. This ubiquitous device is the result of a globally coordinated industry value chain of different products and services:

- The raw materials to make your cell phone, such as chemicals, ceramics, metals, oil for plastic, and so on, are commodities. In each of these commodity businesses are different companies, such as DuPont (U.S.), BASF (Germany), Kyocera (Japan), and ExxonMobil (U.S.).

EXHIBIT 8.4 / Backward and Forward Vertical Integration along an Industry Value Chain

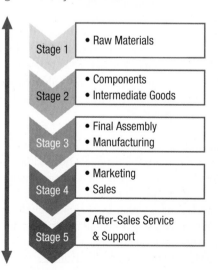

UPSTREAM INDUSTRIES

BACKWARD VERTICAL INTEGRATION

Stage 1 • Raw Materials

Stage 2 • Components • Intermediate Goods

Stage 3 • Final Assembly • Manufacturing

Stage 4 • Marketing • Sales

Stage 5 • After-Sales Service & Support

DOWNSTREAM INDUSTRIES

FORWARD VERTICAL INTEGRATION

- *Intermediate goods and components* such as integrated circuits, displays, touchscreens, cameras, and batteries are provided by firms such as ARM Holdings (UK), Jabil Circuit (U.S.), Intel (U.S.), LG Display (Korea), Altek (Taiwan), and BYD (China).

- *Original equipment manufacturing firms (OEMs)* such as Flextronics (Singapore) or Foxconn (China) typically assemble cell phones under contract for consumer electronics and telecommunications companies such as BlackBerry (Canada), Ericsson (Sweden), Motorola (U.S.), Nokia (Finland), Samsung (South Korea), and others. If you look closely at an iPhone, for example, you'll notice it says "Designed by Apple in California. Assembled in China."

- Finally, to get wireless data and voice service, you pick a *service provider* such as AT&T, Sprint, T-Mobile, or Verizon in the United States; América Móvil in Mexico; Oi in Brazil; Orange in France; T-Mobile or Vodafone in Germany; NTT Docomo in Japan; Airtel in India; or China Mobile in China, among others.

All of these companies—from the raw-materials suppliers to the service providers—comprise the global industry value chain that, as a whole, delivers you a working cell phone. Determined by their corporate strategy, each firm decides where in the industry value chain to participate. This in turn defines the vertical boundaries of the firm.

TYPES OF VERTICAL INTEGRATION

Along the industry value chain, there are varying degrees of vertical integration. Some firms participate in only one or a few stages of the industry value chain, while others comprise many if not all stages.

LO 8-3

Describe the two types of vertical integration along the industry value chain: backward and forward vertical integration.

Weyerhaeuser, one of the world's largest paper and pulp companies, is *fully vertically integrated:* all activities are conducted within the boundaries of the firm. Weyerhaeuser owns forests, grows and cuts its timber, mills it, manufactures a variety of different paper and construction products, and distributes them to retail outlets and other large customers. Weyerhaeuser's value added is 100 percent. Weyerhaeuser, therefore, competes in a number of different industries along the entire vertical value chain. As a consequence, it faces different competitors in each stage of the industry value chain.

On the other end of the spectrum are firms that are more or less *vertically disintegrated with a low degree of vertical integration.* These firms focus on only one or a few stages of the industry value chain. Apple, for example, focuses only on design, marketing, and retailing; all other value chain activities are outsourced.

Be aware that *not all industry value chain stages are equally profitable.* Apple captures significant value by designing mobile devices through integration of hardware and software in novel ways, but it outsources the manufacturing to generic OEMs. The logic behind these decisions can be explained by applying Porter's five forces model and the VRIO model. The many small cell phone OEMs are almost completely interchangeable and are exposed to the perils of perfect competition. However, Apple's competencies in innovation, system integration, and marketing are valuable, rare, and unique (non-imitable) resources, and Apple is organized to capture most of the value it creates. Apple's continued innovation through new products and services provides it with a string of temporary competitive advantages. Even so, competitors are not sitting idle.

To compete with Apple's iOS operating system powering its iPhones, and Google's Android dominance in mobile operating systems, Microsoft launched the Accord in 2012, a smartphone that uses Windows 8, Microsoft's latest operating system. Microsoft, at its heart a software company, chose to have HTC of Taiwan manufacture the product's hardware. Exhibit 8.5 displays part of the value chain for smartphones. In this figure, note

EXHIBIT 8.5 / HTC's Backward and Forward Integration along the Industry Value Chain in the Smartphone Industry

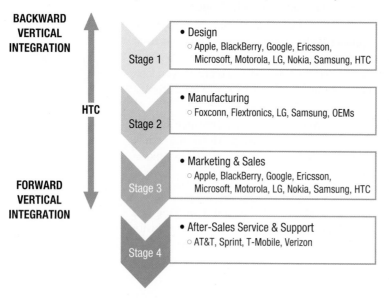

BACKWARD VERTICAL INTEGRATION

HTC

FORWARD VERTICAL INTEGRATION

Stage 1
- Design
  - Apple, BlackBerry, Google, Ericsson, Microsoft, Motorola, LG, Nokia, Samsung, HTC

Stage 2
- Manufacturing
  - Foxconn, Flextronics, LG, Samsung, OEMs

Stage 3
- Marketing & Sales
  - Apple, BlackBerry, Google, Ericsson, Microsoft, Motorola, LG, Nokia, Samsung, HTC

Stage 4
- After-Sales Service & Support
  - AT&T, Sprint, T-Mobile, Verizon

HTC's transformation from a no-name OEM manufacturer in stage 2 of the value chain, to a significant player in the design, manufacture, and sale of smartphones (stages 1 and 3). It now offers a lineup of innovative and high-performance smartphones under the HTC label.[24]

Over time, HTC was able to upgrade its capabilities from merely manufacturing smartphones to also designing products.[25] In doing so, HTC engaged in **backward vertical integration**—moving ownership of activities upstream to the originating inputs of the value chain. Moreover, by moving downstream into sales and increasing its branding activities, HTC has also engaged in **forward vertical integration**—moving ownership of activities closer to the end customer. Although HTC has long benefitted from *economies of scale* as an OEM, it is now also benefitting from *economies of scope* through participating in different stages of the industry value chain. For instance, it now is able to share competencies in product design, manufacturing, and sales, while at the same time attempting to reduce transaction costs.

BENEFITS AND RISKS OF VERTICAL INTEGRATION

LO 8-4

Identify and evaluate benefits and risks of vertical integration.

To decide the degree and type of vertical integration to pursue, managers need to understand the possible benefits and risks of vertical integration.

BENEFITS OF VERTICAL INTEGRATION. Vertical integration, either backward or forward, can have a number of benefits, including:[26]

backward vertical integration Changes in an industry value chain that involve moving ownership of activities upstream to the originating (inputs) point of the value chain.

forward vertical integration Changes in an industry value chain that involve moving ownership of activities closer to the end (customer) point of the value chain.

- Securing critical supplies and distribution channels
- Lowering costs
- Improving quality
- Facilitating scheduling and planning
- Facilitating investments in specialized assets

As noted earlier, HTC started as an OEM for brand-name mobile device companies such as Motorola and Nokia, or telecom service providers such as AT&T and T-Mobile. It backwardly integrated into smartphone design by acquiring One & Co., a San Francisco–based design firm.[27] The acquisition allowed HTC to secure scarce design talent and capabilities that it leveraged into the design of smartphones with superior quality and features built in, enhancing the differentiated appeal of its products. Moreover, HTC can now design phones that leverage its low-cost manufacturing capabilities.

Likewise, forward integration into distribution and sales allows companies to more effectively plan for and respond to changes in demand. HTC's forward integration into sales enables it to offer its products directly to wireless providers such as AT&T, Sprint, and Verizon. HTC even offers unlocked phones directly to the end consumer via its own website. With ownership and control of more stages of the industry value chain, HTC is now in a much better position to respond if, for example, demand for its latest phone should suddenly pick up.

PepsiCo's corporate strategy highlights several benefits to vertical integration. In 2009, PepsiCo forwardly integrated by buying its bottlers in order to obtain more control over its quality, pricing, distribution, and in-store display. This $8 billion purchase reversed a 1999 decision in which PepsiCo sold its bottlers in order to focus on marketing. CEO Indra Nooyi revised Pepsi's strategic intent to broaden its menu of offerings to include noncarbonated beverages such as flavored water enhanced with vitamins and fruit juices. With an integrated value chain, Ms. Nooyi hoped to improve decision making and enhance flexibility to bring these innovative products to market faster, while reducing costs by more than $400 million.[28]

Because of the strategic interdependence of companies in an oligopoly (as studied in Chapter 3), it came as no surprise that only a few months later, in early 2010, Pepsi's archrival Coca-Cola responded with its own forward integration move and purchased its bottlers for $12 billion. Coca-Cola also indicated that more control of manufacturing and distribution was the key driver behind this deal. Moreover, Coca-Cola pegged the expected cost savings at $350 million. Like PepsiCo, Coca-Cola's forward integration represented a major departure from its decade-old business model with large independent bottlers and distributors.[29]

Vertical integration allows firms to increase operational efficiencies through improved coordination and the fine-tuning of adjacent value chain activities. Keeping the downstream value chain activities independent worked well for PepsiCo and Coca-Cola during the 1980s and 1990s, when consumption of soda beverages was on the rise. However, independent bottlers are cost-effective only when doing large-volume business of a few, limited product offerings. With Pepsi's and Coke's more diversified portfolio of noncarbonated and healthier drinks, the costs of outsourcing bottling and distribution to independent bottlers increased significantly. Some of the independent bottlers even lacked the specialized equipment needed to produce the niche drinks now in demand. In addition, the independent bottlers' direct store-delivery system adds significant costs. To overcome this problem, the soft drink giants had begun to deliver some of their niche products such as Pepsi's Gatorade and SoBe Lifewater and Coke's Powerade and Glacéau directly to warehouse retailers such as Sam's Club and Costco. By owning the bottlers, both companies can deliver all products through one channel, thus lowering the overall cost of distribution.

Given the increase in costs of using independent bottlers (or the market), the forward integration of Pepsi and Coca-Cola is in line with predictions derived from transaction cost economics. Controlling the delivery part of the value chain also enhances the soft drink giants' bargaining power when negotiating product price, placement, and promotion. Looking at Porter's five forces model, Pepsi and Coke are reducing the bargaining power of buyers and thus shifting the industry structure in their favor. End consumers are likely to benefit from Coke's and Pepsi's forward integration in the form of a wider variety of niche drinks. Taken together, vertical integration can increase differentiation and reduce costs, thus strengthening a firm's strategic position as the gap between value creation and costs widens.

Vertical integration along the industry value chain can also facilitate *investments in specialized assets*. What does this mean? **Specialized assets** have a high opportunity cost: They have significantly more value in their intended use than in their next-best use.[30] They can come in several forms:[31]

- *Site specificity.* Assets are required to be co-located, such as the equipment necessary for mining bauxite and aluminum smelting.
- *Physical-asset specificity.* Assets whose physical and engineering properties are designed to satisfy a particular customer, such as bottling machinery for Coca-Cola and

specialized assets
Unique assets with high opportunity cost: They have significantly more value in their intended use than in their next-best use. They come in three types: site specificity, physical-asset specificity, and human-asset specificity.

PepsiCo. Since the bottles have different and often trademarked shapes, they require unique molds. Cans, in contrast, do not require physical-asset specificity because they are generic.

■ *Human-asset specificity.* Investments made in human capital to acquire unique knowledge and skills, such as mastering the routines and procedures of a specific organization, which are not transferable to a different employer.

Why do investments in specialized assets tend to incur high opportunity costs? Making the specialized investment opens up the threat of *opportunism* by one of the partners. Opportunism is defined as self-interest seeking with guile.[32] Backward vertical integration is often undertaken to overcome the threat of opportunism and in securing key raw materials.

In an effort to secure supplies and reduce the costs of jet fuel, Delta was the first airline to acquire an oil refinery. In 2012, it purchased a Pennsylvania-based facility from ConocoPhillips. Delta estimates that this backward vertical integration move not only will allow it to provide 80 percent of its fuel internally, but will also save it some $300 million in costs annually. Fuel costs are quite significant for airlines; for Delta, they are almost 40 percent of its total operating cost.[33]

RISKS OF VERTICAL INTEGRATION. Depending on the situation, vertical integration has several risks, including:[34]

■ Increasing costs
■ Reducing quality
■ Reducing flexibility
■ Increasing the potential for legal repercussions

A higher degree of vertical integration can lead to increasing costs for a number of reasons. In-house suppliers tend to have higher cost structures because they are not exposed to market competition. Knowing there will always be a buyer for their products reduces their incentives to lower costs. In contrast, suppliers in the open market, because they serve a much larger market, can achieve economies of scale that elude in-house suppliers. Organizational complexity increases with higher levels of vertical integration, thereby increasing administrative costs such as determining the appropriate transfer prices between an in-house supplier and buyer. Administrative costs are part of internal transaction costs and arise from the coordination of multiple divisions, political maneuvering for resources, the consumption of company perks, or simply from employees slacking off.

The knowledge that there will always be a buyer for their products not only reduces the incentives of in-house suppliers to lower costs, but also can reduce the incentive to increase quality or come up with innovative new products. Moreover, given their larger scale and greater exposure to more customers, external suppliers often can reap higher learning and experience effects and so develop unique capabilities or quality improvements.

A higher degree of vertical integration can also reduce a firm's strategic flexibility, especially when faced with changes in the external environment like fluctuations in demand and technological change.[35] For instance, when technological process innovations enabled significant improvements in steel-making, mills such as U.S. Steel and Bethlehem Steel were tied to their fully integrated business models and were thus unable to switch technologies, leading to the bankruptcy of many integrated steel mills. Non-vertically integrated mini-mills such as Nucor and Chaparral, on the other hand, invested in the new steel-making process and grew their business by taking market share away from the less flexible integrated producers.[36]

U.S. regulators such as the Federal Trade Commission (FTC) and the Justice Department (DOJ) tend to allow vertical integration, arguing that it generally makes firms more efficient and lowers costs, which in turn can benefit customers. However, due to monopoly concerns, vertical integration has not gone entirely unchallenged.[37] The FTC, for example, carefully reviewed PepsiCo's plan to reintegrate its two largest bottlers, which gives the firm full control of about 80 percent of its North American distribution. Before engaging in vertical integration, therefore, managers need to be aware that this corporate strategy can increase the potential for legal repercussions.

ALTERNATIVES TO VERTICAL INTEGRATION

Ideally, one would like to find alternatives to vertical integration that provide similar benefits without the accompanying risks. Are there such alternatives?

TAPER INTEGRATION. One alternative to vertical integration is **taper integration**. It is a way of orchestrating value activities in which a firm is backwardly integrated, but it also relies on outside-market firms for some of its supplies, and/or is forwardly integrated but also relies on outside-market firms for some if its distribution.[38] Exhibit 8.6 illustrates the concept of taper integration along the vertical industry value chain. Here, the firm sources intermediate goods and components from in-house suppliers as well as outside suppliers. In a similar fashion, a firm sells its products through company-owned retail outlets and through independent retailers. Both Apple and Nike, for example, use taper integration: They own retail outlets but also use other retailers, both the brick-and-mortar type and online.

Taper integration has several benefits:[39]

- It exposes in-house suppliers and distributors to market competition so that performance comparisons are possible. Rather than hollowing out its competencies by relying too much on outsourcing, taper integration allows a firm to retain and fine-tune its competencies in upstream and downstream value chain activities.[40]

- Taper integration also enhances a firm's flexibility. For example, when adjusting to fluctuations in demand, a firm could cut back on the finished goods it delivers to external retailers while continuing to stock its own stores.

- Using taper integration, firms can combine internal and external knowledge, possibly paving the path for innovation.

Based on a study of 3,500 product introductions in the computer industry, researchers have provided empirical evidence that taper integration can be beneficial.[41] Firms that pursued taper integration achieved superior performance in both innovation and financial performance when compared with firms that relied more on vertical integration or strategic outsourcing.

STRATEGIC OUTSOURCING. Another alternative to vertical integration is **strategic outsourcing**, which involves moving one or more internal value chain activities outside the firm's boundaries to other firms in the industry value chain. A firm that engages in strategic outsourcing reduces its level of vertical integration. Rather than developing their own human resource

LO 8-5

Describe and examine alternatives to vertical integration.

taper integration
A way of orchestrating value activities in which a firm is backwardly integrated but also relies on outside-market firms for some of its supplies, and/or is forwardly integrated but also relies on outside-market firms for some of its distribution.

strategic outsourcing
Moving one or more internal value chain activities outside the firm's boundaries to other firms in the industry value chain.

EXHIBIT 8.6 / Taper Integration along the Industry Value Chain

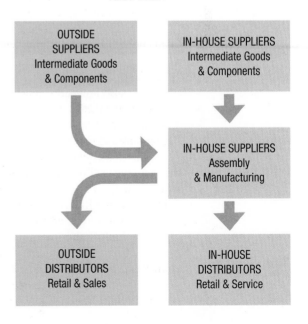

management systems, for instance, some firms outsource these non-core activities to companies such as PeopleSoft (owned by Oracle), EDS (owned by HP), or Perot Systems (owned by Dell), which can leverage their deep competencies and produce scale effects.

In the popular media and in everyday conversation, you may hear the term "outsourcing" used to mean sending jobs out of the country. Actually, when outsourced activities take place outside the home country, the correct term is *off-shoring* (or *off-shore outsourcing*). By whatever name, it is a *huge* phenomenon. For example, Infosys, one of the world's largest technology companies and providers of IT services to many Fortune 100 companies, is located in Bangalore, India. The global off-shoring market is estimated to be $1.4 trillion, and is expected to grow at a compound annual growth rate of 15 percent. Banking and financial services, IT, and health care are the most active sectors in such off-shore outsourcing.[42] More recently, U.S. law firms began to off-shore low-end legal work, such as drafting standard contracts and background research, to India.[43] We discuss *global strategy* in detail in Chapter 10.

8.4 Corporate Diversification: Expanding Beyond a Single Market

Early in the chapter, we listed three questions related to corporate strategy and, in particular, the boundaries of the firm. We discussed the first question defining corporate strategy (*In what stages of the industry value chain should the firm participate?*) in detail earlier when discussing vertical integration. We now turn to the second and third questions that determine corporate strategy and the boundaries of the firm.

The second of those questions relates to the firm's *degree of diversification:* What range of products and services should the firm offer? In particular, why do some companies compete in a single product market, while others compete in several different product markets? Coca-Cola, for example, focuses on soft drinks and thus on a *single* product market. Its archrival PepsiCo competes directly with Coca-Cola by selling a wide variety of soft drinks and other beverages, and also offering different types of chips such as Lay's, Doritos, and Cheetos, as well as Quaker Oats products such as oatmeal and granola bars. Although PepsiCo is more diversified than Coca-Cola, it has reduced its level of diversification in recent years.

The third and final of the key questions defining corporate strategy concerns the question of *where to compete* in terms of regional, national, or international markets. This decision determines the firm's geographic focus. For example, why do some firms compete beyond state boundaries, while others are content to focus on the local market? Why do some firms compete beyond their national borders, while others prefer to focus on the domestic market?

Kentucky Fried Chicken (KFC), the world's largest quick-service chicken restaurant chain, operates more than 5,200 outlets in the U.S., and more than 15,000 outlets internationally in 109 countries.[44] It is particularly popular in China, where it has over 4,000 restaurants and about the same revenues as in the U.S. We noted in ChapterCase 2 that Indra Nooyi, PepsiCo's CEO, was instrumental in spinning out KFC, as well as Pizza Hut and Taco Bell, to reduce PepsiCo's level of diversification. In 1997, the three fast-food chains were established as an independent company under the name Yum Brands. In 2012, Yum Brands had annual revenues of $13 billion. The world's second-largest quick-service chicken restaurant is Chick-fil-A.[45] KFC and Chick-fil-A are direct competitors in the United States. Not only do they both compete in the fast-food industry; they also both specialize in chicken. In 2012, Chick-fil-A operated over 1,700 locations in 39 U.S. states with sales of $4.6 billion.

Why are KFC and Chick-fil-A pursuing different corporate strategies? Although both companies were founded roughly in the same time period (KFC in 1930 and Chick-fil-A in 1946), one big difference between KFC and Chick-fil-A is the ownership structure. KFC is a publicly traded stock company, as part of Yum Brands; Chick-fil-A is privately owned. Public companies are often expected by shareholders to achieve profitable growth as fast as possible to result in an appreciation of the stock price and thus an increase in shareholder value (see the discussion in Chapter 5). In contrast, private companies generally grow slower than public companies because their growth is mostly financed through retained earnings and debt rather than equity. Prior to an initial public offering, private companies do not have the option to sell shares (equity) to the public to fuel growth. This is one explanation why KFC focuses on international markets, especially China, where future expected growth continues to be high, while Chick-fil-A focuses on the domestic U.S. market.

Answers to questions about the number of markets to compete in and where to compete geographically relate to the broad topic of **diversification**. A firm that engages in diversification increases the variety of products and services it offers or markets and the geographic regions in which it competes. A *non-diversified company* focuses on a single market, whereas a *diversified company* competes in several different markets simultaneously.[46]

There are various general diversification strategies:

- A firm that is active in several different product markets is pursuing a **product diversification strategy**.

- A firm that is active in several different countries is pursuing a **geographic diversification strategy**.

- A company that pursues *both* a product *and* a geographic diversification strategy simultaneously follows a **product–market diversification strategy**.

Because shareholders expect continuous growth from public companies, managers frequently turn to product and geographic diversification to achieve it. It is therefore not surprising that the vast majority of the Fortune 500 companies are diversified to some degree. Achieving performance gains through diversification, however, is not guaranteed. Some forms of diversification are more likely to lead to performance improvements than others. We now discuss which diversification types are more likely to lead to a competitive advantage, and why.

TYPES OF CORPORATE DIVERSIFICATION

To understand the different types and degrees of corporate diversification, Richard Rumelt developed a helpful classification scheme, depicted in Exhibit 8.7:

LO 8-6

Describe and evaluate different types of corporate diversification.

- A *single-business firm* derives 95 percent or more of its revenues from one business. Although Google is active in many different businesses, it obtains more than 95 percent of its revenues ($50 billion in 2012) from online advertising.[47]

---

diversification An increase in the variety of products and services a firm offers or markets and the geographic regions in which it competes.

product diversification strategy Corporate strategy in which a firm is active in several different product markets.

geographic diversification strategy Corporate strategy in which a firm is active in several different countries.

product–market diversification strategy Corporate strategy in which a firm is active in several different product markets *and* several different countries.

EXHIBIT 8.7 / Different Types of Diversification

Type of Diversification	Revenues from Primary Activity	Sample Firms	Graphic Representation
Single Business	>95%	Coca-Cola Google Facebook	A
Dominant Business	70–95% *Dominant business shares competencies in products, services, technology, or distribution*	Harley-Davidson Nestlé UPS	A — B
Related Diversification			
1. *Related-constrained*	<70% *All businesses share competencies in products, services, technology, or distribution*	ExxonMobil Johnson & Johnson Nike	A, B, C (all connected)
2. *Related-linked*	<70% *Only some businesses share competencies in products, services, technology, or distribution*	Amazon Disney GE	A, B, C (A–B, B–C)
Unrelated Diversification	<70% *No competency linkages in products, services, technology, or distribution between businesses*	Berkshire Hathaway Yamaha Tata Group	A B C

SOURCE: Adapted from R. P. Rumelt (1974), *Strategy, Structure, and Economic Performance* (Boston, MA: Harvard Business School Press).

■ A *dominant-business firm* derives between 70 and 95 percent of its revenues from a single business, but it pursues at least one other business activity. The dominant business shares competencies in products, services, technology, or distribution. Although Harley-Davidson is primarily a motorcycle manufacturer, it derives some 10 percent of its annual revenues from Harley-Davidson branded motorcycle clothing and attire, as well as from licensing its brand.[48]

A firm follows a **related diversification strategy** when it derives less than 70 percent of its revenues from a single business activity and obtains revenues from other lines of business linked to the primary business activity (see Exhibit 8.7). The rationale behind related diversification is to benefit from economies of scale and scope: These multibusiness firms can pool and share resources as well as leverage competencies across different business lines.

ExxonMobil's strategic move into natural gas is an example of related diversification. In 2009, ExxonMobil bought XTO Energy, a natural gas company, for $31 billion.[49] XTO Energy is known for its core competency to extract natural gas from unconventional places such as shale rock—the type of deposits currently being exploited in the United States. ExxonMobil hopes to leverage its core competency in the exploration and commercialization of oil into natural gas extraction. The company is producing nearly equal amounts of crude oil and natural gas, making it the world's largest producer of natural gas. The company believes that roughly 50 percent of the world's energy for the next 50 years will continue to come from fossil fuels, but that its diversification into natural gas, the cleanest of the fossil fuels in terms of greenhouse gas emissions, will pay off. ExxonMobil's strategic scenario may be right on the mark. Because of major technological advances in hydraulic fracking to extract oil and natural gas from shale rock by companies such as XTO Energy, the United States has emerged as the world's richest country in natural gas resources and the third-largest producer of crude oil, just behind Saudi Arabia and Russia.[50]

We can further identify two types of related diversification strategy: related-constrained and related-linked (see Exhibit 8.7). When executives consider business opportunities only where they can leverage their existing competencies and resources, the firm is using *related-constrained diversification.* The choices of alternative business activities are limited—constrained—by the fact that they need to be related through common resources, capabilities, and competencies. ExxonMobil's diversification move into natural gas is an example of related-constrained diversification.

If executives consider new business activities that share only a limited number of linkages, the firm is using *related-linked diversification.* For example, Amazon began business by selling only one product: books. Over time, it expanded into CDs and later gradually leveraged its online retailing capabilities into a wide array of product offerings. As the world's largest online retailer, and given the need to build huge data centers to service its peak holiday demand, Amazon decided to leverage spare capacity into cloud computing, again benefitting from economies of scope and scale. Amazon now also offers its Kindle line of tablet computers and proprietary content, as well as instant video streaming via its Prime service. Amazon follows a related-linked diversification strategy.

A firm follows an **unrelated diversification strategy** when less than 70 percent of its revenues comes from a single business and there are few, if any, linkages among its businesses (see Exhibit 8.7). A company that combines two or more strategic business units under one overarching corporation and follows an unrelated diversification strategy is called a **conglomerate.** Some research evidence suggests that an unrelated diversification strategy can be advantageous.[51] This arrangement helps firms gain and sustain competitive advantage because it allows the conglomerate to overcome institutional weaknesses in emerging economies, such as a lack of capital markets and well-defined legal systems and property rights. Companies such as Berkshire Hathaway, the South Korean LG chaebol, and the Yamaha group are all considered conglomerates due to their unrelated diversification strategy. Strategy Highlight 8.2 features the Tata Group of India, a conglomerate that follows an unrelated diversification strategy.

---

related diversification strategy Corporate strategy in which a firm derives less than 70 percent of its revenues from a single business activity and obtains revenues from other lines of business that are linked to the primary business activity.

unrelated diversification strategy Corporate strategy in which a firm derives less than 70 percent of its revenues from a single business activity and there are few, if any, linkages among its businesses.

conglomerate A company that combines two or more strategic business units under one overarching corporation; follows an unrelated diversification strategy.

Strategy Highlight 8.2

The Tata Group: Integration at the Corporate Level

Founded in 1868 as a trading company by then 29-year-old entrepreneur Jamsetji Nusserwanji Tata, the Tata Group today has roughly 500,000 employees and $100 billion in annual revenues. A widely diversified multinational conglomerate, headquartered in Mumbai, India, it is active in industries ranging from tea, to hospitality, steel, IT, communications, power, and automobiles. Some of its strategic business units are giants in their own right. The Tata Group includes Asia's largest software company (TCS) and India's largest steelmaker. It also owns the renowned Taj Hotels Resorts & Palaces.

In 2008, Tata Motors attracted attention in the automotive world when it bought Jaguar and Land Rover from Ford for $2.3 billion. In 2009, the Indian Tata Motors attracted even more attention when it unveiled its Tata Nano car. The Nano is the lowest-priced car in the world. It accommodates passengers just over six feet tall, goes from zero to 60 mph in 30 seconds, and gets 67 mpg, beating the Toyota Prius for fuel consumption. The Tata Nano, clearly a no-frills car, exemplifies a focused low-cost strategy. The rear hatch can't be opened, it doesn't have a radio or glove compartment, and its top speed is a little over 60 mph. Nonetheless, being about 50 percent cheaper than the

next-lowest-cost car, Tata Motors hopes to find tens of millions of customers in the Indian and Chinese markets. Initial sales were disappointing, however. Apparently low cost alone was not sufficient to lure new buyers into the market. The first Nano models might have provided too little along the value dimension. Tata Motors is now attempting to revive Nano sales by adding features to newer models such side-view mirrors, a music system with Bluetooth connectivity, chrome trim, and wheel covers.

The Tata Group is attempting to carve out different strategic positions in its different segments of the automotive industry. Moreover, the Tata Group hopes to integrate distinctly different business strategies at the corporate level. In particular, the luxury division of Tata Motors, with the Jaguar and Land Rover brands, is pursuing a focused differentiation strategy; the Nano car division is pursuing a focused cost-leadership strategy. Although their respective strategic profiles are basically the opposite of one another (differentiation versus low-cost), both business-level strategies are aimed at a specific segment of the market. Jaguar and Land Rover are luxury brands in their respective categories and appeal to buyers in the developed world; the Nano is clearly a low(est)-cost offering, focused on a very specific market niche. Indeed, the Nano focuses on *non-consumption:* Buyers of the Nano will not be replacing other vehicles. They will be first-time car buyers moving up from bicycles and mopeds. By offering the Nano, Tata Motors is still hoping to bring millions of new car buyers from emerging countries into the market and thus increase the size of the automobile market. Taken together, Tata's corporate strategy is attempting to integrate different strategic positions, pursued by different strategic business units, each with its own profit and loss responsibility.[52]

LEVERAGING CORE COMPETENCIES FOR CORPORATE DIVERSIFICATION

LO 8-7

Apply the core competence–market matrix to derive different diversification strategies.

In Chapter 4, when looking inside the firm, we introduced the idea that competitive advantage can be based on core competencies. Core competencies are unique strengths embedded deep within a firm. They allow companies to increase the perceived value of their product and service offerings and/or lower the cost to produce them.[53] Examples of core competencies are:

- Walmart's ability to effectively orchestrate a globally distributed supply chain at low cost.
- Infosys's ability to provide high-quality information technology services at a low cost by leveraging its global delivery model. This implies taking work to the location where

it makes the best economic sense, based on the available talent and the least amount of acceptable risk and lowest cost.

To survive and prosper, companies need to grow. This mantra holds especially true for publicly owned companies, because they create shareholder value through profitable growth. Managers respond to this relentless growth imperative by leveraging their existing core competencies to find future growth opportunities. Gary Hamel and C. K. Prahalad advanced the **core competence–market matrix**, depicted in Exhibit 8.8, as a way to guide managerial decisions in regard to diversification strategies. The first task for managers is to identify their existing core competencies and understand the firm's current market situation. When applying an existing or new dimension to core competencies and markets, four quadrants emerge, each with distinct strategic implications.

The lower-left quadrant combines existing core competencies with existing markets. Here, managers must come up with ideas of how to leverage existing core competencies to improve the firm's current market position. Bank of America is one of the largest banks in the United States and has at least one customer in 50 percent of U.S. households.[54] Some 20 years ago, Bank of America had been North Carolina National Bank (NCNB), a regional bank in North Carolina. One of NCNB's unique core competencies was identifying, appraising, and integrating acquisition targets. In particular, it bought smaller banks to supplement its organic growth throughout the 1970s and 80s, and from 1989 to 1992, NCNB purchased over 200 regional community and thrift banks, to further improve its market position. It then turned its core competency to national banks, with the goal of becoming the first nationwide bank. Known as NationsBank in the 1990s, it purchased Barnett Bank, BankSouth, FleetBank, LaSalle, CountryWide Mortgages, and its namesake Bank of America. This example illustrates how NationsBank, rebranded as Bank of America since 1998, honed and deployed its core competency of selecting, acquiring, and integrating other commercial banks and dramatically grew in size and geographic scope to emerge as one of the leading banks in the United States. As a key vehicle of corporate strategy, we study acquisitions in more detail in Chapter 9.

The lower-right quadrant of Exhibit 8.8 combines existing core competencies with new market opportunities. Here, managers must strategize about how to redeploy and recombine existing core competencies to compete in future markets. At the height of the financial crisis in the fall of 2008, Bank of America bought the investment bank Merrill Lynch for

core competence–market matrix
A framework to guide corporate diversification strategy by analyzing possible combinations of existing/new core competencies and existing/new markets.

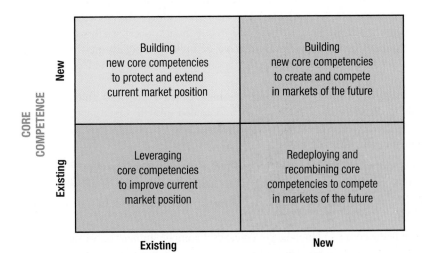

EXHIBIT 8.8

The Core Competence–Market Matrix

SOURCE: Adapted from G. Hamel and C. K. Prahalad (1994), *Competing for the Future* (Boston, MA: Harvard Business School Press).

$50 billion.[55] Although many problems ensued for Bank of America following the Merrill Lynch acquisition, it is now the bank's investment and wealth management division. Bank of America's corporate managers applied an existing competency (acquiring and integrating) into a new market (investment and wealth management). The combined entity is now leveraging economies of scope through cross-selling when, for example, consumer banking makes customer referrals for investment bankers to follow up.[56]

The upper-left quadrant combines new core competencies with existing market opportunities. Here, managers must come up with strategic initiatives to build new core competencies to protect and extend the company's current market position. For example, in the early 1990s, Gatorade dominated the market for sports drinks, a segment in which it had been the original innovator. Some 25 years earlier, medical researchers at the University of Florida had created the drink to enhance the performance of the Gators, the university's football team, thus the name Gatorade. Stokely-Van Camp commercialized and marketed the drink, and eventually sold it to Quaker Oats. PepsiCo brought Gatorade into its lineup of soft drinks when it acquired Quaker Oats in 2001.

By comparison, Coca-Cola had existing core competencies in marketing, bottling, and distributing soft drinks, but had never attempted to compete in the sports-drink market. Over a 10-year R&D effort, Coca-Cola developed competencies in the development and marketing of its own sports drink, Powerade, which launched in 1990. In 2012, Powerade held about 25 percent of the sports drink-market, making it a viable competitor to Gatorade, which still holds about 70 percent of the market.[57]

Finally, the upper-right quadrant combines new core competencies with new market opportunities. Hamel and Prahalad call this combination "mega opportunities"—those that hold significant future-growth opportunities. At the same time, it is likely the most challenging diversification strategy because it requires building new core competencies to create and compete in future markets.

Salesforce.com, for example, is a company that employs this diversification strategy well.[58] In recent years, Salesforce experienced tremendous growth, the bulk of it coming from the firm's existing core competency in delivering customer relationship management (CRM) software to its clients. Salesforce's product distinguished itself from the competition by providing software as a service via cloud computing: Clients did not need to install software or manage any servers, but could easily access the CRM through a web browser (a business model called *software as a service,* or *SaaS*). In 2007, Salesforce recognized an emerging market for *platform as a service (PaaS)* offerings, which would enable clients to build their own software solutions that are accessed the same way as the Salesforce CRM. Seizing the opportunity, Salesforce developed a new competency in delivering software development and deployment tools that allowed its customers to either extend their existing CRM offering or build completely new types of software. Today, Salesforce's Force.com offering is one of the leading providers of PaaS tools and services.

Taken together, the core competence–market matrix provides guidance to executives on how to diversify in order to achieve continued growth. Once managers have a clear understanding of their firm's core competencies (see Chapter 4), they have four options to formulate corporate strategy:

1. Leverage existing core competencies to improve current market position.
2. Build new core competencies to protect and extend current market position.
3. Redeploy and recombine existing core competencies to compete in markets of the future.
4. Build new core competencies to create and compete in markets of the future.

CORPORATE DIVERSIFICATION AND FIRM PERFORMANCE

Corporate managers pursue diversification to gain and sustain competitive advantage. But does corporate diversification indeed lead to superior performance? To answer this question, we can evaluate the performance of diversified companies. The critical question to ask when doing so is whether the individual businesses are worth more under the company's management than if each were managed individually.

The diversification-performance relationship is a function of the underlying type of diversification. A cumulative body of research indicates an inverted U-shaped relationship between the type of diversification and overall firm performance, as depicted in Exhibit 8.9.[59] High and low levels of diversification are generally associated with lower overall performance, while moderate levels of diversification are associated with higher firm performance. This implies that companies that focus on a single business, as well as companies that pursue unrelated diversification, often fail to achieve additional value creation. Firms that compete in single markets could potentially benefit from economies of scope by leveraging their core competencies into adjacent markets.

Firms that pursue unrelated diversification are often unable to create additional value. They experience a **diversification discount** in the stock market: The stock price of such highly diversified firms is valued at less than the sum of their individual business units.[60] This finding, however, depends on the institutional context. Although it holds in developed economies with developed capital markets, some research evidence suggests that an unrelated diversification strategy can be advantageous in emerging economies (as mentioned when discussing the Tata Group).[61] Here, unrelated diversification may help firms gain and sustain competitive advantage because it allows the conglomerate to overcome institutional weaknesses in emerging economies such as a lack of a functioning capital market.

In contrast, companies that pursue related diversification are more likely to improve their performance. They create a **diversification premium**: the stock price of related-diversification firms is valued at greater than the sum of their individual business units.[62]

Why is this so? At the most basic level, a corporate diversification strategy enhances firm performance when its value creation is greater than the costs it incurs. Exhibit 8.10 lists the sources of value creation and costs for different corporate strategies, for vertical integration as well as related and unrelated diversification. For diversification to enhance firm performance, it must do at least one of the following:

- Provide *economies of scale,* which reduces costs.
- Exploit *economies of scope,* which increases value.
- Reduce costs *and* increase value.

We discussed these drivers of competitive advantage—economies of scale, economies of scope, and

LO 8-8

Explain when a diversification strategy creates a competitive advantage and when it does not.

diversification discount Situation in which the stock price of highly diversified firms is valued at less than the sum of their individual business units.

diversification premium Situation in which the stock price of related-diversification firms is valued at greater than the sum of their individual business units.

EXHIBIT 8.9 / The Diversification-Performance Relationship

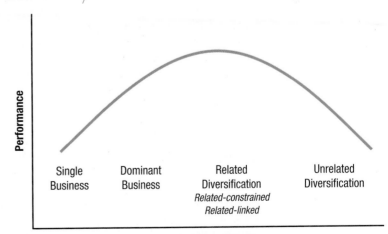

SOURCE: Adapted from L. E. Palich, L. B. Cardinal, and C. C. Miller (2000), "Curvilinearity in the diversification-performance linkage: An examination of over three decades of research," *Strategic Management Journal* 21: 155–174.

EXHIBIT 8.10 / Vertical Integration and Diversification: Sources of Value Creation and Costs

Corporate Strategy	Sources of Value Creation (*V*)	Sources of Costs (*C*)
Vertical Integration	• Securing critical supplies and distribution channels • Lowering costs • Improving quality • Facilitating scheduling and planning • Facilitating investments in specialized assets	• Increasing costs • Reducing quality • Reducing flexibility • Increasing potential for legal repercussions

Related Diversification	• Economies of scope
	• Economies of scale
	• Financial economies
	  ▪ Restructuring
	  ▪ Internal capital markets
		• Coordination costs
		• Influence costs

Unrelated Diversification	• Financial economies
	  ▪ Restructuring
	  ▪ Internal capital markets
		• Influence costs

increase in value and reduction of costs—in depth in Chapter 6 in relation to business strategy. In addition to these criteria, firms may enhance their performance when following a diversification strategy by benefitting from:

■ *Financial economies,* including:

   ◆ Restructuring

   ◆ Using internal capital markets

RESTRUCTURING. *Restructuring* describes the process of reorganizing and divesting business units and activities to refocus a company in order to leverage its core competencies more fully. ChapterCase 8 highlighted the restructuring that has taken place at GE to leverage its core competency in management processes and industrial engineering. The Belgium-based Anheuser-Busch InBev recently sold Busch Entertainment, its theme park unit that owns SeaWorld and Busch Gardens, to a group of private investors for roughly $3 billion. This strategic move allows InBev to focus more fully on its core business and to pay for its 2008 acquisition of Anheuser-Busch, which cost $52 billion.[63]

Corporate executives can restructure the portfolio of their firm's businesses, much like an investor can change a portfolio of stocks. One helpful tool to guide corporate portfolio planning is the **Boston Consulting Group (BCG) growth-share matrix**, shown in Exhibit 8.11.[64] This matrix locates the firm's individual SBUs in two dimensions: relative market share (horizontal axis) and speed of market growth (vertical axis). The firm plots its SBUs into one of four categories in the matrix: dog, cash cow, star, and question mark. Each category warrants a different investment strategy. All four categories shape the firm's corporate strategy.

SBUs identified as *dogs* are relatively easy to identify: They are the underperforming businesses. Dogs hold a small market share in a low-growth market; they have low and unstable earnings, combined with neutral or negative cash flows. The strategic

Boston Consulting Group (BCG) growth-share matrix A corporate planning tool in which the corporation is viewed as a portfolio of business units, which are represented graphically along relative market share (horizontal axis) and speed of market growth (vertical axis). SBUs are plotted into four categories (dog, cash cow, star, and question mark), each of which warrants a different investment strategy.

EXHIBIT 8.11

Restructuring the Corporate Portfolio: The Boston Consulting Group Growth-Share Matrix

recommendations are either to divest the business or to *harvest* it. This implies stopping investment in the business and squeezing out as much cash flow as possible before shutting it down or selling it.

Cash cows, in contrast, are SBUs that compete in a low-growth market but hold considerable market share. Their earnings and cash flows are high and stable. The strategic recommendation is to invest enough into cash cows to hold their current position, and to avoid having them turn into dogs (as indicated by the arrow).

A corporation's *star* SBUs hold a high market share in a fast-growing market. Their earnings are high and either stable or growing. The recommendation for the corporate strategist is to invest sufficient resources to hold the star's position or even increase investments for future growth. As indicated by the arrow, stars may turn into cash cows as the market in which the SBU is situated slows down due to reaching the maturity stage of the industry life cycle.

Finally, some SBUs are *question marks:* It is not clear whether they will turn into dogs or stars. Their earnings are low and unstable, but they might be growing. The cash flow, however, is negative. Ideally, corporate executives want to invest in question marks to increase their relative market share so they turn into stars. If market conditions change, however, or the overall market growth slows down, then a question-mark SBU is likely to turn into a dog. In this case, executives would want to harvest the cash flow or divest the SBU.

USING INTERNAL CAPITAL MARKETS. *Internal capital markets* can be a source of value creation in a diversification strategy if the conglomerate's headquarters does a more efficient job of allocating capital through its budgeting process than what could be achieved in external capital markets. Based on private information, corporate managers are in a position to discover which of their strategic business units will provide the highest return on invested capital. In addition, internal capital markets may allow the company to access capital at a lower cost.

Until recently, for example, GE Capital brought in close to $70 billion in annual revenues, and generated more than half of GE's profits.[65] In combination with GE's triple-A debt rating, having access to such a large finance arm allowed GE to benefit from a lower cost of capital, which in turn was a source of value creation in itself. In 2009, GE lost its AAA debt rating and is now in the process of downsizing its finance unit. The lower debt rating and the smaller finance unit are likely to result in a higher cost of capital, and thus a potential loss in value creation through internal capital markets.

A strategy of related-constrained or related-linked diversification is more likely to enhance corporate performance than either a single or dominant level of diversification or an unrelated level of diversification. The reason is that the sources of value creation include not only restructuring, but more fundamentally, the potential benefits of economies of scope and scale. To create additional value, however, the benefits from these sources of incremental value creation must outweigh their costs. A related-diversification strategy entails two additional types of costs: coordination and influence costs. *Coordination costs* are a function of the number, size, and types of businesses that are linked to one another. *Influence costs* occur due to political maneuvering by managers to influence capital and resource allocation and the resulting inefficiencies stemming from suboptimal allocation of scarce resources.[66]

8.5 ◀▶ Implications for the Strategist

An effective corporate strategy increases a firm's chances to gain and sustain a competitive advantage. By formulating corporate strategy, executives make important choices along three dimensions that determine the boundaries of the firm:

- The degree of vertical integration—in what stages of the industry value chain to participate.
- The type of diversification—what range of products and services to offer.
- The geographic scope—where to compete.

As an executive, you will have the opportunity to proactively shape the company's corporate strategy in order to take advantage of external opportunities and mitigate threats.

As discussed in ChapterCase 8, Jeffrey Immelt formulated a new corporate strategy to take advantage of future business opportunities in clean-tech and health care, while reducing the exposure to global financial markets.

Corporate strategy needs to be dynamic over time. As firms grow, they tend to diversify and globalize to capture additional growth opportunities. Exhibit 8.12 shows the dynamic nature of corporate strategy through decisions made by two top competitors in the sports footwear and apparel industry: Nike and adidas.

Adidas was founded in 1924 in Germany. It began its life in the laundry room of a small apartment. Two brothers focused on one product: athletic shoes. Initially, adidas was a fairly integrated manufacturer of athletic shoes. The big breakthrough for the company came in 1954 when the underdog West Germany

EXHIBIT 8.12 / Dynamic Corporate Strategy: Nike versus adidas

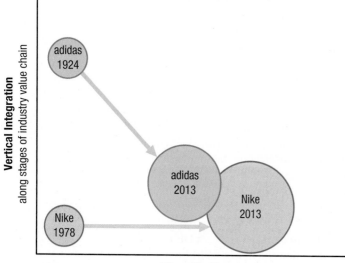

won the soccer World Cup in adidas cleats. As the world markets globalized and became more competitive in the decades after World War II, adidas not only vertically disintegrated to focus mainly on the design of athletic shoes but also diversified into sports apparel. By 2013, adidas was a diversified company active across the globe in sports shoes (40 percent of revenues), sports apparel (50 percent of revenues), and sports equipment (10 percent of revenues). The change in adidas' corporate strategy from a small, highly integrated single business to a disintegrated and diversified global company is shown in Exhibit 8.12.

Nike, the world's leader in sports shoes and apparel, was featured in ChapterCase 4. Founded in 1978, and thus much younger than adidas, Nike was vertically disintegrated from the very beginning. After moving beyond importing Japanese shoes to the U.S., Nike focused almost exclusively on R&D, design, and marketing of running shoes. Although Nike diversified into different lines of business, it stayed true to its vertical disintegration by focusing on only a few activities (see Exhibit 8.12). In 2013, Nike was a global company and its revenues came from sports shoes (50 percent) and apparel (25 percent), as well as sports equipment and other businesses, such as affiliate brands Cole Haan, Converse, Hurley, and Umbro. The changes in the strategic positions shown in Exhibit 8.12 highlight the dynamic nature of corporate strategy. Also, keep in mind that the relationship between diversification strategy and competitive advantage depends on the *type of diversification*. There exists an inverted U-shaped relationship between the level of diversification and performance improvements. On average, related diversification (either related-constrained or related-linked such as in the Nike and adidas example) is most likely to lead to superior performance because it taps into multiple sources of value creation (economies of scale and scope; financial economies). To achieve a net positive effect on firm performance, however, related diversification must overcome additional sources of costs such as coordination and influence costs.

CHAPTER**CASE 8** / Consider This . . .

AS DISCUSSED IN the ChapterCase, General Electric has been refocusing its businesses through aggressive corporate divestitures and restructuring. It divested NBC Universal, chemicals, and insurance. It also restructured GE Capital.

GE's focus on clean-tech seems to be bearing some fruit, with the industrial sector experiencing double-digit earnings growth in the last few years. The GE Energy division grew to almost $50 billion in annual revenues, partly through acquisitions, making up roughly one-third of GE's total revenues. Because GE management believes the energy business has become too big to be managed effectively, it continued its corporate restructuring and split the energy business into three standalone strategic business units in 2012: Power and Water; Oil and Gas; and Energy Management. This move comes in response

to external trends as well as internal needs.

Externally, it is GE's response to the shale gas revolution that is reshaping America's energy industry. For example, lower gas prices drive up demand for GE's gas turbines as more and more power providers retire coal-fired plants and replace them with gas-fired power plants. Internally, this restructuring was motivated to create three more CEO positions for the new SBUs for training a potential successor for Jeffrey Immelt. After running GE for more than a decade, Mr. Immelt needs to begin grooming a number of potential successors since the company tends to recruit its CEOs internally.

GE has also been increasing its global footprint. International sales have soared from 19 percent of sales in 1980, to 34 percent in 2000, to over 52 percent in 2012. Immelt believes that tackling big problems on a global scale is a strength of conglomerates such as GE. An example of a large-scale problem is the fact that according to the United Nations, nearly one-fourth of the world's population lives without access to reliable power. In India, one of the fastest-growing economies in the world, the electrical coverage rate is about 65 percent. India has set a goal to provide electricity to all its citizens using a combination of national-scale power systems for the major cities and smaller "micro grids" for rural areas. India and other rapidly developing nations are seeking to replicate a "leap frog" approach in energy similar to that used in telecommunications. Instead of investing in vast quantities of landline communications wires, India built extensive mobile capabilities for communication needs. In energy, this means using software-enabled "smart grid" electrical systems and smaller-scale but numerous renewable generation (such as wind, solar, and biomass) locations across the country. The Indian government is

also encouraging smaller investments in order to improve the efficiency of existing fossil-fuel–based generators. When completed, this energy infrastructure is likely to be more economical and robust than most systems in the "more developed" Western economies.[67]

Questions

1. Where do *ecomagination* and *healthymagination* fit on the core competence–market matrix for GE? (See Exhibit 8.8.)

2. Take either the energy or health care industry and draw the industry value chain. What areas of potential vertical integration should GE consider?

3. What related diversification would you suggest for GE in reference to its focus for the future?

4. How do GE's corporate strategic initiatives of clean-tech, health care, and globalization reinforce each other? How might they generate conflicts in the company?

TAKE-AWAY CONCEPTS

This chapter defined corporate strategy and then looked at two fundamental corporate strategy topics— vertical integration and diversification—as summarized by the following learning objectives and related take-away concepts.

LO 8-1 / Define corporate strategy and describe the three dimensions along which it is assessed.

- Corporate strategy addresses "where to compete." Business strategy addresses "how to compete."

- Corporate strategy concerns the boundaries of the firm along three dimensions: (1) industry value chain, (2) products and services, and (3) geography (regional, national, or global markets).

- To gain and sustain competitive advantage, any corporate strategy must support and strengthen a firm's strategic position, regardless of whether it is a differentiation, cost-leadership, or integration strategy.

LO 8-2 / Describe and evaluate different options firms have to organize economic activity.

- Transaction cost economics help managers decide what activities to do in-house ("make") versus what services and products to obtain from the external market ("buy").

- When the costs to pursue an activity in-house are less than the costs of transacting in the market $(C_{in\text{-}house} < C_{market})$, then the firm should vertically integrate.

- Principal–agent problems and information asymmetries can lead to market failures, and thus situations where internalizing the activity is preferred.

- A principal–agent problem arises when an agent performing activities on behalf of a principal pursues his or her own interests.

- Information asymmetries arise when one party is more informed than another because of the possession of private information.

- Moving from less integrated to more fully integrated forms of transacting, alternatives include short-term contracts, strategic alliances (including long-term contracts, equity alliances, and joint ventures), and parent–subsidiary relationships.

LO 8-3 / Describe the two types of vertical integration along the industry value chain: backward and forward vertical integration.

- Vertical integration denotes a firm's value added—what percentage of a firm's sales is generated by the firm within its boundaries.
- Industry value chains (vertical value chains) depict the transformation of raw materials into finished goods and services. Each stage typically represents a distinct industry in which a number of different firms are competing.
- Backward vertical integration involves moving ownership of activities upstream nearer to the originating (inputs) point of the industry value chain.
- Forward vertical integration involves moving ownership of activities closer to the end (customer) point of the value chain.

LO 8-4 / Identify and evaluate benefits and risks of vertical integration.

- Benefits of vertical integration include securing critical supplies and distribution channels, lowering costs, improving quality, facilitating scheduling and planning, and facilitating investments in specialized assets.
- Risks of vertical integration include increasing costs, reducing quality, reducing flexibility, and increasing the potential for legal repercussions.

LO 8-5 / Describe and examine alternatives to vertical integration.

- Taper integration is a strategy in which a firm is backwardly integrated but also relies on outside-market firms for some of its supplies, and/or is forwardly integrated but also relies on outside-market firms for some if its distribution.
- Strategic outsourcing involves moving one or more value chain activities outside the firm's boundaries to other firms in the industry value chain. Off-shoring is the outsourcing of activities outside the home country.

LO 8-6 / Describe and evaluate different types of corporate diversification.

- A single-business firm derives 95 percent or more of its revenues from one business.
- A dominant-business firm derives between 70 and 95 percent of its revenues from a single business, but pursues at least one other business activity.
- A firm follows a related diversification strategy when it derives less than 70 percent of its revenues from a single business activity, but obtains revenues from other lines of business that are linked to the primary business activity. Choices within a related diversification strategy can be related-constrained or related-linked.
- A firm follows an unrelated diversification strategy when less than 70 percent of its revenues come from a single business, and there are few, if any, linkages among its businesses.

LO 8-7 / Apply the core competence–market matrix to derive different diversification strategies.

- When applying an existing/new dimension to core competencies and markets, four quadrants emerge, as depicted in Exhibit 8.8.
- The lower-left quadrant combines existing core competencies with existing markets. Here, managers need to come up with ideas of how to leverage existing core competencies to improve their current market position.
- The lower-right quadrant combines existing core competencies with new market opportunities. Here, managers need to think about how to redeploy and recombine existing core competencies to compete in future markets.
- The upper-left quadrant combines new core competencies with existing market opportunities. Here, managers must come up with strategic initiatives of how to build new core competencies to protect and extend the firm's current market position.
- The upper-right quadrant combines new core competencies with new market opportunities. This is likely the most challenging diversification strategy because it requires building new core competencies to create and compete in future markets.

LO 8-8 / **Explain when a diversification strategy creates a competitive advantage and when it does not.**

- The diversification-performance relationship is a function of the underlying type of diversification.
- The relationship between the type of diversification and overall firm performance takes on the shape of an inverted U (see Exhibit 8.9).
- Unrelated diversification often results in a diversification discount: the stock price of such highly diversified firms is valued at less than the sum of their individual business units.
- Related diversification often results in a diversification premium: the stock price of related-diversification firms is valued at greater than the sum of their individual business units.
- In the BCG matrix, the corporation is viewed as a portfolio of businesses, much like a portfolio of stocks in finance (see Exhibit 8.11). The individual SBUs are evaluated according to relative market share and the speed of market growth, and are plotted using one of four categories: dog, cash cow, star, and question mark. Each category warrants a different investment strategy.
- Both low levels and high levels of diversification are generally associated with lower overall performance, while moderate levels of diversification are associated with higher firm performance.

KEY TERMS

Backward vertical integration
Boston Consulting Group (BCG) growth-share matrix
Conglomerate
Core competence–market matrix
Corporate strategy
Credible commitment
Diversification
Diversification discount
Diversification premium
External transaction costs

Forward vertical integration
Franchising
Geographic diversification strategy
Industry value chain
Information asymmetries
Internal transaction costs
Joint venture
Licensing
Principal–agent problem
Product diversification strategy

Product–market diversification strategy
Related diversification strategy
Specialized assets
Strategic alliances
Strategic outsourcing
Taper integration
Transaction cost economics
Transaction costs
Unrelated diversification strategy
Vertical integration

DISCUSSION QUESTIONS

1. When Walmart decided to incorporate grocery stores into some locations and created "supercenters," was this a business-level strategy of differentiation or a corporate strategy of diversification? Why? Explain your answer.

2. How can related diversification create a competitive advantage for the firm? Keeping the advantages of related diversification in mind, think back to the example in the chapter of Delta's vertical integration decision to acquire an oil refinery—clearly an

unrelated diversification move. What challenges might Delta confront in operating this refinery? Think of the strategic concepts you have learned and how they can help you evaluate Delta's decision.

3. Franchising is widely used in the casual dining and fast-food industry, yet Starbucks is quite successful with a large number of company-owned stores. How do you explain this difference? Is Starbucks bucking the bandwagon effect, or is something else going on?

ETHICAL/SOCIAL ISSUES

1. The chapter notes that some firms choose to outsource their human resource management systems. If a firm has a core value of respecting its employees and rewarding top performance with training, raises, and promotions, does outsourcing HR management show a lack of commitment by the firm? HR management systems are software applications that typically manage payroll, benefits, hiring and training, and performance appraisal. What are the advantages and disadvantages of this decision? Think of ways that a firm can continue to show its commitment to treat employees with respect.

2. Nike is a large and successful firm in the design of athletic shoes. It could easily decide to forward-integrate to manufacture the shoes it designs. Therefore, the firm has a credible threat over its current manufacturers. If Nike has no intention of actually entering the manufacturing arena, is its supply chain management team being ethical with the current manufacturers if the team mentions this credible threat numerous times in annual pricing negotiations? Why or why not? What aspects of Nike's agreement with its manufacturing partners do you believe they emphasize in negotiations?

SMALL-GROUP EXERCISES

//// Small-Group Exercise 1

Agriculture is one of the largest and oldest industries in the world. In the U.S. and many other countries, farmers often struggle to turn a profit given the variances of weather and commodity prices. Some working farms are turning to tourism as an additional and complementary revenue source. A study from the U.S. Census of Agriculture in 2007 found nearly 25,000 farms providing some level of agri-tourism and recreation services. There were 2.2 million farms in the census, almost triple the number from 2002. In 2010, the Department of Agriculture announced a new grant program aimed at providing public access to private farms for such purposes. Small farms worldwide are participating in this trend by offering "pick your own" crops in season, as well as small bed-and-breakfast experiences.

Perhaps one of the most successful large companies leading this marriage of industries is a dairy farm in Indiana: Fair Oaks Farms (http://www.fofarms.com/en/home). Fair Oaks Farms is home to 30,000 cows and produces enough milk to feed 8 million people. Fair Oaks is also participating in the education market as a popular destination for school field trips. Other attractions include the "Birthing Barn," where calf births can be viewed live; the Cheese Factory; and Mooville—a themed outdoor play area. Fair Oaks Farms hosts some 500,000 tourists each year, who come to see the hands-on adventure center and the working milking operations. A video of the operation is available at www.youtube.com/watch?v=JJRy82i8e5Q. Such ingenious business diversification can offer many benefits to the agriculture industry.[68]

1. What other industrial or commercial industries could benefit from such potential tourist or recreational revenues? Discuss what new and complementary capabilities would need to be developed in order to succeed.

2. In your group, list other industry combinations you have seen be successful. Consider why you think the combination has been a success.

//// Small-Group Exercise 2

Target and Walmart are significant rivals in the retailing industry. Though Walmart is the world's largest company (2012 sales of $466 billion), Target had been growing faster than Walmart until the 2008 recession. From 2003 to 2007, same-store sales at Target grew an average of 4.6 percent, while Walmart's comparable growth was 2.9 percent.

However, in 2008 Target's same-store sales fell 2.6 percent, while Walmart's rose 3.3 percent. What drove this difference? Product mix seems to be a large factor. Target devotes less than 20 percent of its space to consumables such as health and beauty products and food. Walmart, by contrast, has 45 percent of its shelf space for consumables, with groceries being a major component.

Though an obvious answer for Target is to continue following Walmart into groceries, consider that the average net profit of the grocery industry was less than 1.4 percent from 2002 to 2008. As a team, assume you've been called in to consult with Target on the problem.[69]

1. What should Target do to get back on a growth track?

2. Is Target's problem strategy or execution?

3. What action plan would you recommend?

STRATEGY TERM PROJECT

//// Module 8: Vertical Integration

In this section, you will study the boundaries of the firm you have selected for your strategy project in reference to the vertical value chain activities of its industry.

1. Draw out the vertical value chain for your firm's industry. List the major firms in each important activity along the chain (see Exhibits 8.4 and 8.5 as examples). Note that a firm's name may appear multiple times in the value chain. This indicates some level of vertical integration by the firm. If your firm is in many different industries (e.g., GE), then choose the dominant industry or the one that intrigues you the most and use only that one for this analysis.

2. Is your firm highly vertically integrated? If yes, does it also employ taper integration?

3. Are any of the vertical value chain operations off-shored? If so, list some of the pros and cons

of having this part of the value chain outside the home country.

4. Use the preceding vertical value chain to identify the corporate strategy of the firm. In other words, where within the industry has the firm chosen to compete? Based on where it competes, describe what you now see as its corporate strategy.

5. In Module 2, you were asked to identify the mission and major goals for your selected company. Go back to that information now and compare the mission and goals to what you have found as the corporate strategy. Are the mission, goals, and corporate strategy in alignment? Do you see any holes or conflicts among these three elements? Can you relate the performance of the firm to this finding in any way? (If all three are consistent, is this a well-performing unit?) If there is a conflict between the corporate strategy and the mission, does this lack of alignment contribute to performance problems? Why or why not?

my STRATEGY

How Diversified Are You?

When someone asks a manager about diversification, the questioner may be referring to the manager's overall portfolio of savings and retirement investments. While that is an important personal financial consideration, here we are asking you to think about diversification a bit differently.

Corporations diversify by investing time and resources into new areas of business. As individuals, each of us makes choices about how to spend our time and energies. Typically, we could

divide our time between school, work, family, sleep, and play. During high-stress work projects, we likely devote more of our time to work; when studying for final exams or a professional board exam (such as the CPA exam), we probably spend more time and effort in the "student learning" mode. This manner of dividing our time can be thought of as "personal diversification." Just as companies can invest in related or unrelated activities, we make similar choices. While we attend college, we may choose to engage in social and leisure activities with campus colleagues, or we may focus on classwork at school and spend our "play time" with an entirely separate set of people.

Using Exhibit 8.7 as a guide, list each of your major activity areas. Think of each of these as a business. (If you are literally "all work and no play," you are a single-business type of personal diversification.) Instead of revenues, estimate the percentage of *time* you spend per week in each activity. (Most people will be diversified, though some may be dominant perhaps in school or work.) To assess your degree of *relatedness* and *unrelatedness,* consider the subject matter and community involved

with each activity. For example, if you are studying ballet and working as an accountant, those would be largely unrelated activities (unless you are an accountant for a ballet company!).

1. What conclusions do you derive based on your personal diversification strategy?

2. Do you need to make adjustments to your portfolio of activities? Explain the reasons for your answer.

ENDNOTES

1. Jeffrey Immelt, quoted in "Ecomagination: Inside GE's power play," by J. Makower, May 8, 2005, www.worldchanging.com/archives/002669.html.

2. This ChapterCase is based on: "A slipping crown," *The Economist,* March 13, 2009; "Comcast, GE strike deal; Vivendi to sell NBC stake," *The Wall Street Journal,* December 4, 2009; "Ecomagination: Inside GE's power play," *Worldchanging,* May 8, 2005; "GE: How clean (and not-so-clean) tech drives ecomagination," *The Wall Street Journal,* May 27, 2009; "GE launches 'healthymagination'; will commit $6 billion to enable better health focusing on cost, access and quality," GE press release, May 7, 2009; "GE may shed storied appliance unit," *The Wall Street Journal,* May 15, 2008; "GE's chief declines $12 million bonus amid crisis," *The Wall Street Journal,* February 19, 2009; "Comcast buys rest of NBC's parent," *The Wall Street Journal,* February 13, 2013; www.ge.com; and www.wolframalpha.com.

3. Collis, D. J. (1995), "The scope of the corporation," *Harvard Business School Note,* 9-795-139.

4. 2010 Letter to Shareholders in 2009 GE Annual Report.

5. Kogut, B., and U. Zander (1992), "Knowledge of the firm, combinative capabilities, and the replication of technology," *Organization Science* 3: 383–397; O'Connor, G. C., and M. Rice (2001), "Opportunity recognition and breakthrough innovation in large firms," *California Management Review* 43: 95–116; O'Connor, G. C., and R. W. Veryzer (2001), "The nature of market visioning for technology-based radical innovation," *Journal of Product Innovation Management* 18: 231–224.

6. The literature on transaction cost economics is rich and expanding. For important

theoretical and empirical contributions, see: Folta, T. B. (1998), "Governance and uncertainty: The trade-off between administrative control and commitment," *Strategic Management Journal* 19: 1007–1028; Klein, B., R. Crawford, and A. Alchian (1978), "Vertical integration, appropriable rents, and the competitive contracting process," *Journal of Law and Economics* 21: 297–326; Leiblein, M. J., and D. J. Miller (2003), "An empirical examination of transformation- and firm-level influences on the vertical boundaries of the firm," *Strategic Management Journal* 24: 839–859; Leiblein, M. J., J. J. Reuer, and F. Dalsace (2002), "Do make or buy decisions matter? The influence of organizational governance on technological performance," *Strategic Management Journal* 23: 817–833; Mahoney, J. (1992), "The choice of organizational form: Vertical financial ownership versus other methods of vertical integration," *Strategic Management Journal* 13: 559–584; Mahoney, J. T. (2005), *Economic Foundations of Strategy* (Thousand Oaks, CA: Sage); Williamson, O. E. (1975), *Markets and Hierarchies,* (New York: Free Press); Williamson, O. E. (1981), "The economics of organization: The transaction cost approach," *American Journal of Sociology* 87: 548–577; and Williamson, O. E. (1985), *The Economic Institutions of Capitalism* (New York: Free Press).

7. This draws on: Mahoney, J. T. (2005), *Economic Foundations of Strategy* (Thousand Oaks, CA: Sage); Williamson, O. E. (1975), *Markets and Hierarchies* (New York: Free Press); Williamson, O. E. (1981), "The economics of organization: The transaction cost approach," *American Journal of Sociology* 87: 548–577; Williamson, O. E. (1985), *The Economic Institutions of Capitalism* (New York: Free Press); and Hart, O., and O. Moore (1990), "Property rights and the nature of

the firm," *Journal of Political Economy* 98: 1119–1158.

8. Highlighting the relevance of research on transaction costs, both Ronald Coase (1991) and Oliver Williamson (2009), who further developed and refined Coase's initial insight, were each awarded a Nobel Prize in economics.

9. Levy, S. (2011), *In the Plex: How Google Thinks, Works, and Shapes Our Lives* (New York: Simon & Schuster).

10. This is based on: Berle, A., and G. Means (1932), *The Modern Corporation and Private Property* (New York: Macmillan); Jensen, M., and W. Meckling (1976), "Theory of the firm: Managerial behavior, agency costs and ownership structure," *Journal of Financial Economics* 3: 305–360; and Fama, E. (1980), "Agency problems and the theory of the firm," *Journal of Political Economy* 88: 375–390.

11. Berle, A., and G. Means (1932), *The Modern Corporation and Private Property.*

12. This discussion draws on: Zenger, T. R., and W. S. Hesterly (1997), "The disaggregation of corporations: Selective intervention, high-powered incentives, and molecular units," *Organization Science* 8: 209–222; and Zenger, T. R., and S. G. Lazzarini (2004), "Compensating for innovation: Do small firms offer high-powered incentives that lure talent and motivate effort," *Managerial and Decision Economics* 25: 329–345.

13. This discussion draws on: Akerlof, G. A. (1970), "The market for lemons: Quality uncertainty and the market mechanism," *Quarterly Journal of Economics* 94: 488–500.

14. Pisano, G. P. (1997), "R&D performance, collaborative arrangements, and the market-for-know-how: A test of the 'lemons' hypothesis in biotechnology," *Working Paper No. 97-105,* Harvard Business School; Lerner, J., and

R. P. Merges (1998), "The control of technology alliances: An empirical analysis of the biotechnology industry," *Journal of Industrial Economics* 46: 125–156; Huston, J. H., and R. W. Spencer (2002), "Quality, uncertainty and the Internet: The market for cyber lemons," *The American Economist* 46: 50–60; Rothaermel, F. T., and D. L. Deeds (2004), "Exploration and exploitation alliances in biotechnology: A system of new product development," *Strategic Management Journal* 25: 201–221; Downing, C., D. Jaffee, and N. Walla (2009), "Is the market for mortgage-backed securities a market for lemons?" *Review of Financial Studies* 22: 2457–2494.

15. This discussion draws on: Williamson, O. E. (1991), "Comparative economic organization: The analysis of discrete structural alternatives," *Administrative Science Quarterly* 36: 269–296.

16. Since short-term contracts are unlikely to be of strategic significance, they are not subsumed under the term strategic alliances, but rather are considered to be mere contractual arrangements.

17. Dyer, J. H. (1997), "Effective interfirm collaboration: How firms minimize transaction costs and maximize transaction value," *Strategic Management Journal* 18: 535–556.

18. This is based on: Gulati, R. (1998), "Alliances and networks," *Strategic Management Journal* 19: 293–317; Ireland, R. D., M. A. Hitt, and D. Vaidyanath (2002), "Alliance management as a source of competitive advantage," *Journal of Management* 28: 413–446; Hoang, H., and F. T. Rothaermel (2005), "The effect of general and partner-specific alliance experience on joint R&D project performance," *Academy of Management Journal* 48: 332–345; and Lavie, D. (2006), "The competitive advantage of interconnected firms: An extension of the resource-based view," *Academy of Management Review* 31: 638–658.

19. This Strategy Highlight is based on "Toyota sets pact on lithium," *The Wall Street Journal,* January 20, 2010; and "Toyota predicts hybrid majority," *The Wall Street Journal Japan Edition,* April 18, 2013.

20. www.dowcorning.com.

21. "Rising from the ashes in Detroit," *The Economist,* August 19, 2010.

22. "Small cars, big question," *The Economist,* January 21, 2010.

23. Tucker, I., and R. P. Wilder (1977), "Trends in vertical integration in the U.S. manufacturing sector," *Journal of Industrial Economics* 26: 81–97; Harrigan, K. R. (1984), "Formulating vertical integration strategies," *Academy of Management Review* 9: 638–652; Harrigan, K. R. (1986), "Matching

vertical integration strategies to competitive conditions," *Strategic Management Journal* 7: 535–555; Rothaermel, F. T., M. A. Hitt, and L. A. Jobe (2006), "Balancing vertical integration and strategic outsourcing: Effects on product portfolios, new product success, and firm performance," *Strategic Management Journal* 27: 1033–1056.

24. "HTC clones Nexus One, launches 3 new phones," *Wired.com,* February 16, 2010.

25. www.htc.com.

26. Harrigan, K. R. (1984), "Formulating vertical integration strategies," *Academy of Management Review* 9: 638–652; Harrigan, K. R. (1986), "Matching vertical integration strategies to competitive conditions," *Strategic Management Journal* 7: 535–555.

27. "HTC clones Nexus One, launches 3 new phones," *Wired.com,* February 16, 2010.

28. "Companies more prone to go vertical," *The Wall Street Journal,* December 1, 2009.

29. This is based on: "Pepsi bids $6 billion for largest bottlers, posts flat profit," *The Wall Street Journal,* April 20, 2009; "PepsiCo buys bottlers for $7.8 billion," *The Wall Street Journal,* August 5, 2009; "Companies more prone to go vertical," *The Wall Street Journal,* December 1, 2009; and "Coca-Cola strikes deal with bottler," *The Wall Street Journal,* February 25, 2010.

30. Williamson, O. E. (1975), *Markets and Hierarchies* (New York: Free Press); Williamson, O. E. (1981), "The economics of organization: The transaction cost approach," *American Journal of Sociology* 87: 548–577; Williamson, O. E. (1985), *The Economic Institutions of Capitalism* (New York: Free Press); Poppo, L., and T. Zenger (1998), "Testing alternative theories of the firm: Transaction cost, knowledge based, and measurement explanations for make or buy decisions in information services," *Strategic Management Journal* 19: 853–878.

31. Williamson, O. E. (1975), *Markets and Hierarchies* (New York: Free Press); Williamson, O. E. (1981), "The economics of organization: The transaction cost approach," *American Journal of Sociology* 87: 548–577; Williamson, O. E. (1985), *The Economic Institutions of Capitalism* (New York: Free Press).

32. Williamson, O. E. (1975), *Markets and Hierarchies* (New York: Free Press).

33. "Delta to buy refinery in effort to lower jet-fuel costs," *The Wall Street Journal,* April 30, 2012.

34. Harrigan, K. R. (1984), "Formulating vertical integration strategies," *Academy of Management Review* 9: 638–652; Harrigan, K. R. (1986), "Matching vertical integration

strategies to competitive conditions," *Strategic Management Journal* 7: 535–555; Afuah, A. (2001), "Dynamic boundaries of the firm: Are firms better off being vertically integrated in the face of a technological change?" *Academy of Management Journal* 44: 1211–1228; Rothaermel, F. T., M. A. Hitt, and L. A. Jobe (2006), "Balancing vertical integration and strategic outsourcing: Effects on product portfolios, new product success, and firm performance," *Strategic Management Journal* 27: 1033–1056.

35. Afuah, A. (2001), "Dynamic boundaries of the firm: Are firms better off being vertically integrated in the face of a technological change?"

36. Ghemawat, P. (1993), "Commitment to a process innovation: Nucor, USX, and thin slab casting," *Journal of Economics and Management Strategy* 2: 133–161; Christensen, C. M., and M. E. Raynor (2003), *The Innovator's Solution: Creating and Sustaining Successful Growth* (Boston, MA: Harvard Business School Press).

37. "Companies more prone to go vertical," *The Wall Street Journal,* December 1, 2009.

38. Harrigan, K. R. (1984), "Formulating vertical integration strategies," *Academy of Management Review* 9: 638–652.

39. This is based on: Harrigan, K. R. (1984), "Formulating vertical integration strategies"; and Harrigan, K. R. (1986), "Matching vertical integration strategies to competitive conditions," *Strategic Management Journal* 7: 535–555.

40. This is based on the following: Prahalad and Hamel argued that a firm that outsources too many activities risks hollowing out ("unlearning") its core competencies because the firm no longer participates in key adjacent value chain activities. A similar argument has been made by Teece (1986); Prahalad, C. K., and G. Hamel (1990), "The core competence of the corporation," *Harvard Business Review,* May–June; and Teece, D. J. (1986), "Profiting from technological innovation: Implications for integration, collaboration, licensing and public policy," *Research Policy* 15: 285–305.

41. Rothaermel, F. T., M. A. Hitt, and L. A. Jobe (2006), "Balancing vertical integration and strategic outsourcing: Effects on product portfolios, new product success, and firm performance," *Strategic Management Journal* 27: 1033–1056.

42. "Global outsourcing market to be worth $1,430bn by 2009," *Computer Business Review,* August 2007.

43. "Passage to India," *The Economist,* June 26, 2010.

44. KFC and Yum Brands data drawn from 2012 Yum Brands Annual Report (http://yum.com/annualreport/) and www.kfc.com/about/.

45. Chick-fil-A data drawn from http://www.chick-fil-a.com/Company/Highlights-Fact-Sheets.

46. This section is based on: Rumelt, R. P. (1974), *Strategy, Structure, and Economic Performance* (Boston, MA: Harvard Business School Press); Montgomery, C. A. (1985), "Product-market diversification and market power," *Academy of Management Review* 28: 789–798.

47. Google Annual Reports.

48. Harley-Davidson Annual Reports.

49. This is based on: ExxonMobil Annual Reports; "Oil's decline slows Exxon, Chevron profit growth," *The Wall Street Journal,* January 30, 2009; "The greening of ExxonMobil," *Forbes,* August 24, 2009; Friedman, T. L. (2008), *Hot, Flat, and Crowded. Why We Need a Green Revolution—And How It Can Renew America* (New York: Farrar, Straus and Giroux); "Exxon to acquire XTO Energy in $31 billion stock deal," *The Wall Street Journal,* December 14, 2009; and "ExxonMobil buys XTO Energy," *The Economist,* December 17, 2009.

50. "The shale revolution: What could go wrong?" *The Wall Street Journal,* September 6, 2012; and "U.S. oil notches record growth," *The Wall Street Journal,* June 12, 2013.

51. This is based on: Peng, M. W., and P. S. Heath (1996), "The growth of the firm in planned economies in transitions: Institutions, organizations, and strategic choice," *Academy of Management Review* 21: 492–528; Peng, M. W. (2000), *Business Strategies in Transition Economies* (Thousand Oaks, CA: Sage); and Peng, M. W. (2005), "What determines the scope of the firm over time? A focus on institutional relatedness," *Academy of Management Review* 30: 622–633.

52. The history of the Tata Group is documented at: http://www.tata.com/htm/heritage/HeritageOption1.html; "The Tata group," *The Economist,* March 3, 2011; "Ratan Tata's legacy," *The Economist,* December 1, 2012; and "A new boss at Tata," *The Economist,* December 1, 2012. See also, Sean McLaing, "Why the world's cheapest car flopped," *The Wall Street Journal,* October 14, 2013.

53. Prahalad, C. K., and G. Hamel (1990), "The core competence of the corporation."

54. This discussion is based on: Burt, C., and F. T. Rothaermel (2013), "Bank of America and the new financial landscape," case study, in Rothaermel, F. T., *Strategic Management* (Burr Ridge IL: McGraw-Hill), http://mcgrawhillcreate.com/rothaermel, ID# MHE-FTR-07-0077645065.

55. Bank of America had long coveted Merrill Lynch, a premier investment bank. Severely weakened by the global financial crisis, Merrill Lynch became a takeover target, and Bank of America made a bid. In the process, Bank of America learned that Merrill Lynch's exposure to subprime mortgages and other exotic financial instruments was much larger than previously disclosed. Other problems included Merrill Lynch's payments of multimillion-dollar bonuses to many employees, despite the investment bank's having lost billions of dollars (in 2008). After learning this new information, Bank of America (under its then-CEO Ken Lewis) attempted to withdraw from the Merrill Lynch takeover. The Federal Reserve Bank, under the leadership of its chairman, Ben Bernanke, insisted that Bank of America fulfill the agreement, noting that the takeover was part of a grand strategy to save the financial system from collapse. Once Bank of America shareholders learned that CEO Ken Lewis had not disclosed the problems at Merrill Lynch, they first stripped him of his chairmanship of the board of directors, and later fired him as CEO. For a detailed and insightful discussion on the Merrill Lynch takeover by Bank of America, see Lowenstein, R. (2010), *The End of Wall Street* (New York: Penguin Press).

56. "Bank of America and Merrill Lynch," *The Economist,* April 14, 2010.

57. "In Gatorade war, Pepsi seems to have deliberately given up market share to Coke," *Business Insider,* February 1, 2012.

58. "Oracle vs. salesforce.com," Harvard Business School Case Study, 9-705-440; "How to innovate in a downturn," *The Wall Street Journal,* March 18, 2009; and Dyer, J., H. Gregersen, and C. M. Christensen (2011), *The Innovator's DNA: Mastering the Five Skills of Disruptive Innovators* (Boston, MA: Harvard Business Review Press).

59. Palich, L. E., L. B. Cardinal, and C. C. Miller (2000), "Curvilinearity in the diversification-performance linkage: An examination of over three decades of research," *Strategic Management Journal* 21: 155–174.

60. This is based on: Lang, L.H.P., and R. M. Stulz (1994), "Tobin's *q,* corporate diversification, and firm performance," *Journal of Political Economy* 102: 1248–1280; Martin, J. D., and A. Sayrak (2003), "Corporate diversification and shareholder value: A survey of recent literature," *Journal of Corporate Finance* 9: 37–57; and Rajan, R., H. Servaes, and L. Zingales (2000), "The cost of diversity: The diversification discount and inefficient investment," *Journal of Finance* 55: 35–80.

61. This is based on: Peng, M. W., and P. S. Heath (1996), "The growth of the firm in planned economies in transitions: Institutions, organizations, and strategic choice," *Academy of Management Review* 21: 492–528; Peng, M. W. (2000), *Business Strategies in Transition Economies* (Thousand Oaks, CA: Sage); and Peng, M. W. (2005), "What determines the scope of the firm over time? A focus on institutional relatedness," *Academy of Management Review* 30: 622–633.

62. Villalonga, B. (2004), "Diversification discount or premium? New evidence from the business information tracking series," *Journal of Finance* 59: 479–506.

63. This section is based on: "U.S. clears InBev to buy Anheuser," *The Wall Street Journal,* November 15, 2008; and "Blackstone nears deal," *The Wall Street Journal,* October 5, 2009.

64. Boston Consulting Group (1970), *The Product Portfolio* (Boston, MA); and Shay, J. P., and F. T. Rothaermel (1999), "Dynamic competitive strategy: Towards a multi-perspective conceptual framework," *Long Range Planning* 32: 559–572; and Kiechel, W. (2010), *The Lords of Strategy: The Secret Intellectual History of the New Corporate World* (Boston, MA: Harvard Business School Press).

65. GE Annual Reports.

66. Milgrom, P., and J. Roberts (1990), "Bargaining costs, influence costs, and the organization of economic activity," in Alt, J., and K. Shepsle (eds.), *Perspectives on Positive Political Economy* (Cambridge, UK: Cambridge University Press).

67. GE Annual Reports; Heintzelman, D. (2010), "India's path to renewable power," *Bloomberg Businessweek,* Viewpoint Column, May 27 (Mr. Heintzelman is president and CEO of GE Oil & Gas); and "GE shake-up will audition new leaders," *The Wall Street Journal,* July 20, 2012.

68. This Small-Group Exercise is based on: The Rural Community Building website produced by the American Farm Bureau Federation; *America's Heartland* "Episode 311"; and Fair Oaks Farms Dairy (www.fofarms.com).

69. This Small-Group Exercise is based on: Gregory, S. (2009), "Walmart vs. Target: No contest in the recession," *Time,* March 14; and Food Marketing Institute Annual Financial Report, December 2008.

Corporate Strategy: Mergers and Acquisitions, Strategic Alliances

Learning Objectives

After studying this chapter, you should be able to:

LO 9-1 Differentiate between mergers and acquisitions, and explain why firms would use either as a vehicle for corporate strategy.

LO 9-2 Define horizontal integration and evaluate the advantages and disadvantages of this corporate-level strategy.

LO 9-3 Explain why firms engage in acquisitions.

LO 9-4 Evaluate whether mergers and acquisitions lead to competitive advantage.

LO 9-5 Define strategic alliances, and explain why they are important corporate strategy vehicles and why firms enter into them.

LO 9-6 Describe three alliance governance mechanisms and evaluate their pros and cons.

LO 9-7 Describe the three phases of alliance management and explain how an alliance management capability can lead to a competitive advantage.

LO 9-8 Apply the build-borrow-or-buy framework to guide corporate strategy.

How Buzz Lightyear, Iron Man, and Darth Vader Joined Mickey's Family

WITH $45 BILLION in annual revenues, Disney is the world's largest media company. In recent years, Disney has grown through a number of high-profile acquisitions, including Pixar (2006), Marvel (2009), and Lucasfilm (2012), the creator of Star Wars. Let's take a closer look at how an alliance with Pixar turned into an acquisition, and how Disney then rounded out its brand portfolio with subsequent acquisitions.

Pixar started out as a computer hardware company producing high-end graphic display systems. One of its customers was Disney. To demonstrate the graphic display systems' capabilities, Pixar produced short, computer-animated movies. In the beginning, though, despite being sophisticated, Pixar's computer hardware was not selling well, and the new venture was hemorrhaging money. In rode not Buzz Lightyear, but Steve Jobs to the rescue. Shortly after being ousted from Apple in 1986, Jobs bought the struggling hardware company for $5 million and founded Pixar Animation Studios, investing another $5 million into the company. The Pixar team then transformed the company into a computer animation film studio.

To finance and distribute its newly created computer-animated movies, Pixar entered a strategic alliance with Disney. Disney's distribution network and its stellar reputation in animated movies were critical complementary assets that Pixar needed to commercialize its new type of films. In turn, Disney was able to rejuvenate its floundering product lineup, retaining the rights to the newly created Pixar characters and to any sequels.

Pixar became successful beyond imagination as it rolled out one blockbuster after another: *Toy Story (1, 2,* and *3), A Bug's Life, Monsters, Inc., Finding Nemo,* and *The Incredibles,* grossing several billion dollars. Given Pixar's huge success and Disney's abysmal performance with its own releases during this time, the bargaining power in the alliance shifted dramatically. Renegotiations of the Pixar–Disney alliance broke down altogether in 2004, reportedly because of personality conflicts between Steve Jobs and then–Disney Chairman and CEO Michael Eisner.

After Eisner left Disney in the fall of 2005, Disney acquired Pixar for $7.4 billion. The success of the alliance demonstrated that the two entities' complementary assets matched, and gave Disney an inside perspective on the value of Pixar's core competencies in the creation of computer-animated features. In 2009, Disney turned to acquisitions again in order to address the problem of poor performance in its internal movie creation efforts. The acquisition of Marvel Entertainment for $4 billion added *Spiderman, Iron Man, The Incredible Hulk,* and *Captain America* to its lineup of characters. Marvel's superheroes grossed a cumulative $14 billion at the box office, with *The Avengers* bringing in more than $1.5 billion.

In 2012, Mickey's newly extended family was joined by Darth Vader, Obi-Wan Kenobi, Princess Leia, and Luke Skywalker when Disney acquired Lucasfilm for over $4 billion. Continued success in movies depends more and more on owning a vast library of valuable content. Using alliances and acquisitions, Disney has amassed an impressive family of superheroes.[1]

After reading the chapter, you will find more about this case, with related questions, on page 296.

⒜ **DISNEY IS ACTIVE** in a wide array of business activities, from cable and network television stations (ABC, ESPN, and others) and movies to amusement parks, cruises, and retailing. It became the world's leading media company to a large extent by pursuing a corporate strategy of related-linked diversification (see discussion in Chapter 8). This is because some, but not all, of Disney's business activities share some common resources, capabilities, and competencies. As detailed in the ChapterCase, Disney's executives implemented its corporate strategy through the use of strategic alliances and acquisitions.

In addition to internal organic growth, firms have two critical strategic options to pursue common interests, enhance competitiveness, and increase revenues: acquisitions and alliances. We devote this chapter to the study of these fundamental pathways through which to implement corporate strategy. We begin by taking a closer look at mergers and acquisitions before studying strategic alliances. We conclude with *Implications for the Strategist*, in which we discuss practical applications. Here, we apply the "build-borrow-buy" framework to guiding corporate strategy in deciding whether and when to grow internally (build), use alliances (borrow), or make acquisitions (buy).

9.1 Mergers and Acquisitions

LO 9-1

Differentiate between mergers and acquisitions, and explain why firms would use either as a vehicle for corporate strategy.

A popular vehicle for executing corporate strategy is mergers and acquisitions (M&A). Thousands of mergers and acquisitions occur each year, with a cumulative value in the trillions of dollars.[2] Although people sometimes use the terms interchangeably, and usually in tandem, mergers and acquisitions are, by definition, distinct from each other. A **merger** describes the joining of two independent companies to form *a combined entity*. Mergers tend to be friendly; in mergers, the target firm would like to be acquired. Disney's acquisition of Pixar, for example, was a friendly one, in which both management teams believed that joining the two companies was a good idea.

An **acquisition** describes the purchase or takeover of one company by another. Acquisitions can be friendly or unfriendly. When a target firm does not want to be acquired, the acquisition is considered a **hostile takeover**. British telecom company Vodafone's acquisition of Germany-based Mannesmann, a diversified conglomerate with holdings in telephony and Internet services, at an estimated value of $150 billion, was a hostile one.

In defining mergers and acquisitions, size can matter as well. The combining of two firms of comparable size is often described as a merger even though it might in fact be an acquisition. For example, the integration of Daimler and Chrysler was pitched as a merger, though in reality Daimler acquired Chrysler and later sold it. After emerging from bankruptcy restructuring, Chrysler is now majority-owned by Fiat, an Italian auto manufacturer.

In contrast, when large, incumbent firms such as the Tata Group, GE, or Microsoft buy startup companies, the transaction is generally described as an acquisition. Although there is a distinction between mergers and acquisitions, many observers simply use the umbrella term "mergers and acquisitions" or M&A.

LO 9-2

Define horizontal integration and evaluate the advantages and disadvantages of this corporate-level strategy.

MERGING WITH COMPETITORS

In contrast to vertical integration, which concerns the number of activities a firm participates in up and down the industry value chain (as discussed in Chapter 8), **horizontal integration**

---

merger The joining of two independent companies to form a combined entity.

acquisition The purchase or takeover of one company by another; can be friendly or unfriendly.

hostile takeover Acquisition in which the target company does not wish to be acquired.

horizontal integration The process of merging with competitors, leading to industry consolidation.

is the process of merging with a competitor at the same stage of the industry value chain. Horizontal integration is a type of corporate strategy that can improve a firm's strategic position in a single industry. An industry-wide trend toward horizontal integration leads to industry consolidation. The pharmaceutical industry has seen considerable consolidation, with Pfizer merging with Wyeth, and Merck and Schering-Plough merging in 2009. In the event-promotion business, the only remaining segment in the music industry in which revenues are increasing, Live Nation acquired Ticketmaster in 2010.

There are three main benefits to a horizontal integration strategy:

- Reduction in competitive intensity
- Lower costs
- Increased differentiation

Exhibit 9.1 previews the sources of value creation and costs in horizontal integration, which we discuss next.

REDUCTION IN COMPETITIVE INTENSITY. Looking through the lens of Porter's five forces model with a focus on rivalry among competitors (introduced in Chapter 3), horizontal integration changes the underlying industry structure in favor of the surviving firms. Excess capacity is taken out of the market, and competition tends to decrease as a consequence of horizontal integration, assuming no new entrants. As a whole, the industry structure becomes more consolidated and potentially more profitable. If the surviving firms find themselves in an oligopolistic industry structure and maintain a focus on non-price competition (e.g., R&D spending, customer service, or advertising), the industry can indeed be quite profitable, and rivalry would likely decrease among existing firms. Recent horizontal integration in the U.S. airline industry, for example, provided several benefits to the surviving carriers. By reducing excess capacity, the mergers between Delta and Northwest Airlines (in 2008), United Airlines and Continental (in 2010), Southwest and AirTran (in 2010), and American and US Airways (proposed in 2013 but put on hold by the U.S. Department of Justice) lowered competitive intensity in the industry overall.

Horizontal integration can favorably affect several of Porter's five forces for the surviving firms: strengthening bargaining power vis-à-vis suppliers and buyers, reducing the threat of entry, and reducing rivalry among existing firms. Because of the potential to reduce competitive intensity in an industry, government authorities such

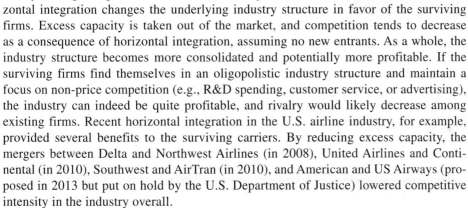

Corporate Strategy	Sources of Value Creation (*V*)	Sources of Costs (*C*)
Horizontal integration through M&A	• Reduction in competitive intensity • Lower costs • Increased differentiation	• Integration failure • Reduced flexibility • Increased potential for legal repercussions

EXHIBIT 9.1

Sources of Value Creation and Costs in Horizontal Integration as the FTC and/or the European Commission usually must approve any large horizontal integration activity. For example, the FTC did not approve the proposed merger between Staples and Office Depot, arguing that the remaining industry would have only two competitors (the other being Office Max). Staples and Office Depot argued that the market for office supplies needed to be defined more broadly to include large retailers such as Walmart and Target. The U.S. courts sided with the FTC, which argued that the prices for end consumers would be significantly higher if the market had only two category killers.[3]

LOWER COSTS. Research provides empirical evidence that firms use horizontal integration to lower costs through economies of scale, enhance their economic value creation, and in turn their performance.[4] In industries that have high fixed costs, achieving economies of scale through large output is critical in lowering costs. The dominant pharmaceutical companies such as Pfizer, Roche, and Novartis, for example, maintain large sales forces ("detail people") who call on doctors and hospitals to promote their products. These specialized sales forces often number 10,000 or more, and thus are a significant fixed cost to the firms, even though part of their compensation is based on commissions. Maintaining such a large and sophisticated sales force (many with MBAs) is costly if the firm has only a few drugs it can show the doctor. As a rule of thumb, if a pharma company does not possess a blockbuster drug that brings in more than $1 billion in annual revenues, it cannot maintain its own sales force.[5] When existing firms such as Pfizer and Wyeth merge, they join their drug pipelines and portfolios of existing drugs. They are likely to have one sales force for the combined portfolio, consequently reducing the size of the sales force and lowering the overall cost of distribution.

INCREASED DIFFERENTIATION. Horizontal integration through M&A can help firms strengthen their competitive positions by increasing the differentiation of their product and service offerings. In particular, horizontal integration can do this by filling gaps in a firm's product offering, allowing the combined entity to offer a complete suite of products and services. To enhance its differentiated appeal, Oracle acquired PeopleSoft for $10 billion in 2005. This horizontal integration joined Oracle, the world's leading enterprise software company, whose core competency is in database management systems, with PeopleSoft, a market leader in human resource management systems. This move allowed Oracle to offer its customers a complete suite of enterprise software systems to optimize their entire internal value chains.

WHY DO FIRMS MAKE ACQUISITIONS?

LO 9-3

Explain why firms engage in acquisitions.

When first defining the terminology at the beginning of the chapter, we noted that an *acquisition* describes the purchase or takeover of one company by another. Why do firms make acquisitions? Three main reasons stand out:

- To gain access to new markets and distribution channels.
- To gain access to a new capability or competency.
- To preempt rivals.

Firms sometimes make acquisitions to overcome entry barriers. Merging with competitors can allow firms to gain access to new markets and distribution channels. Strategy Highlight 9.1 discusses Kraft's acquisition of Cadbury to tap into new distribution channels in both the U.S. and fast-growing international markets.

Larger firms—such as GE, Cisco, Siemens, and Microsoft—often engage in serial acquisitions to maintain a window on the latest technology developments. These companies

Strategy Highlight 9.1

Food Fight: Kraft's Hostile Takeover of Cadbury

In 2010, Kraft Foods bought its UK-based competitor Cadbury PLC for close to $20 billion in a hostile takeover. Unlike the more diversified food-products company Kraft, Cadbury was focused solely on candy and gum. Hailing back to 1824, Cadbury established itself in markets across the globe, in concert with the British Empire.

Kraft was attracted to Cadbury due to its strong position in countries such as India, Egypt, and Thailand and in fast-growing markets in Latin America. Cadbury held 70 percent of the market share for chocolate in India, with more than one billion people. Children there specifically ask for "Cadbury chocolate" instead of just plain "chocolate." It is difficult for outsiders like Kraft to break into emerging economies because earlier entrants have developed and perfected their distribution systems to meet the needs of millions of small, independent vendors. To secure a strong strategic position in these fast-growing emerging markets, therefore, Kraft felt that horizontal integration with Cadbury was critical. Kraft continues to face formidable competitors in global markets, including Nestlé and Mars (which is especially strong in China where its famous Snickers bar was the official chocolate of the 2008 Olympic Games in Beijing).

In the U.S. market, the Cadbury acquisition allows Kraft greater access to convenience stores, gives it a new distribution channel, and opens a market for it that is growing fast and tends to have high profit margins. To achieve a stronger strategic position in the domestic market, Kraft has to compete with The Hershey Company, the largest U.S. chocolate manufacturer. This battle is intense because Hershey's main strategic focus is on the domestic market. With the U.S. population growing slowly and becoming more health conscious, however, Hershey decided to enter the Chinese market in 2013, the world's fastest-growing candy market. Since its founding in 1894, Hershey's entry into China is the company's first new product launch outside the United States. With Hershey's attention on China, Kraft could have a window of opportunity for gaining market share in the U.S. market.

In 2012, Kraft Foods announced a restructuring. It separated its North American grocery-food business from its fast-growing global snack-food and candy business (including Oreos and Cadbury chocolate), which is now Mondeléz International.[6]

acquire small startups not only to gain access to a new capability or competency, but also to preempt rivals from doing so.

Let's look at the acquisitions made by some of the leading Internet companies: Google, Facebook, and Yahoo.[7] Google, the leader in online search and advertisement, engaged in a number of smaller acquisitions of tech ventures to fill gaps in its competency lineup. In 2006, Google bought YouTube, the video-sharing website, for $1.65 billion. Also motivated by the desire to gain a new capability, Facebook acquired Instagram, a photo and video-sharing social media site, for $1 billion in 2012. Likewise, Yahoo is attempting to fill a gap in its social networking capabilities by acquiring Tumblr for $1.1 billion in 2013.

In 2013, Google purchased the Israeli startup company Waze for $1 billion. Google acquired Waze to gain access to a new capability and to prevent rivals from gaining access. Waze's claim to fame is its interactive mobile map app. Google is already the leader in online maps and wanted to extend this capability to mobile devices. Perhaps even more importantly, Google's intent was to preempt its competitors Apple and Facebook from buying Waze. Apple and Facebook are each comparatively weaker than Google in the increasingly important interactive mobile map and information services segment.

Google engaged in a somewhat larger acquisition when it bought Motorola's cell phone unit for $12.5 billion (in 2011). This was done to gain access to Motorola's valuable patent holdings in mobile technology. The Motorola acquisition also enables Google to integrate hardware and software (Android OS) more seamlessly. In turn, this positions Google better to compete with Apple and Samsung in mobile devices.

M&A AND COMPETITIVE ADVANTAGE

LO 9-4

Evaluate whether mergers and acquisitions lead to competitive advantage.

Do mergers and acquisitions create competitive advantage? Despite their popularity, the answer, surprisingly, is that in most cases they do not. In fact, the M&A performance track record is rather mixed. Most mergers destroy shareholder value because the antici-pated synergies never materialize.[8] If there is any value creation, it generally accrues to the shareholders of the firm that was taken over (the acquiree), because acquirers often pay a premium when buying the target company.[9] Indeed, sometimes companies get involved in a bidding war for an acquisition; the winner may end up with the prize but may have over-paid for the acquisition—thus falling victim to the *winner's curse.*

Given that mergers and acquisitions, on average, destroy rather than create shareholder value, why do we see so many mergers? Reasons include:

■ Principal–agent problems

■ The desire to overcome competitive disadvantage

■ Superior acquisition and integration capability

PRINCIPAL–AGENT PROBLEMS. When discussing diversification in the previous chapter, we noted that some firms diversify through acquisitions due to principal–agent problems.[10] Managers, as agents, are supposed to act in the best interest of the principals, the shareholders. However, managers may have incentives to grow their firms through acquisitions—not for anticipated shareholder value appreciation, but to build a larger empire, which is positively correlated with prestige, power, and pay. Besides providing higher compensation and more corporate perks, a larger organization may also provide more job security, especially if the company pursues unrelated diversification.

managerial hubris
A form of self-delusion in which managers convince themselves of their superior skills in the face of clear evidence to the contrary.

A related problem is **managerial hubris**, a form of self-delusion in which managers convince themselves of their superior skills in the face of clear evidence to the contrary.[11] Managerial hubris comes in two forms:

1. Managers of the acquiring company convince themselves that they are able to manage the business of the target company more effectively and, therefore, create additional share-holder value. This justification is often used for an unrelated diversification strategy.

2. Although most top-level managers are aware that the majority of acquisitions destroy rather than create shareholder value, they see themselves as the exceptions to the rule.

Managerial hubris has led to many ill-fated deals, destroying billions of dol-lars. For example, Quaker Oats Company acquired Snapple because its manag-ers thought Snapple was another Gatorade, which was a successful previous acquisition.[12] The difference was that Gatorade had been a standalone company and was easily integrated, but Snapple relied on a decentralized network of independent distributors and retailers who did not want Snapple to be taken over and who made it difficult and costly for Quaker Oats Company to inte-grate Snapple. The acquisition failed—and Quaker Oats itself was taken over by PepsiCo. Snapple was spun out and eventually ended up being part of the Dr Pepper Snapple Group.

THE DESIRE TO OVERCOME COMPETITIVE DISADVANTAGE. In some instances, mergers are not motivated by gaining competitive advantage, but by overcoming a competitive disadvantage. For example, to compete more successfully with Nike, the worldwide leader in sports shoes and apparel, adidas (#2) acquired Reebok (#3) for $3.8 billion in 2006. This acquisition allowed the now-larger adidas group to benefit from economies of scale and scope that were unachievable when adidas and Reebok operated independently. Overcoming its competitive disadvantage against Nike in turn strengthened adidas' competitive position. Indeed, overcoming a competitive disadvantage may put an organization on the road to gaining a competitive advantage.

SUPERIOR ACQUISITION AND INTEGRATION CAPABILITY. Acquisition and integration capabilities are not equally distributed across firms. Although there is strong evidence that mergers and acquisitions, *on average,* destroy rather than create shareholder value, it does not exclude the possibility that *some* firms are consistently able to identify, acquire, and integrate target companies to strengthen their competitive positions. Since it is valuable, rare, and difficult to imitate, a superior acquisition and integration capability, together with past experience, can lead to competitive advantage.

Cisco Systems, a networking and telecommunications company, is one such firm with an exemplary acquisitions record.[13] To position itself more strongly after the 2001 bursting of the Internet and tech stock bubble, Cisco embarked on an acquisitions-led growth strategy in which it acquired more than 150 technology companies.[14] Through this process, it diversified from computer networking routers to local area networking switching, Voice over IP (Internet telephony), and home networks. While Cisco acquired mainly smaller technology companies, it also acquired several larger firms including Linksys, Scientific Atlanta, and WebEx, now each multibillion-dollar business units in their own right. Cisco buys successful companies, provides them with important complementary assets, and then lets them continue to be successful more or less on their own. Cisco has developed a template to monitor, evaluate, select, buy, and integrate technology ventures. It benefits from learning- and experience-curve effects accumulated through its large number of acquisitions. Because of this superior integration template, Cisco kept the management of the larger firms it acquired and managed the relationships more like strategic alliances than acquisitions.[15]

In stark contrast to Cisco, HP did not have as much expertise in selecting, pricing, and integrating technology acquisitions. HP wrote off completely some of its recent technology acquisitions, taking billions of dollars in losses. In 2011, HP acquired Palm, a pioneer in personal digital assistants (PDAs).[16] HP's strategic intent was to leverage the Palm's webOS mobile operating system into a stronger position in the fast-growing smartphone and tablet-computer markets in order to compete more effectively with Apple's lead. Not even a year later, HP wrote off almost $2 billion and declared the Palm OS acquisition a failure. HP capitulated to Apple, and decided to exit the mobile device industry. Even more disastrous was HP's acquisition of the UK-based enterprise-software company Autonomy. In 2011, HP spent a whopping $11 billion for the company, only to write down $9 billion some two years later.[17]

We now turn to discussing strategic alliances as the second key vehicle for corporate strategy.

9.2 Strategic Alliances

Strategic alliances are voluntary arrangements between firms that involve the sharing of knowledge, resources, and capabilities with the intent of developing processes, products, or services.[18] Firms enter many types of alliances, from small contracts that have no bearing on a firm's competitiveness to multibillion-dollar joint ventures that can make or break the company. An alliance, therefore, qualifies as *strategic* only if it has the potential to affect a firm's competitive advantage.

LO 9-5

Define strategic alliances, and explain why they are important corporate strategy vehicles and why firms enter into them.

strategic alliance A voluntary arrangement between firms that involves the sharing of knowledge, resources, and capabilities with the intent of developing processes, products, or services.

The use of strategic alliances to implement corporate strategy has exploded since the 1980s, with thousands forming each year.[19] Strategic alliances may join complementary parts of a firm's value chain, such as R&D and marketing, or they may focus on joining the same value chain activities. Strategic alliances are attractive because they enable firms to achieve goals faster and at lower costs than going it alone. Globalization has also contributed to an increase in cross-border strategic alliances.

A strategic alliance has the potential to help a firm gain and sustain a competitive advantage when it joins together resources and knowledge in a combination that obeys the VRIO principles (introduced in Chapter 4).[20] The locus of competitive advantage is often not found within the individual firm but within a strategic partnership. According to this **relational view of competitive advantage**, critical resources and capabilities frequently are embedded in strategic alliances that span firm boundaries. Applying the VRIO framework introduced in Chapter 4, we know that the basis for competitive advantage is formed when a strategic alliance creates resource combinations that are valuable, rare, and difficult to imitate, and the alliance is organized appropriately to allow for value capture. In support of this perspective, over 80 percent of Fortune 1000 CEOs indicated in a recent survey that more than one-quarter of their firm's revenues were derived from strategic alliances.[21]

> **relational view of competitive advantage**
> Strategic management framework that proposes that critical resources and capabilities frequently are embedded in strategic alliances that span firm boundaries.

Using a strategic alliance, HP and DreamWorks Animation SKG created the Halo Collaboration Studio, which makes virtual communication possible around the globe.[22] Halo's conferencing technology gives participants the vivid sense that they are in the same room. The conference rooms of clients match, down to the last detail, giving participants the impression that they are sitting together at the same table. DreamWorks produced the computer-animated movie *Shrek 2* using this new technology for its meetings. People with different creative skills—script writers, computer animators, directors—though dispersed geographically, were able to participate as if in the same room, even seeing the work on each other's laptops. Use of the technology enabled faster decision making, enhanced productivity, reduced (or even eliminated) travel time and expense, and increased job satisfaction. Neither HP nor DreamWorks would have been able to produce this technology breakthrough alone, but moving into the videoconferencing arena together via a strategic alliance allowed both partners to pursue related diversification. Moreover, HP's alliance with DreamWorks Animation SKG enabled HP to compete head on with Cisco's high-end videoconferencing solution, TelePresence.[23]

WHY DO FIRMS ENTER STRATEGIC ALLIANCES?

To affect a firm's competitive advantage, an alliance must promise a positive effect on the firm's economic value creation through increasing value and/or lowering costs (see discussion in Chapter 5). This logic is reflected in the common reasons why firms enter alliances.[24] They do so to:

- Strengthen competitive position.
- Enter new markets.
- Hedge against uncertainty.
- Access critical complementary assets.
- Learn new capabilities.

STRENGTHEN COMPETITIVE POSITION. Firms can use strategic alliances to change the industry structure in their favor.[25] Firms frequently use strategic alliances when competing in so-called battles for industry standards (see discussion in Chapter 7).

Strategy Highlight 9.2

Strategic Alliances to Challenge Amazon

In 2007, Amazon established its Kindle device as the dominant e-reader by offering content (e-books, newspapers, and magazines) for instant download at heavily discounted prices. Kindle users paid $9.99 for e-books, including new releases and *The New York Times'* best sellers. Amazon lost money on each e-book sold, because it had to pay publishers between $12.99 and $14.99 per e-book. Still, it was able to leverage this pricing strategy to establish Kindle as the dominant e-reader with 90 percent market share.

Selling below cost is the same pricing strategy Amazon had used successfully when it first established itself as the leading e-tailer in sales of printed books. Amazon's e-book pricing strategy, however, did not sit well with content providers. They did not want to set an expectation in consumers' minds that all e-books should be priced at $9.99. Also, anchoring the e-book prices clearly would have negative repercussions for the sale of printed books, which are priced higher.

Apple crafted a different e-book business model. To attack Amazon's stronghold, Apple orchestrated a web of strategic alliances with major publishing houses such as HarperCollins, Macmillan, McGraw-Hill, and Simon & Schuster prior to launching its iPad product. To incentivize the publishers, Apple offered to let the content providers set the sales prices directly for the end consumers. These alliances aided Apple in populating its iBookstore with much needed content for iPad when it launched in 2010.

The publishers liked this deal. They retained pricing power over e-books, which allowed them to break the customer expectation that e-books should be priced at $9.99. In this agency model, publishers set the retail prices and Apple would take a 30 percent cut. Their alliances with Apple also gave the publishers much needed leverage in negotiations with Amazon. Applying industry structural analysis, the bargaining power of suppliers—in this case, the content providers—increased from Amazon's perspective. In fact, book publishers even threatened to withhold or delay book titles if Amazon would not change its pricing structure. As a result, Amazon reluctantly changed its e-book pricing strategy and now charges between $12.99 and $14.99 for some new releases.

The U.S. Department of Justice suspected collusion between Apple and the book publishers. It alleged that they conspired to fix prices, which is illegal. Although the book publishers settled with the Department of Justice, Apple and the publishers maintained their innocence. Amazon's market share in the e-book readers has dropped from 90 to 60 percent. In July 2013, a federal judge ruled that Apple colluded with five major publishers to drive up prices of e-books.[26]

Or they may also initiate these alliances by themselves to challenge market leaders and thus change the underlying market structure. Strategy Highlight 9.2 shows how Apple orchestrated a web of strategic alliances with publishing houses to challenge Amazon's early lead in the delivery of e-content.

ENTER NEW MARKETS. Firms may use strategic alliances to enter new markets, either in terms of geography or products and services.[27] In some instances, governments such as Saudi Arabia or China may require that foreign firms have a local joint venture partner before doing business in their countries. These cross-border strategic alliances have both benefits and risks. While the foreign firm can benefit from local expertise and contacts, it is exposed to the risk that some of its proprietary know-how may be appropriated by the foreign partner. We will address such issues in the next chapter when studying global strategy.

Microsoft, though the leader in PC-based software, has been struggling for years to gain a foothold in the online search and advertising market. As personal computing moves more and more into the cloud, and PC-based software can be replaced by free online offerings such as Google Docs, it is critical for Microsoft to establish future revenue streams. The new cloud computing market, in which money is made, for example, from the accompanying online advertising, reached $30 billion in 2013.[28]

Although Yahoo's co-founder and then-CEO Jerry Yang rebuffed Microsoft's $48 billion acquisition bid for Yahoo in 2008, Microsoft was able to get a much better deal through a subsequent strategic alliance. In early 2009, Yahoo appointed Carol Bartz as its new CEO, and she almost immediately rekindled negotiations with Microsoft's CEO Steve Ballmer, who suggested a strategic alliance between the two companies. Yahoo and Microsoft formed a partnership through which Yahoo's searches are powered by Microsoft's search engine, Bing. In return, Yahoo gets a portion of the revenues from the search ads sold on its sites. With its technology now powering some 30 percent of all online searches, Microsoft is able to fine-tune Bing. Microsoft can strengthen its competitive position against Google's dominance in online search and advertisement.[29] In the end, this strategic alliance was a low-cost alternative to an acquisition for Microsoft.

But why did Yahoo agree to the deal? It entered this alliance because it had not generated the cash flow necessary to continuously update its own search technology. As a consequence of the lack of adequate cash flow, Yahoo suffered years of a competitive disadvantage, especially in comparison to online search leader Google. Yahoo also churned through a number of CEOs. Carol Bartz was let go in 2011 and replaced by a number of short-term (interim) CEOs. In 2012, Yahoo appointed Marissa Mayer as CEO. Ms. Mayer was hired away from Google, which she had joined in 1999 as employee number 20. When departing for Yahoo, Marissa Mayer was a vice president at Google.

Marissa Mayer, CEO of Yahoo.

HEDGE AGAINST UNCERTAINTY. In dynamic markets, strategic alliances allow firms to limit their exposure to uncertainty in the market.[30] For instance, in the wake of the biotechnology revolution, incumbent pharmaceutical firms such as Pfizer, Novartis, and Roche entered into hundreds of strategic alliances with biotech startups.[31] These alliances allowed the big pharma firms to make small-scale investments in many of the new biotechnology ventures that were poised to disrupt existing market economics. In some sense, the pharma companies were taking *real options* in these biotechnology experiments, providing them with the right but not the obligation to make further investments when new drugs were introduced from the biotech companies.

A **real-options perspective** to strategic decision making breaks down a larger investment decision (such as whether to enter biotechnology or not) into a set of smaller decisions that are staged sequentially over time. This approach allows the firm to obtain additional information at predetermined stages. At each stage, after new information is revealed, the firm evaluates whether or not to make further investments. In a sense, a real option, which is the right, but not the obligation, to continue making investments allows the firm to buy time until sufficient information for a go versus no-go decision is revealed. Once the new biotech drugs were a known quantity, the uncertainty was removed, and the incumbent firms could react accordingly.

For example, in 1990 the Swiss pharma company Roche initially invested $2.1 billion in an equity alliance to purchase a controlling interest (> 50 percent) in the biotech startup Genentech. In 2009, after witnessing the success of Genentech's drug discovery and development projects in subsequent years, Roche spent $47 billion to purchase the remaining minority interest in Genentech, making it a wholly owned subsidiary.[32] Taking a wait-and-see approach by entering strategic alliances allows incumbent firms to buy time and wait for the uncertainty surrounding the market and technology to fade. Many firms in fast-moving markets subscribe to this rationale. Besides biotechnology, it has also been documented in nanotechnology, semiconductors, and other dynamic markets.[33]

ACCESS CRITICAL COMPLEMENTARY ASSETS. The successful commercialization of a new product or service often requires complementary assets such as marketing, manufacturing, and after-sale service.[34] In particular, new firms are in need of complementary assets to complete the value chain from upstream innovation to downstream commercialization. This implies that a new venture that has a core competency in R&D, for example, will need to access distribution channels and marketing expertise to complete the value chain. Building downstream complementary assets such as marketing and regulatory expertise or a sales force is often prohibitively expensive and time-consuming, and thus frequently not an option for new ventures. Strategic alliances allow firms to match complementary skills and resources to complete the value chain. Moreover, licensing agreements of this sort allow the partners to benefit from a division of labor, allowing each to efficiently focus on its core competency.

LEARN NEW CAPABILITIES. Firms enter strategic alliances because they are motivated by the desire to learn new capabilities from their partners.[35] When the collaborating firms are also competitors, *co-opetition* ensues.[36] **Co-opetition** is a portmanteau describing cooperation by competitors. They may cooperate to create a larger pie but then might compete about how the pie should be divided. Such co-opetition can lead to **learning races** in strategic alliances,[37] a situation in which both partners are motivated to form an alliance for learning, but the rate at which the firms learn may vary. The firm that learns faster and accomplishes its goal more quickly has an incentive to exit the alliance or, at a minimum, to reduce its knowledge sharing. Since the cooperating firms are also competitors, learning races can have a positive effect on the winning firm's competitive position vis-à-vis its alliance partner.

NUMMI (New United Motor Manufacturing, Inc.) was the first joint venture in the U.S. automobile industry, formed between GM and Toyota in 1984. Recall from Chapter 8 that joint ventures are a special type of a strategic alliance in which two partner firms create a third, jointly owned entity. In the NUMMI joint venture, each partner was motivated to learn new capabilities: GM entered the strategic alliance to learn the lean manufacturing system pioneered by Toyota in order to produce high-quality, fuel-efficient cars at a profit. Toyota entered the alliance to learn how to implement its lean manufacturing program with an American work force. NUMMI was a test-run for Toyota before building fully owned *greenfield plants* (new manufacturing facilities) in Alabama, Indiana, Kentucky, Texas, and West Virginia. In this 25-year history, GM and Toyota built some seven million high-quality cars at the NUMMI plant. In fact, NUMMI was transformed from worst performer

---

real-options perspective Approach to strategic decision making that breaks down a larger investment decision into a set of smaller decisions that are staged sequentially over time. This approach allows the firm to obtain additional information in pre-determined stages.

co-opetition Cooperation by competitors to achieve a strategic objective.

learning races Situations in which both partners in a strategic alliance are motivated to form an alliance for learning, but the rate at which the firms learn may vary; the firm that accomplishes its goal more quickly has an incentive to exit the alliance or reduce its knowledge sharing.

(under GM ownership prior to the joint venture) to GM's highest-quality plant in the U.S. In the end, as part of GM's bankruptcy reorganization during 2009–2010, it pulled out of the NUMMI joint venture.

The joint venture between GM and Toyota can be seen as a learning race. Who won? Strategy scholars argue that Toyota was faster in accomplishing its alliance goal—learning how to manage U.S. labor—because of its limited scope.[38] Toyota had already perfected lean manufacturing; all it needed to do was learn how to train U.S. workers in the method and transfer this knowledge to its subsidiary plants in the U.S. On the other hand, GM had to learn a completely new production system. GM was successful in transferring lean manufacturing to its newly created Saturn brand (which was discontinued in 2010 as part of GM's reorganization), but it had a hard time implementing lean manufacturing in its *existing* plants. These factors suggest that Toyota won the learning race with GM, which in turn helped Toyota gain and sustain a competitive advantage over GM in the U.S. market.

Also, note that different motivations for forming alliances are not necessarily independent and can be intertwined. For example, firms that collaborate to access critical complementary assets may also want to learn from one another to subsequently pursue vertical integration. In sum, alliance formation is frequently motivated by leveraging economies of scale, scope, specialization, and learning.

GOVERNING STRATEGIC ALLIANCES

LO 9-6

Describe three alliance governance mechanisms and evaluate their pros and cons.

In Chapter 8, we showed that strategic alliances lie in the middle of the make-or-buy continuum (see Exhibit 8.3). Alliances can be governed by the following mechanisms—contractual agreements for:

- Non-equity alliances
- Equity alliances
- Joint ventures[39]

Exhibit 9.2 provides an overview of the key characteristics of the three alliance types, including their advantages and disadvantages.

non-equity alliance Partnership based on contracts between firms. The most frequent forms are *supply agreements, distribution agreements,* and *licensing agreements.*

explicit knowledge Knowledge that can be codified (e.g., information, facts, instructions, recipes); concerns *knowing about* a process or product.

NON-EQUITY ALLIANCES. The most common type of alliance is a **non-equity alliance**, which is based on contracts between firms. The most frequent forms of non-equity alliances are *supply agreements, distribution agreements,* and *licensing agreements.* As suggested by their names, these contractual agreements are vertical strategic alliances, connecting different parts of the industry value chain. In a non-equity alliance, firms tend to share **explicit knowledge**—knowledge that can be codified. Patents, user manuals, fact sheets, and scientific publications are all ways to capture explicit knowledge, which concerns the notion of *knowing about* a certain process or product.

Licensing agreements are contractual alliances in which the participants regularly exchange codified knowledge. The biotech firm Genentech licensed its newly developed drug Humulin (human insulin) to the pharmaceutical firm Eli Lilly for manufacturing, facilitating approval by the Food and Drug Administration (FDA), and distribution. This partnership was an example of a vertical strategic alliance: one partner (Genentech) was positioned upstream in the industry value chain focusing on R&D, while the other partner (Eli Lilly) was positioned downstream focusing on manufacturing and distribution. This type of vertical arrangement is often described as a "hand-off" from the upstream partner to the downstream partner, and is possible because the underlying knowledge is largely explicit and can be easily codified. When Humulin reached the market in 1982, it was the first approved genetically engineered human therapeutic worldwide.[40] Subsequently, Humulin became a billion-dollar blockbuster drug.

EXHIBIT 9.2 / Key Characteristics of Different Alliance Types

Alliance Type	Governance Mechanism	Frequency	Type of Knowledge Exchanged	Pros	Cons	Examples
Non-equity (supply, licensing, and distribution agreements)	Contract	Most common	Explicit	• Flexible • Fast • Easy to initiate and terminate	• Weak tie • Lack of trust and commitment	• Genentech–Lilly (exclusive) licensing agreement for Humulin • Microsoft–IBM (non-exclusive) licensing agreement for MS-DOS
Equity (purchase of an equity stake or corporate venture capital, CVC investment)	Equity investment	Less common than non-equity alliances, but more common than joint ventures	Explicit; exchange of tacit knowledge possible	• Stronger tie • Trust and commitment can emerge • Window into new technology (option value)	• Less flexible • Slower • Can entail significant investments	• Renault–Nissan alliance based on cross equity holdings, with Renault owning 44.4% in Nissan; and Nissan owning 15% in Renault • Roche's equity investment in Genentech (prior to full integration)
Joint venture (JV)	Creation of new entity by two or more parent firms	Least common	Both tacit and explicit knowledge exchanged	• Strongest tie • Trust and commitment likely to emerge • May be required by institutional setting	• Can entail long negotiations and significant investments • Long-term solution • JV managers have double reporting lines (2 bosses)	• Hulu, JV owned by NBC, Fox, and ABC • Dow Corning, JV owned by Dow Chemical and Corning

Because of their contractual nature, non-equity alliances are flexible and easy to initiate and terminate. However, because they can be temporary in nature, they also sometimes produce weak ties between the alliance partners, which can result in a lack of trust and commitment.

EQUITY ALLIANCES. In an **equity alliance**, at least one partner takes partial ownership in the other partner. Equity alliances are less common than contractual, non-equity alliances because they often require larger investments. Because they are based on partial

equity alliance
Partnership in which at least one partner takes partial ownership in the other.

ownership rather than contracts, equity alliances are used to signal stronger commitments. Moreover, equity alliances allow for the sharing of **tacit knowledge**—knowledge that cannot be codified.[41] Tacit knowledge concerns *knowing how* to do a certain task. It can be acquired only through actively participating in the process. In an equity alliance, therefore, the partners frequently exchange personnel to make the acquisition of tacit knowledge possible.

Toyota is using an equity alliance with Tesla Motors, a designer and developer of electric cars, to learn new knowledge and gain a window into new technology. In 2010, Toyota made a $50 million equity investment in the California startup company. In the same year, Tesla Motors purchased the NUMMI plant in Fremont, California, where it now manufactures its Model S sedan. Tesla's CEO Elon Musk stated, "The Tesla factory effectively leverages an ideal combination of hardcore Silicon Valley engineering talent, traditional automotive engineering talent and the proven Toyota production system."[42] Toyota in turn hopes to infuse its company with Tesla's entrepreneurial spirit. Toyota President Akio Toyoda commented that "by partnering with Tesla, my hope is that all Toyota employees will recall that 'venture business spirit' and take on the challenges of the future."[43] Mr. Toyoda hopes that a transfer of tacit knowledge will take place, in which Tesla's entrepreneurial spirit reinvigorates Toyota.[44]

Another governance mechanism that falls under the broad rubric of equity alliances is **corporate venture capital (CVC)** investments, which are equity investments by established firms in entrepreneurial ventures.[45] The value of CVC investments is estimated to be in the double-digit billion-dollar range each year. Larger firms frequently have dedicated CVC units, such as Dow Venture Capital, Siemens Venture Capital, Kaiser Permanente Ventures, and Johnson & Johnson Development Corporation. Rather than hoping primarily for financial gains, as venture capitalists traditionally do, CVC investments create real options in terms of gaining access to new, and potentially disruptive, technologies.[46] Strategy scholars find that CVC investments have a positive impact on value creation for the investing firm, especially in high-tech industries such as semiconductors, computing, and the medical-device sector.[47]

Taken together, equity alliances tend to produce stronger ties and greater trust between partners than non-equity alliances do. They also offer a window into new technology that, like a real option, can be exercised if successful or abandoned if not promising. Equity alliances are frequently stepping stones toward full integration of the partner firms either through

---

tacit knowledge
Knowledge that cannot be codified; concerns *knowing how* to do a certain task and can be acquired only through active participation in that task.

corporate venture capital (CVC) Equity investments by established firms in entrepreneurial ventures; CVC falls under the broader rubric of equity alliances.

joint venture A standalone organization created and jointly owned by two or more parent companies.

alliance management capability A firm's ability to effectively manage three alliance-related tasks concurrently: (1) partner selection and alliance formation, (2) alliance design and governance, and (3) post-formation alliance management.

a merger or an acquisition. Essentially, they are often used as a "try before you buy" strategic option.[48] The downside of equity alliances is the amount of investment that can be involved, as well as a possible lack of flexibility and speed in putting together the partnership.

JOINT VENTURES. A **joint venture** (JV) is a standalone organization created and jointly owned by two or more parent companies (as discussed in Chapter 8). For example, Hulu (a video-on-demand service) is jointly owned by NBC, ABC, and Fox. Since partners contribute equity to a joint venture, they are making a long-term commitment. Exchange of both explicit and tacit knowledge through interaction of personnel is typical. Joint ventures are also frequently used to enter foreign markets where the host country requires such a partnership to gain access to the market in exchange for advanced technology and know-how. In terms of frequency, joint ventures are the least common of the three types of strategic alliances.

The advantages of joint ventures are the strong ties, trust, and commitment that can result between the partners. However, they can entail long negotiations and significant investments. If the alliance doesn't work out as expected, undoing the JV can take some time and involve considerable cost. A further risk is that knowledge shared with the new partner could be misappropriated by opportunistic behavior. Finally, any rewards from the collaboration must be shared between the partners.

ALLIANCE MANAGEMENT CAPABILITY

Strategic alliances create a paradox for managers. Although alliances appear to be necessary to compete in many industries, between 30 and 70 percent of all strategic alliances do not deliver the expected benefits, and are considered failures by at least one alliance partner.[49] Given the high failure or, at least, disappointment rate, effective alliance management is critical to gaining and sustaining a competitive advantage, especially in high-technology industries.[50]

Alliance management capability is a firm's ability to effectively manage three alliance-related tasks concurrently, often across a portfolio of many different alliances (see Exhibit 9.3):[51]

- Partner selection and alliance formation
- Alliance design and governance
- Post-formation alliance management

PARTNER SELECTION AND ALLIANCE FORMATION. When making the business case for an alliance, the expected benefits of the alliance must exceed its costs. When one or more of the five reasons for alliance formation are present—to strengthen competitive position, enter new markets, hedge against uncertainty, access critical complementary resources, or learn new capabilities—the firm must select the best possible alliance partner.

LO 9-7

Describe the three phases of alliance management and explain how an alliance management capability can lead to a competitive advantage.

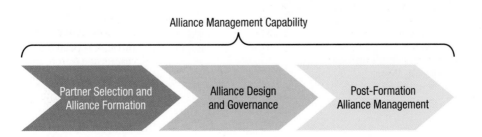

EXHIBIT 9.3

Alliance Management Capability

Partner compatibility and partner commitment are necessary conditions for successful alliance formation.[52] *Partner compatibility* captures aspects of cultural fit between different firms. *Partner commitment* concerns the willingness to make available necessary resources and to accept short-term sacrifices to ensure long-term rewards.

ALLIANCE DESIGN AND GOVERNANCE. Once two or more firms agree to pursue an alliance, managers must then design the alliance and choose an appropriate governance mechanism from among the three options: non-equity contractual agreement, equity alliances, or joint venture. For example, in a study of over 640 alliances, researchers found that the joining of specialized complementary assets increases the likelihood that the alliance is governed hierarchically. This effect is stronger in the presence of uncertainties concerning the alliance partner as well as the envisioned tasks.[53]

In addition to the formal governance mechanisms, *inter-organizational trust* is a critical dimension of alliance success.[54] Because all contracts are necessarily incomplete, trust between the alliance partners plays an important role for effective post-formation alliance management. Effective governance, therefore, can be accomplished only by skillfully combining formal and informal mechanisms.

POST-FORMATION ALLIANCE MANAGEMENT. The third phase in a firm's alliance management capability concerns the ongoing management of the alliance. To be a source of competitive advantage, the partnership needs to create resource combinations that obey the VRIO criteria. As shown in Exhibit 9.4, this can be most likely accomplished if the alliance partners *make relation-specific investments, establish knowledge-sharing routines,* and *build interfirm trust.*[55]

Trust is a critical aspect of any alliance. Interfirm trust entails the expectation that each alliance partner will behave in good faith and develop norms of reciprocity and fairness.[56] Such trust helps ensure that the relationship survives and thereby increases the possibility of meeting the intended goals of the alliance. Interfirm trust is also important for fast decision making.[57] Several firms such as Eli Lilly, HP, Procter & Gamble, and IBM compete to obtain trustworthy reputations in order to become the alliance "partner of choice" for small technology ventures, universities, and individual inventors.

Indeed, the systematic differences in firms' alliance management capability can be a source of competitive advantage.[58] But how do firms go about building alliance management capability? The answer is to build capability through repeated experiences over time. In support of this idea, several empirical studies have shown that firms move down the learning curve and become better at managing alliances through repeated alliance exposure.[59]

The "learning-by-doing" approach has value for small ventures in which a few key people coordinate most of the firms' activities.[60] However, there

EXHIBIT 9.4 / How to Make Alliances Work

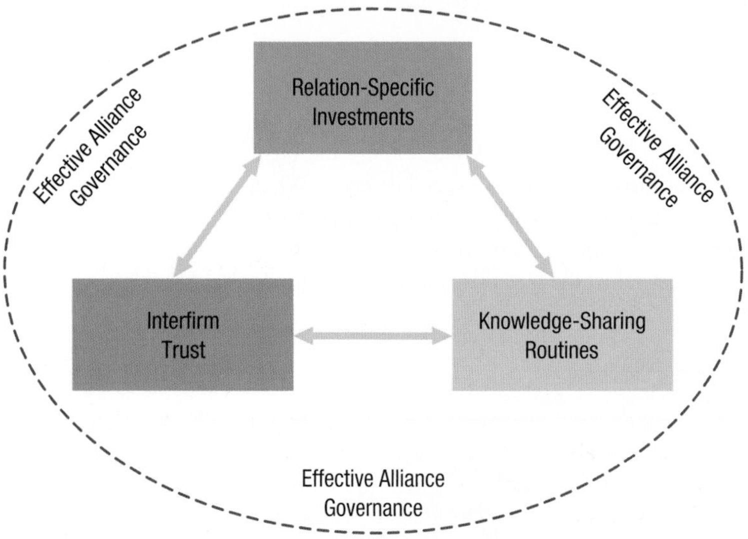

SOURCE: Adapted from J. H. Dyer and H. Singh (1998), "The relational view: Cooperative strategy and the sources of intraorganizational advantage," *Academy of Management Review* 23: 660–679.

are clearly limitations for larger companies. Firms such as ABB, GE, Philips, or Siemens are engaged in hundreds of alliances simultaneously. In fact, if alliances are not managed from a portfolio perspective at the corporate level, serious negative repercussions can emerge.[61] Groupe Danone, a large French food conglomerate, lost its leading position in the highly lucrative and fast-growing Chinese market because its local alliance partner, Hangzhou Wahaha Group, terminated their long-standing alliance.[62] Wahaha accused different Danone business units of subsequently setting up partnerships with other Chinese firms that were a direct competitive threat to Wahaha. This example makes it clear that although alliances are important pathways by which to pursue business-level strategy, they are best managed at the corporate level.

To accomplish effective alliance management, strategy scholars suggest that firms create a *dedicated alliance function,*[63] led by a vice president or director of alliance management and endowed with its own resources and support staff. The dedicated alliance function should be given the tasks of coordinating all alliance-related activity in the entire organization, taking a corporate-level perspective. It should serve as a repository of prior experience and be responsible for creating processes and structures to teach and leverage that experience and related knowledge throughout the rest of the organization across all levels. Research shows that firms with a dedicated alliance function are able to create value from their alliances above and beyond what could be expected based on experience alone.[64]

Pharmaceutical company Eli Lilly is an acknowledged leader in alliance management.[65] Lilly's Office of Alliance Management, led by a director and endowed with several managers, manages its far-flung alliance activity across all hierarchical levels and around the globe. Lilly's process prescribes that each alliance is managed by a three-person team: an alliance champion, alliance leader, and alliance manager.

- The *alliance champion* is a senior, corporate-level executive responsible for high-level support and oversight. This senior manager is also responsible for making sure that the alliance fits within the firm's existing alliance portfolio and corporate-level strategy.

- The *alliance leader* has the technical expertise and knowledge needed for the specific technical area and is responsible for the day-to-day management of the alliance.

- The *alliance manager,* positioned within the Office of Alliance Management, serves as an alliance process resource and business integrator between the two alliance partners, and provides alliance training and development, as well as diagnostic tools.

Some companies are also able to leverage the relational capabilities obtained through managing alliance portfolios into a successful acquisition strategy.[66] As detailed earlier, Eli Lilly has an entire department at the corporate level devoted to managing its alliance portfolio. Following up on an earlier 50/50 joint venture formed with Icos, maker of the $1 billion-plus erectile-dysfunction drug Cialis, Lilly acquired Icos in 2007. Just a year later, Eli Lilly outmaneuvered Bristol-Myers Squibb to acquire biotech venture ImClone for $6.5 billion. ImClone discovered and developed the cancer-fighting drug Erbitux, also a $1 billion blockbuster in terms of annual sales. The acquisition of these two smaller biotech ventures allowed Lilly to address its problem of an empty drug pipeline.[67]

Strategy researchers, therefore, have suggested that corporate-level managers should not only coordinate the firm's portfolio of alliances, but also leverage their relationships to successfully engage in mergers and acquisitions.[68] That is, rather than focusing on developing an alliance management capability in isolation, firms should develop a *relational capability* that allows for the successful management of both strategic alliances *and* mergers and acquisitions.

9.3 ◀▶ Implications for the Strategist

LO 9-8

Apply the build-borrow-or-buy framework to guide corporate strategy.

The business environment is constantly changing.[69] New opportunities come and go quickly. Firms often need to develop new resources, capabilities, or competencies to take advantage of opportunities. Examples abound. Traditional book publishers must transform themselves into digital content companies. Old-line banking institutions with expensive networks of branches must now offer seamless online banking services. They must make them work between a set of traditional and non-traditional payment services on a mobile platform. Energy providers are in the process of changing their coal-fired power plants to gas-fired ones in the wake of the shale gas boom. Pharmaceutical companies need to take advantage of advances in biotechnology to drive future growth. Food companies are now expected to offer organic, all natural, gluten-free products.

The strategist also knows that firms need to grow to survive and prosper, especially if they are publicly traded stock companies. A firm's corporate strategy is critical in pursuing growth. To be able to grow as well as gain and sustain a competitive advantage, a firm must not only possess VRIO resources but also be able to leverage existing resources and build new ones. The question of how to build new resources, capabilities, and competencies to grow your enterprise lies at the center of corporate strategy.

As a strategist, you have three options at your disposal to drive firm growth: organic growth through internal development, external growth through alliances, or external growth through acquisitions. Laurence Capron and Will Mitchell have developed an insightful step-by-step decision model to guide strategists in selecting the most appropriate corporate strategy vehicle.[70] Selecting the most appropriate vehicle for corporate strategy in response to a specific strategic challenge also makes implementation success more likely.

build-borrow-or-buy framework
Conceptual model that aids strategists in deciding whether to pursue internal development (build), enter a contract arrangement or strategic alliance (borrow), or acquire new resources, capabilities, and competencies (buy).

The **build-borrow-or-buy framework** provides a conceptual model that aids strategists in deciding whether to pursue internal development (*build*), enter a contract arrangement or strategic alliance (*borrow*), or acquire new resources, capabilities, and competencies (*buy*). Firms that are able to learn how to select the right pathways to obtain new resources are more likely to gain and sustain a competitive advantage. Note that in the borrow-build-or-buy model, the term *resources* is defined broadly to also include capabilities and competencies. Exhibit 9.5 shows the *build-borrow-or-buy* decision framework.

The starting point is management's identification of a strategic resource gap that will impede future growth. The resource gap is *strategic* because closing this gap is likely to lead to a competitive advantage. Also, as we learned in Chapter 4, the required resources with the potential to lead to competitive advantage cannot be simply bought on the open market. This is because any firm could buy this simple resource, negating any potential for competitive advantage. The options to close the strategic resource gap are, therefore, to build, borrow, or buy (through an acquisition).

After a strategic resource gap has been identified, the first decision question the strategist needs to pose is: *Are the firm's internal resources relevant?* The strategist first needs to consider the firm's existing resources. As shown in Exhibit 9.5, if the firm's internal resources are highly relevant, the firm should itself build the new resources needed, through internal development. How does the strategist know whether the firm's resources are relevant in addressing the new challenge or opportunity? A firm's internal resources are relevant if they are (1) *similar to those you need to develop* and (2) *superior to those of competitors in the targeted area.*[71] If both conditions are met, then the firm's internal resources are relevant and the strategist should pursue internal development.

Let's look at both conditions. Often strategists are misled by the first test because things that might appear similar at the surface are actually quite different deep down.[72] Moreover, managers have a tendency to focus on the similarities they know rather than on the

EXHIBIT 9.5 / How to Implement Corporate Strategy: The Build-Borrow-or-Buy Framework

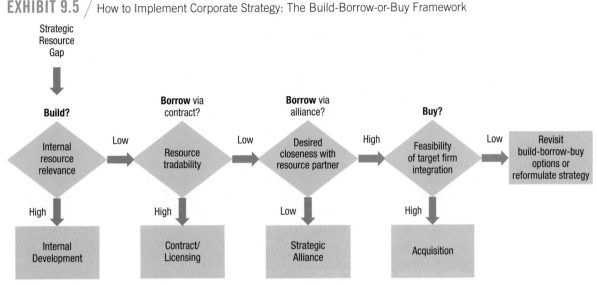

SOURCE: Adapted from L. Capron and W. Mitchell (2012), *Build, Borrow, or Buy: Solving the Growth Dilemma* (Boston, MA: Harvard Business Review Press).

differences. They often don't know how the resources needed for the existing and new business opportunity differ. A strategist in a newspaper publisher might conclude that the researching, reporting, writing, and editing for a printed newspaper are identical to those activities for an online one. Although there are some similarities, there are also some major differences. The underlying business model and technology for online publishing are radically different from traditional print media. Managing the community interactions of online publishing as well as applying data analytics to understand website traffic are also elements that are entirely new. To make the challenge greater, online news reporting is required in real time, 24/7, 365 days a year.

The second test, *whether your internal resources are superior to those of competitors in the targeted area,* can best be assessed by applying the VRIO framework (see Exhibit 4.6). In the case of the print publisher, the answer to both questions is likely a "no." This implies that building the new resource through internal development is not an option. The strategist then needs to consider external—borrow or buy—options. This then leads us to the next question.

As shown in Exhibit 9.5, the second decision question the strategist needs to pose is: *Are the targeted resources tradable?* The term *tradable* implies that you are able to source the resource externally through a contract that allows for the transfer of ownership or use of the resource. Short-term as well as long-term contracts such as licensing or franchising are a way to *borrow* resources from another company (see discussion in Chapter 8). As detailed earlier, Eli Lilly has commercialized several breakthrough biotech drugs using licensing agreements with new ventures. For the strategist, the implication is that if a resource is highly tradable (such as transfer from R&D to manufacturing in the biotech-pharma example), then the resource should be *borrowed* via a licensing agreement or other contractual agreement. If the resource in question is not easily tradable, then the strategist needs to consider either a deeper strategic alliance or an outright acquisition.

The third decision question is (see Exhibit 9.5): *How close do you need to be with your resource partner?* Many times, firms are able to obtain the required resources to fill the strategic gap through more integrated strategic alliances such as equity alliances or joint ventures (see Exhibit 8.3) rather than through outright acquisition. As discussed earlier, mergers and acquisitions are the most costly, complex, and difficult to reverse strategic option. This implies that only if extreme closeness to the resource partner is necessary in order to understand and obtain its underlying knowledge should M&A be considered the *buy* option. Regardless, the strategist should always first consider *borrowing* the necessary resources through integrated strategic alliances before looking at M&A.

The final decision question is (see Exhibit 9.5): *Can you integrate the target firm?* Many firms fail with post-merger integration. The list of post-integration failure, often due to cultural differences, is long. We briefly highlighted the Daimler-Chrysler integration failure; other costly integration failures include AOL and TimeWarner, HP and Autonomy, and Bank of America and Merrill Lynch.

Only if the three prior conditions shown in the decision tree in Exhibit 9.5 are met should the strategist consider M&A: If the firm's internal resources are insufficient to *build, and* the resource needed to fill the strategic gap cannot be *borrowed* through a strategic alliance, *and* closeness to the resource partner is needed, then the final question for the strategist to consider is whether the integration of the two firms in M&A will be successful. In all other cases, the firms should consider finding a less costly *borrow* arrangement when *building* is not an option.

We now have concluded our discussion of corporate strategy. Acquisitions and alliances are the key vehicles to execute corporate strategy, each with its distinct advantages and disadvantages. It is also clear from this chapter that mergers and acquisitions, as well as strategic alliances, are a global phenomenon. In the next chapter, we discuss strategy in a global world.

CHAPTER**CASE 9** / Consider This . . .

UNDER CEO ROBERT IGER, Disney has followed an acquisition-led growth strategy. This corporate strategy turned Disney into a more diversified company. Revenue streams from its various activities (box office, home entertainment, theme parks, cable TV, toys, licensing, and so on) have become more stable and predictable. Being more diversified also allowed Disney to compensate more easily for losses from flops such as the sci-fi movie *John Carter*.

Disney has also shown superior post-merger integration capabilities after acquiring Pixar, Marvel, and Lucasfilm. Disney managed its new subsidiaries more like alliances rather than attempting full integration (which could have destroyed the unique value of the acquisitions). In Pixar's case, Disney kept the entire creative team in place and allowed them to continue to work in Pixar's headquarters near San Francisco with minimum interference. The hands-off approach paid huge dividends: Although Disney paid a steep $7.4 billion for Pixar, it made

some $10 billion on Pixar's *Toy Story 3* franchise revenues alone. As a consequence, Disney has gained a competitive advantage over its rivals such as Sony, and has also outperformed the Dow Jones Industrial Average over the last few years by a wide margin.

There are clouds on the horizon, however. The media industry is being disrupted: People spend much less time and money watching movies on the large screen, and spend more time consuming content online via YouTube, Netflix, Hulu, and other streaming services. The only large-screen movies that have done well recently are sequels in existing franchises such as Sony's *Skyfall*, the 23rd installment in the James Bond saga, Warner Bros.' Batman sequel *The Dark Knight Rises,* and Disney's own sequels in the Pixar and Marvel brands. Soon Disney will be adding the next installment in the *Star Wars* trilogy.

Questions

1. Why do you think Disney was so successful with the Pixar and Marvel acquisitions, while other media interactions such as Sony's acquisition of Columbia Pictures or News Corp.'s acquisition of MySpace were much less successful?

2. Given the "build-borrow-or-buy" framework discussed in the *Implications for the Strategist* section, do you think Disney should pursue alternatives to acquisitions? Why or why not?

3. Do you think Disney's acquisition-led growth strategy is sustainable? Are there sufficient "Mini-Disneys" that Disney can acquire?

4. What effects do you expect from the continued disruption of the media industry on Disney? How should Disney respond?

TAKE-AWAY CONCEPTS

This chapter discussed two mechanisms of corporate-level strategy (acquisitions and alliances), as summarized by the following learning objectives and related take-away concepts.

LO 9-1 / Differentiate between mergers and acquisitions, and explain why firms would use either as a vehicle for corporate strategy.

- A merger describes the joining of two independent companies to form a combined entity.

- An acquisition describes the purchase or takeover of one company by another. It can be friendly or hostile.

- Although there is a distinction between mergers and acquisitions, many observers simply use the umbrella term "mergers and acquisitions," or M&A.

- Firms can use M&A activity for competitive advantage when they possess a superior relational capability, which is often built on superior alliance management capability.

LO 9-2 / Define horizontal integration and evaluate the advantages and disadvantages of this corporate-level strategy.

- Horizontal integration is the process of merging with competitors, leading to industry consolidation.

- As a corporate strategy, firms use horizontal integration to (1) reduce competitive intensity, (2) lower costs, and (3) increase differentiation.

LO 9-3 / Explain why firms engage in acquisitions.

- Firms engage in acquisitions to (1) access new markets and distributions channels, (2) gain access to a new capability or competency, and (3) preempt rivals.

LO 9-4 / Evaluate whether mergers and acquisitions lead to competitive advantage.

- Most mergers and acquisitions destroy shareholder value because anticipated synergies never materialize.

- If there is any value creation in M&A, it generally accrues to the shareholders of the firm that is taken over (the acquiree), because acquirers often pay a premium when buying the target company.

- Mergers and acquisitions are a popular vehicle for corporate-level strategy implementation for three reasons: (1) because of principal–agent problems, (2) the desire to overcome competitive disadvantage, and (3) the quest for superior acquisition and integration capability.

LO 9-5 / Define strategic alliances, and explain why they are important corporate strategy vehicles and why firms enter into them.

- Strategic alliances have the goal of sharing knowledge, resources, and capabilities in order to develop processes, products, or services.

- An alliance qualifies as strategic if it has the potential to affect a firm's competitive advantage by increasing value and/or lowering costs.

- The most common reasons why firms enter alliances are to (1) strengthen competitive position, (2) enter new markets, (3) hedge against uncertainty, (4) access critical complementary resources, and (5) learn new capabilities.

LO 9-6 / Describe three alliance governance mechanisms and evaluate their pros and cons.

- Alliances can be governed by the following mechanisms: contractual agreements for non-equity alliances, equity alliances, and joint ventures.

- Exhibit 9.2 presents the pros and cons of each alliance governance mechanism.

LO 9-7 / Describe the three phases of alliance management and explain how an alliance management capability can lead to a competitive advantage.

- An alliance management capability can be a source of competitive advantage.

- An alliance management capability consists of a firm's ability to effectively manage three alliance-related tasks concurrently: (1) partner selection and alliance formation, (2) alliance design and governance, and (3) post-formation alliance management.

- Firms build a superior alliance management capability through "learning-by-doing" and by establishing a dedicated alliance function.

LO 9-8 / Apply the build-borrow-or-buy framework to guide corporate strategy.

- The build-borrow-or-buy framework provides a conceptual model that aids strategists in deciding whether to pursue internal development (build), enter a contract arrangement or strategic alliance (borrow), or acquire new resources, capabilities, and competencies (buy).

- Firms that are able to learn how to select the right pathways to obtain new resources are more likely to gain and sustain a competitive advantage.

KEY TERMS

Acquisition
Alliance management capability
Build-borrow-or-buy framework
Co-opetition
Corporate venture capital (CVC)
Equity alliance

Explicit knowledge
Horizontal integration
Hostile takeover
Joint venture
Learning races
Managerial hubris
Merger

Non-equity alliance
Real-options perspective
Relational view of competitive advantage
Strategic alliance
Tacit knowledge

DISCUSSION QUESTIONS

1. Horizontal integration has benefits to the firms involved. Consider the consolidation in the event-promotion business when Live Nation bought Ticketmaster. List some specific advantages of this acquisition for Live Nation. Do you see any downside to the merger?

2. The chapter distinguishes between "merging with competitors" (or horizontal integration) and the acquisitions of smaller companies, often tech ventures. Do you expect there to be a difference in the failure rate? Why or why not? Which concepts introduced in Chapter 6 (when discussing cost drivers) could help in lowering the failure rate of serial acquisitions?

3. The chapter identifies three governing mechanisms for strategic alliances: non-equity, equity, and joint venture. Provide the benefits and downsides for each of these mechanisms.

4. An alliance's purpose can affect which governance structure is optimal. Compare a

pharmaceutical R&D alliance with a prescription-drug marketing agreement, and recommend a governing mechanism for each. Provide reasons for your selections.

5. Alliances are often used to pursue business-level goals, but they may be managed at the corporate level. Explain why this portfolio approach to alliance management would make sense.

ETHICAL/SOCIAL ISSUES

1. If mergers and acquisitions quite often end up providing a competitive disadvantage, why do so many of them take place? Given the poor track record, is the continuing M&A activity a result of principal–agent problems and managerial hubris? What can be done to overcome principal–agent problems? Are there other reasons for poor performance?

2. Alliances and acquisitions can sometimes lead to less access or higher prices for consumers. Comcast bought NBC Universal (from GE). When one content provider and the Internet access provider are the same, will this lead to some content being favored over others on the Internet? For example, will Comcast want to send Universal movies (which it owns) with faster download capabilities than it sends, say, a Harry Potter movie from Warner Brothers (which it doesn't own)? If you were a Comcast executive, would you want to favor the speed of your own content delivery versus other content providers, including Netflix?[73]

3. IKEA is the world's largest furniture retailer. It has many non-equity alliances with suppliers and manufacturers around the world. IKEA also makes strategic use of non-equity alliances and stakeholder partnerships to participate in finding solutions to social and environmental challenges. For example, IKEA has had long-standing relationships with Save the Children, UNICEF (United Nations Children's Fund), and the WWF (World Wildlife Fund, the global conservation organization). Go to IKEA's website and use your Internet search expertise to find more information about these and other active partnerships. In what ways does IKEA participate? What projects have shown success? How do these partnerships relate to maintaining IKEA's competitive advantage as the world's largest furniture retailer?

SMALL-GROUP EXERCISES

//// Small-Group Exercise 1

In this chapter, we studied horizontal integration and the build-borrow-or-buy framework. One industry currently anticipating a wave of consolidation is the furniture manufacturing industry, with thousands of manufacturers and suppliers. Manufacturers range from large recognizable brands such as Baker, Steelcase, and La-Z-Boy, to small family-owned companies. Demand for both office furniture and residential furniture is beginning to experience post-recession growth. Analysts have observed that companies are shopping for acquisitions just as consumers are shopping for furniture.

The Charter Group in Grand Rapids, Michigan, is a mergers and acquisitions adviser helping companies initiate, negotiate, and close deals on one company's purchase of another. To take advantage of the increase in M&A activity in the furniture manufacturing industry, The Charter Group launched a dedicated furniture practice in 2013. Western Michigan is home to the top three office furniture manufacturers, which is a key segment of the industry. The sales of the top three make up half of the industry's $10 billion market.

The Charter Group has hired your small consulting team to do the basic research regarding a client that has recently approached them. The client is a small manufacturer of office furniture in a medium-sized town in Michigan. The managers are seeking advice as they decide whether to upgrade capabilities in order to expand sales, to find a partner with complementary skills, or to sell to a larger company. The owner has stated that the firm is like a family, and he feels a sense of loyalty to the workers and the community. The firm has had steady sales over its history, although it experienced a slight dip in sales during the recession. The company is aware that other office furniture manufacturers are beginning to integrate technology into the furniture. For example, one competitor is building wireless technology into desk surfaces to power several devices at one time and avoid the need to plug them in. The owner sees the integration of technology as a game changer.

Using the build-borrow-or-buy framework and other strategic concepts, develop a set of questions to ask the managers of this small business in order to gather information to inform the decision as to whether to hire new employees with more sophisticated technology expertise in order to build capabilities in-house or whether to partner with another firm that already has these capabilities. Alternatively, consider information that could help the owner decide whether this is the time to sell to a larger company. Your consulting team will need adequate information to help put a value on the firm in order to advise The Charter Group if/when it initiates a search for a partner or buyer.

//// Small-Group Exercise 2

The global public relations and communications firm Burson-Marsteller conducted its first study of how the Fortune Global 100 used social media in 2010. It found that 79 percent of the 100 largest companies used Twitter, Facebook, YouTube, or corporate blogs to communicate corporate messages to customers and other stakeholders. Burson-Marsteller wanted to learn how the largest global companies had changed their usage of social media after two years of experience and conducted *The Global Social Media Check-Up 2012.*

The 2012 study focused on the Fortune Global 100 companies' social media activity on Twitter, Facebook, YouTube, Google Plus, and Pinterest. The findings show that companies have gained experience and adapted quickly. Twitter is the most popular platform, as tweets have exploded from 50 million tweets per day in 2010 to 340 million per day in 2012 (over 1 billion every three days). Because of this popularity, 82 percent of the companies have Twitter accounts (up from 65 percent in 2010), and 79 percent are actively engaged in retweeting or @mentions. YouTube has seen the most growth in

company usage—79 percent of companies create original content to use on YouTube (up from 50 percent) and average 2 million viewers. Companies are also reacting faster to new social media platforms; Google Plus was launched in November 2011, and 48 percent of the largest companies had accounts by March 2012. Another new platform, Pinterest, is joined by invitation, and 48 percent of the Global 100 have accounts.

The study found that companies now have more accounts on each platform. For example, they may have many Twitter accounts or Facebook pages established in order to communicate more effectively to different stakeholder interests and to highlight different products or services. The companies can provide general news or more specific information about career opportunities or customer service.

The research firm also observed changes in its findings by region (North America, Europe, Asia-Pacific, and Latin America) and network. Twitter is now the most popular platform for Latin American companies, used by 53 percent of them (up from 32 percent in 2010), and 65 percent use at least one social media platform (up from 49 percent in 2010). Europe has more challenges in efficiently using social media because of multiple languages; however, Vodafone has separate Facebook accounts for each country, while others engage in more common languages, such as English and French. Asia-Pacific companies are catching up, but tend to use different social media, such as micro blogs, social networks, corporate blogs, and video sharing. Video sharing allows visual storytelling and can be used across countries.[74]

In your group, select three firms and research their social media web presence. If you select firms from the same industry, you can more directly compare and contrast their social media expertise.

1. Do the firms seem to do a good job of managing their web identity? If you chose firms from the same industry, is it evident how each firm's web content relates to its competitive position?

2. What differences do you find among the three firms? For example, do some tailor their message for different stakeholders? Are some firms more creative in generating YouTube content?

3. Pinterest is newer than the other platforms and requires an invite to join. Do any of the three firms you selected have a Pinterest account?

STRATEGY TERM PROJECT

//// Module 9: Strategic Alliance and M&A Strategy

In this section, you will study your selected firm's use of acquisitions and alliances to grow or change its business.

1. Has your firm participated in any mergers or acquisitions in the past three years? What was the nature of these actions? Did they result in a consolidation of competitors?

2. Research what strategic alliances your firm has entered in the past three years. If there are several of these, choose the three you identify as the most important for further analysis. Based on company press releases and business journal reports for each alliance, what do you find to be the main reason the firm entered these alliances?

3. Do you think each of the three alliances achieves the original intent, and therefore is successful? Why or why not?

4. Does your firm have an identifiable alliance management organization? Can you find any evidence that this organization improves the likelihood of success for these alliances? What responsibilities does this alliance management organization have in your firm?

5. Go to LinkedIn (www.linkedin.com) and see what executive officers or groups your firm may have set up on the professional networking site. Next, look to see if the firm has a "fan page" on Facebook. Is there also a "detractors page" for your firm? How would you assess your firm's use of web networks and social media for its business?

my STRATEGY

What Is Your Network Strategy?

Most of us participate in one or more popular social networks online such as Facebook, LinkedIn, Pinterest, Tumblr, or Twitter. While many of us spend countless hours in these social networks, you may not have given a lot of thought to your network strategy.

Social networks describe the relationships or ties between individuals linked to one another. An important element of social networks is the *different strengths of ties* between individuals. Some ties between two people in a network may be very strong (e.g., "soul mates" or "best friends"), while others are weak (mere acquaintances—"I talk to her briefly in my yoga class"). As a member of a social network, you have access to *social capital,* which is derived from the connections within and between social networks. It is a function of whom you know, and what advantages you can create through those connections. Social capital is an important concept in business. Remember the old adage: *What matters is not what you know, but whom you know.*

Some Facebook users claim to have 2,000 or more "friends." With larger networks, one expects to have greater social capital, right? Though this seems obvious, academic research suggests that humans have the brain capacity to maintain a functional network of only about 150 people. This so-called *Dunbar number* was derived by extrapolating from the brain sizes and social networks of primates.

Far-fetched? Not necessarily. You may have a lot more than 150 friends on Facebook, but researchers call that number the *social core* of any network. Why is this the case? Even though it takes only a split second to accept a new friend request on Facebook, friendships still need to be "groomed." To develop a meaningful relationship, you need to spend some time with this new friend, even in cyberspace. Recent data from Facebook provide support for the concept of a social core, that the average number of friends a user has is 120, with women having more friends than men. However, the number of friends a Facebook user frequently interacts with is a lot smaller, and tends to be stable over time. The more frequent the exchanges among friends, the smaller the inner core. For example, on average, men leave comments for 17 friends and communicate with 10, while women leave comments for 26 friends and communicate with 16.

Social networking sites allow users to broadcast their lives and to passively keep track of more people. They enlarge their social networks, even though many of those ties tend to be weak. It may come as a surprise, however, to learn that research shows new opportunities such as job offers tend to come from weak ties, because it is these weak ties that allow you to access non-redundant and novel information. This phenomenon is called *strength of weak ties.* So, in thinking about how to leverage your social capital more fully as part of your network strategy, rather than always communicating with the same people, it may pay off for you to invest a bit more time in grooming your weak ties.[75]

1. Create a list of up to 12 people at your university with whom you regularly communicate (in person, electronically, or both). Draw your network (place names or initials next to each node), and connect every node where people you communicate with also talk to one another (i.e., indicate friends of friends). Can you identify strong and weak ties in your network?

2. What is the *degree of closure* in your network? The density of your network reflects the degree of closure. Network density can be calculated in three simple steps.

    Step 1: Create a simple matrix in which you list the names of the people in your network on both the horizontal and vertical axis. (This can be easily done in an Excel spreadsheet.) Then put an X in each box, indicating who knows whom in your network. Each X corresponds to a social tie in your network. Count the total number of Xs in your matrix. Let's assume X = 8.

    Step 2: If your network contains 12 people (including yourself), N = 12. The maximum network density is

calculated by the following formula: $[N \times (N - 1)] / 2$. If your network size is 12, then your maximum network density is $[12 \times (12 - 1)] / 2 = 66$. This is the maximum number of ties in your network when everybody knows everybody.

    Step 3: To calculate your actual network density, divide X by N: Network density = (X/N). In the example with 8 ties in a network of 12 people, the network density is 0.67. The closer this number is to 1, the denser the network.

3. Network density is bound by 0 and 1. Is a network density that approaches 1 the most beneficial? Why or why not? Think about weak ties, which can also be indirect connections.

4. Compare your network to that of your group members (two to four people in your class). Do you find any commonalities in your networks? Who has the greatest social capital, and why? What can you do to "optimize" your network structure?

5. Can you draw the joint network of your study group?

6. In this joint (study group) network, can you identify different network positions such as those discussed in the chapter, centrally located person(s) and broker(s), or a person who connects different clusters? Can you identify people with high and low social capital? Are there any dense clusters in this network? Would that indicate the existence of cliques? Is it a small-world network? What other implications can you draw?

ENDNOTES

1. This ChapterCase is based on: Disney Annual Reports; Paik, K. (2007), *To Infinity and Beyond!: The Story of Pixar Animation Studies* (New York: Chronicle Books); "Marvel superheroes join the Disney family," *The Wall Street Journal,* August 31, 2009; Isaacson, W. (2011), *Steve Jobs* (New York: Simon & Schuster); "Disney buys out George Lucas, the creator of 'Star Wars,'" *The Economist,* November 3, 2012; and "Superman v Spider-Man," *The Economist,* January 15, 2013.

2. Hitt, M. A., R. D. Ireland, and J. S. Harrison (2001), "Mergers and acquisitions: A value creating or value destroying strategy?" in Hitt, M. A., R. E. Freeman, and J. S. Harrison, *Handbook of Strategic Management* (Oxford, UK: Blackwell-Wiley): 384–408.

3. Allen, W. B., N. A. Doherty, K. Weigelt, and E. Mansfield (2005), *Managerial Economics,* 6th ed. (New York: Norton); and Breshnahan, T., and P. Reiss (1991), "Entry and competition in concentrated markets," *Journal of Political Economy* 99: 997–1009.

4. Brush, T. H. (1996), "Predicted change in operational synergy and post-acquisition performance of acquired businesses," *Strategic Management Journal* 17: 1–24.

5. Tebbutt, T. (2010), "An insider's perspective of the pharmaceutical industry," presentation in "Competing in the Health Sciences," Georgia Institute of Technology, January 29. Mr. Tebbutt is former president of UCB Pharma.

6. This Strategy Highlight is based on: Kraft Foods Annual Reports; The Hershey Company Annual Reports; "Cadbury rejects Kraft's $16.73 billion bid," *The Wall Street Journal,* September 7, 2009; "Food fight," *The Economist,* November 5, 2009; "Cadbury accepts fresh Kraft offer," *The Wall Street Journal,* January 19, 2010; "Kraft wins a reluctant Cadbury with help of clock, hedge funds," *The Wall Street Journal,* January 20, 2010; "Analysts bullish on Mondeléz ahead of Kraft split," *The Wall Street Journal,* October 1, 2012; "Mondeléz can slim way to success," *The Wall Street Journal,* May 28, 2013; and the author's personal communication with Dr. Narayanan Jayaraman, Georgia Institute of Technology.

7. Examples are drawn from: "Google in talks to buy YouTube for $1.6 billion," *The Wall Street Journal,* October 7, 2006; "Google's $12.5 billion gamble," *The Wall Street Journal,* August 16, 2011; Insta-rich: $1 billion for Instagram," *The Wall Street Journal,* April 10, 2012; and "Google buys Waze," *The Economist,* June 15, 2013.

8. Capron, L. (1999), "The long-term performance of horizontal acquisitions," *Strategic Management Journal* 20: 987–1018; Capron, L., and J. C. Shen (2007), "Acquisitions of private vs. public firms: Private information, target selection, and acquirer returns," *Strategic Management Journal* 28: 891–911.

9. Jensen, M. C., and R. S. Ruback (1983), "The market for corporate control: The scientific evidence," *Journal of Financial Economics* 11: 5–50.

10. This discussion is based on: Finkelstein, S., and D. C. Hambrick (1989), "Chief executive compensation: A study of the intersection of markets and political processes, *Strategic Management Journal* 10: 121–134; Lambert, R. A., D. F. Larcker, and K. Weigelt (1991), "How sensitive is executive compensation to organizational size?" *Strategic Management Journal* 12: 395–402; and Finkelstein, S. (2003), *Why Smart Executives Fail, and What You Can Learn from Their Mistakes* (New York: Portfolio).

11. This discussion is based on: Finkelstein, S. (2003), *Why Smart Executives Fail, and What You Can Learn from Their Mistakes;* and Finkelstein, S., J. Whitehead, and A. Campbell (2009), *Think Again: Why Good Leaders Make Bad Decisions and How to Keep It from Happening to You* (Boston, MA: Harvard Business School Press).

12. The examples are drawn from: Finkelstein, S. (2003), *Why Smart Executives Fail, and What You Can Learn from Their Mistakes;* and Finkelstein, S., J. Whitehead, and A. Campbell (2009), *Think Again: Why Good Leaders Make Bad Decisions and How to Keep It from Happening to You.*

13. Dyer, J. H., P. Kale, and H. Singh (2004), "When to ally and when to acquire," *Harvard Business Review,* July–August; Mayer, D., and M. Kenney (2004), "Ecosystems and acquisition management: Understanding Cisco's strategy," *Industry and Innovation* 11: 299–326.

14. "Silicon Valley survivor," *The Wall Street Journal,* July 28, 2009.

15. Kale, P., H. Singh, and A. P. Raman (2009), "Don't integrate your acquisitions, partner with them," *Harvard Business Review,* December.

16. "HP gambles on ailing Palm," *The Wall Street Journal,* April 29, 2010.

17. "HP affirms commitment to Autonomy," *The Wall Street Journal,* April 10, 2013.

18. Gulati, R. (1998), "Alliances and networks," *Strategic Management Journal* 19: 293–317.

19. J. Hagedoorn (2002), "Inter-firm R&D partnerships: An overview of major trends and patterns since 1960," *Research Policy* 31: 477–492; and Schilling, M. A. (2009), "Understanding the alliance data," *Strategic Management Journal* 30: 233–260.

20. This discussion draws on: Dyer, J. H., and H. Singh (1998), "The relational view: Cooperative strategy and the sources of interorganizational advantage," *Academy of Management Review* 23: 660–679.

21. Kale, P., and H. Singh (2009), "Managing strategic alliances: What do we know now, and where do we go from here?" *Academy of Management Perspectives* 23: 45–62.

22. The author participated in the HP demo; and "HP unveils Halo collaboration studio: Life-like communication leaps across geographic boundaries," HP Press Release, December 12, 2005.

23. "Bank of America taps Cisco for Tele Presence," *InformationWeek,* March 30, 2010.

24. For a review of the alliance literature, see: Gulati, R. (1998), "Alliances and networks," *Strategic Management Journal* 19: 293–317; Dyer, J. H., and H. Singh (1998), "The relational view: Cooperative strategy and the sources of interorganizational advantage," *Academy of Management Review* 23: 660–679; Inkpen, A. (2001), "Strategic alliances," in Hitt, M. A., R. E. Freeman, and J. S. Harrison, *Handbook of Strategic Management;* Ireland, R. D., M. A. Hitt, and D. Vaidyanath (2002), "Alliance management as a source of competitive advantage," *Journal of Management* 28: 413–446; Lavie, D. (2006), "The competitive advantage of interconnected firms: An extension of the resource-based view," *Academy of Management Review* 31: 638–658; Kale, P., and H. Singh (2009), "Managing strategic alliances: What do we know now, and where do we go from here?" *Academy of Management Perspectives* 23: 45–62.

25. Kogut, B. (1991), "Joint ventures and the option to expand and acquire," *Management Science* 37: 19–34.

26. "U.S. alleges e-book scheme," *The Wall Street Journal,* April 11, 2012; "Apple's 30% e-book commission is 100% legal," *The Wall Street Journal,* June 9, 2013; "Throwing the book at Apple," *The Wall Street Journal,* June 12, 2013; and "U.S. judge rules Apple colluded on e-books," *The Wall Street Journal,* July 10, 2013, http://online.wsj.com/article/ SB100014241278873244252045785974530 53469898.html.

27. Markides, C. C., and P. J. Williamsen (1994), "Related diversification, core competences, and performance," *Strategic Management Journal* 15: 149–165 (Summer Special Issue); Kale, P., and H. Singh (2009), "Managing strategic alliances: What do we know now, and where do we go from here?" *Academy of Management Perspectives* 23: 45–62.

28. "The real market size of public cloud services," *Wired,* March 4, 2013.

29. "Microsoft, Yahoo tout ad alliance," *The Wall Street Journal,* July 30, 2009.

30. Tripsas, M. (1997), "Unraveling the process of creative destruction: Complementary assets and incumbent survival in the typesetter industry," *Strategic Management Journal* 18: 119–142.

31. Rothaermel, F. T. (2001), "Incumbent's advantage through exploiting complementary assets via interfirm cooperation," *Strategic Management Journal* 22: 687–699; Rothaermel, F. T. (2001), "Complementary assets, strategic alliances, and the incumbent's advantage: An empirical study of industry and firm effects in the biopharmaceutical industry," *Research Policy* 30: 1235–1251; Hill, C.W.L., and F. T. Rothaermel (2003), "The performance of incumbent firms in the face of radical technological innovation," *Academy of Management Review* 28: 257–274; Rothaermel, F. T., and C.W.L. Hill (2005), "Technological discontinuities and complementary assets: A longitudinal study of industry and firm performance," *Organization Science* 16: 52–70.

32. Arthaud-Day, M. L., F. T. Rothaermel, and W. Zhang (2013), "Genentech: After the Acquisition by Roche," case study, in Rothaermel, F. T. *Strategic Management* (Burr Ridge, IL: McGraw-Hill). http:// mcgrawhillcreate.com/rothaermel, ID# MHE-FTR-014-0077645065.

33. Jiang, L., J. Tan, and M. Thursby (2011), "Incumbent firm invention in emerging fields: Evidence from the semiconductor industry," *Strategic Management Journal;* Rothaermel, F. T., and M. Thursby (2007), "The nanotech vs. the biotech revolution: Sources of incumbent productivity in research," *Research Policy* 36: 832–849.

34. This discussion is based on: Teece, D. J. (1986), "Profiting from technological innovation: Implications for integration, collaboration, licensing and public policy," *Research Policy* 15: 285–305; Tripsas, M. (1997), "Unraveling the process of creative destruction: Complementary assets and incumbent survival in the typesetter industry"; Rothaermel, F. T. (2001), "Incumbent's advantage through exploiting complementary assets via interfirm cooperation," *Strategic*

Management Journal 22 (6–7): 687–699; Ceccagnoli, M., and F. T. Rothaermel (2008), "Appropriating the returns to innovation," *Advances in Study of Entrepreneurship, Innovation, and Economic Growth* 18: 11–34; Rothaermel, F. T., and W. Boeker (2008), "Old technology meets new technology: Complementarities, similarities, and alliance formation," *Strategic Management Journal* 29 (1): 47–77; and Hess, A. M., and F. T. Rothaermel (2011), "When are assets complementary? Star scientists, strategic alliances and innovation in the pharmaceutical industry," *Strategic Management Journal* 32: 895–909.

35. Mowery, D. C., J. E. Oxley, and B. S. Silverman (1996), "Strategic alliances and interfirm knowledge transfer," *Strategic Management Journal* 17: 77–91 (Winter Special Issue).

36. Brandenburger, A. M., and B. J. Nalebuff (1996), *Co-opetition* (New York: Currency Doubleday); Gnyawali, D., and B. Park (2011), "Co-opetition between Giants: Collaboration with competitors for technological innovation," *Research Policy;* Gnyawali, D., J. He, and R. Madhaven (2008), "Co-opetition: Promises and challenges," in Wankel, C. (ed.), *21st Century Management: A Reference Handbook* (Thousand Oaks, CA: Sage): 386–398.

37. This discussion is based on: Hamel, G., Y. Doz, and C. K. Prahalad (1989), "Collaborate with your competitors—and win," *Harvard Business Review* (January–February): 190–196; Hamel, G. (1991), "Competition for competence and interpartner learning within international alliances," *Strategic Management Journal* 12: 83–103 (Summer Special Issue); Khanna, T., R. Gulati, and N. Nohria (1998), "The dynamics of learning alliances: Competition, cooperation, and relative scope," *Strategic Management Journal* 19: 193–210; Larsson, R., L. Bengtsson, K. Henriksson, and J. Sparks (1998), "The interorganizational learning dilemma: Collective knowledge development in strategic alliances," *Organization Science* 9: 285–305; and Kale, P., and H. Perlmutter (2000), "Learning and protection of proprietary assets in strategic alliances: Building relational capital," *Strategic Management Journal* 21: 217–237.

38. Nti, K. O., and R. Kumar (2000), "Differential learning in alliances," in Faulkner, D., and M. de Rond (eds.), *Cooperative Strategy. Economic, Business, and Organizational Issues* (Oxford, UK: University Press): 119–134. For an opposing viewpoint, see: Inkpen, A. C. (2008), "Knowledge transfer and international joint ventures: The case of NUMMI and General Motors," *Strategic Management Journal* 29: 447–453.

39. This discussion is based on: Gulati, R. (1998), "Alliances and networks," *Strategic Management Journal* 19: 293–317; Ireland, R. D., Hitt, M. A., and Vaidyanath D. (2002), "Alliance management as a source of competitive advantage," *Journal of Management* 28: 413–446; Hoang, H., and F. T. Rothaermel (2005), "The effect of general and partner-specific alliance experience on joint R&D project performance," *Academy of Management Journal* 48: 332–345; and Lavie, D. (2006), "The competitive advantage of interconnected firms: An extension of the resource-based view," *Academy of Management Review* 31: 638–658.

40. This is based on: Pisano, G. P., and Mang P. (1993), "Collaborative product development and the market for know-how: Strategies and structures in the biotechnology industry," in Rosenbloom, R., and R. Burgelman (eds.), *Research on Technological Innovation, Management, and Policy* (Greenwich, CT: J.A.I. Press) 109–136; and Hoang, H., and F. T. Rothaermel (2010), "Leveraging internal and external experience: Exploration, exploitation, and R&D project performance," *Strategic Management Journal* 31 (7): 734–758.

41. The distinction of explicit and tacit knowledge goes back to the seminal work by Polanyi, M. (1966), *The Tacit Dimension* (Chicago, IL: University of Chicago Press). For more recent treatments, see: Spender, J.-C. (1996), "Managing knowledge as the basis of a dynamic theory of the firm," *Strategic Management Journal* 17: 45–62 (Winter Special Issue); Spender, J.-C., and R. M. Grant (1996), "Knowledge and the firm," *Strategic Management Journal* 17: 5–9 (Winter Special Issue); and Crossan, M. M., H. W. Lane, R. E. White (1999), "An organizational learning framework: From intuition to institution," *Academy of Management Review* 24: 522–537.

42. "Toyota and Tesla partnering to make electric cars," *The Wall Street Journal,* May 21, 2010.

43. Ibid.

44. Ibid.

45. For an insightful treatment of CVC investments, see: Dushnitsky, G., and M. J. Lenox (2005a), "When do incumbent firms learn from entrepreneurial ventures? Corporate venture capital and investing firm innovation rates," *Research Policy* 34: 615–639; Dushnitsky, G., and M. J. Lenox (2005b), "When do firms undertake R&D by investing in new ventures?" *Strategic Management Journal* 26: 947–965; Dushnitsky, G., and M. J. Lenox (2006), "When does corporate venture capital investment create value?" *Journal of Business Venturing* 21: 753–772;

and Wadhwa, A., and S. Kotha (2006), "Knowledge creation through external venturing: Evidence from the telecommunications equipment manufacturing industry," *Academy of Management Journal* 49: 1–17.

46. Benson, D., and R. H. Ziedonis (2009), "Corporate venture capital as a window on new technology for the performance of corporate investors when acquiring startups," *Organization Science* 20: 329–351.

47. Dushnitsky, G., and M. J. Lenox (2006), "When does corporate venture capital investment create value?" *Journal of Business Venturing* 21: 753–772.

48. Higgins, M. J., and D. Rodriguez (2006), "The outsourcing of R&D through acquisition in the pharmaceutical industry," *Journal of Financial Economics* 80: 351–383; Benson, D., and R. H. Ziedonis (2009), "Corporate venture capital as a window on new technology for the performance of corporate investors when acquiring startups," *Organization Science* 20: 329–351.

49. Reuer, J. J., M. Zollo, and H. Singh (2002), "Post-formation dynamics in strategic alliances," *Strategic Management Journal* 23: 135–151.

50. This discussion is based on: Dyer, J. H., and H. Singh (1998), "The relational view: Cooperative strategy and the sources of interorganizational advantage," *Academy of Management Review* 23: 660–679; Ireland, R. D., M. A. Hitt, and D. Vaidyanath (2002), "Alliance management as a source of competitive advantage," *Journal of Management* 28: 413–446; and Lavie, D. (2006), "The competitive advantage of interconnected firms: An extension of the resource-based view," *Academy of Management Review* 31: 638–658.

51. For an insightful discussion of alliance management capability and alliance portfolios, see: Rothaermel, F. T., and D. L. Deeds (2006), "Alliance type, alliance experience, and alliance management capability in high-technology ventures," *Journal of Business Venturing* 21: 429–460; Hoffmann, W. (2007), "Strategies for managing a portfolio of alliances," *Strategic Management Journal* 28: 827–856; Schreiner, M., P. Kale, and D. Corsten (2009), "What really is alliance management capability and how does it impact alliance outcomes and success?" *Strategic Management Journal* 30: 1395–1419; Ozcan, P., and K. M. Eisenhardt (2009), "Origin of alliance portfolios: Entrepreneurs, network strategies, and firm performance," *Academy of Management Journal* 52: 246–279; and Schilke, O., and A. Goerzten (2010), "Alliance management capability: An investigation of the construct and its measurement," *Journal of Management* 36: 1192–1219.

52. Kale, P., and H. Singh (2009), "Managing strategic alliances: What do we know now, and where do we go from here?" *Academy of Management Perspectives* 23: 45–62.

53. Santoro, M. D., and J. P. McGill (2005), "The effect of uncertainty and asset co-specialization on governance in biotechnology alliances," *Strategic Management Journal* 26: 1261–1269.

54. This is based on: Gulati, R. (1995), "Does familiarity breed trust? The implications of repeated ties for contractual choice in alliances," *Academy of Management Journal* 38: 85–112; and Poppo, L., and T. Zenger (2002), "Do formal contracts and relational governance function as substitutes or complements?" *Strategic Management Journal* 23: 707–725.

55. Dyer, J. H., and H. Singh (1998), "The relational view: Cooperative strategy and the sources of interorganizational advantage," *Academy of Management Review* 23: 660–679.

56. Zaheer, A., B. McEvily, and V. Perrone (1998), "Does trust matter? Exploring the effects of interorganizational and interpersonal trust on performance," *Organization Science* 8: 141–159.

57. Covey, S.M.R. (2008), *The Speed of Trust: The One Thing That Changes Everything* (New York: Free Press).

58. Dyer, J. H., and H. Singh (1998), "The relational view: Cooperative strategy and the sources of interorganizational advantage," *Academy of Management Review* 23: 660–679; Ireland, R. D., M. A. Hitt, and D. Vaidyanath (2002), "Alliance management as a source of competitive advantage," *Journal of Management* 28: 413–446; Lavie, D. (2006), "The competitive advantage of interconnected firms: An extension of the resource-based view," *Academy of Management Review* 31: 638–658.

59. This is based on: Anand, B., and T. Khanna (2000), "Do firms learn to create value?" *Strategic Management Journal* 21: 295–315; Sampson, R. (2005), "Experience effects and collaborative returns in R&D alliances," *Strategic Management Journal* 26: 1009–1031; Hoang, H., and F. T. Rothaermel (2005), "The effect of general and partner-specific alliance experience on joint R&D project performance," *Academy of Management Journal* 48: 332–345; and Rothaermel, F. T., and D. L. Deeds (2006), "Alliance type, alliance experience, and alliance management capability in high-technology ventures," *Journal of Business Venturing* 21: 429–460.

60. Rothaermel, F. T., and D. L. Deeds (2006), "Alliance type, alliance experience, and alliance management capability in high-technology ventures," *Journal of Business Venturing* 21: 429–460.

61. Hoffmann, W. (2007), "Strategies for managing a portfolio of alliances," *Strategic Management Journal* 28: 827–856.

62. Wassmer, U., P. Dussage, and M. Planellas (2010), "How to manage alliances better than one at a time," *MIT Sloan Management Review*, Spring: 77–84.

63. Dyer, J. H., P. Kale, and H. Singh (2001), "How to make strategic alliances work," *MIT Sloan Management Review*, Summer: 37–43.

64. Kale, P., J. H. Dyer, and H. Singh (2002), "Alliance capability, stock market response, and long-term alliance success: The role of the alliance function," *Strategic Management Journal* 23: 747–767.

65. Gueth A., N. Sims, and R. Harrison (2001), "Managing alliances at Lilly," *In Vivo: The Business & Medicine Report* (June): 1–9; Rothaermel, F. T., and D. L. Deeds (2006), "Alliance type, alliance experience, and alliance management capability in high-technology ventures," *Journal of Business Venturing* 21: 429–46.

66. Dyer, J. H., Kale, P., Singh, H. (2004), "When to ally and when to acquire," *Harvard Business Review*, July–August.

67. Rothaermel, F. T., and A. Hess (2010), "Innovation strategies combined," *MIT Sloan Management Review*, Spring: 12–15.

68. Dyer, J. H., Kale, P., Singh, H. (2004), "When to ally and when to acquire," *Harvard Business Review*, July–August.

69. This section is based on: Capron, L., and W. Mitchell (2012), *Build, Borrow, or Buy: Solving the Growth Dilemma* (Boston, MA: Harvard Business Review Press).

70. Ibid.

71. Ibid., p. 16.

72. Hoang, H., and Rothaermel, F. T. (2010), "Leveraging internal and external experience: Exploration, exploitation, and R&D project performance," *Strategic Management Journal* 31: 734–758; and Gick, M. L., and K. J. Holyoak (1987), "The cognitive basis of knowledge transfer," in Cormier, S. M., and J. D. Hagman (eds.), *Transfer of Learning* (New York: Academic Press): 9–46.

73. If so, this would violate a "net-neutrality" policy that has generally been honored—that all information on the Internet is treated equally as far as speed and cost per size of content. Data sourced from "The FCC's crusade to keep the Internet free," *Bloomberg Businessweek*, August 16, 2010.

74. Data from "Global social media check up" by Burson-Marsteller PR firm, 2010.

75. This *my*Strategy section is based on: Granovetter, M. (1973), "The strength of weak ties," *American Journal of Sociology* 78: 1360–1380; and "Primates on Facebook," *The Economist*, February 26, 2009.

Global Strategy: Competing Around the World

Learning Objectives

After studying this chapter, you should be able to:

LO 10-1   Define globalization, multinational enterprise (MNE), foreign direct investment (FDI), and global strategy.

LO 10-2   Explain why companies compete abroad, and evaluate the advantages and disadvantages of a global strategy.

LO 10-3   Apply the CAGE distance framework to explain which countries MNEs enter.

LO 10-4   Compare and contrast the different options MNEs have to enter foreign markets.

LO 10-5   Apply the integration-responsiveness framework to evaluate the four different strategies MNEs can pursue when competing globally.

LO 10-6   Apply Porter's diamond framework to explain why certain industries are more competitive in specific nations than in others.

Hollywood Goes Global

HOLLYWOOD MOVIES HAVE always been a quintessentially American product. Globalization, however, has changed the economics of the movie industry. Foreign ticket sales for Hollywood blockbusters made up 50 percent of worldwide totals in 2000. By 2012, they had jumped to over 70 percent. Of the total $35 billion that Hollywood movies grossed in 2012, over $24 billion came from outside the United States! Today, largely due to the collapse of DVD/Blu-ray sales, Hollywood would be unable to continue producing big-budget movies without foreign revenues. Foreign sales can make or break the success of newly released big-budget movies.

Look at Exhibit 10.1, which depicts the lifetime revenues (domestic and foreign) of recent Hollywood blockbuster movies. *Avatar* is the highest-grossing movie to date, earning over $2.7 billion since its release in 2009. It may surprise you to learn that non-U.S. box office

sales account for almost 75 percent of that number. *Avatar* was hugely popular in Asia, especially in China, where the government gave permission to increase the number of movie theaters showing the film from 5,000 to 35,000. Another of James Cameron's popular films, *Titanic*, grossed almost 70 percent of its $1.8 billion in overseas markets. The only billion-dollar blockbuster to receive a majority of ticket receipts from domestic audiences was the second installment in the Batman trilogy, *The Dark Knight* (2008).

EXHIBIT 10.1 / Lifetime Revenues of Hollywood Blockbuster Movies, > $800 million
(release year in parentheses)

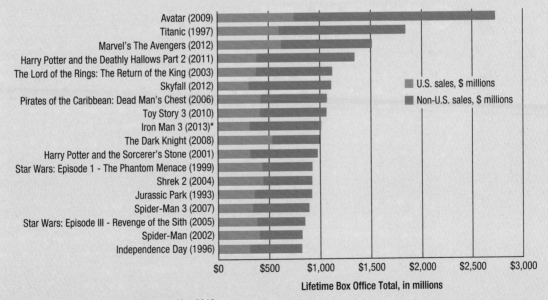

* through May 2013

SOURCE: Adapted from "Plot change: Foreign forces transform Hollywood films," *The Wall Street Journal*, August 2, 2010, and updated with data from http://boxofficemojo.com for years 2010–2013.

Given the increasing importance of non-U.S. box-office sales, Hollywood studios are changing their business models. Rob Moore, vice chairman of Paramount Pictures, explains: "We need to make movies that have the ability to break out internationally. That's the only way to make the economic puzzle of film production work today."[1] As a result, studios are adapting scripts to appeal to global audiences, casting foreign actors in leading roles, and pulling the plug on projects that seem too U.S.-centric. For example, the film *G.I. Joe: The Rise of Cobra* prominently featured South Korean movie star Byung-hun Lee and South African actor Arnold Vosloo. On the other hand, Disney's *Wedding Banned,* a romantic comedy about a divorced couple trying to prevent their daughter from getting married, was axed in the advanced production stage despite several marquee stars (Robin Williams, Anna Faris, and Diane Keaton) because of perceptions that it would not succeed outside the American market. Some mega releases such as Disney's *Monsters University* (the prequel to *Monsters, Inc.*) premier first in foreign markets before being shown in the U.S. Similarly, many scripts are altered or movie studios produce multiple versions of the same movie.

Disney's Marvel studio produced two versions of the 2013 box office hit *Iron Man 3.* One version of the film was produced for general release, and another version specifically targeted the 1.3 billion Chinese that make up the second-largest film market in the world. This version included bonus footage in Beijing and guest appearances by Chinese movie stars. *Iron Man 3* grossed roughly 70 percent of its box office sales overseas, or almost $700 million. Other studios are also realizing the significance of the Chinese market. Movies such as the latest James Bond film *Skyfall, Men in Black 3, Pirates of the Caribbean: At World's End,* and *Mission Impossible 3* have all been edited so they would be permitted to screen in China.

Globalization also puts pressure on the pay of Hollywood stars. Given the importance of international audiences and the availability of foreign stars and movies, the days are over when stars like Tom Hanks, Eddie Murphy, and Julia Roberts could demand 20 percent royalties on total ticket sales.[2]

After reading the chapter, you will find more about this case, with related questions, on page 332.

HOLLYWOOD HAS ALWAYS obtained some of its revenues from international sales, but it is now a truly global enterprise, with the vast majority of revenues coming from outside the United States. Moreover, the huge opportunities in the global movie market have also attracted new entrants. Besides wanting to cater to international audiences, Hollywood film studios are also feeling squeezed by low-cost foreign competition. For example, Bollywood, the Indian movie industry, creates its own productions and brings in low-cost but high-impact actors such as Freida Pinto and Dev Patel, who played the lead roles in the mega-success *Slumdog Millionaire. Slumdog*'s budget was merely $14 million, but the movie grossed almost $400 million and won eight Oscars. By comparison, Hollywood's budget for *Home Alone,* a similar success in terms of revenues, was nearly five times as large.

The shift in revenue sources away from the U.S. market, as well as the opportunities for future growth in emerging economies, is changing the global strategy of many U.S. firms, not just Hollywood moviemakers. Firms from a wide variety of industries—such as Apple, Caterpillar, GE, Intel, and IBM—are global enterprises. They not only manage global supply chains, but also obtain the majority of their revenues from outside their home market. Once-unassailable U.S. firms now encounter formidable foreign competitors such as Brazil's Embraer (aerospace), China's Haier (home appliances) and Lenovo (PCs), India's ArcelorMittal (steel), Infosys (IT services) and Reliance Group (conglomerate), Mexico's Cemex (cement), Russia's Gazprom (energy), South Korea's LG and Samsung (both in electronics and appliances), and Sweden's IKEA (home furnishings), to name just a few. This chapter is about how firms gain and sustain competitive advantage when competing around the world.

The competitive playing field is becoming increasingly global, as the ChapterCase about the movie industry indicates. This globalization provides significant opportunities for individuals, companies, and countries. Indeed, you can probably see the increase in globalization on your own campus. The number of students enrolled at universities outside their native countries tripled between 1980 (about one million students) to 2010 (three million students).[3] The country of choice for foreign students remains the United States, with some 600,000 enrolled per year, followed by the UK with some 360,000 foreign university students.

In Chapter 8, we looked at the first two dimensions of corporate strategy: managing the degree of vertical integration, and deciding which products and services to offer (the degree of diversification). The question of how to compete effectively around the world is the third dimension of corporate strategy. The world's marketplace—made up of some 200 countries—is a staggering $70 trillion in gross domestic product (GDP), of which the U.S. market is roughly $15 trillion, or about 21 percent.[4]

We begin this chapter by defining globalization and presenting stages of globalization. We then tackle a number of questions that the strategist must answer: Why should the company go global? Where and how should it compete? We present the CAGE[5] distance model to answer the question of where the firm should compete globally. In a next step, we present the integration-responsiveness framework to link a firm's options of how to compete globally with the different business strategies introduced in Chapter 6 (cost leadership, differentiation, and integration). We then debate the question of why world leadership in specific industries is often concentrated in certain geographic areas. We conclude with practical *Implications for the Strategist.*

10.1 What Is Globalization?

Globalization is a process of closer integration and exchange between different countries and peoples worldwide, made possible by falling trade and investment barriers, advances in telecommunications, and reductions in transportation costs.[6] Combined, these factors reduce the costs of doing business around the world, opening the doors to a much larger market than any one home country. Globalization also allows companies to source supplies at lower costs and to further differentiate products. Consequently, the world's market economies are becoming more integrated and interdependent.

Globalization has led to significant increases in living standards in many economies around the world. Germany and Japan, countries that were basically destroyed after World War II, turned into industrial powerhouses, fueled by export-led growth. The Asian Tigers—Hong Kong, Singapore, South Korea, and Taiwan—turned themselves from underdeveloped countries into advanced economies, enjoying some of the world's highest standards of living. The BRIC countries (Brazil, Russia, India, and China), with more than 40 percent of the world's population and producing roughly half of the world's economic growth over the last decade, continue to offer significant business opportunities.[7] Indeed, China with $7.5 trillion in GDP has become the second-largest economy worldwide after the United States (with $15 trillion in GDP), in absolute terms.[8]

The engine behind globalization is the **multinational enterprise (MNE)**—a company that deploys resources and capabilities in the procurement, production, and distribution of goods and services in at least two countries. By making investments in value chain activities abroad, MNEs engage in **foreign direct investment (FDI)**.[9] For example, the European aircraft maker Airbus is investing $600 million in Mobile, Alabama, to build jetliners.[10] It's doing so in order to avoid voluntary import restrictions, to take advantage of business-friendly conditions such as lower taxes, labor cost, and cost of living, as well as

LO 10-1

Define globalization, multinational enterprise (MNE), foreign direct investment (FDI), and global strategy.

globalization The process of closer integration and exchange between different countries and peoples worldwide, made possible by falling trade and investment barriers, advances in telecommunications, and reductions in transportation costs.

multinational enterprise (MNE) A company that deploys resources and capabilities in the procurement, production, and distribution of goods and services in at least two countries.

foreign direct investment (FDI) A firm's investments in value chain activities abroad.

global strategy Part
of a firm's corporate
strategy to gain and
sustain a competitive
advantage when
competing against
other foreign and
domestic companies
around the world.

other incentives provided by host states in the southern United States, and to be closer to customers in North America. For similar reasons, German carmaker Volkswagen invested $1 billion in its Chattanooga, Tennessee, plant.[11] MNEs need an effective **global strategy** that enables them to gain and sustain a competitive advantage when competing against other foreign and domestic companies around the world.[12]

In the digital age, some companies are even *born global*—their founders start them with the intent of running global operations. Internet-based companies such as Amazon, eBay, Google, and LinkedIn by nature have a global presence. Indeed, Facebook, with over one billion users around the globe, would—if it were a country—be the third-most populous country worldwide after China (1.4 billion) and India (1.2 billion). To better customize their websites to suit local preferences and cultures, these companies still tend to establish offices and maintain computer servers in different countries.[13] Amazon.com, for example, customizes its offerings for different markets (see country-specific sites at: www.amazon.cn for China, www.amazon.de for Germany, and www.amazon.com.br for Brazil).

U.S. MNEs have a disproportionately positive impact on the U.S. economy.[14] Well-known U.S. multinational enterprises include Boeing, Caterpillar, Coca-Cola, GE, John Deere, Exxon Mobil, IBM, P&G, and Walmart. They make up less than 1 percent of the number of total U.S. companies, but they:

- Account for 11 percent of private-sector employment growth since 1990.
- Employ 19 percent of the work force.
- Pay 25 percent of the wages.
- Account for 31 percent of the U.S. gross domestic product (GDP).
- Make up 74 percent of private-sector R&D spending.

STAGES OF GLOBALIZATION

Since the beginning of the 20th century, globalization has proceeded through three notable stages.[15] Each stage presents a different global strategy pursued by MNEs headquartered in the United States.

GLOBALIZATION 1.0: 1900–1941. Globalization 1.0 took place from about 1900 through the early years of World War II. In that period, basically all the important business functions were located in the home country. Typically, only sales and distribution operations took place overseas—essentially exporting goods to other markets. In some instances, firms procured raw materials from overseas. Strategy formulation and implementation, as well as knowledge flows, followed a one-way path—from domestic headquarters to international outposts. This time period saw the blossoming of the idea of MNEs. It ended with the U.S. entry into World War II.

GLOBALIZATION 2.0: 1945–2000. With the end of World War II came a new focus on growing business—not only to meet the needs that went unfulfilled during the war years but also to reconstruct the damage from the war. From 1945 to the end of the 20th century, in the Globalization 2.0 stage, MNEs began to create smaller, self-contained copies of themselves, with all business functions intact, in a few key countries (notably, Western European countries, Japan, and Australia).

This strategy required significant amounts of foreign direct investment. Although it was costly to duplicate business functions in overseas outposts, doing so allowed for greater local responsiveness to country-specific circumstances. While the corporate headquarters back in the U.S. set overarching strategic goals and allocated resources through the capital budgeting process, local mini-MNE replicas had considerable leeway in day-to-day operations. Knowledge flow back to U.S. headquarters, however, remained limited in most instances.

GLOBALIZATION 3.0: 21ST CENTURY. We are now in the Globalization 3.0 stage. MNEs that had been the vanguard of globalization have since become global-collaboration networks (see Exhibit 10.2). Such companies now freely locate business functions anywhere in the world based on an optimal mix of costs, capabilities, and PESTEL factors. Huge investments in fiber-optic cable networks around the world have effectively reduced communication distances, enabling companies to operate 24/7, 365 days a year. When an engineer in Minneapolis, Minnesota, leaves for the evening, an engineer in Mumbai, India, begins her workday. In the Globalization 3.0 stage, the MNE's strategic objective changes. The MNE reorganizes from a multinational company with self-contained operations in a few selected countries to a more seamless global enterprise with centers of expertise. Each of these centers of expertise is a hub within a global network for delivering products and services. Consulting companies, for example, can now tap into a worldwide network of experts in real time, rather than relying on the limited number of employees in their local offices.

Creating a global network of local expertise is beneficial not only in service industries, but also in the industrial sector. To increase the rate of low-cost innovation that can then be used to disrupt existing markets, GE organizes local growth teams in China, India, Kenya, and many other emerging countries.[16] GE uses the slogan "in country, for country" to describe the local growth teams' autonomy in deciding which products and services to develop, how to make them, and how to shape the business model. Many of these low-cost innovations that were developed to serve local market needs such as the Vcan (a handheld ultrasound device, developed in China), the Mac 400 (an ECG device, developed in India—more details later in the chapter), and the 9100c (an anesthesia system developed in Kenya) were developed in emerging economies, and then introduced as disruptive innovations in Western markets.[17]

Some new ventures organize as global-collaboration networks (shown in Exhibit 10.2) from the start. Logitech, the maker of wireless peripherals such as computer mice, presentation "clickers," and video game controllers, started in Switzerland but quickly established offices in Silicon Valley, California.[18] Pursuing a global strategy right from the

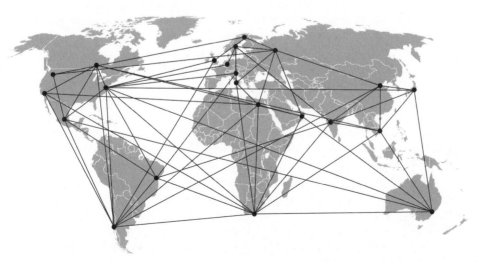

EXHIBIT 10.2 /

Globalization 3.0:
21st Century

Based on an optimal mix of costs, skills, and PESTEL factors, MNEs are organized as global-collaboration networks that perform business functions throughout the world.

SOURCE: Adapted from IBM (2009), *A Decade of Generating Higher Value at IBM*, IBM report, www.ibm.com.

start allowed Logitech to tap into the innovation expertise contained in Silicon Valley.[19] In 2012, Logitech had sales of over $2 billion, with offices throughout the Americas, Asia, and Europe. Underlying Logitech's innovation competence is a network of best-in-class skills around the globe. Moreover, Logitech can organize work continuously because its teams in different locations around the globe can work 24/7.

The trend toward global-collaboration networks during the Globalization 3.0 stage indeed raises the interesting question, "What defines a U.S. company?" If it's the address of the headquarters, then IBM, GE, and others are U.S. companies—despite the fact that a majority of their employees work outside the United States. On the other hand, non-U.S. companies such as carmakers from Japan (Toyota, Honda, and Nissan) and South Korea (Hyundai and Kia) and several engineering companies (Siemens from Germany, and ABB, a Swiss-Swedish MNE) all have made significant investments in the United States and created a large number of well-paying jobs.

As a business student, you have several reasons to be interested in MNEs. Not only can these companies provide interesting work assignments in different locations throughout the world, but they also frequently offer the highest-paying jobs for college graduates. Even if you don't want to work for an MNE, chances are that the organization you will be working for will do business with one, so it's important to understand how they compete around the globe.

Before we delve deeper into the question of why and how firms compete for advantage globally, a cautionary note concerning *globalization* is in order. Although many large firms are more than 50 percent globalized—meaning that more than half of their revenues are from outside the home country—the world itself is far from being globalized.[20] If we look at a number of different indicators, the level of globalization is no more than 10 to 25 percent. For example, only:

- 2 percent of all voice-calling minutes are cross-border.[21]
- 3 percent of the world's population are first-generation immigrants.
- 9 percent of all investments in the economy are foreign direct investments.
- 15 percent of patents list at least one foreign inventor.
- 18 percent of Internet traffic crosses national borders.

These data indicate that the world is not quite flat yet,[22] but at best *semi-globalized.*[23] Pankaj Ghemawat reasons that many more gains in social welfare and living standards can be had through further globalization if future integration is managed effectively through coordinated efforts by governments.[24] The European Union is an example of coordinated economic and political integration by 28 countries, of which 17 use the euro as a common currency. This coordinated integration took place over several decades following World War II, precisely to prevent future wars in Europe. The EU now encompasses more than 500 million people. This makes it one of the largest economic zones in the world. Further coordinated integration appears to be one solution to the current Eurozone crisis. Although the EU has monetary authority (administered through the European Central Bank), it does not have fiscal (i.e., budgetary) authority. This important responsibility remains with national governments, leading to the sovereign debt crisis (discussed in detail in Chapter 2). Further coordinated integration may not only solve this problem, but also create more business opportunities for companies to gain and sustain competitive advantage.

Continued economic development across the globe has two consequences for MNEs. First, rising wages and other costs are likely to negate any benefits of access to low-cost input factors. Second, as the standard of living rises in emerging economies, MNEs are hoping that increased purchasing power will enable workers to purchase the products they used to make for export only.[25] China's labor costs, for example, are steadily rising in tandem with an improved standard of living, especially in the coastal regions, where wages have risen 50 percent since 2005.[26] Some MNEs have boosted wages an extra 30 percent following the recent labor unrest. Many now offer bonuses to blue-collar workers and are taking other measures to avoid sweatshop allegations that have plagued companies such as Nike, Apple, and Levi Strauss. Rising wages, fewer workers due to the effects of China's one-child-per-family policy, and appreciation of the Chinese currency now combine to lessen the country's advantage in low-cost manufacturing.[27] This shift is in alignment with the Chinese government's economic policy, which wants to see a move from "Made in China" to "Designed in China," to capture more of the value added.[28] The value added of manufacturing an iPad (by Foxconn in China) is only about 5 percent.[29] We next discuss in more detail the reasons why firms "go global."

10.2 Going Global: Why?

Clearly, the decision to pursue a global strategy comes from the firm's assessment that doing so will enhance its competitive advantage and that the benefits of globalization will exceed the costs. Simply put, firms expand beyond their domestic borders if they can increase their economic value creation $(V - C)$ and enhance competitive advantage. As detailed in Chapter 5, firms enlarge their competitive advantage by increasing a consumer's willingness to pay through higher perceived value based on differentiation and/or lower production and service delivery costs. Here we consider both the advantages and disadvantages of expanding beyond the home market.

LO 10-2

Explain why companies compete abroad, and evaluate the advantages and disadvantages of a global strategy.

ADVANTAGES OF EXPANDING INTERNATIONALLY

Why do firms expand internationally? The main reasons firms expand abroad are to:

- Gain access to a larger market.
- Gain access to low-cost input factors.
- Develop new competencies.

GAIN ACCESS TO A LARGER MARKET. Becoming an MNE provides significant opportunities for U.S. companies, given *economies of scale* and *scope* that can be reaped by participating in a much larger and more diverse market. At the same time, some countries with relatively weak domestic demand, such as China, Germany, South Korea, and Japan, focus on export-led economic growth, which in turn drives many of their domestic businesses to become MNEs.

For companies based in smaller economies, becoming an MNE may be necessary to achieve growth or to gain and sustain competitive advantage. Examples include Acer (Taiwan), Casella Wines (Australia), Nestlé (Switzerland), Novo Nordisk (Denmark), Philips (Netherlands), Samsung (South Korea), and Zara (Spain). Unless companies in smaller economies expand internationally, their domestic markets are often too small for them to reach significant economies of scale to compete effectively against other MNEs.

In contrast, given the sheer size of the U.S. automotive market, GM needed to focus mainly on its domestic market only to do well. GM once held more than 50 percent market share and was the leader in global car sales between 1931 and 2008. In its heyday, GM employed 350,000 U.S. workers and was an American icon. More and more, however, GM's future depends on its performance outside the U.S. In particular, the Chinese market is becoming more and more important to GM's performance, as Strategy Highlight 10.1 discusses.

Strategy Highlight 10.1

Does GM's Future Lie in China?

With a population of 1.4 billion and currently only one vehicle per 100 people—compared with a vehicle density of 94 per 100 in the U.S.—China offers tremendous growth opportunities for the automotive industry. Since China joined the World Trade Organization (WTO) in 2001, its domestic auto market has been growing at double digits annually and has now overtaken the U.S. as the largest in the world.

GM entered China in 1997 through a joint venture with Shanghai Automotive Industrial Corp (SAIC). Today, the Chinese market already accounts for 25 percent of GM's total revenues. Moreover, GM's China operation has been cost-competitive from day one. The company operates about the same number of assembly plants in China as in the U.S., but sells more vehicles while employing about half the number of employees. Chinese workers cost only a fraction of what U.S. workers do, and GM is not weighed down by additional health care and pension obligations.

GM's Buick brand is considered a luxury vehicle in China. GM's best-selling model in China, however, is the Wuling Sunshine, a small, boxy, purely functional vehicle (a so-called "micro van") priced between $5,000 and $10,000 depending on what options the customer chooses. The SAIC-GM joint venture sold more than 1.4 million

Wuling vehicles in China in 2012. In the same year, GM held almost 15 percent market share in China. The Wuling Sunshine may help GM further penetrate the Chinese market; it also may be an introductory car for other emerging markets, such as India. GM's low-cost strategy with this vehicle has been so successful that the firm is planning to expand the Wuling product line and offer the vehicle globally. GM already sells the Wuling Sunshine in Brazil under the Buick nameplate. In total, GM earns over 70 percent of its revenues annually from outside the United States! This is quite a high level of globalization for a company that once was focused more or less domestically on the U.S. market.

Indeed, GM is betting its future on China and other emerging economies in Asia, Latin America, and the Middle East as it strives to become a lean and low-cost manufacturer of profitable small cars. To back up its strategic intent, GM has quadrupled its engineering and design personnel in China and is investing a quarter-billion dollars to build a cutting-edge R&D center on its Shanghai campus, home of its international headquarters. With GM's growth in the double digits in China and rebounding in the U.S., the company confidently declared: "GM's greatest strengths today are our market-leading positions in the United States and China, the world's two largest markets."[30]

GAIN ACCESS TO LOW-COST INPUT FACTORS. Access to low-cost raw materials such as lumber, iron ore, oil, and coal was a key driver behind Globalization 1.0 and 2.0. During Globalization 3.0, firms have expanded globally to benefit from lower labor costs in manufacturing and services. India carved out a competitive advantage in business process outsourcing (BPO), not only because of low-cost labor but because of an abundance of well-educated, English-speaking young people. Infosys, TCS, and Wipro are some of the more well-known Indian IT service companies. Taken together, these companies employ close to 250,000 people and provide services to many of the Global Fortune 500. Many MNEs have close business ties with Indian IT firms. Some, such as IBM, are engaged in foreign direct investment through equity alliances or building their own IT and customer service centers in India. More than a quarter of Accenture's work force, a consultancy specializing in technology and outsourcing, is now in Bangalore, India.[31]

Likewise, China has emerged as a manufacturing powerhouse because of low labor costs and an efficient infrastructure. An American manufacturing worker costs about 20 times more in wages alone than a similarly skilled worker in China.[32] A significant cost differential exists not only for low-skilled labor, but for high-skilled labor as well. A Chinese engineer trained at Purdue University, for example, works for only a quarter of the salary in his native country compared with an engineer working in the U.S.[33] Of course, this absolute wage disparity also reflects the relative difference in the two countries' cost of living.

DEVELOP NEW COMPETENCIES. Some MNEs pursue a global strategy in order to develop new competencies.[34] These companies are making foreign direct investments to be part of *communities of learning,* which are often contained in specific geographic regions.[35] AstraZeneca, a Swiss-based pharmaceutical company, relocated its research facility to Cambridge, Massachusetts, to be part of the Boston biotech cluster, in hopes of developing new R&D competencies in biotechnology.[36] Cisco is investing more than $1 billion to create an Asian headquarters in Bangalore, in order to be right in the middle of India's top IT location.[37] Unilever's new-concept center is located in downtown Shanghai, China, attracting hundreds of eager volunteers to test the firm's latest product innovations onsite, while Unilever researchers monitor consumer reactions. In these examples, AstraZeneca, Cisco, and Unilever all reap **location economies**—benefits from locating value chain activities in optimal geographies for a specific activity, wherever that may be.[38]

> **location economies**
> Benefits from locating value chain activities in the world's optimal geographies for a specific activity, wherever that may be.

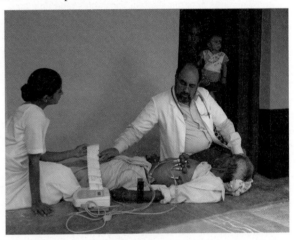

The GE Mac 400 device is small, portable, and enables doctors to do an ECG test in non-hospital settings and at low cost. It is now making its entry as a disruptive innovation in Western markets.

Many MNEs now are replacing the one-way innovation flow from Western economies to developing markets with a *polycentric innovation strategy*—a strategy in which MNEs now draw on multiple, equally important innovation hubs throughout the world (characteristic of Globalization 3.0; see Exhibit 10.2). GE Global Research, for example, orchestrates a "network of excellence" with facilities in Niskayuna, New York (USA), Bangalore (India), Shanghai (China), and Munich (Germany). Indeed, emerging economies are becoming hotbeds for low-cost innovations that find their way back to developed markets. In Bangalore, GE researchers developed the Mac 400, a handheld electrocardiogram (ECG).[39] The device is small, portable, and runs on batteries. Although a conventional ECG costs $2,000, this handheld version costs $800 and enables doctors to do an ECG test at a cost of only $1 per patient. The Mac 400 is now making its entry as a disruptive innovation into the U.S. and other Western markets, with anticipated widespread use in the offices of general practitioners and emergency ambulances.

DISADVANTAGES OF EXPANDING INTERNATIONALLY

Companies expanding internationally must carefully weigh the benefits and costs of doing so. Disadvantages to "going global" include:

- The liability of foreignness
- Loss of reputation
- Loss of intellectual property

THE LIABILITY OF FOREIGNESS. In international expansion, firms also face some risks. In particular, MNEs doing business abroad also must overcome the **liability of foreignness**. This liability consists of the additional costs of doing business in an unfamiliar cultural and economic environment, and of coordinating across geographic distances.[40] Strategy Highlight 10.2 illustrates how Walmart underestimated its liability of foreignness when entering and competing in Germany.

> **liability of foreignness**
> Additional costs of doing business in an unfamiliar cultural and economic environment, and of coordinating across geographic distances.

Strategy Highlight 10.2

Walmart Retreats from Germany

In late 1997, facing a saturated U.S. market, Walmart entered Germany, then the third-largest economy in the world behind the U.S. and Japan. At that time, the big-box retailer was already active in six foreign countries, with some 500 stores outside the United States. Given the intense pressure for cost reductions in the retail industry and Walmart's superior strategic position as the dominant cost leader in the U.S., executives decided to pursue a similar low-cost strategy in Germany. In 2006, however, Walmart exited Germany, after losing billions of dollars. This massive failure came as a shock to a company that was used to success. What went wrong?

To enter Germany, Walmart acquired the 21-store Wertkauf chain and 74 hypermarkets from German retailer Spar Handels AG. Next, Walmart attempted to implement its U.S. personnel policies and procedures: the Walmart cheer, a door greeter, every associate within 10 feet of a customer smiling and offering help, bagging groceries at the checkout, video surveillance, a prohibition against dating co-workers, and so on. German employees, however, simply refused to accept these policies. There were no door greeters in the German Walmart stores. The front-line employees behaved as gruffly as they do in other retail outlets in Germany. It also didn't help that the first Walmart boss in Germany was installed from Walmart headquarters in Bentonville, Arkansas. The executive didn't speak any German, and simply decreed that English would be the official in-house language.

Significant cultural differences aside, one of the biggest problems Walmart faced in Germany was that, lacking its usual economies of scale and efficient distribution centers, it couldn't get its costs down far enough to successfully implement its trademark cost-leadership strategy. Higher required wages and restrictive labor laws further drove up costs. As a result, the prices at Walmart in Germany were not "always low" as the company slogan suggested, but fell in the medium range. Germany was already home to retail discount powerhouses such as Aldi and Lidl, with thousands of smaller outlets offering higher convenience combined with lower prices. Walmart was unable to be cost-competitive against such tough domestic competition. It also faced Metro, a dominant large-box retailer, that upon entering Germany immediately initiated a price war against Walmart. In the end, a defeated Walmart sold its stores to—guess who?—Metro![41]

LOSS OF REPUTATION. One of the most valuable resources that a firm may possess is its reputation. A firm's reputation can have several dimensions, including a reputation for innovation, customer service, or brand reputation. Apple's brand, for example, stands for innovation and superior customer experience. Apple's brand reputation is also one of its most important resources. Apple's brand is valued at $185 billion, making it the most valuable in the world.[42] We detailed in Chapter 4 that a brand can lead to competitive advantage if it is valuable, rare, and difficult to imitate.

Globalizing a supply chain, for example, can have unintended side effects. These in turn can lead to a loss of reputation and diminish the MNE's competitiveness. A possible loss in reputation can be a considerable risk and cost for doing business abroad. Because Apple's stellar consumer reputation is critical to its competitive advantage, it should be very concerned about any potential negative exposure from its global activities. Problems at Apple's main supplier, Foxconn, brought this concern to the fore.

Low wages, long hours, and poor working and living conditions contributed to a spate of suicides at Foxconn, Apple's main supplier in China.[43] The Taiwanese company, which employs more than one million people, manufactures computers, tablets, smartphones, and other consumer electronics for Apple and other leading consumer electronics companies. The backlash against alleged sweatshop conditions in Foxconn prompted Apple to work with its main supplier to improve working conditions and wages. Tim Cook, Apple's CEO, visited Foxconn in China to personally inspect its manufacturing facility and workers' living conditions. Although conditions at Foxconn have been improving,[44] Apple started to diversify its supplier base by adding Pegatron, another Taiwanese original equipment manufacturer (OEM).[45]

There have also been some tragic effects of the MNEs' search for low-cost labor, often in a context where local governments are corrupt and unwilling or unable to enforce a minimum of safety standards. The textile industry is notorious for sweatshop conditions, and many Western companies such as the Gap (U.S.), H&M (UK), and Carrefour (France) have taken a big hit to their reputation in recent factory accidents in Bangladesh and elsewhere in Southeast Asia. Hundreds of factory workers were killed when a textile factory collapsed on the outskirts of Dhaka, Bangladesh.[46] Although much of the blame lies with the often corrupt host governments not enforcing laws, regulations, and building codes, the MNEs that source their textiles in these factories also receive some of the blame with negative consequences for their reputation. The MNEs are accused of exploiting workers and being indifferent to their working conditions and safety, all in an unending quest to drive down costs.

This challenge directly concerns the MNEs' *corporate social responsibility (CSR),* discussed in Chapter 2. Since some host governments are either unwilling or unable to enforce regulation and safety codes, MNEs need to rise to the challenge.[47] Walmart responded by posting a public list of "banned suppliers" on its website. These are suppliers that do not meet adequate safety standards and working conditions. Prior to the Rana Plaza accident, Walmart had already launched a working and fire-safety academy in Bangladesh to train textile workers.

Given the regulatory and legal void that local governments often leave, several Western MNEs have proposed a concerted action to finance safety efforts and worker training as well as structural upgrades to factory buildings. After earlier revelations about the frequent practice of child labor in many developing countries, Western MNEs in the textile industry worked together to ban their suppliers from using child labor. Ensuring "ethical sourcing" of raw materials and supplies is becoming ever more important. Besides a moral responsibility, MNEs have a market incentive to protect their reputations given the public backlash in the wake of factory accidents, child labor, worker suicides, and other horrific externalities.

LOSS OF INTELLECTUAL PROPERTY. Finally, the issue of protecting intellectual property in foreign markets also looms large. The software, movie, and music industries have long lamented large-scale copyright infringements in many foreign markets. In addition, when required to partner with a foreign host firm, companies may find their intellectual property being siphoned off and reverse-engineered.

Japanese and European engineering companies entered China, for example, to participate in building the world's largest network of high-speed trains worth billions of dollars.[48] Companies such as Kawasaki Heavy Industries (Japan), Siemens (Germany), and Alstom (France) were joint venture partners with domestic Chinese companies. These firms now allege that the Chinese partners built on the Japanese and European partners' advanced technology to create their own, next-generation high-speed trains. To make matters worse, they also claim that the Chinese companies now compete against them in other lucrative foreign markets, such as Saudi Arabia, Brazil, and even California, with trains of equal or better capabilities but at much lower prices. This example highlights the *intellectual property exposure* that firms can face when expanding overseas.

10.3 Going Global: Where and How?

LO 10-3

Apply the CAGE distance framework to explain which countries MNEs enter.

After discussing why companies expand internationally, we now turn our attention to the question of which countries MNEs choose to enter, and how they do so.

WHERE IN THE WORLD TO COMPETE? THE CAGE DISTANCE FRAMEWORK

The question of where to compete geographically is, besides vertical integration and diversification, the third dimension of determining a firm's corporate strategy. The primary drivers behind firms expanding beyond their domestic market are to gain access to larger markets and low-cost input factors and to develop new competencies. Often, however, several countries and locations score similarly on *absolute* metrics. Ireland and Portugal, for example, have similar cost structures, and both provide access to the 500 million customers in the European Union. In such cases, how does an MNE decide? Rather than looking at absolute measures such as the combination of market size (e.g., per capita fast-food consumption) and consumer purchasing power (e.g., proxied by per capita income) when conducting a country portfolio analysis, MNEs need to consider *relative distance*.

CAGE distance framework A decision framework based on the *relative* distance between home and a foreign target country along four dimensions: cultural distance, administrative and political distance, geographic distance, and economic distance.

To aid MNEs in deciding where in the world to compete, Pankaj Ghemawat introduced the **CAGE distance framework**. CAGE is an acronym for *C*ultural, *A*dministrative and political, *G*eographic, and *E*conomic distance.[49] Most of the costs and risks involved in expanding beyond the domestic market are created by *distance*. Distance not only denotes geographic distance (in miles or kilometers), but also includes, as the CAGE acronym points out, cultural distance, administrative and political distance, and economic distance. The CAGE distance framework breaks distance into different relative components between any two country pairs that affect the success of FDI.

Although absolute metrics such as country wealth or market size matter to some extent (for example, a 1 percent increase in country wealth leads to a 0.8 percent increase in international trade), the relative factors captured by the CAGE distance model matter more. For instance, countries that are 5,000 miles apart trade only 20 percent of the amount traded among countries that are 1,000 miles apart. Cultural distance matters even more. A common language increases trade between two countries by 200 percent over country pairs that do not share a common language. In the earlier example regarding which EU country to select for FDI, a U.S. MNE would pick Ireland, while a Brazilian MNE would select Portugal. In the latter case, Brazil and Portugal also share a historic colony–colonizer relationship. This tie increases the expected trade intensity between these two countries by yet another 900 percent in comparison to country pairs where this link is absent. Other CAGE distance factors that are significant in predicting the amount of trade between two countries include whether they belong to the same regional trading bloc (+330 percent; e.g., the U.S. and Mexico in NAFTA, or the 28 member states of the European Union) and whether the two countries use the same currency (+340 percent; e.g., the euro is used in 17 of 28 EU countries as the common currency).

Exhibit 10.3 presents the CAGE distance model. In particular, it details factors that increase the distance between two countries and how distance affects different industries or products along the CAGE dimensions.[50] Next, we briefly discuss each of the CAGE distance dimensions.[51]

national culture The collective mental and emotional "programming of the mind" that differentiates human groups.

CULTURAL DISTANCE. In his research, Geert Hofstede defined and measured **national culture**, the collective mental and emotional "programming of the mind" that differentiates human groups.[52] Culture is made up of a collection of social norms and mores,

EXHIBIT 10.3 / The CAGE Distance Framework

	C **Cultural Distance**	*A* **Administrative and Political Distance**	*G* **Geographic Distance**	*E* **Economic Distance**
Distance between two countries increases with . . .	• Different languages, ethnicities, religions, social norms, and dispositions • Lack of connective ethnic or social networks • Lack of trust and mutual respect	• Absence of trading bloc • Absence of shared currency, monetary or political association • Absence of colonial ties • Political hostilities • Weak legal and financial institutions	• Lack of common border, waterway access, adequate transportation, or communication links • Physical remoteness • Different climates and time zones	• Different consumer incomes • Different costs and quality of natural, financial, and human resources • Different information or knowledge
Distance most affects industries or products . . .	• With high linguistic content (TV) • Related to national and/or religious identity (foods) • Carrying country-specific quality associations (wines)	• That a foreign government views as staples (electricity), as building national reputations (aerospace), or as vital to national security (telecommunications)	• With low value-to-weight ratio (cement) • That are fragile or perishable (glass, meats) • In which communications are vital (financial services)	• For which demand varies by income (cars) • In which labor and other cost differences matter (textiles)

SOURCE: Adapted from P. Ghemawat (2001), "Distance still matters: The hard reality of global expansion," *Harvard Business Review*, September: 137–147.

beliefs, and values. Culture captures the often unwritten and implicitly understood rules of the game.

Although there is no one-size-fits-all culture that accurately describes any nation, Hofstede's work provides a useful tool to proxy cultural distance. Based on data analysis from more than 100,000 individuals from many different countries, four dimensions of culture emerged: *power distance, individualism, masculinity–femininity,* and *uncertainty avoidance.*[53] Hofstede's data analysis yielded scores for the different countries, for each dimension, on a range of zero to 100, with 100 as the high end. More recently, Hofstede added a fifth cultural dimension: *long-term orientation.*[54]

Cultural differences find their expression in language, ethnicity, religion, and social norms. They directly affect customer preferences (see Exhibit 10.3). Because of their religious beliefs, for example, Hindus do not eat beef, while Muslims do not eat pork. In terms of content-intensive service, cultural and language differences are also the reason why global Internet companies such as Amazon or Google offer country-specific variations of their sites. Despite these best efforts, they are often outflanked by native providers because of their deeper cultural understanding. For example, in China the leading websites are domestic ones: Alibaba in e-commerce, and Baidu in online search. In Russia, the leading e-commerce site is Ozon, while the leading search engine is Yandex.

Hofstede's national-culture research becomes even more useful for managers by combining the four distinct dimensions of culture into an aggregate measure for each country. MNEs then can compare the national-culture measures for any two country pairings to

When Starbucks entered the Chinese market in 2000, it sought to reduce cultural distance by handing out keychains to help new customers learn how to order. Layered cylinders on the mini coffee cup represent drink options—caffeinated or not, number of espresso shots, type of syrup, and so on. The customer spins the choices into the desired position and hands the keychain to the barista.

cultural distance
Cultural disparity between an internationally expanding firm's home country and its targeted host country.

inform their entry decisions.[55] The difference between scores indicates **cultural distance**, the cultural disparity between the internationally expanding firm's home country and its targeted host country. A firm's decision to enter certain international markets is influenced by cultural differences. A greater cultural distance can increase the cost and uncertainty of conducting business abroad. In short, greater cultural distance increases the liability of foreignness.

If we calculate the cultural distance from the U.S. to various countries, for example, we find that some countries are culturally very close to the U.S. (e.g., Australia has an overall cultural distance score of 0.02), while others are culturally quite distant (e.g., Russia has an overall cultural distance score of 4.42). As can be expected, English-speaking countries such as Canada (0.12), Ireland (0.35), New Zealand (0.26), and the UK (0.09) all exhibit a low cultural distance to the United States. Since culture is embedded in language, it comes as no surprise that cultural and linguistic differences are highly correlated.

Culture even matters in the age of Facebook with its global reach of over one billion users. Turns out that most Facebook friends are local rather than across borders. This makes sense when one considers that the online social graph that Facebook users develop in their network of friends is actually a virtual network laid above a (pre)existing social network, rather than forming one anew.[56]

ADMINISTRATIVE AND POLITICAL DISTANCE.

Administrative and political distances are captured in factors such as the absence or presence of shared monetary or political associations, political hostilities, and weak legal and financial institutions.[57] The 17 European countries in the Eurozone, for example, not only share the same currency but are also integrated politically to some extent. It should come as no surprise then that most cross-border trade between European countries takes place within the EU. Germany, one of the world's largest exporters, conducts roughly 75 percent of its cross-border business within the EU.[58] Similarly, Canada and Mexico partner with the United States in the North American Free Trade Agreement (NAFTA), increasing trade in goods and services between the three countries. Colony–colonizer relationships also have a strong positive effect on bilateral trade between countries. British companies continue to trade heavily with businesses from its former colonies in the Commonwealth; Spanish companies trade heavily with Latin American countries; and French businesses trade with the franc zone of West Africa.

Many foreign (target) countries also erect other political and administrative barriers, such as tariffs, trade quotas, FDI restrictions, and so forth, to protect domestic competitors. In many instances, China, for example, requests the sharing of technology in a joint venture when entering the country. This was the case in the high-speed train developments discussed earlier. Other countries, such as the U.S. or those in the EU, protect national champions like Boeing or Airbus from foreign competition. Industries that are considered critical to national security such as domestic airlines or telecommunications are often protected. Finally, strong legal and ethical pillars as well as well-functioning economic institutions like capital markets and an independent central bank reduce distance. Strong institutions, both formal and informal, reduce uncertainty, and thus reduce transaction costs.[59]

GEOGRAPHIC DISTANCE.

The costs to cross-border trade rise with geographic distance. It is important to note, however, that geographic distance does not simply capture how far two countries are from each other but also includes additional attributes such as the country's physical size (Canada versus Singapore), whether the countries are contiguous to one another, have access to waterways to the ocean, the within-country distances to its borders, the country's topography, and its time zones. The country's infrastructure such as road, power, and telecommunications networks also plays a role in determining geographic distance. Geographic distance is particularly relevant when trading products with low value-to-weight ratios such as steel, cement, or other bulk products and fragile and perishable products such as glass or fresh meats and fruits.

ECONOMIC DISTANCE. The wealth and per capita income of consumers is the most important determinant of economic distance. Wealthy countries engage in relatively more cross-border trade than poorer ones. Rich countries tend to trade with other rich countries; in addition, poor countries also trade more frequently with rich countries than with other poor countries. Companies from wealthy countries benefit in cross-border trade with other wealthy countries when their competitive advantage is based on *economies of experience, scale, scope,* and *standardization.* This is because replication of an existing business model is much easier in a country where the incomes are relatively similar and resources, complements, and infrastructure are of roughly equal quality. Although Walmart in Canada is a virtual carbon copy of the Walmart in the United States, Walmart in India is very different.[60] *The Wall Street Journal* captured Walmart's difficulties in replicating its finely tuned supply chain with the overarching aim to minimize cost in the headline "Bad Roads, Red Tape, Burly Thugs Slow Walmart's Passage in India."[61] These are all key reasons why India would score as very distant from the U.S. using the CAGE model. In contrast, Walmart's successful expansion into Canada was a simple *replication.*

Companies from wealthy countries also trade with companies from poor countries to benefit from *economic arbitrage.* The textile industry (discussed earlier) is a prime example. We also highlighted economic arbitrage as one of the main benefits of "going global": access to low-cost input factors.

In conclusion, although the CAGE distance framework helps determine the attractiveness of foreign target markets in a more fine-grained manner based on relative differences, it is necessarily only a first step. A deeper analysis requires looking inside the firm (as done in Chapter 4) to see how a firm's strengths and weaknesses work to increase or reduce distance from specific foreign markets. A company with a large cadre of cosmopolitan managers and a diverse work force will be much less affected by cultural differences, for example, than a company with a more insular and less diverse culture with all managers from the home country. Although technology may make the world seem smaller, the costs of distance along all its dimensions are real. The costs of distance in expanding internationally are often very high. Ignoring these costs can be very costly (see Walmart's adventure in Germany, discussed in Strategy Highlight 10.2) and lead to a competitive disadvantage.

HOW DO MNEs ENTER FOREIGN MARKETS?

Assuming an MNE has decided why and where to enter a foreign market, the remaining decision is *how* to do so. Exhibit 10.4 displays the different options managers have when entering foreign markets, along with the required investments necessary and the control they can exert. On the end of the continuum (left in Exhibit 10.4) are vehicles of foreign expansion that require low investments but also allow for a low level of control. On the right are foreign entry modes that require a high level of investments in terms of capital and other resources, but also allow for a high level of control. Foreign entry modes with a high level of control such as foreign acquisitions or greenfield plants reduce the firm's exposure to two particular downsides of global business: loss of reputation and loss of intellectual property.

LO 10-4

Compare and contrast the different options MNEs have to enter foreign markets.

EXHIBIT 10.4 / Modes of Foreign-Market Entry along the Investment and Control Continuum

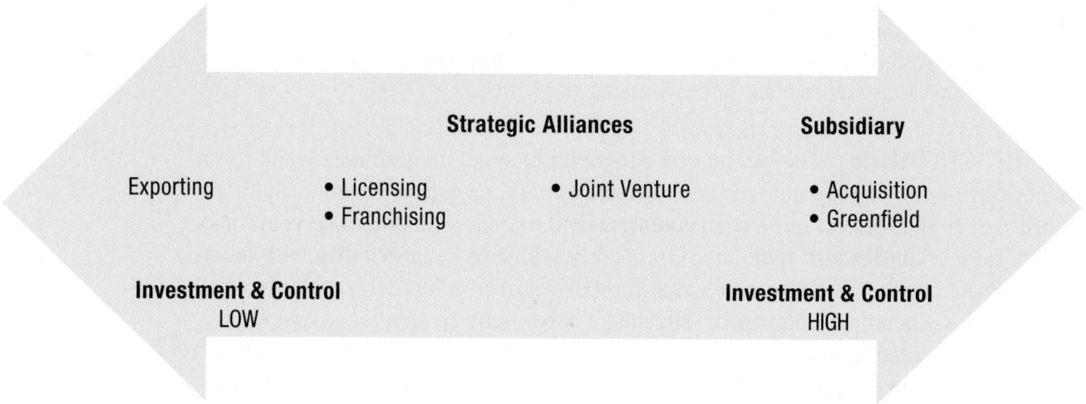

Strategic Alliances   **Subsidiary**

Exporting   • Licensing   • Joint Venture   • Acquisition
                    • Franchising   • Greenfield

Investment & Control   **Investment & Control**
LOW   HIGH

Exporting—producing goods in one country to sell in another—is one of the oldest forms of internationalization (part of Globalization 1.0). It is often used to test whether a foreign market is ready for a firm's products. When studying vertical integration and diversification (in Chapter 8), we discussed in detail different forms along the make-or-buy continuum. As discussed in Chapter 9, acquisitions and strategic alliances (including licensing, franchising, and joint ventures) are popular vehicles for entry into foreign markets. Since we discussed these organizational arrangements in detail in previous chapters, we therefore keep this section on foreign entry modes brief.

The framework illustrated in Exhibit 10.4, moving from left to right, has been suggested as a *stage model* of sequential commitment to a foreign market over time.[62] Though it does not apply to globally born companies, it is relevant for manufacturing companies that are just now expanding into global operations. In some instances, companies are required by the host country to form joint ventures in order to conduct business there, while some MNEs prefer *greenfield operations* (building new plants and facilities from scratch), as Motorola did when it entered China in the 1990s.[63]

10.4 Cost Reductions vs. Local Responsiveness: The Integration-Responsiveness Framework

LO 10-5

Apply the integration-responsiveness framework to evaluate the four different strategies MNEs can pursue when competing globally.

When discussing business strategy (in Chapter 6), we noted that an effective integration strategy must resolve the inherent trade-offs between cost and differentiation. In much the same fashion, MNEs face two opposing forces when competing around the globe: *cost reductions* versus *local responsiveness*. Indeed, cost reductions achieved through a global-standardization strategy often reinforce a cost-leadership strategy at the business level. Similarly, local responsiveness increases the differentiation of products and services, reinforcing a differentiation strategy at the business level.

One of the core drivers for globalization is to expand the total market of firms in order to achieve economies of scale and drive down costs. For many business executives, the move toward globalization was based on the **globalization hypothesis**, which states that consumer needs and preferences throughout the world are converging and thus becoming increasingly homogenous.[64] Theodore Levitt stated: "Nothing confirms [the globalization hypothesis] as much as the success of McDonald's from [the] Champs-Élysées to Ginza, of Coca-Cola in Bahrain and Pepsi-Cola in Moscow, and of rock music, Greek salad, Hollywood movies, Revlon cosmetics, Sony televisions, and Levi jeans everywhere."[65]

In support of the globalization hypothesis, Toyota is selling its hybrid Prius vehicle successfully in 80 countries. Most vehicles today are built on global platforms and modified (sometimes only cosmetically) to meet local tastes and standards.

The strategic foundations of the globalization hypothesis are based primarily on cost reduction. One key competitive weapon is lower price, and MNEs attempt to reap significant cost reductions by leveraging economies of scale and by managing global supply chains to access the lowest-cost input factors.

Although there seems to be some convergence of consumer preferences across the globe, national differences remain, due to distinct institutions and cultures. For example, in the 1990s, Ford Motor Company followed this one-size-fits-all strategy by offering a more or less identical car throughout the world: the Ford Mondeo, sold as the Ford Contour and the Mercury Mystique in North America. Ford learned the hard way (lack of sales) that consumer preferences were not converging sufficiently to allow it to ignore regional differences.[66] In some instances, MNEs therefore experience pressure for **local responsiveness**—the need to tailor product and service offerings to fit local consumer preferences and host-country requirements. McDonald's, for example, uses mutton instead of beef in India and offers a teriyaki burger in Japan, even though its basic business model of offering fast food remains the same the world over. Local responsiveness generally entails higher cost, and sometimes even outweighs cost advantages from economies of scale and lower-cost input factors.

Given the two opposing pressures of cost reductions versus local responsiveness, scholars have advanced the **integration-responsiveness framework**, shown in Exhibit 10.5.[67] This framework juxtaposes the opposing pressures for cost reductions and local responsiveness to derive four different strategies to gain and sustain competitive advantage when competing globally. The four strategies, which we will discuss in the following sections, are:

- International strategy
- Multidomestic strategy
- Global-standardization strategy
- Transnational strategy[68]

At the end of that discussion, Exhibit 10.7 summarizes each global strategy.

INTERNATIONAL STRATEGY

An **international strategy** is essentially a strategy in which a company sells the same products or services in both domestic and foreign markets. It enables MNEs to leverage their home-based core competencies in foreign markets. An international strategy is one

---

globalization hypothesis Assumption that consumer needs and preferences throughout the world are converging and thus becoming increasingly homogenous.

local responsiveness The need to tailor product and service offerings to fit local consumer preferences and host-country requirements; generally entails higher costs.

integration-responsiveness framework Strategy framework that juxtaposes the pressures an MNE faces for cost reductions and local responsiveness to derive four different strategies to gain and sustain competitive advantage when competing globally: international strategy, multidomestic strategy, global-standardization strategy, and transnational strategy.

international strategy Strategy that involves leveraging home-based core competencies by selling the same products or services in both domestic and foreign markets; advantageous when the MNE faces low pressures for both local responsiveness and cost reductions.

EXHIBIT 10.5

The Integration-Responsiveness Framework: Global Strategy Positions and Representative MNEs

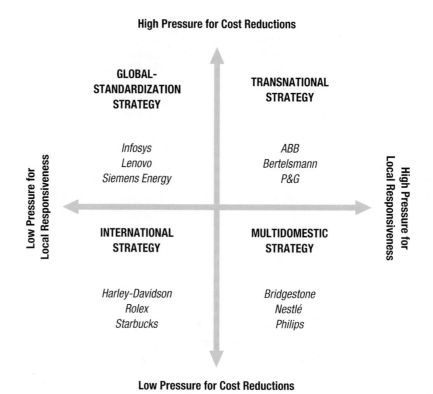

High Pressure for Cost Reductions

GLOBAL-STANDARDIZATION STRATEGY

Infosys
Lenovo
Siemens Energy

TRANSNATIONAL STRATEGY

ABB
Bertelsmann
P&G

Low Pressure for Local Responsiveness

High Pressure for Local Responsiveness

INTERNATIONAL STRATEGY

Harley-Davidson
Rolex
Starbucks

MULTIDOMESTIC STRATEGY

Bridgestone
Nestlé
Philips

Low Pressure for Cost Reductions

of the oldest types of global strategies (Globalization 1.0) and is frequently the first step companies take when beginning to conduct business abroad. As shown in the integration-responsiveness framework, it is advantageous when the MNE faces low pressures for both local responsiveness and cost reductions.

An international strategy is often used successfully by MNEs with relatively large domestic markets, and strong reputations and brand names. These MNEs, capitalizing on the fact that foreign customers want to buy the original product, tend to use differentiation as their preferred business strategy. For example, bikers in Shanghai, China, like their Harley-Davidson motorcycles to roar just like the ones ridden by the Hells Angels in the United States. Similarly, a Brazilian entrepreneur importing machine tools from Germany expects superior engineering and quality. An international strategy tends to rely on exporting or the licensing of products and franchising of services to reap economies of scale by accessing a larger market.

A strength of the international strategy—its limited local responsiveness—is also a weakness in many industries. For example, when an MNE sells its products in foreign markets with little or no change, it leaves itself open to the expropriation of intellectual property (IP). Looking at the MNE's products and services, pirates can reverse-engineer the products to discover the intellectual property embedded in them. In Thailand, for example, a flourishing market for knockoff luxury sports cars (e.g., Ferraris, Lamborghinis, and Porsches) has sprung up.[69] Besides the risk of exposing IP, MNEs following an international strategy are highly affected by exchange-rate fluctuations. Given increasing globalization, however, fewer and fewer markets correspond to this situation—low pressures for local responsiveness *and* cost reductions—that gives rise to the international strategy.

MULTIDOMESTIC STRATEGY

MNEs pursuing a **multidomestic strategy** attempt to maximize local responsiveness, hoping that local consumers will perceive them to be domestic companies. This strategy arises out of the combination of high pressure for local responsiveness and low pressure for cost reductions. MNEs frequently use a multidomestic strategy when entering host countries with large and/or idiosyncratic domestic markets, such as Japan or Saudi Arabia. This is one of the main strategies MNEs pursued in the Globalization 2.0 stage.

A multidomestic strategy is common in the consumer products and food industries. For example, Swiss-based Nestlé, the largest food company in the world, is well known for customizing its product offerings to suit local preferences, tastes, and requirements. Given the strong brand names and core competencies in R&D, and the quality in their consumer products and food industries, it is not surprising that these MNEs generally pursue a differentiation strategy at the business level. An MNE following a multidomestic strategy, in contrast with an international strategy, faces reduced exchange-rate exposure because the majority of the value creation takes place in the host-country business units, which tend to span all functions.

On the downside, a multidomestic strategy is costly and inefficient because it requires the duplication of key business functions across multiple countries. Each country unit tends to be highly autonomous, and the MNE is unable to reap economies of scale or learning across regions. The risk of IP appropriation increases when companies follow a multidomestic strategy. Besides exposing codified knowledge embedded in products, as is the case with an international strategy, a multidomestic strategy also requires exposing tacit knowledge because products are manufactured locally. Tacit knowledge that is at risk of appropriation may include, for example, the process of how to create consumer products of higher perceived quality.

> **multidomestic strategy** Strategy pursued by MNEs that attempts to maximize local responsiveness, with the intent that local consumers will perceive them to be domestic companies; the strategy arises out of the combination of high pressure for local responsiveness and low pressure for cost reductions.

GLOBAL-STANDARDIZATION STRATEGY

MNEs following a **global-standardization strategy** attempt to reap significant economies of scale and location economies by pursuing a global division of labor based on wherever best-of-class capabilities reside at the lowest cost. The global-standardization strategy arises out of the combination of high pressure for cost reductions and low pressure for local responsiveness. MNEs who use this strategy are often organized as networks (Globalization 3.0). This lets them strive for the lowest cost position possible. Their business-level strategy tends to be cost leadership. Because there is little or no differentiation or local responsiveness (because products are standardized), price becomes the main competitive weapon.

MNEs that manufacture commodity products such as computer hardware or offer services such as business process outsourcing generally pursue a global-standardization strategy. Lenovo, the Chinese computer manufacturer, is now the maker of the ThinkPad line of laptops, which it acquired from IBM in 2005. To keep track of the latest developments in computing, Lenovo's research centers are located in Beijing and Shanghai in China, in Raleigh, North Carolina (in the Research Triangle Park), and in Japan.[70] To benefit from low-cost labor and to be close to its main markets in order to reduce shipping costs, Lenovo's manufacturing facilities are in Mexico, India, and China. The company describes the benefits of its global-standardization strategy insightfully: "Lenovo organizes its worldwide operations with the view that a truly global company must be able to quickly capitalize on new ideas and opportunities from anywhere. By forgoing a traditional headquarters model and focusing on centers of excellence around the world, Lenovo makes the maximum use of its resources to create the best products in the most efficient and effective way possible."[71]

> **global-standardization strategy** Strategy attempting to reap significant economies of scale and location economies by pursuing a global division of labor based on wherever best-of-class capabilities reside at the lowest cost.

One of the advantages of the global-standardization strategy—obtaining the lowest cost point possible by minimizing local adaptations—is also one of its key weaknesses. The American MTV network cable channel started out with a global-standardization strategy.[72] The main inputs—music videos by vocal artists—were sourced more or less globally based on the prevailing music hits. MTV reasoned that music videos were a commodity product that would attract worldwide audiences. MTV was wrong! As indicated by the CAGE distance model, cultural distance most affects products with high linguistic content such as TV. Even in a music video channel, audiences have a distinct preference for at least some local content.

Keep in mind that strategic positions are not constant; they can change over time. Exhibit 10.6 shows how MTV changed its strategic positions over time. To be more responsive to local audiences, MTV then implemented a multidomestic strategy to meet the need for local responsiveness. This turn led to a loss of all possible scale effects, especially rolling out expensive content over a large installed base of viewers. In a next move, MTV shifted its strategic position away from a multidomestic strategy and is now pursuing a transnational strategy.

TRANSNATIONAL STRATEGY

MNEs pursuing a **transnational strategy** attempt to combine the benefits of a localization strategy (high local responsiveness) with those of a global-standardization strategy (lowest cost position attainable). This strategy arises out of the combination of high pressure for local responsiveness and high pressure for cost reductions. A transnational strategy is generally used by MNEs that pursue an integration strategy at the business level by attempting to reconcile product and/or service differentiations at low cost.

transnational strategy
Strategy that attempts to combine the benefits of a localization strategy (high local responsiveness) with those of a global-standardization strategy (lowest cost position attainable).

EXHIBIT 10.6 /

Dynamic Strategic Positioning: The MTV Music Chanel

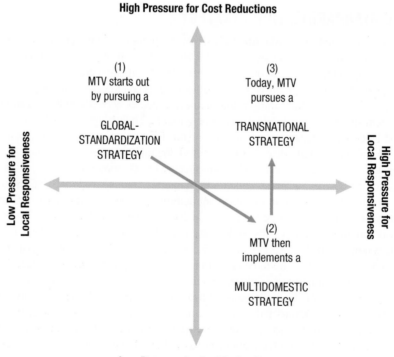

Besides harnessing economies of scale and location, a transnational strategy also aims to benefit from global learning. MNEs typically implement a transnational strategy through a global matrix structure. That structure combines economies of scale along specific product divisions with economies of learning attainable in specific geographic regions. The idea is that best practices, ideas, and innovations will be diffused throughout the world, regardless of their origination. The managers' mantra is to *think globally, but act locally.*

Although a transnational strategy is quite appealing, the required matrix structure is rather difficult to implement because of the organizational complexities involved. High local responsiveness typically requires that key business functions are frequently duplicated in each host country, leading to higher costs. Further compounding the organizational complexities is the challenge of finding managers who can dexterously work across cultures in the ways required by a transnational strategy. We'll discuss organizational structure in more depth in the next chapter.

The German multimedia conglomerate Bertelsmann attempts to follow a transnational strategy. Bertelsmann employs over 100,000 people, with two-thirds of that work force outside its home country. In particular, Bertelsmann operates in more than 60 countries throughout the world, and owns many regional leaders in their specific product categories, including Random House Publishing in the U.S. and RTL Group, Europe's second-largest TV, radio, and production company (after the BBC). Bertelsmann operates its over 500 regional media divisions as more or less autonomous profit-and-loss centers; global learning and human resource strategies for executives are coordinated at the network level.[73]

As a summary, Exhibit 10.7 (next page) provides a detailed description of each of the four global strategies in the integration-responsiveness framework.

10.5 National Competitive Advantage: World Leadership in Specific Industries

Globalization, the prevalence of the Internet and other advances in communications technology, and transportation logistics can lead us to believe that firm location is becoming increasingly less important.[74] Because firms can now, more than ever, source inputs globally, many believe that location must be diminishing in importance as an explanation of firm-level competitive advantage. This idea is called the **death-of-distance hypothesis**.[75]

Despite an increasingly globalized world, however, it turns out that high-performing firms in certain industries *are* concentrated in specific countries.[76] For example, the leading biotechnology, software, and Internet companies are headquartered in the United States. Some of the world's best computer manufacturers are in China and Taiwan. Many of the leading consumer electronics companies are in South Korea and Japan. The top mining companies are in Australia. The leading business process outsourcing (BPO) companies are in India. Some of the best engineering and car companies are in Germany. The world's top fashion designers are in Italy. The best wineries are in France. The list goes on. Although globalization lowers the barriers to trade and investments and increases human capital mobility, one key question remains: *Why are certain industries more competitive in some countries than in others?* This question goes to the heart of the issue of **national competitive advantage**, a consideration of world leadership in specific industries. That

death-of-distance hypothesis Assumption that geographic location alone should not lead to firm-level competitive advantage because firms are now, more than ever, able to source inputs globally.

national competitive advantage World leadership in specific industries.

EXHIBIT 10.7 / International, Multidomestic, Global-Standardization, and Transnational Strategies: Characteristics, Benefits, and Risks

	Characteristics	Benefits	Risks

International Strategy	• Often the first step in internationalizing.
	• Used by MNEs with relatively large domestic markets or strong exporters (e.g., MNEs from the U.S., Germany, Japan, South Korea).
	• Well-suited for high-end products with high value-to-weight ratios such as machine tools and luxury goods that can be shipped across the globe.
	• Products and services tend to have strong brands.
	• Main business-level strategy tends to be differentiation because exporting, licensing, and franchising add additional costs.
		• Leveraging core competencies.
		• Economies of scale.
		• Low-cost implementation through:
		  ▪ Exporting or licensing (for products)
		  ▪ Franchising (for services)
		  ▪ Licensing (for trademarks)
			• No or limited local responsiveness.
			• Highly affected by exchange-rate fluctuations.
			• IP embedded in product or service could be expropriated.

Multidomestic Strategy	• Used by MNEs to compete in host countries with large and/or lucrative but idiosyncratic domestic markets (e.g., Germany, Japan, Saudi Arabia). • Often used in consumer products and food industries. • Main business-level strategy is differentiation. • MNE wants to be perceived as local company.	• Highest-possible local responsiveness. • Increased differentiation. • Reduced exchange-rate exposure.	• Duplication of key business functions in multiple countries leads to high cost of implementation. • Little or no economies of scale. • Little or no learning across different regions. • Higher risk of IP expropriation.
Global-Standardization Strategy	• Used by MNEs that are offering standardized products and services (e.g., computer hardware or business process outsourcing). • Main business-level strategy is cost leadership.	• Location economies: global division of labor based on wherever best-of-class capabilities reside at lowest cost. • Economies of scale and standardization.	• No local responsiveness. • Little or no product differentiation. • Some exchange-rate exposure. • "Race to the bottom" as wages increase. • Some risk of IP expropriation.
Transnational Strategy	• Used by MNEs that pursue an integration strategy at the business level by simultaneously focusing on product differentiation and low cost. • Mantra: Think globally, act locally.	• Attempts to combine benefits of localization and standardization strategies simultaneously by creating a global matrix structure. • Economies of scale, location, experience and learning.	• Global matrix structure is costly and difficult to implement, leading to high failure rate. • Some exchange-rate exposure. • Higher risk of IP expropriation.

issue, in turn, has a direct effect on firm-level competitive advantage. Companies from home countries that are world leaders in specific industries tend to be the strongest competitors globally.

PORTER'S DIAMOND FRAMEWORK

Michael Porter advanced a framework to explain national competitive advantage—why are some nations outperforming others in specific industries. This framework is called Porter's diamond of national competitive advantage, and is shown in Exhibit 10.8. It consists of four interrelated factors:

■ Factor conditions

■ Demand conditions

■ Competitive intensity in focal industry

■ Related and supporting industries/complementors

FACTOR CONDITIONS. *Factor conditions* describe a country's endowments in terms of natural, human, and other resources. Interestingly, natural resources are often not needed to generate world-leading companies, because competitive advantage is often based on human capital and know-how. Several of the world's most resource-rich countries (such as Afghanistan,[77] Iran, Iraq, Russia, Saudi Arabia, and Venezuela) are not home to any

LO 10-6

Apply Porter's diamond framework to explain why certain industries are more competitive in specific nations than in others.

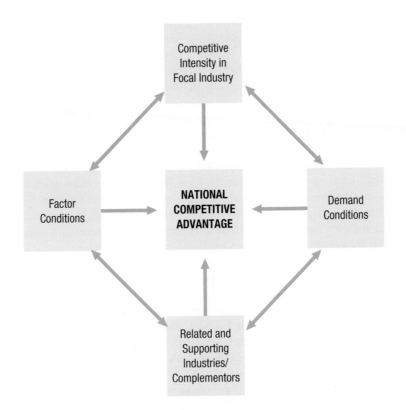

EXHIBIT 10.8

Porter's Diamond of National Competitive Advantage

SOURCE: Adapted from M. E. Porter (1990), "The competitive advantage of nations," *Harvard Business Review*, March–April: 78.

of the world's leading companies, even though some (though not all) do have in place institutional frameworks allowing them to be a productive member of world commerce. In contrast, countries that lack natural resources (e.g., Denmark, Finland, Israel, Japan, Singapore, South Korea, Switzerland, Taiwan, and the Netherlands) often develop world-class human capital to compensate.[78] Other important factors include capital markets, a supportive institutional framework, research universities, and public infrastructure (airports, roads, schools, health care system), among others.

DEMAND CONDITIONS. *Demand conditions* are the specific characteristics of demand in a firm's domestic market. A home market made up of sophisticated customers who hold companies to a high standard of value creation and cost containment contributes to national competitive advantage. Moreover, demanding customers may also clue firms in to the latest developments in specific fields and may push firms to move research from basic findings to commercial applications for the marketplace.

For example, due to dense urban living conditions, hot and humid summers, and high energy costs, it is not surprising that Japanese customers demand small, quiet, and energy-efficient air conditioners. In contrast to the Japanese, Finns have a sparse population living in a more remote countryside. A lack of land lines for telephone service has resulted in the Finnish demand for high-quality wireless services, combined with reliable handsets (and long-life batteries) that can be operated in remote, often hostile, environments. Cell phones have long been a necessity for survival in rural areas of Finland. This situation enabled Nokia to become an early leader in cell phones.[79]

COMPETITIVE INTENSITY IN A FOCAL INDUSTRY. Companies that face a highly competitive environment at home tend to outperform global competitors that lack such intense domestic competition. Fierce domestic competition in Germany, for example, combined with demanding customers and the no-speed-limit Autobahn make a tough environment for any car company. Success requires top-notch engineering of chassis and engines, as well as keeping costs and fuel consumption ($9-per-gallon gas prices) in check. This extremely tough home environment amply prepared German car companies such as Volkswagen (which also owns Audi and Porsche), BMW, and Daimler for global competition.

RELATED AND SUPPORTING INDUSTRIES/COMPLEMENTORS. Leadership in related and supporting industries can also foster world-class competitors in downstream industries. The availability of top-notch *complementors*—firms that provide a good or service that leads customers to value the focal firm's offering more when the two are combined—further strengthens national competitive advantage. Switzerland, for example, leveraged its early lead in industrial chemicals into pharmaceuticals. A sophisticated health care service industry sprang up alongside as an important complementor, to provide further stimulus for growth and continuous improvement and innovation.

The effects of sophisticated customers and highly competitive industries ripple through the industry value chain to create top-notch suppliers and complementors. Toyota's global success in the 1990s and early 2000s was based to a large extent on a network of world-class suppliers in Japan.[80] This tightly knit network allowed for fast two-way knowledge sharing—this in turn improved Toyota's quality and lowered its cost, which it leveraged into a successful integration strategy at the business level.

It is also interesting to note that by 2010, Toyota's supplier advantage had disappeared.[81] It was unable to solve the trade-off between drastically increasing its volume and maintaining superior quality. Toyota's rapid growth to becoming the world's leader in volume required quickly bringing on new suppliers outside Japan, and quality standards couldn't be maintained. Part of the problem lies in path dependence (discussed in Chapter 4), because Chinese and other suppliers could not be found quickly enough, nor could most foreign suppliers build at the required quality levels fast enough. The cultural distance between Japan and China exacerbated these problems. Combined, these factors explain the quality problems Toyota experienced recently, and serve to highlight the importance of related and supporting industries to national competitive advantage.

10.6 ◄► Implications for the Strategist

In addition to determining the degree of vertical integration and level of diversification, the strategist needs to decide if and how the firm should compete beyond its home market. Decisions along all three dimensions formulate the firm's corporate strategy. Because of increasing global integration in products and services as well as capital markets, the benefits of competing globally outweigh the costs for more and more enterprises. This is not just true for large MNEs, but also for small and medium ones (SMEs). Even small startups are now able to leverage technology such as the Internet to compete beyond their home market.

The strategist has a number of frameworks at his or her disposal to make global strategy decisions. The CAGE framework allows for a detailed analysis of any country pairing. Rather than looking at simple absolute measures such as market size, the strategist can determine the *relative* distance or closeness of a target market to the home market along cultural, administrative/political, geographic, and economic dimensions. Once the strategist has decided which countries to enter, the mode of foreign entry needs to be determined. Considerations of the degree of investment and level of control help in this decision. Higher levels of control, and thus greater protection of IP and a lower likelihood of any loss in reputation, go along with more investment-intensive foreign entry modes such as acquisitions or greenfield plants.

A firm's business-level strategy (discussed in Chapter 6) provides an important clue to possible strategies pursued globally. A cost leader, for example, is more likely to have the capabilities to be successful with a global-standardization strategy. In contrast, a differentiator is more likely to be successful in pursuing an international or multidomestic strategy. The same caveats raised concerning an integration strategy at the business level apply at the corporate level: Although attractive on paper, a transnational strategy combining high pressures for cost reductions with high pressures for local responsiveness is difficult to implement because of inherent trade-offs.

Finally, the strategist must be aware of the fact that despite globalization and the emergence of the Internet, firm geographic location has actually maintained its importance. Critical masses of world-class firms are clearly apparent in *regional geographic clusters*. Think of computer technology firms in Silicon Valley, medical device firms in the Chicago area, and biotechnology firms in and around Boston. This is not only a U.S. phenomenon, it holds worldwide. Known for their engineering prowess, car companies such as Daimler, BMW, Audi, and Porsche are clustered in southern Germany. Many fashion-related companies (clothing, shoes, and accessories) are located in northern Italy. Singapore is a well-known cluster for semiconductor materials, and India's leading IT firms are in Bangalore. Porter captures this phenomenon succinctly: "Paradoxically, the enduring competitive advantages in a global economy lie increasingly in local things—knowledge, relationships, and motivation that distant rivals cannot match."[82]

This concludes our discussion of global strategy. Moreover, we have now completed our study of the first two pillars of the AFI framework—*Strategy Analysis* (Chapters 1–5) and *Strategy Formulation* (Chapters 6–10). Next, we turn to the third and final pillar of the AFI framework—*Strategy Implementation*. In Chapter 11, we'll study what managers can do to implement their carefully crafted strategies successfully and how to avoid failure. In Chapter 12, we study corporate governance and business ethics.

CHAPTER**CASE** 10 / Consider This . . .

THE HOLLYWOOD FILM INDUSTRY garners a surprisingly large percentage of its revenues (nearly 75 percent) from foreign sales, as discussed in the ChapterCase. This number is surprisingly large given several constraints that U.S. films have when selling internationally. First, there are numerous piracy concerns. Even in the European Union (EU), where countries like Britain and France impose fines on producers and buyers of pirated content, other countries such as Spain have long been havens for the distribution of illegal movies and music. In February 2011, Spain passed a new law to provide better protection of copyrighted material, but enforcement may be difficult in a country where nearly 50 percent of all Internet users admit to illegally downloading copyrighted content (twice the EU average rate).[83]

China is infamous for its rampant business in illegal materials. In 2010, a Chinese government report found that the market for pirated DVDs was $6 billion. As a comparison, the *total* box-office revenues in China in 2010 were $1.5 billion.[84] One reason is that ticket prices for movies in China are steep and movies are considered luxury entertainment that few can afford. Another reason that "black-market" sales in China are so high is that legitimate sales often are not allowed. China allows only about 20 new non-Chinese movies into its theaters each year. Additionally, it has strict licensing rules on the sale of home-entertainment goods. Chinese censors are not likely to approve the sale of official DVDs for movies such as *Lara Croft Tomb Raider: The Cradle of Life, Black Swan,* and *The Social Network.* As a result there is often no legitimate product competing with the bootlegged offerings available via DVD and the Internet in China.[85]

Movie studios are moving to simultaneous worldwide releases of expected block-busters in part to try to cut down on the revenues lost to piracy. International growth is expected to continue and take increasing shares of Hollywood film revenues, especially in the face of falling U.S. DVD sales. China is reportedly building new cinema screens at a rate of three per *day* in 2011. Yet growth in China (and elsewhere) is not as profitable as traditional releases in the United States. For example, film distributors typically earn 50 to 55 percent of box-office revenues in America. The average in many other countries is closer to 40 percent (the rest goes to the cinema owner). But in China, a typical Hollywood film distributor gets only 15 percent of the box-office ticket revenue.[86]

Questions

1. Given the forces on the Hollywood movie industry, is it likely we will see a decrease in the production of regional- and U.S.-centered movies, or will small independent movie producers pick up a higher share of the domestic U.S. market? Please explain.

2. What alternatives could movie producers develop to help combat the piracy of first-run movies and follow-on DVD and Internet releases?

3. How would you prioritize which nations to expand distribution into if you were working for a major Hollywood movie studio?

TAKE-AWAY CONCEPTS

This chapter discussed the roles of MNEs for economic growth; the stages of globalization; why, where, and how companies go global; four strategies MNEs use to navigate between cost reductions and local responsiveness; and national competitive advantage, as summarized by the following learning objectives and related take-away concepts.

LO 10-1 / Define globalization, multinational enterprise (MNE), foreign direct investment (FDI), and global strategy.

- Globalization involves closer integration and exchange between different countries and peoples worldwide, made possible by factors such as falling trade and investment barriers, advances in telecommunications, and reductions in transportation costs.

- A multinational enterprise (MNE) deploys resources and capabilities to procure, produce, and distribute goods and services in at least two countries.

- Many MNEs are more than 50 percent globalized; they receive the majority of their revenues from countries other than their home country.

- Product, service, and capital markets are more globalized than labor markets. The level of everyday activities is roughly 10 to 25 percent integrated, and thus *semi-globalized.*

- Foreign direct investment (FDI) denotes a firm's investments in value chain activities abroad.

LO 10-2 / Explain why companies compete abroad, and evaluate the advantages and disadvantages of a global strategy.

- Companies expand beyond their home market if the benefits outweigh the risks.

- Advantages to competing internationally include gaining access to a larger market, gaining access to low-cost input factors, and developing new competencies.

- Disadvantages to competing internationally include the liability of foreignness, the possible loss of reputation, and the possible loss of intellectual capital.

LO 10-3 / Apply the CAGE distance framework to explain which countries MNEs enter.

- Most of the costs and risks involved in expanding beyond the domestic market are created by *distance.*

- The CAGE distance framework determines the *relative* distance between home and foreign target country along four dimensions: cultural distance, administrative and political distance, geographic distance, and economic distance.

LO 10-4 / Compare and contrast the different options MNEs have to enter foreign markets.

- The strategist has the following foreign entry modes available: exporting, strategic alliances (licensing for products, franchising for services), joint venture, and subsidiary (acquisition or greenfield).

- Higher levels of control, and thus a greater protection of IP and a lower likelihood of any loss in reputation, go along with more investment-intensive foreign entry modes such as acquisitions or greenfield plants.

LO 10-5 / Apply the integration-responsiveness framework to evaluate the four different strategies MNEs can pursue when competing globally.

- To navigate between the competing pressures of cost reductions and local responsiveness, MNEs have four strategy options: international, multidomestic, global-standardization, and transnational.

- An international strategy leverages home-based core competencies into foreign markets, primarily through exports. It is useful when the MNE faces low pressures for both local responsiveness and cost reductions.

- A multidomestic strategy attempts to maximize local responsiveness in the face of low pressure for cost reductions. It is costly and inefficient because it requires the duplication of key business functions in multiple countries.

- A global-standardization strategy seeks to reap economies of scale and location by pursuing a global division of labor based on wherever best-of-class capabilities reside at the lowest cost. It involves little or no local responsiveness.

- A transnational strategy attempts to combine the high local responsiveness of a localization strategy with the lowest cost position attainable from a global-standardization strategy. It also aims to benefit from global learning. Although appealing, it is difficult to implement due to the organizational complexities involved.

LO 10-6 / Apply Porter's diamond framework to explain why certain industries are more competitive in specific nations than in others.

- National competitive advantage, or world leadership in specific industries, is created rather than inherited.

- Four interrelated factors explain national competitive advantage: (1) factor conditions, (2) demand conditions, (3) competitive intensity in a focal industry, and (4) related and supporting industries/complementors.

- Even in a more globalized world, the basis for competitive advantage is often local.

KEY TERMS

CAGE distance framework
Cultural distance
Death-of-distance hypothesis
Foreign direct investment (FDI)
Global-standardization strategy
Global strategy
Globalization

Globalization hypothesis
Integration-responsiveness framework
International strategy
Liability of foreignness
Local responsiveness
Location economies

Multidomestic strategy
Multinational enterprise (MNE)
National competitive advantage
National culture
Transnational strategy

DISCUSSION QUESTIONS

1. Think about the last movie you saw in a movie theater. What aspects of the movie had international components in it (e.g., the plot line, locations, cast, and so on)? Are there more international elements included than compared to your favorite movie from a decade ago?

2. Multinational enterprises (MNEs) have an impact far beyond their firm boundaries. Assume you are working for a small firm that supplies a product or service to an MNE. How might your relationship change as the MNE moves from Globalization 2.0 to Globalization 3.0 operations?

3. Professor Pankaj Ghemawat delivered a TED talk entitled "Actually, the World Isn't Flat." Do you agree with his assessment that the world is at most *semi-globalized,* and that we need to be careful not to fall victim to "globalony"? View the talk at: http://www.ted.com/talks/pankaj_ghemawat_actually_the_world_isn_t_flat.html [17.04 min].

4. "Licensing patented technology to a foreign competitor is likely to reduce or eliminate the firm's competitive advantage." True or false? Write a paragraph discussing this statement.

ETHICAL/SOCIAL ISSUES

1. A "race-to-the-bottom" process may set in as MNEs search for ever-lower-cost locations. Discuss the trade-offs between the positive effects of raising the standard of living in some of the world's poorest countries with the drawbacks of moving jobs established in one country to another. Does your perspective change in light of the recent accidents in textile factories in Bangladesh, Cambodia, and elsewhere, where the cumulative death was over 1,000 workers? What responsibilities do MNEs have?

2. Will the Globalization 3.0 strategy persist through the 21st century? If not, what will Globalization 4.0 look like? Several American companies such as Apple and GE have realized that they miscalculated the full cost of managing far-flung production operations and are bringing production back to the United States. *Forbes* magazine put the blame on managers who were focused on maximizing shareholder value rather than emphasizing the long-term future of the firm.[87] That is, some managers looked only at labor costs and ignored the hidden costs of time and money trying to communicate quality and design concerns to workers across countries as well as unexpected costs to the supply chain from natural disasters or political threats. These factors combined with the new economics of energy (e.g., growing supply of natural gas) and new technologies (robotics, artificial intelligence, 3D printing, and nanotechnology) are rapidly changing manufacturing and management decisions.

   Discuss the factors that managers of Apple or GE may consider as they focus on continuous innovation rather than the cost of manufacturing. How might governments with an interest in generating employment opportunities try to influence the decisions of firms? What other stakeholders may have an interest in bringing jobs back onshore and thus try to influence the decisions of firms? Consider the persuasive arguments and deals that might be struck. With changes to the location of production, what might Globalization 4.0 look like?

SMALL-GROUP EXERCISES

//// Small-Group Exercise 1
(Ethical/Social Issues)

Many U.S. companies have become global players. The technology giant IBM employs over 465,000 people and has revenues of roughly $100 billion. Although IBM's headquarters is in Armonk, New York, the vast majority of its employees (more than 70 percent) actually work outside the United States. IBM, like many other U.S.-based multinationals, now earns the majority of its revenues (roughly two-thirds) outside the United States (as shown in Exhibit 1.6).[88] IBM's revenues in the BRIC countries have been growing at between 20 and 40 percent per year, while they have grown by only about 1 to 3 percent in developed markets such as the United States. IBM's goal is to obtain 35 percent of its total revenue from fast-growing emerging economies such as the BRIC countries by 2015. To capture these opportunities, IBM (along with many other multinational companies) has been reducing the U.S. headcount while increasing employment in emerging economies such as India.[89]

1. Given that traditional U.S. firms such as IBM have over 70 percent of their employees outside the U.S. and earn almost two-thirds of their revenues from outside the U.S., what is an appropriate definition of a "U.S. firm"?

2. Is there any special consideration a firm should have for its "home country"? Is it ethical to lay off workers in the U.S. while hiring overseas? What about keeping profits outside the U.S. in offshore accounts to avoid paying corporate taxes?

//// Small-Group Exercise 2

In this exercise, we want to apply the four types of global strategy. Imagine your group works for Clif Bar (www.clifbar.com). Founded in 1992, the firm makes nutritious, all natural food and drinks for sport and healthy snacking. Clif Bar is a privately held company with some 200 employees. About 20 percent of the company is owned by the employees through an employee-stock-ownership program (ESOP). The vast majority of Clif Bar's sales are in the United States. The firm has some distribution set up in Canada (since 1996) and the United Kingdom (since 2007). As of 2013, Clif Bar sells its products via the website in six countries: Austria, Canada, Germany, Japan, New Zealand, and Switzerland.

Review the company's website for more information about the firm and its products.

1. Apply the CAGE distance framework to the six international countries where Clif Bar is operating. What is the *relative* distance of each to the United States? Rank the order of the six countries in terms of *relative* distance.

2. Given the results from the CAGE model, do the six chosen countries make sense? Why or why not?

3. Can you recommend three or four other countries Clif Bar should enter? Support your recommendations.

4. What entrance strategy should the firm employ in expanding the business to new countries? Why?

STRATEGY TERM PROJECT

//// Module 10: Global Strategy

In this section, you will study your firm's global strategy, or a strategy it should pursue globally.

If your firm is already engaged in international activities, answer the following questions:

1. Is your company varying its product or service to adapt to differences in countries? Is the marketing approach different among the nations involved? Should it be?

2. Is your firm working internationally to access larger markets? To gain low-cost input factors? To develop new competencies? Is its approach in all three areas appropriate?

3. Which of the four global strategies is the firm using? Is this the best strategy for it to use? Why or why not? (Exhibit 10.7 provides a summary of the four global strategies.)

If your firm is not now engaged internationally, answer the following questions:

1. Would your firm's product or service need to be modified or marketed differently if it expanded beyond the home country?

2. Does your firm have the potential to access larger markets by expanding internationally? Does it have the possibility of lowering input factors with such expansion? Please explain why or why not.

3. If your firm decided to expand internationally, where does the firm reside on the integration-responsiveness framework? (Refer to Exhibit 10.5 if needed.) What does this result say about the "best" global strategy for your firm to use for international expansion?

my STRATEGY

How Do You Develop a Global Mind-Set?

How can you develop the skills needed to succeed as an international leader? Researchers have developed a personal strategy for building a global mind-set that will facilitate success as an effective manager in a different cultural setting. A global mind-set has three components: *intellectual capital,* the understanding of how business works on a global level; *psychological capital,* openness to new ideas and experiences; and *social capital,* the ability to build connections with people and to influence stakeholders from a different cultural background.[90]

Intellectual capital is considered the easiest to gain if one puts forth the effort. You can gain global business acumen by taking courses, but you can learn a great deal on your own by reading publications with an international scope such as

The Economist, visiting websites that provide information on different cultures or business operations in foreign countries, or simply watching television programs with an international news or culture focus. Working in global industries with people from diverse cultures is also a complex assignment, requiring the ability to manage complexity and uncertainty.

Psychological capital is gained by being receptive to new ideas and experiences and appreciating diversity. It may be the most difficult to develop, because your ability to change your personality has limits. If you are enthusiastic about adventure and are willing to take risks in new environments, then you have the attitudes needed to be energized by a foreign assignment. It takes self-confidence and a sense of humor to adapt successfully to new environments.

Social capital is based on relationships and is gained through experience. You can gain experience with diversity simply by widening your social circle, volunteering to work with international students, or by traveling on vacation or through a study abroad experience.

Now that you have a description of the three components of a global mind-set and a few ideas about how to develop the attributes necessary for global success, consider some ways you can develop a personal strategy that can be implemented during your college career.

1. So that you have a better idea of where you stand now, draw up a list of your strengths and weaknesses for each component.

2. Identify your weakest area, and make a list of activities that will help you improve your capital in that area. After generating your own list, check out http://hbr.org/globalize-yourself-list. You will be amazed at the possibilities.

3. Identify courses you could take in international business, economics, politics, history, or art history. While you may be required to be proficient in at least one foreign language, learn a few words in other languages that can help you navigate any new countries you visit.

4. Make a list of at least six activities you could do this week in order to get started. For example, you could choose to work with international students on group projects in class. Or, move on to having lunch with them. What questions could you ask that would help you learn about their culture and about doing business in their country? You could go to a museum with an exhibit from another culture, an international movie, or a restaurant with cuisine that is new to you.

If you are interested in more information, go to http://globalmindset.thunderbird.edu/, where you can also take a sample survey to get an idea of the degree to which you have the attributes needed for global success.

ENDNOTES

1. "Plot change: Foreign forces transform Hollywood films," *The Wall Street Journal,* August 2, 2010.

2. This ChapterCase is based on: "Plot change: Foreign forces transform Hollywood films," *The Wall Street Journal;* "Hollywood squeezes stars' pay in slump," *The Wall Street Journal,* April 2, 2009; "News Corporation," *The Economist,* February 26, 2009; and "Slumdog Millionaire wins eight Oscars," *The Wall Street Journal,* February 23, 2009; "China gets its OWN VERSION of Iron Man 3 after Disney allows the country's film censors onto the set," *MailOnline,* April 14, 2012; "'Hobbit' to break $1 billion," *Daily Variety,* January 22, 2013.

3. "Foreign university students," *The Economist,* August 7, 2010.

4. World Bank (2013), *World Development Indicators,* http://data.worldbank.org/data-catalog/world-development-indicators.

5. CAGE is an acronym for *C*ultural, *A*dministrative and political, *G*eographic, and *E*conomic distance. The model was introduced by Ghemawat, P. (2001), "Distance still matters: The hard reality of global expansion," *Harvard Business Review,* September.

6. Stiglitz, J. (2002), *Globalization and Its Discontents* (New York: Norton).

7. "BRICs, emerging markets and the world economy," *The Economist,* June 18, 2009.

8. World Bank (2013), *World Development Indicators,* http://data.worldbank.org/data-catalog/world-development-indicators.

9. Caves, R. (1996), *Multinational Enterprise and Economic Analysis* (New York: Cambridge University Press); and Dunning, J. (1993), *Multinational Enterprises and the Global Economy* (Reading, MA: Addison-Wesley).

10. "Airbus's new push: Made in the U.S.A.," *The Wall Street Journal,* July 2, 2012.

11. "GM's latest nemesis: VW," *The Wall Street Journal,* August 4, 2010.

12. Following Peng (2010: 18), we define global strategy as a "strategy of firms around the globe—essentially various firms' theories about how to compete successfully." This stands in contrast to a narrower alternative use of the term "global strategy," which implies a global cost leadership strategy in standardized products. We follow Peng to denote this type of strategy as *global-standardization strategy* (Peng, 2010: 20); Peng, M. W. (2010), *Global Strategy,* 2nd ed. (Mason, OH: Cengage).

13. Kotha, S., V. Rindova, and F. T. Rothaermel (2001), "Assets and actions: Firm-specific factors in the internationalization of U.S. Internet firms," *Journal of International Business Studies* 32: 769–791.

14. McKinsey Global Institute (2010), *Growth and Competitiveness in the United States: The Role of Its Multinational Companies* (London).

15. IBM (2009), *A Decade of Generating Higher Value at IBM,* IBM report, www.ibm. com.

16. Immelt, J. R., V. Govindarajan, and C. Trimble (2009), "How GE is disrupting itself," *Harvard Business Review,* October; Author's interviews with Michael Poteran of GE Healthcare (10/30/09 and 11/04/09); and "Vscan handheld ultrasound: GE unveils 'stethoscope of the 21st century,'" *Huffington Post,* October 20, 2009; and Govindarajan, V., and C. Trimble (2012), *Reverse Innovation: Create Far from Home, Win Everywhere* (Boston, MA: Harvard Business Review Press).

17. This process is also referred to as reverse innovation. Govindarajan, V., and C. Trimble (2012), *Reverse Innovation: Create Far from Home, Win Everywhere.*

18. www.logitech.com. Its two founders, one Swiss and the other Italian, each held master's degrees from Stanford University.

19. Saxenian, A. (1994), *Regional Advantage* (Cambridge, MA: Harvard University Press); and Rothaermel, F. T., and D. Ku (2008), "Intercluster innovation differentials: The role of research universities," *IEEE Transactions on Engineering Management* 55: 9–22.

20. Ghemawat, P. (2011), *World 3.0: Global Prosperity and How to Achieve It* (Boston, MA: Harvard Business Review Press). The data presented are drawn from Ghemawat (2011) and his TED talk "Actually, the world isn't flat," June 2012. It is an excellent talk. You can view it at: http://www.ted.com/talks/ pankaj_ghemawat_actually_the_world_isn_t_ flat.html.

21. The number rises to 6–7 percent if VoIP (such as Skype) is included; Ghemawat, P. (2012), "Actually, the world isn't flat," TED talk.

22. Friedman, T. L. (2005), *The World Is Flat: A Brief History of the Twenty-First Century* (New York: Farrar, Strauss, and Giroux).

23. Ghemawat, P. (2011), *World 3.0: Global Prosperity and How to Achieve It.*

24. Ibid.

25. "The rising power of the Chinese worker," *The Economist,* July 29, 2010.

26. "Supply chain for iPhone highlights costs in China," *The New York Times,* July 5, 2010.

27. Ibid.

28. This is based on: Friedman, T. L. (2005), *The World Is Flat: A Brief History of the Twenty-First Century;* "Supply chain for iPhone highlights costs in China," *The New York Times;* and "The rising power of the Chinese worker," *The Economist.*

29. Ghemawat, P. (2011), *World 3.0: Global Prosperity and How to Achieve It* (Boston: Harvard Business Review Press).

30. This Strategy Highlight is based on: quote from "2012 GM Annual Report," p. 6 (www.gm.com); "Can China save GM?" *Forbes,* May 10, 2010; and Tao, Q. (2009), "Competition in the Chinese automobile industry," in Peng, M. W. (2010), *Global Strategy,* pp. 419–425; "GM 2012 global sales rise 2.9 percent on strong Chevy demand," *Reuters,* January 14, 2013.

31. "A special report on innovation in emerging markets," *The Economist,* April 15, 2010.

32. "The rising power of the Chinese worker," *The Economist,* July 29, 2010.

33. Friedman, T. L. (2005), *The World Is Flat: A Brief History of the Twenty-First Century.*

34. Chang, S. J. (1995), "International expansion strategy of Japanese firms: Capability building through sequential entry," *Academy of Management Journal* 38: 383–407; Vermeulen, F., and H. G. Barkema (1998), "International expansion through start-up or acquisition: A learning perspective," *Academy of Management Journal* 41: 7–26; Vermeulen, F., and H. G. Barkema (2002), "Pace, rhythm, and scope: Process dependence in building a profitable multinational corporation," *Strategic Management Journal* 23: 637–653; and Ghemawat, P. (2011), *World 3.0: Global Prosperity and How to Achieve It.*

35. Brown, J. S., and P. Duguid (1991), "Organizational learning and communities-of-practice: Toward a unified view of working, learning, and innovation," *Organization Science* 2: 40–57.

36. Owen-Smith, J., and W. W. Powell (2004), "Knowledge networks as channels and conduits: The effects of spillovers in the Boston biotech community," *Organization Science* 15: 5–21.

37. Examples drawn from: "A special report on innovation in emerging markets," *The Economist,* April 15, 2010.

38. Dunning, J. H., and S. M. Lundan (2008), *Multinational Enterprises and the Global Economy,* 2nd ed. (Northampton, MA: Edward Elgar).

39. "A special report on innovation in emerging markets," *The Economist,* April 15, 2010.

40. Zaheer, S. (1995), "Overcoming the liability of foreignness," *Academy of Management Journal* 38: 341–363.

41. This Strategy Highlight is based on: Knorr, A., and A. Arndt (2003), "Why did Wal-Mart fail in Germany?" in Knorr, A., A. Lemper, A. Sell, and K. Wohlmuth (eds.), *Materialien des Wissenschaftsschwerpunktes "Globalisierung der Weltwirtschaft,"* vol. 24 (IWIM—Institute for World Economics and International Management, Universität Bremen, Germany); the author's onsite observations at Walmart stores in Germany; and "Hair-shirt economics: Getting Germans to open their wallets is hard," *The Economist,* July 8, 2010. For a recent discussion of Walmart's global efforts, see: "After early errors, Wal-Mart thinks locally to act globally," *The Wall Street Journal,* August 14, 2009.

42. Top 100 Most Valuable Global Brands 2013," report by Millward Brown, WPP.

43. "The Foxconn suicides," *The Wall Street Journal,* May 27, 2010.

44. "When workers dream of a life beyond the factory gates," *The Economist,* December 15, 2012.

45. "Apple shifts supply chain away from Foxconn to Pegatron," *The Wall Street Journal,* May 29, 2013.

46. "Disaster at Rana Plaza," *The Economist,* May 4, 2013; "The Bangladesh disaster and corporate social responsibility," *Forbes,* May 2, 2013.

47. Ibid.

48. This example is drawn from: "Train makers rail against China's high-speed designs," *The Wall Street Journal,* November 17, 2010.

49. This section is based on: Ghemawat, P. (2001), "Distance still matters: The hard reality of global expansion," *Harvard Business Review,* September; see also Ghemawat, P. (2011), *World 3.0: Global Prosperity and How to Achieve It.*

50. To obtain scores for any two country pairings and to view interactive CAGE distance maps, go to www.ghemawat.com.

51. The discussion of the CAGE distance frameworks and the attributes thereof is based on: Ghemawat, P. (2001), "Distance still matters: The hard reality of global expansion"; see also Ghemawat, P. (2011), *World 3.0: Global Prosperity and How to Achieve It.*

52. Hofstede, G. H. (1984), *Culture's Consequences: International Differences in Work-Related Values* (Beverly Hills, CA: Sage), p. 21. The description of Hofstede's four cultural dimensions is drawn from: Rothaermel, F. T., S. Kotha, and H. K. Steensma (2006), "International market entry by U.S. Internet firms: An empirical analysis of country risk, national culture, and market size," *Journal of Management* 32: 56–82.

53. The *power-distance dimension* of national culture focuses on how a society deals with inequality among people in terms of physical and intellectual capabilities and how those methods translate into power distributions within organizations. High power-distance cultures, like the Philippines (94/100, with 100 = high), tend to allow inequalities among people to translate into inequalities in opportunity, power, status, and wealth. Low power-distance cultures, like Austria (11/100), on the other hand, tend to intervene to create a more equal distribution among people within organizations and society at large.

The *individualism dimension* of national culture focuses on the relationship between individuals in a society, particularly in regard to the relationship between individual and collective pursuits. In highly individualistic cultures, like the U.S. (91/100), individual freedom and achievements are highly valued. As a result, individuals are only tied loosely to one another within society. In less-individualistic cultures, like Venezuela (12/100), the collective good is emphasized over the individual, and members of society are strongly tied to one another throughout their lifetimes by virtue of birth into groups like extended families.

The *masculinity–femininity dimension* of national culture focuses on the relationship between genders and its relation to an individual's role at work and in society. In more "masculine" cultures, like Japan (95/100), gender roles tend to be clearly defined and sharply differentiated. In "masculine" cultures, values like competitiveness, assertiveness, and exercise of power are considered cultural ideals, and men are expected to behave accordingly. In more "feminine" cultures, like Sweden (5/100), values like cooperation, humility, and harmony are guiding cultural principles. The masculinity–femininity dimension uncovered in Hofstede's research is undoubtedly evolving over time, and values and behaviors are converging to some extent.

The *uncertainty-avoidance dimension* of national culture focuses on societal differences in tolerance toward ambiguity and uncertainty. In particular, it highlights the extent to which members of a certain culture feel anxious when faced with uncertain or unknown situations. Members of high uncertainty-avoidance cultures, like Russia (95/100), value clear rules and regulations as well as clearly structured career patterns, lifetime employment, and retirement benefits. Members of low uncertainty-avoidance cultures, like Singapore (8/100), have greater tolerance toward ambiguity and thus exhibit less emotional resistance to change and a greater willingness to take risks.

54. The available data on that fifth dimension is not, at this point, as comprehensive as for the four original dimensions.

55. This is based on: Kogut, B., and H. Singh (1988), "The effect of national culture on the choice of entry mode," *Journal of International Business Studies* 19: 411–432; Rothaermel, F. T., S. Kotha, and H. K. Steensma (2006), "International market entry by U.S. Internet firms: An empirical analysis

of country risk, national culture, and market size"; cultural distance from the United States, for example, is calculated as follows: where I_{ij} stands for the index for the ith cultural dimension and jth country, V_i is the variance of the index of ith dimension, u indicates the United States, and CD_j is the cultural distance difference of the jth country from the United States.

56. Ghemawat, P. (2012), "Actually, the world isn't flat," TED talk, http://www.ted.com/talks/pankaj_ghemawat_actually_the_world_isn_t_flat.html; and Ghemawat, P. (2011), *World 3.0: Global Prosperity and How to Achieve It.*

57. Ghemawat, P. (2001), "Distance still matters: The hard reality of global expansion."

58. See statistics provided by Eurostat at: http://epp.eurostat.ec.europa.eu.

59. Williamson, O. E. (1975), *Markets and Hierarchies* (New York: Free Press); Williamson, O. E. (1981), "The economics of organization: The transaction cost approach," *American Journal of Sociology* 87: 548–577; and Williamson, O. E. (1985), *The Economic Institutions of Capitalism* (New York: Free Press).

60. Ghemawat, P. (2001), "Distance still matters: The hard reality of global expansion."

61. "Bad roads, red tape, burly thugs slow Walmart's passage in India," *The Wall Street Journal,* January 11, 2013.

62. Johanson, J., and J. Vahlne (1977), "The internationalization process of the firm," *Journal of International Business Studies* 4: 20–29.

63. Fuller, A. W., and F. T. Rothaermel (2008), "The interplay between capability development and strategy formation: Motorola's entry into China," Georgia Institute of Technology Working Paper.

64. Levitt, T. (1983), "The globalization of markets," *Harvard Business Review,* May–June: 92–102.

65. Ibid., p. 93.

66. Mol, M. (2002), "Ford Mondeo: A Model T world car?" in Tan, F. B. (ed.), *Cases on Global IT Applications and Management: Successes and Pitfalls,* pp. 69–89.

67. Prahalad, C. K., and Y. L. Doz (1987), *The Multinational Mission* (New York: Free Press); and Roth, K., and A. J. Morrison (1990), "An empirical analysis of the integration-responsiveness framework in global industries," *Journal of International Business Studies* 21: 541–564.

68. Bartlett, C. A., S. Ghoshal, and P. W. Beamish (2007), *Transnational Management: Text, Cases and Readings in Cross-Border Management,* 5th ed. (Burr Ridge, IL: McGraw-Hill).

69. "Ditch the knock-off watch, get the knock-off car," *The Wall Street Journal Video,* August 8, 2010.

70. www.lenovo.com/lenovo/US/en/locations.html.

71. Ibid.

72. Ghemawat, P. (2011), *World 3.0: Global Prosperity and How to Achieve It.*

73. Mueller, H.-E. (2001), "Developing global human resource strategies," paper presented at the European International Business Academy, Paris, December 13–15; Mueller, H.-E. (2001), "Wie Global Player den Kampf um Talente führen," *Harvard Business Manager* 6: 16–25.

74. This section draws on: Rothaermel, F. T., and D. Ku (2008), "Intercluster innovation differentials: The role of research universities," *IEEE Transactions on Engineering Management* 55: 9–22.

75. This is based on: Buckley, P. J., and P. N. Ghauri (2004), "Globalisation, economic geography and the strategy of multinational enterprises," *Journal of International Business Studies* 35: 81–98; Cairncross, F. (1997), *The Death of Distance: How the Communications Revolution Will Change Our Lives* (Boston, MA: Harvard Business School Press); and Friedman, T. L. (2005), *The World Is Flat: A Brief History of the Twenty-First Century.* For a counterpoint, see: Ghemawat, P. (2001), "Distance still matters: The hard reality of global expansion"; Ghemawat, P. (2007), *Redefining Global Strategy: Crossing Borders in a World Where Differences Still Matter* (Boston, MA: Harvard Business School Press); and Ghemawat, P. (2011), *World 3.0: Global Prosperity and How to Achieve It.*

76. This section is based on: Porter, M. E. (1990), "The competitive advantage of nations," *Harvard Business Review,* March–April: 73–91; and Porter, M. E. (1990), *The Competitive Advantage of Nations* (New York: Free Press).

77. "U.S. identifies vast mineral riches in Afghanistan," *The New York Times,* June 13, 2010.

78. For an insightful recent discussion, see: Breznitz, D. (2007), *Innovation and the State: Political Choice and Strategies for Growth in Israel, Taiwan, and Ireland* (New Haven, CT: Yale University Press).

79. More recently, however, Nokia has ceded leadership to RIM (Canada). Currently, Apple and Samsung (South Korea) are the leaders in the smartphone industry.

80. Dyer, J. H., and K. Nobeoka (2000), "Creating and managing a high-performance knowledge-sharing network: The Toyota case," *Strategic Management Journal* 21: 345–367.

81. This discussion is based on: "Toyota slips up," *The Economist,* December 10, 2009; "Toyota: Losing its shine," *The Economist,* December 10, 2009; "Toyota heir faces crises at the wheel," *The Wall Street Journal,* January 27, 2010; "Toyota's troubles deepen," *The Economist,* February 4, 2010; "The humbling of Toyota," *Bloomberg Businessweek,* March 11, 2010; and "Inside Toyota, executives trade blame over debacle," *The Wall Street Journal,* April 13, 2010.

82. Porter, M. E. (1990), *The Competitive Advantage of Nations* (New York: Free Press), p. 77.

83. "Ending the open season on artists," *The Economist,* February 17, 2011.

84. Levin, D., and J. Horn (2011), "DVD pirates running rampant in China," *Los Angeles Times,* March, 22.

85. Ibid.

86. "Bigger abroad," *The Economist,* February 17, 2011.

87. "Why Apple and GE are bringing back manufacturing," *Forbes,* December 7, 2012.

88. IBM Annual Reports, various years.

89. "IBM to cut U.S. jobs, expand in India," *The Wall Street Journal,* March 26, 2009.

90. This *my*Strategy item is based on an article by Javidan, M., M. Teagarden, and D. Bowen, (2010), "Making it overseas," *Harvard Business Review,* April, vol. 88 (4): 109–113.

Strategy Implementation

The AFI Strategy Framework

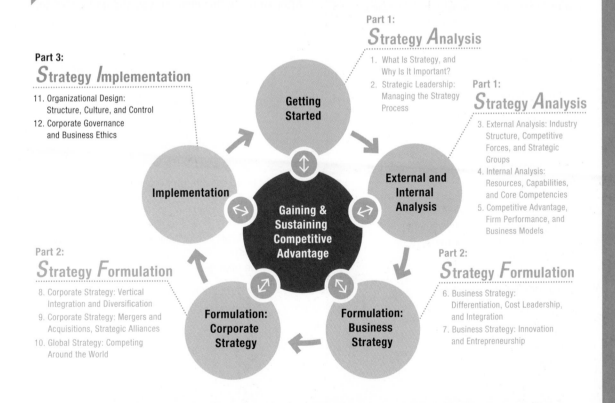

Part 3:
*S*trategy *I*mplementation

11. Organizational Design: Structure, Culture, and Control
12. Corporate Governance and Business Ethics

Part 1:
*S*trategy *A*nalysis

1. What Is Strategy, and Why Is It Important?
2. Strategic Leadership: Managing the Strategy Process

Part 1:
*S*trategy *A*nalysis

3. External Analysis: Industry Structure, Competitive Forces, and Strategic Groups
4. Internal Analysis: Resources, Capabilities, and Core Competencies
5. Competitive Advantage, Firm Performance, and Business Models

Part 2:
*S*trategy *F*ormulation

8. Corporate Strategy: Vertical Integration and Diversification
9. Corporate Strategy: Mergers and Acquisitions, Strategic Alliances
10. Global Strategy: Competing Around the World

Part 2:
*S*trategy *F*ormulation

6. Business Strategy: Differentiation, Cost Leadership, and Integration
7. Business Strategy: Innovation and Entrepreneurship

Getting Started

External and Internal Analysis

Implementation

Gaining & Sustaining Competitive Advantage

Formulation: Corporate Strategy

Formulation: Business Strategy

Chapter 11

Organizational Design: Structure, Culture, and Control

Learning Objectives

After studying this chapter, you should be able to:

LO 11-1 Define organizational design and list its three components.

LO 11-2 Explain how organizational inertia can lead established firms to failure.

LO 11-3 Define organizational structure and describe its four elements.

LO 11-4 Compare and contrast mechanistic versus organic organizations.

LO 11-5 Describe different organizational structures and match them with appropriate strategies.

LO 11-6 Describe the elements of organizational culture, and explain where organizational cultures can come from and how they can be changed.

LO 11-7 Compare and contrast different strategic control-and-reward systems.

Zappos: Designed to Deliver Happiness

DELIVERING HAPPINESS is the title of *The New York Times* bestseller by Tony Hsieh, CEO of Zappos, the online shoe and clothing store (www.zappos.com). Delivering happiness is also Zappos' mission. To make its customers, employees, and other stakeholders happy, Tony Hsieh and other Zappos leaders designed a unique organization.

To live up to its mission, Zappos decided that exceptional customer service should be its core competency. They put several policies and procedures in place to "deliver WOW through service"—the first of its 10 core values (see Exhibit 11.1). For example, shipments to and from customers within the U.S. are free of charge, allowing customers to order several pairs of shoes and send back (within a liberal 365 days) those that don't fit or are no longer wanted. Repeat customers are automatically upgraded to complimentary express shipping. One of the most important lessons Hsieh learned is "Never outsource your core competency!"[1] Customer service, therefore, is done exclusively in-house. Perhaps even more importantly, Zappos does not provide a script

or measure customer service reps' call times. Rather, the company leaves it up to the individual "Customer Loyalty Team" member to deliver exceptional customer service: "We want our reps to let their true personalities shine during each phone call so that they can develop a personal emotional connection with the customer."[2] In fact, one customer service phone call lasted almost six hours! The same trust in the customer service reps applies to e-mail communication. Zappos' official communication policy is to "be real and use your best judgment."[3] Most of Zappos' over 1,500 employees are in some type of sales function, to maintain constant contact with the customer. The customer call centers are staffed 24/7, seven days a week, 365 days a year.

As Zappos grew, its managers realized that it was critical to explicitly define a set of core values from which to develop the company's culture, brand, and strategy. It wanted to make sure that, in a time of fast growth, all employees understood the same set of

EXHIBIT 11.1 / Zappos' 10 Core Values

1.	Deliver WOW through service.
2.	Embrace and drive change.
3.	Create fun and a little weirdness.
4.	Be adventurous, creative, and open-minded.
5.	Pursue growth and learning.
6.	Build open and honest relationships with communication.
7.	Build a positive team and family spirit.
8.	Do more with less.
9.	Be passionate and determined.
10.	Be humble.

SOURCE: T. Hsieh, (2010), *Delivering Happiness: A Path to Profits, Passion, and Purpose* (New York: Business Plus), pp. 157–160.

values and expected behaviors. Zappos' list of 10 core values was crafted through a bottom-up initiative, in which all employees were invited to participate. Zappos also restructured its performance-evaluation system to give these values "teeth": The firm rewards employees who apply the values well in their day-to-day decision making. In this way, Zappos' managers directly connected the informal cultural control system to the formal reward system. CEO Tony Hsieh states, "Ideally, we want all 10 core values to be reflected in everything we do, including how we interact with each other, how we interact with our customers, and how we interact with our vendors and business partners. . . . Our core values should always be the framework from which we make all of our decisions."[4]

When establishing customer service as a core competency, one of the hardest decisions Tony Hsieh made was to pull the plug on drop-shipment orders. These are orders for which Zappos would be the intermediary, relaying them to particular shoe vendors who then ship directly to the customer. Such orders were very profitable because Zappos would not have to stock all the shoes. They were also appealing because the fledgling startup was still losing money. The problem was twofold. The vendors were slower than Zappos in filling orders. In addition, they did not accomplish the reliability metric that Zappos wanted for exceptional service: 95 percent accuracy was simply not good enough! Instead, Zappos decided to forgo drop shipments and instead built a larger warehouse in Kentucky to stock a full inventory. This move enabled the firm to achieve close to 100 percent accuracy in its shipments, many of which were overnight. Unlike other online retailers, Zappos stocks everything it sells in its own warehouses—this is the only way to get the merchandise as quickly as possible with 100 percent accuracy to the customer.

In addition to making customers happy, Zappos also works to keep its own employees happy. Although it employs more than 1,500 people, Zappos' organizational structure is extremely flat. Once an employee has mastered a job, he or she is rotated to a different job, often horizontally. This system allows Zappos to create a large pool of trained talent, and makes it easier to promote from within. In keeping with another of its core values, "Create fun and a little weirdness," the Las Vegas–based startup offers employees "free" lunches, employer-paid health care benefits, a designated nap room, concierge service, an onsite life coach who is also a chiropractor, a library of books on happiness (along with other bestsellers), onsite seminars on personal growth, and fun events such as pajama parties at work. In 2011, Zappos was ranked #6 in *Fortune*'s "100 Best Companies to Work For" list (the highest ranking for a relatively young firm).

Finally, Zappos has also made its investors happy. In 2008, just 10 years after its founding, Zappos achieved over $1 billion in annual sales. In 2009, Amazon acquired the startup in a deal valued at $1.2 billion. Although now a subsidiary of Amazon, Zappos continues to operate as an independent brand. Indeed, Zappos has grown so much—receiving 10 million website hits a day—that it reorganized to continue to offer the best customer service possible. To keep the organization flat and responsive to customers, Zappos restructured into 10 separate units such as Zappos.com, Zappos Gift Cards, Zappos IP, and 6pm.com, among others. Today, Zappos.com stocks over three million shoes, handbags, and clothing items from some 1,200 brands.[5]

After reading the chapter, you will find more about this case, with related questions, on page 367.

---

strategy implementation The part of the strategic management process that concerns the organization, coordination, and integration of how work gets done. It is key to gaining and sustaining competitive advantage.

▲ **ZAPPOS' CEO, TONY** Hsieh, believes that soon 30 percent of all retail transactions in the U.S. will be online, and that people will buy from the company with the best customer service and best selection. The strategic intent for Zappos is to be that online store. Tony Hsieh and other Zappos employees thought long and hard about what type of structure, culture, and processes to put in place that would support the firm's strategic goals. They proactively designed a flat organization that enabled them to implement its differentiation strategy effectively. Zappos' managers further refined their organizational design through trial-and-error, being transparent, and soliciting bottom-up feedback, while making the tough strategic decisions of what not to do.

ChapterCase 11 brings us to the final piece of the AFI framework: strategy implementation. **Strategy implementation** concerns the organization, coordination, and integration of how work gets done. It is key to gaining and sustaining competitive advantage. Although the discussion of strategy formulation (what to do) is distinct from strategy implementation (how to do it), formulation and implementation must be part of an interdependent, reciprocal process in order to ensure continued success. That need for interdependence is why the AFI framework is illustrated as a circle, rather than a linear diagram. The design of an organization, the matching of strategy and structure, and its control-and-reward systems determine whether an organization that has chosen an effective strategy will thrive or wither away.

In this chapter, we study the three key levers that managers have at their disposal when designing their organizations for competitive advantage: structure, culture, and control. We begin our discussion with organizational structure. We discuss different types of organizational structures as well as why and how they need to change over time as successful firms grow in size and complexity. We highlight the critical need to match strategy and structure, and then dive into corporate culture. An organization's culture can either support or hinder its quest for competitive advantage.[6] We next study strategic control systems, which allow managers to receive feedback on how well a firm's strategy is being implemented. We conclude our discussion of how to design an organization for competitive advantage with practical implications for the strategist.

Managers employ these three levers—structure, culture, and control—to coordinate work and motivate employees across different levels, functions, and geographies. How successful they are in this endeavor determines whether they are able to translate their chosen business, corporate, and global strategies into strategic actions and business models, and ultimately whether the firm is able to gain and sustain a competitive advantage.

11.1 How to Organize for Competitive Advantage

Organizational design is the process of creating, implementing, monitoring, and modifying the structure, processes, and procedures of an organization. The key components of organizational design are structure, culture, and control. The goal is to design an organization that allows managers to effectively translate their chosen strategy into a realized one. Simply formulating an effective strategy is a necessary but not sufficient condition for gaining and sustaining competitive advantage. Some argue that strategy execution is more important.[7] Often, managers do a good job of analyzing the firm's internal and external environments to formulate a promising business, corporate, and global strategy, but then fail to implement the chosen strategy successfully. That is why some scholars refer to implementation as the "graveyard of strategy."[8]

Not surprisingly, the inability to implement strategy effectively is the number-one reason boards of directors fire CEOs.[9] Yahoo's co-founder and CEO Jerry Yang was ousted in 2008 precisely because he failed to implement necessary strategic changes after Yahoo lost its competitive advantage.[10] In the two years leading up to his exit, Yahoo lost more than 75 percent of its market value. Mr. Yang was described as someone who preferred consensus among his managers to making tough strategic decisions needed to change Yahoo's structure. That preference, though, led to bickering and infighting. Jerry Yang's failure to make the necessary changes to the Internet firm's organizational structure not only led to a destruction of billions in shareholder value and thousands of layoffs, but also cost him his job. Once a leader in online search, Yahoo is struggling to make a comeback. A number of short-term and interim CEOs followed Jerry Yang without much success. In 2012, former Google executive Marissa Mayer was appointed president and CEO of Yahoo. Ms. Mayer's turnaround efforts at Yahoo are focused on improving the user experience, thus driving online advertising revenues.[11]

LO 11-1

Define organizational design and list its three components.

organizational design The process of creating, implementing, monitoring, and modifying the structure, processes, and procedures of an organization.

Because strategy implementation transforms strategy into actions and business models, it often requires changes within the organization. However, strategy implementation often fails because managers are unable to make the necessary changes due to its effects on resource allocation and power distribution within an organization.[12]

As demonstrated by business historian Alfred Chandler in his seminal book *Strategy and Structure,* organizational structure must follow strategy in order for firms to achieve superior performance: "Structure can be defined as the design of organization through which the enterprise is administered . . . the thesis deduced [from studying the administrative history of DuPont, GM, Sears Roebuck, and Standard Oil from the early to mid-1900s] is that *structure follows strategy.*"[13] This tenet implies that to implement a strategy successfully, organizational design must be flexible enough to accommodate the formulated strategy and future growth and expansion. Featured in the ChapterCase, Zappos provides an example of a company with flexible organizational structure. To maintain its core competency of providing a superior customer experience in the face of explosive growth, Zappos split the organization into 10 standalone units.

ORGANIZATIONAL INERTIA AND THE FAILURE OF ESTABLISHED FIRMS

LO 11-2

Explain how organizational inertia can lead established firms to failure.

In reality, however, a firm's strategy often follows its structure.[14] This reversal implies that some managers consider only strategies that do not change existing organizational structures; they do not want to confront the inertia that often exists in established organizations.[15] *Inertia,* a firm's resistance to change the status quo, can set the stage for the firm's subsequent failure. Successful firms often plant the seed of subsequent failure: They optimize their organizational structure to the current situation. That tightly coupled system can break apart when internal or external pressures occur.

Exhibit 11.2 shows how success in the current environment can lead to a firm's downfall in the future, when the tightly coupled system of strategy and structure experiences internal or external shifts.[16] First, the managers achieve a mastery of, and fit with, the firm's current environment. Second, the firm often defines and measures success by financial metrics, with a focus on short-term performance. (See the discussion of firm performance in Chapter 5.) Third, the firm puts in place metrics and systems to accommodate and manage increasing firm size due to continued success. Finally, as a result of a tightly coupled (albeit successful) system, organizational inertia sets in—and with it, resistance to change.

organizational structure A key building block of organizational design that determines how the work efforts of individuals and teams are orchestrated and how resources are distributed.

Such a tightly coupled system is prone to break apart when external and internal shifts put pressure on the system.[17] In Exhibit 11.2, the blue arrows show the firm's tightly coupled organizational design. The light gray arrows indicate pressures emanating from internal shifts such as accelerated growth, a change in the business model, entry into new markets, a change in the top management team (TMT), or mergers and acquisitions. The dark gray arrows indicate external pressures, which can stem from any of the PESTEL forces (political, economic, sociocultural, technological, ecological, and legal, as discussed in Chapter 3). Strong external or internal pressure can break apart the current system, which may lead to firm failure.

THE KEY ELEMENTS OF ORGANIZATIONAL STRUCTURE

LO 11-3

Define organizational structure and describe its four elements.

Some of the key decisions managers must make when designing effective organizations pertain to the firm's **organizational structure**. That structure determines how the work efforts of individuals and teams are orchestrated and how resources are distributed. In particular, an organizational structure defines how jobs and tasks are divided and integrated, delineates the reporting relationships up and down the hierarchy, defines formal communication channels, and

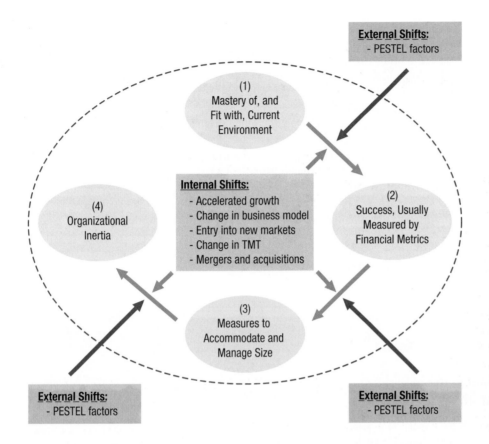

EXHIBIT 11.2 /

Organizational Inertia
and the Failure of
Established Firms
When External or
Internal Environments
Shift

specialization An element of organizational structure that describes the degree to which a task is divided into separate jobs (i.e., the division of labor).

formalization An element of organizational structure that captures the extent to which employee behavior is steered by explicit and codified rules and procedures.

prescribes how individuals and teams coordinate their work efforts. The key building blocks of an organizational structure are *specialization, formalization, centralization,* and *hierarchy.*

Specialization describes the degree to which a task is divided into separate jobs—that is, the *division of labor.* Larger firms, such as Fortune 100 companies, tend to have a high degree of specialization; smaller entrepreneurial ventures tend to have a low degree of specialization. For example, an accountant for a large firm may specialize in only one area (e.g., internal audit), whereas an accountant in a small firm needs to be more of a generalist and take on many different things (e.g., not only internal auditing, but also payroll, accounts receivable, financial planning, and taxes). Specialization requires a trade-off between breadth and depth of knowledge. While a high degree of the division of labor increases productivity, it can also have unintended side-effects such as reduced employee job satisfaction due to repetition of tasks.

Formalization captures the extent to which employee behavior is steered by explicit and codified rules and procedures. Formalized structures are characterized by detailed written rules and policies of what to do in specific situations. These are often codified in employee handbooks. McDonald's, for example, uses detailed standard operating procedures throughout the world to ensure consistent quality and service. Don Thompson, McDonald's Corporation President and CEO, formalized the company's strategy by focusing on three key priorities in the company's Plan to Win: to optimize the menu, modernize the customer experience, and broaden restaurant accessibility.[18]

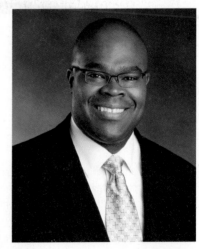

Don Thompson, McDonald's
Corporation President and CEO

Formalization, therefore, is not necessarily negative; often it is necessary to achieve consistent and predictable results. Airlines, for instance, must rely on a high degree of formalization to instruct pilots on how to fly their airplanes in order to ensure safety and reliability. Yet a high degree of formalization *can* slow decision making, reduce creativity and innovation, and hinder customer service.[19] Most customer service reps in call centers, for example, follow a detailed script. This is especially true when call centers are outsourced to overseas locations. As highlighted in the ChapterCase, Zappos deliberately avoided this approach when it made customer service its core competency. W. L. Gore uses an extremely *informal* organizational structure to foster employee satisfaction, retention, and creativity, as discussed in Strategy Highlight 11.1.

centralization An element of organizational structure that refers to the degree to which decision making is concentrated at the top of the organization.

Centralization refers to the degree to which decision making is concentrated at the top of the organization. Centralized decision making often correlates with slow response time and reduced customer satisfaction. In decentralized organizations such as W. L. Gore or Zappos, decisions are made and problems solved by empowered lower-level employees who are closer to the sources of issues. Different strategic management processes (discussed in Chapter 2) match with different degrees of centralization. Top-down strategic

Strategy Highlight 11.1

W. L. Gore & Associates: Informality and Innovation

W. L. Gore & Associates is the inventor of path-breaking new products such as breathable GORE-TEX fabrics, Glide dental floss, and Elixir guitar strings. Bill Gore, a former long-time employee of chemical giant DuPont, founded the company with the vision to create an organization "devoted to innovation, a company where imagination and initiative would flourish, where chronically curious engineers would be free to invent, invest, and succeed."[20] When founding the company in 1958, Bill Gore articulated four core values that still guide the company and its associates to this day:

1. Fairness to each other and everyone with whom the firm does business

2. Freedom to encourage, help, and allow other associates to grow in knowledge, skill, and scope of responsibility

3. The ability to make one's own commitments and keep them

4. Consultation with other associates before undertaking actions that could cause serious damage to the reputation of the company ("blowing a hole below the waterline")

W. L. Gore & Associates is organized in an informal and decentralized manner: It has no formal job titles, job descriptions, chains of command, formal communication channels, written rules or standard operating procedures. Face-to-face communication is preferred over e-mail. There is no organizational chart. In what is called a *lattice* or *boundaryless* organizational form, everyone is empowered and encouraged to speak to anyone else in the organization. People who work at Gore are called "associates" rather than employees, indicating professional expertise and status. Gore associates organize themselves in project-based teams that are led by sponsors, not bosses. Associates invite other team members based on their expertise and interests in a more or less ad hoc fashion. Peer control in these multidisciplinary teams further enhances associate productivity. Group members evaluate each other's performance annually, and these evaluations determine each associate's level of compensation. Moreover, all associates at W. L. Gore are also shareholders of the company, and thus are part owners sharing in profits and losses.

Gore's freewheeling and informal culture has been linked to greater employee satisfaction and retention, higher personal initiative and creativity, and innovation at the firm level. Although W. L. Gore's organizational structure may look like something you might find in a small, high-tech startup company, the company has 10,000 employees and over $2.5 billion in revenues, making Gore one of the largest privately held companies in the United States. W. L. Gore is consistently ranked in the top 25 of *Fortune*'s "100 Best Companies to Work For" list (#21 in 2013), and has been included in every edition of that prestigious ranking.[21]

planning takes place in highly centralized organizations, whereas planned emergence is found in more decentralized organizations.

Whether centralization or decentralization is more effective depends on the specific situation. During the Gulf oil spill in 2010, BP's response was slow and cumbersome because key decisions were initially made in its UK headquarters and not onsite. In this case, centralization reduced response time and led to a prolonged crisis. In contrast, the FBI and the CIA were faulted in the 9/11 Commission Report for *not being centralized enough.*[22] The report concluded that although each agency had different types of evidence that a terrorist strike in the U.S. was imminent, their decentralization made them unable to put together the pieces to prevent the 9/11 attacks.

Hierarchy determines the formal, position-based reporting lines and thus stipulates *who reports to whom.* Let's assume two firms of roughly equal size: Firm A and Firm B. If many levels of hierarchy exist between the front-line employee and the CEO in Firm A, it has a *tall structure.* In contrast, if there are few levels of hierarchy in Firm B, it has a *flat structure.*

The number of levels of hierarchy, in turn, determines the managers' **span of control**—how many employees directly report to a manager. In tall organizational structures (Firm A), the span of control is narrow. In flat structures (Firm B), the span of control is wide, meaning one manager supervises many employees. In recent years, firms have de-layered by reducing the headcount (often middle managers), making themselves flatter and more nimble. This, however, puts more pressure on the remaining managers who have to supervise and monitor more direct reports due to an increased span of control.[23] Recent research suggests that managers are most effective at an intermediate point where the span of control is not too narrow or too wide.[24]

ASSEMBLING THE PIECES: MECHANISTIC VS. ORGANIC ORGANIZATIONS

Several of the building blocks of organizational structure frequently show up together, creating distinct organizational forms—organic and mechanistic organizations.[25]

Zappos and W. L. Gore are both examples of **organic organizations**. Such organizations have a low degree of specialization and formalization, a flat organizational structure, and decentralized decision making.[26] Organic structures tend to be correlated with the following: a fluid and flexible information flow among employees in both horizontal and vertical directions; faster decision making; and higher employee motivation, retention, satisfaction, and creativity. Organic organizations also typically exhibit a higher rate of entrepreneurial behaviors and innovation. Organic structures allow firms to foster R&D and/or marketing, for example, as a core competency. Thus, firms that pursue a differentiation strategy at the business level frequently employ an organic structure. Exhibit 11.3 highlights the key features of organic organizations.

Due to significant advances in information technology, organic organizations frequently use *virtual teams.* In these teams, geographically dispersed team members are able to collaborate through electronic communications such as e-mail, instant messaging, intranets, and teleconferencing.[27] Given time differences, virtual teams often organize work flow so that projects can be pushed forward 24 hours a day, seven days a week. Use of virtual work

LO 11-4

Compare and contrast mechanistic versus organic organizations.

---

hierarchy An element of organizational structure that determines the formal, position-based reporting lines and thus stipulates who reports to whom.

span of control The number of employees who directly report to a manager.

organic organization Organizational form characterized by a low degree of specialization and formalization, a flat organizational structure, and decentralized decision making.

EXHIBIT 11.3 / Mechanistic vs. Organic Organizations: The Building Blocks of Organizational Structure

	Mechanistic Organizations	**Organic Organizations**
Specialization	• High degree of specialization • Rigid division of labor • Employees focus on narrowly defined tasks	• Low degree of specialization • Flexible division of labor • Employees focus on "bigger picture"
Formalization	• Intimate familiarity with rules, policies, and processes necessary • Deep expertise in narrowly defined domain required • Task-specific knowledge valued	• Clear understanding of organization's core competencies and strategic intent • Domain expertise in different areas • Generalized knowledge of how to accomplish strategic goals valued
Centralization	• Decision power centralized at top • Vertical (top-down) communication	• Distributed decision making • Vertical (top-down and bottom-up) as well as horizontal communication
Hierarchy	• Tall structures • Low span of control • Clear lines of authority • Command and control	• Flat structures • High span of control • Horizontal as well as two-way vertical communication • Mutual adjustment
Business Strategy	• Cost-leadership strategy • Examples: McDonald's; Walmart	• Differentiation strategy • Examples: W. L. Gore, Zappos

and collaboration technologies has enabled companies to be more nimble and to employ flatter and more decentralized organizational structures. Research data show that the largest 30 companies by market capitalization used networked digital technologies to double productivity per employee, despite more than doubling the number of employees. In the decades prior to the widespread use of computer-mediated work, employee productivity remained more or less flat.[28]

mechanistic organization Organizational form characterized by a high degree of specialization and formalization, and a tall hierarchy that relies on centralized decision making.

Mechanistic organizations are characterized by a high degree of specialization and formalization, and a tall hierarchy that relies on centralized decision making. The fast-food chain McDonald's fits this description quite well. Each step of every job (such as deep-frying fries) is documented in minute detail (e.g., what kind of vat, the quantity of oil, how many fries, what temperature, how long, and so on). Decision power is centralized at the top of the organization: McDonald's headquarters provides detailed instructions to each of its franchisees so that they provide comparable quality and service across the board (although with some local menu variations). Communication and authority lines are top-down and well defined. To ensure standardized operating procedures and consistent food quality throughout the world, McDonald's operates Hamburger University, a state-of-the-art teaching facility in a Chicago suburb, where 50 full-time instructors teach courses in chemistry, food preparation, and marketing. In 2010, McDonald's opened a second Hamburger University campus in Shanghai, China. Mechanistic structures allow for standardization and economies of scale, and often are used when the firm pursues a cost-leadership strategy at the business level (again, see Exhibit 11.3).

Although at first glance organic organizations may appear to be more attractive than mechanistic ones, their relative effectiveness depends on context. McDonald's, with its over 34,000 restaurants across the globe, would not be successful with an organic structure. Similarly, a mechanistic structure would not allow Zappos or W. L. Gore to develop and hone their respective core competencies in customer service and product innovation.

The key point is this: To gain and sustain competitive advantage, structure must follow strategy. Moreover, the chosen organizational form must match the firm's business strategy. We will expand further on the required strategy-structure relationship in the next section.

11.2 Matching Strategy and Structure

The important and interdependent relationship between strategy and structure directly impacts a firm's performance. Moreover, the relationship is dynamic—changing over time in a predictable pattern as firms grow in size and complexity. Successful new ventures generally grow first by increasing sales, then by obtaining larger geographic reach, and finally by diversifying through vertical integration and entering into related and unrelated businesses.[29] Different stages in a firm's growth require different organizational structures. This important evolutionary pattern is depicted in Exhibit 11.4. As we will discuss next, organizational structures range from simple to functional to multidivisional to matrix.

SIMPLE STRUCTURE

A **simple structure** generally is used by small firms with low organizational complexity. In such firms, the founders tend to make all the important strategic decisions and run the day-to-day operations. Examples include entrepreneurial ventures such as Facebook in 2004, when the startup operated out of Mark Zuckerberg's dorm room, and professional service firms such as smaller advertising, consulting, accounting, and law firms, as well as family-owned businesses. Simple structures are flat hierarchies operated in a decentralized fashion. They exhibit a low degree of formalization and specialization. Typically, neither professional managers nor sophisticated systems are in place, which often leads to an overload for the founder and/or CEO when the firms experience growth.

FUNCTIONAL STRUCTURE

As sales increase, firms generally adopt a **functional structure**, which groups employees into distinct functional areas based on domain expertise. These functional areas often correspond to distinct stages in the company value chain such as R&D, engineering and manufacturing, and marketing and sales, as well as supporting areas such as human resources, finance, and accounting. Exhibit 11.5 shows a functional structure, with the lines indicating reporting and authority relationships. The department head of each functional area reports to the CEO, who coordinates and integrates the work of each function. A business school student generally majors in one of these

LO 11-5

Describe different organizational structures and match them with appropriate strategies.

simple structure
Organizational structure in which the founders tend to make all the important strategic decisions as well as run the day-to-day operations.

functional structure
Organizational structure that groups employees into distinct functional areas based on domain expertise.

EXHIBIT 11.4 / Changing Organizational Structures and Increasing Complexity as Firms Grow

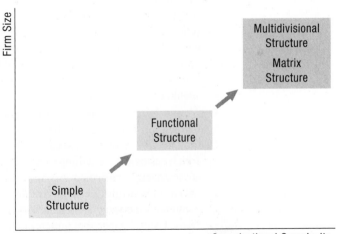

EXHIBIT 11.5

Typical Functional Structure

functional areas such as finance, accounting, IT, marketing, operations, or human resources, and is then recruited into a corresponding functional group.

W. L. Gore began as a company by operating out of Bill Gore's basement and using a simple structure. Two years after its founding, the company received a large manufacturing order for high-tech cable that it could not meet with its ad hoc basement operation. At that point, W. L. Gore reorganized itself into a functional structure. A simple structure could not provide the effective division, coordination, and integration of work required to accommodate future growth.

A functional structure allows for a higher degree of specialization and deeper domain expertise than a simple structure. Higher specialization also allows for a greater division of labor, which is linked to higher productivity.[30] While work in a functional structure tends to be specialized, it is centrally coordinated by the CEO (see Exhibit 11.5). A functional structure allows for an efficient top-down and bottom-up communication chain between the CEO and the functional departments, and thus relies on a relatively flat structure.

USE WITH VARIOUS BUSINESS STRATEGIES. A functional structure is recommended when a firm has a fairly narrow focus in terms of product/service offerings (i.e., low level of diversification) combined with a small geographic footprint. It matches well, therefore, with the different *business* strategies discussed in Chapter 6: cost leadership, differentiation, and integration. Although a functional structure is the preferred method for implementing business strategy, different variations and contexts require careful modifications in each case:

- The goal of a *cost-leadership strategy* is to create a competitive advantage by reducing the firm's cost below that of competitors while offering acceptable value. The cost leader sells a no-frills, standardized product or service to the mainstream customer. To effectively implement a cost-leadership strategy, therefore, managers must create a functional structure that contains the organizational elements of a *mechanistic structure*—one that is centralized, with well-defined lines of authority up and down the hierarchy. Using a functional structure allows the cost leader to nurture and constantly upgrade necessary core competencies in manufacturing and logistics. Moreover, the cost leader needs to create incentives to foster process innovation in order to drive down cost. Finally, because the firm services the average customer, and thus targets the largest market segment possible, it should focus on leveraging economies of scale to further drive down costs.

- The goal of a *differentiation strategy* is to create a competitive advantage by offering products or services at a higher perceived value, while controlling costs. The differentiator, therefore, sells a non-standardized product or service to specific market segments in which customers are willing to pay a higher price. To effectively implement a differentiation strategy, managers rely on a functional structure that resembles an *organic organization*. In particular, decision making tends to be decentralized to foster and incentivize continuous innovation and creativity as well as flexibility and mutual adjustment across areas. Using a functional structure with an organic organization allows the differentiator to nurture and constantly upgrade necessary core competencies in R&D, innovation, and marketing. Finally, the functional structure should be set up to allow the firm to reap economies of scope from its core competencies, such as by leveraging its brand name across different products or its technology across different devices.

■ A successful *integration strategy* requires reconciliation of the trade-offs between differentiation and low cost. To effectively implement an integration strategy, the firm must be both efficient and flexible. For example, the integrator must balance centralization (to control costs) with decentralization (to foster creativity and innovation). Managers must, therefore, attempt to combine the advantages of the functional-structure variations used for cost leadership and differentiation while mitigating their disadvantages. Moreover, the integrator needs to develop several distinct core competencies to both drive up perceived value and lower cost. It must further pursue both product and process innovations in an attempt to reap economies of scale and scope. All of these challenges make it clear that although an integration strategy is attractive at first glance, it is quite difficult to implement given the range of important trade-offs that must be addressed.

Exhibit 11.6 presents a detailed match between different business strategies and their corresponding functional structures.

EXHIBIT 11.6 / Matching Business Strategy and Structure

Business Strategy	Structure
Cost leadership	Functional • Mechanistic organization • Centralized • Command and control • Core competencies in efficient manufacturing and logistics • Process innovation to drive down cost • Focus on economies of scale
Differentiation	Functional • Organic organization • Decentralized • Flexibility and mutual adjustment • Core competencies in R&D, innovation, and marketing • Product innovation • Focus on economies of scope
Integration	Functional • Ambidextrous organization • Balancing centralization with decentralization • Multiple core competencies along the value chain required: R&D, manufacturing, logistics, marketing, etc. • Process and product innovations • Focus on economies of scale and scope

Strategy Highlight 11.2

USA Today: Leveraging Ambidextrous Organizational Design

The newspaper *USA Today*, published by Gannett Company, has one of the widest print circulations in the United States (close to 2 million). Though highly profitable, in the mid-1990s the newspaper faced the emerging threat of online news media, which is mostly free for the end user. Gannett decided to create a competing online offering—*USA Today.com,* making it independent from the namesake newspaper. The online news unit hired staff from the outside, and its first general manager put in place an organizational structure with fundamentally different roles and incentives and a different culture. *USA Today.com*'s culture was that of a new high-tech venture, whereas the print media *USA Today* had a more conservative corporate culture. Physically and structurally separated from the print newspaper, *USA Today.com* resembled an online startup company in the media business more than a traditional newspaper outlet. Roughly 80 percent of the online news originated from sources other than the print version.

Although *USA Today.com* successfully attracted readers and advertising dollars, Gannett starved the fledgling startup by draining resources. As a result, *USA Today.com* lost some key editorial talent because it could not provide competitive compensation packages. To solve this problem, *USA Today.com*'s general manager pushed for even greater independence and for profit-and-loss responsibility. That decision further isolated the startup from the print-news unit.

By 2000, Gannett decided it was time to integrate *USA Today.com* with the newspaper in order to create synergies between the two news outfits. Duplication of all editorial functions and separate creation of content no longer made sense. Given the strained relationship and large cultural differences between the print newspaper and the online business, however, this seemed a daunting task.

The newly appointed general manager of *USA Today .com* put in place an ambidextrous organizational structure, keeping the online unit somewhat independent but integrating important functions at the top through joint editorial meetings and senior management teams. To support this integration, the president of *USA Today* shifted compensation incentives for both senior teams to accomplish *joint* goals rather than to focus solely on each business unit's performance. General managers of each unit implemented further integration through weekly meetings of lower-level editorial staff. The general managers of each unit, therefore, were the key integrating linchpins between formerly independent business units, allowing for synergies to emerge.[34]

---

exploitation Applying current knowledge to enhance firm performance in the short term.

exploration Searching for new knowledge that may enhance future performance.

As mentioned in Chapter 6, managers can implement an integration strategy by building an *ambidextrous* organization, which attempts to balance and harness different activities in trade-off situations.[31] One example is the attempt to balance **exploitation**—applying current knowledge to enhance firm performance in the short term—with **exploration**—searching for new knowledge that may enhance future performance.[32] To transform a functional structure into an ambidextrous organization, the CEO or a team of top executives must personally take responsibility for the integration and coordination across different functional areas. Strategy scholars found that ambidextrous organizations were most effective in executing continuous innovation.[33] Strategy Highlight 11.2 shows how *USA Today* used an ambidextrous organizational design to successfully reintegrate its independent online unit.

DRAWBACKS. While certainly attractive, the functional strategy is not without significant drawbacks. One is that, although the functional strategy facilitates rich and extensive communication between members of the *same* department, it frequently lacks effective communication channels *across* departments. (Notice in Exhibit 11.5 the lack of links between different functions.) The lack of linkage between functions is the reason, for example, why R&D managers often do not communicate directly with marketing managers. In an ambidextrous organization, a top-level manager such as the CEO must take on the necessary coordination and integration work.

To overcome the lack of cross-departmental collaboration in a functional structure, a firm can set up *cross-functional teams*. In these temporary teams, members come from different functional areas to work together on a specific project or product, usually from start to completion. Each team member reports to two supervisors: the team leader and the respective functional department head. As we saw in Strategy Highlight 11.1, W. L. Gore employs cross-functional teams successfully.

A second critical drawback of the functional structure is that it cannot effectively address a higher level of diversification, which often stems from further growth.[35] This is the stage at which firms find it effective to evolve and adopt a multidivisional or matrix structure, both of which we will discuss next.

MULTIDIVISIONAL STRUCTURE

Over time, as a firm diversifies into different product lines and geographies, it implements a multidivisional or a matrix structure (as shown in Exhibit 11.4). The **multidivisional structure** (or **M-form**) consists of several distinct strategic business units (SBUs), each with its own profit-and-loss (P&L) responsibility. Each SBU is operated more or less independently from one another, and each is led by a CEO (or equivalent general manager) who is responsible for the unit's business strategy and its day-to-day operations. The CEOs of each division in turn report to the corporate office, which is led by the company's highest-ranking executive (titles vary and include president or CEO for the entire corporation). Because most large firms are diversified to some extent across different product lines and geographies, the M-form is a widely adopted organizational structure.

> **multidivisional structure (M-form)** Organizational structure that consists of several distinct strategic business units (SBUs), each with its own profit-and-loss (P&L) responsibility.

For example, Zappos is an SBU under Amazon, which employs a multidivisional structure. Also, W. L. Gore uses a multidivisional structure to administer its differentiation and related diversification strategies. It has four product divisions (electronic products, industrial products, medical products, and fabrics division) with manufacturing facilities in the U.S., China, Germany, Japan, and Scotland, and business activities in 30 countries across the globe.[36]

A typical M-form is shown in Exhibit 11.7. In this example, the company has four SBUs, each led by a CEO. Corporations may use SBUs to organize around different businesses and product lines or around different geographic regions. Each SBU represents a self-contained business with its *own* hierarchy and organizational structure. In Exhibit 11.7, SBU 2 is organized using a functional structure, while SBU 4 is organized using a matrix structure. The CEO of each SBU must determine which organizational structure is most appropriate to implement the SBU's business strategy.

A firm's corporate office is supported by company-wide staff functions such as human resources, finance, and corporate R&D. These staff functions support all of the company's SBUs, but are centralized at corporate headquarters to benefit from economies of scale and to avoid duplication within each SBU. Since most of the larger enterprises are publicly held stock companies, the president reports to a board of directors who represents the interests of the shareholders (indicated by the dashed line in Exhibit 11.7).

The president, with help from corporate headquarters staff, monitors the performance of each SBU and determines how to allocate resources across units.[37] Corporate headquarters add value by functioning as an internal capital market. The goal is to be more efficient at allocating capital through its budgeting process than what could be achieved in external capital markets. This can be especially effective if the corporation overall

EXHIBIT 11.7

Typical Multidivisional (M-Form) Structure

(Note that SBU 2 uses a functional structure, and SBU 4 uses a matrix structure.)

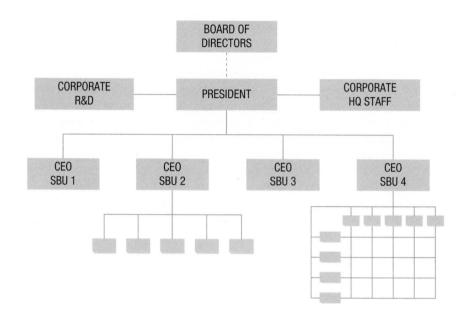

can access capital at a lower cost than competitors due to a favorable (AAA) debt rating. Corporate headquarters can also add value through restructuring the company's portfolio of SBUs by selling low-performing businesses and adding promising businesses through acquisitions.

USE WITH VARIOUS CORPORATE STRATEGIES. To achieve an optimal match between strategy and structure, different *corporate* strategies require different organizational structures. In Chapter 8, we identified four types of corporate diversification (see Exhibit 8.7): *single business, dominant business, related diversification*, and *unrelated diversification*. Each is defined by the percentage of revenues obtained from the firm's primary activity. Firms that follow a single-business or dominant-business strategy at the corporate level gain at least 70 percent of their revenues from their primary activity; they generally employ a functional structure. For firms that pursue either related or unrelated diversification, the M-form is the preferred organizational structure. Exhibit 11.8 matches different corporate strategies and their corresponding organizational structures.

Managers using the M-form organizational structure to support a *related-diversification* strategy should ideally concentrate decision making at the top of the organization. Doing so allows a high level of integration. It also helps corporate headquarters leverage and transfer across different SBUs the core competencies that form the basis for a related diversification. *Co-opetition* among the SBUs is both inevitable and necessary. They compete with one another for resources such as capital and managerial talent, but they also need to cooperate to share competencies.

In contrast, corporate executives using the M-form structures to support an *unrelated-diversification* strategy should decentralize decision making. Doing so allows general managers to respond to specific circumstances, and leads to a low level of integration at corporate headquarters. Since each SBU is evaluated as a standalone profit-and-loss center, SBUs end up in *competition* with each other. A high-performing SBU might be rewarded with greater capital budgets and strategic freedoms; low-performing businesses might be spun off. As explained in Chapter 8, the BCG growth-share matrix helps corporate executives when making these types of decisions.

EXHIBIT 11.8 / Matching Corporate Strategy and Structure

Corporate Strategy	Structure
Single business	Functional structure
Dominant business	Functional structure
Related diversification	Cooperative multidivisional (M-form) • Centralized decision making • High level of integration at corporate headquarters • Co-opetition among SBUs 　▪ Competition for resources 　▪ Cooperation in competency sharing
Unrelated diversification	Competitive multidivisional (M-form) • Decentralized decision making • Low level of integration at corporate headquarters • Competition among SBUs for resources

MATRIX STRUCTURE

To reap the benefits of both the M-form and the functional structure, many firms employ a mix of these two organizational forms, called a **matrix structure**. Exhibit 11.9 shows an example. In it, the firm is organized according to SBUs (along a horizontal axis, like in the M-form), but also has a second dimension of organizational structure (along a vertical axis). In this case, the second dimension consists of different geographic areas, each of which generally would house a full set of functional activities. The idea behind the matrix structure is to combine the benefits of the M-form (domain expertise, economies of scale, and the efficient processing of information) with those of the functional structure (responsiveness and decentralized focus).

The horizontal and vertical reporting lines between SBUs and geographic areas intersect, creating nodes in the matrix. Exhibit 11.9 highlights one employee, represented by the purple node. This employee works (in a group with other employees) in SBU 2 (the company's health care unit) for the Europe division in France. Therefore, this employee has two bosses—the CEO of the health care SBU and the general manager (GM) for the Europe division. Both supervisors in turn report to corporate headquarters, which is led by the president of the corporation (indicated in Exhibit 11.9 by the reporting lines from the SBUs and geographic units to the president).

The specific organizational configuration depicted in Exhibit 11.9 is a *global matrix structure*. Firms tend to use it to pursue a *transnational strategy*, in which the firm combines the benefits of a multidomestic strategy (high local responsiveness) with those of a global-standardization strategy (lowest cost position attainable). In a global matrix structure, the geographic divisions are charged with local responsiveness and learning. At the same time, each SBU is charged with driving down costs through economies of scale and other efficiencies. A global matrix structure also allows the firm to feed local learning back to different SBUs and thus diffuse it throughout the organization.

The matrix structure is quite versatile, because managers can assign different groupings along the vertical and horizontal axes. A common form of the matrix structure uses different projects or products on the vertical axis, and different functional areas on the horizontal

matrix structure
Organizational structure that combines the functional structure with the M-form.

EXHIBIT 11.9

Typical Matrix Structure with Geographic and SBU Divisions

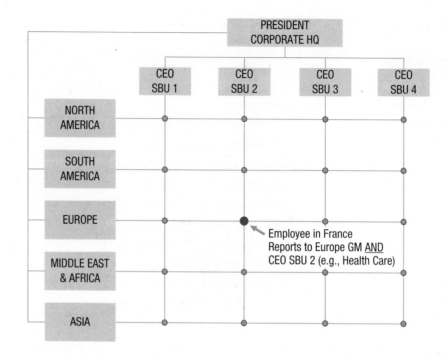

axis. In that traditional matrix structure, *cross-functional* teams work together on different projects. In contrast to the cross-functional teams discussed earlier in the W. L. Gore example, the teams in a matrix structure tend to be more permanent rather than project-based.

Though it is appealing in theory, the matrix structure does have shortcomings. It is usually difficult to implement: Implementing two layers of organizational structure creates significant organizational complexity and increases administrative costs. Also, reporting structures in a matrix are often not clear. In particular, employees can have trouble reconciling goals presented by their two (or more) supervisors. Less-clear reporting structures can undermine accountability by creating multiple principal–agent relationships. This can make performance appraisals more difficult. Adding a layer of hierarchy can also slow decision making and increase bureaucratic costs.

Given the advances in computer-mediated collaboration tools, some firms have replaced the more rigid matrix structure with a *network structure*. A network structure allows the firm to connect centers of excellence, whatever their global location (see Exhibit 10.2).[38] The firm benefits from *communities of practice*, which store important organizational learning and expertise. To avoid undue complexity, however, these network structures need to be supported by corporate-wide procedures and policies to streamline communication, collaboration, and the allocation of resources.[39]

USE WITH VARIOUS GLOBAL STRATEGIES. We already noted that a global matrix structure fits well with a transnational strategy. To complete the strategy-structure relationships in the global context, we also need to consider the international, multidomestic, and standardization strategies discussed in Chapter 10. Exhibit 11.10 shows how different global strategies best match with different organizational structures.

In an *international strategy,* the company leverages its home-based core competency by moving into foreign markets. An international strategy is advantageous when the company faces low pressure for both local responsiveness and cost reductions. Companies pursue an

EXHIBIT 11.10 / Matching Global Strategy and Structure

Global Strategy	Structure
International	Functional
Multidomestic	Multidivisional
	• Geographic areas
	• Decentralized decision making
Global Standardization	**Multidivisional**
	• Product divisions
	• Centralized decision making
Transnational	Global matrix
	• Balance of centralized and decentralized decision making
	• Additional layer of hierarchy to coordinate both:
	▪ Geographic areas
	▪ Product divisions

international strategy through a differentiation strategy at the business level. The best match for an international strategy is a *functional* organizational structure, which allows the company to leverage its core competency most effectively. This approach is similar to matching a business-level differentiation strategy with a functional structure (discussed in detail earlier).

When a multinational enterprise (MNE) pursues a *multidomestic strategy,* it attempts to maximize local responsiveness in the face of low pressures for cost reductions. An appropriate match for this type of global strategy is the *multidivisional* organizational structure. That structure would enable the MNE to set up different divisions based on geographic regions (e.g., by continent). The different geographic divisions operate more or less as standalone SBUs to maximize local responsiveness. Decision making is decentralized.

When following a *global-standardization strategy,* the MNE attempts to reap significant economies of scale as well as location economies by pursuing a global division of labor based on wherever best-of-class capabilities reside at the lowest cost. Since the product offered is more or less an undifferentiated commodity, the MNE pursues a cost-leadership strategy. The optimal organizational structure match is, again, a *multidivisional* structure. Rather than focusing on geographic differences as in the multidomestic strategy, the focus is on driving down costs due to consolidation of activities across different geographic areas.

11.3 Organizational Culture: Values, Norms, and Artifacts

Organizational culture is the second key building block when designing organizations for competitive advantage. Just as people have distinctive personalities, so too do organizations have unique cultures that capture "how things get done around here." **Organizational culture** describes the collectively shared values and norms of an organization's members.[40] *Values* define what is considered important. Zappos' 10 core values (shown in Exhibit 11.1) are important to its employees; they define their identity of what it means to be working at Zappos.[41] *Norms* define appropriate employee attitudes and behaviors.[42]

organizational culture The collectively shared values and norms of an organization's members; a key building block of organizational design.

LO 11-6

Describe the elements of organizational culture, and explain where organizational cultures can come from and how they can be changed.

EXHIBIT 11.11 / The Elements of Organizational Culture: Values, Norms, and Artifacts

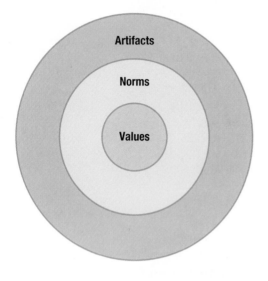

Employees learn about an organization's culture through *socialization,* a process whereby employees internalize an organization's values and norms through immersion in its day-to-day operations.[43] Successful socialization, in turn, allows employees to function productively and to take on specific roles within the organization. *Strong cultures* emerge when the company's core values are widely shared among the firm's employees and when the norms have been internalized.

Corporate culture finds its expression in *artifacts.* Artifacts include elements such as the design and layout of physical space (e.g., cubicles or private offices); symbols (e.g., the type of clothing worn by employees); vocabulary; what stories are told (see the Zappos example that follows); what events are celebrated and highlighted; and how they are celebrated (e.g., a formal dinner versus a company BBQ when the firm reaches its sales target).

Exhibit 11.11 depicts the elements of organizational culture—values, norms, and artifacts—in concentric circles. The most important yet least visible element—values—is in the center. As we move outward in the figure, from values to norms to artifacts, culture becomes more observable. Understanding what organizational culture is, and how it is created, maintained, and changed, can help you be a more effective manager. A unique culture that is strategically relevant can also be the basis of a firm's competitive advantage.

WHERE DO ORGANIZATIONAL CULTURES COME FROM?

founder imprinting A process by which the founder defines and shapes an organization's culture, which can persist for decades after his or her departure.

Often, company founders define and shape an organization's culture, which can persist for many decades after their departure. This phenomenon is called **founder imprinting.**[44] Firm founders set the initial strategy, structure, and culture of an organization by transforming their vision into reality. Famous founders who have left strong imprints on their organizations include Steve Jobs (Apple), Walt Disney (Disney), Michael Dell (Dell), Sergei Brin and Larry Page (Google), Oprah Winfrey (Harpo Productions and *OWN,* the Oprah Winfrey Network), Bill Gates (Microsoft), Larry Ellison (Oracle), Ralph Lauren (Polo Ralph Lauren), Martha Stewart (Martha Stewart Living Omnimedia), and Herb Kelleher (Southwest Airlines).

Walmart's founder Sam Walton personified the retailer's cost-leadership strategy. At one time the richest man in America, Sam Walton drove a beat-up Ford pickup truck, got $5 haircuts, went camping for vacations, and lived in a modest ranch home in Bentonville, Arkansas.[45] Everything Sam Walton did was consistent with the low-cost strategy. Walmart stays true to its founder's tradition. Home to one of the largest companies on the planet, the company's Arkansas headquarters in Bentonville was described by Thomas Friedman in his book *The World Is Flat* as follows: "[Walmart's corporate headquarters] are crammed into a reconfigured warehouse . . . a large building made of corrugated metal, I figured it was the maintenance shed."[46]

groupthink A situation in which opinions coalesce around a leader without individuals critically evaluating and challenging that leader's opinions and assumptions.

The culture that founders initially imprint is reinforced by their strong preference to recruit, retain, and promote employees who subscribe to the same values. In turn, more people with similar values are attracted to that organization.[47] As the values and norms held by the employees become more similar, the firm's corporate culture becomes stronger and more distinct. This in turn can have a serious negative side-effect: **groupthink,** a situation in which opinions coalesce around a leader without individuals critically evaluating and challenging that leader's opinions and assumptions. Cohesive, non-diverse groups are highly susceptible to groupthink, which in turn can lead to flawed decision making with potentially disastrous consequences.

In addition to founder imprinting, a firm's culture also flows from its values, especially when they are linked to the company's reward system. For example, Zappos established its unique organizational culture through explicitly stated values that are connected to its reward system (see Exhibit 11.1). To recruit people that fit with the company's values, Tony Hsieh has all new-hires go through a four-week training program. It covers such topics as company history, culture, and vision, as well as customer service.[48] New-hires also spend two weeks on the phone as customer service reps. What's novel about Zappos' approach is that at the end of the first week, the company offers any new hire $2,000 to quit (plus pay for the time already worked). This offer stands until the end of the fourth week, when the training program is completed. Individuals who choose to stay on despite the enticing offer tend to fit well with and strengthen Zappos' distinct culture.[49]

HOW DOES ORGANIZATIONAL CULTURE CHANGE?

An organization's culture can be one of its strongest assets, but also its greatest liability. An organization's culture can turn from a core competency into a **core rigidity** if a firm relies too long on the competency without honing, refining, and upgrading as the firm and the environment change.[50] Over time, the original core competency is no longer a good fit and turns from an asset into a liability, and thus a *core rigidity*.

For example, GM's bureaucratic culture, combined with its innovative M-form structure, was once hailed as the key to superior efficiency and management.[51] However, that culture became a liability when the external environment changed following the oil-price shocks in the 1970s and the entry of Japanese carmakers into the U.S.[52] As a consequence, GM's strong culture led to organizational inertia. This resulted in a failure to adapt to changing customer preferences for more fuel-efficient cars, and prevented higher quality and more innovative designs. GM lost customers to foreign competitors that offered these features. In such times, corporate culture may need to be changed to address a breakdown in the culture-environment fit.

The primary avenues of culture change (often combined with changes in strategy and structure) include bringing in new leadership and mergers and acquisitions (M&As). Leaders and top executives shape corporate culture in the way they communicate and make decisions regarding an organization's structure, resource-allocation process, and reward system.

core rigidity A former core competency that turned into a liability because the firm has failed to hone, refine, and upgrade the competency as the environment changed.

ORGANIZATIONAL CULTURE AND COMPETITIVE ADVANTAGE

Can organizational culture be the basis of a firm's (sustainable) competitive advantage? For this to occur, according to the resource-based view of the firm, the resource—in this case, organizational culture—must be valuable, rare, difficult to imitate, and the firm must be organized to capture the value created. That is, the VRIO principles must hold (see Chapter 4).[53]

Let's look at two examples of how culture affects employee behavior and ultimately firm performance:

- If you have flown with Southwest Airlines (SWA), you may have noticed that things are done a little differently there. Flight attendants might sing a song about the city you're

landing in, or they might slide bags of peanuts down the aisle at takeoff. Employees celebrate Halloween in a big way by wearing costumes to work. Some argue that SWA's business strategy—being a cost leader in point-to-point air travel—is fairly simple, and that SWA's competitive advantage actually comes from its unique culture.[54] It's not all fun and games, though: Friendly and highly energized employees work across functional and hierarchical levels. Even Southwest's pilots pitch in to help load baggage quickly when needed. As a result, SWA's turn time between flights is only 15 minutes, whereas competitors frequently take two to three times as long.

■ Zappos' number-one core value is to "deliver WOW through service." CEO Tony Hsieh shares the following story to illustrate this core value in action: "I was in Santa Monica, California, a few years ago at a Skechers sales conference. . . . [In the early hours of the morning], a small group of us headed up to someone's hotel room to order some food. My friend from Skechers tried to order a pepperoni pizza from the room-service menu but was disappointed to learn that the hotel did not deliver hot food after 11:00 p.m. We had missed the deadline by several hours. . . . A few of us cajoled her into calling Zappos to try to order a pizza. She took us up on our dare, turned on the speakerphone, and explained to the (very) patient Zappos rep that she was staying in a Santa Monica hotel and really craving a pepperoni pizza, that room service was no longer delivering hot food, and that she wanted to know if there was anything Zappos could do to help. The Zappos rep was initially a bit confused by the request, but she quickly recovered and put us on hold. She returned two minutes later, listing the five closest places in the Santa Monica area that were still open and delivering pizzas at that time."[55]

In the SWA example, the company's unique culture helps it keep costs low by turning around its planes faster, thus keeping them flying longer hours (among many other activities that lower SWA's cost structure).[56] In the Zappos example, providing a "wow" customer experience by "going the extra mile" didn't save Zappos money, but in the long run superior experience does increase the company's perceived value and thereby its economic value creation. Indeed, Tony Hsieh makes it a point to conclude the story with the following statement: "As for my friend from Skechers? After that phone call, she's now a customer for life."[57]

Let's consider how an organization's culture can have a strong influence on employee behavior.[58] A positive culture motivates and energizes employees by appealing to their higher ideals. Internalizing the firm's values and norms, employees feel that they are part of a larger, meaningful community attempting to accomplish important things. When employees are intrinsically motivated this way, the firm can rely on fewer levels of hierarchy; thus close monitoring and supervision are not needed as much. Moreover, motivating through inspiring values allows the firms to tap employees' emotions so they use both their heads and their hearts when making business decisions. Strong organizational cultures that are strategically relevant, therefore, align employees' behaviors more fully with the organization's strategic goals. In doing so, they better coordinate work efforts, and they make cooperation more effective. They also strengthen employee commitment, engagement, and effort. Effective alignment in turn allows the organization to develop and refine its core competencies, which can form the basis for competitive advantage.

Applying the VRIO principles to the SWA and Zappos examples, we see that both cultures are valuable (lowering costs for SWA and increasing perceived value created for Zappos), rare (none of their competitors has an identical culture), non-imitable (despite attempts by competitors), and organized to capture some part of the incremental economic value created due to their unique cultures. It appears that at both SWA and Zappos, a unique organizational culture can in fact provide the basis for a (sustained) competitive advantage. These cultures, of course, need to be in sync with and in support of the respective business strategies pursued (cost leadership for SWA and differentiation for Zappos). Moreover, as the firms grow and external economic environments change, these cultures must be flexible enough to adapt.

Once it becomes clear that a firm's culture is a source of competitive advantage, some competitors will attempt to imitate that culture. Therefore, only a culture that cannot be easily copied can provide a competitive advantage. However, it can be difficult, at best, to imitate the cultures of successful firms, for two reasons: *causal ambiguity* and *social complexity*. While one can observe that a firm has a unique culture, the causal relationships among values, norms, artifacts, and the firm's performance may be hard to establish, even for people who work within the organization. For example, employees may become aware of the effect culture has on performance only after significant organizational changes occur. Moreover, organizational culture is socially complex. It encompasses not only interactions among employees across layers of hierarchy, but also the firm's outside relationships with its customers and suppliers.[59] Such a wide range of factors is difficult for any competing firm to imitate.

It is best to develop a strong and strategically relevant culture in the first few years of a firm's existence. Strategy scholars have documented that the initial structure, culture, and control mechanisms established in a new firm can be a significant predictor of later success.[60] In other empirical research, founder CEOs had a stronger positive imprinting effect than non-founder CEOs.[61] This stronger imprinting effect, in turn, resulted in higher performance of firms led by founder CEOs. In addition, consider that the vehicles of cultural change—changing leadership and growing through M&As—do not have a stellar record of success.[62] Indeed, researchers estimate that only about 20 percent of organizational change attempts are successful.[63] Thus, it is even more important to get the culture right from the beginning and then adapt it as the business evolves.

By combining theory and empirical evidence, we can see that organizational culture can help a firm gain and sustain competitive advantage *if* the culture makes a positive contribution to the firm's economic value creation and obeys the VRIO principles. Organizational culture is an especially effective lever for new ventures due to its malleability. Firm founders, early-stage CEOs, and venture capitalists, therefore, should be proactive in attempting to create a culture that leads to or at least supports a firm's competitive advantage.

11.4 Strategic Control-and-Reward Systems

Strategic control-and-reward systems are the third and final key building block when designing organizations for competitive advantage. **Strategic control-and-reward systems** are internal-governance mechanisms put in place to align the incentives of principals (shareholders) and agents (employees). These systems allow managers to specify goals, measure progress, and provide performance feedback. In Chapter 5, we discussed how firms can use the balanced-scorecard framework as a strategic control system. Here, we discuss additional control-and-reward systems: organizational culture, input controls, and output controls.

As just demonstrated, *organizational culture* can be a powerful motivator. It also can be an effective control system. Norms, informal and tacit in nature, act as a social control mechanism. Zappos, for example, achieves organizational control partly through an employee's peer group: Each group member's compensation, including the supervisor's, depends in part on the group's *overall productivity*. Peer control, therefore, exerts a

LO 11-7

Compare and contrast different strategic control-and-reward systems.

strategic control-and-reward systems A key building block of organizational design; internal-governance mechanisms put in place to align the incentives of principals (shareholders) and agents (employees).

powerful force on employee conformity and performance.[64] Values and norms also provide control by helping employees address unpredictable and irregular situations and problems (common in service businesses). In contrast, rules and procedures (e.g., codified in an employee handbook) can address only circumstances that can be predicted.

INPUT CONTROLS

input controls
Mechanisms in a strategic control-and-reward system that seek to define and direct employee behavior through a set of explicit, codified rules and standard operating procedures that are considered prior to the value-creating activities.

Input controls seek to define and direct employee behavior through a set of explicit, codified rules and standard operating procedures. Firms use input controls when the goal is to define the ways and means to reach a strategic goal and to ensure a predictable outcome. They are called input controls because management designs these mechanisms so they are considered *before* employees make any business decisions; thus, they are an input into the value-creation activities.

The use of *budgets* is key to input controls. Managers set budgets before employees define and undertake the actual business activities. For example, managers decide how much money to allocate to a certain R&D project before the project begins. In diversified companies using the M-form, corporate headquarters determines the budgets for each division. Public institutions, like some universities, also operate on budgets that must be balanced each year. Their funding often depends to a large extent on state appropriations and thus fluctuates depending on the economic cycle. During recessions, budgets tend to be cut, and they expand during boom periods.

Standard operating procedures, or policies and rules, are also a frequently used mechanism when relying on input controls. In our discussion on formalization, we described how McDonald's relies on detailed operating procedures to ensure consistent quality and service worldwide. The goal is to specify the conversion process from beginning to end in great detail to guarantee standardization and minimize deviation. This is important when a company operates in different geographies and with different human capital throughout the globe but needs to deliver a standardized product or service.

OUTPUT CONTROLS

output controls
Mechanisms in a strategic control-and-reward system that seek to guide employee behavior by defining expected results (outputs), but leave the means to those results open to individual employees, groups, or SBUs.

Output controls seek to guide employee behavior by defining expected results (outputs), but leave the means to those results open to individual employees, groups, or SBUs. Firms frequently tie employee compensation and rewards to predetermined goals, such as a specific sales target or return on invested capital. When factors internal to the firm determine the relationship between effort and expected performance, outcome controls are especially effective. At the corporate level, outcome controls discourage collaboration among different strategic business units. They are therefore best applied when a firm focuses on a single line of business or pursues unrelated diversification.

These days, more and more work requires creativity and innovation, especially in highly developed economies.[65] As a consequence, so-called *results-only-work-environments (ROWEs)* have attracted significant attention. ROWEs are output controls that attempt to tap intrinsic (rather than extrinsic) employee motivation, which is driven by the employee's interest in and the meaning of the work itself. In contrast, extrinsic motivation is driven by external factors such as awards and higher compensation, or punishments like demotions and layoffs (the *carrot-and-stick approach*). According to a recent synthesis of the strategic human resources literature, intrinsic motivation in a task is highest when an employee has autonomy (about what to do), mastery (how to do it), and purpose (why to do it).[66]

Today, 3M is best known for its adhesives and other consumer and industrial products.[67] But its full name reflects its origins: 3M stands for Minnesota Mining and Manufacturing

Company. Over time, 3M has relied on the ROWE framework and has morphed into a highly science-driven innovation company. At 3M, employees are encouraged to spend 15 percent of their time on projects of their *own choosing.* If any of these projects look promising, 3M provides financing through an internal venture capital fund and other resources to further develop their commercial potential. In fact, several of 3M's flagship products, including Post-It Notes and Scotch Tape, were the results of serendipity (see Chapter 2). To foster continued innovation, moreover, 3M requires each of its divisions to derive at least 30 percent of their revenues from products introduced in the past four years.

11.5 ◄► Implications for the Strategist

Daniel Pink's book on motivation *(Drive: The Surprising Truth About What Motivates Us)* discusses the limits of the carrot-and-stick approach versus the motivational impact of autonomy.

This chapter has a clear practical implication for the strategist: Formulating an effective strategy is a necessary but not sufficient condition for gaining and sustaining competitive advantage; strategy *execution* is at least as important for success. Successful strategy implementation requires managers to design and shape structure, culture, and control mechanisms. In doing so, they execute a firm's strategy as they put its accompanying business model into action. Strategy formulation and strategy implementation, therefore, are iterative and interdependent activities.

Organizing for competitive advantage, moreover, is a dynamic and not a static process. As seen in the Zappos example, to maintain competitive advantage, companies need to restructure as they grow and the competitive environment changes. In Chapter 4, we introduced the SWOT analysis as a helpful tool for the strategist to combine the results of a thorough external and internal analysis. We applied a SWOT analysis based on four strategic questions to McDonald's, the results of which were shown Exhibit 4.10.

We are now in a position to provide more guidance in terms of how to implement the recommendations over time and apply the resources necessary. Exhibit 11.12 shows this framework. The left panel is a repeat of the results from the SWOT analysis conducted in Chapter 4. The right panel shows resource requirements (low $, medium $$, and high $$$) on the horizontal axis, and time horizon (short term, medium term, and long term) on the vertical axis. Translating the findings from the left panel into the right panel, the strategist concludes that the first recommendation—to launch new locations in China and Mexico (S1, S2, O1)—requires a high level of investment and is a long-term proposition. The second recommendation—to show new ads highlighting the ease and speed of the McDonald's drive-thru for take-home orders (W1, T2)—requires a low amount of funding and can be achieved in the short term. The third recommendation—to launch a line of McDonald's frozen food in grocery chains (S2, S3, T2)—requires a medium investment and likely needs a longer time horizon to be accomplished. Finally, the fourth recommendation—to develop and emphasize more healthy food menu items (W1, W2, O2)—needs a medium level of resources and can be accomplished in the medium term. This exercise helps make the results of strategy analysis and formulation more concrete, and allows for a detailed list of action items outlining required investment levels and time horizons. In sum, the implementation matrix shown in Exhibit 11.12 provides helpful guidance for the strategist to operationalize strategy implementation.

This concludes our discussion of organizational design. We now move on to our concluding chapter, where we study corporate governance and business ethics.

EXHIBIT 11.12 / Strategy Implementation: Turning a SWOT Analysis into Action

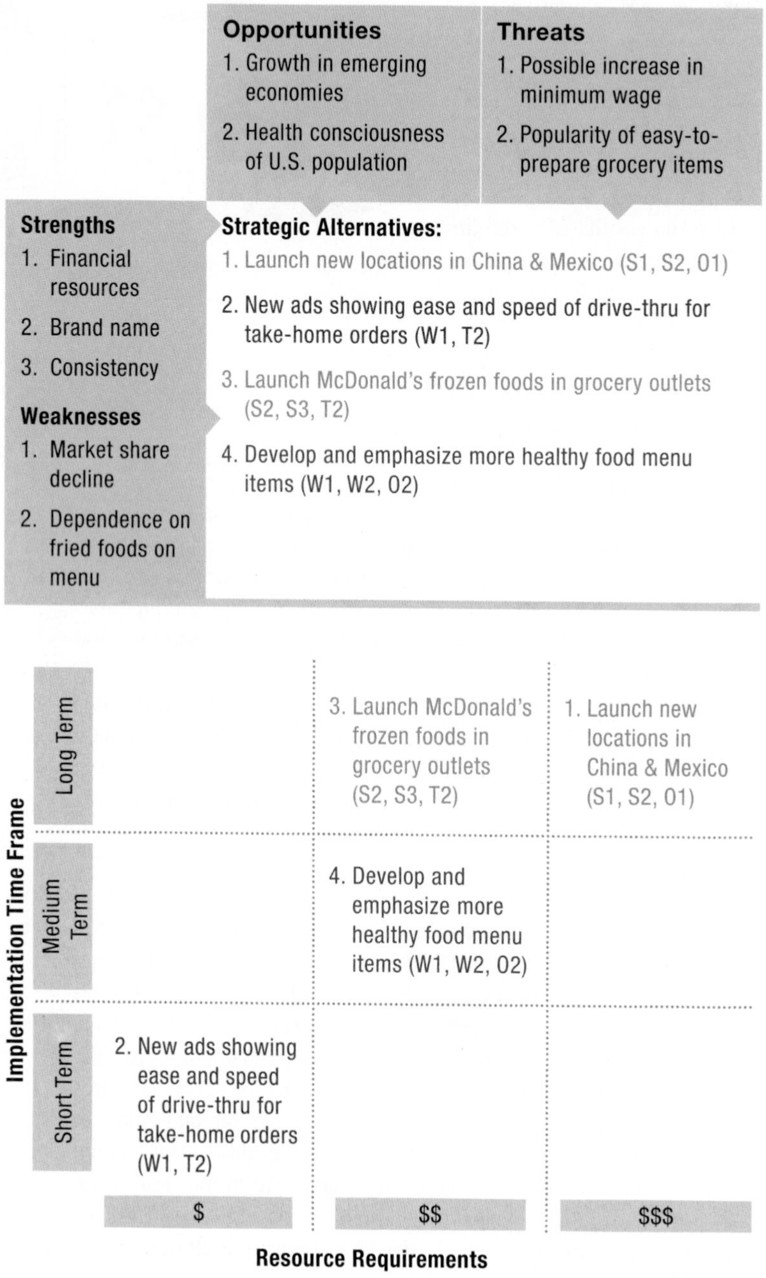

Opportunities
1. Growth in emerging economies
2. Health consciousness of U.S. population

Threats
1. Possible increase in minimum wage
2. Popularity of easy-to-prepare grocery items

Strengths
1. Financial resources
2. Brand name
3. Consistency

Weaknesses
1. Market share decline
2. Dependence on fried foods on menu

Strategic Alternatives:
1. Launch new locations in China & Mexico (S1, S2, O1)
2. New ads showing ease and speed of drive-thru for take-home orders (W1, T2)
3. Launch McDonald's frozen foods in grocery outlets (S2, S3, T2)
4. Develop and emphasize more healthy food menu items (W1, W2, O2)

Implementation Time Frame	$	$$	$$$
Long Term		3. Launch McDonald's frozen foods in grocery outlets (S2, S3, T2)	1. Launch new locations in China & Mexico (S1, S2, O1)
Medium Term		4. Develop and emphasize more healthy food menu items (W1, W2, O2)	
Short Term	2. New ads showing ease and speed of drive-thru for take-home orders (W1, T2)		

Resource Requirements

CHAPTER**CASE 11** / Consider This . . .

ZAPPOS WANTS TO "deliver WOW through service." We saw an example of this culture in the story of the Zappos customer service rep who provided contacts for local pizza delivery to an out-of-town guest. Though it is a memorable story, providing the pizza 411-service did not involve significant cost to the employee or the firm for delivering "WOW through service." However, at midnight on Friday, May 21, 2010, Zappos created a problem that required a significant financial cost to deliver that "WOW." Due to a programming error in its pricing engine, Zappos accidentally capped the sales price at $49.95 for all products sold on its subsidiary site (www.6pm.com). The mistake was not discovered until 6 a.m., and Zappos pulled down the site to correct the pricing problem. Once fixed, there remained a question of what to do about the products sold with the erroneous prices.

Zappos' terms and conditions clearly state that the firm is under no obligation to fulfill orders placed due to pricing mistakes. However, Zappos decided to honor every sale made in the time frame between midnight and 6 a.m.—resulting in a loss of over $1.6 million. That's putting your money where your "WOW" is![68]

Amazon, which owns Zappos, had its own pricing mistake just two months prior to the Zappos incident. Best Buy and Dell have also both had online pricing errors.[69] None of these firms handled the situation as smoothly as Zappos.

Questions

1. What elements of an organic organization are apparent from the chapter material on Zappos? (Refer to Exhibit 11.3.)

2. How does the Zappos business strategy match its organizational structure?

3. Which strategic control-and-reward system discussed in the chapter would be most appropriate for Zappos?

4. Do you think Zappos' decision to honor every sale, despite its explicit business terms and conditions that would allow it not to do so, was a sound one? Why or why not?

TAKE-AWAY CONCEPTS

In this chapter, we studied the three key levers that managers have at their disposal when designing their firms for competitive advantage—structure, culture, and control—as summarized by the following learning objectives and related take-away concepts.

LO 11-1 / Define organizational design and list its three components.

- Organizational design is the process of creating, implementing, monitoring, and modifying the structure, processes, and procedures of an organization.
- The key components of organizational design are structure, culture, and control.

- The goal is to design an organization that allows managers to effectively translate their chosen strategy into a realized one.

LO 11-2 / Explain how organizational inertia can lead established firms to failure.

- Organizational inertia can lead to the failure of established firms when a tightly coupled system of strategy and structure experiences internal or external shifts.
- Firm failure happens through a dynamic, four-step process (see Exhibit 11.2).

LO 11-3 / Define organizational structure and describe its four elements.

- An organizational structure determines how firms orchestrate employees' work efforts and distribute resources. It defines how firms divide and integrate tasks, delineates the reporting relationships up and down the hierarchy, defines formal communication channels, and prescribes how employees coordinate work efforts.

- The four building blocks of an organizational structure are specialization, formalization, centralization, and hierarchy (see Exhibit 11.3).

LO 11-4 / Compare and contrast mechanistic versus organic organizations.

- Organic organizations are characterized by a low degree of specialization and formalization, a flat organizational structure, and decentralized decision making.

- Mechanistic organizations are described by a high degree of specialization and formalization, and a tall hierarchy that relies on centralized decision making.

- The comparative effectiveness of mechanistic versus organic organizational forms depends on the context.

LO 11-5 / Describe different organizational structures and match them with appropriate strategies.

- To gain and sustain competitive advantage, not only must structure follow strategy, but also the chosen organizational form must match the firm's business strategy.

- The strategy-structure relationship is dynamic, changing in a predictable pattern—from simple to functional structure, then to multidivisional (M-form) and matrix structure—as firms grow in size and complexity.

- In a simple structure, the founder tends to make all the important strategic decisions as well as run the day-to-day operations.

- A functional structure groups employees into distinct functional areas based on domain expertise. Its different variations are matched with different business strategies: cost leadership, differentiation, and integration (see Exhibit 11.6).

- The multidivisional (M-form) structure consists of several distinct SBUs, each with its own profit-and-loss responsibility. Each SBU operates more or less independently from one another, led by a CEO responsible for the business strategy of the unit and its day-to-day operations (see Exhibit 11.7).

- The matrix structure is a mixture of two organizational forms: the M-form and the functional structure (see Exhibit 11.9).

- Exhibits 11.8 and 11.10 show how best to match different corporate and global strategies with respective organizational structures.

LO 11-6 / Describe the elements of organizational culture, and explain where organizational cultures can come from and how they can be changed.

- Organizational culture describes the collectively shared values and norms of its members.

- Values define what is considered important, and norms define appropriate employee attitudes and behaviors.

- Corporate culture finds its expression in artifacts, which are observable expressions of an organization's culture.

LO 11-7 / Compare and contrast different strategic control-and-reward systems.

- Strategic control-and-reward systems are internal governance mechanisms put in place to align the incentives of principals (shareholders) and agents (employees).

- Strategic control-and-reward systems allow managers to specify goals, measure progress, and provide performance feedback.

- In addition to the balanced-scorecard framework, managers can use organizational culture, input controls, and output controls as part of the firm's strategic control-and-reward systems.

- Input controls define and direct employee behavior through explicit and codified rules and standard operating procedures.

- Output controls guide employee behavior by defining expected results, but leave the means to those results open to individual employees, groups, or SBUs.

KEY TERMS

Centralization	Input controls	Simple structure
Core rigidity	Matrix structure	Span of control
Exploitation	Mechanistic organization	Specialization
Exploration	Multidivisional structure (M-form)	Strategic control-and-reward systems
Formalization	Organic organization	Strategy implementation
Founder imprinting	Organizational culture	
Functional structure	Organizational design	
Groupthink	Organizational structure	
Hierarchy	Output controls	

DISCUSSION QUESTIONS

1. Why is it important for an organization to have alignment between its strategy and structure?

2. The chapter describes the role of culture in the successful implementation of strategy. Consider an employment experience of your own or of someone you have observed closely (e.g., a family member). Describe to the best of your ability the values, norms, and artifacts of the organization. What was the socialization process of embedding the culture? Do you consider this to be an example of an effective culture for contributing to the organization's competitive advantage? Why or why not?

3. Strategy Highlight 11.1 discusses the informal organizational structure of W. L. Gore & Associates. Go to the firm's website (www.gore.com) and review the company's product scope.

   a. What commonalities across the products would likely be enhanced by flexible cross-functional teams?

   b. What would be your expectations of the type of norms found at W. L. Gore?

ETHICAL/SOCIAL ISSUES

1. As noted in Chapter 5, many public firms are under intense pressure for short-term (such as quarterly) financial improvements. How might such pressure, in combination with output controls, lead to unethical behaviors?

2. Cultural norms and values play a significant role in all organizations, from businesses in the economic sector to religious, political, and sports organizations. Strong organizational cultures can have many benefits, such as those described in the Zappos example. However, sometimes a strong organizational culture is less positive. Vince Lombardi, renowned coach of the Green Bay Packers, is often quoted as saying, "Winning isn't everything; it's the only thing." Many sports teams from junior sports to professional sports have either explicitly or implicitly touted this attitude as exemplary. Others, however, argue that this attitude is what's wrong with sports and leads to injury, minor misbehavior, and criminal behavior. It encourages players to do whatever it takes to win—from tripping a player or other unsportsmanlike conduct during middle-school sports to throwing a game as part of gambling.

   When a player hears the message as "any action will be tolerated as long as you are winning," there can be serious consequences on and off the field. Recent examples include high-school football players convicted of rape, yet Jen Floyd Engel of Fox Sports noticed "a shocking lack of outrage" within the community as they continued to support their football heroes.[70]

How could leaders of sports organizations communicate the will to win and develop the necessary skills while maintaining ethical behavior? Think of examples of coaches who coaxed players to play by the rules and maintain high personal ethical standards. What other socialization experiences could a coach use? What is the role of team leaders in encouraging high ethical standards while building the desire to win? Name some other examples of organizational culture leading to business failure, criminal behavior, or civil legal actions.

3. What makes some strong cultures helpful in gaining and sustaining a competitive advantage, while other strong cultures are a liability to achieving that goal?

SMALL-GROUP EXERCISES

//// Small-Group Exercise 1

Your classmates are a group of friends who have decided to open a small retail shop. The team is torn between two storefront ideas. The first idea is to open a high-end antique store selling household items used for decorations in upscale homes. Members of the team have found a location in a heavily pedestrian area near a local coffee shop. The store would have many items authenticated by a team member's uncle, who is a certified appraiser.

In discussing the plan, however, two group members suggest shifting to a drop-off store for online auctions such as eBay. In this business model, customers drop off items they want to sell, and the retail store does all the logistics involved—listing and selling the items on eBay, and then shipping them to buyers—for a percentage of the sales price. They suggest that a quick way to get started is to become a franchisee for a group such as "I Sold It" (www.877isoldit.com).

1. What is the business strategy for each store concept?

2. How would the organizational structure be different for the concepts?

3. What would likely be the cultural differences in the two store concepts?

4. How would the control-and-reward systems be different?

//// Small-Group Exercise 2
(Ethical/Social Issues)

The chapter describes Daniel Pink's ROWE theory of motivation, in which he argued that the most powerful motivation occurs when there is an interest in the work and the work itself has meaning. Intrinsic motivation is highest when an employee has *autonomy* (about what to do), *mastery* (how to do it), and *purpose* (why to do it). Assume your group has been asked by your university to brainstorm ways that the university might apply the ROWE theory. Discuss whether you would be more motivated and better educated if you had more autonomy in designing your program of study, could determine the best way for you to learn and gain mastery, and could develop your own statement of purpose as to why you were pursuing a particular program of study.

1. How might this change the university's allocation of resources (e.g., would more trained advisers and career counselors be required, and how would they be evaluated)?

2. If large numbers of students decided they would learn some of the core materials best by taking an online course, how might this affect the university's revenue stream? How might this change the way professors teach courses?

3. Have each group member explain how this approach might change his/her program of study.

4. Consider the potential pitfalls of such an approach and how these might be addressed.

STRATEGY TERM PROJECT

//// Module 11: Organizational Implementation Processes

In this module, you will study the organizational implementation processes of your selected firm. You will again rely on annual reports, news articles, and press releases for information to analyze and formulate your answers. You will identify a major strategic change the firm should seriously consider implementing, and then follow a six-step process to study the implementation impacts.

Implementation is a critical step in putting a planned action into effect. It often introduces change into the organization and can be met with strong resistance. The six stages outlined in Exhibit 11.13 can help leaders and organizations determine *how* to implement a particular plan.[71] These questions provide a framework for the strategic change. You may be able to find a prior successful strategic change the firm undertook and use this prior implementation as a guide for your suggested change.

As you progress through the six stages, reflect on what you have learned about your firm in the prior modules. In some cases, you will need to make educated guesses for the answer since you are looking at the implementation from outside the organization. However, over the 10 modules you have completed, you have already learned much about the firm. Answer the following questions for your selected organization.

1. From your knowledge of the firm, identify a major strategic change the firm should seriously consider. Briefly describe what the goal of the initiative is for the organization.

2. Work your way through the six stages in Exhibit 11.13, answering as many of the questions as you can for the proposed strategic change. As you develop the project plans with specifics for each of the stages, the plan should provide flexibility, allowing for unexpected contingencies to emerge.

EXHIBIT 11.13 / Implementation Framework

Implementation Stage	Key Questions to Ask in This Stage
Stage 1 People, skills, and organizational structure	• When must the strategy/strategic initiative be implemented? (How flexible is that date?) • Who is going to do it? What human skills are needed? • Do affected employees understand their roles? • Will the organization need to hire or lay off people? If so, how should we go about it? • How should the firm be organized? What structure should be implemented? Why and how?
Stage 2 Organizational culture	• What culture in the organization is required for the implementation to be successful? • If the current culture differs from the culture needed for the success of the strategy implementation, how should the firm go about changing its culture?
Stage 3 Reward system	• Is a reward structure in place to accomplish the task? • If not, what type of reward structure needs to be introduced to ensure successful strategy implementation?
Stage 4 Resource requirements	• What resources (financial and otherwise) are needed? • Are they in place? • If not, how can the firm obtain the required resources?
Stage 5 Supporting activities	• How is the implementation to be supported? • What policies, procedures, and IT support are needed? • Does the firm need external help (e.g., consulting services)? If so, what kind of services would the firm need, and why?
Stage 6 Strategic leadership	• What types of strategic leaders are required to make the change happen? • Does the firm have them in-house? • Should the firm hire some strategic leaders from outside? • How should the firm train its managers to create a pipeline of strategic leaders?

my STRATEGY

For What Type of Organization Are *You* Best-Suited?

A s noted in the chapter, firms can have very distinctive cultures. Recall that Zappos has a standing offer to pay any new hire $2,000 to quit the company during the first month. Zappos makes this offer to help ensure that those who stay with the company are comfortable in its "create fun and a little weirdness" environment.

You may have taken a personality test such as Myers-Briggs or The Big Five. These tests may be useful in gauging compatibility of career and personality types. They are often available for both graduate and undergraduate students at university career-placement centers. In considering the following questions, think about your next job and your longer-term career plans.

1. Review Exhibit 11.3 and circle the organizational characteristics you find appealing. Cross out those factors you think you would not like. Do you find a trend toward either the mechanistic or organic organization?

2. Have you been in school or work situations in which your values did not align with those of your peers or colleagues? How did you handle the situation? Are there certain values or norms important enough for you to consider as you look for a new job?

3. As you consider your career after graduation, which control-and-reward system discussed in the concluding section of the chapter would you find most motivating? Is this different from the controls used at some jobs you have had in the past?

ENDNOTES

1. Hsieh, T. (2010), *Delivering Happiness: A Path to Profits, Passion, and Purpose* (New York: Business Plus), p. 130.

2. Ibid., p. 145.

3. Ibid., p. 177.

4. Ibid., pp. 157–160.

5. This ChapterCase is based on: Hsieh, T. (2010), *Delivering Happiness: A Path to Profits, Passion, and Purpose;* and http://about.zappos.com.

6. Barney, J. B. (1986), "Organizational culture: Can it be a source of sustained competitive advantage?" *Academy of Management Review* 11: 656–665.

7. Bossidy, L., R. Charan, and C. Burck (2002), *Execution: The Discipline of Getting Things Done* (New York: Crown Business); and Hrebiniak, L. G. (2005), *Making Strategy Work: Leading Effective Execution and Change* (Philadelphia: Wharton School Publishing).

8. Grundy, T. (1998), "Strategy implementation and project management," *International Journal of Project Management* 16: 43–50.

9. Bossidy, L., R. Charan, and C. Burck (2002), *Execution: The Discipline of Getting Things Done;* and Herold, D. M., and D. B. Fedor (2008), *Change the Way You Lead Change: Leadership Strategies That Really*

Work (Palo Alto, CA: Stanford University Press).

10. "Yang's exit doesn't fix Yahoo," *The Wall Street Journal,* November 19, 2008.

11. "Yahoo's ad struggles persist," *The Wall Street Journal,* April 16, 2013.

12. Herold, D. M., and D. B. Fedor (2008), *Change the Way You Lead Change.*

13. Chandler, A. D. (1962), *Strategy and Structure: Chapters in the History of American Industrial Enterprise* (Cambridge, MA: MIT Press), p. 14 (italics added).

14. Hall, D. J., and M. A. Saias (1980), "Strategy follows structure!" *Strategic Management Journal* 1: 149–163.

15. Hill, C.W.L., and F. T. Rothaermel (2003), "The performance of incumbent firms in the face of radical technological innovation," *Academy of Management Review* 28: 257–274.

16. I gratefully acknowledge Professor Luis Martins' input on this exhibit.

17. In his insightful book, Finkelstein (2003) identifies several key transition points that put pressure on an organization and thus increase the likelihood of subsequent failure. See Finkelstein, S. (2003), *Why Smart Executives Fail: And What You Can Learn from Their Mistakes* (New York: Portfolio).

18. http://www.aboutmcdonalds.com/mcd/our_company/leadership/don_thompson.html.

19. Fredrickson, J. W. (1986), "The strategic decision process and organizational structure," *Academy of Management Review* 11: 280–297; Eisenhardt, K. M. (1989), "Making fast strategic decisions in high-velocity environments," *Academy of Management Journal* 32: 543–576; and Wally, S., and R. J. Baum (1994), "Strategic decision speed and firm performance," *Strategic Management Journal* 24: 1107–1129.

20. Hamel, G. (2007), *The Future of Management* (Boston, MA: Harvard Business School Press), p. 84.

21. This Strategy Highlight is based on: Hamel, G. (2007), *The Future of Management;* Collins, J. (2009), *How the Mighty Fall: And Why Some Companies Never Give In* (New York: HarperCollins); Collins, J., and M. Hansen (2011), *Great by Choice: Uncertainty, Chaos, and Luck—Why Some Thrive Despite Them All* (New York: HarperCollins); and www.gore.com.

22. *The 9/11 Report. The National Commission on Terrorist Attacks Upon the United States* (2004), http://govinfo.library.unt.edu/911/report/index.htm.

23. Child, J., and R. G. McGrath (2001), "Organization unfettered: Organizational forms in the information-intensive economy," *Academy of Management Journal* 44: 1135–1148; and Huy, Q. N. (2002), "Emotional balancing of organizational continuity and radical change: The contribution of middle managers," *Administrative Science Quarterly* 47: 31–69.

24. Theobald, N. A., and S. Nicholson-Crotty (2005), "The many faces of span of control: Organizational structure across multiple goals," *Administration and Society* 36: 648–660.

25. This section draws on: Burns, T., and G. M. Stalker (1961), *The Management of Innovation* (London: Tavistock).

26. This section draws on: Burns, T., and G. M. Stalker (1961), *The Management of Innovation;* Perry-Smith, J. E., and C. E. Shalley (2003), "The social side of creativity: A static and dynamic social network perspective," *Academy of Management Review* 28: 89–106; and Shalley, C. E., and J. E. Perry-Smith (2008), "The emergence of team creative cognition: The role of diverse outside ties, sociocognitive network centrality, and team evolution," *Strategic Entrepreneurship Journal* 2: 23–41.

27. Hagel III, J., J. S. Brown, and L. Davison (2010), *The Power of Pull: How Small Moves, Smartly Made, Can Set Big Things in Motion* (Philadelphia: Basic Books); Majchrzak, A., A. Malhotra, J. Stamps, and J. Lipnack (2004), "Can absence make a team grow stronger?" *Harvard Business Review,* May: 137–144; and Malhotra, A., A. Majchrzak, and B. Rosen, (2007), "Leading far-flung teams," *Academy of Management Perspectives* 21: 60–70.

28. Bryan, L. L., and C. I. Joyce (2007), "Better strategy through organizational design," *The McKinsey Quarterly* 2: 21–29.

29. Chandler, A. D. (1962), *Strategy and Structure: Chapters in the History of American Industrial Enterprise.*

30. Ibid. Also, for a more recent treatise across different levels of analysis, see Ridley, M. (2010), *The Rational Optimist: How Prosperity Evolves* (New York: HarperCollins).

31. Rothaermel, F. T., and M. T. Alexandre (2009), "Ambidexterity in technology sourcing: The moderating role of absorptive capacity," *Organization Science* 20: 759–780.

32. Levinthal, D. A., and J. G. March (1993), "The myopia of learning," *Strategic Management Journal* 14: 95–112; and March, J. G. (1991), "Exploration and exploitation in organizational learning," *Organization Science* 2: 319–340.

33. Tushman, M., W. K. Smith, R. C. Wood, and G. Westerman (2010), "Organizational designs and innovation streams," *Industrial and Corporate Change* 19: 1331–1366.

34. Ibid.

35. Chandler, A. D. (1962), *Strategy and Structure: Chapters in the History of American Industrial Enterprise.*

36. www.gore.com.

37. Williamson, O. E. (1975), *Markets and Hierarchies* (Free Press: New York); and Williamson, O. E. (1985), *The Economic Institutions of Capitalism* (Free Press: New York).

38. Bryan, L. L., and C. I. Joyce (2007), "Better strategy through organizational design"; Hagel III, J., J. S. Brown, and L. Davison (2010), *The Power of Pull: How Small Moves, Smartly Made, Can Set Big Things in Motion;* Majchrzak, A., A. Malhotra, J. Stamps, and J. Lipnack (2004), "Can absence make a team grow stronger?"; Malhotra, A., A. Majchrzak, and B. Rosen (2007), "Leading far-flung teams."

39. Brown, J. S., and P. Duguid (1991), "Organizational learning and communities-of-practice: Toward a unified view of working, learning, and innovation," *Organization Science* 2: 40–57.

40. This section draws on: Barney, J. B. (1986), "Organizational culture: Can it be a source of sustained competitive advantage?"; Chatman, J. A., and S. Eunyoung Cha (2003), "Leading by leveraging culture," *California Management Review* 45: 19–34; Kerr, J., and J. W. Slocum (2005), "Managing corporate culture through reward systems," *Academy of Management Executive* 19: 130–138; O'Reilly, C. A., J. Chatman, and D. L. Caldwell (1991), "People and organizational culture: A profile comparison approach to assessing person-organization fit," *Academy of Management Journal* 34: 487–516; and Schein, E. H. (1992), *Organizational Culture and Leadership* (San Francisco: Jossey-Bass).

41. In this video, Zappos employees speak about what the 10 core values mean to them: http://about.zappos.com/our-unique-culture/zappos-core-values [3.50 min].

42. Chatman, J. A., and S. Eunyoung Cha (2003), "Leading by leveraging culture," pp. 19–34

43. Chao, G. T., A. M. O'Leary-Kelly, S. Wolf, H. J. Klein, and P. D. Gardner (1994), "Organizational socialization: Its content and consequences," *Journal of Applied Psychology* 79: 730–743.

44. Nelson, T. (2003), "The persistence of founder influence: Management, ownership, and performance effects at initial public offering," *Strategic Management Journal* 24: 707–724.

45. A&E Biography Video (1997), *Sam Walton: Bargain Billionaire.*

46. Friedman, T. L. (2005), *The World Is Flat. A Brief History of the 21st Century* (New York: Farrar, Straus and Giroux), pp. 130–131.

47. Schneider, B., H. W. Goldstein, and D. B. Smith (1995), "The ASA framework: An update," *Personnel Psychology* 48: 747–773.

48. Hsieh, T. (2010), *Delivering Happiness. A Path to Profits, Passion, and Purpose,* p. 145.

49. Less than 1 percent of new hires take Zappos up on the $2,000 offer to quit during the training program.

50. Leonard-Barton, D. (1995), *Wellsprings of Knowledge: Building and Sustaining the Sources of Innovation* (Boston, MA: Harvard Business School Press).

51. Chandler, A. D. (1962), *Strategy and Structure: Chapters in the History of American Industrial Enterprise.*

52. Birkinshaw, J. (2010), *Reinventing Management. Smarter Choices for Getting Work Done* (Chichester, West Sussex, UK: Jossey-Bass).

53. This section is based on: Barney, J. B. (1986), "Organizational culture: Can it be a source of sustained competitive advantage?"; Barney, J. (1991), "Firm resources and sustained competitive advantage," *Journal of Management* 17: 99–120; and Chatman, J. A., and S. Eunyoung Cha (2003), "Leading by leveraging culture," pp. 19–34.

54. Hoffer Gittel, J. (2003), *The Southwest Airlines Way* (Burr Ridge, IL: McGraw-Hill); and O'Reilly, C., and J. Pfeffer (1995), "Southwest Airlines: Using human resources for competitive advantage," case study, Graduate School of Business, Stanford University.

55. Hsieh, T. (2010), *Delivering Happiness. A Path to Profits, Passion, and Purpose,* p. 146.

56. See discussion in Chapter 4 on SWA's activities supporting its cost-leadership strategy. Recently, SWA has experienced problems with the fuselage of its 737 cracking prematurely. See: "Southwest's solo flight in crisis," *The Wall Street Journal,* April 8, 2011.

57. Hsieh, T. (2010), *Delivering Happiness. A Path to Profits, Passion, and Purpose,* p. 146.

58. Chatman, J. A., and S. Eunyoung Cha (2003), "Leading by leveraging culture," pp. 19–34.

59. Hoffer Gittel, J. (2003), *The Southwest Airlines Way* (Burr Ridge, IL: McGraw-Hill).

60. Baron, J. N., M. T. Hannan, and M. D. Burton (2001), "Labor pains: Change in organizational models and employee turnover in young, high-tech firms," *American Journal of Sociology* 106: 960–1012; and Hannan, M. T., M. D. Burton, and J. N. Baron (1996), "Inertia and change in the early years: Employment relationships in young, high technology firms," *Industrial and Corporate Change* 5: 503–537.

61. Nelson, T. (2003), "The persistence of founder influence: Management, ownership, and performance effects at initial public offering," *Strategic Management Journal* 24: 707–724.

62. See the section "*Gaining & Sustaining Competitive Advantage:* Mergers and Acquisitions" in Chapter 9.

63. Herold, D. M., and D. B. Fedor (2008), *Change the Way You Lead Change: Leadership Strategies That Really Work.*

64. Hsieh, T. (2010), *Delivering Happiness: A Path to Profits, Passion, and Purpose* (New York: Business Plus).

65. Pink, D. H. (2009), *Drive: The Surprising Truth about What Motivates Us* (New York: Riverhead Books).

66. Ibid.

67. 3M Company (2002), *A Century of Innovation: The 3M Story* (Maplewood, MN: The 3M Company).

68. The ChapterCase 11 information is based on "Zappos screws up pricing and sells products at $1.6M below costs . . . Then honors the sales!" *Business Insider,* May 23, 2010; and "6pm.com pricing mistake," *The Zappos Family Blog,* May 21, 2010.

69. "Zappos will honor $1.6 million pricing mistake," *MSN MoneyCentral,* May 25, 2010; and "Amazon wields $25 gift certificates to pacify frustrated comic book fans," *TechCrunch.com,* March 9, 2010.

70. http://www.cleveland.com/steubenville-rape-case/, March 18, 2013.

71. Input for this module is used with the permission of Blaine Lawlor, strategic management professor, University of West Florida.

Corporate Governance and Business Ethics

Learning Objectives

After studying this chapter, you should be able to:

LO 12-1 Describe the shared value creation framework and its relationship to competitive advantage.

LO 12-2 Explain the role of corporate governance.

LO 12-3 Apply agency theory to explain why and how companies use governance mechanisms to align interests of principals and agents.

LO 12-4 Evaluate the board of directors as the central governance mechanism for public stock companies.

LO 12-5 Evaluate other governance mechanisms.

LO 12-6 Explain the relationship between strategy and business ethics.

HP's Boardroom Soap Opera Continues

WITH SOME $120 BILLION in annual revenues, Hewlett-Packard (HP) is still one of the largest technology companies in the world. Within a short 18-month period, however, HP's market value dropped by almost 80 percent, from some $105 billion in April 2010 to a mere $23 billion by November 2012, wiping out $82 billion in shareholder wealth. It turns out that a perfect storm of corporate-governance problems, combined with repeated ethical shortcomings, had been brewing at HP for a decade.

This development is even more astonishing given that, at one point, HP was much admired for its corporate culture—known as "the HP Way." The core values of the HP Way include "business conduct with uncompromising integrity," as well as "trust and respect for individuals," among others (see Exhibit 12.1). The HP Way guided the company since its inception in 1938, when it was founded with some $500 of initial investment in Dave Packard's garage in Palo Alto, California. As one of the world's most successful technology companies (think "laser printing"), HP initiated the famous technology cluster known as Silicon Valley. Over the last decade, however, HP's board of directors—a group of individuals that is supposed to represent the interests of the firm's shareholders and oversee the CEO—seemed to forget the HP Way as it violated its core values time and time again. In the process, HP's board of directors acted out a sordid "soap opera," with the season finale not yet in sight.

The first episode "aired" in 2006. The online technology site CNET published an article on HP's strategy. Quoting an anonymous source, the article disclosed sensitive details that could have only come from one of the directors or senior executives at HP. Eager to discover the identity of the leaker, Patricia Dunn, then chair of the board, launched a covert investigation. She hired an outside security firm to conduct surveillance on HP's board members, selected employees, and even some journalists. Although it is common practice for companies to monitor phone and computer use of their employees, HP's investigation went above and beyond. The private investigators used an illegal spying

technique called "pretexting" (impersonating the targets) to obtain phone records by contacting the telecom service providers. The security firm obtained some 300 telephone records covering mobile, home, and office phones of all directors (including Ms. Dunn), nine journalists, and several HP employees. Not to leave anything to chance, the security firm also obtained phone records of the spouses and even the children of suspected HP board members and employees. The firm also conducted physical surveillance of the suspected leaker—board member George Keyworth and his spouse—as well as two other directors.

In a May 2006 board meeting, Ms. Dunn presented the evidence gathered, implicating Mr. Keyworth as the source of the leak. Ms. Dunn's disclosure of the investigation infuriated HP director Thomas Perkins, a prominent venture capitalist, so much that he resigned on the spot. Mr. Perkins called the HP-initiated surveillance "illegal, unethical, and a misplaced corporate priority."[1] Mr. Perkins also forced HP to disclose the spying campaign to the SEC (and thus the public) as his reason for resigning. Ms. Dunn and Mr. Keyworth were dismissed from the board along with six senior HP managers. Despite the boardroom drama, HP came out unscathed financially, largely due to the superior performance of then-CEO Mark Hurd.

Mark Hurd was appointed Hewlett-Packard's CEO in the spring of 2005. He began his business career 25 years earlier as an entry-level salesperson with NCR, a U.S. technology company best known for its bar code scanners in retail outlets and automatic teller machines (ATMs). By the time he worked his way up to the role of CEO at NCR, he had earned a reputation as a low-profile, no-nonsense manager focused on flawless strategy execution. When he was appointed HP's CEO, industry analysts praised its

EXHIBIT 12.1 / The HP Way

We have trust and respect for individuals.

- We approach each situation with the belief that people want to do a good job and will do so, given the proper tools and support. We attract highly capable, diverse, innovative people and recognize their efforts and contributions to the company. HP people contribute enthusiastically and share in the success that they make possible.

We focus on a high level of achievement and contribution.

- Our customers expect HP products and services to be of the highest quality and to provide lasting value. To achieve this, all HP people, especially managers, must be leaders who generate enthusiasm and respond with extra effort to meet customer needs. Techniques and management practices which are effective today may be outdated in the future. For us to remain at the forefront in all our activities, people should always be looking for new and better ways to do their work.

We conduct our business with uncompromising integrity.

- We expect HP people to be open and honest in their dealings to earn the trust and loyalty of others. People at every level are expected to adhere to the highest standards of business ethics and must understand that anything less is unacceptable. As a practical matter, ethical conduct cannot be assured by written HP policies and codes; it must be an integral part of the organization, a deeply ingrained tradition that is passed from one generation of employees to another.

We achieve our common objectives through teamwork.

- We recognize that it is only through effective cooperation within and among organizations that we can achieve our goals. Our commitment is to work as a worldwide team to fulfill the expectations of our customers, shareholders and others who depend upon us. The benefits and obligations of doing business are shared among all HP people.

We encourage flexibility and innovation.

- We create an inclusive work environment which supports the diversity of our people and stimulates innovation. We strive for overall objectives which are clearly stated and agreed upon, and allow people flexibility in working toward goals in ways that they help determine are best for the organization. HP people should personally accept responsibility and be encouraged to upgrade their skills and capabilities through ongoing training and development. This is especially important in a technical business where the rate of progress is rapid and where people are expected to adapt to change.

SOURCE: Hewlett-Packard Alumni Association, http://www.hpalumni.org/hp_way.htm.

board of directors. Moreover, investors hoped that Mr. Hurd would run an efficient and lean operation at HP and return the company to its former greatness and, above all, profitability.

Mr. Hurd did not disappoint. By all indications, he was highly successful at the helm of HP. The company became number one in desktop computer sales and increased its lead in inkjet and laser printers to more than 50 percent market share. Through significant cost-cutting and streamlining measures, Mr. Hurd turned HP into a lean operation. For example, he oversaw large-scale layoffs and a pay cut for all remaining employees as he reorganized the company. Wall Street rewarded HP shareholders with an almost 90 percent stock price appreciation during Mr. Hurd's tenure (see Exhibit 12.2), outperforming the S&P 500 composite index by a wide margin.

Yet, in the summer of 2010, HP aired the second season of its boardroom soap opera. The HP board found itself caught "between a rock and a hard place," with no easy options in sight. Jodie Fisher, a former adult-movie actress, filed a lawsuit against Mr. Hurd, alleging sexual harassment. As an independent contractor, she worked as a hostess at HP-sponsored events. In this function, she screened attending HP customers and personally ensured that Mr. Hurd would spend time with the most important ones. With another ethics scandal looming despite Mr. Hurd's stellar financial results for the company, HP's board of directors forced him to resign. He left HP in August 2010 with an exit package worth $35 million.

The third season of HP's soap opera began in the fall of 2010 when HP announced Leo Apotheker as its new CEO. Mr. Apotheker, who came to HP after being let go from the German enterprise software company SAP, proposed a new corporate strategy for HP. He suggested that the company focus on enterprise software solutions and spin out its low-margin consumer hardware business. HP's consumer hardware business resulted from the $25 billion legacy acquisition of Compaq during the

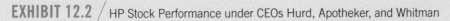

EXHIBIT 12.2 / HP Stock Performance under CEOs Hurd, Apotheker, and Whitman

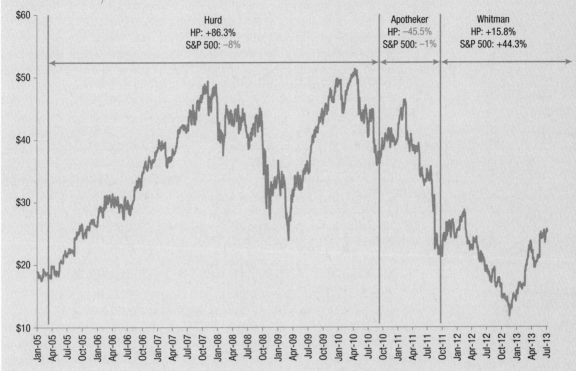

Hurd	Apotheker	Whitman
HP: +86.3%	HP: −45.5%	HP: +15.8%
S&P 500: −8%	S&P 500: −1%	S&P 500: +44.3%

SOURCE: Author's depiction of data drawn from Yahoo Finance.

tumultuous tenure of CEO Carly Fiorina (prior to Mark Hurd). The hardware business had grown to 40 percent of HP's total revenues. Under Mr. Apotheker, HP also exited from the mobile device industry, most notably tablet computers. Many viewed this move as capitulating to Apple's dominance with the iPad.

As part of his new corporate strategy, Mr. Apotheker acquired the British software company Autonomy for $11 billion, which analysts saw as grossly overvalued. Shortly thereafter, HP took an almost $9 billion write-down due to alleged "accounting inaccuracies" at Autonomy. HP's stock went into free fall. Under Mr. Apotheker's short

11 months at the helm of HP, the share price dropped by almost 50 percent (see Exhibit 12.2). Moreover, after Mr. Apotheker was let go, HP did not conduct a search for its next CEO. Instead, in September 2011, the board appointed one of its directors, Meg Whitman, as CEO because the board members were "too exhausted by the fighting."[2] She was formerly the CEO at eBay, had been appointed to HP's board of directors in 2011, and was a director when the Autonomy acquisition was approved.[3]

After reading the chapter, you will find more about this case, with related questions, on page 396.

HP'S SOAP OPERA illustrates how intricate and intertwined corporate governance and business ethics issues can be. The ChapterCase demonstrates the difficult decisions that a board of directors must make when governing a public company: How should a company deal with a situation in which internal stakeholders leak sensitive information to outsiders? Should the board force a highly successful CEO to resign when ethical shortcomings are discovered but before an investigation proves or disproves illegal behavior? Would the company, and the stockholders, have been better served by just reprimanding the CEO? On the other hand, would a mere reprimand communicate to the employees and other stakeholders that performance trumps ethics? What due diligence should a board of directors apply when approving a multibillion-dollar acquisition or appointing a new CEO? The ChapterCase highlights how failure in corporate governance and ethical shortcomings by executives can dramatically affect firm performance. Many observers place the blame for HP's loss in competitive advantage and stellar reputation squarely on its board of directors because of major strategic errors committed over the last decade.[4]

In this chapter, we wrap up our discussion of strategy implementation and close the circle in the AFI framework by studying two important areas: corporate governance and business ethics. To be effective as a strategist, you must understand and appreciate the link between business and society. This chapter first introduces the *shared value creation framework* to illuminate the link between strategic management, competitive advantage, and society more fully. We then discuss effective *corporate-governance* mechanisms to direct and control the enterprise, which a firm must put in place to ensure pursuit of its intended goals. Next, we study *business ethics,* which enable managers to think through complex decisions in an increasingly dynamic, interdependent, and global marketplace. We conclude with practical implications for the strategist.

12.1 The Shared Value Creation Framework

LO 12-1

Describe the shared value creation framework and its relationship to competitive advantage.

The shared value creation framework provides guidance to managers about how to reconcile the economic imperative of gaining and sustaining competitive advantage with corporate social responsibility (introduced in Chapter 1).[5] It helps managers create a larger pie that benefits both shareholders and other stakeholders. To develop the shared value creation framework, though, we first must understand the role of the public stock company.

PUBLIC STOCK COMPANIES AND SHAREHOLDER CAPITALISM

The public stock company is an important institutional arrangement in modern, free-market economies. It provides goods and services as well as employment, pays taxes, and increases the standard of living. There exists an implicit contract based on trust between society and the public stock company. Society grants the right to incorporation, but in turn expects companies to be good citizens by adding value to society.

Exhibit 12.3 depicts the levels of hierarchy within a public stock company. The state (or society) grants a charter of incorporation to the company's shareholders—its owners, who legally own stock in the company. The shareholders appoint a board of directors to govern and oversee the firm's management. The managers in turn hire, supervise, and coordinate employees to manufacture products and provide services. The public stock company enjoys four characteristics that make it an attractive corporate form:[6]

1. *Limited liability for investors.* This characteristic means that the shareholders who provide the risk capital are liable only to the capital specifically invested, and not for other investments they may have made or for their personal wealth. Limited liability encourages investments by the wider public and entrepreneurial risk-taking.

2. *Transferability of investor ownership* through the trading of shares of stock on exchanges such as the New York Stock Exchange (NYSE) and NASDAQ,[7] or exchanges in other countries. Each share represents only a minute fraction of ownership in a company, thus easing transferability.

3. *Legal personality*—that is, the law regards a non-living entity such as a for-profit firm as similar to a person, with legal rights and obligations. Legal personality allows a firm's continuation beyond the founder or the founder's family.

4. *Separation of legal ownership and management control.*[8] In publicly traded companies, the stockholders (the principals, represented by the board of directors) are the legal owners of the company, and they delegate decision-making authority to professional managers (the agents).

The public stock company has been a major contributor to value creation since its inception as a new organizational form over one hundred years ago. Michael Porter and others, however, argue that many public companies have defined value creation too narrowly in terms of financial performance.[9] This in turn has contributed to some of the *black swan events* discussed in Chapter 1, such as large-scale accounting scandals and the global financial crisis. Managers' pursuit of strategies that define value creation too narrowly may have negative consequences for society at large, as evidenced during the global financial crisis. This narrow focus has contributed to the loss of trust in the corporation as a vehicle for value creation, not only for shareholders but also other stakeholders and society.

Nobel laureate Milton Friedman stated his view of the firm's social obligations: "There is one and only one social responsibility of business—to use its resources and engage in activities designed to increase its profits so long as it stays within the rules of the game, which is to say, engages in open and free competition without deception or fraud."[10] This notion is often captured by the term *shareholder capitalism.* According to this perspective, shareholders—the providers of the necessary risk capital and the legal owners of public companies—have the most legitimate claim on profits. When introducing the notion of *corporate social responsibility* (CSR) in Chapter 1, though, we noted that a firm's obligations frequently go beyond the economic responsibility to increase profits, extending to ethical and philanthropic expectations that society has of the business enterprise.[11]

A recent survey measured attitudes toward business responsibility in various countries. The survey asked the top 25 percent of income earners holding a university degree in each country surveyed whether they agree with Milton Friedman's philosophy that "the *social responsibility* of business is to increase its profits."[12] The results, displayed in Exhibit 12.4, revealed some intriguing national differences. The United Arab Emirates (UAE), a small and business-friendly federation of seven emirates, had the highest level of agreement, at 84 percent. The top five also included a number of Asian countries (Japan, India, South Korea, and Singapore), where roughly two-thirds agreed.

The countries where the fewest people agreed with Friedman's philosophy were China, Brazil, Germany, Italy, and Spain; fewer than 40 percent of respondents in those countries supported an exclusive focus on shareholder capitalism. Although they have achieved a high standard of living, European countries such as Germany have tempered the free-market system with a strong social element, leading to so-called *social market economies.* The respondents from these countries seemed to be more supportive of a *stakeholder strategy* approach to business. Some critics, however, would argue that too strong a focus on the social dimension contributed to the European debt crisis because sovereign governments such as Greece, Italy, and Spain took on nonsustainable debt levels to fund social programs such as early retirement plans, government-funded health care, and so on. The United States placed roughly in the middle of the continuum. In particular, a bit more than half (56 percent) of U.S. respondents subscribed to Friedman's philosophy.

CREATING SHARED VALUE

In contrast to Milton Friedman, Porter argues that executives should not concentrate exclusively on increasing firm profits. Rather, the strategist should focus on creating *shared value,* a concept that involves creating economic value for shareholders while also creating

EXHIBIT 12.3

The Public Stock Company: Hierarchy of Authority

STATE CHARTER

↓

SHAREHOLDERS

↓

BOARD OF DIRECTORS

↓

MANAGEMENT

↓

EMPLOYEES

EXHIBIT 12.4

Global Survey of Attitudes Toward Business Responsibility

The bar chart indicates the percentage of members of the "informed public" who "strongly agree/somewhat agree" with Milton Friedman's philosophy, "the social responsibility of business is to increase its profits."

SOURCE: Author's depiction of data from Edelman's (2011) Trust Barometer as included in "Milton Friedman goes on tour," *The Economist*, January 27, 2011.

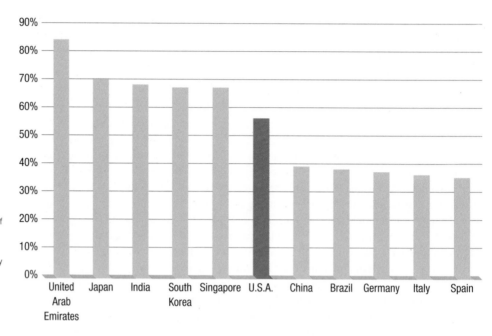

shared value creation framework
A model proposing that managers have a dual focus on shareholder value creation and value creation for society.

social value by addressing society's needs and challenges. He argues that managers need to reestablish the important relationship between superior firm performance and societal progress. This dual point of view, Porter argues, will not only allow companies to gain and sustain a competitive advantage but also reshape capitalism and its relationship to society.

The **shared value creation framework** proposes that managers maintain a dual focus on shareholder value creation and value creation for society. It recognizes that markets are defined not only by economic needs but also by societal needs. It also advances the perspective that *externalities* such as pollution, wasted energy, and costly accidents actually create *internal costs,* at least in lost reputation if not directly on the bottom line. Rather than pitting economic and societal needs in a trade-off, Porter suggests that the two can be reconciled to create a larger pie. The shared value creation framework seeks to enhance a firm's competitiveness by identifying connections between economic and social needs, and then creating a competitive advantage by addressing these business opportunities.

GE, for example, has strengthened its competitiveness by creating a profitable business with its "green" *ecomagination* initiative. *Ecomagination* is GE's strategic initiative to provide cleaner and more efficient sources of energy, provide abundant sources of clean water anywhere in the world, and reduce emissions.[13] Jeffrey Immelt, GE's CEO, is fond of saying: "Green is green,"[14] meaning that addressing ecological needs offers the potential of gaining and sustaining a competitive advantage for GE. Through applying strategic innovation, GE is providing solutions for some tough environmental challenges, while driving company growth at the same time. *Ecomagination* solutions and products allow GE to increase the perceived value it creates for its customers while lowering costs to produce and deliver the "green" products and services. *Ecomagination* allows GE to solve the trade-off between increasing value creation and lower costs at the same time. This in turn enhances GE's economic value creation and its competitive advantage. Moreover, *ecomagination* products and services also create value for society in terms of reducing emissions and lowering energy consumption, among other benefits. In 2012, GE's *ecomagination* strategic initiative alone generated $25 billion in revenues. Just to put this in perspective, if GE's *ecomagination* were a standalone company, it would rank at roughly #110 in the Fortune 500 of largest public companies in the U.S., approximately equal in size to Rite Aid and Staples.[15]

To ensure that managers can reconnect economic and societal needs, Michael Porter recommends that managers focus on three things within the shared value creation framework:[16]

1. Expand the customer base to bring in *nonconsumers* such as those at the *bottom of the pyramid*—the largest but poorest socioeconomic group of the world's population. The bottom of the pyramid in the global economy can yield significant business opportunities, which—if satisfied—could improve the living standard of the world's poorest. Muhammad Yunus, Nobel Peace Prize winner, founded Grameen Bank in Bangladesh to provide small loans (termed microcredit) to impoverished villagers, who used the funding for entrepreneurial ventures that would help them climb out of poverty. Other businesses have also found profitable opportunities at the bottom of the pyramid. In India, Arvind Mills offers jeans in a ready-to-make kit that costs only a fraction of the high-end Levi's. The Tata Group sells its Nano car for around 150,000 rupees (less than $2,500), enabling more Indian families to move from mopeds to cars and adding up to a substantial business.

2. Expand traditional internal firm value chains to include more nontraditional partners such as *nongovernmental organizations* (NGOs). NGOs are nonprofit organizations that pursue a particular cause in the public interest, and are independent of any governments. Habitat for Humanity and Greenpeace are examples of NGOs.

3. Focus on creating new *regional clusters*, such as Silicon Valley in the U.S., Electronic City in Bangalore, India, and Chilecon Valley in Santiago, Chile.

In line with *stakeholder theory* (discussed in Chapter 1), Porter argues that these strategic actions will in turn lead to a larger pie of revenues and profits that can be distributed among a company's stakeholders. General Electric, for example, recognizes a convergence between shareholders and stakeholders to create shared value. It states in its Governance Principles: "Both the board of directors and management recognize that the long-term interests of shareowners are advanced by responsibly addressing the concerns of other stakeholders and interested parties, including employees, recruits, customers, suppliers, GE communities, government officials and the public at large."[17] To ensure that convergence indeed takes place, companies need effective governance mechanisms, which we discuss next.

12.2 Corporate Governance

Corporate governance concerns the mechanisms to direct and control an enterprise in order to ensure that it pursues its strategic goals successfully and legally.[18] Corporate governance is about checks and balances and about asking the tough questions at the right time. The accounting scandals of the early 2000s and the global financial crisis of 2008 and beyond got so out of hand because the enterprises involved did not practice effective corporate governance.

Corporate governance attempts to address the *principal–agent problem* (introduced in Chapter 8), which can occur any time an agent performs activities on behalf of a principal.[19] This problem can arise whenever a principal delegates decision making and control over resources to agents, with the expectation that they will act in the principal's best interest. We mentioned earlier that the separation of ownership and control is one of the major advantages of the public stock companies. This benefit, however, is also the source of the

> **LO 12-2**
>
> Explain the role of corporate governance.
>
> **corporate governance**
> A system of mechanisms to direct and control an enterprise in order to ensure that it pursues its strategic goals successfully and legally.

principal–agent problem. In publicly traded companies, the stockholders are the legal owners of the company, but they delegate decision-making authority to professional managers. The conflict arises if the agents pursue their own personal interests, which can be at odds with the principals' goals. For their part, agents may be more interested in maximizing their total compensation, including benefits, job security, status, and power. Principals desire maximization of total returns to shareholders.

The risk of opportunism on behalf of agents is exacerbated by *information asymmetry:* the agents are generally better informed than the principals. Exhibit 12.5 depicts the principal–agent relationship.

Managers, executives, and board members tend to have access to *private information* concerning important company developments that outsiders, especially investors, are not privy to. Often this informational advantage is based on timing—insiders are the first to learn about important developments before the information is released to the public. Although possessing insider information is not illegal and indeed is part of an executive's job, what *is* illegal is acting upon it through trading stocks or passing on the information to others who might do so. Insider-trading cases, therefore, provide an example of egregious exploitation of information asymmetry. The hedge fund Galleon Group (holding assets worth $7 billion under management at its peak) was engulfed in an insider-trading scandal involving private information about important developments at companies such as Goldman Sachs, Google, IBM, Intel, and P&G.[20] Galleon Group's founder, Raj Rajaratnam, the mastermind behind a complex network of informants, was sentenced to 11 years in prison and fined over $150 million. In one instance, an Intel manager had provided Rajaratnam with internal Intel data such as orders for processors and production runs. These data indicated that demand for Intel processors was much higher than analysts had expected. Galleon bought Intel stock well before this information was public to benefit from the anticipated share appreciation.

In another instance, Rajaratnam benefitted from insider tips provided by Rajat Gupta, a former McKinsey chief executive who served on Goldman Sachs' board. Often within seconds after a Goldman Sachs board meeting ended, Gupta called Rajaratnam. In one of these phone calls, Gupta revealed the impending multibillion-dollar liquidity injection by Warren Buffett into Goldman Sachs during the midst of the global financial crisis. This information allowed the Galleon Group to buy Goldman Sachs shares before the official announcement about Buffett's investment was made, profiting from the subsequent stock appreciation. In another call, Gupta informed Rajaratnam that the investment bank would miss earnings estimates. Based on this insider information, the Galleon Group was able to sell its holdings in Goldman Sachs' stock prior to the announcement, avoiding a multimillion-dollar loss.[21]

Information asymmetry also can breed *on-the-job consumption,* perquisites, and excessive compensation. Although use of company funds for golf outings, resort retreats, attending professional sporting events, or having elegant dinners and other entertainment is an everyday manifestation of on-the-job consumption, other forms are more extreme. Dennis Kozlowski, former

EXHIBIT 12.5 / The Principal–Agent Problem

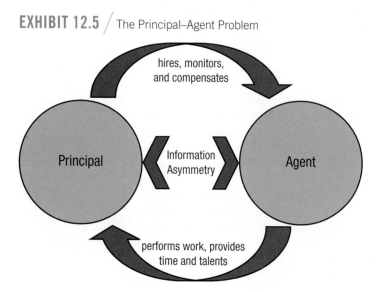

CEO of Tyco, a diversified conglomerate, used company funds for his $30 million New York City apartment (the shower curtain alone was $6,000) and for a $2 million birthday party for his second wife.[22] John Thain, former CEO of Merrill Lynch, spent $1.2 million of company funds on redecorating his office, while he demanded cost cutting and frugality from his employees.[23] Such uses of company funds, in effect, mean that shareholders pay for those items and activities. Mr. Thain also allegedly requested a bonus in the range of $10 to $30 million in 2009 despite Merrill Lynch having lost billions of dollars and being unable to continue as an independent company. (Merrill Lynch was later acquired by Bank of America.)

AGENCY THEORY

The principal–agent problem is a core part of **agency theory,** which views the firm as a nexus of legal contracts.[24] In this perspective, corporations are viewed merely as a set of legal contracts between different parties. Conflicts that may arise are to be addressed in the legal realm. Agency theory finds its everyday application in employment contracts, for example.

Besides dealing with the relationship between shareholders and managers, principal–agent problems also cascade down the organizational hierarchy (shown in Exhibit 12.3). Senior executives, such as the CEO, face agency problems when they delegate authority of strategic business units to general managers. Employees who perform the actual operational labor are agents who work on behalf of the managers. Such front-line employees often enjoy an informational advantage over management. They may tell their supervisor that it took longer to complete a project or serve a customer than it actually did, for example. Some employees may be tempted to use such informational advantage for their own self-interest (e.g., spending time on Facebook during work hours, watching YouTube videos, or using the company's computer and Internet connection for personal business).

The managerial implication of agency theory relates to the management functions of organization and control: The firm needs to design work tasks, incentives, and employment contracts and other control mechanisms in ways that minimize opportunism by agents. Such governance mechanisms are used to align incentives between principals and agents. These mechanisms need to be designed in such a fashion as to overcome two specific agency problems: *adverse selection* and *moral hazard.*

ADVERSE SELECTION. In general, **adverse selection** occurs when information asymmetry increases the likelihood of selecting inferior alternatives. In principal–agent relationships, for example, adverse selection describes a situation in which an agent misrepresents his or her ability to do the job. Such misrepresentation is common during the recruiting process. Once hired, the principal may not be able to accurately assess whether the agent can do the work for which he or she is being paid. The problem is especially pronounced in team production, when the principal often cannot ascertain the contributions of individual team members. This in turn creates an incentive for opportunistic employees to free-ride on the efforts of others.

MORAL HAZARD. In general, **moral hazard** describes a situation in which information asymmetry increases the incentive of one party to take undue risks or shirk other responsibilities because the costs incur to the other party. For example, bailing out homeowners from their mortgage obligations or bailing out banks from the consequences of undue risk-taking in lending are examples of moral hazard. The costs of default are rolled over to society. Knowing that there is a high probability of being bailed out ("too big to fail") increases moral hazard. In this scenario, any profits occurring due to a competitive advantage remain private, while losses become public.

LO 12-3

Apply agency theory to explain why and how companies use governance mechanisms to align interests of principals and agents.

agency theory A theory that views the firm as a nexus of legal contracts.

adverse selection A situation that occurs when information asymmetry increases the likelihood of selecting inferior alternatives.

moral hazard A situation in which information asymmetry increases the incentive of one party to take undue risks or shirk other responsibilities because the costs incur to the other party.

In the principal–agent relationship, moral hazard describes the difficulty of the principal to ascertain whether the agent has really put forth a best effort. In this situation, the agent is *able* to do the work but may decide not to do so. For example, a company scientist at a biotechnology company may decide to work on his own research project, hoping to eventually start his own firm, rather than on the project he was assigned.[25] While working on his own research on company time, he might also use the company's laboratory and technicians. Given the complexities of basic research, it is often challenging, especially for nonscientist principals, to ascertain which problem a scientist is working on.[26] To overcome these principal–agent problems, firms put several governance mechanisms in place. We shall discuss several of them next, beginning with the board of directors.

THE BOARD OF DIRECTORS

LO 12-4

Evaluate the board of directors as the central governance mechanism for public stock companies.

The shareholders of public stock companies appoint a **board of directors** to represent their interests. The board of directors is the centerpiece of corporate governance in such companies. The shareholders' interests, however, are not uniform. The goals of some shareholders, such as institutional investors (e.g., retirement funds, governmental bodies, and so on), are generally the long-term viability of the enterprise combined with profitable growth. Long-term viability and profitable growth should allow consistent dividend payments and result in stock appreciation over time. The goals of other shareholders, such as hedge funds, are often to profit from short-term movements of stock prices. These more proactive investors often demand changes in a firm's strategy, such as spinning out certain divisions or splitting up companies into parts to enhance overall performance. Votes at shareholder meetings, generally in proportion to the amount of ownership, determine whose representatives are appointed to the board of directors.

The ChapterCase illustrated that a board of directors may not always act in the best interests of shareholders. In the case of HP, one can argue that poor strategic decisions taken by the board led to billions of dollars of shareholder value destruction. Indeed, shareholders have filed lawsuits against HP's board of directors in conjunction with Mark Hurd's forced resignation and for allegedly misleading statements by Leo Apotheker about HP's commitment to mobile devices (a segment which HP later exited under Apotheker).

The day-to-day business operations of a publicly traded stock company are conducted by its managers and employees, under the direction of the chief executive officer (CEO) and the oversight of the board of directors. The board of directors is composed of inside and outside directors who are elected by the shareholders:[27]

- **Inside directors** are generally part of the company's senior management team, such as the chief financial officer (CFO) and the chief operating officer (COO). They are appointed by shareholders to provide the board with necessary information pertaining to the company's internal workings and performance. Without this valuable inside information, the board would not be able to effectively monitor the firm. As senior executives, however, inside board members' interests tend to align with management and the CEO rather than the shareholders.

- **Outside directors,** on the other hand, are not employees of the firm. They frequently are senior executives from other firms or full-time professionals, who are appointed to a board and who serve on several boards simultaneously. Given their independence, they are more likely to watch out for the interests of shareholders.

The board is elected by the shareholders to represent their interests. Each director has a *fiduciary responsibility* toward the shareholders because of the trust placed in him or her. Prior to the annual shareholders' meeting, the board proposes a slate of nominees, although shareholders can also directly nominate director candidates. In general, large institutional investors support their favored candidates through their accumulated proxy votes. The board members meet several times a year to review and evaluate the company's performance and to assess its future strategic plans as well as opportunities and threats. In addition to general strategic oversight and guidance, the board of directors has other, more specific functions, including:

- Selecting, evaluating, and compensating the CEO. The CEO reports to the board. Should the CEO lose the board's confidence, the board may fire him or her.

- Overseeing the company's CEO succession plan. Both HP and Apple have been criticized for poor succession planning. HP's board was apparently unprepared to deal with the unexpected departure of Mark Hurd.[28] Likewise, institutional shareholders criticized Apple's board for not (publicly) addressing CEO succession in light of Steve Jobs' repeated medical leaves.[29]

- Providing guidance to the CEO in the selection, evaluation, and compensation of other senior executives.

- Reviewing, monitoring, evaluating, and approving any significant strategic initiatives and corporate actions such as large acquisitions.

- Conducting a thorough risk assessment and proposing options to mitigate risk. The boards of directors of the financial firms at the center of the global financial crisis were faulted for not noticing or not appreciating the risks the firms were exposed to.

- Ensuring that the firm's audited financial statements represent a true and accurate picture of the firm.

- Ensuring the firm's compliance with laws and regulations. The boards of directors of firms caught up in the large accounting scandals were faulted for being negligent in their company oversight and not adequately performing several of the functions listed here.

Board independence is critical to effectively fulfilling a board's governance responsibilities. Given that board members are directly responsible to shareholders, they have an incentive to ensure that the shareholders' interests are pursued. If not, they can experience a loss in reputation or can be removed outright. More and more directors are also exposed to legal repercussions should they fail in their fiduciary responsibility. To perform their strategic oversight tasks, board members apply the strategic management theories and concepts presented herein, among other more specialized tools such as those originating in finance and accounting. Strategy Highlight 12.1 takes a closer look at the composition and workings of General Electric's board of directors.

---

board of directors
The centerpiece of corporate governance, composed of inside and outside directors who are elected by the shareholders.

inside directors
Board members who are generally part of the company's senior management team; appointed by shareholders to provide the board with necessary information pertaining to the company's internal workings and performance.

outside directors
Board members who are not employees of the firm, but who are frequently senior executives from other firms or full-time professionals. Given their independence, they are more likely to watch out for shareholder interests.

Strategy Highlight 12.1

GE's Board of Directors

The GE board is composed of individuals from the business world (chairpersons and CEOs of Fortune 500 companies spanning a range of industries), academia (business school and science professors, deans, and provosts), and government (SEC).[30] Including the board's chairperson, there are 17 members on GE's board. Experts in corporate governance consider an appropriate number of directors for a company of GE's size (roughly $250 billion in market capitalization as of summer 2013). In contrast, Apple's board of directors has only eight members, while its market capitalization is about $425 billion. Indeed, Apple's board of directors has been criticized for having become too insular in recent years.[31]

At GE (as of 2013), 16 of the 17 board members (94 percent) are independent outside directors. To achieve board independence, experts in corporate governance recommend that two-thirds of its directors be outsiders. GE's board has only one inside director, Jeffrey Immelt, GE's CEO, who also acts as chairman of the board. In roughly one half of U.S. public firms, the CEO of the company also serves as chair of the board of directors.

This practice of *duality*—holding both the role of CEO and chairperson of the board—has been declining somewhat in recent years. Arguments can be made both for and against splitting the roles of CEO and chairman of the board. On the one hand, the CEO has invaluable inside information that can help in chairing the board effectively. On the other hand, the chairperson may influence

the board unduly through setting the meeting agendas or suggesting board appointees who are friendly toward the CEO. The recent trend toward *separation of CEO/chair duality* is likely to continue. Because one of the key roles of the board is to monitor and evaluate the CEO's performance, there can be a conflict of interest when the CEO actually chairs the board.

GE's board of directors meets a dozen or more times annually. With increasing board accountability in recent years, boards now tend to meet more often. Moreover, many firms limit the number and type of directorships a board member may hold concurrently.[32] To accomplish their responsibilities, boards of directors are usually organized into different committees. GE's board has five committees, each with its own chair: the audit committee; the management development and compensation committee; the nominating, corporate governance and public responsibilities committee; the risk committee; and the science and technology committee.

In general, women and minorities remain underrepresented on boards of directors across the U.S. and throughout most of the world. GE's board is actually fairly diverse when compared with other Fortune 500 companies, which averaged less than 16 percent women on their boards (versus 28 percent for GE). Diversity in backgrounds and expertise in the boardroom is considered an asset: More diverse boards are less likely to fall victim to *groupthink*, a situation in which opinions coalesce around a leader without individuals critically challenging and evaluating that leader's opinions and assumptions.

LO 12-5

Evaluate other governance mechanisms.

stock options An incentive mechanism to align the interests of shareholders and managers, by giving the recipient the right to buy a company's stock at a predetermined price sometime in the future.

OTHER GOVERNANCE MECHANISMS

While the board of directors is the central governance piece for a public stock company, several other corporate mechanisms are also used to align incentives between principals and agents, including:

- Executive compensation
- The market for corporate control
- Financial statement auditors, government regulators, and industry analysts

EXECUTIVE COMPENSATION. The board of directors determines executive compensation packages. To align incentives between shareholders and management, the board may grant **stock options** as part of the compensation package. This incentive mechanism gives the recipient the right to buy a company's stock at a predetermined price sometime in the future. If the company's share price rises above the negotiated strike price, which is often the price on the day when compensation is negotiated, the executive stands to reap significant gains.

Executive compensation—CEO pay, in particular—has attracted significant attention in recent years. Two issues are at the forefront: (1) the absolute size of the CEO pay package compared with the pay of the average employee, and (2) the relationship between firm performance and CEO pay. The ratio of CEO to average employee pay in the U.S. is about 300 to 1, up from roughly 40 to 1 in 1980.[33] In 2012, the average compensation for a CEO of a Fortune 500 company was $11 million.[34] The top three earners in terms of annual compensation were Larry Ellison of Oracle ($96 million), Robert Kotick of Activision Blizzard ($64 million), and Leslie Moonves of CBS ($60 million).[35] In 2013, McKesson's CEO John Hammergren made headlines by setting the all-time record with $159 million pension package.[36] Mr. Hammergren is also one of the highest-paid CEOs, averaging $50 million in annual compensation.[37]

In some instances, the relationship between executive pay and firm performance is strong; in others it is nonexistent or even negative.[38] Mr. Hammergren's compensation and pension package, for example, was closely tied to performance. Since he was appointed CEO in 2001, McKesson's stock price more than tripled, outperforming the overall market by a wide margin. Specifically, McKesson's stock appreciated by roughly 325 percent under Mr. Hammergren's leadership, while the S&P 500 index rose merely 40 percent.[39] On the other hand, as CEO of The Home Depot, Robert Nardelli earned annual compensation packages of over $200 million, while the company's stock remained flat under his tenure (2000–2007). In comparison, the share price of The Home Depot's main competitor, Lowe's, nearly doubled during that time. In another example in which executive pay did not reflect performance, after only 11 months on the job and almost losing one half of the company's total market value, HP's former CEO Leo Apotheker left with a $25 million compensation package.[40]

Responding to shareholder criticism, the GE board recently revised the compensation package for Jeffrey Immelt, GE's CEO and chairman of the board.[41] His compensation package was changed to include a stronger performance-related equity component. In particular, GE's board attached strings on stock options already granted to Mr. Immelt. The revised compensation package now stipulates more stringent performance conditions: The stock options will vest only if GE's stock and dividend performance in its industrial businesses (energy, health care, and technology infrastructure) is equal to or better than the performance of the Standard & Poor 500 stock index. In addition, half of the options will vest only if GE achieves at least $55 billion in cash flow from operating activities between 2011 and 2014. This unusual move by GE's board of directors underscores the increasing clout of vocal shareholders who have expressed dissatisfaction with GE's stock performance over the last decade. They expect that linking compensation to specific performance measures tied to GE's core competency in industrial engineering will result in improved stock performance.

Some recent experiments in *behavioral economics* caution that incentives that are too high-powered (e.g., outsized bonuses) may have a negative effect on job performance.[42] That is, when the incentive level is very high, an individual may get distracted from strategic activities because too much attention is devoted to the outsized bonus to be enjoyed in the near future. This in turn can further increase job stress and negatively impact job performance.

THE MARKET FOR CORPORATE CONTROL. Whereas the board of directors and executive compensation are *internal* corporate-governance mechanisms, the *market for corporate control* is an important *external* corporate-governance mechanism. It consists of activist investors who seek to gain control of an underperforming corporation by buying shares of its stock in the open market. To avoid such attempts, corporate managers strive to protect shareholder value by delivering strong share-price performance or putting in place poison pills (discussed later).

Here's how the market for corporate control works: If a company is poorly managed, its performance suffers and its stock price falls as more and more investors sell their shares. Once shares fall to a low enough level, the firm may become the target of a *hostile takeover* (as discussed in Chapter 9) when new bidders believe they can fix the internal problems that are causing the performance decline. Besides competitors, so-called *corporate raiders* (e.g., Carl Icahn and T. Boone Pickens) or *private equity firms* and *hedge funds* (e.g., The Blackstone Group and Soros Fund Management) may buy enough shares to exert control over a company.

leveraged buyout (LBO) A single investor or group of investors buys, with the help of borrowed money (leveraged against the company's assets), the outstanding shares of a publicly traded company in order to take it private; the private owners often will restructure the company and eventually take it public again.

In a **leveraged buyout (LBO),** a single investor or group of investors buys, with the help of borrowed money (leveraged against the company's assets), the outstanding shares of a publicly traded company in order to take it private. In short, an LBO changes the ownership structure of a company from public to private. The expectation is often that the private owners will restructure the company and eventually take it public again through an initial public offering (IPO).

Private companies enjoy certain benefits that public companies do not. Private companies are not required to disclose financial statements. They experience less scrutiny from analysts and can often focus more on long-term viability. In a classic example, Harley-Davidson underwent an LBO in 1981 as the company was struggling against Japanese competitors. By implementing a "back to its roots retro style" and improving product quality and labor relations, Harley-Davidson is considered one of the most successful corporate turnarounds: The company went public again in 1987 and remains so today.[43]

In 2013, computer maker Dell Inc. became a takeover target of famed corporate raider Carl Icahn.[44] He jumped into action after Dell's founder and its largest shareholder, Michael Dell, announced in January of that year that he intended a *leveraged buyout* with the help of Silverlake Partners, a private equity firm, to take the company private. In the Dell buyout battle, many observers, including Mr. Icahn who is the second-largest shareholder of Dell, saw the attempt by Mr. Dell to take the company private as the "ultimate insider trade."

This view implied that Mr. Dell, who is also CEO and chairman, had private information about the future value of the company, and that his offer was too low. Dell Inc., which had $57 billion in revenues in its fiscal year 2013, has been struggling in the ongoing transition from personal computers such as desktops and laptops to mobile devices and services. Between December 2004 and February 2009, Dell (which until just a few years ago was the number-one computer maker) lost more than 80 percent of its market capitalization, dropping from some $76 billion to a mere $14 billion. In the the fall of 2013, Dell's shareholders approved Mr. Dell's $25 billion offer to take the company private, thus avoiding a hostile takeover.

If a hostile takeover attempt is successful, however, the new owner frequently replaces the old management and board of directors in order to manage the company in a way that creates more value for shareholders. In some instances, the new owner will break up the company and sell off its pieces. In either case, since a firm's existing management faces the threat of losing their jobs and their reputations as effective executives if the firm sustains a competitive disadvantage, the market for corporate control is a credible governance mechanism.

To avoid being taken over against their consent, some firms put in place *poison pills.* These are defensive provisions that kick in should a buyer reach a certain level of share ownership without top management approval. For example, a poison pill could allow existing shareholders to buy additional shares at a steep discount. Those additional shares would in turn make any takeover attempt much more expensive and function as a deterrent. With the rise of actively involved institutional investors, poison pills have become rare because they retard an effective function of equity markets.

Although poison pills are becoming rarer, the market for corporate control is alive and well, as shown in the battle over control of Dell Inc. or the hostile takeover of Cadbury by Kraft (featured in Strategy Highlight 9.1). However, the market for corporate control is a last resort because it comes with significant transaction costs. To succeed in its hostile takeover bid, buyers generally pay a significant premium over given share price. This often leads to overpaying for the acquisition and subsequent shareholder value destruction—the so-called *winner's curse.* The market for corporate control is useful, however, when internal corporate-governance mechanisms have not functioned effectively and the company is underperforming.

AUDITORS, GOVERNMENT REGULATORS, AND INDUSTRY ANALYSTS.

Auditors, government regulators, and industry analysts serve as additional external-governance mechanisms. All public companies listed on the U.S. stock exchanges must file a number of financial statements with the *Securities and Exchange Commission (SEC),* a federal regulatory agency whose task it is to oversee stock trading and enforce federal securities laws. To avoid the misrepresentation of financial results, all public financial statements must follow *generally accepted accounting principles (GAAP)*[45] and be audited by certified public accountants.

As part of its disclosure policy, the SEC makes all financial reports filed by public companies available electronically via the EDGAR database.[46] This database contains more than 7 million financial statements, going back several years. Industry analysts scrutinize these reports in great detail, trying to identify any financial irregularities and assess firm performance. Given recent high-profile oversights in accounting scandals and fraud cases, the SEC has come under pressure to step up its monitoring and enforcement.

Industry analysts often base their buy, hold, or sell recommendations on financial statements filed with the SEC and business news published in *The Wall Street Journal, Bloomberg Businessweek, Fortune, Forbes,* and other business media such as CNBC. Researchers have questioned the independence of industry analysts and credit-rating agencies that evaluate companies (such as Fitch, Moody's, and Standard & Poor's),[47] because the investment banks and rating agencies frequently have lucrative business relationships with the companies they are supposed to evaluate, creating conflicts of interest. A study of over 8,000 analysts' ratings of corporate equity securities, for example, revealed that investment bankers rated their own clients more favorably.[48]

In addition, an industry has sprung up around assessing the effectiveness of corporate governance in individual firms. Research outfits such as GovernanceMetrics International (now GMI Ratings)[49] provide independent corporate governance ratings. The ratings from these external watchdog organizations inform a wide range of stakeholders, including investors, insurers, auditors, regulators, and others.

Corporate-governance mechanisms play an important part in aligning the interests of principals and agents. They enable closer monitoring and controlling, as well as provide incentives to align interests of principals and agents. Perhaps even more important are the "most internal of control mechanisms": *business ethics*—a topic we discuss next.

12.3 Strategy and Business Ethics

LO 12-6

Explain the relationship between strategy and business ethics.

Multiple, high-profile accounting scandals and the global financial crisis have placed business ethics center stage in the public eye. **Business ethics** is an agreed-upon code of conduct in business, based on societal norms. Business ethics lay the foundation and provide training for "behavior that is consistent with the principles, norms, and standards of business practice that have been agreed upon by society."[50] These principles, norms, and standards of business practice differ to some degree in different cultures around the globe. But a large number of research studies have found that some notions—such as fairness, honesty, and reciprocity—are universal norms.[51] As such, many of these values have been codified into law.

Law and ethics, however, are not synonymous. This distinction is important. Staying within the law is a *minimum acceptable standard.* A note of caution is therefore in order, though: A manager's actions can be completely legal, but ethically questionable. For example, consider the actions of mortgage-loan officers who—being incentivized by commissions—persuaded unsuspecting consumers to sign up for exotic mortgages, such as "option ARMs." These mortgages offer borrowers the choice to pay less than the required interest, which is then added to the principal while the interest rate can adjust upward. Such actions may be legal, but they are unethical, especially if there are indications that the borrower might be unable to repay the mortgage once the interest rate moves up.[52]

business ethics An agreed-upon code of conduct in business, based on societal norms.

To go beyond the minimum acceptable standard codified in law, many organizations have explicit *codes of conduct.* These codes go above and beyond the law in detailing how the organization expects an employee to behave and to represent the company in business dealings. Codes of conduct allow an organization to overcome moral hazards and adverse selections as they attempt to resonate with employees' deeper values of justice, fairness, honesty, integrity, and reciprocity. Since business decisions are not made in a vacuum but are embedded within a societal context that expects ethical behavior, managers can improve their decision making by also considering:

- When facing an ethical dilemma, a manager can ask whether the intended course of action falls within the *acceptable norms of professional behavior* as outlined in the organization's code of conduct and defined by the profession at large.

- The manager should imagine whether he or she would feel *comfortable explaining and defending the decision in public.* How would the media report the business decision if it were to become public? How would the company's stakeholders feel about it?

Strategy Highlight 12.2 features Goldman Sachs, which has come under close scrutiny and faced some tough questions pertaining to its business dealings in the wake of the financial crisis.

In the aftermath of the Abacus debacle (discussed in Strategy Highlight 12.2), Goldman Sachs revised its code of conduct. A former Goldman Sachs employee, Greg Smith, published a book in 2012 chronicling his career at the investment bank, from a lowly summer intern to head of Goldman Sachs' U.S. equity derivatives business in Europe, the Middle East, and Africa.[53] Mr. Smith's thesis was that the entire ethical climate within Goldman Sachs changed over that period of time. For its first 130 years, Goldman Sachs was organized as a professional partnership, like most law firms. In this organizational form, a selected group of partners are joint owners and directors of the professional service firm. After years of superior performance, associates in the professional service firms may "make partner"—being promoted to joint owner. During the time when organized as a

Strategy Highlight 12.2

Did Goldman Sachs and the "Fabulous Fab" Commit Securities Fraud?

In April 2010, the SEC sued Goldman Sachs and one of its employees, Mr. Fabrice Tourre, for securities fraud. The SEC's case focused on one specific, mortgage-related deal during the financial crisis. The deal began in 2006 during the height of the real estate bubble in the United States. The assumption at this time was that house prices could only go up, after years of consistent real estate appreciation. Indeed, real estate prices in the United States had surged, and a speculative bubble had emerged. The real estate bubble was fueled by cheap mortgages, many of them extended to home buyers who really couldn't afford them. John Paulson, founder of the hedge fund Paulson & Co., approached Goldman Sachs with a trading idea to place a billion-dollar bet that the real estate bubble was about to burst. This would occur when borrowers began to default on their mortgages in large numbers. House prices would collapse as distressed borrowers attempted to unload their properties at fire sale prices, and banks foreclosed in large numbers. That is exactly what happened.

To benefit from his timely insight, Mr. Paulson asked Goldman Sachs to create an investment instrument, later named "Abacus." Goldman Sachs agreed and assigned Mr. Tourre to put Abacus together. This investment vehicle was a *collateralized debt obligation (CDO)*. CDOs are made up of thousands of mortgages bundled together into bonds. These bonds provide stable and regular interest payments as long as the borrowers make mortgage payments. CDOs were considered to be much safer investment choices than regular, standalone mortgages because defaults by a few borrowers would not matter much. To make matters worse, rating agencies such as Standard & Poor's, Fitch, and Moody's frequently rated such CDOs as "triple A," which is the highest-quality rating. A triple A rating indicates an "extremely strong capacity" for the borrower to meet its financial obligation. Only a few companies, such as Exxon, Johnson & Johnson, and Microsoft, hold a triple A rating. Given that the Abacus investment vehicle received a triple A rating, many institutional investors such as pension funds bought into it. Everything looked great: Abacus was offered by Goldman Sachs, the number-one investment bank in the world with a stellar reputation, and it had a triple A rating.

But, according to internal e-mails, Mr. Paulson and several Goldman Sachs employees, including Mr. Tourre, knew otherwise. For example, Mr. Tourre earned his nickname "fabulous Fab" based on an e-mail he sent describing the anticipated burst of the real estate bubble: "The entire building is at risk of collapse at any moment. Only potential survivor, the fabulous Fab (. . . even though there is nothing fabulous about me . . .) standing in the middle of all these complex, highly leveraged, exotic trades he created without necessarily understanding all the implications of these monstrosities."[54]

Messrs. Paulson and Tourre worked together in selecting highly risky CDOs to roll them into Abacus. Goldman Sachs then turned around and sold the Abacus CDOs to unsuspecting clients—without, of course, revealing the motivation behind Abacus. Nor did Goldman Sachs reveal that Mr. Paulson helped in selecting the riskiest CDOs to be bundled into Abacus. Mr. Paulson then took a "short position" in Abacus—meaning he bought into it at a low price when first issued but sold his holdings when the price was bid up by institutional investors, often long-term Goldman clients, who believed that Abacus was a great investment opportunity. When the real estate bubble burst, Mr. Paulson made more than $1 billion from his position in Abacus.

The question that immediately arose was whether Goldman Sachs defrauded investors—as the SEC believed. The SEC argued that the investment bank knowingly misled investors by not revealing their motives in putting Abacus together and not informing them about John Paulson's role in this transaction. Basically, the SEC alleged that Goldman violated its *fiduciary responsibility* and defrauded its clients. Mounting a strong legal defense, Goldman Sachs argued that it is up to the clients to assess the risks involved in any investments. As public pressure mounted, however, Goldman Sachs settled the lawsuit with the SEC by paying a $550 million fine without admitting any wrongdoing. Mr. Tourre declined a settlement, and his case went to court. In August 2013, Mr. Tourre was convicted of securities fraud.[55]

professional partnership, Goldman Sachs earned a reputation as the best investment bank in the world. It had the best people and put its clients' interests first. Mr. Smith describes how Goldman's culture—and with it, employee attitudes—changed after the firm went public (in 1999), from "we are here to serve our clients as honorable business partners, and we have our clients best interest in mind," to "we [Goldman Sachs and our clients] are all grown-ups and just counter parties to any transaction."[56] In the latter perspective, unsuspecting clients in the Abacus deal were seen just as "counter parties to a transaction," who should have known better.

Some people believe that unethical behavior is limited to a few "bad apples" in organizations.[57] The assumption is that the vast majority of the population—and by extension, organizations—are good, and that we need only safeguard against abuses by a few bad actors. According to agency theory, it's the "bad agents" who act opportunistically, and principals need to be on guard against bad actors.

However, research indicates that it is not just the few "bad apples" but entire organizations that can create a climate in which unethical, even illegal behavior is tolerated.[58] While there clearly are some people with unethical or even criminal inclinations, in general one's ethical decision-making capacity depends very much on the organizational context. Research shows that if people work in organizations that expect and value ethical behavior, they are more likely to act ethically.[59] The opposite is also true. Enron's *stated* key values included respect and integrity, and its mission statement proclaimed that all business dealings should be open and fair.[60] Yet, the ethos at Enron was all about creating an inflated share price at any cost, and its employees observed and followed the behavior set by their leaders.

Sometimes, it's the bad barrel that can spoil the apples! This is precisely what Mr. Smith argues in regard to Goldman Sachs: The ethical climate had changed for the worse, so that seeing clients as mere "counter parties" to transactions made deals like Abacus possible. One could argue that Mr. Tourre simply followed the values held within Goldman Sachs ("profit is king" and "clients are grown-ups"). As a mid-level employee, many view Mr. Tourre as the scapegoat in the Abacus case.[61]

Employees take cues from their environment on how to act. Therefore, ethical leadership is critical, and strategic leaders set the tone for the ethical climate within an organization. This is one of the reasons the HP board removed Mark Hurd, even without proof of illegal behavior or violation of the company's sexual-harassment policy. The Chapter-Case illustrates that strategic leaders, such as CEOs of Fortune 500 companies, are under constant public scrutiny and ought to adhere to the highest ethical standards. If they do not, they cannot rationally expect their employees to behave ethically. Unethical behavior can quickly destroy the reputation of a CEO, one of the most important assets he or she possesses.

To foster ethical behavior in employees, top management must create an organizational structure, culture, and control system that values and encourages desired behavior. Furthermore, a company's formal and informal cultures must be aligned, and executive behavior must be in sync with the formally stated vision and values. Employees will quickly see through any duplicity. Actions by executives speak louder than words in vision statements.

Other leading professions have accepted codes of conduct (e.g., the bar association in the practice of law and the Hippocratic oath in medicine); management has not.[62] Some argue that management needs an accepted code of conduct,[63] holding members to a high professional standard and imposing consequences for misconduct. Misconduct by an attorney, for example, can result in being disbarred and losing the right to practice law. Likewise, medical doctors can lose their professional accreditations if they engage in misconduct.

EXHIBIT 12.6 /

The MBA Oath
SOURCE: www.mbaoath.org.

As a business leader I recognize my role in society.

>> *My purpose is to lead people and manage resources to create value that no single individual can create alone.*

>> *My decisions affect the well-being of individuals inside and outside my enterprise, today and tomorrow.*

Therefore, I promise that:

>> *I will manage my enterprise with loyalty and care, and will not advance my personal interests at the expense of my enterprise or society.*

>> *I will understand and uphold, in letter and spirit, the laws and contracts governing my conduct and that of my enterprise.*

>> *I will refrain from corruption, unfair competition, or business practices harmful to society.*

>> *I will protect the human rights and dignity of all people affected by my enterprise, and I will oppose discrimination and exploitation.*

>> *I will protect the right of future generations to advance their standard of living and enjoy a healthy planet.*

>> *I will report the performance and risks of my enterprise accurately and honestly.*

>> *I will invest in developing myself and others, helping the management profession continue to advance and create sustainable and inclusive prosperity.*

In exercising my professional duties according to these principles, I recognize that my behavior must set an example of integrity, eliciting trust and esteem from those I serve. I will remain accountable to my peers and to society for my actions and for upholding these standards.

This oath I make freely, and upon my honor.

To anchor future managers in professional values and to move management closer to a truly professional status, a group of Harvard Business School students developed an MBA oath (see Exhibit 12.6).[64] Since 2009, over 6,000 MBA students from over 300 institutions around the world have taken this voluntary pledge. The oath explicitly recognizes the role of business in society and its responsibilities beyond shareholders. It also holds managers to a high ethical standard based on more or less universally accepted principles in order to "create value responsibly and ethically."[65] Having the highest personal integrity is of utmost importance to one's career. It takes decades to build a career, but sometimes just a few moments to destroy one. The voluntary MBA oath sets professional standards, but its effect on behavior is unknown, and it does not impose any consequences for misconduct.

12.4 ◄► Implications for the Strategist

An important implication for the strategist is the recognition that effective corporate governance and solid business ethics are critical to gaining and sustaining competitive advantage.

A variety of corporate governance mechanisms can be effective in addressing the principal–agent problem. These mechanisms tend to focus on monitoring, controlling, and providing incentives, and they must be complemented by a strong code of conduct and strategic leaders who act with integrity. The strategist must help employees to "walk the talk"; leading by ethical example often has a stronger effect on employee behavior than words alone.

IBM is a company that emphasizes its values—"the dignity of the individual, excellence, and service"—to its employees worldwide. Stephen Covey, author of the best-selling leadership and business ethics book *The 7 Habits of Highly Effective People* describes how IBM acted upon this belief system:

> Once I was training a group of people for IBM in New York. It was a small group, about 20 people, and one of them became ill. He called his wife in California, who expressed concern because his illness required special treatment. The IBM people responsible for the training session arranged to have him taken to an excellent hospital with medical specialists in the disease. But they could sense that his wife was uncertain and really wanted him home where their personal physician could handle the problem. So they decided to get him home. Concerned about the time in driving him to the airport and waiting for a commercial plane, they brought in a helicopter, flew him to the airport, and hired a special plane just to take this man to California.[66]

It is interesting to note that this expensive evacuation ("walking the talk") did not come as a surprise for any of the IBMers present—they knew that the company would act upon its belief system and do the same for any of them, regardless of circumstance or geography.

The strategist needs to look beyond shareholders and apply a stakeholder perspective to ensure long-term survival and success of the firm. A firm that does not respond to stakeholders beyond stockholders in a way that keeps them committed to its vision will not be successful. Stakeholders want fair treatment even if not all of their demands can be met. A minimum of fairness and transparency is critical to maintaining good relationships within the network of stakeholders the firm is embedded in.

Finally, the large number of glaring ethical lapses over the last decade or so makes it clear that ethical values and a code of conduct are key to the continued professionalization of management.

CHAPTER**CASE 12** / Consider This . . .

HP WAS ONCE so successful that it was featured as one of a handful of visionary companies in the business bestseller *Built to Last,* published in 1994.[67] These select companies outperformed the stock market by a wide margin over several decades. *Built to Last* opens with a quote by HP's co-founder Bill Hewlett:

> As I look back on my life's work, I'm probably most proud of having helped to create a company that by virtue of its values, practices, and success has had a tremendous impact on the way companies are managed around the world. And I'm particularly proud that I'm leaving behind an ongoing organization that can live on as a role model long after I'm gone.[68]

Bill Hewlett passed away in 2001. Much has changed since then. Although generally CEOs are blamed for a company's poor performance, it appears that in the case of HP much of the blame is to be laid on the board of directors. The board is a key corporate governance mechanism that is supposed to act in the best interests of shareholders, but many of the HP board's decisions contributed to the destruction of $82 billion in shareholder value. For the last decade, it appears that HP's board of directors was dysfunctional. It started with the pretexting affair, followed by the handling of the Mark Hurd ethics scandal, the appointment of Leo Apotheker, and the botched Autonomy acquisition. In order to appoint a successor to Apotheker quickly, the board made the controversial decision not to engage in an open search for the next CEO but rather appoint Meg Whitman, who was serving as an HP board member at the time.

A closer look, for example, at the Autonomy acquisition in which HP lost some $9 billion shows that the due diligence process by the board was flawed. The process itself was truncated. Moreover, the HP board did not heed the red flags thrown up by Deloitte, Autonomy's auditor. Indeed, a few days before the Autonomy acquisition was finalized, Deloitte auditors asked to meet with the board to inform them about a former Autonomy executive who accused the company of accounting irregularities. Deloitte also added that it investigated the claim and did not find any irregularities.

Perhaps most problematic, the board fell victim to *groupthink*, rallying around Mr. Apotheker as CEO and Ray Lane, the board chair, who strongly supported him. Mr. Apotheker was eager to make a high-impact acquisition to put his strategic vision of HP as a software and service company into action. In the wake of the Mark Hurd ethics scandal, an outside recruiting firm

had identified Mr. Apotheker as CEO and Ray Lane as the new chair of HP's board of directors. The full board never met either of the men before hiring them into key strategic positions!

The HP board of directors experienced a major shakeup after the Mark Hurd ethics scandal and then again after the departure of Leo Apotheker. Mr. Lane stepped down as chairman of HP's board in spring 2013, but remains a director.[69]

Questions

1. Who is to blame for HP's shareholder value destruction—the CEO, the board of directors, or both? What recourse, if any, do shareholders have?

2. You are brought in as (a) a corporate governance consultant or (b) a business ethics consultant by HP's CEO. What recommendations would you give the new CEO, Meg Whitman? How would you go about implementing them? Be specific.

3. Discuss the general lessons in terms of corporate governance and business ethics that can be drawn from ChapterCase 12.

TAKE-AWAY CONCEPTS

In this final chapter, we looked at stakeholder strategy, corporate governance, business ethics, and strategic leadership, as summarized by the following learning objectives and related take-away concepts.

LO 12-1 / Describe the shared value creation framework and its relationship to competitive advantage.

- By focusing on financial performance, many companies have defined value creation too narrowly.

- Companies should instead focus on creating *shared value*, a concept that includes value creation for both shareholders and society.

- The shared value creation framework seeks to identify connections between economic and social needs, and then leverage them into competitive advantage.

LO 12-2 / Explain the role of corporate governance.

- Corporate governance involves mechanisms used to direct and control an enterprise in order to ensure that it pursues its strategic goals successfully and legally.

- Corporate governance attempts to address the principal–agent problem, which describes any situation in which an agent performs activities on behalf of a principal.

LO 12-3 / Apply agency theory to explain why and how companies use governance mechanisms to align interests of principals and agents.

- Agency theory views the firm as a nexus of legal contracts.
- The principal–agent problem concerns the relationship between owners (shareholders) and managers and also cascades down the organizational hierarchy.
- The risk of opportunism on behalf of agents is exacerbated by information asymmetry: Agents are generally better informed than the principals.
- Governance mechanisms are used to align incentives between principals and agents.
- Governance mechanisms need to be designed in such a fashion as to overcome two specific agency problems: adverse selection and moral hazard.

LO 12-4 / Evaluate the board of directors as the central governance mechanism for public stock companies.

- The shareholders are the legal owners of a publicly traded company and appoint a board of directors to represent their interests.
- The day-to-day business operations of a publicly traded stock company are conducted by its managers and employees, under the direction of the chief executive officer (CEO) and the oversight of the board of directors. The board of directors is composed of inside and outside directors, who are elected by the shareholders.
- Inside directors are generally part of the company's senior management team, such as the chief financial officer (CFO) and the chief operating officer (COO).
- Outside directors are not employees of the firm. They frequently are senior executives from other firms or full-time professionals who are appointed to a board and who serve on several boards simultaneously.

LO 12-5 / Evaluate other governance mechanisms.

- Other important corporate mechanisms are executive compensation, the market for corporate control, and financial statement auditors, government regulators, and industry analysts.
- Executive compensation has attracted significant attention in recent years. Two issues are at the forefront: (1) the absolute size of the CEO pay package compared with the pay of the average employee and (2) the relationship between firm performance and CEO pay.
- The board of directors and executive compensation are internal corporate-governance mechanisms. The market for corporate control is an important external corporate-governance mechanism. It consists of activist investors who seek to gain control of an underperforming corporation by buying shares of its stock in the open market.
- All public companies listed on the U.S. stock exchanges must file a number of financial statements with the Securities and Exchange Commission (SEC), a federal regulatory agency whose task it is to oversee stock trading and enforce federal securities laws. Auditors and industry analysts study these public financial statements carefully for clues of a firm's future valuations, financial irregularities, and strategy.

LO 12-6 / Explain the relationship between strategy and business ethics.

- The ethical pursuit of competitive advantage lays the foundation for long-term superior performance.
- Law and ethics are not synonymous; obeying the law is the minimum that society expects of a corporation and its managers.
- A manager's actions can be completely legal, but ethically questionable.
- Some argue that management needs an accepted code of conduct that holds members to a high professional standard and imposes consequences for misconduct.

KEY TERMS

Adverse selection

Agency theory

Board of directors

Business ethics

Corporate governance

Inside directors

Leveraged buyout (LBO)

Moral hazard

Outside directors

Shared value creation
    framework

Stock options

DISCUSSION QUESTIONS

1. How can a top management team lower the chances that key managers will pursue their own self-interests at the expense of stockholders? At the expense of the employees? At the expense of other key stakeholders?

2. The Business Roundtable has recommended that the CEO should not also serve as the chairman of the board. Discuss the disadvantages for building a sustainable competitive advantage if the two positions are held by one person. What are the disadvantages for stakeholder management? Are there situations where it would be advantageous to have one person in both positions?

3. The shared value creation framework provides help in making connections between economic needs and social needs in a way that transforms into a business opportunity. Taking the role of consultant to Nike Inc., discuss how Nike might move beyond selling high-quality footwear and apparel and utilize its expertise to serve a social need. Give Nike some advice on actions the company could take in different geographic markets that would connect economic and social needs.

ETHICAL/SOCIAL ISSUES

1. Assume you work in the accounting department of a large software company. Toward the end of December, your supervisor tells you to change the dates on several executive stock option grants from March 15 to July 30. Why would she ask for this change? What should you do?

2. As noted in the chapter, the average compensation for a CEO of a Fortune 500 company was $11 million, and CEO pay was 300 times the average worker pay. This contrasts with historic values of between 25 and 40 times the average pay.

   a. What are the potentially negative effects of this increasing disparity in CEO pay?

   b. Do you believe that current executive pay packages are justified? Why or why not?

3. The MBA oath (shown in Exhibit 12.6) says in part, "My decisions affect the well-being of

individuals inside and outside my enterprise, today and tomorrow." This echoes what John Mackey of Whole Foods has in recent years called *conscious capitalism.*[70]

   One example of a large firm reorienting toward this approach is PepsiCo. In the last few years, PepsiCo has been contracting directly with small farmers in impoverished areas (for example, in Mexico). What started as a pilot project in PepsiCo's Sabritas snack food division has now spread to over 1,000 farmers providing potatoes, corn, and sunflower oil to the firm. Pepsi provides a price guarantee for farmers' crops that is higher and much more consistent than the previous system of using intermediaries. The farmers report that since they have a firm market, they are planting more crops. Output is up about 160 percent, and farm incomes have tripled in the last three years.[71] The program has benefits for Pepsi as well. A shift to sunflower oil for its Mexican products will replace the 80,000 tons of palm oil it currently imports to Mexico from Asia and Africa, thus slashing transportation and storage costs.

a.   What are the benefits of this program for PepsiCo? What are its drawbacks?

b.   What other societal benefits could such a program have in Mexico?

c.   If you were a PepsiCo shareholder, would you support this program? Why or why not?

d.   Can you find other examples of firms employing "conscious capitalism"?

SMALL-GROUP EXERCISES

//// Small-Group Exercise 1

1.   Discuss in your group the contrasting perspectives of "shareholder versus stakeholder" governance. What benefits and drawbacks can you find in each view?

2.   Next, go online to find two sets of examples: (a) firms in the U.S. or Britain saving jobs by offering reduced hours to workers rather than having layoffs, and (b) large firms in Germany or Japan laying off employees or closing plants. What do the results of your search say about the impact of governance structure on corporate decisions?

3.   Developments after the global financial crisis moved the U.S. away from being one of the most free-market economies in the world toward an economy with much more active and stronger government involvement (e.g., the "Patient Protection and Affordable Care Act," commonly known as "Obama-care," requires employers to spend more on health care, including smaller firms). What implications does this shift in the political and economic environment in the United States have for large firms (such as GE or IBM) versus small firms (mom-and-pop entrepreneurs and technology startups)? How does this change the competitive landscape and affect a firm's strategy formulation and implementation?

//// Small-Group Exercise 2
(Ethical/Social Issues)

It is not unusual for even large corporate boards to have no women or minorities on them. In the U.S., women held 16 percent of board seats at Fortune 500 companies in 2012.[72] In her 2013 book, *Lean In,* Sheryl Sandberg points out that this number has been flat for 10 years—or, as she puts it, there has been no progress in the past 10 years.[73] In Europe, of the total number of board members in Britain, only 12 percent were women; Spain, France, and Germany all had less than 10 percent.[74] In Norway, by contrast, female members comprised 40 percent of the boards.

So how did Norway do it? In 2005, the government of Norway gave public firms two years to change their boards' composition from 9 percent female to 40 percent female. Is this a good idea? Spain, Italy, France, and the Netherlands must think so: Each country is considering implementing a similar quota (though generally with more than two years to implement it).

1.   Discuss in your group to what extent it is a problem that women are proportionally underrepresented on corporate boards. Provide the rationale for your responses.

2.   Why has representation by women on U.S. boards not increased over the past 10 years? What actions could be taken by companies to increase participation? What actions could be taken by women who seek to be directors?

3.   Would a regulatory quota be a good solution? Why or why not?

4.   What other methods could be used to increase female and minority participation on corporate boards? Should it be perceived as a problem when a company seeks minority women as directors so that both statistics rise? What data would you gather in order to verify that such appointments are sincere?

STRATEGY TERM PROJECT

//// Module 12: Corporate Governance

In this section, you will study the governance structure of your selected firm. This is also our concluding module, so we will have final questions for you to consider about your firm overall.

1. Find a list of the members of the board of directors for your firm. How large is the board? How many independent (non-employee) members are on the board? Are any women or minorities on the board? Is the CEO also the chair of the board?

2. Who are the largest stockholders of your firm? Is there a high degree of employee ownership of the stock?

3. In reviewing press releases and news articles about your firm over the past year, can you find examples of any actions the firm has taken that, though legal, may be ethically questionable?

4. You have now completed 12 modular assignments about your selected firm. You know a lot about its mission, strategies, competitive advantage, and organization. Is this a company you would like to work for? If you had $1,000 to invest in a firm, would you invest it in the stock of this firm? Why or why not?

my STRATEGY

Are You Part of Gen Y, or Will You Manage Gen-Y Workers?

Generation Y (born between 1980 and 2001) is entering the work force and advancing their careers now, as the Baby Boomers of their parents' generation begin to retire in large numbers. Given the smaller size of Gen Y compared to the Baby Boomers, this generation received much more individual attention from their immediate and extended families. Classes in school were much smaller than in previous generations. The parents of Gen-Y members placed a premium on achievement, both academically and socially. Gen Y grew up during a time of unprecedented economic growth and prosperity, combined with an explosion in technology (including laptop computers, cell phones, the Internet, e-mail, instant messaging, and online social networks). Gen Yers are connected 24/7 and are able to work anywhere, frequently multitasking. Due to the unique circumstances of their upbringing, they are said to be tech-savvy, family- and friends-centric, team players, achievement-oriented, but also attention-craving.[75]

Some have called Generation Y the "trophy kids," due in part to the practice of giving all Gen-Y children trophies in competitive activities, not wanting to single out winners and losers. When coaching a group of Gen-Y students for job interviews, a consultant asked them how they believe future employers view them. She gave them a clue to the answer: the letter E. Quickly, the students answered confidently: *excellent, enthusiastic,* and *energetic.* The answer the consultant was looking for was "entitled." Baby Boomers believe that Gen Y has an overblown sense of entitlement.

When they bring so many positive characteristics to the workplace, why do Baby Boomers view Gen-Y employees as entitled? Many managers are concerned that these young workers have outlandish expectations when compared with other employees: They often expect higher pay, flexible work schedules, promotions and significant raises every year, and generous vacation and personal time.[76] Managers also often find that for Gen-Y employees, the traditional annual or semiannual performance evaluations are not considered sufficient. Instead, Gen-Y employees seek more immediate feedback, ideally daily or at least weekly. For many, feedback needs to come in the form of positive reinforcement rather than as a critique.

The generational tension seems a bit ironic, since the dissatisfied Baby Boomer managers are the same indulgent parents who raised Gen Yers. Some companies, such as Google, Intel, and Sun Microsystems (Sun), have leveraged this tension into an opportunity. Google, for example, allows its engineers to spend one day a week on any project of their own choosing, thus meeting the Gen-Y need for creativity and self-determination. Executives at Intel have learned to motivate Gen-Y employees by sincerely respecting their contributions as colleagues rather than relying on hierarchical or position power. The network-computing company Sun accommodates Gen Yers' need for flexibility through drastically increasing work-from-home and telecommunicating arrangements, so that basically all employees now have a "floating office."

1. As you and your cohort enter the work force, do you expect to see a different set of business ethics take hold?

2. Are efforts such as the MBA oath (discussed in this chapter) reflections of a different approach that Gen Y will take to the business environment, compared with prior generations?

ENDNOTES

1. "Suspicions and spies in Silicon Valley," *Newsweek,* September 17, 2006.

2. "How Hewlett-Packard lost its way," *CNN Money,* May 8, 2012.

3. This ChapterCase, developed by Frank T. Rothaermel and Carrie Yang (GT MBA, MSc.), is based on: Packard, D. (1995), *HP Way: How Bill Hewlett and I Built Our Company* (New York: Collins); "Corporate governance: Spying and leaking are wrong," *The Economist,* September 14, 2006; "Corporate governance: Pretext in context," *The Economist,* September 14, 2006; "HP CEO Mark Hurd resigns after sexual-harassment probe," *The Huffington Post,* August 6, 2010; "The curse of HP," *The Economist,* August 12, 2010; "HP shakes up board in scandal's wake," *The Wall Street Journal,* January 21, 2011; "How Hewlett-Packard lost its way," *CNN Money,* May 8, 2012; "Inside HP's missed chance to avoid a disastrous deal," *The Wall Street Journal,* January 21, 2013; and "The HP Way out," *The Economist,* April 5, 2013.

4. "Inside HP's missed chance to avoid a disastrous deal," *The Wall Street Journal,* January 21, 2013; and "The HP Way out," *The Economist,* April 5, 2013.

5. Porter, M. E., and M. R. Kramer (2006), "Strategy and society: The link between competitive advantage and corporate social responsibility," *Harvard Business Review,* December: 80–92; Porter, M. E., and M. R. Kramer (2011), "Creating shared value: How to reinvent capitalism—and unleash innovation and growth," *Harvard Business Review,* January–February.

6. "The endangered public company," *The Economist,* March 19, 2012; and the classic work by Berle, A., and G. Means (1932), *The Modern Corporation & Private Property* (New York: Macmillan); and Monks, R.A.G., and N. Minow (2008), *Corporate Governance,* 4th ed. (West Sussex, UK: Wiley).

7. NASDAQ was originally an acronym for National Association of Securities Dealers Automated Quotations, but it is now a stand-alone term.

8. Berle, A., and G. Means (1932), *The Modern Corporation & Private Property* (New York: Macmillan); and Monks, R.A.G., and N. Minow (2008), *Corporate Governance,* 4th ed. (West Sussex, UK: Wiley).

9. This section is based on: Porter, M. E., and M. R. Kramer (2006), "Strategy and society: The link between competitive advantage and corporate social responsibility," *Harvard Business Review,* December: 80–92; Porter, M. E., and M. R. Kramer (2011), "Creating shared value: How to reinvent capitalism—and unleash innovation and growth," *Harvard Business Review,* January–February.

10. Friedman, M. (1962), *Capitalism and Freedom* (Chicago, IL: University of Chicago Press), quoted in Friedman, M. (1970), "The social responsibility of business is to increase its profits," *The New York Times Magazine,* September 13.

11. Carroll, A. B., and A. K. Buchholtz (2012), *Business & Society. Ethics, Sustainability, and Stakeholder Management* (Mason, OH: South-Western Cengage).

12. "Milton Friedman goes on tour," *The Economist,* January 27, 2011.

13. For detailed data and descriptions on the GE *ecomagination* initiative, see http://www.ge.com/about-us/ecomagination.

14. "GE to invest more in 'green' technology," *The New York Times,* May 10, 2005.

15. 2012 *Fortune 500* ranking, see http://money.cnn.com/magazines/fortune/fortune500/index.html.

16. Porter, M. E., and M. R. Kramer (2011), "Creating shared value: How to reinvent capitalism—and unleash innovation and growth," *Harvard Business Review,* January–February.

17. *GE Governance Principles,* p. 1, www.ge.com.

18. Monks, R.A.G., and N. Minow (2008), *Corporate Governance,* 4th ed. (West Sussex, UK: Wiley).

19. Berle, A., and G. Means (1932), *The Modern Corporation & Private Property* (New York, Macmillan); Jensen, M., and W. Meckling (1976), "Theory of the firm: Managerial behavior, agency costs and ownership structure," *Journal of Financial Economics* 3: 305–360; and Fama, E. (1980), "Agency problems and the theory of the firm," *Journal of Political Economy* 88: 375–390.

20. "Fund titan found guilty," *The Wall Street Journal,* May 12, 2011.

21. Ibid.

22. "Top 10 crooked CEOs," *Time,* June 9, 2009.

23. "Thain ousted in clash at Bank of America," *The Wall Street Journal,* January 23, 2009.

24. Agency theory originated in finance; see Jensen, M., and W. Meckling (1976), "Theory of the firm: Managerial behavior, agency costs and ownership structure," *Journal of Financial Economics* 3: 305–360; and Fama, E. (1980), "Agency problems and the theory of the firm," *Journal of Political Economy* 88: 375–390. For an application to strategic management, see Eisenhardt, K. M. (1989), "Agency theory: An assessment and review," *Academy of Management Review* 14: 57–74; and Mahoney, J. T. (2005), *Economic Foundations of Strategy* (Thousand Oaks, CA: Sage).

25. Fuller, A.W., and F. T. Rothaermel (2012), "When stars shine: The effects of faculty founders on new technology ventures," *Strategic Entrepreneurship Journal,* 6: 220–235.

26. Eisenhardt, K. M. (1989), "Agency theory: An assessment and review," *Academy of Management Review* 14: 57–74.

27. This section draws on: Monks, R.A.G., and N. Minow (2008), *Corporate Governance,* 4th ed. (West Sussex, UK: Wiley); Williamson, O. E. (1984), "Corporate governance," *Yale Law Journal* 93: 1197–1230; and Williamson, O. E. (1985), *The Economic Institutions of Capitalism* (New York: Free Press).

28. "HP looks beyond its ranks," *The Wall Street Journal,* August 9, 2010.

29. "Apple chief to take leave," *The Wall Street Journal,* January 18, 2010.

30. For the latest listing, see www.ge.com/company/leadership/directors.html.

31. "On Apple's board, fewer independent voices," *The Wall Street Journal,* March 24, 2010.

32. This Strategy Highlight is based on: "2010 Catalyst census: Fortune 500 women board directors," www.catalyst.org; Baliga, B. R., R. C. Moyer, and R. S. Rao (1996), "CEO duality and firm performance: What's the fuss," *Strategic Management Journal* 17: 41–53; Brickley, J. A., J. L. Coles, and G. Jarrell (1997), "Leadership structure: Separating the CEO and chairman of the board," *Journal of Corporate Finance* 3: 189–220; Daily, C. M., and D. R. Dalton (1997), "CEO and board chair roles held jointly or separately," *Academy of Management Executive* 3: 11–20; "GE governance principles," www.ge.com; Irving, J. (1972), *Victims of Groupthink. A Psychological Study of Foreign-Policy Decisions and Fiascoes* (Boston, MA: Houghton Mifflin); Jensen, M. C. (1993), "The modern industrial revolution, exit, and the failure of internal control systems," *Journal of Corporate Finance* 48: 831–880; "On Apple's board, fewer independent voices," *The Wall Street Journal,* March 24, 2010; "Strings attached to options grant for GE's Immelt," *The Wall Street Journal,* April 20, 2011; Westphal, J. D., and E. J. Zajac (1995), "Who shall govern? CEO board power, demographic similarity and new director selection," *Administrative Science Quarterly* 40: 60–83; and Westphal, J. D., and I. Stern (2007), "Flattery will get you everywhere (especially if you are male Caucasian): How ingratiation, boardroom behavior, and demographic minority status affect additional board appointments at U.S. companies," *Academy of Management Journals* 50: 267–288.

33. www.faireconomy.org.

34. http://www.forbes.com/pictures/eggh45jef/highest-paid-bosses/.

35. "Executive pay by the numbers," *The New York Times,* June 23, 2013.

36. "For McKesson's CEO, a pension of $159 million," *The Wall Street Journal,* June 24, 2013.

37. Ibid.

38. Heineman, B. W. (2008), "The fatal flaw in pay for performance," *Harvard Business Review,* June; and Kaplan, S. N. (2008), "Are U.S. CEOs overpaid?" *Academy of Management Perspectives* 22: 5–20.

39. "Executive pay: Because he's worth it," *The Economist,* July 6, 2013.

40. "HP's ousted CEO will take home $25 million," *CNNMoneyTech,* September 22, 2011.

41. "Strings attached to options grant for GE's Immelt," *The Wall Street Journal,* April 20, 2011.

42. Ariely, D. (2010), *The Upside of Irrationality: The Unexpected Benefits of Defying Logic at Work and at Home* (New York: HarperCollins).

43. "Have investors learned their LBO lessons?" *BusinessWeek,* December 3, 2007.

44. The Dell LBO battle is described in: "Dell buyout pushed to brink," *The Wall Street Journal,* July 18, 2013; and "Monarchs versus managers. The battle over Dell raises the question of whether tech firms' founders make the best long-term leaders of their creations," *The Economist,* July 27, 2013.

45. www.fasb.org: "The term 'generally accepted accounting principles' has a specific meaning for accountants and auditors. The AICPA Code of Professional Conduct prohibits members from expressing an opinion or stating affirmatively that financial statements or other financial data 'present fairly . . . in conformity with generally accepted accounting principles,' if such information contains any departures from accounting principles promulgated by a body designated by the AICPA Council to establish such principles. The AICPA Council designated FASAB as the body that establishes generally accepted accounting principles (GAAP) for federal reporting entities."

46. www.secfilings.com.

47. Lowenstein, R. (2010), *The End of Wall Street* (New York: Penguin Press).

48. Hayward, M.L.A., and W. Boeker (1998), "Power and conflicts of interest in professional firms: Evidence from investment banking," *Administrative Science Quarterly* 43: 1–22.

49. http://www2.gmiratings.com/.

50. This section draws on and the definition is from: Treviño, L. K., and K. A. Nelson (2011), *Managing Business Ethics: Straight Talk About How to Do It Right,* 5th ed. (Hoboken, NJ: Wiley).

51. Several such studies, such as the "ultimatum game," are described in: Ariely, D. (2008), *Predictably Irrational: The Hidden Forces That Shape Our Decisions* (New York: HarperCollins); and Ariely, D. (2010), *The Upside of Irrationality: The Unexpected Benefits of Defying Logic at Work and at Home* (New York: HarperCollins).

52. Lowenstein, R. (2010), *The End of Wall Street* (New York: Penguin Press).

53. Smith, G. (2012), *Why I Left Goldman Sachs. A Wall Street Story* (New York: Grand Central Publishing).

54. Quoted in "'Fab' trader liable in fraud," *The Wall Street Journal,* August 2, 2013.

55. This Strategy Highlight is based on: Smith, G. (2012), *Why I Left Goldman Sachs. A Wall Street Story* (New York: Grand Central Publishing); "The trial of Fabrice Tourre. Not so fabulous," *The Economist,* July 20, 2013; "'Fab' trader liable in fraud," *The Wall Street Journal,* August 2, 2013; and "The Abacus trial. No longer fabulous," *The Economist,* August 2, 2013.

56. Smith, G. (2012), *Why I Left Goldman Sachs. A Wall Street Story.*

57. This section draws on: Treviño, L. K., and K. A. Nelson (2011), *Managing Business Ethics.*

58. Treviño, L., and A. Youngblood (1990), "Bad apples in bad barrels: A causal analysis of ethical-decision behavior," *Journal of Applied Psychology* 75: 378–385.

59. Ibid. Also, for a superb review and discussion of this issue, see Treviño, L. K., and K. A. Nelson (2011), *Managing Business Ethics.*

60. McLean, B., and P. Elkind (2004), *The Smartest Guys in the Room: The Amazing Rise and Scandalous Fall of Enron* (New York: Portfolio).

61. "The trial of Fabrice Tourre. Not so fabulous," *The Economist,* July 20, 2013; "'Fab' trader liable in fraud," *The Wall Street Journal,* August 2, 2013; and "The Abacus trial. No longer fabulous," *The Economist,* August 2, 2013.

62. Khurana, R. (2007), *From Higher Aims to Hired Hands: The Social Transformation of American Business Schools and the Unfulfilled Promise of Management as a Profession* (Princeton, NJ: Princeton University Press).

63. Khurana, R., and N. Nohria (2008), "It's time to make management a true profession," *Harvard Business Review,* October: 70–77.

64. For a history of the MBA oath and other information, see www.mbaoath.org.

65. www.mbaoath.org.

66. Covey, S. R. (1989), *The 7 Habits of Highly Effective People. Powerful Lessons in Personal Change* (New York: Fire Side), pp. 139–140.

67. Collins, J. C., and J. I. Porras (1994), *Built to Last: Successful Habits of Visionary Companies* (New York: HarperCollins).

68. Bill Hewlett, HP co-founder, as quoted in Collins, J. C., and J. I. Porras (1994), *Built to Last: Successful Habits of Visionary Companies,* p. 1.

69. "HP shakes up board in scandal's wake," *The Wall Street Journal,* January 21, 2011; and "Inside HP's missed chance to avoid a disastrous deal," *The Wall Street Journal,* January 21, 2013.

70. "The conscience of a capitalist," *The Wall Street Journal,* October 3, 2009.

71. "For Pepsi, a business decision with social benefit," *The New York Times,* February 21, 2011.

72. "Catalyst 2012 census of Fortune 500: No change for women in top leadership," http://www.catalyst.org/media/catalyst-2012-census-fortune-500-no-change-women-top-leadership.

73. Sandberg, S. (2013), *Lean In: Women, Work, and the Will to Lead* (New York: Knopf).

74. "Skirting the issue," *The Economist,* March 11, 2010.

75. This *my*Strategy module is based on: "The 'trophy kids' go to work," *The Wall Street Journal,* October 21, 2008; and Alsop, R. (2008), *The Trophy Kids Grow Up: How the Millennial Generation Is Shaking Up the Workplace* (Hoboken, NJ: Jossey-Bass).

76. Survey by CareerBuilder.com.

MiniCases

Does Facebook Have a Strategy?

FACEBOOK WAS FOUNDED in a dorm room at Harvard in 2004 by 19-year-old Mark Zuckerberg and three college pals. What began as a hobby to let college students socialize online is now the world's largest social networking site, with more than 1.1 billion users and over $5 billion in revenues (in 2012). As of summer 2013, Facebook is the most popular website globally, even more popular than Google. Zuckerberg sees online social networking as the "most powerful and transformative social change" in recent history, and the biggest invention since Gutenberg's printing press.[1] Indeed, it's made him the world's youngest billionaire.

Before Facebook became a global phenomenon, it had to overcome the first-mover advantage held by Myspace. Launched in 2003, Myspace was an early leader in social networking. Its success attracted the attention of News Corp. and other media outlets. News Corp. acquired Myspace for $580 million in 2005. As a subsidiary of a publicly owned company, Myspace's revenues and profitability became more pressing issues after the acquisition. Myspace's business model shifted from accumulating more users to growing revenues and profits by focusing on a few ad-heavy markets such as the U.S., UK, Germany, France, and Japan. Myspace was hit hard by the global economic downturn that began in 2008. A year later, it laid off 45 percent of its staff.

Facebook, on the other hand, remained a private company until May 2012. Among other investors, Microsoft purchased a $240 million equity stake in 2007, and a Russian investment group added $200 million in 2009. Facebook's managers had less pressure to produce bottom-line results than did Myspace. This allowed the company to pursue a different business model: more users first, profits later. While Myspace concentrated on a few developed markets, Facebook pursued a truly global strategy. More than 70 percent of its users are outside the United States. In 2008, Facebook displaced Myspace as the most popular social networking site. Facebook's new challengers in the social media space include Google+, LinkedIn, Pinterest, and Twitter.

Facebook's business model is based on three pillars:

1. *News Feed.* Launched in September 2006, this quickly became a core feature of Facebook. It is at the heart of a user's homepage and provides regular updates of friends' posts, photos, events, group memberships, and other subjects. The priority of items displayed in the News Feed is based on a complex algorithm.
2. *Timeline.* This is an updated version of the profile pages and was launched in September 2011. It allows each user to paint a complete life story on his or her profile. Users can select what information is shared and with whom they share it.
3. *Graph Search.* Zuckerberg calls the network of connections between people the "social graph." Graph Search is an attempt to map the global social graph in the form of a massive database. Introduced in January 2013, it is a search bar that hovers at the top of Facebook's web page, acting as a title for the content of that page and allowing a user to query the portion of the social graph that is connected to and filled in by the user.

As Exhibit MC1.1 shows, in May 2012 Facebook went public with an initial share price of $38, making the company worth more than $100 billion. Just a year later, in the summer of 2013, Facebook was valued at around $60 billion. In an interview, Mark Zuckerberg conceded, "The performance of the stock has obviously been disappointing."[2]

Frank T. Rothaermel prepared this MiniCase from public sources. It is developed for the purpose of class discussion. It is not intended to be used for any kind of endorsement, source of data, or depiction of efficient or inefficient management. All opinions expressed, and all errors and omissions, are entirely the author's. © Rothaermel, 2014.

EXHIBIT MC1.1 / Facebook's Share Price May 18, 2012, at IPO ($38.00) to July 4, 2013 ($24.52)

SOURCE: MSN Money, http://money.msn.com/.

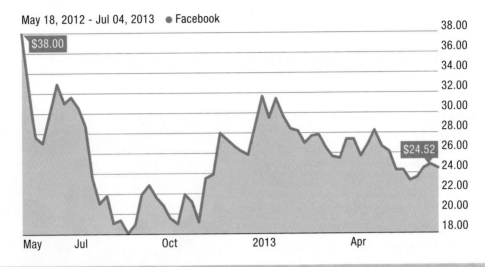

May 18, 2012 - Jul 04, 2013   ● Facebook

DISCUSSION QUESTIONS

Review Chapter 1: What Is Strategy, and Why Is It Important?

1. Why is Facebook the number-one social media company, and not Myspace which enjoyed a first-mover advantage?

2. Given the hallmarks of good and bad strategy (discussed in Chapter 1), do you think Facebook has a good strategy? Why or why not?

3. The first step in creating a good strategy is to diagnose the competitive challenge. What do you believe is Facebook's number-one competitive challenge?

4. What top-three recommendations would you give Mr. Zuckerberg? Why? Support your arguments.

Endnotes

1. "Facebook CEO in no rush to 'friend' Wall Street," *The Wall Street Journal,* March 3, 2010.

2. Quote from: "Zuckerberg admits to missteps," *The Wall Street Journal,* September 11, 2012.

Sources: This MiniCase is based on "Facebook's land grab in the face of a downturn," *Bloomberg Businessweek,* November 20, 2008; "A special report on social networking," *The Economist,* January 30, 2010; "Facebook CEO in no rush to 'friend' Wall Street," *The Wall Street Journal;* "The world's billionaires," *Forbes,* March 10, 2010; "Facebook wants to know more than just who your friends are," *The Wall Street Journal;* "Facebook's Washington problem," *Bloomberg Businessweek,* May 13, 2010; "Lives of others," *The Economist,* May 20, 2010; www.comscore.com; www.facebook.com; and www.myspace.com. For an in-depth discussion of Facebook, see: Case Study MHHE-FTR-0021 "Facebook: Will Wall Street hit the 'Like' button?" by Frank T. Rothaermel and Seth Taylor (2014).

Michael Phelps: The Greatest Olympian

MICHAEL PHELPS, nicknamed MP, is the most decorated Olympian of all time. Competing in four Olympic Games,[1] the American swimmer won 22 Olympic medals, including 18 gold medals! In 2000 at the Sydney Olympics, Michael Phelps was, at the age of 15, the youngest U.S. athlete in almost seven decades. In 2008, at the Beijing Olympics, Phelps won an unprecedented eight gold medals, and while doing so set seven new world records. Eight short days changed Olympic history and Michael Phelps' life forever, making MP one of the greatest athletes of all time. Immediately after the event, *The Wall Street Journal* reported that Phelps would be likely to turn the eight gold medals into a cash flow stream of more than $100 million through several product and service endorsements.[2] Phelps did not rest on his laurels, however. In 2012 at the London Summer Olympics, Michael Phelps added another four gold and two silver medals, elevating him to superstardom. One interesting fact is that Michael Phelps became an Olympic hero against significant odds. So, how did he become so successful?

In his youth, MP was diagnosed with attention deficit hyperactivity disorder (ADHD). Doctors prescribed swimming to help him release his energy. It worked! Between 2004 and 2008, Michael Phelps attended the University of Michigan, studying marketing and management. He had already competed quite successfully in the 2004 Athens Summer Olympics, where he won eight medals: six gold and two bronze. Right after the Athens Games, the then-19-year-old sat down with his manager, Peter Carlisle, and his long-time swim coach, Bob Bowman, to map out a detailed strategy for the next four years. The explicit goal was to win nothing less than a gold medal in each of the events in which he would compete in Beijing.[3]

Bob Bowman was responsible for getting MP into the necessary physical shape needed for Beijing and nurturing the mental toughness required to break Mark Spitz's 36-year record of seven gold medals won in the

1972 Munich Olympic Games. Peter Carlisle, meanwhile, conceived of a detailed strategy to launch MP as a world superstar during the Beijing Games. While MP spent six hours a day in the pool, Carlisle focused on exposing MP to the Asian market, the largest consumer market in the world, with a special emphasis on the Chinese consumer. MP's wide-ranging presence in the real world was combined with a huge exposure in the virtual world. Phelps posts and maintains his own Facebook page, with 7.5 million "phans." MP is also a favorite of Twitter, YouTube, and online blogs, garnering worldwide exposure to an extent never

Frank T. Rothaermel prepared this MiniCase from public sources. It is developed for the purpose of class discussion. It is not intended to be used for any kind of endorsement, source of data, or depiction of efficient or inefficient management. All opinions expressed, and all errors and omissions, are entirely the author's. © Rothaermel, 2014.

before achieved by an Olympian.[4] The gradual buildup of Phelps over a number of years enabled manager Peter Carlisle to launch MP as a superstar right after he won his eighth gold medal at the Beijing Games. By then, MP had become a worldwide brand.

A successful strategy can be based on leveraging unique resources and capabilities. Accordingly, some suggest that MP's success can be explained by his unique physical endowments: his long thin torso, which reduces drag; his arm span of 6 feet 7 inches (204 cm), which is disproportionate to his 6-foot-4-inch (193 cm) height; his relatively short legs for a person of his height; and his size-14 feet which work like flippers due to hypermobile ankles.[5] While MP's physical attributes are a *necessary* condition for winning, they are *not sufficient*. Many other swimmers, like the Australian Ian Thorpe (who has size-17 feet) or the German "albatross" Michael Gross (with an arm span of 7 feet, or 213 cm), also brought extraordinary resource endowments to the swim meet. Yet neither of them won eight gold medals in a single Olympics.

DISCUSSION QUESTIONS

Review Chapter 1: What Is Strategy, and Why Is It Important?

1. Olympians generally do not turn into global phenomena. One reason is that they are highlighted only every four years (e.g., not too many people follow competitive swimming or downhill skiing [think Lindsey Vonn] outside the Olympics). How did Michael Phelps transform his competitive advantage as an athlete into a "global brand"?

2. Following the Beijing Olympics, a photo published by a British tabloid showed Michael Phelps using a "bong," a device for smoking marijuana, at a party in South Carolina. Kellogg's withdrew Phelps' endorsement contract. What does this incident tell you about maintaining and increasing brand value over time?

3. According to a study by two economics professors at the University of California, Davis,[6] another example of an athlete who lost significant "brand value" is Tiger Woods, who destroyed an estimated $12 billion in stock market value of the firms sponsoring him—Accenture, Gillette, Nike, PepsiCo (Gatorade), and Electronic Arts (EA). As a manager, what lessons about celebrity endorsements can you draw from the examples of Phelps and Woods? What are some general take-aways that a strategist should keep in mind?

Endnotes

1. Sydney in 2000; Athens in 2004; Beijing in 2008; and London in 2012.

2. "Now, Phelps chases gold on land," *The Wall Street Journal*, August 18, 2008.

3. Ibid.

4. "Michael Phelps' agent has been crafting the swimmer's image for years," *Associated Press*, September 14, 2008.

5. "Profile: Michael Phelps—A normal guy from another planet," *Telegraph*, August 15, 2008.

6. Knittel, C. R., and V. Stango (2008), "Celebrity endorsements, firm value and reputation risk: Evidence from the Tiger Woods scandal," working paper, University of California, Davis, http://faculty.gsm.ucdavis.edu/~vstango/tiger007.pdf.

Teach For America: Inspiring Future Leaders

TEACH FOR AMERICA (TFA) is a nonprofit organization that recruits college graduates and professionals to teach for two years in economically disadvantaged communities in the United States. The idea behind Teach For America was developed in 1989 by then-21-year-old Wendy Kopp as her senior thesis at Princeton. Kopp was convinced young people today are searching for meaning in their lives by making a positive contribution to society. In the first four months after creating TFA, Kopp received more than 2,500 applicants. Her "marketing" tool was flyers under dorm rooms at this time. Corporate America donated $2.5 million in seed grants during TFA's first year. In 2012, TFA's operating budget was $250 million. Teach For America describes itself as "the growing movement of leaders who work to ensure that kids growing up in poverty get an excellent education."[1]

The genius of Kopp's idea was to turn on its head the social perception of teaching—to make what appeared to be an unattractive, low-status job into a high-prestige professional opportunity. Kopp established a mission for the organization she had in mind: to eliminate educational inequality by enlisting our nation's most promising future leaders in the effort. Her underlying assumption was that significant numbers of young people have a desire to take on meaningful responsibility in order to have a positive impact on the lives of others. To be chosen for TFA is a badge of honor. In 2012, TFA received some 48,000 applications for only about 5,000 positions across the country (paying the same as all other first-year teachers, ranging from $30,000 to $51,500 a year). This translates to a mere 10 percent acceptance rate. Since each TFA cohort teaches for two years, in the 2012–2013 school year, more than 10,000 corps members taught 750,000 students.

Persuading highly qualified teachers to take up jobs in some inner cities and rural areas has been an elusive goal for many decades. Making TFA highly selective changed the social perception of teaching in underprivileged areas. Suddenly, it was an honor (and

great résumé builder) to be chosen for TFA. More than 60 percent of TFA's more than 20,000 alumni are still working in the field of education today.

TFA is not without critics, however. Some traditional teachers have charged that hiring college students who are given only seven weeks of teacher training and who are committed to a community for only two years takes jobs away from traditionally trained teachers and thus is detrimental to a community.

DISCUSSION QUESTIONS

Review Chapter 2: Strategic Leadership: Managing the Strategy Process.

1. How did an undergraduate student accomplish what the Department of Education, state and local school boards, and the national Parent-Teacher Association were unable to achieve despite trying for decades and spending billions of dollars in the process?

2. Respond to the charge that TFA teachers take jobs away from teachers with degrees in education. Is

Frank T. Rothaermel prepared this MiniCase from public sources. It is developed for the purpose of class discussion. It is not intended to be used for any kind of endorsement, source of data, or depiction of efficient or inefficient management. All opinions expressed, and all errors and omissions, are entirely the author's. © Rothaermel, 2014.

using TFA teachers a way for school corporations to lower costs by hiring younger teachers at entry-level salaries?

3. Applying the Level-5 leadership pyramid, in what ways is Wendy Kopp an effective leader?

4. What are your personal leadership take-aways from Wendy Kopp and the TFA MiniCase?

Endnote

1. http://www.teachforamerica.org.

Strategy and Serendipity: A Billion-Dollar Bonanza

ABOUT 20 MILLION U.S. MEN experience some form of male erectile dysfunction (MED), and treating the disorder with prescription drugs is a business worth more than $3 billion a year. Was this great pharmaceutical success the result of smart strategic planning? Far from it. Without serendipity, there would be no success story. Here is how two modern blockbuster drugs were discovered.

In the 1990s, researchers at Pfizer developed the compound UK-95,480 as a potential drug to treat heart disease. In their research, they focused on two things: preventing blood clots and enhancing blood flow. The drug did not achieve the desired effects in human trials, but some men in the test group reported an unexpected side-effect: prolonged erections. Pfizer's managers were quick to turn this unintended result into the blockbuster drug Viagra.

Although the old adage says lightning never strikes the same place twice, it did so in the area of MED drugs. In the mid-1990s, the biotech firm Icos was developing a new treatment for hypertension. Code named IC-351, the drug moved quickly to clinical trials because of encouraging lab results. Then, unexpected things happened. First was the unusually high compliance rate of patients who took the medication required by the trial, especially males in their fifties, despite the fact that IC-351 turned out to be ineffective in treating hypertension. The second surprise was that many male patients refused to return their surplus pills. The reason: their improved sex life. Icos' IC-351 had failed to treat hypertension but succeeded in treating MED. Marketed as Cialis, it is a major competitor to Viagra, and its success led Lilly to acquire Icos for $2.3 billion in 2007.

DISCUSSION QUESTIONS

Review Chapter 2: Strategic Leadership: Managing the Strategy Process.

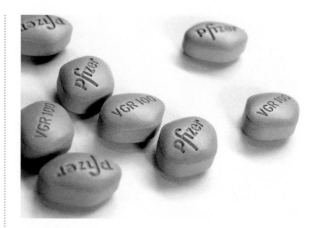

1. Do you think "serendipity is random," as some say? Why or why not?

2. What does the "discovery" of Viagra and Cialis tell us about the strategic management process? About the role of strategic initiatives?

3. Which model of strategy process best explains the Viagra/Cialis story? Why?

4. Does the Viagra/Cialis story influence how you would design a strategic management process? Why or why not? If yes, what process would you design?

Frank T. Rothaermel prepared this MiniCase from public sources. It is developed for the purpose of class discussion. It is not intended to be used for any kind of endorsement, source of data, or depiction of efficient or inefficient management. All opinions expressed, and all errors and omissions, are entirely the author's. © Rothaermel, 2014.

Sources: This MiniCase is based on Mestel, R. (1999), "Sexual chemistry," *Discover*, January: 32; "Eli Lilly says Icos acquisition complete," *Reuters*, January 29, 2007; and Deeds, D. L., and F. T. Rothaermel (2003), "Honeymoons and liabilities: The relationship between alliance age and performance in R&D alliances," *Journal of Product Innovation Management* 20, no. 6: 468–484.

The Wonder from Sweden: Is IKEA's Success Sustainable?

THE WORLD'S MOST SUCCESSFUL GLOBAL RETAILER, in terms of profitability, is not Walmart or the French grocery chain Carrefour, but IKEA—a privately owned home-furnishings company with origins in Sweden. In 2012, IKEA had more than 330 stores worldwide in 38 countries, employed some 140,000 people, and earned revenues of 33 billion euros. IKEA's revenues by geographic region are 70 percent from Europe, with the rest from North America (16 percent), Asia and Australia (8 percent), and Russia (6 percent) (Exhibit MC5.1). Although IKEA's largest market is in Germany (14 percent of total sales), its fastest-growing markets are the United States, China, and Russia. Exhibit MC5.2 shows IKEA's growth in the number of stores and revenues worldwide since 1974. Known today for its iconic blue-and-yellow big-box retail stores, focusing on flat-pack furniture boxes combined with a large DIY component, IKEA started as a small retail outlet in 1943 by then-17-year-old Ingvar Kamprad.

Though IKEA has become a global phenomenon, it was initially slow to internationalize. It took 20 years before the company expanded beyond Sweden to its neighboring country of Norway. After honing and refining its core competencies of designing modern functional home furnishings at low prices and offering a unique retail experience in its home market, IKEA followed an *international strategy,* expanding first to Europe, and then beyond. Using an international strategy allowed IKEA to sell the same types of home furnishings across the globe with little adaptation (although it does make some allowances for country preferences). Because IKEA focuses on low cost, it shifted more recently from an international strategy to a global-standardization strategy, in which it attempts to achieve economies of scale through effectively managing a global supply chain. Although

EXHIBIT MC5.1 / IKEA's Sales by Geographic Region (2012)

SOURCE: Author's depiction of data from "IKEA's Yearly Summary FY 2012" (www.ikea.com).

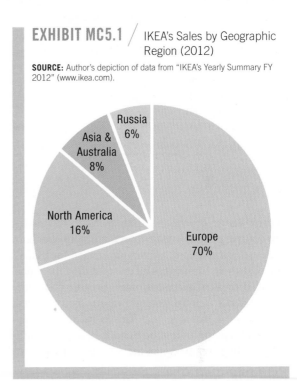

Asia accounts currently for only 8 percent of its sales, IKEA sources 32 percent of its inputs (mostly timber) from this region. To drive costs down further, IKEA has begun to implement production techniques from auto and electronics industries, in which cutting-edge technologies are employed to address complexity while achieving flexibility and low cost.

Despite its success, IKEA faces significant challenges going forward. Opening new stores is critical

EXHIBIT MC5.2 / IKEA Stores and Revenues, 1974–2012

SOURCES: Author's depiction of data from "The secret of IKEA's success," *The Economist*, February 24, 2011, and various IKEA "Yearly Summaries" (www.ikea.com).

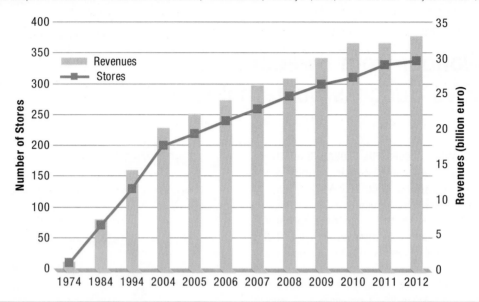

to drive future growth (see Exhibit MC5.2). Finding new sources of supply to support more store openings, however, is a challenge. Although demand for IKEA's low-cost home furnishings increased during the global financial crisis as more customers became price conscious, IKEA's annual store growth has slowed to less than five new stores a year. This is because its supply chain has become a bottleneck. IKEA has difficulty finding suppliers that are a strategic fit with its highly efficient operations. Related to this issue is the fact that wood remains one of IKEA's main input factors, and the world's consumers are becoming more sensitive to the issue of deforestation and its possible link to global warming. In the near future, IKEA must find low-cost replacement materials for wood. In addition, powerful competitors have taken notice of IKEA's success. Although IKEA is growing in North America, it holds less than 5 percent of the home-furnishings market. In some European markets, IKEA holds 30 percent market share. To keep IKEA at bay in the U.S., Target has recently recruited top designers and launched a wide range of low-priced furnishings. Kmart, likewise, has enrolled Martha Stewart to help with the design of its offerings of home furnishings.

Besides these external challenges, IKEA also faces significant internal ones. Since the company's founding in 1943, no strategic decisions have been made without Mr. Kamprad's involvement and explicit approval. In 2013, Mr. Kamprad (now in his late 80s) announced he is stepping down from chairing Inter IKEA, the foundation that owns the company. Many observers compare Mr. Kamprad's influence on IKEA's culture and organization to that of the legendary Sam Walton at Walmart. Mr. Kamprad's three sons will take on stronger leadership roles at IKEA, with one of them now chairing Inter IKEA.

Moreover, IKEA is privately held (through a complicated network of foundations and holding companies in the Netherlands, Lichtenstein, and Luxembourg). This arrangement provides benefits in terms of reducing tax exposure, but also creates constraints in accessing large sums of capital needed for rapid global expansion. IKEA will need to address these challenges in order to live up to its strategic intent of doubling its number of yearly openings in an attempt to capture a larger slice of fast-growing markets such as the U.S., China, and Russia.

DISCUSSION QUESTIONS

Review Chapter 3: External Analysis: Industry Structure, Competitive Forces, and Strategic Groups.

1. List IKEA's external and internal challenges. Looking at IKEA's challenges, which ones do you think pose the greatest threat? Why? How would you address the challenges?

2. Walmart entered a period of difficulties after Sam Walton stepped down. Do you anticipate IKEA having the same leadership transition challenges? Why or why not?

3. Did it surprise you to learn that both a developed country (the United States) and also emerging economies (i.e., China and Russia) are the fastest-growing international markets for IKEA? Does this fact pose any challenges in the way IKEA ought to compete across the globe? Why or why not?

4. What can IKEA do to continue to drive growth globally, especially given its strategic intent to double annual store openings?

5. Assume you are hired to consult IKEA on the topic of *corporate social responsibility* (see the discussion in Chapter 2). Which areas would you recommend the company be most sensitive to, and how should these be addressed?

Sources: This MiniCase is based on "IKEA: How the Swedish retailer became a global cult brand," *BusinessWeek*, November 14, 2005; "Flat-pack accounting," *The Economist*, May 11, 2006; "Shocking tell-all book takes aim at Ikea," *Bloomberg Businessweek*, November 12, 2009; Peng, M. (2009), *Global Strategy*, 2nd ed. (Mason, OH: South-Western Cengage); "The secret of IKEA's success," *The Economist*, February 24, 2011; "IKEA to accelerate expansion," *The Wall Street Journal*, September 18, 2012; "Ingvar Kamprad steps back," *The Economist*, June 5, 2013; and various IKEA Yearly Summaries (www.ikea.com).

Starbucks: Re-creating Its Uniqueness

INSPIRED BY ITALIAN COFFEE BARS, Starbucks' CEO Howard Schultz set out to provide a completely new consumer experience. The trademark of any Starbucks coffeehouse is its ambience—where music and comfortable chairs and sofas encourage customers to sit and enjoy their beverages. While hanging out at Starbucks (Ticker: SBUX), they can use the complimentary wireless hotspot or just visit with friends. The barista seems to speak a foreign language as she rattles off the offerings: Caffé Misto, Caramel Macchiato, Cinnamon Dolce Latte, Espresso Con Panna, and Starbucks' Mint Mocha Chip Frappuccino are among some 30 different coffee blends. Dazzled and enchanted, customers pay $4 or more for a Venti-sized drink. Starbucks has been so successful in creating its ambience that customers keep coming back for more.

Starbucks' core competency is to create a unique consumer experience the world over. That is what customers are paying for, not the cup of coffee or tea. The consumer experience Starbucks created was a valuable, rare, and costly-to-imitate intangible resource. This allowed the company to gain a competitive advantage.

While core competencies are often built through learning from experience, these competencies can atrophy through forgetting. This is what happened to Starbucks. Between 2004 and 2008, Starbucks expanded operations rapidly by doubling the number of stores from 8,500 to almost 17,000 stores (see Exhibit MC6.1). It also branched out into ice cream, desserts, sandwiches, books, music, and other retail merchandise, straying from its core business. Trying to keep up with its explosive growth in both the number of stores and product offerings, Starbucks began to forget what made it unique. It lost the appeal that made it special, and its unique culture became diluted. For example, baristas used to grind beans throughout the day whenever a new pot of coffee had to be brewed (which was at least every eight minutes). The grinding sounds and fresh coffee aroma were trademarks

of Starbucks stores. Instead, to accommodate its fast growth, many baristas began to grind all of the day's coffee beans in the morning and store them for the rest of the day. To make matters worse, in 2008 the global financial crisis hit. The first items consumers go without during recession are luxury items such as a $4 coffee at Starbucks (see revenue drop in Exhibit MC6.1).

Coming out of an eight-year retirement, Howard Schultz again took the reins as CEO and president in January 2008, attempting to re-create what had made Starbucks special. In 2009, Starbucks introduced Via, its new instant coffee, a move that some worried might further dilute the brand. In the fall of 2010, Schultz rolled out a new guideline: Baristas would no longer multitask, making multiple drinks at the same time, but would instead focus on no more than two drinks at a time, starting a second one while finishing the first. The goal was to bring back the customer experience that built the Starbucks brand. By the summer of 2013, Starbucks operated some 21,000 stores in over 60 countries, bringing in $14 billion in annual revenues.

DISCUSSION QUESTIONS

Review Chapter 4: Internal Analysis: Resources, Capabilities, and Core Competencies.

1. What resources and capabilities formed the basis of the uniqueness of Starbucks in the first place? Why was it so successful?

2. To be a source of competitive advantage over time, core competencies need to be honed and upgraded continuously (see Exhibit 4.4, in Chapter 4).
   a. Why and how did Starbucks lose its uniqueness?
   b. How is Starbucks re-creating its uniqueness? Do you think it will be successful over time? Why or why not?

Frank T. Rothaermel prepared this MiniCase from public sources. It is developed for the purpose of class discussion. It is not intended to be used for any kind of endorsement, source of data, or depiction of efficient or inefficient management. All opinions expressed, and all errors and omissions, are entirely the author's. © Rothaermel, 2014.

EXHIBIT MC6.1 / Total Number of Starbucks Stores, 1971–2013

SOURCES: Author's depiction of data drawn from various Starbucks Annual Reports and "Forty years young: A history of Starbucks," *The Telegraph*, May 11, 2011.

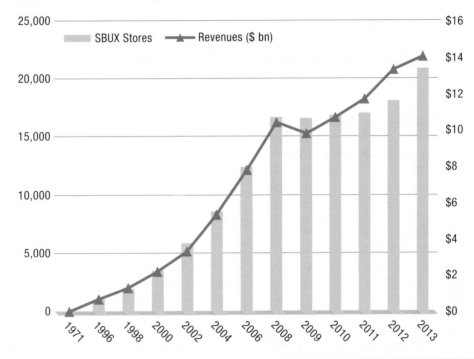

3. What recommendations would you give Howard Schultz to sustain a competitive advantage over time? Support your arguments.

Sources: This MiniCase is based on Schultz, H., and D. J. Yang (1999), *Pour Your Heart into It: How Starbucks Built a Company One Cup at a Time* (New York: Hyperion); Behar, H. (2007), *It's Not About the Coffee: Leadership Principles from a Life at Starbucks* (New York: Portfolio); "Latest Starbucks buzzword: 'Lean' Japanese techniques," *The Wall Street Journal*, August 4, 2009; "At Starbucks, baristas told no more than two drinks," *The Wall Street Journal*, October 13, 2010; "Forty years young: A history of Starbucks," *The Telegraph*, May 11, 2011; and http://investor.starbucks.com.

LVMH in China: Building Its Empire of Desire

IN JULY 2012, Louis Vuitton, the flagship brand of France's Moët Hennessy Louis Vuitton S.A., better known as LVMH, opened its 16th global "Maison" at Shanghai's Plaza 66, a mega luxury mall. The Shanghai Maison houses the entire range of Louis Vuitton collections, from high-fashion clothing and leather goods, to jewelry, watches, cosmetics, and wines and spirits. The grand opening of the Shanghai Maison also coincided with the 20th anniversary of the brand's presence in China; Louis Vuitton had opened its first store in the country in 1992, in Beijing's Peninsula Hotel.

LVMH's sales in Asia accounted for one third of its total revenue by the end of the first quarter of 2013.[1] Those results made Asia the largest region for LVMH in terms of revenues (Exhibit MC7.1). Focusing on countries rather than regions, China is the world's biggest luxury market (Exhibit MC7.2), having achieved an average annual growth rate of 27 percent from 2008 to 2012.

Louis Vuitton loves China, and the Chinese love Louis Vuitton. In a recent Chinese luxury consumer survey published by the Hurun Research Institute, Louis Vuitton topped the list as the number-one and number-two preferred luxury brand by Chinese men and women, respectively. Although the brand's heritage and craftsmanship are attractive characteristics to Chinese consumers, they are not solely responsible for opening the wallets of affluent Chinese. Louis Vuitton's steep prices and glamorous prestige are reflected onto its customers, and Chinese luxury customers value being recognized as wealthy elites with high social status. To stay apart from (or atop) the crowd is what Chinese customers crave in a densely populated and formerly egalitarian (communist) society. The brand's image reinforcement is so powerful that even many in China's middle class aspire to become owners of Louis Vuitton goods. On average, Chinese Louis Vuitton customers are younger than their Western counterparts. Moreover, they spend a significantly higher amount of their disposable income on LVMH's luxury status symbols.

With an eager consumer base and a lack of local competitors, there is probably no stronger tailwind an international brand could hope for in China. LVMH's years of heavy marketing to raise consumer brand recognition have paid off: Goods fly off the shelves, and every single store LVMH has opened in China is profitable.

LVMH managed its growth well. Since its formation in 1987, it has become the world's largest luxury conglomerate, owning more than 60 brands and 3,200 stores worldwide.[2] It has a remarkable track record in Asia: 85 percent of Japanese women own a Louis Vuitton product, for example. With an early entry into China, LVMH was also able to take advantage of the country's increasing growth to become the largest luxury market worldwide. Not only did LVMH capture the luxury lovers in Beijing and Shanghai, but it also opened stores in second-tier provincial capitals and wealthier third-tier cities in the west, where rapid growth was expected.

After nearly a decade of successful expansion, LVMH recently turned more cautious, though. LVMH's concern in China is to "avoid becoming too commonplace."[3] Although the newly rich in second- and third-tier cities still crave luxury goods, consumer tastes in Beijing and Shanghai may be maturing. Chinese in the major cities have become well-traveled global consumers and are shying away from "logo-heavy" mega brands. Increasingly, they are more sophisticated consumers, embracing uniqueness and understatement in luxury items.

To respond to changing consumer tastes, LVMH stopped opening new stores in China and launched the Shanghai Maison with invitation-only floors. It also offers custom made-to-order bags using exotic animal

Frank T. Rothaermel and Carrie Yang (GT MBA, MSc.) prepared this Mini-Case from public sources. It is developed for the purpose of class discussion. It is not intended to be used for any kind of endorsement, source of data, or depiction of efficient or inefficient management. All opinions expressed, and all errors and omissions, are entirely the authors'. © Rothaermel and Yang, 2014.

EXHIBIT MC7.1 / LVMH's Sales by Geographic Region

SOURCE: Authors' depiction of data from LVMH Annual Reports, 2002–Q1 2013.

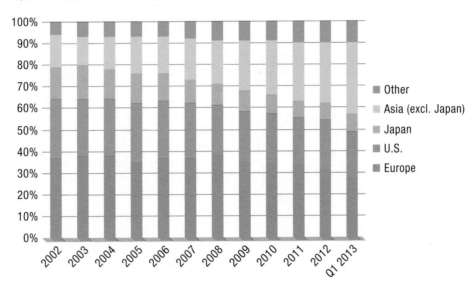

skins, to project exclusivity for the very top-end customers. It began to focus on leather products with high value added rather than the entry-level-priced canvas logo style. In addition, LVMH has promoted a set of "logo-free" handbags targeted exclusively at high-end Chinese customers.

But LVMH's decision to limit store growth may have another reason: The Chinese are more often choosing to buy abroad. The main reasons Chinese consumers cite for shopping overseas are lower prices (due to China's high luxury taxes), better selection, and greater "show-off" value. It is quite common to find busloads of Chinese tourists lining up outside Louis Vuitton's boutique on Avenue des Champs-Elysées in Paris to purchase merchandise.

Although such purchases in the Paris store have created growth for LVMH Europe, they also pose challenges such as managing inventory and providing adequate service. Before a

recent holiday season, for example, Louis Vuitton had to put in drastic measures to slow sales. In its flagship Paris store, LVMH limited the total number of leather products available for purchase for each customer and reduced store hours. In addition, Louis Vuitton's

EXHIBIT MC7.2 / Luxury Market by Consumer Nationality

SOURCE: Authors' depiction of data from "Luxury goods in China: Beyond bling," *The Economist*, June 8, 2013.

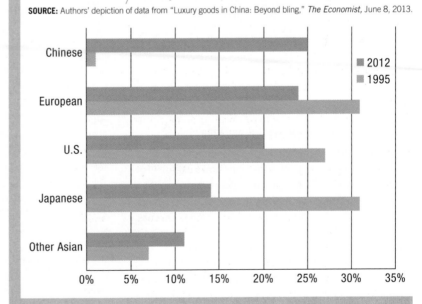

European stores have hired Mandarin-speaking staff who are trained to better meet Chinese needs and better handle the spikes of tour-bus traffic. Meanwhile, LVMH aims to strengthen its relationship with Chinese customers at home by providing premium services and enhancing their shopping experience. As long as the price difference exists, however, stores abroad will continue to be Chinese customers' preferred shopping destinations.

Like all other luxury brands, LVMH has to constantly fight against the counterfeiting of its products, especially the Louis Vuitton brand. China's dominance in manufacturing and its general lack of enforcement of intellectual property laws have made it the location for the manufacture of more than 80 percent of the estimated $300 billion counterfeit industry. To keep some control over its products, LVMH manufactures its leather goods in company-owned factories in France, Switzerland, Germany, Italy, Spain, and the United States. Since the early 2000s, LVMH's Chinese anti-counterfeiting team, together with its global specialists and investigators, has raised public awareness of counterfeits and stemmed the flow of the counterfeits from China to the developed world. It also brought legal actions against pirates who made fake goods, as well as landlords who provided operation locations for the pirates. LVMH has achieved much anti-counterfeiting success in China, including winning several recent cases in Chinese courts. But as long as the popularity of its Louis Vuitton bag lasts, the anti-counterfeiting battle goes on, further contributing to a potential loss of exclusivity.

DISCUSSION QUESTIONS

Review Chapter 4: Internal Analysis: Resources, Capabilities, and Core Competencies.

1. Why is LVMH so successful in China?

2. Louis Vuitton is LVMH's flagship brand. Much of Louis Vuitton's appeal is that it bestows exclusivity on its owners. In the last few years, however, the Louis Vuitton logo has been applied to handbags and accessories at an unprecedented rate. Discuss the challenges to the value of the brand as LVMH responds by introducing more luxury handbags and accessories without displaying the logo.

3. LVMH is also confronting the problem of proliferation of the LV logo through excessive counterfeiting activity. How can LVMH use its strengths to overcome threats from counterfeiters?

4. How does LVMH encourage Chinese customers to purchase LVMH products in China rather than abroad? Do you think these strategic initiatives will be successful? Why or why not? What other ideas do you think LVMH should pursue to encourage Chinese customers to purchase LVMH products in China?

5. Given a backlash in China against *conspicuous consumption* (the spending of money on luxury goods to publicly display wealth and status), what recommendations would you give LVMH?

6. Other luxury brands such as Chanel, Burberry, and Gucci are building a presence in the large luxury-goods market in China. What actions might LVMH take to sustain its strong position in the market?

Endnotes

1. Excluding Japan; LVMH does not break down sales for China separately.

2. LVMH's famous brands include Louis Vuitton (fashion and leather goods), Bulgari and Tag Heuer (watches and jewelry), Moët et Chandon and Dom Pérignon (wines and spirits), and Dior (fashion, perfumes, and cosmetics).

3. "Louis Vuitton slows expansion to protect image," *The Globe and Mail,* January 31, 2013.

Sources: This MiniCase is based on LVMH's Annual Reports, 2002–Q1 2013; "Louis Vuitton's Steven Liew: Protecting IP in China," *Asialaw,* October 2005; "Made in China on the sly," *The New York Times,* November 23, 2007; "LVMH: The empire of desire," *The Economist,* June 2, 2012; "Event watch: Louis Vuitton Shanghai Maison grand opening," *Jing Daily,* July 10, 2012; "LVMH faces dilemma of success," *Financial Times,* October 19, 2012; "Luxury without borders: China's new class of shoppers take on the world," *McKinsey & Company,* December 2012; "Louis Vuitton slows expansion to protect image," *The Globe and Mail,* January 31, 2013; "Has luxury peaked in mainland China," *South China Morning Post,* May 22, 2013; "LVMH rushes to keep up with China's changing tastes," *Jing Daily,* May 27, 2013; "For luxury brands targeting China, expansion to lower-tier cities beckons," *Jing Daily,* June 5, 2013; "Luxury goods in China: Beyond bling," *The Economist,* June 8, 2013; and "Wealthy Chinese love French luxury goods," *South China Morning Post,* June 21, 2013.

GE under Jack Welch vs. Jeffrey Immelt

AN INVESTMENT OF $100 in General Electric (GE) on April 22, 1981, when Jack Welch took over as chairman and CEO would have been worth $6,320 by 2000. Including stock price appreciation plus dividends, GE's total shareholder return was 6,220 percent during this period, equating to an annual compounded growth rate of about 23 percent.

Although the sheer magnitude of GE's total returns to shareholders is impressive, to assess whether GE had a competitive advantage that produced that return, we need a benchmark. Because GE is a widely diversified conglomerate spanning financial and industrial operations across a number of different industries, one common metric for comparison is a broad stock market index such as the Dow Jones Industrial Average (DJIA). The DJIA (or Dow 30) represents an average stock return, based on the stock prices of the 30 most widely held public companies in the U.S. The DJIA was established in 1896, and GE is the only company remaining from its original members (although GE was delisted for a number of years).

Although the DJIA had a return of slightly over 1,000 percent between 1981 and the end of 2000, this return is dwarfed when compared with GE's (see Exhibit MC8.1). This comparison implies that GE outperformed the DJIA by several multiples during this 20-year time period.

When we apply total return to shareholders as a performance metric, GE's total return of 6,220 percent is astonishing. GE clearly enjoyed a *sustained competitive advantage* during the Jack Welch era. This feat is even more impressive for two reasons. First, the calculation was set in a way that both started at 0 percent in 1981. Second, GE is one of the 30 companies included in the DJIA, and thus it is one big reason why the DJIA performed quite well during the 1981–2000 time frame.

Jeffrey Immelt was appointed GE's CEO and chairman on September 7, 2001, just four days before the 9/11 terrorist attacks. Since that tragedy, Mr. Immelt

had spent his time putting out fire after fire. Following 9/11, the U.S. economy went into a recession, and a global economic slowdown began. Several of GE's key industrial sectors such as aviation and energy were especially hard hit. The global financial crisis beginning in 2008 compounded the company's troubles even further. Because the conglomerate relied on its financial services unit, GE Capital, for more than 50 percent of its profits, the company was hit especially hard during the global financial crisis. In 2009, Standard & Poor's downgraded GE's AAA credit rating, further underscoring the market's lost confidence in GE's financial health. GE asked famed investor Warren Buffett for a $15 billion liquidity injection. On March 5, 2009, GE's share price hit an all-time low of $6.66. The performance of GE's stock versus the DJIA during Mr. Immelt's tenure is depicted in Exhibit MC8.2.

DISCUSSION QUESTIONS

Review Chapter 5: Competitive Advantage, Firm Performance, and Business Models.

1. Do you agree with the claim that "GE experienced a *sustained competitive advantage* under Jack Welch, while it experienced a *sustained competitive disadvantage* under Jeffrey Immelt"? Why or why not?

2. How much of the performance difference in the Welch versus Immelt time periods do you believe can be directly attributed to the respective CEO? What other factors might have played an important role in determining firm performance? (Hint: Consider especially the time period since 2001.)

Frank T. Rothaermel prepared this MiniCase from public sources. It is developed for the purpose of class discussion. It is not intended to be used for any kind of endorsement, source of data, or depiction of efficient or inefficient management. All opinions expressed, and all errors and omissions, are entirely the author's. © Rothaermel, 2014.

EXHIBIT MC8.1 / GE under Jack Welch: GE Stock Performance vs. DJIA, April 1981–September 2001

PRICE HISTORY - GE (4/1/1981 - 9/6/2001) ── General Electric Co ── Dow Jones Industrial Average Index

EXHIBIT MC8.2 / GE under Jeffrey Immelt: GE Stock Performance vs. DJIA, September 2001–September 2013

General Electric Company (GE)

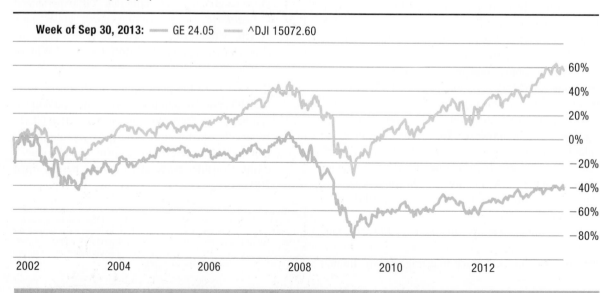

Week of Sep 30, 2013: ── GE 24.05 ── ^DJI 15072.60

3. Shareholder value creation is one of the metrics to assess firm performance. Do you consider this metric to be the most important one? Why or why not?

4. If you were to use a balanced-scorecard or triple-bottom-line approach to assessing firm performance and competitive advantage, how might those approaches change your assessment of the Welch and Immelt eras? If Jack Welch had been more focused on broader measures of firm performance, might GE have been better able to weather the post-2001 changes?

Sources: This MiniCase is based on "GE's Welch will be a tough act to follow; Math shows stock unlikely to repeat its rise," *The New York Times*, November 28, 2000; Glader, P. (2009), "GE's Immelt to cite lessons learned," *The Wall Street Journal*, December 15; and various GE Annual Reports.

Competing on Business Models: Google vs. Microsoft

RIVALS OFTEN USE different business models to compete with one another. Due to competitive dynamics and industry convergence, Google and Microsoft progressively move on to the other's turf. In many areas, Google and Microsoft are now direct competitors. In 2012, Microsoft had $73 billion in revenues and Google $50 billion. Although Google started out as an online search and advertising company, it now offers software applications (Google Docs, word processing, spreadsheet programs, e-mail, interactive calendars, and presentation software) and operating systems (Chrome OS for the Web; Android for mobile applications), among many other online products and services. In contrast, Microsoft began its life by offering an operating system (since 1985, called Windows), then moved into software applications with its Office Suite, and into online search and advertising with Bing, as well as online gaming with Xbox One. The stage is set for a clash of the technology titans.

In competing with each other, Google and Microsoft pursue very different business models, as detailed in Exhibit MC9.1.[1] Google offers its applications software Google Docs for free to induce and retain as many users as possible for its search engine. Although Google's flagship search engine is free for the end user, Google makes money from sponsored links by advertisers. The advertisers pay for the placement of their ad on the results pages and every time a user clicks through an ad (which Google calls a "sponsored link"). Many billions of mini-transactions like this add up to a substantial business. As shown in Exhibit MC9.2, advertising revenues account for close to 90 percent of Google's total revenues.

As indicated in Exhibit MC9.1, Google uses part of the profits earned from its lucrative online advertising business to subsidize Google Docs. Giving away products and services to induce widespread use allows Google to benefit from *network effects*—the increase in the value of a product or service as more people use it. Google can charge advertisers for highly targeted and effective ads, allowing it to subsidize other product offerings that compete directly with Microsoft.

As indicated by the opposing arrows in Exhibit MC9.1, Microsoft's business model is almost the reverse of Google's. Initially, Microsoft focused on creating a large installed base of users for its PC operating system (Windows). It holds some 90 percent market share in operating system software for personal computers worldwide. As shown in Exhibit MC9.3, roughly 50 percent of Microsoft's revenues are based on the Windows franchise. Moreover, the users are locked into a Microsoft operating system (which generally comes preloaded with the computer they purchased), and then want to buy applications that run seamlessly with the operating system. The obvious choice for most users is Microsoft's Office Suite (containing Word, Excel, PowerPoint, Outlook, and Access), but they need to pay several hundred dollars for the latest version. This application software segment (called "Microsoft Business Division," see Exhibit MC9.3) contributes roughly one-third of Microsoft's total revenues. This implies that over 80 percent of Microsoft's revenues are either tied directly or indirectly to its Windows franchise.

As shown in Exhibit MC9.1, Microsoft uses the profits from its application software business to subsidize its search engine Bing, which is—just like Google's—a free product offering for the end user. Given Bing's relatively small market share, however, and the tremendous cost in developing the search

Frank T. Rothaermel prepared this MiniCase from public sources. It is developed for the purpose of class discussion. It is not intended to be used for any kind of endorsement, source of data, or depiction of efficient or inefficient management. All opinions expressed, and all errors and omissions, are entirely the author's. The author is grateful for research assistance by Vivek Viswanathan (GT MBA and MSc.). © Rothaermel, 2014.

EXHIBIT MC9.1 / Competing Business Models: Google vs. Microsoft

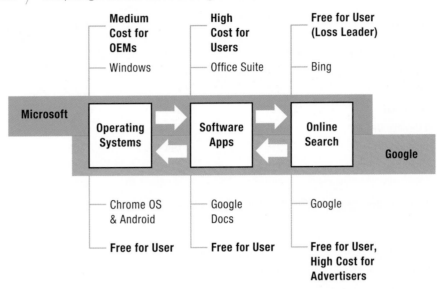

EXHIBIT MC9.2 / Breakdown of Google's Revenues by Business Segment, 2009–2012

Revenues ($ in millions)	2012	2011	2010	2009
Google Websites	$31,221	$26,145	$19,444	$15,723
Google Network Members' Websites	12,465	10,386	8,792	7,166
Total Advertising Revenues	43,686	36,531	28,236	22,889
Other Revenues	2,354	1,374	1,085	762
Total Google Revenues	46,040	37,905	29,321	23,651
Total Motorola Mobile Revenues	4,136	NA	NA	NA
Total Consolidated Revenues	50,175	37,905	29,321	23,651

engine, Microsoft, unlike Google, does not make any money from its online search offering; rather, it is a big money loser.

The logic behind Bing is to provide a countervailing power to Google's dominant position in online search. The logic behind Google Docs is to create a threat to Microsoft's dominant position in application software. Moreover, the computing industry is undergoing a shift away from personal computers to mobile devices. Although Microsoft set the standard and dominates the industry with Windows, Google holds some 75 percent market share in mobile operating systems software with Android, while Microsoft's market share is less than 5 percent. These tactics create *multipoint competition* between the two technology firms.[2] Taken together, Google and Microsoft compete with one another for market share in several different product categories through quite different business models.

DISCUSSION QUESTIONS

Review Chapter 5: Competitive Advantage, Firm Performance, and Business Models.

1. How is a strategy different from a business model? How is it similar?

2. Why are Microsoft and Google becoming increasingly direct competitors?

3. Looking at Exhibits MC9.2 and MC9.3, calculate the annual growth rates for Google's

EXHIBIT MC9.3 / Breakdown of Microsoft's Revenues by Business Segment, 2009–2012

Revenues ($ in millions)	2012	2011	2010	2009
Windows and Windows Live Division	$18,373	$19,033	$19,491	$14,712
Server and Tools (Windows)	18,686	16,680	15,109	14,126
Online Services Division	2,867	2,607	2,294	3,088
Microsoft Business Division	23,991	22,514	19,256	18,894
Entertainment and Devices Division	9,593	8,915	6,079	7,753
Unallocated and Other	213	194	255	145
Total Consolidated Revenues	73,723	69,943	62,484	58,718

and Microsoft's different business segments. What trend emerges? What conclusions can you draw?

4. What recommendations would you give to the CEO of Microsoft to compete more effectively against Google?

5. What recommendations would you give to the CEO of Google to compete more effectively against Microsoft?

Endnotes

1. Anderson, C. (2009), *Free: The Future of a Radical Price* (New York: Hyperion); Levy, S. (2011), *In the Plex: How Google Thinks, Works, and Shapes Our Lives* (New York: Simon & Schuster); Adner, R. (2012), *The Wide Lens. A New Strategy for Innovation* (New York: Portfolio); and "The quest for a third mobile platform," *The Wall Street Journal,* May 6, 2013.

2. Chen, M. J. (1996), "Competitor analysis and interfirm rivalry: Toward a theoretical integration," *Academy of Management Review* 21: 100–134; Gimeno, J. (1999), "Reciprocal threats in multimarket rivalry: Staking out 'spheres of influence' in the U.S. airline industry," *Strategic Management Journal* 20: 101–128; and Gimeno, J., and C. Y. Woo (1999), "Multimarket competition, economies of scale, and firm performance," *Academy of Management Journal* 42: 239–259.

From Good to Great to Gone: The Rise and Fall of Circuit City

IN THE 1990S, Circuit City was the largest and most successful consumer-electronics retailer in the United States. Indeed, Circuit City was so successful it was included as one of only 11 companies featured in Jim Collins' bestseller *Good to Great.* To qualify for this august group of high performers, a company had to attain "extraordinary results, averaging cumulative stock returns 6.9 times the general market in the 15 years following their transition points."[1] Indeed, Circuit City was *the best-performing* company on Collins' good-to-great list, outperforming the stock market 18.5 times during the 1982–1997 period.

How did Circuit City become so successful? The company was able to build and refine a set of core competencies that enabled it to create a higher economic value than its competitors. In particular, Circuit City created world-class competencies in efficient and effective logistics expertise. It deployed sophisticated point-of-sale and inventory-tracking technology, supported by IT investments that enabled the firm to connect the flow of information among geographically dispersed stores. This expertise in turn allowed detailed tracking of customer preferences and enabled Circuit City to respond quickly to changing trends. The company also relied on highly motivated, well-trained sales personnel to provide superior service and thus build and maintain customer loyalty. These core competencies enabled Circuit City to implement a "4S business model"—service, selection, savings, and satisfaction—that it applied to big-ticket consumer electronics with an unmatched degree of consistency throughout the United States.

Perhaps even more important during the company's high-performance run, many capable competitors were unable to replicate Circuit City's core competencies. Further underscoring Circuit City's superior performance is the fact, as Jim Collins described it, that "if you had to choose between $1 invested in Circuit

SOURCE: http://www.wired.com/gadgetlab/2009/03/circuit-city-st/

City or $1 invested in General Electric on the day that the legendary Jack Welch took over GE in 1981 and held [that investment] to January 1, 2000, you would have been better off with Circuit City—by [a factor of]

Frank T. Rothaermel prepared this MiniCase from public sources. It is developed for the purpose of class discussion. It is not intended to be used for any kind of endorsement, source of data, or depiction of efficient or inefficient management. All opinions expressed, and all errors and omissions, are entirely the author's. © Rothaermel, 2014.

six times."[2] In the fall of 2008, however, Circuit City filed for bankruptcy. So what happened?

Circuit City's core competencies lost value because the firm neglected to upgrade and protect them. As a consequence, it was outflanked by Best Buy and online retailers such as Amazon. Moreover, Circuit City's top management team was also distracted by pursuing noncore activities such as the creation of CarMax, a retail chain for used cars, a foray into providing an alternative to video rentals through its proprietary DivX DVD player, and an attempted merger with Blockbuster (which filed for bankruptcy in 2010).

Perhaps the biggest blunder that Circuit City's top-management team committed was to lay off 3,000 of the firm's highest-paid sales personnel. The layoff was done to become more cost-competitive with Best Buy and, in particular, the burgeoning online retailers. The problem was that the highest-paid salespeople were also the most experienced and loyal ones, better able to provide superior customer service. It appears that laying off key human capital—given their valuable, rare, and difficult-to-imitate nature—was a supreme strategic mistake! Not only did Circuit City destroy part of its core competency, it also allowed its main competitor—Best Buy—to recruit Circuit City's top salespeople. With that transfer of personnel to Best Buy went the transfer of important tacit knowledge underlying some of Circuit City's core competencies, which in turn not only eroded Circuit City's advantage but also allowed Best Buy to upgrade its core competencies. In particular, Best Buy went on to develop its innovative "customer-centricity" model, based on a set of skills that allowed its store employees to identify and more effectively serve specific customer segments. Highlighting the dynamic nature of the competitive process, however, Best Buy now faces its own challenges competing with online retailers such as Amazon.

Employees at Circuit City stores and even at the headquarters in Richmond, Virginia, were shocked and devastated when the firm actually ceased operations in March 2009. More than a year after the closing, former headquarters workers noted that the firm had a good, hard-working, and family-friendly atmosphere. They believed to the end that, in the worst case, another firm would buy Circuit City and perhaps reduce its size but not permanently close the business.[3]

DISCUSSION QUESTIONS

Review Chapter 6: Business Strategy: Differentiation, Cost Leadership, and Integration.

1. Why was Circuit City so successful as to be featured in *Good to Great?* What was its strategic position during its successful period? How did it contribute to competitive advantage?

2. Why did Circuit City lose its competitive advantage? What was Circuit City's strategic position during the time of its competitive disadvantage?

3. What could Circuit City's management have done differently?

4. What is the future of Best Buy as the leader in big-box electronics retailing as it faces tough competition with Amazon and other online retailers? What core competencies in big-box retailing are critical not only to survive but also to gain and sustain a competitive advantage?

Endnotes

1. Collins, J. (2001), *Good to Great: Why Some Companies Make the Leap . . . and Others Don't* (New York: HarperCollins), p. 3.

2. Ibid., p. 33.

3. Collins, J. (2001), *Good to Great;* and Collins, J. (2009), *How the Mighty Fall: And Why Some Companies Never Give In* (New York: HarperCollins); and *A Tale of Two Cities: The Circuit City Story,* film documentary by Tom Wulf, released November 2010.

China's Li Ning Challenges Nike and adidas

ALMOST EVERYONE IN CHINA knows Li Ning Company Ltd. The eponymous sportswear company was founded in 1990 by former star gymnast Li Ning, who won six medals (including three golds) at the 1984 Los Angeles Olympics. Riding on the fame of its founder, Li Ning quickly became the largest and best-known Chinese sportswear company. In parallel with China's incredible economic rise, Li Ning did exceptionally well.

The company decided that the 2008 Olympics in Beijing would mark the beginning of overtaking the world leaders in sports shoes and apparel, Nike and adidas. This would happen first in the Chinese market and then globally. To symbolize the company rise, its founder Li Ning, still a popular folk hero, was chosen to light the Olympic flame during the Beijing opening ceremonies. With its home turf advantage, everything seemed to be going in Li Ning's favor. In March 2013, however, Li Ning shocked the business world by announcing a worse-than-expected annual loss of $315 million. This was Li Ning's first ever loss since going public in 2004. Just two years earlier in 2010, Li Ning reported an all-time-high revenue of $1.5 billion, with $182.3 million in net income. What happened?

Li Ning's strategic intent had been from the very beginning to overtake Nike and adidas. The Beijing Olympics were to be the turning point in this "epic battle" for market dominance. In anticipation of the enormous business opportunities that would come with the 2008 Beijing Olympics, Li Ning pushed its penetration into China's second- and third-tier cities via aggressive channel expansion through its distributors, adding almost 1,000 stores a year (Exhibit MC11.1). In 2008 and 2009 alone, more than 80 percent of the new stores were opened in China's second- and third-tier cities.

China's rapid urbanization and the post-Olympics effects echoed Li Ning's vision: from 2005 to 2010, Li Ning tripled its revenue and seemed to be overtaking adidas to become number two in the Chinese market,

just behind Nike (Exhibit MC11.2). Fueled by seemingly unstoppable success, Li Ning began to expand in Southeast Asia. In a brazen move, Li Ning even opened a specialty store across the Pacific in Portland, Oregon, the hometown of Nike.

Li Ning soon found that its local Chinese competitors were pursuing a similar expansion strategy. To make matters worse, even Nike and adidas joined the fray to compete aggressively in second- and third-tier cities. This was a departure from the usual business model where the two world leaders would focus on high-end markets such as Shanghai and Beijing. As the post-Olympic shopping enthusiasm gradually faded, competition further intensified. Realizing that the expansion-fueled growth was not sustainable, Li Ning began fine-tuning its business model: consolidating distributors, upgrading product offerings, and focusing on serving higher-end markets and younger consumers. Li Ning even changed its logo and slogan to promote the new image. Almost overnight, Li Ning's brand marketing campaign swept China's airwaves, towns, and cities.

Despite its best marketing efforts, Li Ning's inventory kept piling up. Against the backdrop of declining sales, Li Ning's cash flow soon drained. Given its financial squeeze, Li Ning had to raise funds from a private equity group and the Government of Singapore Investment Corporation. This led to a shake-up of Li Ning's board of directors, which subsequently put a new top management team in place. The top priority of the new management was to tackle Li Ning's inventory problems. Its management took several drastic steps to revive the sales channel by freeing up distributors' cash flows for introducing new products. Distributors were further consolidated and Li Ning added

Frank T. Rothaermel and Carrie Yang (GT MBA, MSc.) prepared this Mini-Case from public sources. It is developed for the purpose of class discussion. It is not intended to be used for any kind of endorsement, source of data, or depiction of efficient or inefficient management. All opinions expressed, and all errors and omissions, are entirely the authors'. © Rothaermel and Yang, 2014.

429

EXHIBIT MC11.1 / Li Ning's Financials, 2005–2012 ($ figures in millions)

SOURCE: Li Ning's Annual Reports; financial data are converted from Chinese RMB to U.S. dollars.

	2005	2006	2007	2008	2009	2010	2011	2012
Total stores at year-end	3,373	4,297	5,233	6,245	7,249	7,915	8,255	6,434
YoY store change	751	924	936	1,012	1,004	666	340	−1,821
Revenue	$395	$512	$700	$1,077	$1,351	$1,526	$1,438	$1,085
YoY revenue growth	30%	30%	37%	54%	25%	13%	−6%	−25%
Operating profit	$44	$65	$98	$155	$216	$249	$102	−$256
Net income	$30	$48	$76	$117	$156	$182	$66	−$315
Gross profit margin	47%	47%	48%	48%	47%	47%	46%	38%
Operating profit margin	11%	13%	14%	14%	16%	16%	7%	−24%
Average inventory turnover (days)	86	70	70	61	53	52	73	90
Average receivable turnover (days)	44	55	53	48	47	52	76	93
Average payable turnover (days)	68	67	69	69	70	71	97	112

more factory outlets and discount stores to speed up inventory clearance. All stores underwent careful performance evaluation. Eventually, Li Ning closed 1,821 underperforming stores.

In addition, Li Ning started implementing a transformation plan to gradually shift away from the distributor-driven business model to a market-oriented one. In the past, Li Ning's distributors made orders based on their own judgment of retail demand six months ahead at quarterly trade fairs, and so Li Ning would arrange production, deliveries, and marketing campaigns. Under the new plan, Li Ning introduced "A+" Stock Keeping Units (SKUs), as well as customer group–specific SKUs, helping distributors make sound ordering decisions. Once these SKUs hit the stores, Li Ning would collect and monitor

EXHIBIT MC11.2 / China's Sportswear Market Share by Brand Owner

SOURCE: Authors' depiction of data from "Li Ning scaling back after 2012 loss," *The Wall Street Journal*, March 27, 2013.

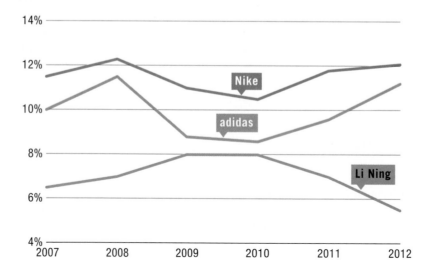

real-time sales data and make inventory adjustments accordingly. Li Ning launched fast-response products that could easily be ordered in between trade fairs in response to changes in market trends. It also redesigned product lines and changed pricing based on the needs of its target customers, which had not been clearly defined before.

The new management team at Li Ning believed that there was a big market between the higher-end Nike and adidas, on the one hand, and most of the low-end local brands, on the other. New products with a wider price range would be launched to capture the consumer in the "middle." Li Ning's transformation is nonetheless costly: revenue in 2012 declined by a whopping 25 percent to $1 billion (versus $26 billion for Nike and $20 billion for adidas). Li Ning's market share ranking in China has dropped to number four from number three (now held by a local competitor, Anta). To avoid bankruptcy, Li Ning had to ask for another round of liquidity injection by its recent backers.

Li Ning's problem of overexpansion is not unique. Slowing sales and high inventories have burdened other sportswear brands in China, including Nike and adidas. The two global brands have gained back their market shares, presumably at Li Ning's expense. Nike and adidas were faster in responding to changes in the market environment. They also further differentiated themselves from the pack through continued innovation and sophisticated marketing. For example, adidas introduced fashionable sportswear such as high-heeled sports shoes in China.

The only sportswear brand in China to post positive growth in 2012 was adidas, and it seems best positioned to gain from the country's $24 billion sportswear business, which is estimated to grow at 15 to 20 percent for the next three years. In contrast, Li Ning is in deep downsizing mode: stores, distributors, and business segments are all up to be cut in 2013. Its proud Portland venture and other overseas stores are long gone, and the company is now refocusing on the Chinese market only.

DISCUSSION QUESTIONS

Review Chapter 6: Business Strategy: Differentiation, Cost Leadership, and Integration.

1. At the close of the case, why was Li Ning experiencing a competitive disadvantage?

2. What are the strategic positions of Nike, adidas, and Li Ning (see Chapter 6)? Do you see a link between strategic position and firm performance? If so, what explains that link?

3. Why is it so difficult for Li Ning to challenge Nike and adidas even in China? Would you expect that the Chinese consumer would be more loyal to a Chinese brand? What moves could the company make that would build customer loyalty? What recommendations would you give Li Ning to achieve a successful turnaround? Explain.

Sources: This MiniCase is based on Li Ning's Annual Reports, 2004–2012; "Nike, adidas readjust marketing strategy," *China Daily*, August 30, 2010; "A year of rebuilding for China's Li Ning," *The Wall Street Journal*, December 2, 2012; "China's sportswear brands nurse Olympics hangover," *China Daily*, July 2, 2012; "Nike notes: Weak China results part of broader strategy," *Portland Business Journal*, December 20, 2012; "Li Ning stumbles over costly makeover plan," *South China Morning Post*, January 26, 2013; "Nike soars but China is its Achilles heel," *Financial Times*, March 21, 2013; "Li Ning scaling back after 2012 loss," *The Wall Street Journal*, March 27, 2013; "adidas sportswear is hot on Nike's heels in China," *The Wall Street Journal*, March 7, 2013.

Which Automotive Technology Will Win?

IN THE ENVISIONED TRANSITION away from gasoline-powered cars, Nissan's CEO Carlos Ghosn firmly believes the next technological paradigm will be electric motors. Mr. Ghosn calls hybrids a "halfway technology" and suggests they will be a temporary phenomenon at best. A number of startup companies, including Tesla Motors in the United States and BYD in China, share Ghosn's belief in this future scenario.

One of the biggest remaining impediments to large-scale adoption of electric vehicles, however, is the lack of appropriate infrastructure: There are few stations on the roads where drivers can recharge their car's battery when necessary. With the mileage range of electric vehicles currently limited to some 200 miles, many consider a lack of recharging stations a serious problem (so called "range anxiety"). Tesla Motors and others, however, are working hard to develop a network of superfast charging stations.

Nissan's Mr. Ghosn believes electric cars will account for 10 percent of global auto sales over the next decade. In contrast, Toyota is convinced gasoline-electric hybrids will become the next dominant technology. These different predictions have significant influence on what technology they decide to back and how much money Nissan and Toyota invest in that technology. Nissan's fully electric vehicle, the Leaf (an acronym for *Leading, Environmentally friendly, Affordable, Family car*), built at a plant in Smyrna, Tennessee, was introduced in 2010 in Japan and in 2011 in Europe, the U.S., and Canada. As of 2013, the Nissan Leaf is the best-selling all-electric car, with global sales of some 100,000 units.

Toyota is expanding its R&D investments in hybrid technology. Toyota has already sold some 4 million of its popular Prius cars since they were first introduced in 1997. By 2020, Toyota plans to offer hybrid technology in all its vehicles. Eventually, the investments made by Nissan and Toyota will yield different returns, depending on which predictions prove more accurate.

An alternative outcome is that neither hybrids nor electric cars will become the next paradigm. To add even more uncertainty to the mix, Honda and BMW are betting on cars powered by hydrogen fuel cells. In sum, many alternative technologies are competing to become the winner in setting a new standard for propelling cars. This situation is depicted in Exhibit MC12.1, where the new technologies represent a swarm of new entries vying for dominance. Only time will tell which technology will win this standard battle.

DISCUSSION QUESTIONS

Review Chapter 7: Business Strategy: Innovation and Entrepreneurship.

1. Do you believe that the internal combustion engine will lose its dominant position in the future? Why or why not? What time horizon are you looking at?

2. Which factors do you think will be most critical in setting the next industry standard for technology in car propulsion? Do you believe it is possible that the new technologies can coexist, or do you think there will be only one industry standard?

3. Which companies do you think are currently best positioned to influence the next industry standard in car-propulsion technology?

4. What would you recommend different competitors (e.g., GM, Toyota, Nissan, and Tesla Motors) do to influence the emerging industry standard?

EXHIBIT MC12.1 / Several Technologies Competing for Dominance

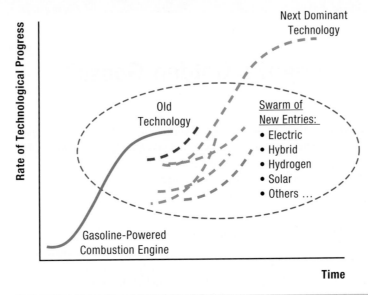

Sources: This MiniCase is based on "Bright sparks," *The Economist,* January 15, 2009; "The electric-fuel-trade acid test," *The Economist,* September 3, 2009; "At Tokyo auto show, hybrids and electrics dominate," *The New York Times,* October 21, 2009; "Risky business at Nissan," *BusinessWeek,* November 2, 2009; "Propulsion systems: The great powertrain race," *The Economist,* April 20, 2013; and "Tesla recharges the battery-car market," *The Economist,* May 10, 2013.

Is Porsche Killing the Golden Goose?

One day a farmer going to the nest of his goose found there an egg all yellow and glittering. He took it and found that the egg was pure gold. The farmer could hardly believe his luck! Every morning the same thing occurred, and the farmer grew richer, day by day. Thinking he could get all the gold at once, he killed the goose. After he opened it, he found nothing.

Aesop's Fable

WHEN PORSCHE REVEALED its 911 sports car design in 1962,[1] it caused a worldwide sensation. Ever since, Porsche has been one of the world's finest performance car manufacturers. The Porsche 911 is a legendary sports car icon. Although focusing on a niche market with a small output every year, Porsche was extremely profitable. Even today, it still enjoys the largest profit margins among all major auto manufacturers, thanks to the hefty premium it can command for its cars.

More than 50 years after its birth, the 911 remains the heart and soul of Porsche. However, it is no longer the company's best-selling model. The number-one spot has been taken by the Cayenne, a five-seat sports utility vehicle (SUV) launched by Porsche in 2002. Porsche views the Cayenne as a way to reduce the company's dependence on the traditional sports models and to provide for future growth in sales and profits. The Cayenne may be the most successful model launch of Porsche since the 911: Porsche sold the 200,000th Cayenne unit only six years after its debut at the Paris Motor Show. In 2012, the Cayenne's worldwide sales reached a record 77,822 units, accounting for more than half of the company's overall sales volume (see Exhibit MC13.1). The popularity of Cayenne is seen across regions, especially in the U.S. and China, the two largest markets of Porsche overall (see Exhibit MC13.2). In fact, China has become the largest market for Cayenne, and the model will continue to be the strategic sales focus of Porsche in that country.

The Cayenne has made Porsche more appealing to people who are not sports-car drivers but are happy to own the sportiest SUV on the market. While the model expansion may upset the purists, Porsche did not stop there. In 2005, Porsche announced its plan to build a new model line Panamera, a premium-category four-seat sports sedan, to extend its customer base. The line was launched on time in 2009 and like Cayenne, it outsold the 911 in the subsequent years. As of 2012, Cayenne and Panamera together accounted for 73 percent of Porsche's total sales volumes.

In the years leading up to the global financial crisis in 2008–2009, Porsche was attempting a hostile takeover of the much larger Volkswagen (VW). Part of the competition was motivated by a bitter family feud resulting from estranged members of the Porsche family holding leading executive positions in both companies. As the global financial crisis took hold, Porsche collapsed under a heavy debt burden caused by the hostile VW takeover attempt. VW turned the tables and took over Porsche in 2012. Now Porsche is clearly gunning for economies of scale as it ramps up unit sales, and VW overall is aiming to overtake GM and Toyota as the word leader in unit sales.

Porsche developed its own growth blueprint, termed "Strategy 2018," as part of Volkswagen group's grand vision: Porsche plans to increase unit sales to 200,000 per year by 2018, up from 30,000 units in 2002. To achieve this goal, Porsche needs to inspire more buyers. It continues to push overseas sales of the Cayenne and the Panamera models, setting up more dealerships where growth is the strongest. To address potential customers' concern over the 911's drivability as an everyday vehicle, Porsche launched an advertising

Frank T. Rothaermel and Carrie Yang (GT MBA, MSc.) prepared this Mini-Case from public sources. It is developed for the purpose of class discussion. It is not intended to be used for any kind of endorsement, source of data, or depiction of efficient or inefficient management. All opinions expressed, and all errors and omissions, are entirely the authors'. © Rothaermel and Yang, 2014.

EXHIBIT MC13.1 / Porsche Annual Sales by Model (units)

SOURCE: Porsche Annual Reports, 2009–2012; pricing is manufacturer's suggested retail price (MSRP) for U.S. 2014 models.

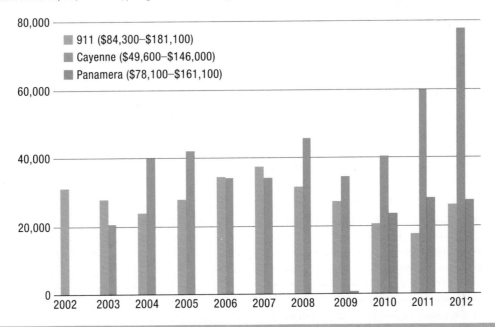

EXHIBIT MC13.2 / Porsche Sales and Deliveries by Region, 2012

SOURCE: Porsche 2012 Annual Report.

	U.S.	China	Germany	Rest of Europe	Rest of World
Total Sales (% of World Total):					
	36,170	33,590	16,090	31,094	26,152
	(25.3%)	(23.5%)	(11.2%)	(21.7%)	(18.3%)
Deliveries by Model (% of Country Total):					
911	8,528	949	5,238	6.654	4,088
	(24.3%)	(3.0%)	(30.0%)	(20.7%)	(16.2%)
Cayenne	15,545	19,959	7,758	16,966	14,535
	(44.4%)	(64.0%)	(44.4%)	(52.8%)	(57.7%)
Panamera	7,614	9,148	2,682	5,262	4,324
	(21.7%)	(29.3%)	(15.3%)	(16.4%)	(17.2%)

campaign titled "Engineered for Magic. Everyday," in the U.S., featuring actual Porsche owners using their sports cars for daily activities, from commuting to work, to picking up their kids and running errands. In 2012, Porsche revealed the name of its fifth model line, Macan—a compact SUV to be launched in 2014. The company is also considering the development of a smaller version of the Panamera.

The essence of a Porsche—a high-performance sports car—seems now to take a back seat. Although the company has built "experience centers" in China and the U.S. to cultivate sports-car enthusiasts, Porsche only sold 26,203 units of the 911 in 2012, or 18 percent of Porsche's total sales volumes. Porsche's expansion success so far largely relies on its reputation as an iconic sports-car maker. At the same time, many of today's Cayenne buyers, such as soccer parents in the U.S. or Chinese businesspeople that like a chauffeur, have no idea about Porsche's true identity as a high-performance sports and race car manufacturer.

DISCUSSION QUESTIONS

Review Chapter 8: Corporate Strategy: Vertical Integration and Diversification.

1. For many decades, Porsche pursued a focused differentiation strategy (see Exhibit 6.2 in Chapter 6). Using a clear strategic profile as a focused differentiator, Porsche was very successful and very profitable. More recently, the Porsche brand is repositioning itself from focused differentiation to broad differentiation by changing its competitive scope. What are the risks inherent in such strategic positioning? What are the benefits? Do you think Porsche will be successful in carving out a new strategic position as a broad differentiator? Why or why not?

2. Volkswagen ranks with GM and Toyota as one of the top-three carmakers in the world today in terms of sales volume (in units). It uses its Volkswagen brand, as well as its entire portfolio of other brands, including the luxury marques of Porsche, Audi, Bentley, Bugatti, and Lamborghini, and at the lower end, the Seat, Skoda, and Scania. What type of diversification is Volkswagen pursuing? What are the advantages and disadvantages in VW's corporate strategy?

3. In the recent past, both GM and Toyota ran into problems as they chased the goal of becoming the world's leader in terms of unit sales. GM achieved this goal but lost billions in the process and ended up in bankruptcy (in 2008). Toyota then pushed output and briefly held the number-one spot in terms of unit sales, but found that the emphasis on increasing output meant that quality issues arose—which then negatively affected its reputation. If you were asked to advise VW, what pitfalls would you point to that may need to be considered when attempting to be the world leader in unit output? How might VW avoid those pitfalls?

4. Porsche is expanding rapidly through both related and geographic diversification. Do you consider this business strategy to be successful? Why, or why not? If you consider Porsche's diversification to be successful, what is the source of Porsche's success?

5. The MiniCase began with Aesop's fable of "The Goose That Laid the Golden Eggs." What is the take-away of this fable? Is Porsche killing its golden goose?

Endnote

1. Originally, the car's name was the Porsche 901, but Porsche had to change this designation because Peugeot claimed trademark infringement using the numbers "901." Porsche settled on 911—and has used that number ever since. See "1964 Porsche 901 prototype classic drive," *Motor Trend,* December 25, 2012.

Sources: This MiniCase is based on Porsche Annual Reports, 2003–2012; "Porsche to develop and produce sports utility vehicle," *Porsche Press Release,* June 4, 1998; "Porsche will build fourth model line: Porsche Panamera," *Porsche Press Release,* July 27, 2005; "The Porsche story: A fierce family feud," *Der Spiegel,* July 21, 2009; "Porsche puts dollars behind sports cars again after pushing SUV, Sedan," *Advertising Age,* April 18, 2011; "Name for new Porsche SUV is Macan," *Porsche Press Release,* February 16, 2012; and "Is Porsche still a sports car maker?" *The Wall Street Journal,* May 29, 2013.

The Rise of Samsung Electronics

IN 2012, SAMSUNG, with $248 billion in revenues, was one of the largest conglomerates globally and the largest *chaebol*[1] in South Korea. A rough comparison would be the U.S. conglomerate General Electric, which had $147 billion in revenues in the same year. Established in 1938 by Lee Byung-chul as a trading company selling noodles and dried seafood, Samsung has since diversified into various industries, such as electronics, chemicals, shipbuilding, financial services, and construction. In particular, Samsung is widely diversified with 83 standalone subsidiaries. The conglomerate accounts for a fifth of all South Korean exports. In 1987, Lee Kun-hee, the youngest son of the founder, took over as chairman of the conglomerate after the death of Lee Byung-chul. By that time, Samsung had become an industry leader in many of its markets.

Samsung Electronics, the flagship subsidiary of Samsung (and best known in the U.S. for its Galaxy line of smartphones and tablets), was initially set up in 1969 to produce home appliances. In 1988, Lee Kun-hee merged Samsung Electronics with Samsung Semiconductors to integrate manufacturing. By 1992, it had become the worldwide market leader in DRAM (dynamic random access memory). Samsung Electronics, however, aspired to be more than a leading supplier and OEM (original equipment manufacturer). Its strategic intent was to be the leader in branded consumer electronics.

Samsung's image, however, was overshadowed by Sony and Motorola, the undisputed world leaders in consumer electronics and mobile phones during this time. In 1988, Samsung Electronics launched its first mobile phone in the South Korean market. It flopped because of the phone's poor quality. In the early 1990s, Samsung Electronics' market share in mobile phones in South Korea was a mere 10 percent compared to Motorola's 60 percent.

The pivotal moment in redefining Samsung Electronics' strategic focus came in early 1995. Samsung's chairman, Mr. Lee, sent out mobile phones as New Year's gifts to hundreds of key business partners. A public embarrassment occurred when Mr. Lee later learned that the phones he had send out as personal gifts didn't work properly. Mr. Lee ordered drastic changes. In front of Samsung's Gami factory with 2,000 employees watching, Mr. Lee set fire to a pile of 150,000 mobile phones to show his disappointment and determination alike. Many Samsung employees credit this day as the beginning of a successful turnaround.

Samsung Electronics increased spending significantly on R&D as well as on marketing and design. Meanwhile, Mr. Lee was undertaking a complete overhaul of the conglomerate's structure in order to change Samsung's culture. To a culture that deeply values seniority, Mr. Lee introduced merit-based pay and promotion. Mr. Lee (who holds an MBA degree from George Washington University) hired Western managers and designers into leading positions and sent home-grown talent to learn the best business practices of other firms around the globe. Mr. Lee also set up the Global Strategic Group to assist non-Korean MBAs and PhDs with a smooth transition into their positions in a largely homogenous cadre of employees.

Mr. Lee appointed a new CEO for Samsung Electronics in 1996, Yun Jong-Yong. Mr. Yun aggressively trimmed costs and sold off unproductive assets during the Asian Financial Crisis in 1997, making the company leaner and more agile. Subsequently, through improved operational efficiency and an integrated manufacturing process, Samsung Electronics shortened the time needed to respond quickly to changes in market trends. It chose to be a fast follower, investing only after a new product category had proven market

Frank T. Rothaermel and Carrie Yang (GT MBA, MSc.) prepared this MiniCase from public sources. It is developed for the purpose of class discussion. It is not intended to be used for any kind of endorsement, source of data, or depiction of efficient or inefficient management. All opinions expressed, and all errors and omissions, are entirely the authors'. © Rothaermel and Yang, 2014.

traction. Once such categories were identified, however, Samsung vastly outspent competitors in order to develop leading electronics products. For example, the company started making batteries for digital gadgets in 2000. Ten years later, it became the world's largest producer of this critical component. In 2001, Samsung started to invest in flat-panel televisions. Just four years later, Samsung was the world's leader in flat-panel TVs. In 2002, Samsung Electronics bet on flash memory, the technology that runs Apple's iPads and iPhones. Providing not only batteries but also flash memory, Samsung is Apple's largest supplier today.

Samsung Electronics applied the same "follow first, innovate second" rule to smartphones. Being a key component vendor to other leading technology companies including Apple, Samsung was able to see easily what directions other companies were taking. It made a range of smartphones tailored to customers in different price categories. Within two short years, it had overtaken Motorola, HTC, BlackBerry, and eventually even Apple to become the number-one vendor of smartphones in the world and the largest technology company by revenues globally (see Exhibits MC14.1 and MC14.2).

Although Samsung has gained a temporary competitive advantage, sustaining it will be even more difficult for a number of reasons. First, Samsung's competitive advantage was built in large part by following its "follow first, innovate second" rule. To keep its number-one spot in the world's technology industry may be a challenge for a company that intends to be a follower rather than a leader. Second, Chinese technology companies such as Lenovo and Huawei are also looking to join the battlefield in smartphones. Third, Apple and Samsung have been locked in ongoing court battles about who infringed the copyrights of whom and in what type of smartphone models. Samsung has already lost a high-profile case against Apple in a California court, where damages were reduced later to some $500 million.

To provide new avenues for future revenue growth, chairman Lee laid out five new business areas in which Samsung plans to invest some $20 billion by 2020. The five areas include (in order of size of investment): LED lighting, solar panels, e-vehicle batteries, biotech drugs, and medical devices.

Succession planning is another challenge Samsung is facing. The family of the late founder, Lee Byung-Chul, still controls a majority of the shares. At 71, Lee Kun-hee has long-groomed his eldest son Jay Y. Lee (43) to be his successor as chairman of

EXHIBIT MC14.1 / Global Smartphone Shipment by Vendor (2009–2012, in millions)

SOURCE: Authors' depiction of data from "How Samsung's rise is reshaping the mobile ecosystem," *Business Insider,* March 14, 2013.

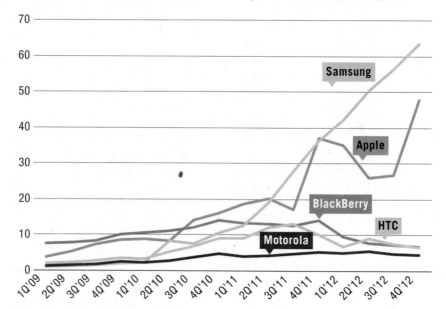

EXHIBIT MC14.2 / Samsung Electronics' Revenues (left vertical axis) and Operating Profits (right vertical axis), in $ billions, 1997–2012

SOURCE: Authors' depiction of data from Samsung's Annual Reports, 2008–2012.

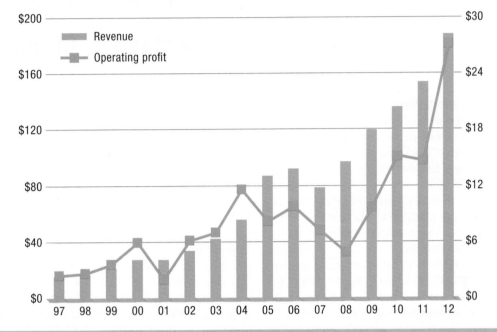

Samsung. It remains to be seen whether the younger Mr. Lee, as grandson of the founder, can maintain Samsung's momentum.

DISCUSSION QUESTIONS

Review Chapter 8: Corporate Strategy: Vertical Integration and Diversification.

1. Describe Samsung as a conglomerate. What type of diversification does Samsung pursue? Identify possible factors such as core competencies, economies of scale, and economies of scope that might underlie its success as a diversified conglomerate (chaebol). Which do you consider its key success factors?

2. How did Mr. Lee turn Samsung Electronics from a sleeping and bureaucratic company into a world leader?

3. What type of global strategy is Samsung Electronics pursuing?

4. What can Samsung Electronics do to sustain its competitive advantage in smartphones? Should Samsung change its "follow first, innovate second" approach as it seeks to build a competitive position in new product areas other than smartphones?

Endnote

1. A *chaebol* denotes a South Korean multinational business conglomerate.

Sources: This MiniCase is based on Khanna, T., J. Song, and K. Lee (2011), "The paradox of Samsung's rise," *Harvard Business Review*, July–August; "Samsung: the next big bet," *The Economist*, October 1, 2011; "Samsung and its attractions: Asia's new model company," *The Economist*, October 1, 2011; "Faster, higher, stronger: the rise and rise of Samsung," *The Sydney Morning Herald*, August 13, 2012; "The rise of Samsung and how it is reshaping ecosystem," *Business Insider*, March 14, 2013; "How Samsung got big," *TechCrunch*, June 1, 2013; various Samsung Annual Reports.

Yummy Yum!'s Competitive Advantage in China

IT MAY SOUND ASTONISHING that a fast-food chain selling fried chicken could conquer a country with a diverse culinary culture rooted in thousands of years of tradition, but the Chinese division of Yum! Brands did just that. Yum! Brands was created in 1997 as a result of PepsiCo spinning off its fast-food operations worldwide, a group that included KFC, Pizza Hut, and Taco Bell. Not only did Yum! China become the biggest restaurant chain in the country, accounting for 4 out of 10 fast-food restaurants; it also now provides half of Yum!'s total revenue and 42 percent of its profits (Exhibit MC15.1). No wonder David Novak, CEO of Yum! Brands, considers China to be "the best restaurant growth opportunity of the 21st century."[1]

When Yum! Brands (then a subsidiary of PepsiCo) opened its first KFC restaurant in Beijing in 1987, there was no other Western-style fast-food chain in China. Being greeted by smiling staff and then dining in an air-conditioned, clean, and brightly lit environment was a novelty to local Chinese, as was a bite of KFC's crispy chicken. Compared to other American fast foods, KFC also has a natural advantage: Chicken is the second most common meat staple in China, just after pork. Based on an understanding and appreciation of the Chinese taste for tradition and variety, KFC introduced dishes that mimicked local cuisines, such as Chinese porridge and dough fritters for breakfast. Its menu in China included more items than on menus in the U.S., and was updated more frequently. In addition, the level of spiciness of the food was adjusted according to regional preferences within China. As a result, a KFC restaurant in China has a much bigger kitchen and employs twice as many people as its U.S. counterpart (although Chinese labor costs are much lower, see Exhibit MC15.2). Given all its efforts in pleasing Chinese diners, KFC no longer positions itself in China as a cheap place for take-outs. Instead, it is seen as a more upscale quick-service restaurant for gatherings of family and friends.

KFC's sister chain, Pizza Hut, also underwent a similar makeover in China. Unlike its image in the West as a cheap, fast-food outlet, Pizza Hut in China has presented itself as a trendy casual dining restaurant since its opening in 1990. Diners at a Pizza Hut restaurant in China are waited on while soothing background music plays, and the menu offers many other Western-style dishes than just pizza.

Yum! China's localization strategy was made possible because Pepsi was busy competing with Coca-Cola in the United States and took a hands-off approach toward managing its overseas restaurant business. When Yum! Brands was spun off from its parent in 1997, Yum! China had already opened 200 restaurants in major cities. But Yum! China's growth strategy is about more than simply adding restaurants. From the very beginning, the company has focused on "building a perfect system which governs every step of the way—from purchasing, to making, to delivering the food and to the quick service."[2] Because a reliable network of distributors in China was nonexistent at the time, Yum! China set up its own distribution arm with company-owned warehouses and a fleet of trucks to cover every province in China. To make sure each new restaurant is properly staffed and offers excellent customer service, Yum! China runs an extensive training program where teams of new employees work side by side with experienced ones in established restaurants. Once trained, these new employees rotate to new restaurants.

The emphasis in the early years on building an efficient operations network nationwide laid a solid foundation for Yum! China's rapid expansion. From 1997 to 2012, Yum! China opened more than 4,000

Frank T. Rothaermel and Carrie Yang (GT MBA, MSc.) prepared this MiniCase from public sources. It is developed for the purpose of class discussion. It is not intended to be used for any kind of endorsement, source of data, or depiction of efficient or inefficient management. All opinions expressed, and all errors and omissions, are entirely the authors'. © Rothaermel and Yang, 2014.

EXHIBIT MC15.1 / Yum! China's Restaurant Numbers

SOURCE: Authors' depiction of data from Yum Brands Annual Reports, 2000–2012.

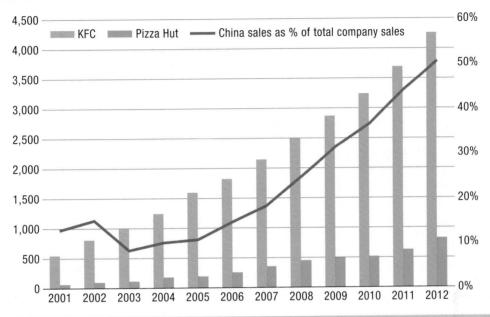

EXHIBIT MC15.2 / Yum! Brands Selected Financials

SOURCE: Yum! Brands Annual Reports, 2006–2012.

	2007	2008	2009	2010	2011	2012
Sales growth						
China	36%	47%	22%	21%	35%	24%
U.S.	−7%	−1%	−13%	−8%	−21%	2%
Rest of world	30%	1%	−12%	4%	23%	−11%
Restaurant margin						
China	20.1%	18.4%	20.2%	22.1%	19.7%	18.1%
U.S.	13.3%	12.5%	13.9%	14.2%	12.1%	16.3%
Rest of world	12.3%	11.1%	11.1%	11.7%	12.3%	12.9%
Cost of labor as % of sales						
China	13.2%	13.8%	13.3%	14.4%	16.2%	18.5%
U.S.	30.5%	30.1%	30.0%	29.6%	30.4%	29.5%
Rest of world	26.1%	26.0%	26.0%	25.2%	25.6%	24.9%

KFC and 800 Pizza Hut restaurants in 850 Chinese cities. Most of the time, Yum! China was the first fast-food chain (let alone international chain) to establish a presence in a city. This enabled Yum! to gain a first-mover advantage by selecting the best locations with strong customer traffic, high visibility, and an

EXHIBIT MC15.3 / Yum! Brands Quarterly Same-Store Sales Growth by Region

SOURCE: Authors' depiction of data from Yum! Brands quarterly earnings releases, Q1 2010–Q1 2013.

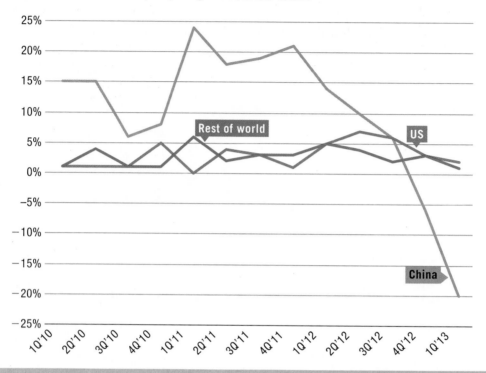

attractive rental rate. Sometimes, being the first also generated free publicity from local officials since the opening of a world-famous fast-food restaurant meant that their city was becoming more cosmopolitan. Also, benefiting from China's lower labor costs, Yum! China has become the only division within Yum! Brands to consistently deliver double-digit sales growth and the highest restaurant margin (see Exhibit MC15.2).

With thousands of stores and a vast distribution network in densely populated areas, Yum! China is vulnerable to many external and internal threats, such as outbreaks of bird flu (a repeat occurrence in China) and food safety scandals. In 2003, the avian flu outbreak caused a 40 percent decline in Yum! China's sales. Two years later, the discovery of a questionable ingredient used in the chicken feeds by one of Yum! China's suppliers brought sales growth down to "only" 11 percent. Although Yum! China recovered quickly from these setbacks, last December Yum! China was again attacked by China's national news service for sourcing from suppliers that use excessive antibiotics in their chicken feeds. Worse yet, just as Yum! China was rebuilding its

bond of trust with Chinese customers, another potential outbreak of avian flu scared more eaters away. Yum! China's same-store sales dropped by 20 percent for the first quarter of 2013, its first quarterly decline in three years (Exhibit MC15.3). But with only two Yum! restaurants per million people in China currently (compared to 58 in the U.S.), Yum! China has no intention of modifying its growth strategy or losing its number-one spot in China's fast-food industry any time soon.

DISCUSSION QUESTIONS

Review Chapter 9: Corporate Strategy: Mergers and Acquisitions, Strategic Alliances.

1. Yum! Brands is the result of a spin-off by PepsiCo, where it sold its fast-food chains KFC, Taco Bell, and Pizza Hut. Do you consider this spin-off successful? Why or why not? Explain.

2. Why is Yum! Brands so much more successful in China than in the U.S., its home country?

3. Why was Yum! Brands KFC so successful in China, while other U.S. fast-food companies—such as

Pizza Hut (also owned by Yum!), McDonald's, and Burger King—were much less successful?

4. Given Yum! Brands recent challenges in China, do you consider this to be a temporary problem or a harbinger of losing its competitive advantage?

5. What recommendations would you give David Novak, Yum! Brands' CEO, to overcome the company's current challenges in China?

Endnotes

1. Yum! Brands 2012 Annual Report.

2. "Competition gearing up in China's fast food industry," *China Daily*, June 30, 2008.

Sources: This MiniCase is based on Yum! Brands Annual Reports, 2000–2012; "Competition gearing up in China's fast food industry," *China Daily*, June 30, 2008; "Fast food in China: Yucky Kentucky," *The Economist*, February 9, 2013; and Bell, D. E., and Shelman, M. L. (2011), "KFC's radical approach to China," *Harvard Business Review*, November.

BYD—"Build Your Dreams" in America

THE CHINESE COMPANY BYD, an acronym for "Build Your Dreams," began life as a manufacturer of rechargeable batteries in 1995. It is now leveraging this expertise into electric vehicles. But why would a battery manufacturer diversify into car manufacturing? Unlike complex gasoline engines, electric cars are powered by simple motors and gearboxes that have very few parts. Electric vehicles are therefore much cheaper and more straightforward to build. BYD's claim to fame is a lithium iron phosphate battery on which cars can run 250 miles on a single three-hour charge. BYD sells plug-in hybrids and all-electric vehicles in China, Africa, the Middle East, and South America. In 2013, it entered the U.S. market.

Given the problems carmakers faced in the aftermath of the global financial crisis, which witnessed the bankruptcies of GM and Chrysler, for a new firm to expand into the auto manufacturing industry doesn't seem advisable. Yet BYD is joining the fray. How can it sidestep such insurmountable entry barriers? The answer: Technology is leveling the playing field. Mr. Wang, founder and chairman of BYD, explains his strategic intent: "It's almost hopeless for a latecomer like us to compete with GM and other established automakers with a century of experience in gasoline engines. With electric vehicles, we're all at the same starting line."[1] Actually, BYD may even have a head start because of its deep experience in batteries, selling them to technology companies such as Motorola, Nokia, and Samsung, and supplying more than 50 percent of the world's global handset batteries. Now it is leveraging its core competencies in batteries, the most critical component of electric vehicles, into car manufacturing.

In 2003, Mr. Wang, who was trained as a chemist, decided to make cars. BYD acquired a state-owned, near-defunct car manufacturer and launched its first self-developed sedan model two years later. The model soon became a national bestseller, and BYD a top-ten auto manufacturer in China. By 2009, BYD's auto division made up more than 50 percent of the company's total revenue (Exhibit MC16.1). Even legendary investor Warren Buffett was so impressed with the company and Wang's entrepreneurial spirit that a subsidiary of Mr. Buffett's Berkshire Hathaway bought a 10 percent equity stake in BYD for $232 million.

Leveraging the company's know-how in making rechargeable batteries, BYD developed an all-electric model, the e6. In 2009, BYD introduced this new model at the North American International Auto Show. The debut generated buzz in the car industry and fueled the company's ambition to promote its brand in America. BYD indicated its plan to start selling the five-seat sedan to fleet customers in the Los Angeles area by 2010. After almost a year of delay, BYD opened its North American headquarters in Los Angeles in 2011. However, the commercialization of the e6 never occurred in the U.S. for a number of reasons: The e6 needed further development; Los Angeles lacked the adequate infrastructure of charging stations required for electric vehicles; and the city did not provide an incentive scheme for green car buyers at the time. In addition, already well-established auto manufacturers launched electric models, such as Nissan's Leaf and General Motor's Volt (a plug-in hybrid), not to mention the popular Toyota Prius (also a plug-in hybrid launched in 2000 in the U.S.). All this has made it much more difficult for BYD to enter the U.S. market successfully.

Given these challenges, BYD is now focusing on making all-electric buses. The primary target market is metropolitan transport authorities, and BYD seems to be gaining momentum. Its all-electric buses are built on the production platform of a Chinese coach manufacturer acquired in 2009. The first all-electric bus model, the K9, rolled off BYD's production line

Frank T. Rothaermel and Carrie Yang (GT MBA, MSc.) prepared this MiniCase from public sources. It is developed for the purpose of class discussion. It is not intended to be used for any kind of endorsement, source of data, or depiction of efficient or inefficient management. All opinions expressed, and all errors and omissions, are entirely the authors'. © Rothaermel and Yang, 2014.

EXHIBIT MC16.1 / BYD Auto Financial Results (2005–2012, $ figures in millions)

SOURCE: BYD Annual Reports, 2004–2012.

	2005	2006	2007	2008	2009	2010	2011	2012
Sales – Auto	$1,046	$2,084	$3,416	$4,314	$6,356	$7,518	$7,458	$7,147
Growth (YoY)*	61.5%	414.2%	50.7%	77.5%	142.8%	2.7%	2.7%	1.9%
Percentage of total sales	9.7%	25.0%	23.0%	32.3%	53.2%	46.2%	47.8%	50.8%
Operating profit – Auto	−$15	$19	$41	$81	$566	$281	$306	$170
Percentage of total operating profit	-	8.3%	12.3%	27.5%	72.9%	48.4%	67.5%	79.2%
Operating margin – Auto	-	3.7%	5.3%	5.8%	16.7%	8.1%	8.6%	4.7%
Number of total vehicles sold	15,993	55,038	85,942	170,000	450,000	500,000	437,000	420,000
YoY growth	7.9%	244.1%	56.2%	97.8%	164.7%	11.1%	−12.6%	−3.9%

*YoY = year over year

in 2010. K9's debut generated immediate commercial interest. In 2012, BYD sold more than 1,200 buses priced at $300,000 each to countries such as Israel, Uruguay, Columbia, Canada, and the Netherlands.

Mr. Wang hasn't given up on his dream of making it big in America, though. To meet the requirements of the "Buy America Act" (which specifies that U.S. government agencies must procure products where U.S.-made parts account for more than 60 percent of total component costs), BYD announced in 2012 its plan to open an electric-bus assembly plant in Lancaster, California. This announcement came right after BYD received a 10-bus order worth $12.1 million from Long Beach Transit, a transport agency serving the communities south of Los Angeles. BYD is now building its buses in the California plant using local labor, and has benefitted from the ability of transport agencies and other public entities in the U.S. to tap federal subsidies that cover up to 80 percent of the cost of buying electric buses. BYD is eyeing other lucrative California markets, also, such as the Los Angeles County Metropolitan Transportation Authority and BART (Bay Area Rapid Transit). BYD plans to deliver between 200 and 300 electric buses to customers in the U.S. by the end of 2014. So, the question remains . . . Will BYD be able to continue building its dream in America?

DISCUSSION QUESTIONS

Review Chapter 10: Global Strategy: Competing Around the World.

1. What type of company is BYD? Is it a battery manufacturer or a car and bus manufacturer? Or is it something else entirely? What is BYD's core competency? How does it leverage its core competency to diversify? (You may want to refer to Exhibit 8.8, "The Core Competence–Market Matrix.")

2. Thinking about the concept of *liability of foreignness,* what would you consider to be BYD's greatest challenge when attempting to compete successfully in the U.S. market? How would you address these challenges?

3. What type of global strategy would you recommend BYD pursue based on the integration-response framework? (See Exhibit 10.5.)

4. Do you think BYD will be successful in America? Why or why not?

Endnote

1. "Technology levels playing field in race to market electric car," *The Wall Street Journal,* January 12, 2009.

Sources: This MiniCase is based on BYD Annual Reports 2003–2012; Fishman, T. C. (2005), *China Inc.: How the Rise of the Next Superpower Challenges America and the World* (New York: Simon & Schuster), p. 215; "Warren Buffett takes charge," *CNN Money,* April 13, 2009; "Hollywood beckons China's BYD," *The Wall Street Journal,* December 10, 2009; "A crowded car industry. From Big Three to magnificent seven," *The Economist,* January 13, 2011; "BYD opens U.S. headquarters in Los Angeles," *Edmunds AutoObserver,* October 25, 2011; "BYD signs South American electric bus deal," *CleanBiz.Asia,* July 23, 2012; "Tel Aviv to get 700 BYD electric buses," *CleanBiz.Asia,* August 28, 2012; "Chasing the dragon: An old relationship presents fresh opportunities," *The Economist,* April 13, 2013.

Alibaba and China's E-Commerce: "Open Sesame" Comes True

IN THE ARABIC TALE of "Ali Baba and the Forty Thieves," Ali Baba, the poor woodcutter, opened the cave with hidden treasure by saying the magic words "Open sesame!" In modern-day China, Alibaba is a family of e-commerce businesses, which *The Wall Street Journal* described as "comparable to eBay, Amazon, and PayPal all rolled into one, with a stake in Twitter-like Weibo thrown in to boot."[1] Alibaba's main trading platforms are Taobao and Tmall; together they processed $170 billion in transactions last year. This is more than Amazon and eBay combined! So, what is Alibaba's magic?

Alibaba had a humble beginning. In 1999, a former English teacher named Jack Ma started the company with a team of 18 in his apartment in Hangzhou, a city some 100 miles southwest of Shanghai. The year 1999 also marked the start of China's explosive growth of Internet users (See Exhibit MC17.1). By 2012, China's Internet users grew to 564 million, a compound annual growth rate (CAGR) of a whopping 37.6 percent.

Initially, Alibaba's website was a business-to-business (B2B) platform where China's small and medium-sized businesses could showcase their products to buyers around the world. Alibaba was not the first company to explore opportunities in introducing China's manufacturing to global demand, but it was the first to do so online. In its first year of operation, Alibaba signed up new members at a rate of 1,200 per day. By 2002, the young startup was already profitable. By 2012, Alibaba facilitated transactions in basically every country in the world.

In 1999, EachNet, another Chinese Internet venture, was founded in Shanghai by two Harvard MBAs who wanted to create a "Chinese eBay," an auction site for locals to sell and bid for goods. By 2003, EachNet had 2 million users and 85 percent market share in China's consumer-to-consumer (C2C) transactions. At the time, eBay was actively looking to expand in China and eventually acquired EachNet as its China operation for $180 million in 2003.

Fearing eBay would lure away small businesses, Alibaba launched a competing C2C platform, Taobao (meaning "digging treasure" in Chinese), as a defensive strategy. Unlike EachNet which charged listing and transaction fees from sellers, Taobao was free for the user. But Taobao's free services did not erode EachNet's loyal customer base. EachNet's dominant market position meant more products and more opportunities for both buyers and sellers to trade. Although EachNet was competing head to head with Taobao on advertising campaigns, eBay made a decision to terminate EachNet's homegrown technology platform and move all EachNet users to eBay's U.S. platform in 2004. Internally, this was called a "migration" at eBay. The intent was to create one global trading platform that would allow eBay users to trade with each other, no matter where they were located.

The problem was that eBay's U.S. platform did not have the set of features that EachNet needed to compete in China. The online data that once freely flowed within China now became cross-border traffic and had to pass the Chinese government's "firewall." The speed to load EachNet's web page slowed significantly. Frustrated users left EachNet in droves and turned to Taobao for a better alternative. While most decisions at EachNet had to go to eBay's U.S. headquarters for approval, Alibaba swiftly launched a number of innovative services to assist transactions on Taobao. One was Aliwangwang, an instant messaging service helping buyers and sellers interact. Another was Alipay, an escrow payment system to reduce online transaction

Frank T. Rothaermel and Carrie Yang (GT MBA, MSc.) prepared this Mini-Case from public sources. It is developed for the purpose of class discussion. It is not intended to be used for any kind of endorsement, source of data, or depiction of efficient or inefficient management. All opinions expressed, and all errors and omissions, are entirely the authors'. © Rothaermel and Yang, 2014.

EXHIBIT MC17.1 / China's Internet Users (in millions)

SOURCE: Authors' depiction of data from China Internet Network Information Center, http://www1.cnnic.cn/.

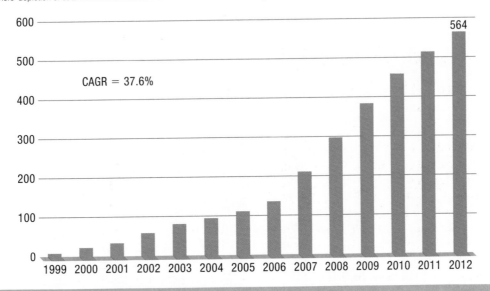

risks. Just three months after eBay's migration, Taobao had captured 60 percent of the C2C market share, leaving EachNet at 30 percent. In 2006, eBay shut down EachNet and folded its China operation altogether.

Alibaba, meanwhile, continued to build its e-commerce venture around Taobao. In 2007, it set up Alisoft, where Taobao sellers could buy customized third-party software to help with their day-to-day operations, and Alimama, where Taobao sellers could post ads on a network of specialized websites. Anticipating a growing share of business-to-consumer (B2C) transactions of online retailing, Taobao launched TMall, a dedicated B2C platform to complement Taobao in 2008. (See Exhibit MC17.2.)

By 2012, Alibaba employed 24,000 people and had over $4 billion in revenues, becoming the clear market share leader in all three e-commerce areas (B2B, C2C, B2C) in China (see Exhibit MC17.3). Alibaba's initial public offering is highly anticipated because the company is valued at somewhere between $55 billion and $120 billion. China's Internet e-commerce market is expected to grow to $600 billion by 2020. The U.S. online search firm Yahoo owns a 24 percent stake in Alibaba.

DISCUSSION QUESTIONS

Review Chapter 10: Global Strategy: Competing Around the World.

1. How was Alibaba able to become the leading online trading platform in China? Think about standards, network effects, and crossing the chasm (from Chapter 7).

2. Apply the CAGE distance framework (see Exhibit 10.3) to help explain why eBay was not successful in the Chinese market. Why do you think Amazon has only 1.9 percent market share in China (see Exhibit MC17.3), while it holds some 26 percent market share of the $226 billion U.S. e-commerce market. What general conclusions do you draw?

3. Review the integration-responsiveness framework shown in Exhibit 10.5. Which global strategy positions would you recommend U.S. e-commerce companies such as eBay, Amazon, and others pursue, and why?

4. Does your recommendation in question 3 support the notion that the "world is flat," or would "semi-globalization" be a more accurate description? Support your arguments.

Endnote

1. "China changes won't faze Alibaba," *The Wall Street Journal*, July 5, 2013.

EXHIBIT MC17.2 / China's Online Retailing Market (2008–2014E*)

SOURCE: Authors' depiction of data from iResearch Global, http://www.iresearchchina.com.

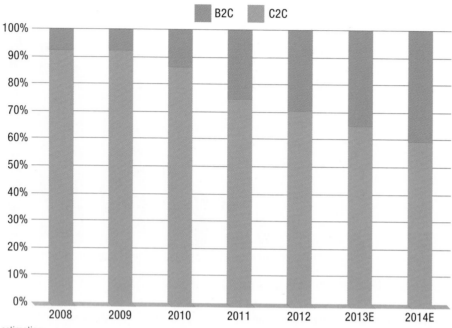

* E indicates an estimation.

EXHIBIT MC17.3 / China's E-Commerce Ranking by Market Share (2012)

SOURCE: iResearch Global, http://www.iresearchchina.com/.

B2B		C2C		B2C*	
Alibaba	39.7%	Taobao (Alibaba)	94.5%	Tmall (Alibaba)	51.3%
Mysteel	5.7%	Tencent Paipai	5.5%	Jd	17.5%
Global Sources	5.4%			Tencent E-Comm.	6.8%
HC360	3.2%			Suning E-Comm.	4.5%
Dhgate	3.0%			Dangdang	2.6%
Made-in-China	2.5%			Gome E-Comm.	2.1%
Global Market	1.2%			Vipshop	1.9%
Toocle	1.1%			Amazon	1.9%
Other	38.0%			Other	11.4%

* Data as of first quarter of 2013.

Sources: This MiniCase is based on company overview, news on Alibaba. com; "The Jack who would be king," *The Economist*, August 24, 2000; "E-commerce with Chinese characteristics," *The Economist*, November 15, 2007; "How eBay lost the China market," *Global Times*, August 10, 2009; "How eBay failed in China," *Forbes*, September 12, 2010; "How Taobao bested eBay in China," *Financial Times*, March 12, 2012; "Yahoo's ad struggles persist," *The Wall Street Journal*, April 16, 2013; "Alibaba: The world's greatest bazaar," *The Economist*, March 23, 2013; "E-commerce in China: The Alibaba phenomenon," *The Economist*, March 23, 2013; "Microsoft considered building e-commerce market," *Fox Business*, June 2013; and "Yahoo's Marissa Mayer hits one-year mark," *The Wall Street Journal*, July 15, 2013.

The Premature Death of a Google Forerunner at Microsoft

IN 1998, 24-YEAR-OLD Sergey Brin and 25-year-old Larry Page founded Google. They met as graduate students in computer science at Stanford University, where they began working together on a web crawler, with the goal of improving online searches. What they developed was the PageRank algorithm, which returns the most relevant web pages more or less instantaneously and ranks them by how often they are referenced on other important web pages. A clear improvement over early search engines such as AltaVista, Overture, and Yahoo, all of which indexed by keywords, the PageRank algorithm is able to consider 500 million variables and 3 billion terms. What started as a homework assignment launched the two into an entrepreneurial venture when they set up shop in a garage in Menlo Park, California.

Today, Google is the world's leading online search and advertising company, with some 70 percent market share of an industry estimated to be worth more than $50 billion a year, and growing quickly. Though Yahoo is a distant second with less than 20 percent share, in 2008 Microsoft's CEO Steve Ballmer offered to buy the runner-up for close to $50 billion to help his company gain a foothold in the paid-search business where Google rules. Yahoo turned down the offer.

What haunts Ballmer is that Microsoft actually had its own working prototype of a Google forerunner, called Keywords, more than a decade earlier. Scott Banister, then a student at the University of Illinois, had come up with the idea of adding paid advertisements to Internet searches. He quit college and drove his Geo hatchback to the San Francisco Bay Area to start Keywords, later joining an online ad company called LinkExchange. In 1998, Microsoft bought LinkExchange for some $265 million (about one two-hundredth the price it would later offer for Yahoo). LinkExchange's managers urged

Microsoft to invest in Keywords. Instead, Microsoft executives shut down LinkExchange in 2000 because they did not see a viable business model in it. One LinkExchange manager actually approached Ballmer himself and explained that he thought Microsoft was making a mistake. But Ballmer said he wanted to manage through delegation and would not reverse a decision made by managers three levels below him, thus bringing an end to Microsoft's first online advertising venture.

In 2003, Microsoft got a second chance to enter the online advertising business when some mid-level managers proposed buying Overture Services, an innovator in combining Internet searches with advertisements. This time, Ballmer, joined by Microsoft's co-founder Bill Gates, decided not to pursue the idea because they thought Overture was overpriced. Shortly thereafter, Yahoo bought Overture for $1.6 billion.

Having missed two huge opportunities to pursue promising strategic initiatives that emerged from

Frank T. Rothaermel prepared this MiniCase from public sources. It is developed for the purpose of class discussion. It is not intended to be used for any kind of endorsement, source of data, or depiction of efficient or inefficient management. All opinions expressed, and all errors and omissions, are entirely the author's. © Rothaermel, 2014.

lower levels within the firm, Microsoft has been playing catch-up in the paid-search business ever since. In the summer of 2009, it launched its own search engine, Bing (an acronym for "Because It's Not Google"). Microsoft and Yahoo subsequently formed a strategic alliance, and Microsoft's new search engine will also power Yahoo searches. These two strategic moves helped Microsoft increase its share in the lucrative online search business to roughly 25 percent, up from just over 8 percent. It remains an open question whether this is sufficient, however, to challenge Google's dominance. In particular, Bing's increase in market share of online searches is obtained at the expense of Yahoo's, and not Google's, market share. Microsoft's CEO Ballmer admits problems in Microsoft's strategic management process: "The biggest mistakes I claim I've been involved with are where I was impatient—because we didn't have a business yet in something, we should have stayed patient. If we'd kept consistent with some of the ideas, we might have been in paid search. We are letting more flowers bloom."[1] In the summer of 2013, Steve Ballmer announced he would retire as Microsoft's CEO by mid-2014.

DISCUSSION QUESTIONS

Review Chapter 11: Organizational Design: Structure, Culture, and Control.

1. Describe the strategic management process at Microsoft. How are strategic decisions made? What are the strengths and weaknesses of this approach?

2. Explain the role of organizational inertia in Microsoft's difficulty in establishing a presence in the online paid-search business. What could Microsoft have done differently? What recommendations pertaining to the strategic management process would you give?

3. How did two college students successfully launch a business in online search and advertising that outperforms Microsoft, one of the world's leading technology companies? Among other issues, consider the role of differences in organizational culture.

4. Why is Google successful in the online search business while Yahoo and Microsoft are struggling?

Endnote

1. Microsoft CEO Steve Ballmer's quote drawn from "Microsoft bid to beat Google builds on a history of misses," *The Wall Street Journal*, January 16, 2009.

Sources: This MiniCase is based on "Yahoo to buy Overture for $1.63 billion," *CNET News*, July 14, 2003; "Microsoft bid to beat Google builds on a history of misses," *The Wall Street Journal*, January 16, 2009; "Yahoo tie-up is latest sign tide turning for Microsoft's Ballmer," *The Wall Street Journal*, July 30, 2009; "Bingoo! A deal between Microsoft and Yahoo!" *The Economist*, July 30, 2009; "Google, Microsoft spar on antitrust," *The Wall Street Journal*, March 1, 2010; Levy, S. (2011), *In the Plex: How Google Thinks, Works, and Shapes Our Lives* (New York: Simon & Schuster); and "Microsoft CEO Steve Ballmer to retire in 12 months," *The Wall Street Journal*, August 23, 2013.

Sony's Structure and Competitive Disadvantage

APPLE'S MARKET CAPITALIZATION in 2001 was $7 billion, while Sony's was $55 billion. Apple introduced the iPod, a portable digital music player, in October 2001 and the iTunes music store 18 months later. Through these two strategic moves Apple redefined the music industry, reinventing itself as not only a mobile-device but also a content-delivery company. Signaling its renaissance, Apple changed its name from Apple Computer, Inc., to simply Apple, Inc. But what happened to Sony—the company that created the portable-music industry by introducing the Walkman in 1979?

Sony's strategy was to differentiate itself through the vertical integration of content and hardware, driven by its 1988 acquisition of CBS Records (later part of Sony Entertainment). This vertical integration strategy contrasted with Sony Music division's desire to protect its lucrative revenue-generating, copyrighted compact discs (CDs). Sony Music's engineers were aggressively combating rampant music piracy by inhibiting the Microsoft Windows Media Player's ability to rip CDs and by serializing discs (assigning unique ID numbers to discs). Meanwhile, Apple's engineers were developing a Digital Rights Management (DRM) system to control and restrict the transfer of copyrighted digital music. Apple's DRM succeeded, protecting the music studio's interests while creating value that enabled consumers to enjoy portable digital music.

Sony had a long history of creating electronics devices of superior quality and design. It had all the right competencies to launch a successful counterattack to compete with Apple: electronics, software, music, and computer divisions. Sony even supplied the batteries for Apple's iPod. Cooperation among strategic business units had served Sony well in the past, leading to breakthrough innovations such as the Walkman, PlayStation, the CD, and the VAIO computer line. In this case, however, the hardware and content divisions each seemed to have their own idea of what needed to be done. Cooperation among the Sony divisions was also hindered by the fact that their centers of operations were spread across the globe: Music operations were located in New York City and electronics design was in Japan, inhibiting face-to-face communications and making real-time interactions more difficult.

Sony's then-CEO Nobuyuki Idei learned the hard way that the Music division managers were focused on the immediate needs of their recordings competing against consumer-driven market forces. In 2002, Mr. Idei shared his frustrations about the cultural differences between the hardware and content divisions:

> The opposite of soft alliances is hard alliances, which include mergers and acquisitions. Since purchasing the Music and Pictures businesses, more than 10 years have passed, and we have experienced many cultural differences between hardware manufacturing and content businesses. . . . This experience has taught us that in certain areas where hard alliances would have taken 10 years to succeed, soft alliances can be created more easily. Another advantage of soft alliances is the ability to form partnerships with many different companies. We aim to provide an open and easy-to-access environment where anybody can participate and we are willing to cooperate with companies that share our vision. Soft alliances offer many possibilities.[1]

In contrast, Apple organized a small, empowered, cross-functional team to produce the iPod in just a few months. Apple successfully outsourced

Frank T. Rothaermel prepared this MiniCase from public sources. A prior version of this MiniCase was prepared in collaboration with Robert Redrow (formerly of Sony Corp.). It is developed for the purpose of class discussion. It is not intended to be used for any kind of endorsement, source of data, or depiction of efficient or inefficient management. All opinions expressed, and all errors and omissions, are entirely the author's. © Rothaermel, 2014.

and integrated many of its components and collaborated across business units. The phenomenal speed and success of the iPod, as well as iTunes' development and seamless integration, became a structural approach that Apple applied to its successful development and launches of other category-defining products such as the iPhone and iPad. By August 2012, Apple's stock market valuation had increased by a factor of 89 times, from $7 billion in 2001 to $623 billion, making it the most valuable public company of all time.[2] In contrast, Sony's market value had declined by almost 80 percent, from $55 billion to $12 billion.

To improve Sony's performance, the company is undergoing a major corporate restructuring. In 2012, Sony's revenues were $72.4 billion, with Sony's Mobile Products and Communications division ($13.0 billion), Entertainment ($12.4 billion), Financial Services ($10.7 billion), and Home Entertainment & Sound ($10.6 billion) being the largest divisions (Exhibit MC19.1). In terms of profitability, however, Sony's core businesses are underperforming (Exhibit MC19.2). Sony's most profitable divisions are non-core businesses such as Financial Services ($1.55 billion) and "Other" business activities ($970 million). The Entertainment unit made only $910 million in net income on over $12 billion in revenues, which represents a meager 0.007 percent return on investment.

As the Japanese economy is undergoing a major transformation under Prime Minister Shinzo Abe, corporate governance at leading Japanese enterprises from Toyota to Sony is also being shaken up. Companies must now rely more on equity financing rather than being able to continually finance operations through debt based on their cozy relationships with banks. This is the result of more than a decade-long competitive disadvantage by once world-leading Japanese companies, especially in the electronics industry (including Sony and Sharp).

Activist investors such as hedge funds are becoming more powerful players in Sony's corporate governance. And with more power, they are becoming more vocal. In particular, they argue that Sony Corp. is spread too thin over too many businesses and that its corporate strategy needs a major refocus. These activist investors are advising Sony to combine its music and movie businesses into one entertainment unit, and then spin it off as a standalone company. Among its assets, Sony Entertainment has music artists such as Justin Timberlake and Pink under contract, and the

EXHIBIT MC19.1 / Sony's Revenues by Segment, 2012 ($ in billions)

SOURCE: Author's depiction of data from "Japan's electronics under siege," *The Wall Street Journal*, May 15, 2013.

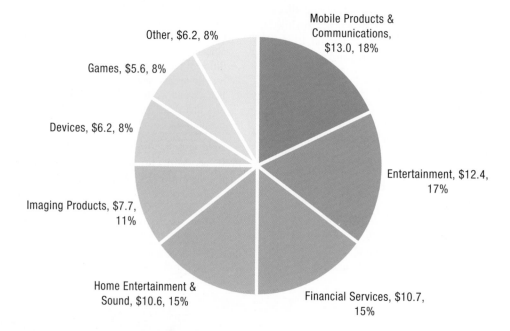

EXHIBIT MC19.2 / Sony's Net Income by Segment, 2012 ($ in billions)

SOURCE: Author's depiction of data from "Japan's electronics under siege," *The Wall Street Journal*, May 15, 2013.

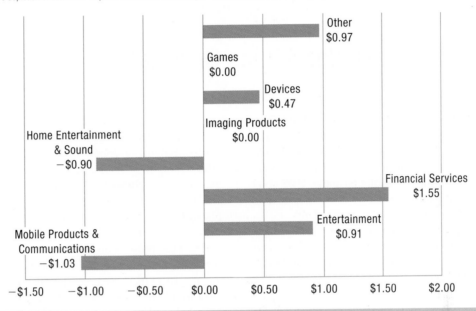

movie *Skyfall,* Sony's latest installment in the James Bond saga, which topped the rankings and grossed over one billion dollars since its release in 2012. This corporate restructuring should allow Sony to focus on its core business in electronics, while unlocking hidden value-creating potential in its entertainment unit.

DISCUSSION QUESTIONS

Review Chapter 11: Organizational Design: Structure, Culture, and Control.

1. Why had Sony been successful in the past (e.g., with the introduction of the Walkman, PlayStation, the CD, and the VAIO computer line)?

2. What was Mr. Idei's assessment of strategic alliances versus M&As? Do you agree or disagree with his conclusion? Support your assessment.

3. Explain how Sony's organizational design (structure, culture, and control) inhibited Sony's ability to respond to the competitive challenge of Apple in the digital portable music industry.

4. What could Sony have done differently to avoid failure? What lessons could be learned?

5. Explain how restructuring (as activist investors are recommending) would produce benefits for Sony. What would be the benefits of splitting up Sony as proposed? What would be its drawbacks?

Endnotes

1. Sony Annual Report 2002, year ended March 31, 2002, Sony Corporation, p. 9.

2. By summer 2013, Apple's stock market valuation had decreased considerably as detailed in ChapterCases 1 and 5.

Sources: This MiniCase is based on Hansen, M. T. (2009), *Collaboration: How Leaders Avoid the Traps, Create Unity, and Reap Big Results* (Cambridge, MA: Harvard Business School Press); Sony Annual Report 2002, year ended March 31, 2002, Sony Corporation, p. 9; "Japan's electronics under siege," *The Wall Street Journal*, May 15, 2013; Sony Corporation Info, www.sony.net/SonyInfo/CorporateInfo/History/sonyhistory-e.html; and Wolfram Alpha, www.wolframalpha.com.

UBS's Billion-Dollar Ethics Scandals

UBS WAS FORMED in 1997 when the Swiss Bank Corporation merged with the Union Bank of Switzerland. After acquiring Paine Webber, a 120-year-old U.S. wealth management firm in 2000, and aggressively hiring for its investment banking business, UBS soon became one of the top financial services companies in the world and the biggest bank in Switzerland.

Between 2008 and 2012, however, UBS's standing was harmed by a series of ethics scandals, detailed next. These scandals cost the bank billions of dollars in fines and lost profits, and severely damaged its reputation (Exhibit MC20.1).

Ethics Scandal #1: U.S. Tax Evasion

Swiss banks have long enjoyed a competitive advantage brought by the Swiss banking privacy laws, making it a criminal offense to share clients' information with any third parties. The exceptions are cases of criminal acts such as accounts linked to terrorists or tax fraud. Merely *not* declaring assets to tax authorities (tax evasion), however, is not considered tax fraud.

After the acquisition of Paine Webber, UBS entered into a Qualified Intermediary (QI) agreement with the Internal Revenue Service (IRS), the federal tax agency of the U.S. government. Like other foreign financial institutions under a QI agreement, UBS agreed to report and withhold taxes on accounts receiving U.S.-sourced income. Reporting on non-U.S. accounts with U.S.-sourced income is done on an aggregate basis. This in turn protects the identity of the non-U.S. account holders.

In mid-2008, it came to light that since 2000, UBS had actively participated in helping its U.S. clients evade taxes. To avoid QI reporting requirements, UBS's Switzerland-based bankers had aided U.S. clients in structuring their accounts to divest U.S. securities and set up sham entities offshore to acquire

non-U.S. account-holder status. Aided by Swiss bank privacy laws, UBS successfully helped its U.S. clients conceal billions of dollars from the IRS. In addition, UBS aggressively marketed its "tax saving" schemes by sending its Swiss bankers to the U.S. to develop clientele, even though those bankers never acquired proper licenses from the U.S. Securities and Exchange Commission (SEC) to do so.

The U.S. prosecutors pressed charges on UBS for conspiring to defraud the United States by impeding the IRS. In a separate suit, the U.S. requested UBS to reveal the names of 52,000 U.S. clients who were believed to be tax evaders. In February 2009, UBS paid $780 million in fines to settle the charges. Although it initially resisted the pressure to turn over clients' information, citing the Swiss bank privacy laws, UBS eventually agreed to disclose 4,450 accounts after intense negotiations involving officials from both countries. Clients left UBS in droves: Operating profit from the bank's wealth management division declined by 60 percent or $4.4 billion in 2008; it declined another 17 percent ($504 million) in 2009.

The UBS case has far-reaching implications for the bank's wealth management business and the Swiss banking industry as a whole, especially for the bank secrecy in which the industry takes such pride. To close loopholes in the QI program and crack down on tax evasion in countries with strict bank-secrecy traditions, President Obama signed into law the Foreign Account Tax Compliance Act (FATCA) in 2010. The law requires all foreign financial institutions to report offshore accounts and activities of their U.S. clients with assets over $50,000, and to impose a 30 percent withholding tax on U.S. investments or

Frank T. Rothaermel and Carrie Yang (GT MBA, MSc.) prepared this MiniCase from public sources. It is developed for the purpose of class discussion. It is not intended to be used for any kind of endorsement, source of data, or depiction of efficient or inefficient management. All opinions expressed, and all errors and omissions, are entirely the authors'. © Rothaermel and Yang, 2014.

EXHIBIT MC20.1 / UBS's Share Prices (12/31/2007–07/02/2013, in $)

SOURCE: Authors' depiction of data from Yahoo Finance, http://finance.yahoo.com.

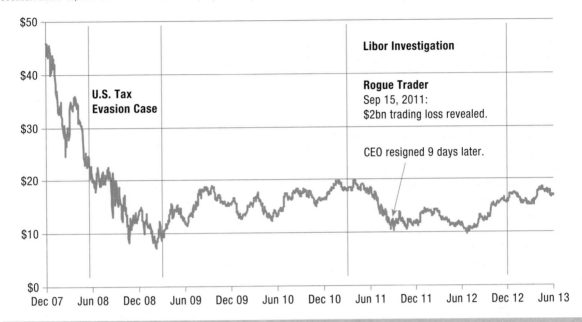

to exit the U.S. business altogether. Switzerland has agreed to implement the FATCA. The annual compliance cost for each Swiss bank is estimated to be $100 million.

Ethics Scandal #2: Rogue Trader

On September 15, 2011, UBS announced that a rogue trader named Kweku Adoboli at its London branch had racked up an unauthorized trading loss of $2.3 billion over a period of three years. Nine days later, UBS's CEO Oswald Grübel resigned "to assume responsibility for the recent unauthorized trading incident."[1]

After more than a year of joint investigation by the UK and Swiss regulators, the case was concluded with findings that systems and controls at UBS were "seriously defective."[2] As a result, Mr. Adoboli, a relatively junior trader, was able to take highly risky positions with vast amounts of money. More alarmingly, all three of Mr. Adoboli's desk colleagues admitted that they knew more or less of his unauthorized trades. Moreover, Mr. Adoboli's two bosses had shown a relaxed attitude toward breaching daily

trading limits. UBS was fined $47.6 million in late 2012.

Ethics Scandal #3: Libor Manipulation

Libor, or the London Interbank Offered Rate, is the interest rate at which international banks based in London lend to each other. Libor is set daily: A panel of banks submits rates to the British Bankers' Association based on their perceived unsecured borrowing cost; the rate is then calculated using a "trimmed" average, which excludes the highest and lowest 25 percent of the submissions. Libor is the most frequently used benchmark reference rate worldwide, setting prices on financial instruments worth about $800 trillion.

UBS, as one of the panel banks, was fined $1.5 billion in December 2012 by the U.S., the UK, and Swiss regulators for manipulating Libor submissions from 2005 to 2010. During that period, UBS traders acted on their own or colluded with interdealer brokers and traders at other panel banks to adjust Libor submissions to benefit UBS's own trading positions. In addition, during the second half of 2008, UBS instructed its Libor submitters to keep submissions low to make the bank look stronger. At least 40 people, including several senior managers at UBS, were involved in the Libor manipulation. In addition to the fine, UBS Japan pleaded guilty to U.S. prosecutors for committing wire fraud. UBS ended the year 2012 with a loss of almost $3 billion, compared with a profit of $4.5 billion for 2011.

DISCUSSION QUESTIONS

Review Chapter 12: Corporate Governance and Business Ethics.

1. MiniCase 20 details three ethics scandals at UBS in recent years. What does that tell you about UBS?

2. Given the UBS ethics failings, who is to blame? The CEO? The board of directors?

3. What lessons in terms of business ethics and competitive advantage can be drawn from the UBS scandals, especially comparing the firm's 2012 and 2011 net income? Looking at Exhibit MC20.1, why do you think the stock market hasn't reacted more strongly to the ethics failings?

4. What can UBS do to (a) avoid more ethics scandals in the future and (b) repair its damaged reputation?

Endnotes

1. "Memo to UBS staff from interim CEO, chairman," *Reuters,* September 24, 2011.

2. "UBS fined £29.7m over rogue trader," *Financial Times,* November 26, 2012.

Sources: This MiniCase is based on UBS Annual Reports, various years; "Tax haven banks and U.S. tax compliance," *United States Senate,* July 17, 2008; "UBS enters into Deferred Prosecution Agreement," *The United States Department of Justice Release,* February 18, 2009; "UBS to give 4,450 names to U.S.," *The Wall Street Journal,* August 20, 2009; Cantley, B. G. (2011), "The U.B.S. case: The U.S. attack on Swiss banking sovereignty," *Brigham Young University International Law & Management Review,* Vol. 7, Spring 2011; available at SSRN: http://ssrn.com/abstract=1554827; "Rogue trader causes $2 billion loss at UBS," *Associated Press,* September 15, 2011; "Ending an era of Swiss banking secrecy: The facts behind FATCA," *American Criminal Law Review,* September 18, 2011; "Swiss and U.S. move forward on tax compliance," *Swissinfo.ch,* June 21, 2012; "The LIBOR scandal: The rotten heart of finance," *The Economist,* July 7, 2012; "UBS fined £30m over rogue trader," *The Guardian,* November 26, 2012; "UBS fined £29.7m over rogue trader," *Financial Times,* November 26, 2012; "Final notice to UBS AG," *Financial Services Authority,* December 19, 2012; "Demise of Swiss banking secrecy heralds new era," *Financial Times,* May 19, 2013; and "UBS ex-official gets 18 months in muni bond-rigging case," *The Wall Street Journal,* July 24, 2013.

How to Conduct a Case Analysis

The case study is a fundamental learning tool in strategic management. We carefully wrote and chose the cases in this book to expose you to a wide variety of key concepts, industries, protagonists, and strategic problems.

In simple terms, cases tell the story of a company facing a strategic dilemma. The firms may be real or fictional in nature, and the problem may be current or one that the firm faced in the past. Although the details of the cases vary, in general they start with a description of the challenge(s) to be addressed, followed by the history of the firm up until the decision point, and then additional information to help you with your analysis. The strategic dilemma is often faced by a specific manager, who wonders what they should do. To address the strategic dilemma, you will use the AFI framework to conduct a case analysis using the tools and concepts provided in this textbook. After careful analysis, you will be able to formulate a strategic response and make recommendations about how to implement it.

Why Do We Use Cases?

Strategy is something that people learn by doing; it cannot be learned simply by reading a book or listening carefully in class. While those activities will help you become more familiar with the concepts and models used in strategic management, the only way to improve your skills in analyzing, formulating, and implementing strategy is to *practice*.

We encourage you to take advantage of the cases in this text as a "laboratory" in which to experiment with the strategic management tools you have been given, so that you can learn more about how, when, and where they might work in the "real world." Cases are valuable because they expose you to a number and variety of situations in which you can refine your strategic management skills without worrying about making mistakes. The companies in these cases will not lose profits or fire you if you miscalculate a financial ratio, misinterpret someone's intentions, or make an incorrect prediction about environmental trends.

Cases also invite you to "walk in" and explore many more kinds of companies in a wider array of industries than you will ever be able to work at in your lifetime. In this textbook alone, you will find cases about companies involved in energy infrastructure development (Siemens), medical products and services (General Electric), electronic equipment (Apple), computer networking (IBM), sustainability consulting (InterfaceRAISE), electric cars (Tesla Motors), book retailing (BetterWorld Books), and consumer products (Cola Wars), to name just a few. Your personal organizational experiences are usually much more limited, defined by the jobs held by your family members or by your own forays into the working world. Learning about companies involved in so many different types of products and services may open up new employment possibilities for you. Diversity also forces us to think about the ways in which industries (as well as people) are both similar and yet distinct, and to critically examine the degree to which lessons learned in one forum transfer to other settings (i.e., to what degree are they "generalizable"). In short, cases are a great training tool, and they are fun to study.

You will find that many of our cases are written from the perspective of the CEO or general manager responsible for strategic decision making in the organization. While you do not need to be a member of a top management team to utilize the strategic-management process, these senior leaders are usually responsible for determining strategy in most of the organizations we study. Importantly, cases allow us to put ourselves "in the shoes" of strategic leaders and invite us to view the issues from their perspective. Having responsibility for the performance of an entire organization is quite different from managing a single project team, department, or functional area. Cases can help you see the *big picture* in a way that most of us are not accustomed to in our daily, organizational lives. We recognize that most undergraduate students and even MBAs do not land immediately in the corporate boardroom. Yet having a basic understanding of the types of conversations going on in the boardroom not only increases your current value as an employee, but improves your chances of getting there someday, should you so desire.

Finally, cases help give us a *long-term* view of the firms they depict. Corporate history is immensely helpful in understanding how a firm got to its present position and why people within that organization think the way they do. Our case authors (both the author of this book and authors of cases from respected third-party sources) have spent many hours poring over historical documents and news reports in order to re-create each company's heritage for you, a luxury that most of us do not have when we are bombarded on a daily basis with homework, tests, and papers or project team meetings, deadlines, and reports. We invite you not just to learn from, but also to savor, reading each company's story.

STRATEGIC CASE ANALYSIS.
The first step in analyzing a case is to *skim it for the basic facts*. As you read, jot down your notes regarding the following basic questions:

- What company or companies is the case about?
- Who are the principal actors?
- What are the key events? When and where do they happen (in other words, what is the timeline)?

Second, go back and reread the case in greater detail, this time with a focus on *defining the problem*. Which facts are relevant and why? Just as a doctor begins by interviewing the patient ("What hurts?"), you likewise gather information and then piece the clues together in order to figure out what is wrong. Your goal at this stage is to identify the "symptoms" in order to figure out which "tests" to run in order to make a definitive "diagnosis" of the main "disease." Only then can you prescribe a "treatment" with confidence that it will actually help the situation. Rushing too quickly through this stage often results in "malpractice" (that is, giving a patient with an upset stomach an antacid when she really has the flu), with effects that range from unhelpful to downright dangerous. The best way to ensure that you "do no harm" is to analyze the facts carefully, fighting the temptation to jump right to proposing a solution.

The third step, continuing the medical analogy, is to determine which analytical tools will help you to most accurately diagnose the problem(s). Doctors may choose to run blood tests or take an x-ray. In doing case analysis,

we follow the steps of the *strategic-management process*. You have any and all of the following models and frameworks at your disposal:

1. Perform an **external environmental analysis** of the:
   - Macrolevel environment (PESTEL analysis)
   - Industry environment (e.g., Porter's five forces)
   - Competitive environment

2. Perform an **internal analysis** of the firm using the resource-based view:
   - What are the firm's resources, capabilities, and competencies?
   - Does the firm possess valuable, rare, costly to imitate resources, and is it organized to capture value from those resources (VRIO analysis)?
   - What is the firm's value chain?

3. Analyze the firm's current **business-level** and **corporate-level** strategies:
   - Business-level strategy (product market positioning)
   - Corporate-level strategy (diversification)
   - International strategy (geographic scope and mode of entry)
   - How are these strategies being implemented?

4. Analyze the firm's **performance:**
   - Use both financial and market-based measures.
   - How does the firm compare to its competitors as well as the industry average?
   - What trends are evident over the past three to five years?
   - Consider the perspectives of multiple stakeholders (internal and external).
   - Does the firm possess a competitive advantage? If so, can it be sustained?

CALCULATING FINANCIAL RATIOS.
Financial ratio analysis is an important tool for assessing the outcomes of a firm's strategy. Although financial performance is not the only relevant outcome measure, long-term profitability is a necessary precondition for firms to remain in business and to be able to serve the needs of all of their stakeholders. Accordingly, at the end of this introductory module, we have provided a table of financial measures that can be used to assess firm performance (see Table 1, pages 463–467).

All of the following aspects of performance should be considered, because each provides a different type of information about the financial health of the firm:

- Profit ratios—how efficiently a company utilizes its resources.
- Activity ratios—how effectively a firm manages its assets.
- Leverage ratios—the degree to which a firm relies on debt versus equity (capital structure).
- Liquidity ratios—a firm's ability to pay off its short-term obligations.
- Market ratios—returns earned by shareholders who hold company stock.

MAKING THE DIAGNOSIS. With all of this information in hand, you are finally ready to *make a "diagnosis."* Describe the problem(s) or opportunity(ies) facing the firm at this point in time and/or in the near future. How are they interrelated? (For example, a runny nose, fever, stomach upset, and body aches are all indicative of the flu.) Support your conclusions with data generated from your analyses.

The following general themes may be helpful to consider as you try to pull all the pieces together into a cohesive summary:

- Are the firm's value chain (primary and support) activities mutually reinforcing?
- Do the firm's resources and capabilities fit with the demands of the external environment?
- Does the firm have a clearly defined strategy that will create a competitive advantage?
- Is the firm making good use of its strengths and taking full advantage of its opportunities?
- Does the firm have serious weaknesses or face significant threats that need to be mitigated?

Keep in mind that "problems" can be positive (how to manage increased demand) as well as negative (declining stock price) in nature. Even firms that are currently performing well need to figure out how to maintain their success in an ever-changing and highly competitive global business environment.

Formulation: Proposing Feasible Solutions

When you have the problem figured out (your diagnosis), the next step is to *propose a "treatment plan"* or solution. There are two parts to the treatment plan:

the *what* and the *why*. Using our medical analogy: The *what* for a patient with the flu might be antiviral medication, rest, and lots of fluids. The *why*: antivirals attack the virus directly, shortening the duration of illness; rest enables the body to recuperate naturally; and fluids are necessary to help the body fight fever and dehydration. *The ultimate goal is to restore the patient to wellness.* Similarly, when you are doing case analysis, your task is to figure out *what* the leaders of the company should do and *why* this is an appropriate course of action. Each part of your proposal should be justifiable based on your analyses.

One word of caution about the formulation stage: By nature, humans are predisposed to engage in "local" and "simplistic" searches for solutions to the problems they face.[1] On the one hand, this can be an efficient approach to problem solving, because relying on past experiences (what worked before) does not "waste time reinventing the wheel." The purpose of doing case analysis, however, is to *look past* the easy answers and to help us figure out not just "what works" (satisficing) but what might be the *best* answer (optimizing). In other words, do not just take the first idea that comes to your mind and run with it. Instead, write down that idea for subsequent consideration but then think about what other solutions might achieve the same (or even better) results. Some of the most successful companies engage in scenario planning, in which they develop several possible outcomes and estimate the likelihood that each will happen. If their first prediction turns out to be incorrect, then they have a "Plan B" ready and waiting to be executed.

Plan for Implementation

The final step in the AFI framework is to develop a plan for implementation. Under formulation, you came up with a proposal, tested it against alternatives, and used your research to support why it provides the best solution to the problem at hand. To demonstrate its feasibility, however, you must be able to explain *how to put it into action.* Consider the following questions:

1. *What activities need to be performed?* The value chain is a very useful tool when you need to figure out how different parts of the company are likely to be affected. What are the implications of your plan with respect to both primary activities (e.g., operations and sales/marketing/service) and support activities (e.g., human resources and infrastructure)?

2. *What is the timeline?* What steps must be taken first and why? Which ones are most critical? Which activities can proceed simultaneously, and which ones are sequential in nature? How long is your plan going to take?

3. *How are you going to finance your proposal?* Does the company have adequate cash on hand, or does it need to consider debt and/or equity financing? How long until your proposal breaks even and pays for itself?

4. *What outcomes is your plan likely to achieve?* Provide goals that are "SMART": specific, measurable, achievable, realistic, and timely in nature. Make a case for how your plan will help the firm to achieve a strategic competitive advantage.

In-Class Discussion

Discussing your ideas in class is often the most valuable part of a case study. Your professor will moderate the class discussion, guiding the AFI process and asking probing questions when necessary. Case discussion classes are most effective and interesting when everybody comes prepared and participates in the exchange.

Actively listen to your fellow students; mutual respect is necessary in order to create an open and inviting environment in which people feel comfortable sharing their thoughts with one another. This does not mean you need to agree with what everyone else is saying, however. Everyone has unique perspectives and biases based on differences in life experiences, education and training, values, and goals. As a result, no two people will interpret the same information in exactly the same way. Be prepared to be challenged, as well as to challenge others, to consider the case from another vantage point. Conflict is natural and even beneficial as long as it is managed in constructive ways.

Throughout the discussion, you should be prepared to support your ideas based on the analyses you conducted. Even students who agree with you on the general steps to be taken may disagree on the order of importance. Alternatively, they may like your plan in principle but argue that it is not feasible for the company to accomplish. You should not be surprised if others come up with an altogether different diagnosis and prescription. For better or worse, a good idea does not stand on its own merit—you must be able to convince your peers of its value by backing it up with sound logic and support.

Things to Keep in Mind While Doing Case Analysis

While some solutions are clearly better than others, it is important to remember that there is no single, correct answer to any case. Unlike an optimization equation or accounting spreadsheet, cases cannot be reduced to a mathematical formula. Formulating and implementing strategy involves people, and working with people is inherently messy. Thus, the best way to get the maximum value from the case-analysis process is to maintain an open mind and carefully consider the strengths and weaknesses of all of the options. Strategy is an iterative process, and it is important not to rush to a premature conclusion.

For some cases, your instructor may be able to share with you what the company actually did, but that does not necessarily mean it was the best course of action. Too often students find out what happened in the "real world" and their creative juices stop flowing. Whether due to lack of information, experience, or time, companies quite often make the most expedient decision. With your access to additional data and time to conduct more detailed analyses, you may very well arrive at a different (and better) conclusion. Stand by your findings as long as you can support them with solid research data. Even Fortune 500 companies make mistakes.

Unfortunately, to their own detriment, students sometimes discount the value of cases based on fictional scenarios or set some time in the past. One significant advantage of fictional cases is that everybody has access to the same information. Not only does this "level the playing field," but it prevents you from being unduly biased by actual events, thus cutting short your own learning process. Similarly, just because a case occurred in the past does not mean it is no longer relevant. The players and technology may change over time, but many questions that businesses face are timeless in nature: how to adapt to a changing environment, the best way to compete against other firms, and whether and how to expand.

Case Limitations

As powerful a learning tool as case analysis can be, it does come with some limitations. One of the most important for you to be aware of is that case analysis relies on a process known as *inductive reasoning*, in which you study specific business cases in order to derive general principles of management. Intuitively, we rely on inductive reasoning across almost every aspect of our lives. We know that we need oxygen to survive, so we assume that all living organisms need oxygen. Similarly, if all the swans we have ever seen are white, we extrapolate this to mean that all swans are white. While such relationships are often built upon a high degree of probability, it is important to remember that they are not empirically proven. We have in fact discovered life forms (microorganisms) that rely on sulfur instead of oxygen. Likewise, just because all the swans you have seen have been white, black swans do exist.

What does this caution mean with respect to case analysis? First and foremost, do not assume that just because one company utilized a joint venture to commercialize a new innovation, another company will be successful employing the same strategy. The first company's success may not be due to the particular organizational form it selected; it might instead be a function of its competencies in managing interfirm relationships or the particularities of the external environment. Practically speaking, this is why the analysis step is so fundamental to good strategic management. Careful research helps us to figure out all of the potential contributing factors and to formulate hypotheses about which ones are most likely critical to success. Put another way, what happens at one firm does not necessarily generalize to others. However, solid analytical skills go a long way toward enabling you to make informed, educated guesses about when and where insights gained from one company have broader applications.

In addition, we have a business culture that tends to put on a pedestal high-performance firms and their leaders. Critical analysis is absolutely essential in order to discern the reasons for such firms' success. Upon closer inspection, we have sometimes found that their image is more a mirage than a direct reflection of sound business practices. Many business analysts have been taken in by the likes of Enron, WorldCom, and Bernie Madoff, only to humbly retract their praise when the company's shaky foundation crumbles. We selected many of the firms in these cases because of their unique stories and positive performance, but we would be remiss if we let students interpret their presence in this book as a whole-hearted endorsement of all of their business activities.

Finally, our business culture also places a high premium on benchmarking and best practices. Although we present you with a sample of firms that we believe are worthy of in-depth study, we would again caution you against uncritical adoption of their activities in the hope of emulating their achievements. Even when a management practice has broad applications, strategy involves far more than merely copying the industry leader. The company that invents a best practice is already far ahead of its competitors on the learning curve, and even if other firms do catch up, the best they can usually hope for is to match (but not exceed) the original firm's success. By all means, learn as much as you can from whomever you can, but use that information to strengthen your organization's *own* strategic identity.

Frequently Asked Questions about Case Analysis

1. *Is it okay to utilize outside materials?*

Ask your professor. Some instructors utilize cases as a springboard for analysis and will want you to look up more recent financial and other data. Others may want you to base your analysis on the information from the case only, so that you are not influenced by the actions actually taken by the company.

2. *Is it okay to talk about the case with other students?*

Again, you should check with your professor, but many will strongly encourage you to meet and talk about the case with other students as part of your preparation process. The goal is not to come to a group consensus, but to test your ideas in a small group setting and revise them based on the feedback you receive.

3. *Is it okay to contact the company for more information?*

If your professor permits you to gather outside information, you may want to consider contacting the company directly. If you do so, it is imperative that you represent yourself and your school in the most professional and ethical manner possible. Explain to them that you are a student studying the firm and that you are seeking additional information, with your instructor's permission. Our experience is that some companies are quite receptive to student inquiries; others are not. You cannot know how a particular company will respond unless you try.

4. *What should I include in my case analysis report?*

Instructors generally provide their own guidelines regarding content and format, but a general outline for a case analysis report is as follows: (1) analysis of the problem; (2) proposal of one or more alternative solutions; and (3) justification for which solution you believe is best and why. The most important thing to remember is not to waste precious space repeating facts from the case. You can assume that your professor has read the case carefully. What he or she is most interested in is your analysis of the situation and your rationale for choosing a particular solution.

Endnotes

1. Cyert, R. M., and March, J. G. (2001), *A Behavioral Theory of the Firm,* 2nd ed. (Malden, MA: Blackwell Publishers Inc.).

TABLE 1 / When and How to Use Financial Measures to Assess Firm Performance

Overview: We have grouped the financial performance measures into five main categories:
Table 1a: Profitability: How profitable is the company?
Table 1b: Activity: How efficient are the operations of the company?
Table 1c: Leverage: How effectively is the company financed in terms of debt and equity?
Table 1d: Liquidity: How capable is the business of meeting its short-term obligations as they fall due?
Table 1e: Market: How does the company's performance compare to other companies in the market?

Table 1a: Profitability Ratios	Formula	Characteristics
Gross margin (or EBITDA, EBIT, etc.)	(Sales − COGS) / Sales	Measures the relationship between sales and the costs to support those sales (e.g., manufacturing, procurement, advertising, payroll, etc.)
Return on assets (ROA)	Net income / Total assets	Measures the firm's efficiency in using assets to generate earnings
Return on equity (ROE)	Net income / Total stockholders' equity	Measures earnings to owners as measured by net assets
Return on invested capital (ROIC)	Net operating profit after taxes / (Total stockholders' equity + Total debt − Value of preferred stock)	Measures how effectively a company uses the capital (owned or borrowed) invested in its operations
Return on revenue (ROR)	Net profits / Revenue	Measures the profit earned per dollar of revenue
Dividend payout	Common dividends / Net income	Measures the percent of earnings paid out to common stockholders

Limitations

1. Static snapshot of balance sheet.
2. Many important intangibles not accounted for.
3. Affected by accounting rules on accruals and timing. One-time non-operating income/expense.
4. Does not take into account cost of capital.
5. Affected by timing and accounting treatment of operating results.

TABLE 1 / When and How to Use Financial Measures to Assess Firm Performance *(continued)*

Table 1b: Activity Ratios	Formula	Characteristics
Inventory turnover	COGS inventory	Measures inventory management
Receivables turnover	Revenue / accounts receivable	Measures the effectiveness of credit policies and the needed level of receivables investment for sales
Payables turnover	Revenue / accounts payable	Measures the rate at which a firm pays its suppliers
Working capital turnover	Revenue / working capital	Measures how much working (operating) capital is needed for sales
Fixed asset turnover	Revenue / fixed assets	Measures the efficiency of investments in net fixed assets (property, plant, and equipment after accumulated depreciation)
Total asset turnover	Revenue / total assets	Represents the overall (comprehensive) efficiency of assets to sales
Cash turnover	Revenue / cash (which usually includes marketable securities)	Measures a firm's efficiency in its use of cash to generate sales
Limitations	Good measures of cash flow efficiency, but with the following limitations:	

1. Limited by accounting treatment and timing (e.g., monthly/quarterly close)
2. Limitations of accrual vs. cash accounting

TABLE 1 / When and How to Use Financial Measures to Assess Firm Performance *(continued)*

Table 1c: Leverage Ratios	Formula	Characteristics
Debt to equity	Total liabilities / Total stockholders' equity	Direct comparison of debt to equity stakeholders and the most common measure of capital structure
Debt to assets	Total liabilities / Total assets	Debt as a percent of assets
Interest coverage (times interest earned)	(Net income + Interest expense + Tax expense) / Interest expense	Direct measure of the firm's ability to meet interest payments, indicating the protection provided from current operations
Long-term debt to equity	Long-term liabilities / Total stockholders' equity	A long-term perspective of debt and equity positions of stakeholders
Debt to market equity	Total liabilities at book value / Total equity at market value	Market valuation may represent a better measure of equity than book value. Most firms have a market premium relative to book value.
Bonded debt to equity	Bonded debt / Stockholders' equity	Measures a firm's leverage in terms of stockholders' equity
Debt to tangible net worth	Total liabilities / (Common equity − Intangible assets)	Measures a firm's leverage in terms of tangible (hard) assets captured in book value
Financial leverage index	Return on equity / Return on assets	Measures how well a company is using its debt
Limitations	Overall good measures of a firm's financing strategy; needs to be looked at in concert with operating results because	
	1. These measures can be misleading if looked at in isolation.	
	2. They can also be misleading if using book values as opposed to market values of debt and equity.	

TABLE 1 / When and How to Use Financial Measures to Assess Firm Performance *(continued)*

Table 1d: Liquidity Ratios	Formula	Characteristics
Current	Current assets / Current liabilities	Measures short-term liquidity. Current assets are all assets that a firm can readily convert to cash to pay outstanding debts and cover liabilities without having to sell hard assets. Current liabilities are a firm's debt and other obligations that are due within a year.
Quick (acid-test)	(Cash + Marketable securities + Net receivables) / Current liabilities	Eliminates inventory from the numerator, focusing on cash, marketable securities, and receivables.
Cash	(Cash + Marketable securities) / Current liabilities	Considers only cash and marketable securities for payment of current liabilities.
Operating cash flow	Cash flow from operations / Current liabilities	Evaluates cash-related performance (as measured from the statement of cash flows) relative to current liabilities
Cash to current assets	(Cash + Marketable securities) / Current assets	Indicates the part of current assets that are among the most fungible (i.e., cash and marketable securities).
Cash position	(Cash + Marketable securities) / Total assets	Indicates the percent of total assets that are most fungible (i.e., cash).
Current liability position	Current liabilities / Total assets	Indicates what percent of total assets the firm's current liabilities represent.
Limitations	Liquidity measures are important, especially in times of economic instability, but they also need to be looked at holistically along with financing and operating measures of a firm's performance. 1. Accounting processes (e.g., monthly close) limit efficacy of these measures when you want to understand daily cash position. 2. No account taken of risk and exposure on the liability side.	

TABLE 1 / When and How to Use Financial Measures to Assess Firm Performance *(continued)*

Table 1e: Market Ratios	Formula	Characteristics
Book value per share	Total stockholders' equity / Number of shares outstanding	Equity or net assets, as measured on the balance sheet
Earnings-based growth models	$P = kE / (r - g)$, where E = earnings, k = dividend payout rate, r = discount rate, and g = earnings growth rate	Valuation models that discount earnings and dividends by a discount rate adjusted for future earnings growth
Market-to-book	(Stock price × Number of shares outstanding) / Total stockholders' equity	Measures accounting-based equity
Price-earnings (PE) ratio	Stock price / EPS	Measures market premium paid for earnings and future expectations
Price-earnings growth (PEG) ratio	PE / Earnings growth rate	PE compared to earnings growth rates, a measure of PE "reasonableness"
Sales-to-market value	Sales / (Stock price × Number of shares outstanding)	A sales activity ratio based on market price
Dividend yield	Dividends per share / Stock price	Direct cash return on stock investment
Total return to shareholders	Stock price appreciation plus dividends	
Limitations	Market measures tend to be more volatile than accounting measures but also provide a good perspective on the overall health of a company when used holistically with the other measures of financial performance. 1. Market volatility/noise is the biggest challenge with these measures. 2. Understanding what is a result of a firm strategy/decision vs. the broader market is challenging.	

PHOTO CREDITS

COMPANY NAME INDEX

Note: Page numbers followed by *n* indicate material in chapter endnotes and source notes

NAME INDEX

Note: Page numbers followed by *n* indicate material in chapter endnotes and source notes.

A

Abe, Shinzo, 452
Abell, D., 195*n*
Abernathy, W. J., 237*n*
Abrahamson, E., 54*n*
Adner, R., 159*n*, 236*n*, 237*n*, 426*n*
Adoboli, Kweku, 455
Aesop, 434, 436
Afuah, A., 93*n*, 196*n*, 274*n*
Agle, B. R., 26*n*
Aime, F., 158*n*
Akerlof, George A., 247, 273*n*
Akers, John, 111
Alchian, A., 273*n*
Alexander, J., 158*n*
Alexandre, M. T., 196*n*, 238*n*, 373*n*
Allen, Paul, 111
Allen, T. J., 238*n*
Allen, W. B., 93*n*, 302*n*
Alsop, R., 404*n*
Alt, J., 275*n*
Alvarez, S., 236*n*
Ambani, Mukesh, 40
Amit, R., 125*n*, 159*n*
Anand, B., 305*n*
Anderson, Chris, 159*n*, 195*n*, 225, 226*n*, 236*n*, 237*n*, 238*n*, 426*n*
Anderson, P., 237*n*
Anderson, R. C., 26*n*, 93*n*, 159*n*, 195*n*
Anderson, Ray, 147
Andrews, P., 126*n*
Apotheker, Leo, 378–379, 386, 389, 397
Appleyard, M. M., 238*n*
Argote, L., 195*n*
Ariely, D., 403*n*
Armstrong, Lance, 98, 120, 205
Arndt, A., 338*n*
Arthaud-Day, M. L., 303*n*
Arthur, W. B., 54*n*, 126*n*, 236*n*

B

Baetz, M. C., 54*n*
Bain, J. S., 93*n*
Baldwin, R., 237*n*
Baliga, B. R., 403*n*
Ballmer, Steve, 111, 286, 426, 449, 450, 450*n*
Bandiera, O., 37*n*, 54*n*
Banister, Scott, 449
Barkema, H. G., 338*n*
Barnett, M., 159*n*
Barney, J. B., 125*n*, 126*n*, 236*n*, 372*n*, 373*n*
Baron, J. N., 373*n*
Bart, C. K., 54*n*
Bartlett, C. A., 339*n*
Bartz, Carol, 286
Baruch, L., 158*n*
Baum, J. A. C., 236*n*
Baum, R. J., 372*n*
Beamish, P. W., 339*n*
Beechy, T., 158*n*
Behar, Howard, 45, 46, 55*n*, 230, 416*n*
Bengtsson, L., 304*n*
Benner, M., 237*n*

Benson, D., 304*n*
Berle, A., 273*n*, 402*n*
Bernanke, Ben, 275*n*
Bernhofen, D., 237*n*
Besanko, D., 93*n*
Bettis, R., 93*n*
Bezos, Jeff, 35, 107, 204
Bingham, C. B., 236*n*
Birkinshaw, J., 196*n*, 373*n*
Blakely, Sara, 211
Boeker, W., 304*n*, 403*n*
Bohmer, R. M., 195*n*–196*n*
Bossidy, L., 372*n*
Bowen, D., 340*n*
Bower, J. L., 54*n*, 55*n*, 237*n*
Bowerman, Bill, 97
Bowman, Bob, 408
Brandenburger, A. M., 54*n*, 93*n*, 237*n*, 304*n*
Branson, Sir Richard, 35, 66
Breshnahan, T., 302*n*
Breznitz, D., 339*n*
Brickley, J. A., 403*n*
Brin, Sergey, 6, 35, 47, 360, 449
Brown, J. L., 373*n*
Brown, J. S., 338*n*
Brown, S. L., 54*n*, 55*n*, 196*n*
Brush, T. H., 302*n*
Bryan, L. L., 373*n*
Bryan Smith, B., 159*n*
Bryant, Kobe, 97, 120
Bryce, D. J., 26*n*
Buchholtz, A. K., 26*n*, 402*n*
Buckley, P. J., 339*n*
Buffett, Warren, 241, 384, 421, 444
Burck, C., 372*n*
Burgelman, R. A., 54*n*–55*n*, 236*n*, 238*n*
Burns, T., 373*n*
Burns, Ursula, 40
Burt, C., 275*n*
Burton, M. D., 373*n*
Buyukkokten, Orkut, 46
Byers, T. H., 237*n*

C

Cairncross, F., 339*n*
Caldwell, D. L., 373*n*
Cameron, James, 306
Cameron, W. B., 158*n*
Camp, S. M., 236*n*
Campbell, A., 303*n*
Cannella, A. A., 54*n*
Cantley, B. G., 454*n*
Capron, Laurence, 294, 295*n*, 303*n*, 305*n*
Cardinal, L. B., 263*n*, 275*n*
Carlisle, Peter, 408, 409
Carlton, D. W., 93*n*
Carroll, A. B., 16*n*, 26*n*, 402*n*
Caves, R. E., 94*n*, 337*n*
Ceccagnoli, M., 237*n*, 304*n*
Cha, S. Eunyoung, 373*n*
Chandler, Alfred D., 346, 372*n*, 373*n*
Chang, S. J., 338*n*

Chao, G. T., 373*n*
Charan, R., 372*n*
Chatman, J. A., 373*n*
Chen, M. J., 426*n*
Chesbrough, H. W., 125*n*, 228*n*, 229*n*, 237*n*, 238*n*
Child, J., 372*n*–373*n*
Christensen, Clayton M., 159*n*, 195*n*, 223, 224, 237*n*, 274*n*, 275*n*
Chung Mong-Koo, 35
Clark, K. B., 237*n*
Clarke, Robert, 144, 159*n*
Coase, Ronald, 244, 273*n*
Cobbold, I., 159*n*
Cohen, W. M., 238*n*
Coles, J. L., 403*n*
Collins, J. C., 38, 38*n*, 39, 54*n*, 147, 159*n*, 372*n*, 403*n*, 404*n*
Collis, D. J., 273*n*
Cook, Tim, 20, 41–42, 113, 152, 215, 317
Cool, K., 94*n*, 115*n*, 126*n*
Cooper, M. B., 54*n*
Corsten, D., 304*n*
Covey, Stephen, 305*n*, 396, 403*n*
Covin, J. G., 236*n*
Crawford, R., 273*n*
Crossan, M. M., 304*n*

D

Daily, C. M., 403*n*
Dalsace, F., 273*n*
Dalton, D. R., 403*n*
Damodaran, A., 26*n*
Darr, E. D., 195*n*
das Graças Silva Foster, Maria, 40
Davis, S. M., 196*n*
Davison, L., 373*n*
De Colle, S., 26*n*
Deeds, D. L., 195*n*, 236*n*, 274*n*, 304*n*, 305*n*, 412*n*
Deephouse, D. L., 94*n*
De Figueireo, R. J. P., 93*n*
DeHart, Jacob, 149
Dell, Michael, 360, 390
Dess, G. G., 196*n*
Dierickx, I., 115*n*, 126*n*
Disney, Walt, 360
Dixit, A., 54*n*, 93*n*
Doherty, N. A., 93*n*, 302*n*
Dorf, R. C., 237*n*
Downing, C., 274*n*
Doz, Y. L., 304*n*, 339*n*
Dranove, E., 93*n*
Dubin, Michael, 150
Duguid, P., 338*n*, 373*n*
Dunn, Brian, 35
Dunn, Patricia, 378
Dunning, J. H., 337*n*, 338*n*
Dushnitsky, G., 304*n*
Dussage, P., 305*n*
Dyer, J. H., 26*n*, 274*n*, 275*n*, 292*n*, 303*n*, 304*n*, 305*n*, 339*n*

SUBJECT INDEX

Note: Page numbers followed by *n* indicate material in chapter endnotes and source notes.

FINANCIAL RATIOS USED IN CASE ANALYSIS

	Formula
Profitability Ratios: "How profitable is the company?"	
Gross Margin (or EBITDA, EBIT, etc.)	(Sales − COGS) / Sales
Return on Assets (ROA)	Net Income / Total Assets
Return on Equity (ROE)	Net Income / Total Stockholders' Equity
Return on Invested Capital (ROIC)	Net Operating Profit After Taxes / (Total Stockholders' Equity + Total Debt − Value of Preferred Stock)
Return on Revenue (ROR)	Net Profits / Revenue
Dividend Payout	Common Dividends / Net Income
Activity Ratios: "How efficient are the operations of the company?"	
Inventory Turnover	COGS / Inventory
Receivables Turnover	Revenue / Accounts Receivable
Payables Turnover	Revenue / Accounts Payable
Working Capital Turnover	Revenue / Working Capital
Fixed Asset Turnover	Revenue / Fixed Assets
Total Asset Turnover	Revenue / Total Assets
Cash Turnover	Revenue / Cash (which usually includes marketable securities)
Leverage Ratios: "How effectively is the company financed in terms of debt and equity?"	
Debt to Equity	Total Liabilities / Total Stockholders' Equity
Financial Leverage Index	Return on Equity / Return on Assets
Debt Ratio	Total Liabilities / Total Assets
Interest Coverage (Times Interest Earned)	(Net Income + Interest Expense + Tax Expense) / Interest Expense
Long-term Debt to Equity	Long-Term Liabilities / Total Stockholders' Equity
Debt to Market Equity	Total Liabilities at Book Value / Total Equity at Market Value
Bonded Debt to Equity	Bonded Debt / Stockholders' Equity
Debt to tangible net worth	Total Liabilities / (Common Equity − Intangible Assets)
Liquidity Ratios: "How capable is the company of meeting its short-term obligations?"	
Current	Current Assets / Current Liabilities
Quick (Acid-Test)	(Cash + Marketable Securities + Net Receivables) / Current Liabilities
Cash	(Cash + Marketable Securities) / Current Liabilities
Operating Cash Flow	Cash Flow from Operations / Current Liabilities
Cash to Current Assets	(Cash + Marketable Securities) / Current Assets
Cash Position	Cash / Total Assets
Current Liability Position	Current Liabilities / Total Assets
Market Ratios: "How does the company's performance compare to other companies?"	
Book Value Per Share	Total Stockholders' Equity / Number Of Shares Outstanding
Earnings-Based Growth Models	$P = kE / (r - g)$, where E = Earnings, k = Dividend Payout Rate, r = Discount Rate, and g = Earnings Growth Rate
Market-to-Book	(Stock Price × Number of Shares Outstanding) / Total Stockholders' Equity
Price-Earnings (PE) Ratio	Stock Price / EPS
Price-Earnings Growth (PEG) Ratio	PE / Earnings Growth Rate
Sales-to-Market Value	Sales / (Stock Price × Number of Shares Outstanding)
Dividend Yield	Dividends per Share / Stock Price
Total Return to Shareholders	Stock Price Appreciation + Dividends

The Strategic Management Process Map

CHAPTER 1
What Is Strategy, and Why Is It Important?

- Gaining and Sustaining Competitive Advantage
- Stakeholder Strategy
- Stakeholder Impact Analysis
- Analysis, Formulation, Implementation (AFI) Framework

CHAPTER 2
Strategic Leadership: Managing the Strategy Process

- Vision, Mission, Values
- Corporate, Business, and Functional Strategy
- Top-Down Strategic Planning
- Scenario Planning
- Strategy as Planned Emergence

CHAPTER 3
External Analysis: Industry Structure, Competitive Forces, and Strategic Groups

- PESTEL Framework
- Porter's Five Forces Model
- Strategic Complements
- Industry Dynamics
- Strategic Groups

CHAPTER 4
Internal Analysis: Resources, Capabilities, and Core Competencies

- Core Competencies
- Resource-Based View (RBV)
- VRIO Framework
- Dynamic Capabilities Perspective
- Value Chain Analysis
- SWOT Analysis: Integrating External & Internal Analyses

CHAPTER 5
Competitive Advantage, Firm Performance, and Business Models

- Accounting Profitability
- Shareholder Value Creation
- Economic Value Creation
- Balanced Scorecard
- Triple Bottom Line
- Business Models

CHAPTER 6
Business Strategy: Differentiation, Cost Leadership, and Integration

- Generic Business Strategies
- Value Drivers and Differentiation Strategy
- Cost Drivers and Cost-Leadership Strategy
- Business Strategy and the Five Forces
- Value Drivers, Cost Drivers, and Integration Strategy
- Dynamics of Competitive Positioning